SENSORY EXPERIENCE, ADAPTATION, AND PERCEPTION

FESTSCHRIFT FOR IVO KOHLER

SENSORY EXPERIENCE, ADAPTATION, AND PERCEPTION

FESTSCHRIFT FOR IVO KOHLER

Edited by

LOTHAR SPILLMANN
Universität Freiburg

BILL R. WOOTEN
Brown University

LEA

1984

LAWRENCE ERLBAUM ASSOCIATES, PUBLISHERS

Hillsdale, New Jersey   London

Copyright © 1984 by Lawrence Erlbaum Associates, Inc.
All rights reserved. No part of this book may be reproduced in
any form, by photostat, microform, retrieval system, or any other
means, without the prior written permission of the publisher.

Lawrence Erlbaum Associates, Inc., Publishers
365 Broadway
Hillsdale, New Jersey 07642

Library of Congress Cataloging in Publication Data

Sensory experience, adaptation, and perception.

   Bibliography: p.
   Includes index.
      1. Visual perception—Addresses, essays, lectures.
2. Perception, Disorders of—Addresses, essays, lectures.
3. Adaptation (Physiology)—Addresses, essays, lectures.
4. Kohler, Ivo—Addresses, essays, lectures.   I. Kohler,
Ivo.   II. Spillmann, Lothar.   III. Wooten, Bill R.
[DNLM: 1. Perception. 2. Adaptation, Physiological.
3. Sensation.   WL 705 S478]
QP487.S46 1984   152.1′4   82-7255
ISBN 0-89859-218-6   AACR2

Printed in the United States of America

10 9 8 7 6 5 4 3 2 1

Contents

QP487
S46
1984
c.2
OPTO

PART II: THEORY

PART III: SPACE PERCEPTION AND BODY ORIENTATION

PART IV: DIRECTIONAL ADAPTATION AND LEARNED REVERSAL

PROFESSOR IVO KOHLER

Preface

While attending the 1981 Spring Meeting of the German Physiological Society in Innsbruck, we learned that the planned *Festschrift* for Professor Ivo Kohler was in jeopardy. Dr. H. Pfister who had started the project the year before was ill, and Dr. G. Lücke who had taken over was busy translating J. J. Gibson's last book. Naturally, we thought of ways to help.

Being long-time admirers of Professor Kohler, and residents of Innsbruck's partner city, Freiburg im Breisgau, we offered to complete the *Festschrift*. The decision was made on top of Mt. Hafelekar, one of the great mountains overlooking the city towards the Stubai Alps. A title and tentative table of contents were quickly drawn up by Dr. W. Ehrenstein who had been overwhelmed by the view (or was it the thin air?), and a phone call was placed to Freiburg to consult with Professor R. Jung.

When we left Innsbruck after five days of glorious skiing and memorable dining, we carried along thirteen of the original manuscripts together with the good wishes of Ms. Helga Faccinelli, our contact at the Psychological Institute. We also brought back fond memories of Professor Kohler, who late at night had taken us into his fascinating world of rare ideas, unusual gadgets, and puzzling phenomena. Needless to say, we felt committed to finish our task as well as we could.

In presenting this *Festschrift* to the public, we hope to have adhered to the high scientific standard characteristic of Professor Kohler's own work. Unfortunately, the time for preparing the book was short. Thanks, however, to the enthusiasm of the contributors and the untiring collaboration of many colleagues, we were able to assemble a collection of some 40 articles which we feel is representative of Professor Kohler's research interests. At the same time they reflect major trends in modern sensory psychology. No attempt was made to systematically cover the field in which Professor Kohler's originality, skill, and pioneering spirit had their greatest impact, the study of visuo-motor disarrangement and rearrangement. This topic has been treated in a number of books (see the listing by M. Ritter, pp. xxiii). Neither were articles included on the neurophysiological and behavioral aspects of sensory plasticity where so many important advances have been made during the last decade. Excellent reviews are available.

In our efforts we were aided by Drs. J. Werner, K. Fuld, A. Ransom-Hogg, and Professor M. Akita who shared in the editorial work while spending time at the Freiburg Psychophysical Laboratory, and by Mr. Franz Rombach who supervised the mailing. Professor R. Jung provided invaluable scientific advice and experience. Professors M. Ritter and A. Hajos were our consultants in matters of *Kohleriana*. We wish to thank them all. The financial costs were borne by the Neurological Clinic of the University of Freiburg, the German Research Council (SFB 70, Brain Research and Sensory Physiology), and the Alexander von Humboldt-Foundation, and their support is much appreciated. We wish to thank Lawrence Erlbaum Associates, Inc., Publishers, for showing unusually great interest in this project. Special thanks go to Mrs. S. Kasmin-Shrader and Mrs. E. Young for editorial help, and to Mr. and Mrs. D. Young for their most generous hospitality.

Lothar Spillmann   *Bill R. Wooten*

ACKNOWLEDGMENTS

The preparation and printing of this book were supported in part by the Austrian Ministry for Science and Research in Vienna. Assistance was also provided by the U. S. Army Research Institute for the Behavioral and Social Sciences through its European Science Coordination Office in London. The opinions expressed in this work are those of the authors and do not necessarily represent those of the above agencies.

For Ivo Kohler: Scientist and Teacher on the Occasion of His 65th Birthday

Anton Hajos
Department of Psychology
University of Gießen

Manfred Ritter
Department of Psychology
University of Marburg
West Germany

Ivo Kohler celebrated his 65th birthday on July 27, 1980. It is no simple task to pay proper homage to such an unconventional scientist and teacher.

One thing is certain: Kohler undoubtedly holds the world record for the duration of a psychological experiment. If we keep in mind that this was an experiment that took place without a single interruption and involved only one subject, Kohler himself, then a period of 124 days is certainly unique in the annals of psychological research. The experiment in question began in November 1946 and continued until March 1947, during which time Kohler wore binocular prisms. This record experiment, together with others that were nearly as long, is described in Kohler's most important work: *Über Aufbau und Wandlungen in der Wahrnehmungswelt. Insbesondere über 'bedingte Empfindungen'* (English: *The Formation and Transformation of the Perceptual World*). At first sight, this work might seem to be only a factual report on observations made by Kohler and other subjects during long periods in which they wore various types of mirror spectacles and goggles with prisms, half-prisms, and colored glasses. However, this was the first comprehensive use of the method of systematically disturbing or biasing perception since its first application by Helmholtz and Stratton. Its goal was to analyze the well-structured organization of the perceptual world by means of that world's own corrective processes.

In the monographs mentioned, maximum performances of the perceptual and motor system were carefully observed and daily recorded in diary form. These observations were accompanied by measurements, which are, however, only of secondary importance. The protocols show how the subjectively disturbed, internal representation of space is reconstructed, how the perceptual system "smoothes out" the visually distorted setting and restores perceptual experiences to their original, accustomed state. For psychologists who expect research re-ports to be replete with data, statistics, correlations, factor analyses, and so forth, this book is highly instructive, but it can be recommended even more to those who are prepared to think about psychology and perception, and who are willing to gain insight into the normal daily function of perception from such extreme conditions. This monograph was published in the proceedings of the Austrian Academy of Sciences, and contains the studies which Kohler submitted for his *Habilitation*. No subsequent theory of perception can afford to ignore the plas-ticity of perception that is so thoroughly documented there.

The book is also outstanding because of the remarkably short time in which its ideas were taken up by international researchers and applied in a multitude of projects. It was one of the few German psychological works of the 1950s to be translated into English and it is still widely cited. Space perception, perceptual constancies, color perception, sensorimotor coordination, the integration of dif-ferent sensory systems, developmental processes in perception—all of these areas were stimulated by Kohler's work.

At the beginning of his article on "*Wahrnehmung*" in Meili and Rohracher's *Lehrbuch der experimentellen Psychologie,* Kohler describes the view advanced by Johannes Müller in 1826 in regard to the three stages of knowledge in science, and thus in psychology: the dogmatic, the empirical, and finally the theoretical. This last, according to Müller, is the highest stage: It is "philosophical and empirical at once, these two aspects influencing and permeating each other, and thus leading to true theory." The work of Ivo Kohler must be assigned to this highest level. The first stage, the dogmatic, was totally disregarded, since a paramount scientific principle of the Innsbruck school was unlimited tolerance towards, and respect for, every opinion. We who knew Kohler, while we were his students and assistants, can testify that his work has always been marked by this tolerance. One of the hardest tasks of his assistants was to keep the talkative at a reasonable distance, since Kohler's willingness to discuss things patiently with others, no matter how bizarre their opinions might appear, was unlimited, and sometimes continued long after his lecture should have begun. In his classes, students who were fond of discussions could easily put an end to Kohler's system-atic presentation, causing him to deviate from his prepared lecture. But at the same time, such impromptu discussions were an opportunity for developing important insights into the basic problems of psychology. For instance, even today we still do not know whether a robot that could completely imitate human behavior would have to have experiences or not. In any case, we learned a great deal from this example in regard to the advantages and disadvantages of intro-spective and behavioral psychology and their interdependence.

Kohler is neither a classical psychophysicist nor a Gestalt psychologist; in-deed, he takes a rather critical attitude towards both views, as is shown in his papers "*Psychophysik heute?*", "*Interne und externe Organisation in der Wahrnehmung*", and "*Gestalt und Mechanismus*". However, Kohler has always succeeded in taking the decisive and the positive from various directions and opinions and incorporating them in his own thinking, but not without taking a critical, sometimes mordantly critical, attitude. His view of classical psychophysics is characterized by his well-known statement: "If we use our senses in measuring our environment, then we are measuring with a rubber band." In other words, Kohler conceives of the rules of relationship between stimuli and perception as being complicated and modifiable.

In regard to Gesalt psychology, Kohler asks the heretical question whether there is such a thing as "Gestalt stimuli"; his answer is, surprisingly at first, "yes". But then follows the sharp comment: "Using the same designation for something that has been experienced and for what the experience is based on . . . is a dangerous linguistic artifact" (in Meili & Rohracher, 1968, p. 100). Thus, it is no wonder that he replaces Gestalt principles ("Gestalt laws") with concepts of information theory, such as redundancy, invariance, and higher orders in the structure of stimuli. This point of view puts Kohler close to J. J. Gibson and G. Johansson, with respect to their concepts of global psychophysics, stimulus gradients, and stimulus dynamics. The Innsbruck school, with Erismann, his assistants, and his successor Ivo Kohler, is typical of non-Gestalt psychology, although Gestalt psychology began in Austria.

In addition to this purely basic research, Kohler's institute was the scene of activity on applied problems, for example, how blind persons orient themselves and how this ability can be proved by the use of technical devices. Some blind persons can obviously develop the ability to localize hindrances from dynamic changes in the sound patterns that are produced by the blind person himself while walking, and that are reflected by the hindrance. The principles on which this is based were analyzed and consistently applied in the construction of new and better aids for the blind.

Furthermore, Kohler suggested numerous dissertation topics and advised the students who were writing them. The problems dealt with came from all possible fields of psychology. In addition to developmental psychology, social psychology, and interdisciplinary areas, perceptual psychology was the main field, with a total of 46 dissertations supervised by Kohler. In these, there are topics regarding the plasticity of perception, selective adaptation, visual space perception, postural control, sensorimotor coordination, reading, time perception, hearing, blind people's sense of distance, and problems of perception in traffic and sport psychology.

Only a modest part of this variety and originality can be explained by the beginnings of Kohler's scientific career. His interests, however, were manifold from the beginning. He interrupted his high school studies to spend a year at the vocational school for locksmiths in Fulpmes, Tyrol, where he was awarded a diploma with honors. Then he began to study theology, but became a pupil of Theodor Erismann, himself originally a physicist who had studied under Albert Einstein but who later taught philosophy and psychology (probably in reverse order) at Innsbruck. Kohler finished his studies there in 1941 with a major in philosophy, including psychology, and a minor in physics. Then, beginning in 1946, he spent 10 years as Theodor Erismann's assistant. In 1956 he was named professor on the basis of his research work and at the same time was appointed chairman of the Institute of Psychology, a position he held until 1980. During these years, he was frequently invited to various American universities as a guest professor.

The overall picture of this scientific career would be incomplete without the essential element of Kohler's inexhaustible stock of new ideas. For him, original ideas, including ideas which occasionally turned out to be merely eccentric or outlandish, and the decisive experiment based on them were of greater importance than a lengthy scientific treatise complete with methodological minutiae. This receptivity towards new ideas is what made Kohler a pioneer in introducing information theory, cybernetics, comparative psychology, ethology, and neurophysiology to perception research and to psychological research in general. His university courses were thus not so much a systematic presentation of certain fields of psychology, but rather, lively encounters with new research ideas, the implications of which remain to be explored. This disappointed those beginning students who expected a systematic presentation of scientific knowledge according to tradition. Thus, one of Kohler's favorite courses was the discussion of trends in contemporary psychology (*"Gegenwartsströmungen in der Psychologie"*).

Some of these topics are enhanced by Kohler's hobby: the construction of electronic devices of every conceivable type, ranging from the automatic babysitter and the "living, sound-sensitive windshield wiper" to the electronic bell hanging on the blackboard in the lecture room, which would ring when Kohler drew the electric circuit in chalk. He is blessed with the ability to convert his ideas by simple means into electronic inventions which are marvels of ingenuity and originality. For everyone who knows Kohler, such demonstrations in his courses remain unforgettable.

On this festive occasion we would like to take one little anecdote, which we are all familiar with, and use it to express our admiration and congratulations in a double manner. During one of his seminars, a note was passed around the room with the message: "There are footprints on the ceiling!"—and everyone immediately looked up! In another sense of this phrase, we all look up to Ivo Kohler, a unique personality who has decisively enriched and deepened the understanding of perceptual processes.

The authors thank L. A. Jones, Marburg, for translating the manuscript into English.

Publications by Professor Ivo Kohler

Original Papers

1941

Kohler, I. *Der Einfluß der Erfahrung in der optischen Wahrnehmung beleuchtet von Versuchen langdauernden Tragens bildverzerrender Prismen*. Phil. Dissertation, Innsbruck 1941.

1948

Kohler, I. Influence of fluctuating stimuli on visual perception. In *Proceedings of the XII. International Congress of Psychology (Edinburgh)*. London: Oliver & Body, 1948.

1951

Kohler, I. Gedanken zur instinktiven Anwendung der Wahrscheinlichkeit. *Studium Generale* 1951, *4*, 110–114.

— Warum sehen wir aufrecht? *Die Pyramide* 1951, *1*, 28–33.

— Über Aufbau und Wandlungen der Wahrnehmungswelt. Insbesondere über 'bedingte Empfindungen.' *Österreichische Akademie der Wissenschaften, Philosophisch-historische Klasse; Sitzungsberichte*, 227. Band, 1. Abhandlung. Wien: Rohrer, 1951.

1952

Kohler, I.   Rohrachers biologische Mikroschwingungen. *Die Pyramide* 1952, *2*, 128–132.

—   Der Fernsinn des Blinden. *Umschau* 1952, *22*, 449–451 u. 700.

—   Es gibt keinen sechsten Sinn (Das Rätsel des Blindensinnes und seine schritt-weise Lösung im Experiment). *Der Kriegsblinde* 1952, *4*, 5–7.

1953

Kohler, I.   Zur Psychologie der euklidischen Axiome und der Anschauung in der Geo-metrie. In A. Wellek (Hrsg.), *Bericht über den 17. und 18. Kongreß der Deutschen Gesellschaft für Psychologie*. Göttingen: Hogrefe Verlag, 1953.

—   Umgewöhnung im Wahrnehmungsbereich. *Die Pyramide* 1953, *3*, 92–96, 109–113, 132–133.

—   Grundsätzliches zur Geometrie der Sinnesräume. *Wiener Zeitschrift für Philo-sophie, Psychologie und Pädagogik*, 1953, *4*, 225–232.

—   Theodor Erismann vollendet das 70. Lebensjahr. *Die Pyramide* 1953, *3*, 181–182.

1954

Kohler, I.   Die Technik im Dienste des Blinden. *Die Pyramide* 1954, *4*, 89–93 (also printed in *Die Auslese* 1955, *3*).

1955

Kohler, I.   Theodor Erismann und die Innsbrucker Brillenversuche. In *Ideen aus Öster-reich. Notring Almanach* (Bd. 2). Wien: Notring der Wissenschaftlichen Verbände Österreichs, 1955.

—   Experiments with prolonged optical distortions. *Acta Psychologica (Pro-ceedings of the XIV. International Congress of Psychology)* 1955, *11*, 176–178.

1956

Kohler, I.   Die Methode des Brillenversuchs in der Wahrnehmungspsychologie mit Bemerkungen zur Lehre von der Adaptation. *Zeitschrift für experimentelle und angewandte Psychologie* 1956, *3*, 381–417.

1957

Kohler, I.   Orientierung durch den Gehörsinn. *Die Pyramide* 1957, *7*, 81–93. (In En-glish: Orientation by aural clues. *Die Pyramide* 1957, *7*, 3–15.)

1958

Kohler, I.   Grenzen der Psychologie. In I. Kohler und H. Windischer (Hrsg.), *Erkenntnis und Wirklichkeit. Festschrift für Richard Strohal. Innsbrucker Beiträge zur Kulturwissenschaft* (Bd. V). Innsbruck: Sprachwissenschaftliches Institut der Universität, 1958.

1959

Kohler, I.   Psychologie als Beruf. *Jahresbericht des Bundesgymnasiums Bregenz* 1958/59, 5–10.

1960

Kohler, I.   und Pissarek, Th.: Brillenversuche zur Vertikalentäuschung. *Psychologische Beiträge* 1960, *5*, 117–140.

—   Gestaltbegriff und Mechanismus. In F. Weinhandl (Hrsg.), *Gestalthaftes Sehen. Ergebnisse und Aufgaben der Morphologie.* (Festschrift zum 100. Geburtstag von Christian v. Ehrenfels.) Darmstadt: Wissenschaftliche Buchgesellschaft, 1960.

1961

Kohler, I.   Pawlow und sein Hund (ein Demonstrationsmodell für den 'bedingten Reflex'). *Kybernetik* 1961, *1*, 54–56.

—   Zentralnervöse Korrekturen in der Wahrnehmung. *Die Naturwissenschaften* 1961, *48*, 259–264.

1962

Kohler, I.   Interne und externe Organisation in der Wahrnehmung. (Festschrift zum 75. Geburtstag von Prof. W. Köhler.) *Psychologische Beiträge*, 1962, *6*, 426–438.

—   In memoriam Univ. Prof. Dr. Theodor Erismann. *Die Pyramide*, 1962, *10*, 49–53.

—   Experiments with goggles. *Scientific American*, 1962, *206/5*, 63–72.

—   Pavlov and his dog. *Journal of Genetic Psychology*, 1962, *100*, 331–335.

—   Reizstatistik und Wahrnehmung. *Acta Psychologica (Bericht über den XVI. Internationalen Kongreß für Psychologie)* 1962, *19*, 536–542.

—   Theodor Erismann. *Psychologische Beiträge* 1962, *7*, 170–177.

1963

Kohler, I.   Wahrnehmung. In R. Meili und H. Rohracher (Hrsg.): *Lehrbuch der experimentellen Psychologie.* Bern: Huber Verlag, 1963.

1964

Kohler, I.   The formation and transformation of the perceptual world. *Psychological Issues*, 1964, 3(4) Monograph 12. New York: International Universities Press.
—   Orientation by aural clues. *Research Bulletin/The American Foundation for the Blind*, 1964, *4*, 14–53.
—   Anpassung der Wahrnehmung an fehlerhafte Gläser. In *Fachvorträge der WVA-Jahrestagung, 1964, Reichenhall*, 14. Sonderdruck der Wissenschaftlichen Vereinigung der Augenoptiker, e.V. Bad Godesberg: 1964.

1965

Kohler, I.   Experiments on sensory cooperation. In E. R. Caianiello (Ed.), *Cybernetics of Neural Processes*. Rom: Consiglio Nazionale delle Ricerche, 1965.
—   Two sensory aids to augment the mobility of the blind. *Research Bulletin/The American Foundation for the Blind* (Proceedings of the Rotterdam Mobility Research Conference) 1965, *May*, 191–197.
—   Gestaltreize, Reizgestalten, Gestaltungsreize—ein Beitrag zur Begriffserklärung. In H. Heckhausen (Hrsg.), *Bericht über den 24. Kongreß der Deutschen Gesellschaft für Psychologie*. Göttingen: Hogrefe Verlag, 1965.

1966

Kohler, I.   Die Zusammenarbeit der Sinne und das allgemeine Adaptationsproblem. In W. Metzger (Hrsg.), *Handbuch der Psychologie. Allgemeine Psychologie*, I/1. Göttingen: Hogrefe Verlag, 1966.
—   Gedanken zu "Die Analytizität der Farbsätze." In P. Weingartner (Hrsg.), *Deskription, Analytizität und Existenz*. Salzburg: Pustet Verlag, 1966.
—   Vestibular guidance. In R. Dufton (Ed.), *Proceedings of the International Conference on Sensory Devices for the Blind*. London: St. Dunstan's, 1966.

1967

Kohler, I.   Der gegenwärtige Stand der Forschung auf dem Gebiet der Erkennung von Objekten durch den Gehörsinn. *Berichte des Naturwissenschaftlich-medizinischen Vereins, Innsbruck*, 1967, *55*, 199–210.
—   Facial vision rehabilitation. In R.-G. Busnel (Ed.), *Animal Sonar Systems, Biology and Bionics* (Vol. I) (Frascati, Italien 1966). (Les Systèmes Sonars Animaux, Biologie et Bionique, Tome I.) Jouy-en-Josas: Laboratoire de Physiologie Acoustique, 1967.

1968

Kohler, I. Wahrnehmung. In R. Meili und H. Rohracher (Hrsg.), *Lehrbuch der experimentellen Psychologie* (2. Auflage). Bern: Huber Verlag, 1968.

— Einige vergleichende Gedanken zum Problem der Willensfreiheit. In E. Oldemeyer (Hrsg.), *Die Philosophie und die Wissenschaften* (Festschrift für S. Moser). Meisenheim: Verlag Hain, 1968.

— Contribution to D. P. Kimble (Ed.), Experience and capacity (Vol. 4). *Proceedings of the Fourth International Interdisciplinary Conference on Learning, Remembering, and Forgetting.* The New York Academy of Sciences: New York, 1968, 129–133.

1971

Kohler, I. Wahrnehmung. In R. Meili und H. Rohracher (Hrsg.), *Lehrbuch der experimentellen Psychologie* (3. Auflage). Bern: Huber Verlag, 1971.

— Ist die Erziehung zur Menschlichkeit heute schon selbstverständlich geworden? *Pädagogische Mitteilungen, Beilage zum Verordnungsblatt des Bundesministeriums für Unterricht und Kunst und des Bundesministeriums für Wissenschaft und Forschung* 1971, *71/10*, 84–85.

1972

Kohler, I. Zur Frage des emotionalen Nachholbedarfs. In V. Satura (Hrsg.), *Jugend im Konflikt.* Innsbruck: Tyrolia Verlag, 1972.

1974

Kohler, I. Past, present, and future of the recombination procedure. *Perception* 1974, *3*, 515–524.

1977

Kohler, I. und Reinelt, T. Entwicklung und Fehlentwicklung optischer Wahrnehmungsprozesse. In E. Berger (Hrsg.), *Teilleistungsschwächen bei Kindern. Arbeiten zur Theorie und Praxis der Rehabilitation in der Medizin, Psychologie und Sonderpädagogik.* Bern: Huber Verlag, 1977.

Kohler, I. Die subjektiven Anforderungen des Schifahrens an Schipisten. In R. Sprung und B. König (Hrsg.), *Das Österreichische Schirecht.* Innsbruck: Wagner, 1977.

1979

Kohler, I. A provisional sensory/motor "complementarity" model for adaptation effects. *The Behavioral and Brain Sciences* 1979, *1*, 73–74.

1981

Kohler, I.   Zur Wahrnehmung pausenlos wiederholter, verzerrter oder unbekannter sprach-lautlicher Äußerungen. In K. Foppa und R. Groner (Hrsg.), *Kognitive Strukturen und ihre Entwicklung*. Bern: Huber Verlag, 1981.

Translations

Gibson, J. J.   *Die Sinne und der Prozeß der Wahrnehmung*. (Original edition: The senses considered as perceptual systems. Boston: Houghton Mifflin, 1966.) Translated by I. Kohler, E. Kohler, and M. Groner. Bern: Huber Verlag, 1973.

Gibson, J. J.   *Wahrnehmung und Umwelt*. (Original edition: The ecological approach to visual perception. Boston: Houghton Mifflin, 1979.) Translated by G. Lücke and I. Kohler. München: Urban & Schwarzenberg, 1981.

Scientific Films

Kohler, I.   und Erismann, Th.   *Die Umkehrbrille und das aufrechte Sehen* (16mm, achromatic film with captions, 120m). Wien: Firma Pacher & Co., 1951 (in English: Upright vision through inverting glasses.) And two introductory manuals in cooperation with Th. Erismann: Die Umkehrbrille und das aufrechte Sehen. Das aufrechte Sehen in Theorie und Experiment.

Kohler, I.   und Erismann, Th.   *Warnung im Dunkeln* (16mm, achromatic, with soundtrack). Wien: Firma Pacher & Co., 1963 (in English: Warning in the dark.)

Kohler, I.   Erismann, Th. und Scheffler, P.: *Verkehrte Welten*. (16mm, achromatic, with soundtrack, 130m). Wien: Firma Pacher & Co., 1955 (in English: Living in a reversed world.)

List of Selected Readings on Perceptual and Sensori-motor Adaptation: Historical Beginnings, Monographs, and Recent Reviews.

Manfred Ritter
University of Marburg
Marburg, West Germany

Helmholtz, H. von *Handbuch der Physiologischen Optik.* Dritter Band. Hamburg und Leipzig: Verlag Voss, 1910. (Originally published, 1866.)

Stratton, G. M. Some preliminary experiments in vision without inversion of the retinal image. *Psychological Review*, 1896, *3*, 611–617.

Stratton, G. M. Vision without inversion of the retinal image. *Psychological Review*, 1897, *4*, 341–360, 463–481.

Stratton, G. M. The spatial harmony of touch and sight. *Mind*, 1899, *8*, 492–502.

Ewert, P. H. A study of the effect of inverted retinal stimulation upon spatially coordinated behavior. *Genetic Psychology Monographs*, 1930, *7*, 177–363.

Gibson, J. J. Adaptation, after-effect and contrast in the perception of curved lines. *Journal of Experimental Psychology*, 1933, *16*, 1–31.

Snyder, F. W. and Pronko, N. H. *Vision with spatial inversion.* Wichita: Wichita Press, 1952.

Kottenhoff, H. *Was ist richtiges Sehen mit Umkehrbrillen und in welchem Sinne stellt sich das Sehen um?* Meisenheim: Verlag A. Hain, 1961.

Smith, K. U., and Smith, W. M. *Perception and motion. An analysis of space-structured behavior.* Philadelphia and London: Saunders Co., 1962.

Taylor, J. B. *The behavioral basis of perception.* New Haven: Yale Univ. Press, 1962.

Harris, C. S. Perceptual adaptation to inverted, reversed and displaced vision. *Psychological Review*, 1965, *72*, 419–444.

Howard, I. P. and Templeton, W. B. *Human spatial orientation.* London: Wiley & Sons, 1966.

Rock, I. *The nature of perceptual adaptation.* New York: Basic Books, Inc., 1966.

Epstein, W. *Varieties of perceptual learning.* New York: McGraw-Hill Book Co., 1967.

Freedman, S. J. (Ed.), *The neuropsychology of spatially oriented behavior*. Homewood, Ill.: Appleton-Century-Crofts, 1969.

Gibson, E. J. *Principles of perceptual learning and development* (ch. 10). New York: Appleton-Century-Crofts, 1969.

Hochberg, J. Space and movement. In J. W. Kling and L. A. Riggs (Eds.), *Woodworth & Schlosberg's experimental psychology* (pp. 532–536). New York: Holt, 1971.

Welch, R. B. Research on adaptation to rearranged vision: 1966–1974. *Perception*, 1974, *3*, 367–392.

Kornheiser, A. S. Adaptation to laterally displaced vision: A review. *Psychological Bulletin*, 1976, *83*, 783–816.

Wallach, H. *On Perception*. New York: Quadrangle, 1976.

Howard, I. P. Effects of exposure to spatially disturbed stimuli. In R. D. Walk and H. L. Pick, Jr. (Eds.), *Perception and experience*. New York: Plenum Press, 1978.

Welch, R. B. *Perceptual modification: Adapting to altered sensory environments*. New York: Academic Press, 1978.

Harris, C. S. (Ed.), *Visual coding and adaptability*. Hillsdale, N.J.: Lawrence Erlbaum Associates, 1980.

Lackner, J. R. Some aspects of sensori-motor control and adaptation in man. In R. D. Walk and H. L. Pick, Jr. (Eds.): *Intersensory perception and sensory integration*. New York: Plenum Press, 1981.

Dolezal, H. *Living in a world transformed*. Perceptual and performatory adaptation to visual distortion. New York: Academic Press, 1982.

Howard, I. P. *Human visual orientation*. Chichester, Sussex: John Wiley, 1982.

Bibliography of Japanese Studies of Disarranged Vision

Tatsuro Makino
Department of Educational Psychology
Waseda University
Tokyo, Japan

Fujihara, M., Nakao, T., Ninomiya, H., & Ikeda, T. A clinical psychological study of inverted visual field by inverting prisms. *The Kyushu Neuropsychiatry,* 1980, *26,* 384–394. (In Japanese with English summary)

Ishii, S., & Wapner, S. Age differences in the effect of lateral displacing prism (base left/20 diopter) on perception and walking. *Bulletin of the Psychonomic Society,* 1977, *9,* 423–426.

Katori, H. Perceptual-motor coordination. In Y. Wada, T. Oyama, & S. Imai (Eds.), *Handbook of psychology of sensation and perception.* Tokyo: Seishinshobo, 1969. (In Japanese)

Makino, T. Perception with spatial inversion. *Jimbun Kenkyu* (Studies in the Humanities), Osaka City University, 1963, *14,* 157–171. (In Japanese)

Makino, T. Orientation of visual space and motion. In T. Oyama (Ed.), *Psychology* (Vol. 4), *Perception.* Tokyo: University of Tokyo Press, 1970. (In Japanese)

Makino, T. Perception of inverted visual field: Ego and "external" world. *Tetsugaku Kaishi* (Philosophical Bulletin), Gakushuin University, 1976, *4,* 1–19. (In Japanese)

Miyakawa, T. Experimental research on the structure of visual space when we bend forward and look backward between the spread legs: On the problem of so-called "matanozoki". *Japanese Journal of Psychology,* 1944, *18,* 289–309. (In Japanese)

Miyakawa, T. Experimental research on the structure of visual space when we been forward and look backward between the spread legs. II *Japanese Journal of Psychology,* 1950, *20(2),* 14–23. (In Japanese, with English summary)

Miyakawa, T. On the change of brightness and color when we bend forward and look backward between the spread legs. *Japanese Journal of Psychology,* 1950, *20(3),* 1–5. (In Japanese with English Summary)

Nakao, T., Ninomiya, H., Fujihara, M., & Ikeda, T. An experimental study of inverted visual field by inverting prisms. *The Kyushu Neuro-psychiatry*, 1980, *26*, 257–265. (In Japanese with English summary)

Nakao, T., Ninomiya, H., Fujiwara, M., & Ikeda, T. Visuo-motor adaptation and change of subjective sense during inverted vision. *The Kyushu Neuro-psychiatry*, 1980, *26*, 266–273. (In Japanese with English summary)

Nakao,T., Ninomiya, H., Fujihara, M., & Ikeda, T. Inverted visual field by inverting prisms: An experimental study. *Seishin Igaku* (Psychiatry), 1981, *23*, 935–393. (In Japanese)

Nakao, T., Ninomiya, H., Fujihara, M., & Ikeda, T. A psycho-physiological study of inverted visual field by inverting prisms. *Electroencephalography and Clinical Neurophysiology*, 1981 *52(3)*, 41–42.

Ohkura, M. Shape constancy measured by the method of single stimuli in the inverted visual field. *Jimbun* (The Humanities), 1976, *22*, 1–25. (In Japanese)

Shigeoka, K. Experimental study of perceptual constancy under the condition of inverted glasses and bodily movements. In Y. Akishige (Ed.), Experimental researches on the structure of the perceptual space. IV. *Bulletin of the Faculty of Literature of Kyushu University*, 1961, *7*, 267–289.

Shimojo, S. A study of inverted and reversed vision experiments. *Japanese Psychological Review*, 1978, *21*, 315–339. (In Japanese with English summary)

Shimojo, S. Adaptation to the reversal of binocular depth cues: Effects of wearing left-right reversing spectacles on stereoscopic depth perception. *Perception*, in press.

Takagi, K., & Doi, T. The influence of torsion of opto-motor system on action. *Japanese Journal of Psychology*, 1935, *10*, 519–544. (In Japanese with English summary)

Tashiro, T. On the studies of displaced vision. *Jimbun Kenkyu* (Studies in the Humanities), Osaka City University, 1967, *19*, 89–109. (In Japanese)

Tashiro, T. Perceptual adaptation to prismatic distortion of form. *Jimbun Kenkyu* (Studies in the Humanities), Osaka City University, 1970, *21*, 1043–1061. (In Japanese)

Tashiro, T. Adaptation to displaced vision: An approach from the reaction time on target pointing. *Jimbun Kenkyu* (Studies in the Humanities), Osaka City University, 1972, *23*, 318–329. (In Japanese)

Tashiro, T. A review of experiments on displaced vision in animals. *Jimbun Kenkyu* (Studies in the Humanities), Osaka City University, 1972, *24*, 372–375. (In Japanese)

Tashiro, T. The effects on eye-hand coordination of visual field during adaptation to prismatic vision. *Jimbun Kenkyu* (Studies in the Humanities), Osaka City University, 1974, *26*, 664–672. (In Japanese)

Tashiro, T. Spatial parameters of eye-hand adaptation to prismatic distortion: Adaptation to vertically split-field wedge prism. *Jimbun Kenkyu* (Studies in the Humanities), Osaka City University, 1976, *28*, 474–497. (In Japanese)

Tashiro, T. A discussion on the conditioning of prismatic adaptation. *Jimbun Kenkyu* (Studies in the Humanities), Osaka City University, 1978, *30*, 784–800. (In Japanese)

Tashiro, T. Adaptation to prismatically rotated visual field: The effects of the imposed rotational size (1). *Jimbun Kenkyu* (Studies in the Humanities), Osaka City University, 1980, *32*, 615–634. (In Japanese)

Tashiro, T. Adaptation to prismatically rotated visual field: The effects of the imposed rotational size (2). *Jimbun Kenkyu* (Studies in the Humanities), Osaka City University, 1981, *33*. (In Japanese)

Yoshimura, H. Visual space as one's environment: A theoretical review of the studies of the mechanisms to stabilize the visual space. *Bulletin of Faculty of Education,* Kyoto University, 1979, *25*, 172–182. (In Japanese)

Yoshimura, H. Some characteristics of eye-head coordination pattern: A study of its difference due to age and its control mechanism. *Japanese Journal of Ergonomics,* 1979, *15*, 265–270. (In Japanese with English summary)

Yoshimura, H., & Ohkura, M. Effects of optical inversion and reversal on walking tasks. *Perception,* in press.

HISTORICAL REVIEWS

Through the Looking Glass and What Ivo Kohler Found There: Contours, Colors and Situational Aftereffects

Alberta S. Gilinsky
University of Bridgeport

ABSTRACT

Kohler's Innsbruck experiments with distorting goggles reulted in variable after-effects and variable degrees of resistance to reconditiong and correct seeing. Recent neurophysiological discoveries based on receptivefield studies of cats and monkeys subjected to "environmental surgery" are her shown to account for Kohler's remarkable research and its fruitful extension in modern psychophysiology. The use of Konorski's theory as a framework intowhich to fit both lines of investigation provides the synthesis of two points of viewdesired by Kohler, that of "situational aftereffects" and "conditioned sensations"

Alice looked round eagerly and found that it was the ed Queen. "She's grown a good deal," was her first remark. She had indeed: wh Alice first found her in the ashes, she had been only three inches high—and he she was, half a head taller than Alice herself. . . .

"I think I'll go and meet her," said Alice, for thigh the flowers were interesting enough, she felt that it would be far grander toave a talk with a real Queen.

"You can't possibly do that," said the Rose. "should advise you to walk the other way."

This sounded nonsense to Alice, so she said nong, but set off at once towards the Red Queen. To her surprise she lost sight of hen a moment, and found herself walking in at the front door again.

A little provoked, she drew back, and after lking everywhere for the Queen (whom she spied out at last, a long way off) she ught she would try the plan this time, of walking in the opposite direction.

It succeeded beautifully. She had not been walking a minute before she found herself face to face with the Red Queen, and full in sight of the hill she had been so long aiming at. (Carroll, 1872, p. 191–192)

Lewis Carroll might have been a subject in one of the Innsbruck experiments (Kohler, 1962; 1964) with goggles. These subjects wore reversing mirrors, prismatic and half-prism spectacles, even split-color goggles to study the effects of these experimental disturbances on behavior and perception. Forward and back are reversed in a mirror, as are left and right; objects are simultaneously enlarged and reduced—in a mirror all asymmetrical objects (objects not superposable on their mirror images) "go the other way."

The prism goggles reverse right and left, and near and far. They also change the sizes of things in a surprising way, depending upon the direction of gaze. When Alice eats the left side of the mushroom she grows larger; the right side has the reverse effect.

The fact that the first verse of the Jabberwocky appeared reversed to Alice is evidence that she herself was not reversed by her passage through the mirror. Martin Gardner (1965) points out that there are new scientific reasons for suspecting that an unreversed Alice could not exist for more than a fraction of a second in a looking glass world composed of "antimatter."

Ivo Kohler and his subjects not only survived long periods of wearing goggles that warp, distort, reverse, invert, and recolor the familiar world, but overcame the disturbances with new habits of both behavior and perception—habits that ran counter to a lifetime of previous experience and activity.

The Innsbruck experiments uncovered an adaptive process of general validity. The most remarkable finding—Ivo Kohler's gay and wonderful discovery that stimulation of the same retinal area could lead not only to a variety of visual aftereffects but that these aftereffects were contingent upon the presence or absence of certain conditions of stimulation—is called both "the situational aftereffect" and "conditional perception."

The discovery was prophetic. Now as the result of a series of remarkable psychophysiological experiments we are beginning to understand the organization of the perceptual system and its modification as the result of experience.

The central finding of the Innsbruck studies was the differential adaptation that occurred in one and the same area of the retina. "It is as though," Kohler wrote, "the particular retinal area had not one but a whole series of subjective standards of reaction for the same visual stimulation" (1964, p. 26).

The problem is to explain the occurrence of variable aftereffects; variable degrees of resistance to the transformation of old habits and the formation of new habits; the lead role of motor behavior and only secondarily, of vision; and complete failure of certain visual phenomena, e.g., the color-stereo effect, to show any adaptation, whatsoever.

Kohler's insight into the value of these experiments as probes to discover the genesis of correct perception and coordinated visual-motor behavior in normal development is now confirmed by new discoveries of the activity and organization of the cerebral cortex.

RECEPTIVE FIELD STUDIES

In the mammalian visual system, the important discovery is that any given retinal area transmits information to the brain in a hierarchy of stages of neural activity, corresponding to increasingly higher orders of abstraction of specific features of stimulation. Especially significant is the finding that single cells in the eye and brain are organized into receptive fields of mutually antagonistic activity. In consequence, the visual system tends to dichotomize perception not only into such opposites as light and dark, black and white, red and green, but also into such spatial opposites as left and right, near and far, above and below, and concave and convex. This opponent organization is maintained by a functional architecture that enables us to respond selectively not to absolute properties of stimulation but to the relations between them.

We find selectivity at every stage. A particular retinal area gives different reactions to the same total stimulation at different times and under different conditions because cells farther upstream select the features to which they respond and reject the others. Some regions react to the onset; others to the offset of stimulation. Individual neurons react to lines, bars or gratings with specific sizes, shapes, orientations, directions of movement, and contrasts, dark against light, or light against dark backgrounds. This selective processing is repeated again and again at progressively higher levels. In this processing, the neural activity sharpens gradations and turns them into contours.

Direction is an important factor in the perception of form since the same contour will look different if it is attached to the right or to the left, above or below the figure it outlines. The receptive field studies show clearly that both the direction of movement and the brightness gradient or spatial phase (light to dark, or dark to light) is critical for the response of a single cortical cell in cat or monkey. Human perception emphasizes this feature of contour also; the one-sided action of contour is fundamental to the discrimination of objects and the segregation of figure and ground.

The apparent paradox of opposite aftereffects arising from one retinal area is no longer bewildering. Having available the data derived from Hubel and Wiesel's (1962; 1979) experiments, we know that the same retinal area sends convergent and divergent impulses to many cells of different receptive field types. Single cell studies using microelectrodes have examined and compared the effective stimuli for cells of the visual pathway from the retina to successive levels of the cortex in cat and monkey. Their results provide a physiological and anatomical basis for understanding the sensory disturbance experiments in animals and human beings.

The visual cortex of cats and monkeys contains sets of neurons that receive information from lower levels of the visual pathways and are either excited or inhibited by slits of light or gratings selectively oriented and placed in the visual field. Within the cortex each region of visual space is ". . . represented over and over again in column after column, first for one receptive field organization and then another" (Hubel & Wiesel, 1962, p. 106). Although there appears to be an initially organized functional architecture ready to work soon after birth, the details of these structures depend strikingly on the previous experience of the individual.

Most neurons in the visual cortex of normal cats and monkeys respond selectively to moving contrasts, lines, or gratings presented to one eye alone or both eyes together. Some cortical cells react preferentially to vertical, some to horizontal, and some to oblique orientations of lines or gratings with all orientations being represented. Cells with similar characteristics are grouped together; their receptive fields are close together also; usually they overlap but each group includes various sizes and some scatter. The important point is that each small region of the retina has input to many cells with different response characteristics and different stimulus requirements. Sweeping an optimally oriented grating across the receptive field of a cell is a powerful stimulus, depending on the direction of movement, although some cells respond to movement in two diametrically opposite directions. The cell soon adapts to continued or repeated stimulation and ceases to respond, although the termination of a stimulus may evoke a burst of excited activity.

Long sequences of cells with the same receptive field orientation are found as the electrode advances through the cortex; then a sudden shift occurs to a new sequence with a common orientation preference. These cell sequences are grouped together in columns containing tens of thousands of cells. Any small region of the retina is represented by many columns subserving different stimulus features. The aggregate fields are linked to eccentricity, or the distance of a cell's receptive field from the center of gaze. "Moving the electrode about 1 or 2 mm in an oblique direction always produces a displacement in the visual field that takes one into an entirely new region. Strongly interconnected cells are grouped together and neighboring regions are not random but systematically related to each other in orderly progression. . . . The column systems are a (possible) solution to the problem of portraying more than two dimensions on a two-dimensional surface . . . the cortex is dealing with at least four sets of values: two for the X and Y position variables in the visual field, one for orientation and one for the different degrees of eye preference" (Hubel & Wiesel, 1979, p. 162).

SENSORY DISTURBANCE EXPERIMENTS

The Innsbruck experiments on the transformation of human perception fit hand in glove with the recent neurophysiological studies of the effects of early distortion of sensory input on the visual system of kittens and monkeys.

Taken together with the research on single cells of the nervous system in various species, these different lines of investigation enable us to understand how the structure and function of the brain are affected by the history of the organism. The ability to undergo long-term alterations as a result of experience is a remarkable property of the nervous system. The factors that influence this relearning or rehabituation are presumably no different than those involved in the initial formation of the perceptual world.

Yet there is one important exception. A brief early experience during a *critical period* of development may cause irreversible effects. In newborn animals the closure of one eye may result in permanent damage even though the neuronal circuits required for vision were already present and ready to work at birth (Hubel & Wiesel, 1963). Kittens are born with the basic wiring already established. Both eyes drive cortical neurons and these cells have receptive fields like those in the adult cat. Some cells are driven better by one eye, some by the other and some are driven equally well by both eyes. What happens when one eye is deprived of all visual experience?

Hubel and Wiesel (1965) tried the experiment on a newborn kitten by sewing the lid of one eye closed for 3 months and then recorded the activity of the cortical cells. The effect in the kitten's visual cortex was extraordinary. Not a single cell could be influenced by the eye that had been closed.

When the previously deprived eye was opened and the experienced eye closed (*reverse suturing*) the kittens were practically blind. They would bump into objects and fall off tables even though no gross defect could be found in the operated eye. But electrical recordings of the responses of cortical cells showed striking changes. Very few cells showed any response to the stimulation of that eye. In short, deprivation of the use of one eye at a critical period of development leads to permanent loss of function in that eye. As little as a day of deprivation at about 4 weeks of age (the height of a "sensitive period") can provoke the permanent reorganization of the visual cortex in the kitten (Movshon & Dürsteler, 1977; Olson & Freeman, 1975).

In the kitten, Blakemore and Van Sluyters (1974) have shown that if the originally experienced eye is closed at the time that the deprived one is reopened there can be virtually total capture of neurons by the newly opened eye. This reverse suturing procedure is more effective the earlier in the sensitive period it is done; at 4 or 5 weeks of age it causes total re-invasion of input from the deprived eye. Blakemore, Garcy, and Vital-Durand (1978) found the same result in monkeys following reverse suturing. After early reverse suturing (5–8 weeks) the newly opened eye gained complete dominance.

EFFECTS OF ABNORMAL VISUAL EXPOSURE

If young kittens are raised during the critical period (3–14 weeks) in a visual environment consisting only of stripes of one orientation, most cortical neurons will be maximally sensitive to orientations within ± 30° of the one to which they had been exposed. That may sound like a wide range until you consider that the hands of the clock between 12 and 1 o'clock are 30° apart.

What are the effects of selective exposure to tilt on *mature* animals? Creutzfeldt and Heggelund (1975) exposed seven adult cats to vertical stripes for 1 hour a day and for the rest of the time kept them in darkness over a period of 2 weeks.

The unexpected result was that cells selectively sensitive to the vertical were *less* frequently found than cells sensitive to horizontal or near horizontal orientations. Unlike newborn kittens, in the adult cats, prolonged exposure to a specific orientation *decreased* sensitivity to the stimulus to which they had been exposed, a finding that supports the idea of neural plasticity in the cortex of the adult animal on the basis of inhibition.

These results are remarkably similar to the orientation–specific effects on adaptation or habituation found in experiments in human perception (Gilinsky, 1967; 1968; Gilinsky & Mayo, 1971). The negative visual aftereffects of tilt, direction of movement, curvature, and color found in the Innsbruck experiments and the many different McCollough effects (McCollough, 1965; Stromeyer, Kronauer, Madsen, & Cohen, 1980) may have a common basis in the underlying neural mechanisms.

In humans, Fiorentini, Ghez and Maffei (1972) found physiological correlates of adaptation to a rotated visual field. Subjects wore prismatic spectacles that tilted the visual field by 30° or 45° for 5–7 days, and all reported progressive diminution of apparent tilt. When the relative contrast thresholds and amplitudes of evoked potentials to vertical and oblique gratings were studied, the adapted subjects showed a surprising departure from the normal human greater sensitivity to vertical contours compared with oblique contours. What was especially interesting was the finding of a decrease in the usual difference between the contrast threshold for vertical and for oblique orientations. Most measures of acuity show that human beings are far better at detecting vertical and horizontal contours than oblique ones. Presumably it is the relative paucity of oblique contours in the environments of individuals raised in technological societies filled with artifacts that emphasize the horizontal and vertical outlines of objects. Following removal of such prisms the expected aftereffect occurs—the world is now distorted in a direction opposite to that of the adaptation prisms.

SQUINT (STRABISMUS)

The most interesting neurophysiological experiment and the one most closely related to the Innsbruck research was on squint (strabismus). An adult who develops squint sees double; an infant or child with squint suppresses vision in one eye. If the squint persists the eye may deteriorate and produce severe loss of vision or blindness.

Hubel (1967) produced a squint in newborn kittens by cutting the medial rectus muscle. The optical axis of the eyes are thereby deflected from normal. Three months later they tested the kittens' vision. Disappointingly the cats had perfectly normal pattern vision in both eyes. But the investigators went ahead to record from the cortex of these animals. To their astonishment they found that few cells could be driven by both eyes; 80% were completely monocular. Squint causes the dominant eye to take over, leading to a complete loss of control from the other eye.

Why should this be? Is it the lack of synergism between the two eyes, or some kind of active antagonism or competition? To answer the question it is necessary to allow both eyes to be used but to prevent their working together.

When the kittens are raised normally but allowed to use only one eye at a time, alternating monocular closure, the same results are found. What is not normal is the time relationships between the impulses from the two eyes. The reduced binocular vision in kittens comes from the eyes not working together.

There is a remarkable correspondence between these findings and those of the Innsbruck squint prisms on human adults. The failure of the color-stereo effect to show any adaptation strengthens the conclusion that normal binocular depth perception requires synergistic cooperation between the two eyes.

Once the two eyes have worked together cooperatively to deliver stereoscopic information to the brain, even if only for a short period of time, the binocular function remains. Those born with cataracts may find that surgery fails them, but the removal of cataracts from older, previously sighted persons does often restore vision.

The child or monkey with amblyopia, unless the amblyopia is overcome early, will rarely recover normal binocular vision (Freeman, Mitchell, & Millodot, 1972; Mitchell, Freeman, & Millodot, 1973). In this regard, the experiments with squint prisms are particularly interesting. In sharp contrast to the occurrence of successful adaptation to other experimental disturbances, the adult subjects in Kohler's experiments with squint prisms experienced a striking color-stereo effect that failed to show the slightest adaptation. Yet when the experimental squint prisms were removed, normal binocular vision returned.

THE COLOR-STEREO EFFECT

How can we explain the fact that the eyes adapt to various intense distortions of geometry and color but not at all to the color-stereo effect? Is it simply that the color-stereo effect "presents the visual mechanism with a random and nearly unpredictable assortment of disparate images" (Kohler, 1962, p. 12)?

Another possibility considered by Kohler offers an attractive alternative hypothesis. Kohler's idea is that chromatic aberration, traditionally regarded as an "optical defect" and "a nuisance to be overcome in visual experimentation," may have persisted together with off-center focus throughout evolution because these "defects" have functional utility. The lack of alignment of the foveae produces prismatic effects that are opposite for the left and right eyes. Kohler speculated that the color-stereo effect may represent a primitive way of identifying colors.

But the function served by chromatic aberration and the related color-stereo effect may be just the reverse; could it not be that we identify "near" and "far" by means of colors? Here is a possible solution to the problem of portraying more than two dimensions on a two-dimensional surface.

Perhaps the normal color-stereo effect provides the visual system with subtle cues for depth perception. Adaptation or habituation to chromatic aberration removes the color fringes from conscious awareness in day-to-day experience, but the persistent color-stereo effect provides excellent cues for depth perception.

If one views the world through goggles with their prism bases pointed in opposite directions, the rainbow fringes are disparate for the two eyes and pseudostereoscopic effects appear, opposite to those normally seen. For example, Kohler explains (1962), a vertical rod viewed with squint glasses, whose prism bases face outward, will appear bent away from the observer; if the bases face inward, the same rod will appear bent toward the observer and plane surfaces seen before as concave will now look convex. (The latter effect is difficult to obtain with prisms because it forces the eyes to extraordinary divergence.)

The reversal of near and far by the prisms dissociates the important cues of disparity and double images from their familiar role.

The receptive field studies using microelectrodes to study the most effective stimuli for single cortical cells in the visual system of the monkey show clearly that different cortical cells are selectively responsive to color, orientation, spatial frequency or size, and to the direction of a brightness gradient, whether a dark stimulus is to the left of a light background, or a light stimulus is to the left of a dark background. This multi-selectivity of polyvalent neurons is probably used as a means of encoding a number of variables simultaneously, a parallel processing strategy that the central nervous system uses to solve the problem of simultaneously processing many separate pieces of information.

THE RIDDLE OF OCULAR DOMINANCE

A major variable disclosed by these electrophysiological studies is that of eye preference. The function of the ocular dominance system, in which neighboring cells prove almost invariably to prefer the same eye, resulting in orderly columns favoring either the right eye or the left eye, but not both, has been a "mystery" (Hubel & Wiesel, 1979, p. 161).

A simple and attractive hypothesis suggests that ocular dominance has something to do with binocular depth perception. This idea has particular interest for our understanding of the color-stereo effect and the functional significance of chromatic aberration.

Binocular vision not only gives disparate views of the object at which one is looking, but it also gives double images of other objects in the field of view which lie nearer or farther than the fixated object. When the eyes are fixed on the near object, the double images of the far object are *uncrossed;* when the eyes fixate the far object, the double images of the near object are *crossed.* Woodworth (1938) noted that ". . . crossed double images of an object are a perfect cue that that object lies nearer than the momentary fixation point, while uncrossed double images indicate the reverse. When attention shifts from one object to another at a different distance, the double images which are already present are perfect cues for the readjustment of convergence to the new object" (p. 662).

Ordinarily we are not aware of these double images, but we clearly use them as cues. We interpret their meaning on the basis of *eye dominance.* Although we cannot introspectively distinguish between crossed and uncrossed double images, "if the right eye is dominant, so that its image is the more *important* of the double images, this important image lies on the right for far objects and on the left for near objects. This eye dominance can afford a cue of relative distance" (Woodworth, 1938, p. 664).

This importance is reversed by prism goggles. The subject must reverse his well-established habit and learn to reinterpret the meaning of right and left images. The associated chromatic fringes that differentiate the left and right edges of objects, and do so independently for each eye (because of the asymmetrical alignment of foveae), must also be reinterpreted. Eye dominance does not change, but now the important image lies to the left for far objects and on the right for near objects.

Clearly, it makes a difference which eye gets a certain view or image. With the stereoscope, interchanging the views presented to the two eyes reverses the depth effect. The prisms also act as pseudoscopes, and just as the microelectrode studies demonstrated, the ocular dominance columns are firmly established in the brain. This functional architecture is fixed; rehabituation can change the meaning of the cues of double images from "near" to "far," and vice versa, by reversing the color code; the adaptation to the color fringes induced by the prisms was remarkable, and vivid negative aftereffects appeared when the spectacles were removed. But the color-stereo effect showed not the slightest adaptation. The reason now seems obvious. The color-stereo effect is a function of the stable ocular dominance system built up by competition between the two eyes in the sensitive early period of visual maturation.

INTERACTION OF CONTOURS AND COLORS

Kohler devised two-toned spectacles in which each eye piece consisted of two halves, a blue left half and a yellow right half, separated by a vertical dividing line down the center of each filter. The arrangement allowed mutually antagonistic stimulation to impinge on the same retinal area and opposite aftereffects to be linked with the direction of gaze, left or right. The amazing result was an alternating adaptation to blue (looking to the left) and to yellow (looking to the right). How can this gaze-contingent aftereffect be explained?

There is undoubtedly an important set of interconnections between eye dominance, eccentricity of gaze, and contours in the visual field.

The remarkable influence of contours in producing brightness and color contrasts is made clearly visible by the use of colored anaglyph or diplopia goggles such as those used by ophthalmologists in which one eye gets a filter of one color, say red, and the other eye, a filter of a different color, approximately complementary in wavelength, say green.

After wearing these anaglyph goggles for a few seconds the initial binocular color rivalry disappears and is replaced by a more nearly neutral appearance of the general illumination. Now natural object colors are seen as long as both eyes remain open and convergence is normal. Close one eye or the other and the color reverts to that passed by the particular filter in front of the seeing eye. Adaptation in the single eye takes place slowly, if at all, but when the spectacles are removed, successive negative contrast effects are clearly evident if each eye is alternately opened and shut.

When one wears the anaglyph goggles and both eyes are open, the fluctuating colors rapidly stabilize, the general illumination appears neutral, and objects resume their natural colors. Adaptation to the red and green filters appears to be complete. The result is color constancy.

But place an object or dividing contour anywhere within normal convergence distance and a remarkable thing happens. At once the field behind the object splits up into two or more distinct color regions. If the filter on the left eye is green and the filter on the right eye is red, then objects to the left of the fixated contour are shifted toward green, and objects to the right of the fixated contour are shifted toward red. The object or contour in the center is seen with its true color. As this object is moved from left to right the green color shifts with it. Conversely, moving the object from right to left carries the red across the field in the opposite direction and eradicates the green. Oblique movements of the object convey the same effects.

A double or multiple contour in the field of binocular convergence gives rise to double or multiple colors. For example, if you look at a sunny window or a bright artificial light through the spread fingers of the hand in front of the eyes, you see alternately green, red, green, red patches of light in the V's formed by your fingers, which themselves maintain their normal flesh tones. The split colors appear in the interstices or behind the near object. Their number and direction depend entirely on the number and direction of contours in the visual field.

The explanation of this phenomenon must be related to the mechanism of binocularly and monocularly driven cells, and the double images of objects which fall on non-corresponding points. When a contour permits proper convergence so that its image falls upon the region of clearest vision at the foveae, then the object is seen entirely as single and with binocularly fused color because the two images fall upon corresponding points of the two retinas. Impulses then converge upon binocular cortical cells. The images of objects farther or nearer than the point of fixation upon which the eyes are converged cannot fall upon corresponding points and therefore do not permit binocular fusion of their individual colors. In consequence the neural messages retain their separate monocular identity. We do not sense them without a particular kind of fixated object. In the absence of a specific contour as a motive for fixation convergence we are not aware of these double images any more than we see them in everyday life where we have learned to suppress them.

The existence of these double images, however, appears to be necessary for contrast colors to be seen, once the split color glasses are removed. The overriding importance of interposition as a cue for depth comes about as a result of this mechanism of binocular vision. The suppression of one of the double images by the dominant eye in response to the kinesthetic command to change binocular convergence is the key to depth perception. In this process, the programmed eye movements, "look to the left," or "look to the right," may become conditioned to color as they are already conditioned to the third dimension of visual space.

REHABITUATION IN PERCEPTION

In the unfamiliar world on the other side of the looking glass, Alice found that her old habits were in the way. They had first to be overpowered before new patterns could prevail.

Kohler's discussion (1964, Part II) of the processes involved in rehabituation makes telling use of introspection as a source of information about the processes of conditioning and reconditioning in behavior and perception.

In this reversed world, the use of the eye to guide walking is dangerous, Kohler points out. "The old habit (of visually guided initiation of movement) continues despite the spectacles but now to the disadvantage of the subject. Subject G. describes his impressions as follows: 'My feet don't go where I want them to . . . but I have the feeling that I'm walking straight ahead; only now and then I get grass under my feet, which I'm quite sorry for. . . .' His path taken with the intention of 'staying in the middle,' appears as a zigzag line. No wonder: the first little deviation was spontaneously 'corrected,' but since the visual field was reversed, the 'correction' was incorrect—until finally the error was obvious and the game (after reorientation) began once more" (p. 147).

"I should see the garden far better," said Alice to herself, "if I could get to the top of that hill: and here's a path that leads straight to it—at least, no, it doesn't do *that*—" (after going a few yards along the path, and turning several sharp corners), "but I suppose it will at last. But how curiously it twists! It's more like a corkscrew than a path! Well, *this* turn goes to the hill, I suppose—no, it doesn't! This goes straight back to the house! Well then I'll try it the other way."

And so she did; wandering up and down, and trying turn after turn, but always coming back to the house, do what she would. Indeed, once, when she turned rather more quickly than usual, she ran against it before she could stop herself. (Carroll, 1872)

In order to approach the Red Queen, Alice "thought she would try the plan, this time, of walking in the opposite direction. It succeeded beautifully" (Carroll, 1872).

Kohler (1964) explains:

. . . To control movements of this type the subject says to himself at every opportunity: "Always do the opposite, head into danger, walk in the direction that you want to turn away from. . . ." By this process he gradually develops a new set of habits and comes eventually to "see correctly." (p. 147)

The overcoming of the disturbance does not begin with vision but rather with touch (p. 149) [and, one must add, with kinesthesis]. Walking, avoiding obstacles, reaching, etc. become better and finally almost faultless after two or three weeks while visual experience—in other words, perception—still remains reversed. In these conditions, one cannot yet speak of perceptual adaptation, but only of a correction of behavior. But it is of greatest interest that the latter becomes a stepping stone for the former. This demonstrates that they are related in some fundamental way. The "how" of this relationship was indeed the primary question of the entire experiment, and the participants always waited expectantly for that moment in the experiment when "correct seeing" occurred for the first time. And this climax always takes place. But a peculiar route, one might almost say a "detour," is taken to get there. (p. 149)

False movements cannot be endured; the immediate necessity is correct behavior. Kohler shows us how this happens and then traces the transition from behavior to "correct seeing."

The process of rehabituation may be codified as a set of rules.

Rule 1. Don't think—*Act!* Conscious reasoning about the reversing spectacles and what was *really* right and *really* left was counter-productive (Kohler, 1964, p. 150).

Rule 2. Go the *other* way. Your first impulse is wrong. Command yourself to do exactly the opposite of what your eyes, on the basis of pre-experimental experience, direct. Head into obstacles, don't avoid them. (p. 151)

Rule 3. Slow down! "An affective tone of 'watch out . . .' does not stop false reactions but it does delay them. From this develops an important area of contact between vision and touch (and *kinesthesis*) which is the basis of the development of a new experience" (p. 151).

Rule 4. Revise *expectations*. "The only thing of relevance is "correct or incorrect," not "right" or "left" (p. 151). ". . . Eventually, there develops a kind of premonition, an expectation about this during the moment of reaching which predicts the result. . . . When dealing with corrections of *expectations*, we are nearing the initiation of correct seeing" (p. 152).

MECHANISMS OF TRANSFORMATION OF CONDITIONED RESPONSES

On what factors do these rules depend? We are beginning to understand the physiological mechanisms that underlie the transformation of conditioned responses. Of particular interest to an explanation of Kohler's discoveries is Konorski's (1967) theory of the formation of separate gnostic fields and their interconnections in the brain.

Konorski's (1967) theory of the formation of associations between different analyzers, especially vision and kinesthesis, provides a useful framework for understanding the rehabituation experiments. The interplay between our visual and proprioceptive afferent systems controls all our visual orientation in space. Even our mental visual images reflect this pervasive influence of proprioceptive associations. With both your eyes closed, observe how difficult, if not impossible, it is to imagine the right side of your room without turning your eyes to the right. The kinesthetic eye movements play a decisive role in visual spatial imagery.

Kohler's subjects had to reverse a lifetime of experience with specific visual-kinesthetic, visual-somesthetic and labyrinthine-spatio-visual associations. They had to form new habits antagonistic to the old firmly established associations or conditioned responses.

What appeared to be truly amazing was that the sensory aftereffects of tilt, curvature, size, shape, and color following prolonged wearing of the distorting spectacles were contingent upon specific eye movements (looking left or right, up or down) and also on specific conditions of stimulation (the general illumination, and the kinds of objects being observed).

"Again and again," Kohler wrote, "standards of size, angulation and movement within a single retinal area were found to vary, even though the stimulus remained the same" (1964, p. 122). Now the crucial question arises, why should this be so?

Although there was a time in the history of sensory psychology when there was a controversy about the validity of these observations—"How can vision ever be partly right, partly reversed?" (Harris, 1965, p. 432)—we now know enough about the physiological properties of the visual system to describe how the visual neural network is organized so as to bring about these situational aftereffects.

Observations that seemed bewildering—the apparently paradoxical split between, on the one hand, small, manipulable objects that normally appear in any position; and on the other hand, printed symbols, asymmetric letters and numerals, that show a greater resistance to rehabituation, are no longer surprising.

According to Konorski's (1967) ideas of the functional organization of the brain, we can discriminate between the formation of gnostic fields clustered around projective areas of each analyzer in various parts of the cerebral cortex and the formation of interconnections by long association pathways between these cortical areas. The gnostic fields, unlike the projective areas, have a categorical and not a topographical organization in the brain. All the possible stimulus patterns impinging upon a given afferent system belong to different categories determined by the elements of which they are composed. Within each category sets of neural units (gnostic units or unitary perceptions) represent the various biologically meaningful objects or patterns that the organism has experienced and recognizes.

The basis for perception is the stored neural representation of familiar patterns in the brain. I should like to call these recognition units "*cognons,*" in order to link *cognition* to the biological units, the *neurons.* These recognition units are divided into particular categories within each modality, sight, hearing, touch, and so on, where they form the subjective standards for perception, judgment and imagination.

For instance, the visual pattern system contains categories representing human beings, animals, small manipulable objects, large movable objects, and far-off scenes, mountains, landscapes. The visual space system categorizes spatial relations giving us near-far, above-below, left-right, in front-behind. The auditory system divides heard sounds into categories also—music, voices, spoken words, and noises of the external world.

Within each category there are a number of equivalent neural units representing the biologically meaningful stimulus patterns and objects that the individual has experienced and stored in memory. Following damage to the brain, a patient may lose the ability to recognize a whole category, human faces, for example, without impairment of visual recognition of other body parts, and with complete retention of auditory and other sensory capacity.

The visual system concerned with the spatial relations between the organism and the environment, and between various parts of the environment is of central interest to the experiments with goggles.

In the day-to-day world of familiar experience the subjective standards are formed under consistent conditions of eye and body position and movement (Kohler, 1964, p. 131). For each object, your hand, the face of a friend, a house, there is a certain "normal viewing distance"; its size at this distance becomes the standard size for this particular object. Not only size, but shape and orientation conform to the normal viewing angle and direction of gaze. When attention is directed to a familiar object, the subjective standard bends the immediate perception to this standard without regard for photographic accuracy. This is what accounts for the constancies of perception.

Under abnormal conditions of stimulation, the old subjective standards no longer fit any but the small, manipulable objects that ordinarily occur in any position, the cup, the clock hands, the chess piece, etc. These objects have no unique location or orientation. They are movable, and they are ordinarily seen not only from various distances, but also from different sides and in different locations in the visual field. However, other categories of objects, the letter B, print in general, faces, feet and shoes, are firmly associated with the subjective left-right, up-down, and normal viewing angle; these asymmetrical objects now "go the other way" (Kohler, 1964, p. 142).

As the subject adapts, his visual perception changes in a piecemeal fashion. Some parts of the visual field are perceived correctly; others remain reversed. "Vehicles driving on the 'right' (and the noise of the motor agreed) carried license numbers in mirror writing. A strange world indeed!" (Kohler, 1964, p. 155).

Yet Subject Grill went beyond this stage and eventually achieved almost completely correct impressions, even where letters and numbers were involved. Mirror reading became well established. Following removal of the spectacles the mirror world returned; "p's were seen as q's, b's as d's, and on a clock face 10:30 was read as 1:30" (p. 160).

This visual-spatial system operates in close correlation with the system of kinesthetic-spatial relations and with the vestibular system. The neurological evidence shows that it is located in the right cerebral hemisphere. Patients with lesions in the right brain lose their spatial images, being unable to locate big cities or familiar landmarks on a contour map, or to sketch their apartments, although the items themselves are well known to them.

The localization of language chiefly in the dominant left hemisphere provides an anatomical separation between verbalization and our visual orientation in space. Here is an explanation of Kohler's finding (1964, p. 150) that words failed to play a helpful role in rehabituation to inverted visual space. Hundreds of times during the day false movements and turns are taken by the subject who naturally seeks methods to control these wrong turns and zigzag paths taken with the intent to walk straight ahead. Like Alice, to succeed, the subject must influence his initial impulse by saying to himself at every opportunity: Always do the opposite, head into danger, walk in the direction that you want to turn away from (Kohler, 1964).

Behavior, no more than vision, is not corrected in one simple step, but in stages. The process of rehabituation teaches us that neither behavior nor perception is unitary—recoordination demands the formation of many separate new associations between voluntary movements and visual experience. Much that has been built up in the course of normal development can be discovered through the rehabituation experiment.

Not conscious reasoning, not talking to oneself about the reversed right and left, or the way things really are (*Rule #1*), but the method of commanding oneself to go where one does not want to; to raise the wrong foot; to run into obstacles head-on—that led to success (*Rule #2*).

Although Konorski (1967) knew Stratton's (1897) experiments and recognized their important value for studying the formation of associations (conditioned responses), it is unlikely that he was acquainted with the Innsbruck research or he certainly would have incorporated these remarkable studies in his 1967 monograph. To Konorski, the "substitution method" as he called it, that Stratton used, was simply to observe the effect of "replacing the expected perception by a quite different one" (Konorski, 1967, p. 218).

Some of the *non-verbal* associations that undoubtedly provided the basis for Stratton's and Kohler's adaptation to strange environments include: stereognostic-visual associations; somesthetic-visual limb associations; kinesthetic-visual associations (objects and signs); auditory-visual associations; and labyrinthine-spatio-visual associations (stabilization of the rubber world).

What is particularly impressive is the demonstration that behavior is corrected first; movements, reaching, walking, avoiding obstacles are adjusted to the changed world and the new motor adaptation becomes a steppingstone for correct *seeing*.

These prism studies clearly demonstrate the existence of what Kohler describes as "the complex interweaving of habits, built up throughout the course of life and almost inextricably 'boxed into' one another" (Kohler, 1964, p. 138).

How do these interconnected habit patterns get disentangled? Kohler's description of the rehabituation experiment shows us how "complex and variously resistant the components of the habit hierarchy can be;" how the "apparently 'simple habit' is built up from a 'network' of components of different 'depths' and how therefore it can never be altered as a whole" (p. 139).

Certain new habits are much easier to establish than others. Why is this so? Konorski's (1967) theory of the transformation of conditioned responses offers a plausible explanation. According to this view, the ease or difficulty of transformations depends on the strength of previous conditioning or past associations. "The so-called 'extinction' of a conditioned response is nothing but the substitution of a new reinforcement for the old one (in that case no- US for US)" (Konorski, 1967, p. 344). Firmly established associations are nearly indestructible; their susceptibility to suppression by fresher associations depends on the substitution of a new reinforcement antagonistic to the old one.

Conversely, it is relatively easy to reestablish or restore the old conditioned response. The old connections on which this conditioned response is built are already there; reverse training consists only in establishing their relative dominance over the newly formed connections.

In this process, whether reconditioning or reversion to the original conditioning, what chiefly matters in establishing an operant or instrumental conditioned response is the active performance of the movement. Of course, it is essential that a drive be present; the conditioned movement must be followed by drive reduction; and the conditioned movement must cease when the drive is satisfied. The formation of an association between two synchronous perceptions may occur only against the background of nonspecific (axodendritic) facilitatory influences exerted upon the neurons receiving the stimuli *(Rule #3)*. As Kohler points out, what is important in the experiments with goggles, is that the hand reaching out to grasp an object gets the object, i.e., that it reaches correctly. If it fails, the subject experiences a strong emotional attitude of annoyance or frustration.

Konorski's ideas about the kinesthetic analyzer are especially relevant here, because this analyzer provides both feedback from self-produced active movements and feed-forward, that is, it plays the role of programming devices for skilled motor acts *(Rule #4)*.

Once the kinesthetic "cognons" for particular acts have been established, these units now begin to function independently of the sensory input to which they owe their formation and can mediate higher order habits without sensory input. Rule #4 evokes William James' idea that the image of a movement (Kohler's "expectations," 1964, p. 152) is an agent eliciting that movement. When the image of a movement is not followed by that movement, it must be because at that moment the corresponding motor units are already engaged, being blocked by antagonistic units.

"In the kinesthetic-spatio-visual association the decisive role is played, not by the *feedback* of the eye movement performed, but by the very programming of that movement in the kinesthetic gnostic field" (Konorski, 1967, p. 222).

Kohler points to some new habits that are much easier to establish than others. The reason for rapid success in such acts as cutting, filing, and soldering is that the subject has never seen *himself* doing certain things and so does not possess the corresponding images in his visual file. Antagonistic expectations are absent. His locomotor behavior, going down the street, turning the corner, whether on foot, bicycle, or skis is controlled, however, by the alternation of visual and kinesthetic images, especially eye movements of his motor acts. These images contradict the required new patterns and Kohler found that it was much easier for his subjects (including himself) to move in a well-known space with their eyes closed than with them open. "There exist movements for which seeing is a luxury" (Kohler, 1964, p. 144).

Similarly, when a retinal image is compared to an expectation formed by experience a deviation from expectation may be interpreted as color. Hohmann and von der Malsburg (1978) offer this explanation for the prismatic fringes and also for the McCollough effect (McCollough, 1965). They write: "Our central nervous system (CNS) possesses in every situation, a precise description of the colour fringes produced by chromatic aberration in the eye. Objective colour near the edges can only be perceived as a deviation from this "expectation". The chromatic fringes change with certain physical parameters which determine the condition of the eye. The CNS must 'know' the functional dependence of the expected colour fringes on these parameters. If this functional dependence is experimentally manipulated, then the brain can readapt by new learning. Subjects with prisms in front of their eyes report seeing color fringes in white light, because chromatic aberration is changed and no longer corresponds to the expectation. After a few days of continued exposure to prisms, the fringes disappear, showing that the CNS is able to return to changed eye optics'' (p. 551).

CONCLUSIONS

If we compare Kohler's experimental alterations of the perceptual world with certain others since tried out with cats and monkeys using monocular alternation and deprivation, reverse suturing, exposure to abnormal environments, and artificial squint, we reach the following conclusions:

1. One can certainly change the organization of the visual system by prolonged deprivation or exposure to certain kinds of stimulation.

2. The effects of these experimental alterations may be permanent or reversible, depending upon the age of the subject and the duration of the critical period of susceptibility. There is no adaption to induced squint that precludes the coordinated activity of the eyes. It is as though the two eyes must have the opportunity to work together to ensure the connections needed for binocular vision.

3. There are strong associations between motor actions, kinesthetic programs, and visual experiences that may have variable optical consequences (such as alterations in the perceived size, form, spatial direction, or color of objects). The conditioned responses established by lifelong experience in the familiar world are more or less resistant, more or less susceptible to reversal by the substitution of antagonistic unconditioned stimuli or reinforcements. Rehabituation can be achieved by the previously experienced organism given the conditions of drive and self-produced activity that satisfies the drive. Changes in preservative and protective motor behavior precede "correct seeing."

4. After removal of the distorting goggles variable aftereffects occur and persist depending on the strength of the newly conditioned responses. Ordinarily, restoration of the original conditioned responses in the mature subject is achieved rapidly relative to the adaptation to the abnormal environment.

5. Situational or conditioned aftereffects do not occur as an all-or-none phenomenon but the changes in "subjective standards" are determined by a wide range of factors involving independent categories of perception units built up by specific experiences.

6. The use of Konorski's theory as a framework into which to fit the results of neurophysiological studies and Kohler's experiments with goggles provides the synthesis of two points of view desired by Kohler, that of *situational aftereffects* and that of *conditoned sensations*. Both lines of investigation show how Alice

gets to the 8th square by twists and turns and the determination to see herself become Queen Alice at last.

7. Kohler's brilliant insight was to see that neither behavior nor perception is unitary; in both motor activity and visual experience the adaptation to a distorted world is stepwise and complex, just as in the formation of the normal perceptual and behavioral world, ". . . the apparently simple habit" is in fact "complex"—"built up from a 'network' of components of different 'depths' and therefore can never be altered as a whole" (Kohler, 1964, p. 139).

REFERENCES

Blakemore, C., Garcy, L. F., & Vital-Durand, F. The physiological effects of monocular deprivation and their reversal in the monkey's visual cortex. *Journal of Physiology*, 1978, *283*, 223–262.

Blakemore, C., & Van Sluyters, R. C. Reversal of the physiological effects of monocular deprivation in kittens: Further evidence for a sensitive period. *Journal of Physiology*, 1974, *237*, 195–216.

Carroll, L. *Through the looking glass and what Alice found there*. Philadelphia: George W. Jacobs Co., 1872.

Creutzfeldt, O. D., & Heggelund, P. Neural plasticity in visual cortex of adult cats after exposure to visual patterns. *Science*, 1975, *188*, 1025–1027.

Fiorentini, A., Ghez, C., & Maffei, L. Physiological correlates of adaptation to a rotated visual field. *Journal of Physiology*, 1972, *227*, 313–322.

Freeman, R. D., Mitchell, D. E., & Millodot, M. Neural effect of partial visual deprivation in humans. *Science*, 1972, *195*, 1384–1386.

Gardner, M. *The annotated Alice by Lewis Carroll*. Great Britain: Fletcher & Son Ltd., Penguin Books, 1965.

Gilinsky, A. S. Masking of contour detectors in the human visual system. *Psychonomic Science* 1967, *8*, 395–396.

Gilinsky, A. S. Orientation-specific effects of adaptation on visual acuity. *Journal of the Optical Society of America*, 1968, *58*, 13–18.

Gilinsky, A.S., & Mayo, T. H. Inhibitory effects of orientational adaptation. *Journal of the Optical Society of America*, 1971, *61*, 1710–1714.

Harris, C. S. Perceptual adaptation to inverted, reversed, and displaced vision. *Psychological Review*, 1965, *72*, 419–444.

Hohmann, A., & von der Malsburg, C. McCollough effect and eye optics, *Perception*, 1978, *7*, 551–555.

Hubel, D. H. Eleventh Bowditch Lecture, Effect of distortion of sensory input on the visual system of kittens. *The Physiologist*, 1967, *10*, 17–45.

Hubel, D. H., & Wiesel, T. N. Receptive fields, binocular interaction and functional architecture in the cat's visual cortex. *Journal of Physiology*, 1962, *160*, 106–154.

Hubel, D. H., & Wiesel, T. N. Receptive fields of cells in striate cortex of very young, visually inexperienced kittens. *Journal of Neurophysiology*, 1963, *26*, 994–1002.

Hubel, D. H., & Wiesel, T. N. Binocular interaction in striate cortex of kittens reared with artificial squint. *Journal of Neurophysiology*, 1965, *28*, 1041–1059.

Hubel, D. H., & Wiesel, T. N. Brain mechanisms of vision. *Scientific American*, 1979, *241*, 150–162.

Kohler, I. Experiments with goggles. *Scientific American*, 1962, *206/15*, 63–72.

Kohler, I. The formation and transformation of the perceptual world. (trans. by H. Fiss) *Psychological Issues,* 1964, 3(4), 1–173, Monograph 12. New York: International Universities Press.

Konorski, J. *Integrative activity of the brain.* Chicago: University of Chicago Press, 1967.

McCollough, C. Color adaptation of edge-detectors in the human visual system. *Science,* 1965, *149,* 1115–1116.

Mitchell, D. E., Freeman, R. D., Millodot, M., & Haegerstrom, G. Meridional amblyopia: Evidence for modification of the human visual system of early visual experience. *Vision Research,* 1973, *13,* 535–558.

Movshon, J. A., & Dürsteler, M. R. Effects of brief periods of unilateral eye closure on the kitten's visual system. *Journal of Neurophysiology,* 1977, *40,* 1255–1265.

Olson, C. R., & Freeman, R. D. Progressive changes in kitten striate cortex during monocular vision. *Journal of Neurophysiology,* 1975, *38,* 26–32.

Stratton, G. M. Vision without inversion of the retinal image. *Psychological Review,* 1897, *4,* 341–60.

Stromeyer, C. F., III, Kronauer, R. E., Madsen, J. C., & Cohen, M. A. Spatial adaptation of short-wavelength pathways on humans. *Science,* 1980, *207,* 555–557.

Woodworth, R. S. *Experimental psychology.* New York: Henry Holt, 1938.

An earlier version of this chapter was printed in *Acta Neurobiol. Exp.* 1981, *41,* 491–408.

2 Ivo Kohler's Poretic Psychology and the Viennese Connection

Erling Eng
Psychology Service
VA Medical Center
Lexington, Kentucky

Erfahrung ist nur die Hälfte der Erfahrung.

—Goethe

Strait is the gate.

—Matt. 7, 14

ABSTRACT

Ivo Kohler's experiments with prolonged wearing of distorting spectacles which alter the habitual integration of visual perception with bodily movement generate a psychology which may be termed "poretic,"[1] from the Greek *poros*, meaning passageway, ford, contrivance. This also relates it to, and differentiates it from the philosophical *aporia*, or impasse, and *hodos*, the beaten path of method, as in "*meta hodos*." A poretic psychology focuses on the process in which the circular interplay of experimental action and vigilant observation constantly secures a path between the equally impossible extremes of repetition and innovation.

Kohler's demonstration of dehabituation and rehabituation as complementary processes in bodily orientation represents an extension of the ideas of Ewald Hering to the sphere of action. A nexus of Kohler's experimental research with depth psychology, which Kohler has suggested, may be seen in the figure and influence of Josef Breuer. Breuer was an early co-worker with Hering, and later, as is well-

---

[1] "Poretic" is my own term for Ivo Kohler's unique contribution to an experimental evolutionary psychology, one implicit in Hering's physiological psychology. Its explicit sense will be developed later in this chapter.

known, with the young Freud. Freud has acknowledged his debt to both Hering and Breuer. Thus it is not surprising that we find certain likenesses between the perceptual action experiments of Kohler and Freud's clinical therapeutic procedures.

THE VIENNESE CONNECTION

Ivo Kohler closes his monograph, *The Formation and Transformation of the Perceptual World* (Kohler, 1964) with these words: "The attentive reader will have noticed that some of the observations described here stand in a peculiarly intimate relation to depth psychology . . . However, this is a topic that deserves its own investigation" (p. 164).

Earlier in the same work Kohler had noted, in discussing his own findings, that "Hering's theory of autoplastic and alloplastic equilibrium in the assimilation of nervous substances serves as a superb model" (p. 25). This reference to "autoplastic and alloplastic" which recalls Freud's and Ferenczi's employment of the same terms in their metapsychological period, provides a clue to the connection of Kohler's work with psychoanalysis.

Let us consider more closely those genealogical connections which link Ivo Kohler's experimental investigations with the clinical discoveries of Freud. This is made possible by new historical evidence that Josef Breuer provided not only a decisive impetus for Freud in his discovery of psychoanalysis, but that he imparted to Freud the scientific approach of Ewald Hering, Breuer's own mentor and co-worker.

Ewald Hering today is far from being as well remembered as his scientific rival, Hermann von Helmholtz. This may derive in large part from the way in which Helmholtz's physical explanation of visual experience, in contrast to Hering's insistence on the autonomy of the physiological, has fitted in better with the preference for spatial and quantitative models in scientific explanation. Hering's insistence on the subjective features of color experience also put him in the company of Goethe, although the poet's observations on the phenomena of color experience had been a source of inspiration for such physiologists as Johannes Müller and Purkinje. Even Helmholtz took up Goethe's *Farbenlehre,* if only to dismiss it.

Ewald Hering (1844–1918) is best known for his theory of color vision. Unlike Helmholtz, who assumed three visual substances corresponding to three basic colors, Hering hypothesized six different colors deriving from three visual substances, each one capable of producing a complementary pair of colors, depending on the relative predominance of an "assimilative" anabolic process, or a "dissimilative" catabolic process. He viewed this kind of complementarity as characteristic of physiological regulation in various functions, for example, bodily temperature, and nerve and muscle action. In opposition to Helmholtz,

Hering also argued that each point of the retina is endowed with three local signs, one for height, another for right and left, and a third for the dimension of depth, either positive or negative, accounting for stereoscopic vision (Boring, 1950, p. 353). Hering's guiding idea, that of the self-regulation of physiological processes, led him to anticipate our present understanding of inhibition and "feedback." This is shown most clearly in his discovery, with Josef Breuer, of respiratory self-regulation through the reflex reaction of the vagus nerve, known to this day as the Hering-Breuer reflex (Porter, 1970). Hering analyzed a wide range of physiological self-regulations in terms of temporal differentiation and integration of latent and active phases of function. His understanding of physiology also included consciousness as a source of relevant data. In accord with the importance he gave to the depth of latent functions in ongoing activity, he considered memory to be a fundamental character of living organisms. This was the theme of Hering's historically famous address to the Imperial Academy of Sciences in Vienna in 1870. His position was that it is indefensible for the neuropsychological investigator of memory to confine himself exclusively to either a physical or a psychological approach, but that he must "take his stand between the physicist and the psychologist" (Hering, 1870/1924, p. 72). From this standpoint, which assumed "the functional interdependence of matter and spirit, it is possible for modern physiology to bring the phenomena of consciousness into the domain of its investigations without leaving the *terra firma* of scientific methods" (p. 73).

If this passage is first of all reminiscent of Freud's neurological prelude to his "psychoanalysis," which he variously located between biology and psychology, or between medicine and philosophy, it is not by chance. There is clear evidence for Freud's continuing interest in and use of Hering's ideas in *Beyond the Pleasure Principle* (Freud, 1920), where he sought to establish the fundamentals of his psychoanalysis: "According to E. Hering's theory, two kinds of processes are constantly at work in living substance, operating in contrary directions, one constructive or assimilatory and the other destructive or dissimilatory. May we venture to recognize in these two directions taken by the vital processes the activity of our two instinctual impulses, the life instincts and the death instincts?" (p. 49). The extent of Hering's importance for Freud is suggested by Freud's remark in his paper on "The Uncanny" (Freud, 1919) from the same period. "Or suppose one is engaged in reading the works of the famous physiologist, Hering, and within the space of a few days receives two letters from two different countries, each from a person called Hering, though one has never before had any dealing with anyone of that name" (p. 238). Another sign of Hering's fundamental importance for Freud is contained in Anna Freud's German translation, published in 1926, of Israel Levine's book, *The Unconscious,* which came out in England in 1923 (Levine, 1923/1926). Freud himself translated one part on Samuel Butler, and then added this explanation of a reference in the text to Hering's 1870 lecture (Strachey, 1926/1957):

German readers, familiar with this lecture of Hering's and regarding it as a master-piece, would not, of course, be inclined to bring into the foreground the considerations based on it by Butler. Moreover, some pertinent remarks are to be found in Hering which allow psychology the right to assume the existence of unconscious mental activity: "Who could hope to disentangle the fabric of our inner life with its thousandfold complexities, if we were willing to pursue its threads only so far as they traverse consciousness? . . . Chains such as these of unconscious material nerve-processes, which end in a link accompanied by a conscious perception, have been described as 'unconscious trains of ideas' and 'unconscious inferences'; and from the standpoint of psychology this can be justified. For the mind would often slip through the fingers of psychology, if psychology refused to keep a hold on the mind's unconscious states." (p. 205)

In this citation by Freud from Hering, the reference to "unconscious material nerve-processes" assumes a standpoint not merely between physics and psychology, as in the earlier passage from Hering, but one that lies between physiology and psychology. This would also parallel Freud's placement of psychoanalysis between biology and psychology (Freud, 1913, p. 182; 1914, pp. 50, 78–79). But even more is entailed in Freud's passage from Hering. Hering's metaphor of linkage, with its shift from "unconscious material nerve processes" to "conscious perception," cannot be understood in a simply linear causal manner. The notion of "unconscious material nerve processes" implicitly includes the conscious perception of the scientist, whether physiologist or psychologist. Hence the analytic term "unconscious material nerve processes" *presupposes* conscious perception. Moreover, conscious perception *also presupposes* analytically distinguishable "unconscious material nerve processes." The physiological, for both Hering and Freud (and as we shall see, for Kohler) is important for the way in which it entails the property of latent complementary function, essential for self-regulating, i.e., autonomous movement.

Although Hering, like Helmholtz, followed in the path of Johannes Müller, his approach differed from that of the biophysical movement of Müller's other disciples such as Brücke, Helmholtz, Ludwig, and Dubois-Reymond, author of the "Ignorabimus" manifesto. For another of Hering's teachers had been G. T. Fechner, founder of "psychophysics", one to whom Freud repeatedly professed indebtedness for his Constancy Principle (Freud, 1920, pp. 8–10; 1923, p. 47; 1924, p. 159; 1925, p. 59). Although Hering, like Brücke, the young Freud's scientific paragon, was also antivitalistic, his approach differed. For Hering it was a matter of "fundamental knowledge, not to view life as a physical and chemical mechanical process, but to do justice to the self-activity, autonomy and purposiveness, and to recover this general characteristic in all specialized expressions" (Tschermak-Seysenegg, 1934, pp. 132–33).

Freud's exposure to Hering's orientation was not limited to his acquaintance with Hering's writing, nor to common influences. More important perhaps was Freud's working relationship with Breuer. After Brücke, it was Ewald Hering who was Breuer's most important teacher and scientific collaborator (Hirschmüller, 1978, pp. 56–57). Considering Hering's approach, in which quantification was combined with phenomenologically informed analysis, it might be expected that this would be most effectively transmitted through personal example in joint research. Hirschmüller (1978), who has made a valuable documentary contribution to the prehistory of psychoanalysis, provides us with this impression of Breuer's scientific style:

> Where do we find the sources of Breuer's conceptions? Naturally they also lie in that physiological way of thinking and experimental instrumentation that he acquired with Brücke and Hering, no less than in his thoroughgoing mathematical-natural science training. But to me what appears decisive is the encounter of these factors with a biological theory which proceeds from the purposive, meaningful structure of organisms, from regulatory processes in the service of optimal functioning. Experimental technique, natural science training, and natural philosophical premises of this sort, brought together in a personality with the patience, preseverance and intellectual capacity of Breuer, are for me the essential sources of his scientific achievement (p. 120).

Elsewhere Hirschmüller refers to experiments by Breuer in which he also acted as subject. This is consistent with his view of the importance of self-regulation and purpose for an adequate understanding of human physiology and psychology. The *Selbstversuch,* incidentally, defines not only the line of descent of Hering, Breuer, and Freud, but also that of Hering, Erismann (who was Kohler's teacher), and Kohler. This tradition extends back through Fechner's ''psychophysics,'' to Johannes Müller's ''phantastic visual appearances,'' and to Goethe's *Farbenlehre.* Such a ''sensitive empiricism'' (Goethe) was converted into a therapeutic method when Freud discovered a way of teaching it to his patients.

PORETIC PSYCHOLOGY: FINDING ONE'S WAY

Ivo Kohler's major contribution to psychology, in the path of Theodor Erismann, has been to show, through ingenuity, precision, and personal courage, the conditions and character of what he has called the ''situational'' or ''conditioned aftereffect.'' Prolonging the period of exposure to experimental conditions far beyond the short-term investigations of Hering, he has demonstrated that long-term habituation to the wearing of visually distorting spectacles produces physiological and psychological responses conditioned to head and eye movements, and by implication to other intentional movements. Retinal processes and positions of the eye are endowed with different significations for behavior, depending on their inclusion in one or another activity pattern of individuals in the everyday world. The issue of nativism versus empiricism, familiar from late nineteenth century thinking about perception, turns out to have been valid for only a relatively superficial level of analysis.

Through Kohler's research these unexpected residuals of unconscious conditioning over extended periods of time are disclosed as lawful, however complexly derived, acquisitions, constituted both ontogenetically and phylogenetically. The quasi-pathological distortions of visual perception represent the aftereffects of various kinds of bodily movement. Meanings attached to particular places and processes of the retina are slowly modified within the context of new, more encompassing patterns of adaptational activity. Kohler's experiments demonstrate how lower order bodily functions are, within limits, modifiable in terms of the meaning with which their participation in one or another structured intentional perspective endows them. Lower order events of the organism change in meaning, in how they are represented, according to the parts they can play in different hierarchically structured activities.

Because of the way Kohler's method of visual interference deconstructs perceptual-motor integrations, it also provides a model for behavioral thinking about psychopathology. Now the latter can be likened to the wide variety of sign representational disorders, with accompanying affects, which occurred both in subjects' adaptation to Kohler's distorting spectacles, and in readaptation after their removal. Careful, resolute, persevering self-movement in the everyday world gradually resulted in the disappearance of the initial perceptual distortions, as they gradually yielded to the behavioral norms of reality. What might have been naively experienced by the subject as "pathological" was shown to be the consequence of the necessarily gradual character of any modification of one's historically structured activity in the historical life world.

Kohler's experiment may be compared with the classical situation in psychoanalysis in a number of ways. First, both involve suspension of customary visual perception. The analysand reclines, while the all but anonymous analyst remains out of view. This has a dehabituating effect, like that produced by Kohler's inverting, reversing, or colored spectacles. Second, Kohler found that the habitual image, which persisted into the newly modified visual situation, functioned as a "resistance" to relearning. Yet, like Freud, he learned that reintegration could be facilitated by providing a cautious kind of assistance, one which facilitated "sublimation" (Kohler, 1964, p. 151). Third, during the period in which the vacillating, "ambivalent" subject suffered from discrepancies both within the visual order and between the information provided by different senses, Kohler, similar to the analyst, escorted the patient (Kohler, 1964, pp. 11, 31, 37). Finally, Kohler's subjects, like analysands, were encouraged to recount as fully as possible their observations both during the dehabituation and rehabituation phases of the experiment.

From a psychoanalytic position, what is omitted from Kohler's account of his experiments is any notice of pathological phenomena which proved resistive to self-correction, any consideration of the importance of the experimenter's presence, or of the behavioral significance of the subjects' self-reports during the experiment.

Kohler's monograph suggests a rather more lucid way of understanding psychoanalysis than is ordinarily the case. Kohler's approach, in the context of evolutionary thought, is consistent with Freud's attempt to account for the therapeutic action of psychoanalysis in his late paper on "Analysis Terminable and Interminable" (Freud, 1937, pp. 209–254). Both approaches assume Hering's view that mechanism and self-regulation are not in conflict, save under exceptional conditions. Ordinarily they supplement each other; self-activity and its context tend to become routine and involuntary, as previous learning flows into emergent patterns of activity. It is only when the situation changes too swiftly, with abrupt alterations of body, others, or world, that dissociation, or "splitting," between new and old activities occurs. This may give rise to contradictory behaviors of the same individual. There is also the likelihood of confusion and dissociated physiological arousal, resulting from breakdown of the self-integrative rhythm of assimilation and dissimilation at one or more levels of organization. Kohler discovered that effective relearning under these conditions calls for deliberate, cautious initiatives, avoiding excessive focus on any single part of the decentered, disorderly field. He would likely also acknowledge that his subjects' acquaintance with their fellows' success in the same situation encouraged them to persevere.

The experiment of Kohler provides a simple model for one way of thinking through the idea of "the unconscious" in psychoanalysis. If we consider Freud's view that Hering's assimilatory and dissimilatory processes are his own "life instincts" and "death instincts," and that these correspond to the nascent activity and habituated past, respectively, of Kohler's analysis, "the unconscious" can then be understood as both creative and destructive, providing new meanings, even while representing norms of reality taken in a broadly biological sense. The "trauma" or "traumatic situation" in psychoanalysis may be seen as corresponding to the estrangement of reality produced by Kohler's distorting spectacles. It is their removal (by the analytic situation) which makes possible the discovery and dissolution of a "traumatic" experience through a derangement of the false perspective. Now a regenerated vision, one of richer reality, emerges through the secondary distortions resulting from the removal of the distorting spectacles, here standing for the perspective of an historically invalidated self. Only then can the earlier "traumatic" effect be identified as the consequence of an incompletely lived-through relationship or situation. The experienced distortions are analogous to those in Kohler's experiment, which resulted from the subjection of perception to fragmentary images in the foreground of attention. Such images are also more assimilatory or autoplastic, than they are dissimilatory or alloplastic, i.e., informative of the world or another. While earlier beliefs are dissolving, bodily urges, both pleasurable and unpleasurable, both originary and defensive, conditioned to intentionalities linked with beliefs, are released into consciousness, sometimes accompanied by inexplicable, confusing, and even uncanny effects.[2]

And yet a decisive biological point has been omitted. Throughout life regulatory norms are constantly changing. The kind of learning and relearning necessitated by growth and aging, and which Freud in part considered in his developmental theory of the libido, was not included in the plan of Kohler's research. It was with the traces and residues of such developmental crises in ontogenetic learning and relearning that Freud was more deeply concerned. These are of particular importance in understanding the possibility of psychosis.

Kohler's monograph reminds us of the extent to which the "wisdom of the body" reaches into the domain of the psychological. It's work reveals the presence in perceptual imagery of the life of the body, both conscious and unconscious. In this way it has a kinship with the contributions of two men with whom Freud's late thought is linked: Sandor Ferenczi and Georg Groddeck. It was from Groddeck that Freud took over the notion of "Id" (das Es), while modifying Groddeck's usage to suit his own tripartite structural-economic theory. Both Ferenczi and Groddeck, like Kohler, emphasized the patient's capacity for self-direction in the analytic situation, dubious of what they saw as the doctor's tendency to dominate the analytic situation (Groddeck, 1950, pp. 208–14). Ferenczi, Freud's longest and closest associate, borrowed the terms "autoplastic" (or assimilative) and "alloplastic" (or dissimilative) from Hering; they served him as physiological equivalents for the life (Eros) and death (Thanatos) instincts of Freud. Ferenczi and Groddeck both saw "trauma" as disturbance in the course of a self-regulative growth process having its own particular direction, within which difficulties are manifested as symptoms (Ferenczi, 1916/1939, pp. 89–94; 1919/1939, pp. 129–147).

The reorganization of the self as bodily movement in Ivo Kohler's work is one of finding one's way between mutually responsive extremes of self and world. Thus, it may be called a "poretic" psychology, i.e., one which focuses on the passage of the embodied individual from one context of creative participation to another. Its root, *poros,* or way, strait, contrivance, not only contrasts with the "aporias" of philosophy, but alludes to Socrates' account of the birth of Eros in the *Symposium.* There we are told that the parents of Eros were Penia (poverty) and Poros (contrivance).[3] Poros as "contrivance" is discovery of the way through an impasse. In a situation of need, it refers to the way found within the

---

[2]Ivo Kohler repeatedly refers to subjects' uncanny feelings in the course of his experiments (Kohler, 1964, pp. 35, 69, 90).

[3]In Greek, "poros" contrasts with the other principal word for way, "hodos," as in "meta hodos" (method). While "poros" refers to ford, strait, passageway, "hodos" is the well-traveled, beaten way, or highway (Becker, 1937, pp. 15–34). In deliberate contrast to the use in philosophy of "aporia" as impasse, I use "poretic" to refer to the improvised narrow way itself, one constituted en route. This is intimately linked with the original Greek sense of "empirical" (Ortega y Gasset, 1971, pp. 152–156).

difficulty itself. A hint of the medieval "homo viator" shines through the empirical analyses of *The Formation and Transformation of the Perceptual World.*

A poretic psychology differs from psychoanalysis in its recognition of forgetting as of no less importance than memory in our preservation of reality. We are continuously reliant on the intentional possibilities of memory as structure. We depend on life having its own memory, as Hering emphasized (Hering, 1870/1924, pp. 82,86,88,94). This was the assumption that underlay his dissimilatory process, which is a kind of forgetting of inner impulsions within a new activity. It also appears to be the sense of Groddeck's notion of the "postconscious" ("nachbewußt") (Groddeck, 1923/1977, pp. 77–81). The "postconscious" is implicit in the outcomes of all training whatsoever, forming the basis of every exceptional human achievement. This is a kind of "storage" on which every genial accomplishment depends, the obverse of that other kind of forgetting marked by relapse to a lower level of accomplishment. Creative achievement involves forgetting in this positive sense. Such self-constitutive forgetting is paramount in Kohler's position, in contrast to the rather more limited way of considering forgetting frequent in psychoanalysis.

THE WAY OF CREATION

Ivo Kohler's relearning experiments reach beyond those of Hering, both through their setting in the everyday world, as well as by virtue of their greatly extended time span. From the other direction, assuming the time span of phylogeny, Freud attempted, in his theory of libidinal evolution, to approach relearning in terms of individual bodily development (Freud, 1905). Ferenczi even attempted a speculative history of phyletic learning in his "Bioanalysis," which Freud differentiated from his own "Psychoanalysis" (Freud, 1933, pp. 228–229). In *Beyond the Pleasure Principle* Freud (1920) speculatively retraced the time of organic memory to the point where life emerged from the pre-organic, Fechner's "cosmorganic" matter, a Rubicon whose trace the organism still retains. It is within such a hierarchical scheme of expanding temporal subjectivities, concentrically organized, that Kohler's researches find their place. Such an evolutionary frame not only points back from Freud to Lamarck, but also forward from Hering to Kohler.[4]

Ivo Kohler has demonstrated how higher order intentionality may instruct bodily process, complementary to the way in which such process also grounds

---

[4]Even Darwin's "Natural Selection" has a place in this hierarchy of self-constituted subjects, namely as the process through which the world persists in time. The emergence of species is evidence for the assimilatory-dissimilatory process in the continuation of the world, Darwin's "Nature." This parallels Hering's self-regulating retinal process, Kohler's self-reorienting experimental subject, or Freud's ontogenetic libido.

intentionally organized action in the life world. He has enriched our differentiated understanding of *Gestalten,* both as considered in Gestalt psychology and as they relate to Husserlian phenomenology.[5] He has shown by experiment the depth to which "being in the world over and beyond the world" (Binswanger, 1953, p. 675ff.) informs bodily activity in everyday life.

REFERENCES

Becker, O. *Das Bild des Weges und verwandte Vorstellungen in frühgriechischem Denken.* (Hermes Einzelschriften, Nr. 4). Berlin: Weidmann, 1937.

Binswanger, L. *Grundformen und Erkenntnis menschlichen Daseins.* Zweite Aufl. Zürich: Max Niehans Verlag, 1953.

Boring, E. *History of experimental psychology.* New York: Appleton-Century-Crofts, 1950.

Ferenczi, S. *Über Pathoneurosen. Bausteine zur Psychoanalyse* (Vol. 3), Bern: Huber, 1916–1939.

Ferenczi, S. *Hysterische Materialisationsphänomene. Bausteine zur Psychoanalyse* (Vol. 3). Bern: Huber, 1919/1939.

Freud, S. *Three essays on the theory of sexuality* (Standard Edition, Vol. 7). London: Hogarth Press, 1905.

Freud, S. *The claims of psychoanalysis to scientific interest* (Standard Edition, Vol. 13). London: Hogarth Press, 1913.

Freud, S. *On narcissism: an introduction* (Standard Edition, Vol. 14). London: Hogarth Press, 1914.

Freud, S. *The uncanny* (Standard Edition, Vol. 17) London: Hogarth Press, 1919.

Freud, S. *Beyond the pleasure principle* (Standard Edition, Vol. 18) London: Hogarth Press, 1920.

Freud, S. *The ego and id* (Standard Edition, Vol. 19) London: Hogarth Press, 1923.

Freud, S. *The economic problem of masochism* (Standard Edition, Vol. 19). London: Hogarth Press, 1924.

Freud, S. *An autobiographical study* (Standard Edition, Vol. 20). London: Hogarth Press, 1925.

Freud, S. *Sandor Ferenczi.* (Standard Edition, Vol. 22) London: Hogarth Press, 1933.

Freud, S. *Analysis terminable and interminable* (Standard Edition, Vol. 23). London: Hogarth Press, 1937.

Groddeck, G. *The meaning of illness.* London: Hogarth Press, 1977. (Originally published, 1923.)

Groddeck, G. *Exploring the unconscious.* London: Vision, 1950.

Hering, E. On memory as a general function of organized matter. In S. Butler (Ed. and trans.), *Collected works* (Vol. 6). London: Cape, 1924. (Originally published, 1870.)

Hirschmüller, A. *Physiologie und Psychoanalyse im Leben und Werk Josef Breuers.* (Jahrbuch der Psychoanalyse, Beiheft 4.) Bern: Huber Verlag, 1978.

Kohler, I. Gestaltbegriff und Mechanismus. In F. Weinhandl (Hrsg.), *Gestalthaftes Sehen Ergebnisse und Aufgaben der Morphologie.* (Festschrift zum 100. Geburtstag von Christian v. Ehrenfels.) Darmstadt: Wissenschaftliche Buchgesellschaft, 1960.

Kohler, I. The formation and transformation of the perceptual world. *Psychological Issues,* 1964, *3* (4), Monograph 12. New York: International Universities Press.

---

[5]Kohler's Gestalt approach to problem solving has an affinity with Max Wertheimer's heuristic Gestalt psychology, though with shift of emphasis to the bodily sphere. With regard to the issue of embodiment, see Zaner's lucid treatment of Husserl's inadequacies in understanding Gestalten (Zaner, 1979). Zaner's interpretation of Husserl's "stratified Gestalten" is also closely akin to Kohler's idea of "Systemgestalten" (Kohler, 1960).

Kohler, I. Gestaltbegriff und Mechanismus. In F. Weinhandl (Ed.), *Gestalthaftes Sehen*. Darmstadt: Wissenschaftliche Buchgesellschaft, 1967.

Levine, I. *The unconscious; an introduction to Freudian psychology*. New York: Macmillan, 1923.

Levine, I. *Das Unbewusste*. Uebersetzung von Anna Freud. Leipzig: Internationaler Psychoanalytischer Verlag, 1926.

Ortega y Gasset, J. *The idea of the principle in Leibnitz and the evolution of deductive theory*. New York: Norton, 1971

Porter, Ruth (Ed.) *Breathing: Hering-Breuer Symposium*. London: Churchill, 1970.

Strachey, J. et al. (Eds.) *Editors appendix A. Freud and Ewald Hering*. (Standard Edition, Vol. 14). London: Hogarth Press, 1926/57.

Tschermak-Seysenegg. Zu Ewald Herings 100. Geburtstag. *Münchener Medizinische Wochenschrift*, 1934, *81*, 132–133.

Zaner, R. The field-theory of experiential organization: A critical appreciation of Aron Gurwitsch. *Journal of the British Society for Phenomenology*, 1979, *10*, 141–152.

THEORY

3 Adaptation in a Peephole: A Texton Theory of Preattentive Vision

Bela Julesz
Bell Laboratories
Murray Hill, New Jersey

ABSTRACT

In preattentive texture perception only conspicuous local features (called textons) of *elongated blobs* (*lines*), with certain orientations, widths, lengths and colors, their *terminators* (*ends of lines*), and their *crossings,* can be perceived; the relative position between these textons is ignored. Thus, outside a narrow peephole of focal attention one cannot distinguish, for example, an *L* from a *T*. What is more, for complex scenes, up-down and left-right reversals have no effect on the textons and their densities; therefore outside the minute disc of attention even without adaptation no perceptual change can be noticed. All the adaptational phenomena of Kohler are probably restricted to this disc of attention. Often this disc is a small fraction of the fovea. This simplification might establish a close link between two seemingly remote paradigms.

INTRODUCTION

We are all students of great men, whether we realize it or not. Indeed, it took me 20 years to become aware of the deep relationships between Ivo Kohler's and my own work. I had assumed that Kohler and I were using totally different methods to investigate virtually unrelated issues. But recent developments in my thinking have revealed that Kohler's ingenious techniques may permit extension of my inquiries into areas that hitherto seemed beyond feasibility. Conversely, some of my conclusions about texture perception may help shed a somewhat different light on some of Kohler's striking discoveries.

Of course, I was a great admirer of Kohler's work when I first encountered it during the period of my metamorphosis from a communication engineer into a psychologist. However, I had discovered the method of computer-generated random-dot stereograms before this metamorphosis (Julesz, 1960). Furthermore, I myself have never worked with mirror or prism goggles. So I was not consciously aware of any connection between Kohler's work and my own until I wrote *Foundations of Cyclopean Perception* (Julesz, 1971). The primary purpose of that book was the exploration of "psychoanatomy," the separation of peripheral processes from central ones, by using cyclopean techniques to operationally by-pass earlier stages and directly stimulate the "cyclopean retina." As I tried to distinguish peripheral (hypocyclopean) phenomena from central (hypercyclopean) ones, I realized that I was following Kohler's precedent, although he used the strength of adaptation effects to perform his version of psychoanatomy. He assumed that the longer lasting ("far-reaching") aftereffects revealed more central phenomena at work than the shorter lasting ("superficial") ones (Kohler, 1964). Only recently, after devising the "texton" theory of preattentive texture perception (Julesz, 1981) in response to a problem that has kept me and my co-workers busy for many years (Julesz, 1962), did I suddenly realize that there may be much deeper relations between my work and Ivo Kohler's. This brief chapter tries to give the flavor of this insight. I hope that it will illustrate the influence that Kohler's beautiful experiments can have on seemingly unrelated domains of inquiry.

TEXTONS AND THE TWO VISUAL SYSTEMS

Let me offer here a brief account, with some demonstrations, of the ideas and phenomena that link my work to Kohler's. (A much more complete account may be found in my recent review article [Julesz, 1981].)

We know from much evidence, collected by workers in perception and cognition, that our vision is carried out by two visual systems. The preattentive visual system processes certain features in our visual environment in parallel, therefore without effort and almost instantaneously. In general, if stimuli are presented in the retinal periphery, or if they are presented in the fovea too briefly to permit scanning, only the preattentive system is engaged. Since it is a parallel system, its operation seems to be independent of the number of visible objects that share those features that have to be detected. The second system, called the attentive visual system, works serially; it can process many objects or certain complex features only by scrutinizing the visual environment in piecemeal fashion, that is scanning it through a small aperture of either focal or focal attention. Therefore, the attentive system's detection time of an element increases with the number of elements in the stimulus array. An excellent treatment of this preattentive/attentive dichotomy is given by Treisman (1979, pp. 301–330) and Treisman and Gelade (1980), with many references.

I had this notion of the "two visual systems" as early as 1962, albeit in implicit form, when I introduced the paradigm of instantaneous, or effortless, texture discrimination as opposed to detailed, element-by- element scrutiny. A texture pair, for example, with different first-order statistics of black, white, and gray picture elements appeared strongly and instantly segregated with well localizable boundaries, whereas a texture pair composed of an array of English words versus nonsense words required word-by-word scrutiny and recognition, and still no boundary could be perceived between the two word arrays (Julesz, 1962). My present version of the "two visual system" is only a refinement of this original dichotomy and shares many ideas with the theory of Treisman (1979, pp. 301–330) and Treisman and Gelade (1980). Treisman, however, derived her theory through the concepts of cognition, and her "features" and their "conjunctions" are not fully specified, whereas in my theory the "textons" and their "interactions" through first-order statistics are precisely defined.

The term "two visual systems" has been explicitly coined by Held, Ingle, Schneider, and Trevarthen (1967–68) to distinguish failures in locating from those of discriminating patterns when lesions in the striate cortex, superior colliculus, or pulvinar were *anatomically* present. In hamsters the distinction between "where" and "what," as mediated by the superior colliculus versus the striate cortex, was impressively demonstrated by Schneider (1969), and Diamond and Hall (1969). The elegant observations by Trevarthen (1968) on split-brain monkeys (with totally split cortical hemispheres but intact subcortical connections in the midbrain) also argue in favor of an ambient/focal dichotomy. However, it is questionable to what extent my *psychologically* defined distinction between preattentive and attentive systems can be related to findings based on *anatomical* concepts involving neural impairments. Furthermore, Trevarthen's ambient midbrain system is a rather crude localizer for vertebrate locomotion and eye-movement control while, as I explain in my preattentive system studies, the texton changes are accurately localized in the visual field (though not their relative positions) and focal attention can be shifted to minute patches even within the fovea when eye movements are prevented. Thus, it is most likely that both our preattentive and attentive systems rely heavily on striate cortex processing.

Regardless of how the various "two-visual system" theories differ, we have a consensus that only in a small patch of focal attention can we tell what patterns we see. This is the basic idea that I try to develop in this chapter.

My texton theory of preattentive vision assumes a parallel system that can instantaneously detect differences in a few conspicuous features, which I have called "textons," without detailed scrutiny. I have shown (Julesz, 1981) that the preattentive system can count only the number of textons and ignores their relative positions, therefore two figures or textures with the same texton content cannot be distinguished without serial search by focal attention. Figure 3.1A clearly demonstrates the focal attention mode used by the two visual systems for processing the feature of "connectivity." In Fig. 3.1A one of the two line drawings is connected, whereas the other is not. However, the complexity of these line drawings prevents us from effortlessly perceiving which of them is the connected one. Instead, we have to scan these stimuli point by point with our limited "disc of attention," and it might take minutes to be able to distinguish the connected line drawing from its disconnected partner. In Fig. 3.1B the two line drawings are less complex, i.e., contain fewer elements; the connected and disconnected line drawings appear to be effortlessly discriminated. However, in an 80 msec brief flash, followed by masking, even these figures cannot be distinguished.

The reason why even the simple line drawings in Fig. 3.1B are not "simple" enough to be preattentively distinguishable are explained at the end of this section. Here, I note only that perceptual simplicity requires that the distinguishable patterns should differ in one or more textons. However, the two line drawings in Fig. 3.1B contain the same textons, so the preattentive system cannot distinguish them. Each focal attention shift requires about 50 msec (Bergen & Julesz, 1981), therefore at least 100 msec is necessary to inspect the two drawings in detail. In order to demonstrate outside the laboratory that these figures

A   B

FIG. 3.1.   Attentive texture discrimination: (A) Deciding which of the two complex figures are "connected" requires detailed scrutiny by focal attention. (From Minsky & Papert, 1968. *Perceptrons,* 1968, p. 73. Reprinted by permission of MIT Press.) (B) When the figures are "simple," deciding which of the two is connected appears effortless, yet in a 80 ms brief presentation cannot be done, since both figures contain the same textons.

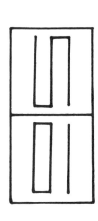

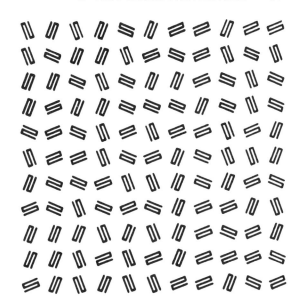

FIG. 3.2. Preattentively indistinguishable texture pair (composed of dual elements depicted in Fig. 3.1B) demonstrating that if the line segments and the number of their terminators (ends-of-lines) agree, their exact positions are ignored. (Julesz, 1980. Reprinted by permission from *Philosophical Transactions of the Royal Society, 1980, B 290, 87.*)

are, indeed, preattentively indistinguishable, let us take the S and 10-shaped figures of Fig. 3.1B and make a texture pair by randomly placing them without overlap as shown in Fig. 3.2 (Julesz, 1962, 1981). Now, the texture pair so derived is preattentively indistinguishable. If we were not told that the array is composed of two apparently distinct elements, we most probably would have perceived it as one uniform texture. Only after element-by-element inspection are we able to tell the two arrays apart. Thus, the preattentive system cannot distinguish textures by the "connectivity" of their elements. Since the S and 10-shaped dual elements differ also in the property of "closed" versus "open," we can conclude that this feature difference does not yield preattentive texture discrimination.

Let me stress that the element-by-element scrutiny in trying to find the S and 10-shaped elements in Fig. 3.2 requires either focal or foveal attention shifts. When the texture array is large and is presented for long durations, foveal scanning by eye movements might suffice. However, a few dozen of the S and 10-shaped elements can be presented scaled down such that they fall entirely on the foveal disc (but the individual elements are still large enough to be resolved separately). Under such "overloading" of the fovea no texture discrimination can be obtained in a brief presentation. Yet, with *focal* attention one can concentrate on a single element within the fovea. Similarly, when the array of Fig. 3.2 is enlarged so that it covers extended portions of the periphery but for only 160 msec or less, and the observer is fixating on the center array, no foveal scanning can occur. Yet, the observer can delegate his focal attention to any desired element in the array in about 50 msec steps, and might detect each one by one. (For details see Bergen and Julesz, 1981.) The important point is that preattentive versus attentive perception should not be confused with peripheral versus foveal vision. This problem is discussed further in the Epilogue.

In 18 years of work with my collaborators we were able to find hundreds of texture pairs that were preattentively indiscriminable, although their elements in isolation appeared very distinct. Here I demonstrate only one other such texture pair (Fig. 3.3) that is especially relevant to this chapter. One texture in Fig. 3.3 consists of *R*'s in any orientation thrown at random, whereas the dual texture is composed of similarly arranged mirror-image *R*'s (Julesz, 1965; Julesz, Gilbert, Shepp, & Frisch, 1973). We have shown in general (Julesz, 1965) that the preattentive system cannot distinguish mirror-image transformation if the num-

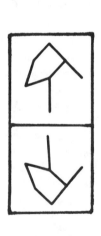

FIG. 3.3.   Preattentively indiscriminable texture pair with identical textons. The dual textures are comprised of *R*'s and their mirror-images, respectively. Thus mirror-imaging (e.g. left-right reversals) is an invariance transformation for preattentive and peripheral vision. (Julesz et al., 1973. Reprinted by permission from *Perception*, 1973, *2*, 397.)

ber of elements is adequately large to form textures. If we simultaneously present a dozen or so micropatterns, we cannot perceive in a brief flash whether one or more of the micropatterns are the mirror-images of the rest.

As of now we have seen indistinguishable texture pairs whose elements looked very different. However, textures in real life usually are easily discriminable. Indeed, there are some very special local properties—the "simple" features of preattentive texture perception I have called "textons" (Julesz, 1980, 1981)—that are conspicuously apparent even in our peripheral vision and regardless of the number of objects if they differ in such textons! So far I have found a few classes of textons: (1) *elongated blobs* (line segments) of specific width, orientation, length and color; (2) *terminators* (ends-of-lines) of these elongated blobs (line segments); and (3) *crossings* of elongated blobs (Bergen & Julesz, 1981). Since local *binocular disparity* changes can be perceived in a brief presentation of 50 msec, and *movement disparity* and *temporal flicker* of local elements can also be perceived during the same brief duration, these three conspicuous local features can be regarded as texton classes, too. However, we restrict ourselves here only to static visual scenes. The preattentive visual system can count only the number (or density) of these textons but ignores their relative positions. Thus, the reason why in Fig. 3.2 the texture pair composed of S and 10-shaped dual elements could not be distinguished was that the dual elements were composed of the same textons. Indeed, the line segments' length, width, and orientation that formed these dual elements were identical, and their numbers (densities) and the number of their ends-of-lines also agreed. Similarly, in Figure 3.3 the mirror-image transformation preserves the density of corresponding textons; only their relative positions to each other change. Since the preattentive visual system ignores the phase (position) information, the texture pair in Figure 3.3 appears indistinguishable.

If the density of these textons changes, then they immediately stand out throughout the visual field. For instance, in Fig. 3.4, a texture pair is shown whose dual elements contain the same line segments, but have two versus five terminators. This difference in texton density renders the texture pair preattentively discriminable (Fig. 3.4). What is more, a texton difference yields such a strong preattentive discrimination that even a few single elements dispersed in a large number of specially chosen dual elements (sharing the same textons but one) are conspicuously apparent. For instance, in Fig. 3.5 the dispersed three-pronged micropatterns are clearly perceivable among many dual triangle-shaped micropatterns because they differ in two textons: first, in the number of their terminators (three versus zero); second, the triangles trigger large blob detectors while their dual partners do not. Obviously, if the micropattern duals differ in the other textons, that is have different line orientations, widths, lengths, or colors, they will also be preattentively perceived anywhere in the visual field regardless of the number of micropatterns.

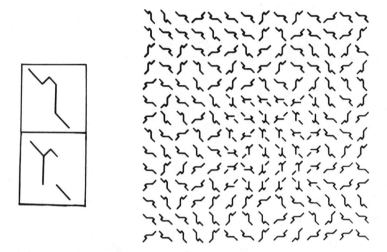

FIG. 3.4. Preattentively discriminable texture pair with identical line segment width, length, orientation, and number, but a different number of terminators (Julesz, 1980. Reprinted by permission from *Philosophical Transactions of the Royal Society*, 1980, *B 290*, 87.)

FIG. 3.5. In case of texton differences (here the number of terminators and elongated blobs), even single elements can be discriminated among many dual elements.

Perhaps the best way to memorize these findings is that a single L or many L's are preattentively indistinguishable when dispersed among many T's (or vice versa), provided the vertical and horizontal line segments that form these figures have the same width, length, and orientation and a small gap is introduced to avoid corners. A typical such indistinguishable texture pair is illustrated by Fig. 3.6. Since the number of their ends-of-lines also agrees, and the "coupling" that locks these texton detectors in their proper positions is missing for the preattentive system, such dual elements are indistinguishable (similar to the cases depicted by Figs. 3.2 and 3.3). *Only in a very small disc of focal attention are the different texton detectors coupled together, enabling us to perceive the relative phase (position) between textons.*

In summary, only those areas in which the textons or their densities differ from their surrounds can be detected by the preattentive system regardless of the complexity (i.e., the number of elements) of the visual environment. However, the relative position between textons cannot be preattentively perceived. One has

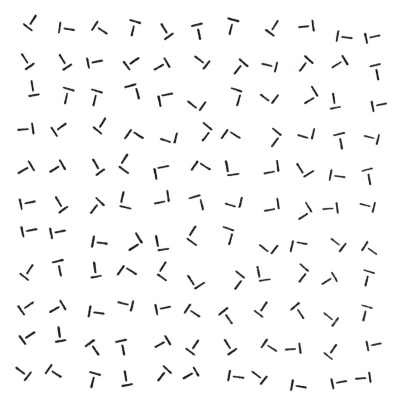

FIG. 3.6.   Indistinguishable texture pair composed of T- and L-shaped micropatterns (with a small gap), showing that relative position between the adjacent perpendicular line segments (textons) is ignored in preattentive vision.

to shift attention to these conspicuous areas and only in a minute disc of focal attention are the textons coupled, permitting us to perceive complex relations, such as, say, the difference between an *R* and its mirror-image, or in general recognize form.

Returning to our question of perceptual "simplicity," very complex perceptual relations can be perceived for the attentive system if the stimulus (that possesses these relations) fits inside a small disc of focal attention. For instance, a Chinese character is such a complex pattern that fits into our disc of attention. During the act of reading one has to inspect such characters one by one as a time-consuming serial process. The preattentive system cannot process complex perceptual relations. As a matter of fact, it cannot even tell an *L* apart from a *T* (Fig. 3.6). Only if the perceptual relation is *simple*, constituting a *texton difference*, can it be easily detected by the preattentive system. The preattentive system can instantaneously detect such texton differences as a parallel system, regardless of the number of textons.

PRISM ADAPTATION AND TEXTONS

In reading Kohler's fascinating accounts of his experiments on adaptation to inverting and reversing goggles, I was always amazed and puzzled by the ability of the visual system to completely "rearrange" itself to recreate normal perception. What a feat it seemed to reconnect all of the many millions of receptors to the many millions of cortical cells! Now, however, my discoveries with textons lead to the suggestion that the amount of rearranging needed may be orders of magnitude less than that. (I am aware that J. R. Harris and C. S. Harris in this volume argue that a very large part of adaptation to reversal is kinesthetic rather than visual. Nevertheless, Kohler's rich and varied observations perhaps still leave room for extensive visual adaptation, especially in the later stages.) When I use "reconnecting," I do not mean some low-level reorganization, and instead "relearning" or "adaptation" could be equally substituted.

What the studies of textons suggest is that instead of functionally reconnecting the entire retina in order to correct reversed perceptions, only a tiny fraction calls for revision . . . because the rest does not yield reversed perceptions even at the start! As we have discussed (and demonstrated) outside the disc of focal or foveal attention, only differences in textons or in their densities can be perceived. For complex visual environments with many objects, up-down and left-right transformations do not change the orientation, width and length of elongated blobs (line segments) or their densities or number of terminators and crossings; therefore the entire visual field can undergo such transformations, and except for a minute disc of attention the observer will be totally unaware of these drastic manipulations. So, when one puts on the mirrors or prisms for the first time, outside a "peephole" of attention no perceptual change should occur. Only in this peephole of attention, where the textons are coupled, is it important to establish new couplings. This "relearning" seems a much less demanding task if it is limited to a very small area, and restricted to rotations and mirror transformations.

Perhaps these findings might correspond to a fascinating observation by Kohler (1951). He reported that after prolonged adaptation to right-left reversal, the observer would still perceive objects under scrutiny as being reversed (e.g. the license plate of a car). Obviously, unscrutinized objects outside our disc of attention are not affected by reversal, particularly if these objects are many and adquately similar to form textures. Some quick bursts of focal attention shifts or foveation by scanning eye movements will reveal that certain objects or texture elements are upside down, but for unfamiliar objects or texture elements these glimpses of reversal are perhaps not as critical as for familiar objects, particularly for letters and numbers.

In all previous arguments I assumed that the observer was surrounded by a rich visual environment, with many objects having a texture-like quality. Obviously, for a giant face, the loci of large texton density changes; for example, where the eyes or the mouth are located would alter their positions when presented upside down (although the skin and hair would retain their texture character). The invariance under reversal for such large and familiar objects cannot be handled directly by my texton theory. Nevertheless, I believe that even for such large stimuli, there are relatively few places of large texton changes that call for serial scrutiny by focal attention. Furthermore, if the strength of texton differences were related to the probability of inspecting the strongest texton changes first, followed by the inspection of the weaker ones in diminishing order, then this order of scanning by focal attention could remain invariant under reversal.

Adaptation to color fringes can be interpreted in a similar vein. The color fringes are adjacent textons of parallel elongated blobs (line segments) of certain colors whose exact position to each other is immaterial outside focal attention. Within the disc of focal attention, the exact order of the color textons is "relearned," new couplings established. Again, only a very limited area of the visual field is affected, and the relearning is also limited to the positional order of a few parallel colored line segments.

This is only a brief sketch of how the texton theory could be applied to various adaptation effects. It would be a lengthy undertaking to work out all the details. For instance, we used the so-called four-disc method (Julesz, Gilbert, Shepp, & Frisch, 1973) to generate indistinguishable texture pairs in spite of very different "open" and "closed" dual elements (see Fig. 3.7A). However, Caelli and I (1978) were able to further open up the "open" micropattern, without affecting the compactness of the "closed" dual partners. This results in a strongly discriminable texture pair (depicted in Fig. 3.7B) based on "quasi-collinear" discs that are absent in the other texture. The critical curvature of the quasi-collinear discs is a well-defined quantity giving the threshold of preattentive texture dis-

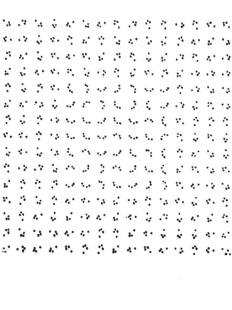

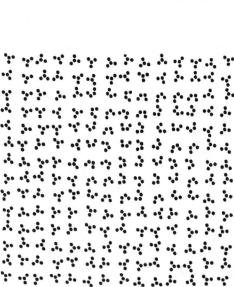

FIG. 3.7. (A) Texture discrimination based on quasi-collinear disks. Just below threshold of preattentive texture discrimination the features have too much curvature; (Julesz et al., 1973 Reprinted by permission from *Perception*, 1973, 2, 397.) (B) Above discrimination threshold; the quasi-collinear features are present in one texture, but absent in the other texture. (Caelli & Julesz, 1978. Reprinted by permission from *Biological Cybernetics*, 1978, 28, 166–69.)

crimination. Here again one might suggest that the weaker wedge prisms of Kohler that cause little curvature of lines with rapid adaptation correspond to the quasi-collinear textons. Since lines and quasi-collinear lines appear similar in preattentive vision, for small wedges, the adaptation effects are again restricted to the focal disc of attention, where initially small curvatures in lines are noticed.

CONCLUSIONS

As of now, it appears that I applied the new theory of textons to explain Kohler's findings. Of course, the possibility that textons might be of use to account for some aspects of his adaptation phenomena is a great satisfaction to me. However, here I want to stress the active contribution of the Kohler paradigm to clarify some of my own problems. For two decades I limited myself to preattentive vision, since I thought that the second visual system of focal attention is too complex for study. Now I see how one can extend the study to focal vision using the Kohler paradigm. If one systematically explores all the transformations that can be adapted to (in a few weeks), a deep understanding of the focal attentional system can be obtained. Obviously, one could extend the transformations beyond up-down and left-right reversals. These transformations kept the textons invariant for *all* possible objects. Perhaps, if one were to limit the visual environment to *specially selected* objects, for instance to objects that possess the same symmetries (e.g. centric or bilateral symmetries, or symmetries for 60 degree rotations), the adaptational requirements could be eased, and new adaptable transformations could be found, or the time of adaptation would be considerably shortened? Perhaps, for an impoverished environment having objects with identical textons, the course of adaptation might reveal how the positional relations between textons are established in the peephole of attention. Since the visual extent of this area can be a thousand times less than the entire visual field, the study of form vision by the attentive system might be a less prodigious feat than I previously believed.

In summary, Kohler placed the most ingenious devices over the eyes to rotate, mirror, split, or alter the spectrum of the visual environment. Perhaps the only trick he has not used was to limit all these manipulations to a small peephole that would either follow our gaze or would be yoked to our shifts of attention. Luckily, such devices need not be built; they are permanently attached to our eyes. The positional insensitivity between textons outside this peephole automatically takes care of all the perceptual invariances under up-down and left-right transformations for complex visual scenes. If this insight of mine is proven correct, an important link will be established between two remote fields of vision. But regardless of whether my speculations are valid, Kohler's beautiful experiments will continue to impress experimentalists and theoreticians for many years to come and will guide researchers to an understanding of attentive perception.

EPILOGUE

Let me clarify a few essential points that could be misunderstood. First, I could give only the flavor of the texton theory, and the interested reader may consult my recent review article (Julesz, 1981). In this review I also compare the texton theory with the "early sketch" model of Marr (1976). Marr used elongated blobs and terminators to construct higher perceptual units he called "place tokens," but did not guess that in preattentive vision no such higher percepts are used since the relative positions between textons are ignored. Nevertheless, I hope that the demonstrations may convince the reader that in complex environments with many objects, those transformations that keep textons invariant are also perceived as being invariant.

Second, and more importantly, my dichotomy of preattentive versus attentive vision should not be confused with peripheral versus foveal vision, although most of the time these two coincide. The "peephole" of attention, therefore, is not always the foveal disc. We have already discussed that the foveal disk can be overloaded by several dozen individually resolvable elements and that at any given instant only a single element can be scrutinized by *focal* attention within the 2 deg arc diameter foveal disc. In such a case the peephole of attention might be only a few minutes of arc in extent (Bergen & Julesz, 1981). This explains why the line drawings of foveal extent in Fig. 3.1A require elaborate scrutiny by focal attention.

When large arrays of elements are presented in the periphery for very brief durations with their afterimages masked, one can still detect a single element at a given location by delegating focal attention to that spot (provided the element is large enough to be resolved). What probably happens is as follows: If the textons that make up the elements are similar (e.g., the same size), then the texton detector pool containing these critical textons will be highly activated, and the observer can inspect in detail any texton in this pool, or some other similar textons in the same neighborhood at a given instant. If these textons are small, then the peephole of focal attention will be small. If the textons are large, then the peephole will be large. So the observer can vary the size of his focal attention to match the size of the elements as long as the elements have similar sizes. Thus, obviously, the "disc" of attention need not be circular, but can be an "aperture" of some shape. If the size of the elements greatly differs, then the observers have great difficulty in attending focally, as the important study by Sperling and Melchner (1978, pp. 675–686) shows. For each additional shift of focal attention 40–60 msec is needed, which is about four times faster than the latency for executing a saccadic eye movement.

In common daily usage, when our visual environment does not change rapidly and the elements to be inspected are not so small to overload the foveal disc, then we can scrutinize with our fovea using eye movements. In this case our peephole has a 2 deg arc diameter.

Thus, our peephole of attention can vary from a few minutes of arc to a few degrees, depending on the detail in the visual field. The important point is that this peephole is always a fraction of the extent of our entire visual field. One might argue that this restriction does not buy us much, since the majority of cortical representation is limited to the central 2 deg arc of the retina. Here again I have to stress that attentive vision is not foveal vision. When the fovea is overloaded only a minute area of the fovea can be in the attentive state.

In essence, I propose the possibility that in the Kohler paradigm subjects can spend long periods in the preattentive state, and very often the object-fragments that drift into their peephole of attention are not adequately familiar to be noticed as being inverted. And, of course, outside this peephole the reversal of objects passes unnoticed.

REFERENCES

Bergen, J., & Julesz, B. Discrimination with brief inspection times. *Journal of the Optical Society of America*, 1981, *71*, 1570

Caelli, T., & Julesz, B. On perceptual analyzers underlying visual texture discrimination: Part I. *Biological Cybernetics*, 1978, *28*, 167–175.

Diamond, I. T., & Hall, W. C. Evolution of neocortex. *Science*, 1969, *164*, 251–262.

Held, R., Ingle, D., Schneider, G. E., & Trevarthen, C. B. Locating and identifying: Two modes of visual processing. *Psychologische Forschung*, 1967–1968, *31*, 44–62; 299–348.

Julesz, B. Binocular depth perception of computer-generated patterns. *Bell System Tech. Journal*, 1960, *39*, 1125–1162.

Julesz, B. Visual pattern discrimination. *IRE Transactions on Information theory*, 1962, *IT-8*, 84–92.

Julesz, B. Texture and visual perception. *Scientific American*, 1965, *212*, 38–48.

Julesz, B. *Foundations of cyclopean perception.* Chicago: University of Chicago Press, 1971.

Julesz, B. Spatial nonlinearities in the instantaneous perception of textures with identical power spectra. *Philosophical Transactions of the Royal Society, London*, 1980, *B 290*, 83–94.

Julesz, B. Textons, the elements of texture perception, and their interactions. *Nature*, 1981, *290*, 91–97.

Julesz, B., Gilbert, E. N., Shepp, L. A., & Frisch, H. L. Inability of humans to discriminate between visual textures that agree in second-order statistics—revisited. *Perception*, 1973, *2*, 391–405.

Kohler, I. Über Aufbau und Wandlungen der Wahrnehmungswelt. Insbesondere über 'bedingte Empfindungen.' "*Österreichische Akademie der Wissenschaften, Philosophisch-historische Klasse; Sitzungsberichte* 227, Band. I. Abhandlung. Wien: Rohrer, 1951.

Kohler, I. The formation and transformation of the perceptual world. *Psychological Issues*, 1964, *3*, 28–46, 116–133, Monograph 12. New York: International Universities Press.

Marr, D. Early processing of visual information. *Philosophical Transactions of the Royal Society, London* B, 1976, *275*, 483–524.

Minsky, M., & Papert S. *Perceptrons.* Cambridge, Mass.: M.I.T. Press, 1968.

Schneider, G. E. Two visual systems: Brain mechanisms for localization and discrimination are dissociated by tectal and cortical lesions. *Science*, 1969, *163*, 895–902.

Sperling, G., & Melchner, M. J. Visual search, visual attention, and the attention operating characteristic. In J. Requin (Ed.), *Attention and performance VII.* Hillsdale, N.J.: L. Erlbaum Associates, 1978.

Treisman, A. The psychological reality of levels of processing. In L. S. Cermak & F. I. M. Craik (Eds.), *Levels of processing and human memory*. Hillsdale, N.J.: L. Erlbaum Associates, 1979.

Treisman, A., & Gelade, G. A feature-integration theory of attention. *Cognitive Psychology*, 1980, *12*, 97–136.

Trevarthen, C. B. Two mechanisms of vision in primates. *Psychologische Forschung*, 1968, *31*, 299–337.

4 Visual Form Perception Based on Biological Filtering

Arthur P. Ginsburg
Aviation Vision Laboratory
Human Engineering Division
Air Force Aerospace Medical Research Laboratory
Wright-Patterson Air Force Base, Ohio

ABSTRACT

A filtering approach to understanding visual perception is shown to provide a framework for understanding certain aspects of how we see contrast, size, and form in simple gratings and letters as well as more complex visual illusions and portraits. Gestalt laws of closure, wholeness, proximity, and similarity are demonstrated using filtered images. Complex variations in the perceived magnitude of Müller-Lyer illusions are well predicted from computer data based on biological filtering. A physics of form perception is used to relate the detection and identification of Snellen type letters to individual contrast sensitivity functions. These results suggest that biologically based filtering and linear systems analysis, typified by Fourier techniques, can provide important tools with which to probe the foundations of our visual world.

INTRODUCTION

There are many physical aspects of vision that must be considered in understanding how we see. The physical properties of the mechanisms that process selected ranges of stimuli provide both the limits and capabilities of vision. The visual system cannot simultaneously process all the information about objects that are seen. For example, the fact that greatest acuity occurs in a region of about only two degrees of visual angle, the fovea, suggests that considerable data reduction occurs at the initial sampling stages in vision. However, even the large amounts of data reduction found in the peripheral retina, which create only a coarse image

53

of our visual world, still provide sufficient information for maintaining contiguity of form. One way to view data reduction is in terms of filtering, that is, the selective processing of certain information. This view raises a question: Can the concept of filtering be useful in understanding the visual system? Measurement of the sine-wave response to quantify the overall filtering characteristics of the visual system has been used extensively by many scientists over the last 15 years (Breitmeyer & Ganz, 1976; Campbell, 1974; DeValois & DeValois, 1980; Robson, 1975; Schade, 1956; Sekuler, 1974). The sine-wave of the visual system, typified by contrast sensitivity functions (CSF: the reciprocal of contrast needed to make sine-wave gratings just visible), have been used to predict the detection of complex one-dimensional waveforms (Campbell, Carpenter, & Levinson, 1969) and checkerboard patterns (Kelly & Magnuski, 1975). Contrast matching and magnitude estimation techniques have also been developed to obtain suprathreshold sensitivity characteristics (Cannon, 1979; Georgeson & Sullivan, 1975; Hamerly, Quick, & Reichert, 1977; Watanabe, Mori, Nagata, & Hiwatashi, 1968). These techniques provide a family of bandpass filter functions for given viewing conditions such as mean luminance, retinal position and display size, from threshold to suprathreshold, which describe the "window" that limits the range of size of objects that can be seen.

The overall filtering characteristics of the visual system embodied by contrast sensitivity data has been related to the visibility of complex two-dimensional objects such as letters, aircraft silhouettes, and faces (Ginsburg, 1973, 1978, 1980; Ginsburg, Evans, Sekuler, & Harp, 1982). Therefore, by keeping the conditions that cause significant changes in the contrast sensitivity function (CSF) reasonably constant, the use of one set of contrast sensitivity data as a modulation transfer function (MTF) appears justified. Indeed, using this approach, an anisotropic two-dimensional MTF was made from one-dimensional contrast sensitivity data (Ginsburg, 1973, 1978, 1980). Some effects of filtering simple and complex objects using this filter will be shown here.

The next question that can be asked about the filtering characteristics of the visual system is whether the overall shape of CSF is the result of one or many filters. Many psychophysical and neurophysiological data have shown that there are quasi-independent, narrow-band mechanisms, called "channels," in the visual system tuned to a bandwidth of about one to two octaves in spatial frequency and about ±15 degrees in orientation (e.g. see recent review by DeValois & DeValois, 1980). Similar to color channels, by which visible light is decomposed into different ranges of spectral information, spatial channels decompose objects into different ranges of spatial information. This further stage of data reduction in the visual system, "spatial channels," can be simulated by bandpass filtering using filter functions that are based on biological data. The effects of channel filtering on a complex object, a portrait, will be shown here.

Fourier techniques are used in this chapter to filter objects biologically and determine bandwidths of perceptually related form information. The use of Fourier techniques by itself does not mean that the brain is doing similar processing. There is evidence, however, suggesting that certain cortical mechanisms may be reasonably described as piece-wise, discrete, local, finite Fourier-like analyzers (see Ginsburg, 1978, 1979, for discussion). Those arguments are not repeated here and the reader is cautioned not to interpret our use of Fourier techniques as evidence for or against a Fourier-like visual process. Further, the use of Fourier analysis and filtering is but one of several possible approaches to the study of vision. Recent reviews by DeValois and DeValois (1980) and Julesz and Schumer (1981) discuss other approaches which involve feature analysis and computational vision. The reader is encouraged to contrast other approaches and results to the data presented here.

In summary, major relevant questions about a filter approach to visual perception are: What are the filter characteristics of visual mechanisms? What are their bandwidths, center frequencies, and weighting functions? How do they extract forms we perceive? How do they combine to create the picture that we see? Once those questions are at least partially answered, How do cognitive processes select and interpret information from those filtered images? These are the kinds of questions that have been previously asked and will be briefly reviewed here in attempting to help solve many long-standing problems of vision: the perception of contrast, size and form, Gestalt laws, visual illusions, and finally, a theory of visual perception based on a hierarchy of filtered images.

PERCEPTION OF CONTRAST

One important and fundamental property of vision requiring understanding is the perception of contrast, the amount of lightness and darkness of the parts that create an object. Although there are many different definitions of contrast, the Michelson definition is typically used in the vision community for gratings: contrast = (Lmax−Lmin)/(Lmax+Lmin) where Lmax and Lmin are the maximum and minimum luminances, respectively. Certain spatial information about the parts of an object can be measured in terms of either size or its reciprocal, spatial frequency. Therefore, one of the most general descriptions about the visibility of an object can be expressed in terms of spatial frequency and contrast. But, does this description have predictive power in understanding how we see objects?

Linear processing of spatial vision has been amply demonstrated at threshold (see Campbell, 1974; DeValois & DeValois, 1980 for reviews). Linearity means that the response of a system to complex stimuli may be calculated simply by taking the sum of the responses of that system to individual simple stimuli. For example, Campbell and Robson (1968) showed that the threshold visibility of a square-wave grating could be predicted from the visibility of only the fundamental sine-wave component of the square-wave. For spatial frequencies above the peak sensitivity (typically about 1 to 5 cycles per degree, cpd), the threshold of a sine-wave grating was shown to be higher than that of a square-wave grating by a factor of $4/\pi$, or 1.27. Since the fundamental Fourier component of a square-wave is 1.27 times the peak-to-peak amplitude of the square-wave, these results suggested that the fundamental sine-wave rather than the peak-to-peak amplitude of the square-wave determined the detection of the square-wave. Although similar results were not found using lower fundamental frequencies, that model did predict the behavior of the visual system at threshold for spatial frequencies greater than those at peak sensitivity.

Although these results are of great interest, most of our perception of the visual world is spent above threshold. The question therefore arises as to how contrast is perceived for suprathreshold levels. Two techniques have generally been used to determine perceived suprathreshold contrast: contrast matching and magnitude estimation. Contrast matching requires the subject to adjust the contrast of one pattern until the perceived contrast matches that of another pattern (e.g. see Georgeson & Sullivan, 1975; Watanabe, Mori, Nagata, & Hiwatashi, 1968). The technique of magnitude estimation requires the observer to assign a number to the perceived contrast of the test object (Kulikowski, 1976; Cannon, 1979). Both techniques have been used to show that perceived contrast is a linear function, at least to a first approximation, of stimulus contrast for single sine-wave gratings over a wide range of contrast and spatial frequency (Kulikowski, 1976; Cannon, 1979).

Recently, these techniques have been used to determine how spatial frequencies and contrast interact in complex objects having more than one frequency component above threshold. Results show that the perceived contrast of a suprathreshold square-wave grating, similar to threshold results, also appears to be extracted in a linear fashion to a first approximation by quasi-independent mechanisms in the visual system (Ginsburg, Cannon, & Nelson, 1980). Both contrast-matching and magnitude-estimation techniques showed that the sine-to-square wave ratio for the equivalent perceived contrast is $4/\pi$ over a large range of contrast and spatial frequency. These results are shown in Fig. 4.1. The data points describe the sine-to-square wave ratio for both contrast-matching (triangles) and magnitude-estimation (circles) experiments. The horizontal dotted line is at amplitude $4/\pi$ in all panels.

These results suggest that there are mechanisms in the visual system able to extract contrast relatively independently of other spatial information found in the higher harmonics of an object. Furthermore, these results suggest that the higher harmonics that are needed for shape and degree of edge sharpness do not contribute greatly to overall contrast perception. Yet, observers perceive such a grating as being square-wave and having sharp edges. This implies that mechanisms in the visual system can selectively filter and use information in different ranges of spatial frequencies of an object depending on the particular task. This ability to select various spatial frequency components from an object supports a filter theory of perception (Ginsburg, 1971, 1978). Thus, one important aspect of form perception, the ability to generalize a form independent of its particular constituent parts, may be the result of attending to the information in one or more filtered

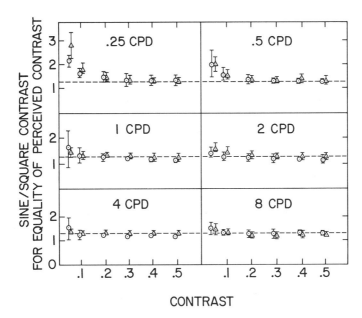

FIG. 4.1.   Data points describing the sine-square ratio for both contrast-matching (triangles) and magnitude-estimation (circles). The horizontal dotted line is at amplitude $4/\pi$ in all panels. These data demonstrate that the ratio is equal to $4/\pi$ over a large range of contrasts and spatial frequencies. These results suggest that supra-threshold contrast perception of square-waves is, to a first approximation, linear (from Ginsburg, Cannon, & Nelson, 1980).

images. This is the visual analogue to the "cocktail party problem" in audition where auditory attention can be shifted at will from speaker to speaker or some background noise. The visual analogue to this superposition of sounds is the superposition of channel-filtered images such as those shown later in Fig. 4.7.

PERCEPTION OF SIZE

Size, like contrast, is an important basic quality of object information. Here we are concerned with the question how the visual system extracts relative size information, the judgment of whether an object is larger or shorter than another, and not how absolute size judgments are made. One reasonable assumption about how size is perceived is to suggest the use of visual mechanisms such as feature detectors which can determine large ranges of size information quite precisely. However, our inability to accurately judge the size of single lines in simple geometric patterns that result in visual illusions has suggested for many years that there is more (really less as we shall see in a later section explicitly devoted to illusions) to size judgments than just measuring distance between the end points of features. This approach to understanding size extends earlier work (Ginsburg,

1971, 1978) that sought to understand perception from the physical information contained in filtered images with which processes such as size judgments must contend. The question asked is, What physical information about relative size is being processed by mechanisms in the visual system? Earlier results suggested that size judgments are made from features contained in relatively low-pass filtered images created from about a one- to two- octave bandwidth (about 2 to 4 cycles per object) (Ginsburg, 1971, 1978). In some examples that will be shown later, the perceived distortions of geometric illusions were found in the images of filtered patterns that create the illusions. These results suggested that size judgments may be based upon information in similar two-octave bandwidth filtered images that provide generalized form information about objects.

The postulate that relative size judgments are based upon extraction of information from filtered images in the cortex (the only known site of narrowband one-to two-octave filters), was recently put to the test to determine how much of the perceived size of a feature of a common illusion could be accounted for by biological filtering (Ginsburg & Evans, 1979). Subjects were required to adjust a line equal to the perceived length of a line in nine variations of the Müller-Lyer illusion shown in Fig. 4.2a. The line lengths of these same patterns were determined from their images produced using filters based on biological data. The rules for determining line lengths were based on the physical peaks, troughs, and midpoints of lines in the filtered images. The ability of the filtered images created from 1.5 octave low-band pass channel filters to predict first the perceived shortening, then the zero illusion point, and finally the perceived lengthening of this line when compared to the subject data, is quite striking. About 79% of the variance of the subject data could be predicted from this simple approach. An even more stringent test was made when the fins were reversed in direction to create nine other variations of the Müller-Lyer illusion shown in Fig. 4.2b. The rules for predicting the line lengths from the filtered images remained the same. Here, 76% of the variance of the perceived distortion could also be predicted. Whether the simple rules for determining line length used will hold for other geometric illusions remains to be seen. If these results hold for other size judgments, then we can see that size is not just a simple measurement of distance between termination points of original features, but rather judgments made from features contained in filtered images.

DETECTING AND IDENTIFYING COMPLEX OBJECTS FROM INDIVIDUAL FILTER CHARACTERISTICS: A PHYSICS OF FORM PERCEPTION

The previous two sections showed how the use of Fourier techniques and spatial filtering provided powerful tools for understanding certain fundamental aspects of contrast and size perception. This section shows the power of those tools in helping to provide a solution to a fundamental problem in vision research, the

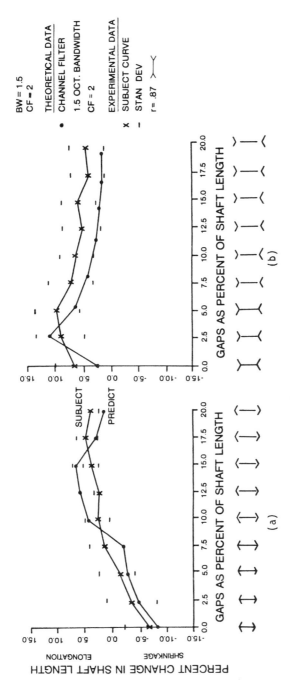

FIG. 4.2. Comparison between the perceived line length of outward-going (a) and inward-going (b) fin configurations of a Müller-Lyer illusion from subjects (x) and the predicted line length from channel-filtered images (•). Note that the channel-filtered images predict about 79% and 76% of the variance of the subject data (from Ginsburg & Evans, 1979).

lack of a physics for form perception. A full argument for the use of linear systems techniques, embodying Fourier analysis as a foundation for a physics of form, is presented elsewhere (Ginsburg, 1982). Here, we simply suggest the need for a physics of form that can describe relevant object information in the same mathematical language as that used to describe the processing of this information by visual mechanisms in a way that is relevant to how objects are seen. An example will demonstrate the power of this general approach. Fourier synthesis will be used to quantify the minimum information to identify complex objects, and the contrast sensitivity function (CSF), as a general description of the threshold filtering characteristics of the visual system. These data will then be used to predict the detection and identification of complex objects from individual CSFs.

There have been attempts to predict the identification of complex objects such as Snellen letters used in common eye charts from the CSF. However, the predictions were not successful when a relationship was attempted between one spatial frequency component of Snellen letters and the cutoff spatial frequency of the CSF (Ginsburg, 1978, 1980). Sufficient information for object indentification has been shown to be contained in low-pass filtered images from previous research (Ginsburg, 1971, 1978). Therefore, a more successful attempt was made by the author based on establishing a relationship between the minimum number of spatial frequency components of Snellen letters that mediated their identification and the threshold contrast of those components specified by the CSF (Ginsburg, 1978, 1980). Using Fourier analysis as a tool, synthesis of the two typical Snellen letters in Fig. 4.3 shows, for example, that an L requires 1.5 cycles per letter width (cpl, which refers to the number of cycles across the width of the letter) and an E requires 2.5 cpl as the minimum number of cycles for identification. Although other bandwidths which contain middle or higher spatial frequencies can also provide sufficient information for identification, those bandwidths produce images of lower contrast, or pass a larger number of spatial frequencies than that of the lowest passband. However, high-pass filtered images do have the interesting property of having almost equal detection and identification thresholds (Howland, Ginsburg, & Campbell, 1978).

It should be noted that the 1.5 cpl, required for correctly identifying the letter $L,$ would not be intuitively obvious from an analysis or computation of letter features such as line length, width or angle. It is this capability of Fourier synthesis to quantify the bandwidth of relevant form information contained in complex objects that promises to provide a foundation for a physics of form. This approach can be used to provide a minimum bandwidth in spatial frequency terms for different amounts of information about any object which in turn can be related to an individual's CSF to determine his ability to see that object.

Threshold contrast for the detection and identification of typical Snellen letters was determined next. The reciprocal of the threshold contrast (contrast sensitivity) is shown in Fig. 4.4. These two curves describe the amount of contrast sensitivity required for the human observer to detect and identify Snellen

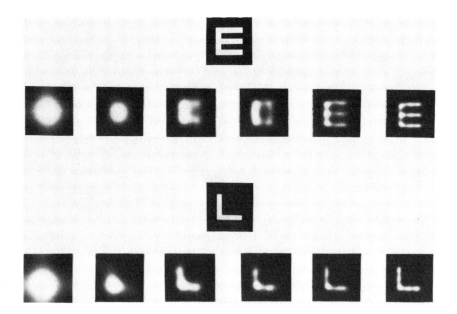

FIG. 4.3.   Fourier synthesis of letters *E* and *L* in .5 cycles per letter width (cpl) increments. From left to right is the original letter, .5, 1.0, 1.5, 2.0, 2.5, and 3.0 cpl. Note that the letter *E* requires 2.5 cpl for minimum recognition whereas the *L* requires only 1.5 cpl. (from Ginsburg, 1978, 1980).

letters whose size ranges from 60 to 5 minutes of arc or whose fundamental frequency (one cycle across the width of the object) ranges from 1 to 12 cpd. Note that for large letters, line 6/60, detection and identification thresholds are very similar. However, for small letters, line 6/5, contrast had to be increased by a factor of five after detection before correct identification occurred. These results are explainable if the detection and identification of the letters require that the low frequency components of each letter, about .5 to 2.5 cpl, reach visual threshold. For example, the size of the largest letter on line 6/60 has a fundamental frequency at 1 cycle per degree (cpd). Since the peak contrast sensitivity of normal vision is about 1 to 5 cpd, the relevant bandwidth of the large letters of line 6/60, will occur at about .5 to 2.5 cpl, and allow identification to occur almost simultaneously with detection. However, the relevant 2.5 cpl for letters at Snellen line 6/6 occurs from 6 to 30 cpd. Since the contrast sensitivity function is a rapidly decreasing monotonic function over that range of spatial frequencies, it is not surprising that much more contrast is required to identify these small Snellen letters after they have been detected. Thus, the amount of contrast required to identify an object after it is detected will depend upon its size.

These results add to the evidence that objects can be correctly identified from only a narrow range of low spatial frequencies. Furthermore, these results show that a particular minimum range of relevant spatial frequencies, that is, a mini-

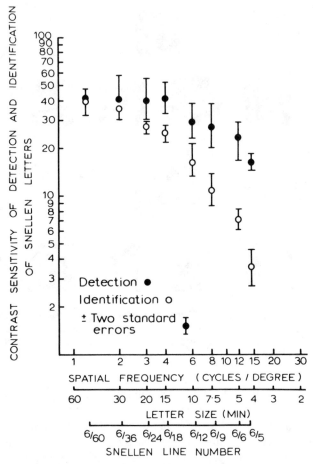

FIG. 4.4. Contrast sensitivity for the detection and identification of at least 50% of the letters on each line of a Snellen visual acuity chart. Contrast sensitivity is defined as the reciprocal of threshold contrast. The abscissa shows the size of the letters in three different ways: the fundamental spatial frequency (one cycle across the letter width), minutes of visual angle, and optometric notation in meters. See text for discussion (from Ginsburg, 1978, 1981).

mum spatial frequency bandwidth used to detect and then identify an object, is based upon the size of the object. The predictive power of this approach was tested by obtaining contrast sensitivity functions from people having impaired vision due to amblyopia and multiple sclerosis. The contrast sensitivity functions obtained from those visual abnormalities ranged from reduced middle, high, or low spatial frequencies and, in one case, a very narrow band loss in sensitivity at middle spatial frequencies (Ginsburg, 1978, 1981,). The corresponding Snellen acuity of these subjects ranged from 6/4 to 6/200. Using the approach that

Snellen acuity requires a narrow band of low spatial frequencies of the letters to reach a certain level of contrast, the Snellen acuity of 17 of 22 eyes was predicted to within one Snellen line from the contrast sensitivity measurements of those visually abnormal subjects. The Snellen acuity of the other five eyes was predicted to within two Snellen lines. Thus, the identification of complex objects, for example, Snellen letters, can be predicted, at least to a first approximation, from individual filtering characteristics of the visual system.

These findings have implications for limiting resolution, the standard method of measuring visual capability. Certain patients having multiple sclerosis complain about the quality of vision between their eyes although their vision is tested as being normal when standard eye charts are used. However, contrast sensitivity differences between the two eyes in such persons can show up quite readily sometimes with factors of more than four difference in sensitivity occurring over large ranges of spatial frequency (Ginsburg, 1981). The point is that typical eye charts used to test the transmission of spatial information in the visual system, by having only one high level of contrast, can provide only limited information. Techniques similar to contrast sensitivity are required for a more complete measure of visual capability. Indeed, a recent study shows that CSF can predict a pilot's ability to detect a semi-isolated air-to-ground target in an aircraft simulator, whereas visual acuity can not (Ginsburg, Evans, Sekuler, & Harp, 1982).

GESTALT LAWS OF PERCEPTION

One of the classic problems of perception the early Gestalt psychologists investigated was how the visual system connects discrete pattern elements (parts) into meaningful units of form information (wholes). Explicit feature analysis approaches have suggested many possible solutions to grouping discrete patterns (e.g. Zahn, 1971). Although many of these solutions are ingenious, they are typically ad hoc and open-ended in the sense that they do not usually form a logical, functional link with known biological properties of visual mechanisms.

In contrast, rather than asking how the visual system is solving the problems of perceptual grouping, the filter approach seeks to find what grouping information about objects can be extracted by existing physical filters in the visual system. In other words, could certain fundamental properties of grouping be a concomitant of basic biological filtering? The answer appears to be yes. Earlier answers to that question showed that the same small bandwidth that captured the generalized form of many solid objects also produced generally homogeneous solid objects even from objects comprised of discrete patterns (Ginsburg, 1971, 1978).

Figure 4.5 a–f shows examples of certain Gestalt laws of perceptual grouping that can be explained in terms of filtering: dot letter G (a), dot letter R in random noise (b), and the patterns that represent examples of grouping properties of

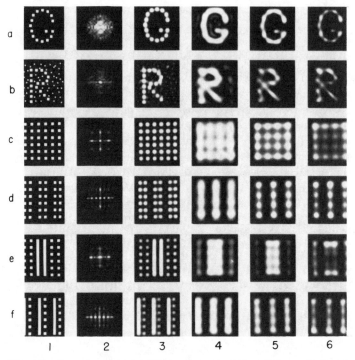

FIG. 4.5. Examples of spatial filtering patterns which exhibit certain Gestalt laws of perceptual grouping: closure (a), closure and figure/ground (b), single whole group (c), three groups due to proximity (d), two similar groups separated by a different central group (e), and three similar groups where proximity overrides the similarity of the pattern features (f). The original patterns (1) have their Fourier spectra biologically filtered by two-dimensional contrast sensitivity (cs) data (2) which are used to create the filtered images in (3). Only the lowest four frequencies are used to create the filtered images without the CS filter in (4) and with the CS pre-filter in (5). Filtered images from only three low frequencies where the fundamental frequency is removed are shown in (6). See text for interpretation of the results (from Ginsburg, 1978).

vision—a single whole group of dots (c), groups of dots separated by an interspace (d) or by a central group of lines (e), three groups where proximity subsumes the similarity of the pattern elements (f). The original patterns in Column 1 have their Fourier magnitude spectra filtered by a two-dimensional anisotropic filter using biological data based on the overall filtering properties of our visual system (Ginsburg, 1973, 1978, 1980). This is shown in Column 2, and results in the filtered image in Column 3. The filtered images created from resynthesizing just the lowest four spatial frequencies which would be similar to information filtered by a channel filter having a two-octave bandwidth, are in Column 4. The effect of using the overall biological filter before passing only the lowest four frequencies is in Column 5. Column 6 contains filtered images where the fundamental frequency or first harmonic is removed to reveal forms comprised of only three low spatial frequencies.

In general, these results show that the overall filtering characteristics of the visual system, under the conditions used here, just smooth the dots. Notice the grey blobs that appear at the intersections of the spaces separating these pictures. The appearance of these grey blobs is called the Hermann grid illusion. A filtering explanation for this kind of illusion is evident from the low contrast grey blobs seen at the intersections within Fig. 4.5c3.

The forms having closure and good continuity perceived in the filtered images of the original patterns contain a range of only three to four spatial frequencies (about 1.5 to 2 octaves bandwidth). Note that one advantage of removing the lowest spatial frequencies by bandpass filtering is that average brightness differences between pattern elements are generally attenuated to create global forms having uniform contrast as seen in Column 6. Therefore, a bank of bandpass filters can separate the average energy or brightness of objects into one channel and separate other information, such as contrast and form, into other channels. This could allow mechanisms of form perception based on contrast to extract similar form information over wide ranges of brightness. Finally, one way to interpret the Fourier magnitude spectra is as idealized maps of the activity of size and orientation channels in the visual system where the light and dark regions represent channels or neurons stimulated maximally and minimally by the pattern. The low frequency or large size channels are represented by the central distributions of the magnitude spectra, and the increasingly higher frequency or small size channels are represented by the magnitude spectra as they radiate outward from the center.

Psychologists such as Ivo Kohler were also concerned with visual perception after optical transformations by goggles, prisms, and mirrors. Perceptual behavior after such transformations of pattern and space provides valuable perceptional information as to limitations, capabilities, and plasticity of visual mechanisms and processes. It is interesting to note that here, too, Fourier techniques may provide a fundamental framework for the analysis of those kinds of transformations. For example, the two-dimensional Fourier transform is not rotationally invariant; it contains information about the orientation of objects. Indeed, a relationship between this lack of rotation invariance in the Fourier transform and human vision was used to correlate observers' identification errors of rotated letters and the Euclidean distance between their rotated and non-rotated low-pass filtered transforms with quite good results (Ginsburg, 1971).

VISUAL ILLUSIONS

In addition to distorting size as discussed earlier, illusions also provide important clues to visual processing because of their ability to demonstrate robust visual "failures" of accurate judgments about brightness, contrast, orientation, and

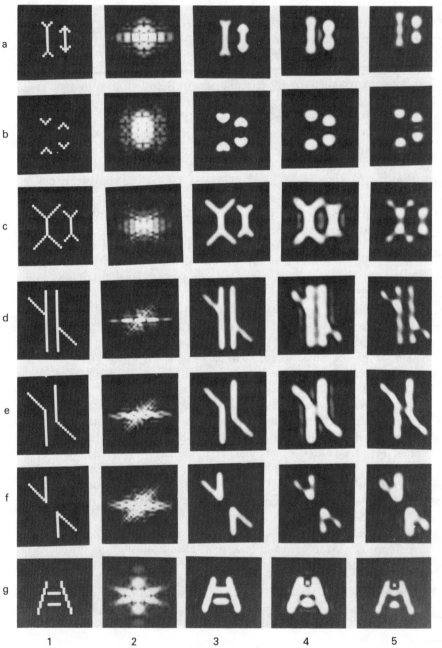

FIG. 4.6. Examples of spatial filtering typical visual illusions: standard Müller-Lyer (a); Müller-Lyer without shafts (b); Müller-Lyer with different sized fins (c); standard Poggendorff figure (d); obtuse angles only Poggendorff variation (e); acute angles only Poggendorff variation (f); standard Ponzo figure (g). See Figure 4.5 on Gestalt perception for details about filtering (from Ginsburg, 1978).

shape. Although a number of theories have been proposed to explain illusions, none seem to provide general, quantitative explanations in a parsimonious manner nor do these theories engage a unified approach to other areas of perception as attempted here for letters and faces (e.g., see Gillam, 1980; Robinson, 1973. The results of investigating visual illusions using spatial filters based on biological data appear to overcome a certain lack of parsimony of these other theories.

Early work on spatial filtering showed that filters capable of producing general forms from the low spatial frequencies of objects also produced physical distortions in visual illusion patterns that compared well to perceived distortions (Ginsburg, 1971, 1978). Examples of subsequent research that extended those early findings and related them more closely to filtering based on biology are shown in Fig. 4.6. These images reveal small spatial distortions similar to perceived distortions. The distortions increase as lower spatial frequencies of the illusion are passed. The subjective distortions seen in these filtered images accurately reflect the objective physical distortions determined from numerical printouts and computer plots of those data used to create these pictures (Ginsburg, 1978). The results of studies determining how much of the perceived distortion of a common illusion, the Müller-Lyer illusion, could be accounted for by the filtering approach was discussed in a previous section on size perception.

Although not shown here, this filtering approach has provided similar results with such contrast illusions as the Hermann grid, Ehrenstein figure, Benussi ring, and the Kanizsa triangle (Ginsburg, 1975, 1978). It should be noted that lateral inhibition alone cannot account for these kinds of distortions. Some of the causes of illusions have been postulated to be due to receptive field inhibition, (e.g. see Spillmann, Fuld & Gerrits, 1976 and recent discussion by Coren & Girgus, 1978). However, that view does not take explicitly into account other important filtering properties of the receptive field, high frequency attenuation and spatial summation, which act over the whole pattern by a large number of overlapping receptive fields whose sizes range from one to two octaves as is being simulated by the filtering shown here (Ginsburg, 1976).

There are other factors that most likely contribute to illusions, such as learning and decreased perceived distortion with repeated exposure, and these factors will have to be incorporated into any final explanation of geometric distortions.

Although it is highly unlikely that there is any unitary theory of visual distortions, these successful initial experiments suggest a strong physiological explanation for visual distortions. What is particularly encouraging is the fact the results from the relative size experiment mentioned earlier show that the data used to predict perceived distortion comes from filtered images using a 1.5 octave bandwidth channel filter, the same general bandwidth that has been found to produce images that correspond to other aspects of vision such as form perceptions (Ginsburg, 1971, 1978). Filters having narrower or broader bandwidths produced data that deviated greatly from the subjects' perception. Thus, the same filtering that seems to provide our capability for rapid form perception appears to exact its toll by distorting simple geometric shapes. The loss of accurate detail

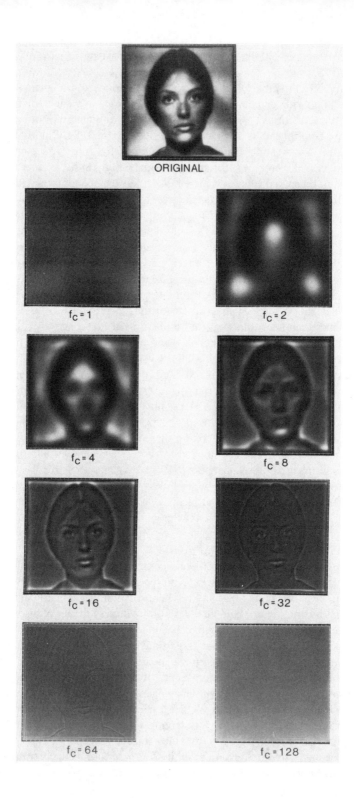

ORIGINAL

$f_C = 1$

$f_C = 2$

$f_C = 4$

$f_C = 8$

$f_C = 16$

$f_C = 32$

$f_C = 64$

$f_C = 128$

that is not needed for the general form of a pattern creates a perceptual problem if that detail is needed to correctly answer a different question about the relative size or distance of parts of the pattern. Since the original pattern must be transmitted throughout the visual system by mechanisms that (by their very nature) create filtered images, it seems likely that filtering plays a major role in perceived distortions.

A HIERARCHY OF FILTERED IMAGES

The results of the previous sections extend a model of visual processing whereby perceptual mechanisms can extract a range of basic attributes about objects such as contrast, size, and form as well as detail using a bank of filters or channels tuned to different ranges of spatial frequencies (Ginsburg, 1971, 1978, 1980). Here we explicitly show what spatial information might lie in such channels. A portrait was filtered into eight different channels whose center frequencies were one octave apart and whose bandwidths were one and two octaves (Ginsburg, 1978, 1980). Portraits filtered to one octave provided only minimal information about the portrait. However, portraits filtered to two octaves provided sufficient information for identification. Such a system of filtering can allow the extraction of degree of spatial detail about an object sufficient to perform most perceptual tasks.

The results of the two-octave filtered portrait are shown in Fig. 4.7. Spatial information transmitted by a two-octave bandwidth having a center frequency of .5 cycles per face width is shown in the picture labeled fc=1. The subsequent picture labels refer to the center frequencies of the filter in terms of cycles per picture width. Cycles per face width is half the cycles per picture width, cpw. The fc=1 filter only passes the very gradual contrast changes that show that something exists. An object having an elliptical shape is clearly present from the information provided by the next higher filter, fc=2, although it is not recognizable as a face. When the filter has a center frequency of 4 cpw, an object that can easily be classified as having head and shoulders are revealed, in agreement with other research on filtered faces (Ginsburg, 1978, 1980; Harmon & Julesz, 1973). The next filtered image, fc=8, shows the portrait of an adult. Definite identification of that adult can be seen in the next filter, fc=16. The details of the portrait, such as the hair over the forehead and eyes are seen from the filter fc=32. Further details about the portrait can be seen in the filtered portraits fc=64 and fc=128. However, the portrait has almost vanished due to low contrast energy content within the bandwidths of those filters.

FIG. 4.7.   A hierarchy of filtered images created from channel filters based on biological data. The original portrait is filtered into eight channels of spatial information having a bandwidth of two octaves and center frequencies one octave apart. See text for discussion (from Ginsburg, 1978, 1980).

This hierarchy of filtered images provides many interesting suggestions as to how the visual system may actually process spatial information. First, note seven filtered images (excluding the last one that shows little useful information) can provide a lexicon of spatial information that agrees well with how objects are described: existence, general form, classification, who or what it is, texture, and edges. Thus, this particular decomposition of spatial information, which is determined from filters that are biologically realizable, partitions spatial information in a meaningful manner. Second, note that only one filter having a two-octave bandwidth centered at 16 cpw is sufficient to identify an individual face. Since in this case, the original picture has 128 cpw, a bandwidth reduction of 28:1 can be easily achieved. Even the next higher filter that might be required to distinguish between identical twins would provide a bandwidth reduction of about 7:1. (This approach to understanding spatial information may have practical importance in maximizing the transmission of spatial information with minimum bandwidth. These results also suggest which spatial bandwidths of displayed information could be used to enhance and cue certain tasks [Ginsburg, 1980].) Third, note that the filtered images having center frequencies of 16 and 32 cpw most resemble the original. Although the 32 cpw filtered image has more detail, the 16 cpw portrait "seems" more like the original. Fourth, note the relative contrast between different filtered portraits which approximates the energy of the features of the original portrait in each bandwidth. Predominant energy can be seen to exist from filters having 2, 4, 8, 16 cpw: the relatively low spatial frequencies of the portrait. The high spatial frequencies captured by the filters having higher center frequencies have greatly reduced energy. This observation further supports the notion that the lower spatial frequencies rather than the higher spatial frequencies convey major information about objects. The lower spatial frequencies will provide high signal-to-noise ratio under certain conditions. For example, subjects can recognize letters that are blurred to 4 cycles per letter as readily as letters having sharp edges (Ginsburg, 1971) and faces containing only 4 cycles per face width can be correctly identified from a set of 12 faces (Woodhouse & Campbell, submitted). Furthermore, similarity judgments of various objects, for example, alpha-numerics, European road and control signs, and certain textures by man and machine correlate well using only low spatial frequencies of the objects (Ginsburg, Carl, Kabrisky, Hall, & Gill, 1976).

Finally, many people have suggested that lateral inhibition from neurophysiological receptive fields serves to "sharpen" the image. These portraits have been filtered using filters with biologically based weighting functions. It is not evident that any edges have been "sharpened" in any filtered image. What is seen is enhanced contrast at the edges. No edge appears any sharper than those in the original portrait. These results suggest that a single receptive field or channel alone cannot sharpen edges. However, non-linear gain mechanisms operating over groups of receptive fields of different sizes or channels could collectively sharpen edges.

The perception of contrast, size and form of various objects has been examined using the concept of filtering. Although any of the individual demonstrations shown could be explained by other approaches, here, a more parsimonious explanation using biological filtering was presented. This approach by itself is not complete. Our ability to analyze objects in complex scenes has not been discussed, nor has mental set or other cognitive factors. However, these kinds of filtered images may also provide a physical data base for more explicit cognitive descriptions and manipulation of object features in complex scenes.

REFERENCES

Breitmeyer, B. G., & Ganz, L. Implications of sustained and transient channels for theories of visual masking, saccadic suppression and information processing. *Psychological Review,* 1976, *83,* 1–33.

Campbell, F. W. The transmission of spatial information through the visual system. In F. O. Schmitt & F. G. Worden, (Eds.), *The neurosciences third study program.* Cambridge, MA.: MIT Press, 1974.

Campbell, F. W., Carpenter, R. H. S., & Levinson, J. Z. Visibility of aperiodic patterns compared with that of sinusoidal gratings. *Journal of Physiology,* London, 1969, *204,* 283–298.

Campbell, F. W., & Robson, J. G. Application of Fourier analysis to the visibility of gratings. *Journal of Physiology,* London, 1968, *197,* 551–566.

Cannon, M. W., Jr. Contrast sensation: A linear function of stimulus contrast. *Vision Research,* 1979, *19,* 1045–1052.

Coren, S., & Girgus, J. S. *Seeing is deceiving: The psychology of visual illusions.* Hillsdale, N.J.: Lawrence Erlbaum Assoc., 1978.

DeValois, R., & DeValois, K. Spatial Vision. *Annual Review of Psychology,* 1980, *31,* 304–341.

Georgeson, M. A., & Sullivan, G. D. Contrast constancy: Deblurring in human vision by spatial frequency channels. *Journal of Physiology,* London, 1975, *252,* 627–656.

Gillam, B. Geometrical illusions. *Scientific American,* 1980, *241,* 102–111.

Ginsburg, A. P. Psychological correlates of a model of the human visual system. Proceedings of the National Aerospace Electronics Conference (NAECON), Dayton, Ohio: *IEEE Transactions on Aerospace and Electronic Systems 71–C–AES,* 1971, 283–290.

Ginsburg, A. P. Pattern recognition techniques suggested from psychological correlates of a model of the human visual system, Proceedings of the National Aerospace Electronics Conference (NAECON), Dayton, Ohio: *IEEE Trans. on Aerospace and Electronic Systems 73–CHO735–1,* 1973, 309–316.

Ginsburg, A. P. Is the illusory triangle physical or imaginary?. *Nature,* 1975, *257,* 219–220.

Ginsburg, A. P. Are negligible illusions under appropriate scaling surprising? *Perception,* 1976, *5,* 119.

Ginsburg, A. P. Visual information processing based on spatial filters constrained by biological data. Dissertation for Ph.D., University of Cambridge, England, 1978 (published as AFAMRL Technical Report TR–78–129).

Ginsburg, A. P. Spatial filtering and mechanism of perception. *Proc. Instr. Soc. Am. Tenth Ann. Pittsburg Conference on Modeling and Simulation,* April 25–27, 1979, 185–192.

Ginsburg, A. P. Specifying relevant spatial information for image evaluation and display design: An explanation of how we see certain objects. *Soc. Info. Display (SID),* 1980, *21,* (3), 210–227.

Ginsburg, A. P. Spatial filtering and vision: Implications for normal and abnormal vision. In L. Proenza, J. Enoch, & A. Jampolski (Eds.), *Applications of psychophysics to clinical problems*

(Proceedings of the Symposium held in San Francisco, Calif., Oct. 1978). New York: The Cambridge University Press, 1981, 70–106.

Ginsburg, A. P. On a filter approach to understanding the perception of visual form. In D. Albrecht (Ed.), *The recognition of pattern and form*. New York: Springer-Verlag, 1982.

Ginsburg, A. P., Cannon, M. W., Jr. & Nelson, M. Suprathreshold processing of complex visual stimuli: Evidence for linearity in contrast perception. *Science*, 1980, *208*, 619–621.

Ginsburg, A. P., Carl, J. W., Kabrisky, M., Hall, C. F., & Gill, R. A. Psychological aspects of a model for the classification of visual images. In J. Rose (Ed.), *Advances in cybernetics and systems*. London: Gordon & Breach, Science Publishers Ltd., 1976.

Ginsburg, A. P., & Evans, D. W. Predicting visual illusions from filtered images based upon biological data. *J. Opt. Soc. Am.*, 1979, *69*, 1443. (Abstract)

Ginsburg, A. P., Evans, D., Sekuler, R., & Harp, S. Contrast sensitivity predicts pilots performance in aircraft simulators. *American Journal of Optometry and Physiological Optics*, 1982, *59*, 105–109.

Hamerly, J. R., Quick, R. F., Jr. & Reichert, T. A. A study of grating contrast judgment. *Vision Research*, 1977, *17*, 201–207.

Harmon, L. D., & Julesz, B. Masking in visual recognition: Effects of two-dimensional filtered noise. *Science*, 1973, *180*, 1194–1197.

Howland, B., Ginsburg, A., & Campbell, F. W. High-pass spatial frequency letters as clinical optotypes. *Vision Research*, 1978, *18*, 1063–1066.

Julesz, B., and Schumer, R. A. Early visual perception, *Annual Review of Psychology*, 1981, *32*, 575–627.

Kelly, D. H., & Magnuski, H. S. Pattern detection and the two-dimensional Fourier transform: Circular targets. *Vision Research*, 1975, *15*, 911–915.

Kulikowski, J. J. Effective contrast constancy and linearity of contrast sensation, *Vision Research*, 1976, *16*, 1419–1431.

Robinson, J. O. *The psychology of visual illusions*. London: Hutchinson, 1973.

Robson, J. G. Receptive fields: Neural representation of the spatial and intensive attributes of the visual image. In E. C. Carterette & M. P. Friedman (Eds.), *Handbook of perception*, New York: Academic Press, 1975.

Schade, O. H., Sr. Optical and photoelectric analog of the eye. *Journal of the Optical Society of America*, 1956, *46*, 721–739.

Sekuler, R. Spatial vision. *Annual Review of Psychology*, 1974, *25*, 195–232.

Spillmann, L., Fuld, K. & Gerrits, H. J. M. Brightness contrast in the Ehrenstein illusion, *Vision Research*, 1976, *16*, 713–719.

Watanabe, A., Mori, T., Nagata, S., & Hiwatashi, K. Spatial sine-wave response of the human visual system. *Vision Research*, 1968, *8*, 1245–1263.

Woodhouse, J. M., & Campbell, F. W. Face recognition: Minimum information requirements. Submitted for publication.

Zahn, C. T. Graph-theoretical methods for determining and describing gestalt clusters. *IEEE Transactions on Computers*, 1971, *C–20*, 68–86.

5 Spatial Mapping and Spatial Vision in Primate Striate and Infero-Temporal Cortex

Eric L. Schwartz
Brain Research Laboratory
New York University
School of Medicine

ABSTRACT

In the present paper, the subject of mapping in the visual cortex will be addressed. Four principal subjects will be covered: (1) A review of the calculus of two-dimensional maps is provided. It is shown that this suggests a mathematical formalism for describing the structure of topographic maps which might occur in the nervous system. (2) This descriptive formalism is applied to summarizing the global and local topographic structures of the primate striate cortex. In particular, areas where current experimental data are uncertain will be emphasized. (3) The functional significance of these patterns of mapping in the visual system are discussed, by briefly reviewing a series of papers which have studied the possible computational significance of striate cortex neuroanatomy. This review includes applications to binocular segmentation, perceptual invariances, visual illusions, and shape analysis. (4) Finally, recent experimental studies of shape analysis by neurons of inferotemporal cortex, which are related to the previous approach, are presented.

MAPPINGS OF TWO-DIMENSIONAL SURFACES INTO TWO-DIMENSIONAL SURFACES

The magnification factor of primate striate cortex is approximately an inverse function of visual field coordinates, between 1 and 20 degrees eccentricity. Recently, much attention has been focused on the precise functional form of the cortical magnification factor, as well as on the two-dimensional structure of the striate cortex map. However, the majority of this work has not addressed the basic mathematical questions which are immediately raised by an attempt to characterize a mapping of a two-dimensional surface into a two-dimensional surface (i.e., the global cortical map). Specifically, the magnification factor itself is not an adequate specification of a general map of this kind. Magnification factor is a scalar (i.e., a number). But, a general map is specified by its matrix of partial derivatives (i.e., the Jacobian matrix), which is a second rank tensor. In other words, a complete analysis of a map, in terms of differential measurements (i.e., magnifications), requires the specification of four coordinate measurements (rather than the single magnification factor) at each point. The following section shows that the magnification tensor can be better understood in terms of two elementary types of mappings. One of these represents a local conformal mapping, and the other represents a shear mapping. In the next section it will be shown that the shear, or non-isotropic component of the primate striate cortical map, is likely to be negligible, according to current data.

Whitney Map Theorem

A broad classification of two-dimensional mappings is provided by the Whitney Mapping Theorem, which states that all stable planar mappings are locally equivalent to either a "fold", a "cusp", or a "regular" mapping (Brocker, 1975). In the following, we ignore the singularities represented by folds and cusps. The class of regular mappings is sufficient to model striate cortex topography. However, it should be noted that some of the complexities in topology of circumstriate cortical mappings might require a more general formalism.

Regular maps are characterized by having a Jacobian matrix of partial derivatives whose determinant is finite and non-zero. In the following section, we regroup the terms of this Jacobian in order to better understand the biological significance of the isotropic (i.e., conformal) and non-isotropic contributions to the structure of cortical maps.

Jacobian Matrix and Magnification Tensor

The (retinal) point (x,y) is taken to a cortical point (f,g) by the functions $f(x,y)$ and $g(x,y)$. The Jacobian of this map (Brocker, 1975) is:

$$J = \begin{pmatrix} \dfrac{\partial f}{\partial x} & \dfrac{\partial f}{\partial y} \\ \dfrac{\partial g}{\partial x} & \dfrac{\partial g}{\partial y} \end{pmatrix} = \begin{pmatrix} f_x & f_y \\ g_x & g_y \end{pmatrix} \tag{1}$$

A common manipulation from the literature of continuum mechanics (and fluid mechanics) will be useful: The Jacobian is rewritten in terms of its symmetrical and anti-symmetrical components:

$$2J = (J + J^t) + (J - J^t) = \begin{pmatrix} 2f_x & f_y + g_x \\ f_y + g_x & 2g_y \end{pmatrix} + \begin{pmatrix} 0 & f_y - g_x \\ g_x - f_y & 0 \end{pmatrix} \quad (2)$$

where the symbol (t) is used to represent the transpose of the Jacobian. The symmetrical part of the Jacobian above may be rewritten in terms of its traceless and diagonal components (Segal, 1977):

$$\begin{pmatrix} 2f_x & f_y + g_x \\ f_y + g_x & 2g_y \end{pmatrix} = \begin{pmatrix} trJ & 0 \\ 0 & trJ \end{pmatrix} + \begin{pmatrix} 2f_x - trJ & f_y + g_x \\ f_y + g_x & 2g_y - trJ \end{pmatrix} \quad (3)$$

where trJ represents the trace of the Jacobian (the sum of its diagonal terms), such that $tr(jacobian) = f_x + g_y$.

The previous analysis thus shows that the most general form of the Jacobian of a regular map is the sum of a traceless symmetric matrix and two other terms, which are a diagonal matrix (i.e., trJ * (unit matrix)) and an antisymmetric matrix. Since the traceless matrix is symmetric (and real), it may be diagonalized by an orthogonal rotation. Thus, the traceless component of the Jacobian matrix is represented by an orientation (i.e., the orientation of its principal axes) and a magnitude (i.e., a magnitude of the shear).

The second rank magnification tensor may be expressed in terms of two conceptually distinct transformations. This is shown in equation (4):

$$2J = \begin{pmatrix} trJ & 0 \\ 0 & trJ \end{pmatrix} + \begin{pmatrix} 0 & f_y - g_x \\ g_x - f_y & 0 \end{pmatrix} + \ldots \begin{pmatrix} 2f_x - trJ & f_y + g_x \\ g_x + f_y & 2g_y - trJ \end{pmatrix} \quad (4)$$

The biological significance of these terms are now outlined by showing that the first two terms represent a conformal (i.e., isotropic) mapping, and that the last term (the traceless symmetric matrix) represents a shear, that is, a squeeze in one direction and an expansion in the other direction, with no change in area. First, the relation of this analysis to the theory of conformal mapping is shown.

A conformal mapping is defined in a number of equivalent ways: if the mapping preserves the shape of infinitesimal triangles (or, equivalently, of local angles), it is conformal. Thus isotropic mappings are conformal. Any analytic function of a complex variable represents a conformal map. A map is conformal if and only if it satisfies the Cauchy-Riemann equations:

$$f_x = g_y$$

$$f_y = -g_x \quad (5)$$

The relation of the sub-class of conformal maps to the class of regular maps can be made explicit: substitute the Cauchy-Riemann equation into the Jacobian of equation (4). The last (i.e., traceless) term is *identically zero*. The conventional physiological magnification factor is the square root of the determinant of the Jacobian matrix, which represents the change, or magnification in a unit length caused by the mapping. If the map is conformal, this magnification factor is equal to $|\nabla f|$ or to $|\nabla g|$.

Thus, if a map is conformal, its Jacobian reduces from a second rank tensor field to a vector field. In particular, the vector magnification factor can be written as the gradient of some scalar (Ahlfors, 1966; Schwartz, 1977b).

The justification for presenting all of this mathematical detail is threefold: (1) Specific experimental consequences follow directly. (2) Several recent analyses, based on one-dimensional fits to cortical magnification factor along several meridians, can be shown to be incomplete (see below). (3) Since the present analysis provides a complete characterization of topologically stable (Segal, 1977), two-dimensional maps, it may be applied to *any* species, or anatomical area, for which the concept of mapping is at all valid. However, one final mathematical tool is still needed.

Riemann Mapping Theorem

The Riemann Mapping Theorem states that a conformal map is *uniquely* specified (for simply connected domains), if it is given on any finite domain (Ahlfors, 1966). This has the following important experimental consequence. If the map of striate cortex were measured, say, along the horizontal meridian *only,* and it was determined that the map was isotropic, then the map would be uniquely determined throughout the entire cortical extent, i.e., by analytic continuation (Ahlfors, 1966). This result has the surprising experimental consequence that *it is not necessary to measure an isotropic map everywhere in order to determine the map function*. As a matter of fact, it is not necessary to measure it by standard physiological point mapping at all. If the map is isotropic (e.g., determined by sampling, with no quantitative data), then the shape of the map alone (i.e., the boundary conditions imposed by the retina and cortex) uniquely determine the map, up to an orientation and a single point in both planes, as guaranteed by the Riemann Mapping Theorem. This fact has been made the basis of a developmental algorithm for neural maps; the connection of this algorithm to classical field theory, in general, and fluid mechanics in particular, is further discussed in this work (Schwartz, 1977b). More significantly, it indicates that a cortical map might be determined uniquely and directly from the anatomy alone, with no physiological measurement, other than the demonstration of isotropy and overall map orientation.

The results outlined above will now be applied to characterizing the global and local topographic map functions of striate cortex.

APPLICATIONS OF TWO-DIMENSIONAL MAPPING
THEORY TO NEURAL TOPOGRAPHY

The analysis provided above represents a complete classification of two dimensional mappings, and relates the concept of conformal mapping to the most general form of two-dimensional map function which can occur. In the following section, this analysis is applied to the problem of describing the structure of the global mapping of primate striate cortex. It is then shown that a particular conformal mapping, of the form $\log(z+a)$, where "a" is a small real constant, provides an excellent fit to current anatomical and physiological data. Currently available data suggest that an isotropic (i.e., conformal) model is in good agreement with the form of this mapping.

Global Topography of Striate Cortex

Fitting Magnification Data.   The magnification factor was first reported in graphical form by Daniel and Whitteridge (1961). A simple fit to their data (Schwartz, 1977a) indicates that between 1° and 20°, magnification factor is approximately proportional to $r^{-0.9}$ (where r represents the spherical polar coordinate of eccentricity, measured in degrees). In other words, magnification factor is approximately proportional to the inverse of visual eccentricity.

Later workers have generally found a similar functional form for the striate cortex magnification factor (for the central 20° of field), that is, roughly an inverse linear function of eccentricity (e.g., Dow et al., 1981; Gattass et al., 1981; Hubel & Freeman, 1977). More precisely, in order to avoid the singularity at zero degrees, the function $1/r$ should be modified to $1/(r+a)$, where "a" is some small constant.

More elaborate fits to the (one-dimensional) curve of magnification factor have been proposed. Dow and his colleagues (1981) and Drasdo (1977) have fit polynomial functions to monkey and human cortical magnification factor, respectively, although the simpler functional form $\log(z+a)$ provides an adequate fit for the central twenty degrees of visual field. This function may be continued to the far periphery (i.e., beyond 20 degrees) using the form $\log(z+a)/(z+b)$, as discussed below. In any case, a simple recipe may be used to find a two-dimensional (conformal) map function which is specified by any form of 1 dimensional magnification factor estimate (e.g., along the horizontal meridian).

Two-Dimensional Conformal Approximation to Cortical Topography.   Suppose that a function of the form $B/(r+a)$ is proposed to fit cortical magnification along the horizontal meridian (e.g., Hubel and Freeman, 1977). By the Riemann Mapping Theorem or, by "analytic continuation" (Ahlfors, 1966), it can be shown that there is one and only one conformal (or isotropic) function which has this functional form along the horizontal meridian, which is the function

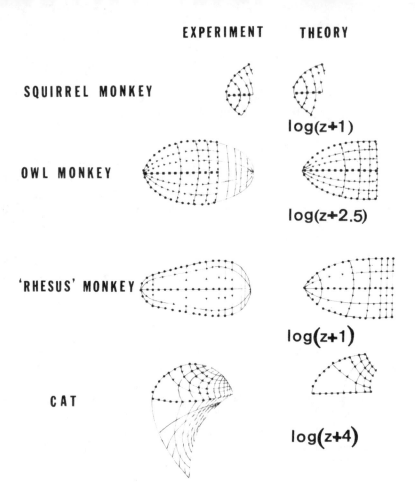

EXPERIMENT   THEORY

SQUIRREL MONKEY

log(z+1)

OWL MONKEY

log(z+2.5)

'RHESUS' MONKEY

log(z+1)

CAT

log(z+4)

FIG. 5.1. A series of computer generated logarithmic mappings are shown which provide the best visual fit to the published retinotopic (striate cortex) mappings of several primate species, as well as the cat. The experimental mappings are shown in the column labeled "experiment," and the complex logarithmic mappings are shown in the column labeled "theory". Only the central 20–40° are presented in the theoretical maps, and the corresponding areas of the experimental maps have been emphasized with the following graphic symbols: circles mark the projection of the horizontal meridian, and squares mark the projection of the vertical meridian. In the cat, it appears that the complex logarithmic approximation is quite good for the upper visual field, as shown, but fails to represent the lower visual field. For the "rhesus" monkey (Daniel & Whitteridge, 1961), the experimental map was drawn as an orthogonal projection, rather than as a flat map, which is the case for the other data. This accounts for the lack of curvature of the circles of constant eccentricity (compare with the owl monkey map [Allman & Kaas, 1971], or the theoretical maps). Also, in this work, a mixture of different primate species was used, in addition to rhesus monkeys. This fact is acknowledged by the use of the quotation marks (i.e., "rhesus"). In summary, this figure demonstrates that it is possible to provide a simple analytic approximation to the global retinotopic mappings of a number of different species, in terms of the general form of a complex logarithmic mapping of a linear function of visual field coordinates, as log(z+a).

More recent work (Dow et al., 1981) suggests that the constant "a" is, for rhesus monkey, equal to .3, rather than 1.0, as used in this figure. (See Fig. 5.3)

$w=B*\log(z+a)$. (The units of the complex variable $z=r*\exp(i\theta)$ are: r measured in degrees of eccentricity; θ measured in degrees of azimuth; B measured in mm/degree.)

Thus, the one-dimensional fit to magnification factor (e.g., along the horizontal meridian) directly gives the two-dimensional (conformal) mapping.

Suppose instead that a polynomial fit is provided for the cortical magnification factor along the horizontal meridian, such as:

$$M = \sum a_n(r+b_n)^N \qquad (6)$$

Then, the two-dimensional map function which corresponds to this function is found immediately by complex integration:

$$w(z) = \sum_{n \neq -1}^{N} \frac{a_n(z+b_n)^{n+1}}{n+1} + a_{-1} \log(z+b_{-1}) \qquad (7)$$

Because of the large expansion of cortical area devoted to the central visual field, the shape of the cortical map function is very dependent on magnification estimates obtained in the central few degrees of visual field.

Figure 5.1, reprinted from earlier work (Schwartz, 1980a), shows approximations of the primary visual cortical maps of several primate species, and the cat. Figure 5.2 shows a didactic illustration of the map function used in this work ($\log(z+1)$). This map function was in good agreement with experimental data at the time that this work was published (Schwartz, 1980a). However, recently, Dow et al. (1981) have provided, for the first time, magnification data for the central foveal projection. They derived a fit to a combination of their own, and previous data, of the form $8.62 \log(r+0.3)$, where r represents eccentricity in degrees. This work suggests that a map function of the form $\log(z+0.3)$ provides a more accurate description of the two-dimensional retinotopic map structure of rhesus striate cortex, as illustrated in Fig. 5.3.

Clearly, the agreement between the model $\log(z+0.3)$ and the data is excellent for the range of 10 minutes of arc to over 20 degrees. Although not shown, the log bilinear mapping of the form $8.62*\log(z+0.3)/(z+60.)$ provides a good fit to these data over the entire visual field.

Also shown in Fig. 5.3 are the anatomical data of LeVay et al. (1975), consisting of a flattened specimen of rhesus monkey striate cortex out to $9°$ eccentricity, superimposed on the map $\log(z+0.3)$. Once again, the fit between the anatomical data of LeVay et al. (1975) and the complex log mapping (i.e., $\log(z+0.3)$ is very good.

Thus, Fig. 5.3, based on the extensive data of Dow et al. (1981) and a calculation of the unique conformal map which fits the magnification factor dependence of the form $1/(r+0.3)$, suggests that the cortical map is reasonably close to being isotropic, in agreement with the original explicit measurements of Daniel and Whitteridge (1961).

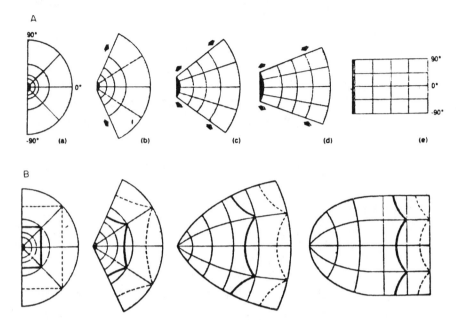

FIG. 5.2.   Graphic simulation of the geometrical properties of the complex log-arithmic mapping, in terms of a series of deformations of an imaginary plastic material. On the top left (a), a logarithmic "radex" is drawn. In figures (b)-(e), this radex, which may be identified with the retina, or the visual field, is smoothly deformed so that its final state, (e), represents the complex logarithmic mapping of the radex. The exponentially spaced concentric circles of (a) have been mapped into parallel, equi-spaced vertical lines; the rays of (a) have been mapped into parallel, equi-spaced horizontal lines. The central black circle of (a) has been stretched into the black band of (e). This black circle represents the singularity of the logarith function. In the lower part of the figure, the singularity is removed by using as mapping function log(1+z). This mapping is quite similar to the log-arithm, except at z=0, where it is finite. Also shown in the figure are the deforma-tion of a large and a small square, under this mapping. It can be seen that the change of shape induced by the mapping is such that the final images are identical in size and shape. A similar property holds for rotation. This is the basis of the pseudo-invariance properties of the complex logarithmic mapping discussed in the text.

Two final remarks may be made at this point concerning the validity of the conformal approximation. First, Sakitt (1982) has recently claimed that "rhesus magnification factor cannot be isotropic". It is difficult to evaluate the map which Sakitt derived, since she did not present it, nor did she present the details of how it was constructed. However, it is clear that Sakitt's conclusion does not logically derive from her arguments. Figure 5.3 shows an example of an iso-tropic (conformal) map which is in excellent agreement with the same anatomical data (LeVay et al., 1975) used by Sakitt. Since the basis of her argument is that, on geometric grounds, it is impossible to find an isotropic map that agrees with current magnification data, and which fits the anatomical data of LeVay et al. (1975), *a single counterexample* is sufficient to disprove this claim. Figure 5.3 shows such a counterexample. The question of whether this map actually is, or is not, isotropic awaits further experimental study. For the time being, the isotropic approximation shown above (in Fig. 5.3) is in good agreement with current data.

If significant shear is found in future work, the mathematical outline presented above indicates how to incorporate it into the description of global topography. In this regard it should be pointed out that LeVay et al. (1975) and Hubel and Freeman (1977) have reported that there is a local anisotropy within ocular dominance columns, caused by a 2:1 compression perpendicular to the ocular dominance column boundary. This shear is *required* if the binocular cortical map is to be isotropic: otherwise, the two sets of ocular input would induce a shear in the overall cortical map. Since it is the average binocular cortical map which has always been measured in cortical magnification experiments, the claim of a local 2:1 shear within ocular dominance columns is consistent with the observed agreement (Fig. 5.3) of an isotropic map with current data.

Recently, Tootell et al., (1982) have observed that the vertical meridian is elongated with respect to the horizontal meridian by a factor of 1.3. They attributed this to a lack of perfect compensation as suggested by LeVay et al. (1975), above, of the ocular dominance column interlacing. However, an elongation of 1.2 of vertical to horizontal meridia is expected from the isotropic function $\log(z+0.3)$ (see above, and Fig. 5.3). Therefore, the apparent shear observed by Tootell et al. (1982) may not, in fact, be due to ocular dominance columns but is very close to the expected result from the isotropic mapping $\log(z+0.3)$.

It is important to emphasize that the map function $\log(z+0.3)$ *does not agree,* in its details, with the polynomial fits of several other workers. Thus, both Drasdo (1977) and Rovamo and Virsu (1979) have provided polynomial fits to retinal ganglion cell density. These fits are similar to published fits to cortical magnification factor, and so these authors have assumed that the retinal data are an accurate predictor of cortical magnification. This assumption is called into question by the following observations: There is a predicted difference in magnification factor along the vertical and horizontal meridians, both from the use of the map $\log(z+a)$, and from the use of the polynomial fits of Drasdo (1977) and Rovamo and Virsu (1979). However, these two approaches to cortical mapping provide *opposite predictions as to this vertical/horizontal magnification difference.* The data of Drasdo (1977) and Rovamo and Virsu (1979) both predict that the magnification factor is larger on the horizontal meridian than on the vertical meridian, and that this difference increases with eccentricity. The map $\log(z+0.3)$ predicts the opposite: magnification factor is larger on the vertical meridian than the horizontal, and the difference decreases with eccentricity. This may be verified, by the interested reader, by direct substitution into the functions published by Drasdo (1977) and Rovamo and Virsu (1979). The magnification factor may be calculated from the function $\log(z+0.3)$ as follows: it is the

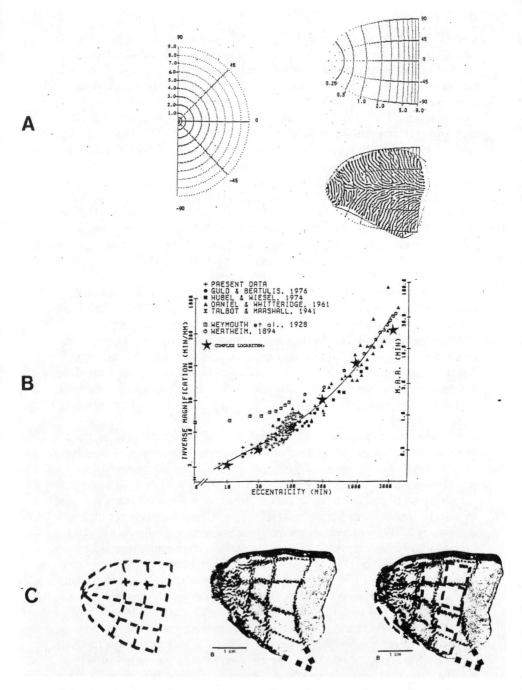

FIG. 5.3. On top left is shown a representation of the visual field (or the surface of the retina). The central 9 deg of field is shown in orthogonal projection. Polar coordinates (r,0) are used to represent the

magnitude of the function $1/(z+0.3)$ (i.e. the derivative of the map function). Thus, a point of ''r'' degrees eccentricity on the vertical meridian, is represented by the complex variable $(0, r*i)$, and its magnification is therefore proportional to $1./\text{sqrt}(r**2+0.009)$. On the other hand, a point of ''r'' degrees eccentricity on the horizontal meridian is represented by the complex variable $(r,0)$, and has a magnification factor proportional to $1/(r+0.3)$.

The total length of the vertical and horizontal meridia may be calculated by integrating these expressions. For integration limits between 0 and 9° (to correspond to the data shown in Fig. 5.3), both Drasdo (1977) and Rovamo and Virsu (1979) predict that the cortical representation of the horizontal meridian is about 15–20% *longer* than the representation of the vertical meridian.

However, the function $\log(z+0.3)$ predicts that the cortical representation of the horizontal meridian is *shorter* than that of the vertical meridian by about 20%. Tootell et al. (1981) have also found, using 2-deoxyglucose mapping, that the horizontal meridian representation of the striate cortex is shorter by 30% than the vertical.

It must be emphasized that this matter is not yet entirely settled. Since the function $\log(z+0.3)$ is in apparently excellent agreement with independent anatomical (LeVay et al., 1975; Tootell et al., 1981) and physiological data (Dow et al., 1981) (see Fig. 5.3), and provides the apparently correct elongation factors of vertical and horizontal meridia, it is proposed that this map function be

---

field. On the right is shown the map of this field representation using the map function $\log(z+0.3)$. This function is derived using the recent fit of Dow et al. (1981) to cortical magnification factor, which provided a best fit to a linear function of inverse magnification factor of the form $\log(z+0.3)$. The two dimensional complex log map is immediately derived from this one dimensional fit of Dow et al. (1981). Also shown is a superposition of the anatomical data of LeVay et al. (1975) showing the central 9 deg of striate cortex (macaque). Clearly, the boundaries of the theoretical map provide a close fit to the boundaries of the anatomical data of LeVay et al. (1975). Thus, an isotropic (i.e. conformal) map of the form $\log(z+0.3)$ provides a good fit to the topography, anatomy, and magnification factor of macaque striate cortex.

In the center is shown a reprint of Dow et al.'s (1981) fit of their own and previous striate cortex magnification data (solid line). Superimposed over this plot of data is the theoretical magnification factor (large stars) calculated from the map function $\log(z+0.3)$. Values at corresponding eccentricities along horizontal and vertical meridians are averaged, in both the theoretical and experimental plots. The agreement is good between 10 minutes and 20 degrees of eccentricity. The far periphery (beyond 20 deg) shows some disagreement, as noted previously (Schwartz, 1977a). However, a function of the form $\log((z+0.3)/(z+60.))$, i.e. the complex logarithm of a bilinear function of visual field, is capable of fitting both central fields (10 min to 20 deg) as well as the far periphery.

On the bottom is shown a superposition of the map function $\log(z+0.3)$, for a stimulus consisting of logarithmically spaced rings and equi-angular rays, as used recently by Tootell et al. (1982), and the corresponding 2-deoxyglucose mapping obtained from macaque striate cortex. The operculum of the cortex is shown (as above, from LeVay et al. (1975). The 2DG map is shown in the center (bottom), and on the right (bottom) is the superposition of this data and the theoretical map function. This map function, which is consistent with the independent experimental data shown in the top and middle parts of this figure, clearly provides a fair prediction for the actual structure of striate cortex topography, as revealed by the 2DG mapping technique of Tootell et al. (1982).

accepted as a candidate for the correct description of striate cortex topography. An additional point is that the function $\log(z+0.3)$ has the advantage that it is an inherently two-dimensional fit, whereas the polynomial fits of Drasdo (1977) and Rovamo and Virsu (1979) are one-dimensional fits along the vertical and horizontal meridia, respectively. The difficulty with these one-dimensional fits is that they do not provide a description of the shape of the map. This may be seen by noting that for Drasdo (1977) and Rovamo and Virsu (1979), both vertical and horizontal meridia have almost identical functional forms, but that the actual data (see Fig. 5.3) have very different curvatures (or shapes) along these two meridia. Although it would be possible to interpolate, if a large number of meridia were fit, it seems that the one-parameter fit provided by a function of the form $\log(z+0.3)$ is a more economical way of presenting these data. The conformal mapping approach allows a direct relationship to be calculated between the observed anatomy (i.e., the shape of striate cortex), and the physiological magnification factor, at all points. Thus, a cross-check on the data may be performed, as done in Fig. 5.3 of this paper. This is important in a field in which the basic data are extremely difficult to obtain, are uncertain, and have tended to waver (in their details) during the past twenty years of study.

Local Functional Architecture of Striate Cortex

Local Architecture of Striate Cortex Modeled by a Local Complex Logarithmic Mapping. The concept of topographic mapping may break down at the level of scale of about 1–2 mm in striate cortex. On this scale, there is a substructure evident which is no longer describable in terms of a simple point mapping. Hubel and Wiesel (1974) have termed this substructure a "hypercolumn". One salient feature of a hypercolumn is that there appears to be a mapping of the orientation of line segments in the visual field to a linear coordinate in the cortex. Specifically, cortical cells which are tuned to lines (or gratings) of a specific orientation are grouped in roughly parallel orientation columns. A full 180° set of these columns occupies about 0.5 mm of rhesus cortex.

Since the retina is only one or two synapses peripheral to this orientation map (in striate cortex), and since the retina presumably represents a more or less strict spatial (x,y) representation of visual data (spatially filtered, but not geometrically reorganized), one may ask the question: Is there a simple map which takes a Cartesian map to an orientation map. If one restricts the possibilities to isotropic regular mappings, then the complex logarithmic provides a prominent candidate (Schwartz, 1976, 1977c).

Figure 5.4 shows an illustration of this model. Parallel lines arranged at equal intervals in the visual field are shown mapped under the function $\log(z+1)$. The reader is reminded that this local map occupies only a tiny piece of the entire cortical surface, and is repeated over and over again across the hypercolumn mosaic.

Several features are evident in this map. A local complex log mapping provides a set of orientation columns, which are quite overlapped. Nevertheless, the mapping of line segment orientation to a linear coordinate, in a roughly parallel fashion, is obvious from Fig. 5.4, top. Conspicuous in this figure is the fact that near the center of the hypercolumn (i.e., where $z=0$), there is increasingly greater overlap of neighboring orientations, and an increasing fuzziness of the column pattern. In other words, near the center ($z=0$), the orientation column pattern is weakened. This effect, due to the singularity near $z=0$, was illustrated in the original discussion of this model (Schwartz, 1977c).

At the time that this model was proposed, there was no evidence of orientation tuning weakening. The data of Hubel and Wiesel (1974) suggested continuous bands of iso-orientation columns. However, recently, Hubel and Livingstone (1981) have reported that near the center of individual ocular dominance columns, there is a noticeable deficit of orientation tuning. This observation is in good agreement with the model of a local complex log geometry.

Thus, the local complex log model outlined above provides a means of spatially organizing afferents to the cortex, so that a simple lateral inhibitory operator and neural summation, will provide a system of orientation columns.

It is important to emphasize that the details of this model, particularly with regard to the local receptive field scatter described by Hubel and Wiesel (1974), have only been addressed in a preliminary fashion (Schwartz, 1977c). This observation of receptive field scatter presents a critical problem for understanding the fine grained spatial functioning of the visual cortex. Hubel and Wiesel (1974) have observed that neighboring cells usually have similar orientation tuning, but may have their receptive field centers scattered by as much as 1–2 mm of cortex. For the central visual cortex, this corresponds to a scatter of about 0.1 degree. But, spatial vision depends on a fidelity of representation which is up to an order of magnitude smaller than this apparent random scatter. Clearly, there must be some ordered structure on this scale of visual cortex which only appears to be random. In the following discussion, it is shown that a particular form of mapping, related to the Radon transform (Herman, 1980), is capable of providing an answer to this puzzle. Although it is not possible to provide a full explanation of this work in the present paper, the basic mathematical results are provided, and several figures are shown to illustrate these ideas. The principal result is that an "inverse back-projection map" seems to be capable of providing a detailed model of local cortical architecture, including the apparent random scatter of receptive fields, but in a way in which perfect spatial fidelity is still preserved.

Receptive Field Scatter and the Radon Map. A suggestion of how to deal with the problem of receptive field scatter in detail is provided by studying the mapping of line segments in Fig. 5.4. It is clear that overlapped parallel bands of equal orientation are constructed. It is also clear that a very rough mapping of

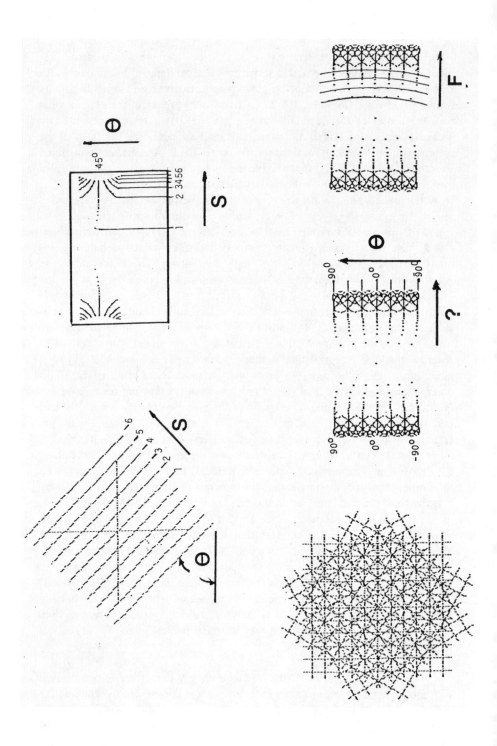

receptive field width (represented by dot spacing in Fig. 5.4) would be created, comparable to spatial frequency columns. However, it is very suggestive that the spatial position (in the cortex) of the lines of Fig. 5.4 is systematically shifted, with increasing distance from the local center of the receptive field. If one recalls that the Radon transform is a map of line integrals such that one coordinate (''s'') represents distance from the origin, and the other coordinate (''θ'') represents orientation, then attention is drawn to the Radon, and related transforms, as a means of modeling the details of summation of afferent input to a cortical hypercolumn.

FIG. 5.4.   This figure is a computer graphic simulation of the symmetric model of a local complex logarithmic mapping representing the structure of a cortical hypercolumn (Schwartz, 1977c).

On the top left, 11 parallel line segments are shown, inclined at a 45 degree angle. Also shown is a pair of vertical and horizontal axes. These line segments may be described by the Radon coordinates (s, θ). The orientation ''θ'' determines the orientation of the lines with respect to the axes. In this case, $\theta = 45$ degrees. The coordinate ''s'' measures the distance of any line from the local origin. Values of ''s'' of 1, 2, 3, 4, 5 and 6, in arbitrary distance units, are indicated. Any line is described by specifying these two coordinates. The area represented by the 11 parallel lines is meant to suggest a small area of retina (i.e., corresponding to a single hypercolumn).

The logarithmic mapping of the 11 line segments, under the function $\log(z+1)$, is shown on the top right. In addition, a uni-directional lateral inhibitory operator has been assumed. The direction of this lateral inhibition is along the ''θ'' axis. The simulation of lateral inhibition has been performed by subtracting neighboring points, within $+ 45°$ of this direction. Note that all of the line segments on the top left have been mapped into the same area of the hypercolumn model on the right. In addition, the Radon coordinate ''s'' indexes the position of these lines on the right. In other words, the local cortical images of the line segments are systematically shifted by the value of their Radon coordinate.

Below, this operation is repeated for 6 different sets of orientations between $+90°$ and $-90°$. It is clear, center and lower right, that a series of ''orientation columns'' are constructed: the images of lines at a given orientation, regardless of their ''s'' coordinate, are mapped into parallel orientation columns. It is evident in this simulation that the center of the hypercolumn model does not possess this property. There is a deficit of orientation mapping in the center of the hypercolumn, as observed recently by Hubel and Livingstone (1981).

Also evident is a systematic ''spatial frequency'' variation, in a direction perpendicular to the orientation axis. This is indicated by the ''F'' axis (lower right) and is consistent with the recent observation of a small variation in spatial frequency sensitivity on the scale of a hypercolumn by Tootell et al. (1981). The reason that this ''F'' axis is also indicated by a ''?'' is to emphasize the uncertainty in the identity of this axis. It is argued in the present paper that the Radon coordinate variation in this direction, rather than the spatial frequency variation in this direction, represents the significant computational aspect of cortical hypercolumn structure.

For reference, the Radon transform, and the inverse Radon transform are stated in equations 8 and 9. The inverse Radon transform is equivalent to the application of three operators: a derivative in the "s" direction, D_s; a Hilbert transform in the "s" direction, H_s; and a backprojection "B". In the following discussion, we consider the possibility that the inverse of the backprojection operator provides a description of hypercolumn architecture, and will outline an experimental test of this hypothesis.

$$m(s,\theta) = [\text{Radon } (g(x,y))](s,\theta) = \int g(s\cos\theta - \mu\sin\theta, s\sin\theta + \mu\cos\theta)d\mu$$
$$g(x,y) = \frac{-1}{2\pi} BH_sD_sm(s,\theta) \tag{8}$$
$$D_s = \frac{\partial}{\partial s}; H_s [m(s, \theta)] = \int \frac{m(s',\theta)ds'}{s' - s}$$

Suppose that, as suggested by Fig. 5.4, the Radon map coordinates (s,θ) represent the local architecture of striate cortex in some layer "A". Figure 5.5 represents a mapping from this layer "A" to another layer "B", in which the inverse backprojection of the image $g(x,y)$ is constructed. This convergence

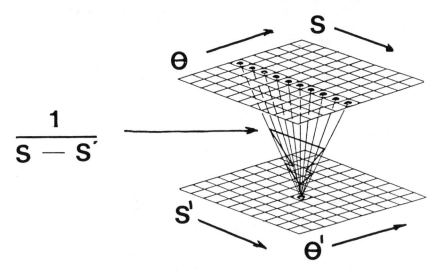

FIG. 5.5.   The top plane shows a Radon map (Plane "A" of the text). The line integral $m(s,\theta)$ is represented at the point (s,θ). Convergence of this plane onto the bottom plane (Plane "B" of the text), with a 1/distance weighting, will result in the Hilbert transform in plane (s',O'). If, in addition, a derivative operator (i.e., via lateral inhibition) is applied prior to convergence, then plane "B" will represent the inverse backprojection of the stimulus. Plane "B" has the phenomenological properties of the local architecture of a cortical hypercolumn, as described in the text.

requires only that an inverse distance weighting to describe the convergence from points in layer A to layer B. This will provide a Hilbert transform. Specifically, if g(x,y) represents the image structure in the retina (i.e., the small patch of retinal projection of the hypercolumn), and if m(s,θ) represents the image in layer A (i.e., a Radon map), then the convergence of Fig. 5.5 will be represented by

$$\rho(s',\theta) \propto B^{-1}g(x,y); \quad B^{-1} = H_s D_s \tag{9}$$

In other words, layer B will be the inverse backprojection of the retinal patch represented by g(x,y).

One can now perform simulated electrophysiological recording in this layer "B" via a *gedanken* experiment. Passing an electrode along the "θ" direction of layer "B" would record cells with oriented "line integral" receptive fields, which had inhibitory flanks due to the derivative operator "D_s" above. This corresponds to orientation columns. Passing an electrode perpendicular to layer "B" would encounter receptive fields at the same orientation, but with scattered "s" coordinates. This scatter is due to the Hilbert transform. The experimental test of the existence of this Hilbert transform would be to determine if the density of the scatter varied as 1/distance from the average center of the receptive fields. It is interesting to note, at this point, that Sanderson (1976) has described just this sort of convolution-like behaviour about LGN projection lines, but with a circularly symmetric rather than a linear structure. If this same result were found in striate cortex, that is, that the apparent scatter of cortical receptive fields within a hypercolumn obeyed a 1/distance weighting with the "s" Radon coordinate (see Fig. 5.5), then the structure of a cortical hypercolumn would resemble that of the inverse backprojection operator, B, of equation (9).

The computational significance of this resemblance of cortical hypercolumn structure to that of the inverse backprojection operator of equation (9) is based on the fact that the sequence of operators which construct the inverse backprojection (derivative and Hilbert transform) are required in order to retain the spatial information which is lost by having elongated "linear" receptive fields. This is of course, the basis of computed tomography (Herman, 1980). But, the visual system appears to use some sort of line integral representation in the form of cortical receptive fields. Thus, the operators associated with the Radon and inverse Radon transforms would be necessary, in order for the cortical map *to retain the details of retinal spatial representation.*

Since visual acuity and vernier acuity are about 10 and 100 times finer, respectively, than the scatter observed by Hubel and Wiesel (1974), it is clear that some form of compensation for this apparently random scatter must occur. The inverse backprojection map suggested above is in agreement with the structure of cortical hypercolumns, including scatter of receptive fields, but provides a solution to the accurate representation of spatial data.

Finally, it should be pointed out that Pollen et al. (1971), in one of the first papers to discuss the relevance of spatial frequency models to cortical physiology, pointed out the resemblance of cortical receptive fields to line integrals, but developed this observation in terms of a Fourier model, rather than the Radon model outlined above. The suggestion of the present paper is that the Radon (and associated) integral transforms may provide a computationally and physiologically plausible alternative to the Fourier transform, as a model of local cortical architecture.

FUNCTIONAL CONSIDERATIONS - COMPUTATIONAL ANATOMY

Global Functional Architecture (Topographic mapping)

Data Compression.   One obvious functional advantage of the non-linear (space-variant) structure of the human visual system is that a wide range of visual resolution is provided, but without the heavy cost that would be incurred by a spatially uniform high resolution system. Since cortical magnification factor decreases by as much as 1.5–2 orders of magnitude from the central fovea to the far periphery, roughly 3–4 more orders of magnitude of surface area would have to be provided if a spatially uniform system, at foveal resolution, were utilized.

This data compression aspect of human vision introduces other problems, however. Eye movement and attentional systems are required in order to utilize the small high acuity area provided by the fovea. In addition, the non-linear map structure of this space-variant system complicates many aspects of pattern recognition. For example, the cortical projection of a stimulus (e.g. a small square) changes as the stimulus moves or as the eye scans (Schwartz, 1980a, Fig. 5.6). Although the conformal nature of the cortical map preserves local angles, distances are distorted. This is a consequence of the non-linear, space-variant structure of the cortical mapping. This aspect of pattern recognition, in terms of the cortical rather than the retinal map of the stimulus, is discussed further below.

Psychophysical 'M' Scaling.   Many workers have pointed out that psychophysical estimates of spatial vision, such as visual acuity and spatial frequency sensitivity, vary with visual eccentricity according to the curve of cortical magnification (Cowan, 1976; Daniel & Whitteridge, 1961; Hubel & Wiesel, 1974; Koenderink & van Doorn, 1978; Ransom-Hogg & Spillmann, 1980; Schwartz, 1976, 1977a; Virsu & Rovamo, 1979). The implication is that visual processing is uniform in the cortical plane. This idea was emphasized by Hubel and Wiesel (1974), who pointed out that the primate visual system behaved as if the same hypercolumn unit was repeated uniformly across the surface of the cortex. Re-

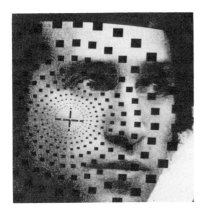 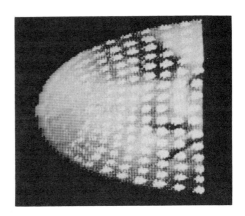

FIG. 5.6.   This figure shows an example of the global complex log mapping. The image on the left (retina) was digitized using a 256 × 256 × 4 bit video display. The image on the right (cortex) was created by mapping this digital image with the topographic map function $\log(z+1)$. Although the map $\log(z+0.3)$ is probably a better estimate for human cortical magnification, as seems to be the case for rhesus monkey data (see p. 83), this map function $\log(z+1)$ will serve to illustrate the topography of the human map, until such time as there are reliable data to indicate the actual topographic structure of this map. Superimposed on the face is a "hypercolumn" grid. The size of these hypercolumns is about 0.1° near the fovea, and about 1–2° at 10° of eccentricity (Ransom-Hogg & Spillmann, 1980). These are indicated by the black squares (in the retina) and the small white blotches (in the cortex). This figure clearly shows the space variant nature of the visual field. Very small areas in the central retina occupy the same amount of cortical space as much larger areas in the periphery. The scale of this figure is such as to roughly mimic the actual relation of cortical hypercolumns to a visual object seen at normal viewing distance. This example provides a didactic illustration of the cortical map function, and the scale of cortical hypercolumns. However, because the aspect ratio of the television differs slightly from 1:1, they should not be used for quantitative purposes. The map of Fig. 5.3 above is quantitatively accurate.

mapping this local hypercolumn unit back to the visual field would result in the "M" scaling (Virsu and Rovamo, 1979) of psychophysical phenomena related to spatial vision. This scaling in terms of the cortical magnification factor seems to accurately summarize the scaling of acuity, spatial frequency sensitivity (Virsu and Rovamo, 1979), and human perceptive field size (Ransom-Hogg and Spillmann, 1980), with the possible exception of the foveal projection (Dow et al., 1981). Fig. 5.6 shows a graphic example of "M" scaling, based on a computer graphic simulation of the topographic structure of striate cortex.

It is important to emphasize that the relationship between retinal ganglion cell density, visual acuity, and cortical magnification factor, requires further detailed investigation. Thus, although these three independent sets of data seem to be approximately proportional to one another, this proportionality may not hold in detail. As outlined above, retinal ganglion cell densities predict a larger magnification factor on the horizontal meridian, compared to the vertical meridian. The opposite difference seems to be the case for actual cortical data. Thus, the detailed nature of "M" scaling requires further experimental and theoretical analysis.

Perceptual Invariances. The complex logarithmic mapping has a well-known invariance property associated with it, which has been the object of extensive study. An example of this size scaling property of the complex log is illustrated in Fig. 5.7. A wrench was digitized with a television camera at three successive distances. The camera was moved along its optical axis. This motion causes the projection of the image onto the camera plane (e.g., the "retina") to increase in size, and, at the same time, to move further into the periphery. The corresponding complex log images are size-invariant, and shift along a straight line, as shown in Fig. 5.7. This property holds for all points of the image plane (beyond the central 1–2 degrees); in other words, the streaming of the visual field, *under motion which lies along the line of sight,* is size-invariant and rectilinear in the complex log plane, while it is radial and size-variant in the image (retinal, or t.v. camera) plane.

Although the present illustration only holds for motion along the line of sight (since other directions of motion include components of shift, instead of pure size streaming), it provides a potential application of the geometric properties of the complex log mapping. Gibson (1966) has discussed this case of motion along the line of sight from the point of view of the image (retinal) plane. It would appear that the complex log plane might simplify the visual streaming pattern for this particular case of motion along the visual axis.

The use of the complex logarithmic mapping in size scaling applications has been extensively discussed in both the biological and machine vision literature (Brousil & Smith, 1967; Casasent & Psaltis, 1976; Schwartz, 1977a; Weiman & Chaiken, 1979). Several of these applications have attempted to avoid the difficulties of the lack of shift invariance of the complex log mapping by providing a preliminary Fourier transform (Brousil & Smith, 1967; Casasent & Psaltis, 1976). It has also been pointed out in the context of biological vision that a combination of a Fourier transform, a complex logarithm, and a final Fourier transform is shift, size and rotation invariant (Cavanagh, 1978; Schwartz, 1978).

Cavanagh (1978) calls the combination of Fourier and complex log mapping a "log polar frequency mapping", and has proposed that either a global, or a local version of this mapping is a basis for human perceptual invariances. Unfortunately, globally this cannot be the case. These mappings yield a visual system which is completely invariant to shift. A small test stimulus (i.e., a Snellen letter) would be equally visible at all positions of the visual field of such a system. Clearly, this is in fundamental disagreement with the space-variant aspects of

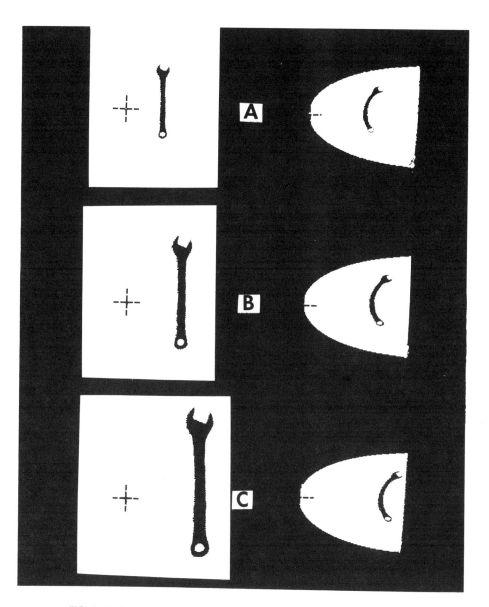

FIG. 5.7.   A wrench was digitized with a television camera, at three distances A, B, C, from the wrench, moving along the optical axis of the camera. The simulated cortical image of the wrench is shown on the right (map function=$\log(z+1)$).
The cortical image is size-invariant, and streams along parallel lines, while the retinal projection is size-variant, and streams along radial lines. This property holds for all stimulus positions, outside of the fovea (about 1–2 degrees with this map function). This simple streaming property does not hold for motion which is off the optical axis, since this introduces components of shift.

human vision (e.g. Ransom-Hogg and Spillmann, 1980). Locally, the log polar frequency mapping is invariant only over the span of a single hypercolumn (which is the region of the proposed initial Fourier transform). Thus, for stimuli which are larger than single hypercolumns, there is in fact no simple invariance property. On the contrary, the problem of patching together the 1000 or so individual log polar frequency mappings, as a stimulus changes size or position across the cortex, is extremely difficult and has not been discussed. Further issues related to the problems associated with the use of Fourier models in human vision are discussed in other work (Schwartz, 1981a). At the present time, it is an open question whether the local hypercolumn structure does, or does not suggest a spatial frequency column structure. As mentioned above, and in previous work (Schwartz, 1977c, Fig. 5), some systematic variation of receptive field width (or spatial frequency tuning) on the scale of a hypercolumn is expected, from the complex log model (Fig. 5.4). On the other hand, the present paper has proposed that integral transforms other than the Fourier transform are potential candidates to describe hypercolumn structure (e.g., the Radon and backprojection transforms discussed above). At the present time, these are open experimental questions.

Computational Anatomy: Applications to Projective Invariance, Stereo Segmentation, and Shape Analysis.   The previous example of the size scaling property of the complex logarithmic mapping provides an example of the term "computational anatomy." The specific forms of spatial mapping which occur in visual cortex may themselves represent, or facilitate, computational aspects of vision. The concept of computational anatomy (Schwartz, 1980a) provides a distinct alternative to the common critique of the neural "homunculus" or "little green man in the brain." This critique seeks to establish that cortical mapping, per se, is not of direct relevance to vision, since this would require a "little man" to "observe" the mappings. The response to this critique is to point out that spatial mapping, from the level of the retina to striate cortex, and beyond, simply provides a means for the visual system to format visual data. Specific formats are provided for specific functions. Computations may be greatly simplified by manipulating these data formats (i.e., by using specific forms of anatomical mapping). This idea is illustrated by briefly citing several additional examples as follows.

Complex Cross Ratio and Global Cortical Topography.   The size scaling properties of the complex logarithm are clearly insufficient, by themselves, to provide a functional model of human perceptual size invariance. This is because of the lack of translation invariance which is caused by the structure of this mapping. As the eye scans over a stimulus, the shape (at the level of striate cortex) of objects in the visual field is continually changing (Schwartz, 1980a,

Fig. 5.6). Because of the conformal nature of this mapping, local angles, and curvature, are preserved. However, the change in the metric properties of the map requires careful discussion. Two approaches to this are briefly reviewed here. First, it can be shown that the *difference map* of a visual scene, for two fixation points, is closely related to the complex cross ratio of the scene (Schwartz, 1981b). For a scan path of "n" fixation points, a generalized complex cross ratio can be defined, which is the net difference map across the set of "n" fixation points. This generalized complex cross ratio is a projective invariant (Schwartz, 1981b). Thus, by combining an algorithm to generate visual scan paths (i.e., by maximum local curvatures of the stimulus), and by considering the net difference map, at the level of striate cortex, a projective invariant representation of the visual field can be obtained (Schwartz, 1981b).

Stereo Segmentation and Ocular Dominance Columns.   One of the principal computational difficulties in stereo vision is the problem of segmentation. Areas of common binocular disparity must be marked, or segmented, in order to continue with any further stereo visual processing. Common computer approaches to this problem involve correlating patches of left and right eye views. Although it is evident that such an algorithm can be made to work, it is a computationally intensive approach. One such algorithm (Marr, 1979) is reported to require over one billion multiplications to converge to a solution with realistic images.

The pattern of interlaced ocular dominance columns suggests that a simpler, and faster, approach may be taken by biological visual systems. In optical information processing, a method of image segmentation based on interlacing two images, which have been projected through optical gratings, is well known (e.g., Pennington et al., 1970). Applications of this method to movement segmentation have been proposed.

The binocular interlacing of input to the cortex, via the ocular dominance column system, is a direct analogue to this method. In this case, the small differences in position, in the projections of the left and right eye, cause a stereo signal to be modulated by the period of the ocular dominance columns. The mathematical details of this are presented in other work (Schwartz, 1982). Figure 5.8 below shows an application of this proposal, using optical simulation, for a photograph, and a random dot stereogram. It can be seen that a stereo segmentation cue is supplied by this difference mapping algorithm.

The interesting aspect of this algorithm is that it may provide a general computational rationale for columnar architecture, which is a feature of many sensory and non-sensory cortical areas (Goldman & Nauta, 1977). The extraction of differences between two similar "views", and their representation as a spatial frequency modulated difference mapping, may be a general computational feature of cortical systems.

FIG. 5.8.   On top, frame C shows a digitized image of a small statue (256 × 256 × 4 bits). Frame D shows this statue filtered with a thresholded 5 point approximation to a difference-of-gaussian filter, providing a sharp high-pass filter which outlines the edges of the stimulus. Frame E shows two slightly shifted versions of the image, interlaced by alternate "ocular dominance columns." The shift between the figures in this case is about half of an ocular dominance column, and the scale of the figure is therefore about 3° from top to bottom. Frame F, G, and H show interlacings corresponding to disparities of 1/3, 1/2 and 1 ocular dominance column, followed by high pass filtering with the D.O.G. filter used in frame D. It is clear that a cue for disparity, in the form of frequency ripples about the stimulus contours, is available. Since the size of Panum's area is about 10 minutes of arc, and since the angular extent of a single human ocular dominance column is about 10 minutes of arc (Schwartz, 1980b), these disparities used in frames F, G, and H correspond to 1/3, 1/2 and 1 unit of Panum's area.

Visual Illusions.   Several visual illusions which have been discussed in terms of the cortical, rather than the retinal, structure of visual stimuli are the fortification illusions associated with migraine headaches (Richards, 1971; Schwartz, 1980a), the Frazer spiral (Schwartz, 1980a), certain visual hallucination patterns (Ermentrout & Cowan, 1979), and the orthogonal afterimage (MacKay, 1970; Schwartz, 1980a, b).

The orthogonal afterimage provides a good example of an effect in which both the local (orientation column) and global (topographic) patterns of the visual cortex contribute to the perceptual effect. This afterimage occurs after prolonged viewing of periodic patterns (Fig. 5.9) and consists of a streaming motion orthogonal to the original stimulus. This illusion has been puzzling, since it would be expected that an afterimage would be the simple spatial complement of the stimulus pattern (Julesz, 1970).

The orientation column pattern of striate cortex, however, provides an immediate solution to this problem. The representation of a line, and its orthogonal complement, differ only by a spatial shift of half of a hypercolumn, at the level of striate cortex. Therefore, a visual pattern, *and its orthogonal complement in the visual field,* consist of spatially complementary patterns at the level of striate cortex. *This is due entirely to the local pattern of periodic orientation columns. Therefore, this effect is not strongly dependent on the momentary position of eye fixation.*

Clearly, this effect should be maximal for visual patterns which project to the cortex in an isotropic fashion, so that the cortical complementarity would be maximal. This appears to be the case for the patterns which MacKay (1970) has used to illustrate the effect: these are approximately logarithmic circles, spirals, and equi-angular rays (Fig. 5.9). But, these are the unique patterns which project to equal isotropic grids at the cortex, due to *the global cortical map* (Schwartz, 1977a).

Thus, the local orientation column pattern seems to provide a general explanation for the association of periodic patterns with their orthogonal complements, while the global cortical map function explains the apparent strength of this illusion for logarithmic patterns (Fig. 5.9), relative to other forms of periodic (e.g. linear) gratings.

INFEROTEMPORAL (IT) CORTEX AND THE ANALYSIS OF CURVATURE

The most striking spatial transformations which occur to the retinal input to striate cortex are the global topographic mapping, the interlacing of the cortical input from the left and right eyes, via the ocular dominance column system, and the regular periodic mapping of orientations which is associated with the orientation column system. In the previous sections, a variety of computational rationales for both the global topographic mapping and the ocular dominance column systems have been discussed. The periodic mapping of contour orientations via the orientation column system is strongly suggestive of an analysis of shape in terms of some aspect of boundary orientation or curvature. In the computer literature, there is a well-known method of shape analysis known as the "Fourier descriptor" approach (e.g., Persoon & Fu, 1977; Zahn and Roskies, 1972). It has been suggested, due to the orientation column mapping of striate cortex, that extrastriate cortex and, in particular, infero-temporal cortex (IT) may analyze the shape of stimuli via an analysis of the spatial texture of the striate cortex map (Schwartz,

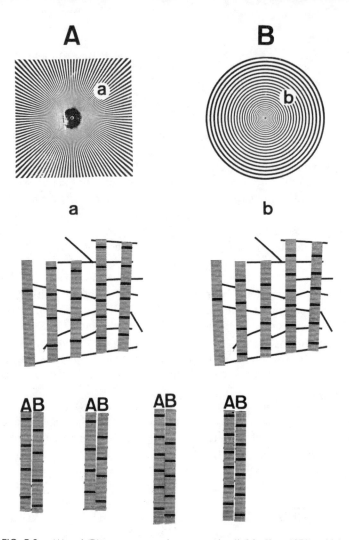

FIG. 5.9. (A) and (B) represent complementary stimuli (MacKay, 1970), which map to equispaced, isotropic patterns under the global mapping log(z+a). A small section of this isotropic cortical pattern is labeled by (a) and (b) in the central panel. The columnar structure of the cortex is suggested by the rows of parallel bars (i.e., orientation columns). The pattern of stimulated orientation columns is indicated by dark bars. Corresponding areas of cortex are reproduced side-by-side on the bottom of the figure. It is clear that the perpendicular contours, in (a) and (b) of the complementary stimuli, are *anatomically complementary at the cortex*. This may be seen also by noting that perpendicular contours in the visual field map to cortical locations (within a hypercolumn) which are exactly half of a hypercolumn shifted with respect to each other. This is illustrated in the figure.

Thus, when image (A) is shown, the cortical complement (or cortical afterimage) is that of (B), and vice-versa.

This effect is presumably strengthened, for these stimuli, due to the fact that the exponential spacing of the circles, and the equi-angular spacing of the rays, causes the patterns to be isotropically mapped to the cortex. This property naturally only holds for central fixation. However, for any fixation point, the local anatomical complementarity still holds, and this seems to provide a simple rationale for the orthogonal afterimage.

1980a). Since spatial intervals in striate cortex correspond to differences in contour orientation (i.e., to curvature), it would be relatively simple for extra-striate visual areas (e.g. IT) to achieve a shape descriptor by "viewing" the striate cortex orientation map through a suitable spatial filtering algorithm. This hypothesis has led to the experimental test that will now be described. This test uses the basic visual patterns associated with the method of Fourier descriptors in order to test the hypothesis that IT cortex may be using a periodic orientation or curvature description of shape (Schwartz et al., 1983; Desimone et al., 1982).

The method of Fourier descriptors assumes that a simple closed contour is represented by its boundary angle function. This is a representation of the orientation of the tangent to the shape at regular intervals around the boundary of the shape. Figure 5.10 shows an example of this boundary angle function for a simple shape such as a hand. Since the boundary angle function represents the shape as a one-dimensional function (parameterized by arc length), a one-dimensional Fourier analysis may be performed. Then, the shape is represented by periodic components of boundary orientation, or Fourier descriptors. Each Fourier descriptor is associated with a frequency "f", and amplitude "a_f", and a phase "α_f". If the boundary angle function is represented as B(1), where 1 represents equal steps of arc length around the perimeter of the shape, then the set of Fourier descriptors, i.e., the Fourier transform of B(1), is given by Zahn and Roskies (1972):

$$a_f e^{i2\pi\alpha_f} = \int_0^L B(1)e^{i2\pi 1 f}dl \qquad (10)$$

Any closed, simple shape is represented by its corresponding set of Fourier descriptors (FD's). A relatively small, truncated set of FD's provides a reasonable estimate of the gestalt of a shape, as shown in Fig. 5.10. FD's thus represent a global approach to shape description which is contingent on a periodic representation of boundary orientation.

Since the striate cortex seems to provide just such a data format (e.g. the periodic orientation column pattern), the hypothesis has been advanced that IT neurons might code shape on the basis of global shape features such as FD's (Schwartz, 1980a).

In order to explore this possibility, a set of visual stimuli was printed onto photographic slides (from a computer graphic display). The inverse transform of a single FD uniquely determines a closed boundary with a specific number of lobes (frequency), lobe indentation (amplitude) and orientation (phase), as shown in Fig. 5.11. These shapes are referred to in the following as FD stimuli.

If IT neurons function as band-pass filters for shape, one would expect different IT neurons to be tuned to different FD's. Furthermore, the tuning should be independent of the size, contrast, and position on the retina (Gross et al., 1972).

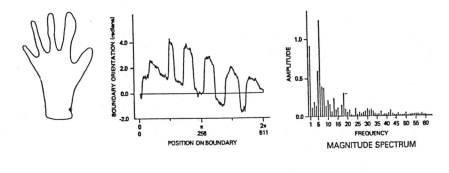

POSITION ON BOUNDARY

MAGNITUDE SPECTRUM

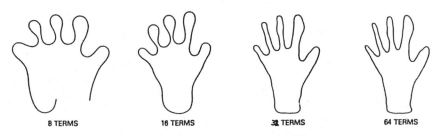

8 TERMS   16 TERMS   32 TERMS   64 TERMS

FIG. 5.10.   On top left is shown a hand. The boundary angle function of this shape is plotted in the center. On the right is the *angular* power spectrum of this boundary angle function. Below are shown several "approximations" of the hand, which are obtained by truncating the set of Fourier descriptors, and then reconstructing the stimulus from the truncated set. This shows that the Fourier descriptors capture the *gestalt* of a shape, even with only a few descriptors.
Note that this constitutes an example of low-pass filtering in the angular or curvature domain. Low-pass filtering, but in the *spatial domain, rather than the curvature domain,* has been discussed by Ginsberg (this volume).

Thus, the activity of a set of such neurons could specify or code any shape, in terms of its boundary curvature.

A total of 234 visually responsive neurons in five macaques were studied with these FD stimuli. All units were tested with slits of light, a set of complex objects (e.g., brushes, dolls, etc.), and a series of FD stimuli. The FD stimuli were white on black patterns projected onto a tangent screen at the center of gaze, and ranged in frequency from 2 to 64 cycles/perimeter in octave steps. For some units, the frequency series was repeated at different sites within the receptive field, with different FD amplitudes, with different stimulus sizes, or with reversed stimulus contrast.

Fifty-four percent of the visually responsive IT neurons were "tuned" to the frequency of FD stimuli (Desimone et al., 1982; Schwartz et al., 1982) with a mean bandwidth of 2 octaves (FWHM). Different cells had different optimal frequencies, and all frequencies were about equally represented although the highest frequency used (Frequency 64) had a reduced incidence. Thus, for about half of the cells in IT, the frequency of FD's appeared to be a relevant stimulus dimension. The remaining neurons either did not respond to the FD stimuli (26%), responded equally well to all of the FD stimuli (13%), or had multi-modal tuning curves (7%).

Thus, although the use of FD methods for the neurophysiological and psycho-physical study of shape perception needs much further work, they seem to offer a promising method of bridging the gap between the local analysis of contrast provided by conventional spatial frequency and edge detection approaches and the global analysis of pattern and shape.

The previous discussion of boundary curvature in IT cortex indicates that the Fourier descriptor method provides a quantitative probe of shape sensitivity in the primate (and human) visual system. It also indicates one way in which an invariant shape description may be achieved, despite the space-variant mapping which occurs early in human visual processing (i.e., at the level of striate cortex). The Fourier descriptors are based on the intrinsic geometry of a shape: they provide a description of curvature parameterized by arc length. This is the reason why they are size and translation invariant. If a similar method of analysis is used in the human visual system, then some form of variable metric, at the

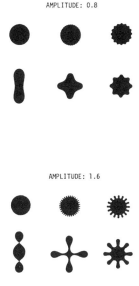

AMPLITUDE: 0.8

AMPLITUDE: 1.6

FIG. 5.11.   The shapes associated with individual Fourier descriptors are shown. On top is a set at ampli-tude 0.8 (units of Zahn & Roskies, 1972), and frequencies 2, 4, 8, 16, 32, 64. On bottom is shown ampli-tude 1.6, at frequencies 2, 4, 8, 16, 32, 64. These shapes were used as stimuli in a recent experiment study-ing the shape sensitivity of in-ferotemporal cortex (Desimone et al., 1982). Read counterclockwise starting from left lower figure in each set.

cortical level, must be employed. Specifically, the IT cells which "view" patterns of cortical orientation columns (through intermediary extrastriate areas) could achieve this form of metric by space-variant filtering which would adjust the measured curvature with respect to position across the cortical surface. In other words, a given spatial interval between stimulated orientation columns would have a curvature value which was determined by the position in the visual field indexed by that particular hypercolumn. By means of a space-variant metric of this kind, the non-linear mapping of early visual processing need not complicate later states of visual computation, could benefit from the data compression inherent in the striate cortex map, yet could provide an invariant description of shape.

SUMMARY

This paper provides a mathematical characterization of the spatial structure of striate cortex topography and proposes several models of the local patterns of functional architecture in striate cortex. A variety of computational applications suggested by these forms of mapping are also proposed. These include applications to visual data compression, stereo segmentation, perceptual invariances, and shape analysis. Finally, recent experimental results concerning shape analysis by higher order cortical processing (i.e., IT cortex) are described.

The principal thrust of this analysis is to view the intricate patterns of functional architecture of striate cortex as one possibility by which the primate (and human) visual system achieves its impressive level of visual performance. The anatomy of the central nervous system may play a direct role in neural computation by providing novel architectures for image representation which greatly simplify the very intensive computations which must occur. In other words, it is argued that in the biology of vision, just as in many other areas of biology, form follows function.

REFERENCES

Ahlfors, L. *Complex Analysis*. McGraw-Hill, New York, 1966.

Allman, J., & Kaas, J. Representation of the striate and adjoining cortex of the owl monkey brain. *Brain Research*, 1971, *35*, 89–106.

Brocker, T. *Differential Germs and Catastrophes*. Cambridge U. Press, New York, 1975.

Brousil, J. K., & Smith, D. R. A threshold logic network for shape invariance. *I.E.E.E. Transactions on Computers* EC-16, 818–828, 1967.

Casasent, D., & Psaltis, D. Position, rotation and scale invariant optical correlation. *Applied Optics* *15*, 1793–1799, 1976.

Cavanagh, P. Size and position invariance in the visual system. *Perception* 1978, *7*, 167–177.

Cowan, J. D. Spatial filtering in the Visual Pathway. In: O. D. Creutzfeldt (Ed.), *Supplement to Afferent and Intrinsic Organization of Laminated Structures in the Brain*. Springer-Verlag, Berlin 1976.

Daniel, M., & Whitteridge, D. The representation of the visual field on the cerebral cortex in monkeys. *Journal of Physiology* 1961, *159*, 203–221.

Desimone, R., Schwartz, E. L., Albright, T. D., & Gross, C. G. Inferior temporal neurons selective for shape. *Investigative Ophthalmology & Visual Science* ARVO Supplement (in press), 1982.

Dow, B. M., Snyder, A. Z., Vautin, R. G., & Bauer, R. Magnification factor and receptive field size in foveal striate cortex of monkey. *Experimental Brain Research* 1981, *44*, 213–228.

Drasdo, N. The neural representation of visual space. *Nature, London,* 1977, *256*, 554–556.

Ermentrout, G. B., & Cowan, J. D. A mathematical theory of visual hallucination patterns. *Biological Cybernetics* 1979, *34*, 137–150.

Gattass, R., Gross, C. G., & Sandell, J. Visual topography of V2 in the macaque. *Journal of Comparative Neurology 201,* 519–539.

Gibson, J. J. *The Senses Considered as Perceptual Systems*. Boston, Mass.: Houghton-Mifflin, 1966.

Goldman, P., & Nauta, W. Columnar distributions of cortico-cortical fibers in frontal association, limbic, and motor cortex of developing rhesus monkey. *Brain Research* 1977, *122*, 393–413.

Gross, C. G., Rocha-Miranda, C. E., & Bender, D. Visual properties of neurons in infertemporal cortex of the macaque. *Journal of Neurophysiology* 1972, *35*, 96–111.

Herman, G. T. *Image Reconstruction from Projections*. New York: Academic Press, 1980.

Hubel, D. H., & Freeman, D. C. Projection into the visual field of ocular dominance columns in macaque monkey. *Brain Research* 1977, *122*, 336–343.

Hubel, D. H., & Livingstone, M. Regions of poor orientation tuning coincide with patches of cytochrome oxidase staining in monkey striate cortex. *Neuroscience Abstracts* 1981, *7*, 357.

Hubel, D. H., & Wiesel, T. N. Sequence regularity and geometry of orientation columns in the monkey striate cortext. *Journal of Comparative Neurology* 1974, *158*, 267–293.

Julesz, B. *Foundations of Cyclopean Perception*. Chicago, Ill.: University of Chicago Press.

Koenderink, J. J., & van Doorn, J. J. Visual detection of spatial contrast; influence of location in the visual field, target extent and illuminance level. *Biological Cybernetics* 1978, *30*, 157–167.

LeVay, S., Hubel, D. H., & Wiesel, T. N. The pattern of ocular dominance columns in macaque visual cortex revealed by a reduced silver stain. *Journal of Comparative Neurology* 1975, *159*, 559–576.

MacKay, D. M. Perception and brain function. In: *Second Neurosciences Study Program*, 305–315. Cambridge, Mass.: M.I.T. Press, 1970.

Marr, D. (Ed.) *Proceedings of Austin Feature Extraction Conference*. New York: Academic Press, 1979.

Pennington, K. S., Will, P. M., & Shelton, G. L. Grid coding: a technique for extraction of differences from scenes. *Optics Communication* 1970, *2*, 113–119.

Persoon, E., & Fu, K. S. Shape discrimination using Fourier descriptors. *I.E.E.E. Transactions on Systems, Man and Cybernetics*, SMC-7, 1977, *3*, 170–179.

Pollen, D., Lee, J. R., & Taylor, J. H. How does the striate cortex begin the reconstruction of the visual world. *Science* 1971, *173*, 74–77.

Ransom-Hogg, A., & Spillmann, L. Perceptive field size in fovea and periphery of the light and dark adapted retina. *Vision Research* 1980, *20*, 221–228.

Richards, W. Fortification illusions associated with migraine headache. *Scientific American* 1971, *78*, 115–120.

Rovamo, J., & Virsu, V. An estimation and application of human cortical magnification factor. *Experimental Brain Research* 1979, *37*, 495–510.

Sakitt, B. Why the cortical magnification factor in rhesus can not be isotropic. *Vision Research* 1982, *22*, 417–421.

Sanderson, K. J. Visual field projection columns and magnification factors in the lateral geniculate body of the cat. *Experimental Brain Research* 1976, *13*, 159–177.

Schwartz, E. L. Analytic structure of the retinotopic mapping of visual cortex and relevance to perception. *Neuroscience Abstracts* #1636, 1976.

Schwartz, E. L. Spatial mapping in primate sensory projection and relevance to perception. *Biological Cybernetics* 1977, *25*, 181–194. (a)

Schwartz, E. L. The development of specific visual connections in the monkey and the goldfish. *Journal of Theoretical Biology* 1977, *69*, 655–683. (b)

Schwartz, E. L. Afferent geometry in primate visual cortex and the generation of neural trigger features. *Biological Cybernetics* 1977, *29*, 1–24. (c)

Schwartz, E. L. Spatial mapping in the visual system. *Journal of the Optical Society of America* 1978, *68*, 1371.

Schwartz, E. L. Computational anatomy and functional architecture of striate cortex: A spatial mapping approach to perceptual coding. *Vision Research* 1980, *20*, 645–669. (a)

Schwartz, E. L. A quantitative model of the functional architecture of human striate cortex with application to visual illusion and texture analysis. *Biological Cybernetics* 1980, *37*, 63–76. (b)

Schwartz, E. L. Cortical anatomy and spatial frequency analysis. *Perception* 1981, *10*, 455–468. (a)

Schwartz, E. L. A projective invariant recursive flow model of visual coding. *Advances in Physiological Sciences* 1981, *16*, 431–436. (b)

Schwartz, E. L. Computational anatomy and columnar architecture in primate striate cortex: Segmentation and feature extraction via spatial frequency coded difference mapping. *Biological Cybernetics* 1982, *42*, 157–168. (a)

Schwartz, E. L., Desimone, R., Albright, T. D., & Gross, C. G. Shape recognition and inferior temporal neurons. Submitted to Proceedings of the National Academy of Science, 1983.

Segal, L. A. *Mathematics Applied to Continuum Mechanics.* New York: Macmillan, 1977.

Tootell, R. B., Silverman, M. S., & De Valois, R. L. Spatial frequency columns in primary visual cortex. *Science* 1981, *214*, 813–815.

Tootell, R., Silverman, M., Switkes, E., & De Valois, R. Deoxyglucose analysis of retinotopic organization in primate striate cortex. *Science 218*, 902–904, 1982.

Virsu, V. & Rovamo, J. Visual resolution, contrast sensitivity and the cortical magnification factor. *Experimental Brain Research* 1979, *37*, 474–494.

Weiman, C. F. R., & Chaiken, G. Logarithmic spiral grids for image processing and display. *Comparative Graphics and Image Processing* 1979, *11*, 197–226.

Zahn, C. R., & Roskies, R. Z. Fourier descriptors for plane closed curves. *I.E.E.E. Transactions on Computers* C-21, 1972, *3*, 269–281.

6 Models of Explanation in Visual Pattern Perception

Kai von Fieandt
University of Helsinki
Helsinki, Finland

ABSTRACT

This chapter is concerned with four models of pattern perception: (a) the Dodwell Model, (b) the System-Theoretical Approach, (c) the Reenpää Model, and (d) the Hoffman Model (LTG/NP—the Lie transformation group approach to neurophysiology).

Three points are stressed in regard to the mathematical descriptions of these models:

1. Progress within the fields of biological research has been extraordinarily rapid, creating a considerable lag in incorporating new achievements. Therefore, parallel biotheoretical models are likely to prevail.

2. There has been much confusion in discussing theoretical models because the levels of description (e.g., metric level, statistical level) have not been kept sufficiently apart. We shall probably never arrive at theories which are truly universal, because of the different explanatory tasks of the models concerned.

3. A false enthusiasm for "universal models" is also rooted in the popularity of reductionism. Hoffman's model, if mathematically valid, has an explanatory value quite independent of whether or not the "geometric orbits or trajectories" can be neurophysiologically interpreted.

INTRODUCTION

What modern neurophysiological research has produced in about three decades in terms of fresh observations and new experimental data is impressive and hard to believe. The abundance of the results is reflected in an increased interest in theoretical models all over the world. Above all, there is the problem of the "integration" of the registered information. What happens to the immediate sensory data, to the "message of the receptors," on its way toward levels of higher neural organization?

In perceptual psychology there has been a tendency to refer discovered regularities and sequences of events to what simultaneously goes on in the CNS. Research in pattern perception in particular has been linked to physiological correlates of immediately observed phenomena. This is how psychological evidence is "reduced" to what we learn about the cytoarchitecture and the biological functions of the brain via the "exact sciences," e.g. physics and chemistry.

The problem is as old as research in perception in general. At several periods, a strong interest has arisen in the potential structural or functional neural correlates of patterned visual experiences. One should not forget the contribution of Gestalt-oriented psychologists e.g. Köhler (1924, 1929), nor the figure-detectors postulated by Hebb (his ideas of cell assemblies and phase-sequences). This vivid interest has been undermined by the lack of knowledge of microscopic structural details and events in the visual cortex. Certainly, the "isomorphism principle" presented by W. Köhler (1929) was exciting; yet, he confined himself to macroscopic descriptions, whereas the most decisive arrangements inside the CNS apparently occur on a cellular level. It was the introduction of "single-cell recordings" (e.g. De Valois, 1971; Hubel & Wiesel 1962, 1965) that completely altered modern explanations of perceptual processes. When searching again for the mechanism of pattern perception, scientists were stimulated not only by advances in the neurophysiology of the CNS; the applications of new mathematical tools (e.g. Bruter, 1977; Hoffman, 1977) have also undergone a revolutionary development. It is quite appropriate to look for mathematically founded explanations of perceptual or cognitive processes. If contemporary perceptual psychology is criticized for lacking a unitary background, such a deficiency is due to disagreements among its representatives about mathematical models that are most suitable for the comprehensive descriptions required. Marr and Poggio (1977), in their evaluation of methodological requirements for explaining biological achievements, have suggested four steps to be taken whenever starting a "natural computation approach":

1. Identify the goal and the givens. What is the desired representation? What data are available?
2. Show theoretically how a reliable representation can be computed. What are the natural constraints that will force the unique interpretation?
3. Design a particular algorithm that correctly interprets the available input information.
4. Test whether the primate visual system uses the particular algorithm. If not, identify which step above is incompatible and reiterate.

It would have been nice if the constructors of various explanatory models had actually adhered to these recommendations by Marr and Poggio. However, "model theorists" have predominantly been guided by their diverging epistemological approaches. In order to understand this background one has to follow their way of presentation. The following discussion is confined to four prevailing models of explanation which have been quite arbitrarily chosen from various alternatives:

1. The Dodwell Model (Hebb, 1949; Hubel & Wiesel, 1962, 1965)
2. The System Theoretical Approach (Kohonen, 1977; Lehtiö & Kohonen, 1978; Wiener, 1961).
3. The Reenpää Model (Hensel, 1966; Keidel, 1961; v. Weizsäcker, 1954)
4. The Hoffman 1977 Model (LTG/NP—the Lie transformation group approach to neurophysiology)

Before discussing these models let us consider the criteria for a good theory of perception, set out by P. C. Dodwell (1977b) in a paper at Marseilles, 1976:

1. A theory must account for the phenomena in question, and it should have depth.
2. A theory must have *predictive* power.
3. A theory should be *extensible*. It gains power by being shown to have application over a range of different situations.
4. A theory should show *originality*. It should bring one to see the facts from a new point of view.
5. A theory should be *parsimonious*. This means involving few explanatory concepts, the power of simplicity.
6. A theory should have *world view compatibility*. It should fit with the general view of the nature of the world accepted by contemporary research.

DODWELL'S MODEL

This explanation may be looked upon as an immediate completion of views represented by Hubel and Wiesel (1962), Boycott (1974), Blakemore and Campbell (1969), Barlow (1975), Campbell and Robson (1968). The simultaneously morphological and functional description which has already been given of the neural procedures could, according to them, be appropriately applied even at the cellular level.

What Hebb was aiming at with his conception of figure extractors has nowadays been specified to represent several systematically investigated types of cells (e.g., orientation, direction and movement detectors). Since his well-known main work, Dodwell (1970) has more recently stressed his point of view in a symposium at Marseilles (1977a).

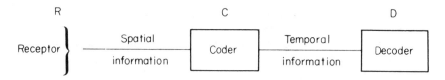

FIG. 6.1.   Schematical drawing of the pattern-coding model. (From Dodwell, 1970. Reprinted by permission from v. Fieandt & Moustgaard, The Perceptual World. London: Academic Press 1977, p. 317.)

The basic model constructed by Dodwell looks, as far as sensory functions are concerned, somewhat like the connections and relationships in the following sketchy diagram (Fig. 6.1).

It has been observed that the contour-information contained in retinal stimulation is transmitted to C as a first stage of communication. At this stage the representation is merely spatial. Mediation of spatial information requires a *topological* correspondence between the input at the R-level and the input at C. Yet, such a correspondence does not necessarily imply a *topographic* identity. It is only at the third stage that the temporal organization of the message is maintained during the transmission procedure from C to D.

When Hubel and Wiesel mapped the receptive fields for single neurons in the cortex of cats, they found some correspondence to the arrangements of the receptive fields at the level of single cells in the geniculate bodies and even at the level of the retina. Yet, the cortical fields turned out to be much more complicated. However, what is surprising is the "economy" and the "simplicity" in the functional solutions of the systems.

Experiments by Hubel and Wiesel (1962, 1965) have justified the conclusion that there might exist a mechanism for extraction of visual linear elements. Dodwell assumes that stimulus-equivalence is at least partly achieved by means of perceptual learning. Although Dodwell took the findings of Hubel and Wiesel (1962, 1965) as his starting point, he is skeptical about single-unit recording techniques providing the *pattern* codes, in addition to the rather obvious *contour* code. So far there is no evidence for units tuned to the detection of elaborate figures, letters, or numerals or even complicated objects ("grandmother cells" etc., see Dodwell 1977a, p. 100).

Interestingly enough, the model elaborated by Dodwell can be used for computer simulations of the activated visual system. What is more, it seems to account for impressive processes of readaptation to optically distorted pattern inputs. Thus, the model provides us with several possibilities for applying the famous distortion experiments carried out by Ivo Kohler (1951, 1974).

Dodwell's model represents many traits which can be found within the framework of general information theory. For instance, the feedback concept plays a predominant role. Incidentally, the information theory of Shannon and Weaver (1949) also made an origin of other explanation models (e.g., *system theory* and *signal-detection theory*).

The theoretical framework of Dodwell's explanations could, of course, be criticized from several points of view. Although he takes into account "the integrative activity of the whole nervous system" (1977a, p. 100), he has not got rid of a few rather Helmholtzian-sounding formulations: "we infer the nature of perceptual space . . ." (1977a, p. 95), object constancies are founded on inferences, etc. It is a mistake to assume that the prevalent notion of constancy should not imply "certain invariances in the perceptual field." In modern perceptual literature, there appears a strong tendency to explain the "classical concept of constancy" in terms of relational invariances (cf. von Fieandt & Moustgaard, 1977, p. 515).

In any case, Dodwell is cautious and modest in his generalizations: ". . . more than one interpretation of the nature of the sensory code for pattern elements is possible, and one cannot say that the matter is decided in any clear way" (1977a, p. 101).

THE SYSTEM-THEORETICAL APPROACH

The basic ideas in this model appeared in the works of two biologically oriented scientists, von Bertalanffy (1950) and N. Wiener (1961), quite independently of each other in the beginning of the 1950s. This chain of thought has until now also been labeled "*cybernetics.*" Most important is the notion that living organisms should be viewed as global systems. This was one of Hegel's favorite ideas. One sign of progress was the introduction of the *feedback* principle. A living global system was further characterized as an *open system.* That is to say it is able to maintain its equilibrium in terms of a continuous interchange of energy with its environment. It prevails in this *steady state,* which is not a state of rest; rather, it is strongly dynamic. A favorite example of an open system is the flame of a burning candle. A popular definition of an open system is a group of elements which together form a connection of prevailing relationships.

The structure and function of an open system may be conveniently represented by the scheme shown in Fig. 6.2.

FIG. 6.2.   Schematical representation of the function of a simple open system.

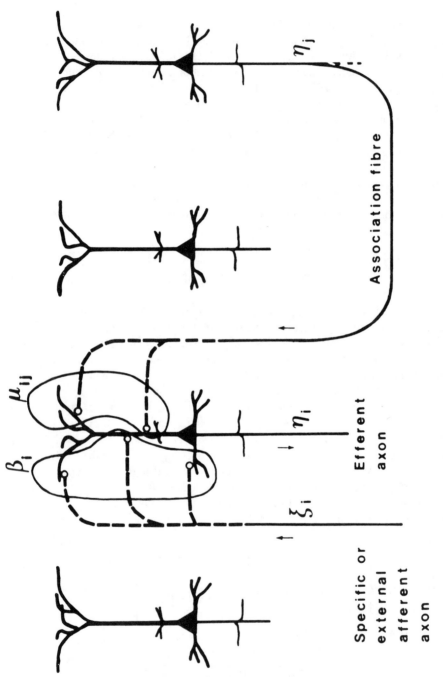

FIG. 6.3. Schematic representation of cortical connectivity discussed with this model; gross structure. Axons marked with dashed lines may be mono- or polysynaptic. Four adjacent functional units are shown, each represented by one pyramidal cell. (From Lehtiö & Kohonen, 1978. Reprinted from Medical Biology, 1978, 56, 112.)

Especially interesting in this context is the recent application of system-theoretical conceptions in studies of pattern recognition by a group of Finnish scholars (Kohonen, 1977; Kohonen, Lehtiö, & Oja, 1979; Lehtiö & Kohonen, 1978). Along with a set of computer demonstrations, they present a model of *neural associative memory* showing the relevance of this model in visual information processing. The model is based upon the hypothesis that adaptive changes in neural networks are mediated by changes in synaptic efficacies. Signal patterns could thus presumably have been stored by gradual changes in the network.

The key contribution of the system-theoretical approach in this connection has been the following assumption: When something gets stored in memory, small changes take place in a large number of modifiable elements. During recall, an integrated effect of those changes gives an output as an approximation of the original pattern.

The neural network model, as presented by Kohonen in 1977 (for a tutorial review, see Lehtiö & Kohonen, 1978), is based on the principle of synaptic plasticity. The neural tissue in the cortex is organized in functional units tentatively identified with columns. Each column consists of a collection of tightly connected neurons. The dynamics of a column are best described at the level of spike activity. In Fig. 6.3, the input spike frequency of each column is denoted by ξ_i and the corresponding output frequency by η_i. The direct connectivity between input and output is described by the coupling coefficient β_i. The figure explicitly shows a long range connection from unit j onto unit i. The modifiable element of this connection is denoted by μ_{ij}. The model is set up to specify how the cross-connection coefficients μ_{ij} (Fig. 6.3) do change as a function of signal activity. On the other hand, the sets of direct short-range connections β_i may show plasticity mainly at the early stage of development. Synaptic modifiability is described in the model by the change of μ_{ij} as a function of spike activity.

If, following the conceptualization by Kohonen, the output of each column i in relation to the input is expressed by a linear function, we end up with the equation

$$\eta_i = \beta_i \, \xi_i + \Sigma_j \, \mu_{ij} \, \eta_j + \eta_b \qquad (1)$$

The dynamics of these network-connections denoted by μ_{ij} is, according to the authors, based on Hebb's idea of pre- and postsynaptic interaction in neuronal efficacy changes. This so-called Hebbian principle, always implies changes in efficacy when pre- and postsynaptic triggering is simultaneous across a synapse. The *law of synaptic modifiability* denoting the Hebbian principle may be quantitatively stated as

$$d\mu_{ij}/dt = \alpha\eta_i(\eta_j\text{-}\eta_b) \qquad (2)$$

where α is a parameter describing the synaptic plasticity. If η_b corresponds to the average background activity, the law states that there is no change in the values μ_{ij} when the average signal activity is equal to the background activity. As stressed by the authors, the law is otherwise similar to that usually expressed for Hebbian synapses, except for the term η_b (Kohonen, 1977, pp. 148–154).

Most exciting is the fact that the adaptive behavior of the neural network can be computed. The computational analysis is based on a rectangular lattice of elementary units simulating the neural network. The mathematical procedure was carried out by Kohonen, and it started with a stepwise solution of Equation 2. After several additions and controls, the authors were able to design a computational program for simulation procedures, including old inputs, lateral inhibition, and virtual reconstruction of the original images.

The validity of the model was demonstrated by a series of simulations. These were carried out with images of human faces as input signal patterns, by means of a TV camera. It turned out that the general collective effects on adaptation could be satisfactorily described by the model concerned.

This example represents just one of the numerous applications of computational analyses as presented by Kohonen in his monograph. The model is still under preparation; its revised version is expected to appear without delay and it seems advisable to present an exhaustive evaluation only after it is completed.

THE REENPÄÄ MODEL

This theory could be appropriately characterized as an attempt to provide a logical axiomatic system of description of our immediate sensory experience. It claims that all statements concerning immediate experiences of the observer have their counterparts in certain axioms on the cognitive level or the conceptual level of the same observer. Thus, any axiom based on phenomenological observations refers to a corresponding axiom on the conceptual level.

"Sensations" are the ultimate real units in Reenpää's (1959) theory. His starting point is with sensations, and he is never concerned with perceptions, imaginations, or "mental images." From the level of sensation he jumps over, as it were, to the conceptual level of thought processes, to a kind of logistic formulation parallel to what had been the content of the sensations. The outcome is a scheme of parallel axiomata, formulated as descriptions of the phenomenological reality on one hand, and of conceptual rules on the other.

The fundamental point in Reenpää's argument is the rejection of causality in stimulus-sensation (Reiz-Empfindung) relationships. All we can experience directly are, according to him, the sensations themselves. "The stimuli, corresponding to some kind of classical 'pure' sensations, can only be established experimentally by inference." (v. Fieandt & Moustgaard, 1977, p. 506; translation from Reenpää 1961) Therefore, this model does not start from the magnitudes of physics, which describe relationships between objects in the external world, because those magnitudes are secondary, based not upon sensations but upon stimuli. The stimulus conception, S, is a derivative construct. It has led to *indirect descriptions of our sensory experience*. In place of them, Reenpää maintains, sensory physiology must create a taxonomy of its own which should be based on the sensory contents of our immediate experience.

The dependency between "stimulus" and "sensation" should thus be described not in terms of causality but as a relation of "reflection" or correspondence. Thus, in this new theory, causal dependence becomes only an equivalence-relationship given in terms of a certain degree of probability.

In 1961, Reenpää developed an autonomous axiomatic system. By means of the so-called analytical reduction method, in which the intentionally goal-directed observer classifies or divides perceived objects into their "qualitative features," Reenpää arrived at the six axioms systematically formalized in Table 6.1. (It would be too far-reaching here to give a detailed survey of Reenpää's interesting symbolic representation. The reader is advised to consult the reference paper [Reenpää, 1961]. The Table is, therefore, given in its original German form and phrasing.)

1. The axiom of simultaneity (Gleichzeitigkeit)
2. The axiom of quantity (Quantität)
3. The axiom of independence (Unabhängigkeit)
4. The axiom of inner discontinuity (Diskontinuität)
5. The axiom of maximal threshold (obere Begrenzung)
6. The axiom of absolute threshold (untere Begrenzung)

Axiom I states: All the various elements of the sensation-content (e.g. time z, space r, quality q and intensity i) are linked by the simultaneity-element g. They always occur at a given moment: "now."

Axiom II means that every experience (e.g., of intensity or of space) is a multiple of a certain minimal experience λ_e.

According to Axiom III, the basic elements of sensory experience, such as the surface area and color of a seen object, vary independently of each other. In Reenpää's analysis of sensations, they thus represent various dimensions: one element may vary without affecting the others. For this reason these dimensions of the basic elements may also be described as an orthogonal system of axes (movement along one axis does not necessarily mean movement along the other). This independence axiom proposed by Reenpää is of great significance in contemporary perceptual psychology, and it will be discussed below.

Axiom IV expresses the "jerky" nature of the dimensions of the multiplicity perceived and thus illustrates the fact that they are not perceived as continua. Here the claim is the same as the well-known affirmation of classical sensory physiology: Sensory dimensions do not occur as unbroken continua. Each just-discriminable step constitutes a discrimination threshold separate from the next.

The last two axioms also deal with a subject long familiar to sensory physio-

TABLE 6.1.

Reenpää's (1961) axiom system in its original form

Phänomenalität:

Axiom der Gleichzeitigkeit:

Axiom I.

$${}_eg = {}_eq : {}_el = {}_el : {}_eq$$
$${}_eg = ({}_eq : {}_ei) : {}_el = {}_eq : ({}_ei : {}_el)$$

Axiom der Quantität:

Axiom II.

$$(\lambda_e e_i) : (\lambda_e e_l) = \lambda({}_e e_i : {}_e e_l)$$
$$(\lambda + \mu)_e e = \lambda_e e : \mu_e e$$
$$\lambda(\mu_e e) = (\lambda\mu)_e e$$

Axiom der Unabhängigkeit:

Axiom III.

$${}_e e_i \xrightarrow{e\underline{l}} ({}_e e_i : {}_e e_l) = ({}_e e_i \xrightarrow{e\underline{l}} {}_e e_l) : ({}_e e_i \xrightarrow{e\underline{l}} {}_e e_i)$$

Axiom der inneren Diskontinuität:

Axiom IV.

$$|{}_e d \vdash {}_i d_n| = {}_e e$$

Axiom der oberen Begrenzung:

Axiom V.

$$({}_e d_{\max} \vdash {}_e d_{\max+1}) = {}_e 0$$

*Axiom der unteren Begrenzung
(der Minimalschwellen):*

Axiom VI.

$$\approx ({}_e e_o = {}_e e_o\blacksquare)$$

Begrifflichkeit:

Axiom der Addition:

$$d = a + b = b + a \qquad \text{Kommutativität}$$
$$d = (a + b) + c = a + (b + c)$$
$$\text{Assoziativität}$$

Axiom der Multiplikation:

$$\left.\begin{array}{l} ma + mb = m(a + b) \\ (m + n)\,a = ma + na \end{array}\right\} \text{Distributivität}$$
$$m(na) = (mn)\,a \qquad \text{Assoziativität}$$

*Axiom des skalaren Produkts
(der Orthogonalität):*

$$[a,(a + b)] = [(a, b) + (a, a)]$$

Axiom der Separation (der Dichte):

$$|{}_i d - {}_i d_n| < \varepsilon \; ; \varepsilon > 0$$

Axiom der Vollständigkeit:

$$({}_i d_{\max} - {}_i d_{\max+1}) \rightarrow 0 \; ; n \rightarrow \infty$$

$${}_c q, {}_e l, {}_e i, {}_e d, \text{ usw.} \rightarrow a, b, c, {}_i d, \text{ usw.}$$
$$: \rightarrow +$$
$$\xrightarrow{e\underline{l}} \xrightarrow{e\underline{l}} \rightarrow,$$

logy: top sensation and sensation threshold. Several dimensions (e.g., that of intensity) have their highest and lowest possible values. The former of these definable values is called the maximal and the latter the minimal or absolute threshold experience.

How does Reenpää's contribution appear in the light of present-day perceptual psychology, and how should it be evaluated from the point of view of the general theory of perception? Presumably something central and significant is lost, if, following Reenpää, perception is simply regarded as nothing more than an intermediate stage when setting up axioms for sensations which should hold well, being parallel to laws of thought. In the empirical descriptive systems of psychology—and indeed in these very systems in particular—the starting point must be precisely in immediate undiscriminated experiences and not in artificial syntactic-logical considerations. (It is actually crucial in Reenpää's way of reasoning to presuppose the perceptual events as concise counterparts of logical processes of thought. The right part of the table is, therefore, indispensable in this regard.)

The illustration of Axiom I,

$$g = q{:}l = l{:}q$$

which is given by Reenpää as the formalized description of the surface color of an object, would not be considered viable today as a statement in perceptual psychology: It states that the *simultaneous* (g) experience of the color quality (q) and the location of the object (1) constitute the surface color.

In the psychological description of surface color, however, it is impossible to present it as the simultaneity of two dimensions. What we directly experience are undiscriminated wholes, such as objects in our environments. If we try a scientific description based on "dimensions" attributed to these objects, such as a certain color and its location, or the shape of this object, we simply forget that those "dimensions" are already a result of sophisticated discrimination. In the psychological description, the objects we perceive do not appear as broken up into their elements in the way postulated by Husserl (1968). We do not experience, for example, "simultaneously red and a location," but the total impression of a particular red object.

In axiomatic sensory *physiology*, the expression given above is acceptable since the conceptual side of Reenpää's description gives the axiom of addition:

$$d = a + b = b + a$$

Such conceptual correspondences would violate the *psychological* description of phenomena. They would also contradict modern sensory physiology.

THE HOFFMAN MODEL

The origin of this theory deserves a brief mention. It so happened that around 15 years ago, an American mathematician, Professor W. C. Hoffman (Oakland University, Rochester, Mich., USA), became deeply interested in neurophysiology and the psychology of perception. His special knowledge of theories and methods of differential analysis led him to stress the suitability of this form of description when studying certain aspects of visual perception. He was especially interested in geometric illusions and the well-known perceptual constancies.

How does Hoffman's Model (1977) fulfill the requirements for a good neurophysiological theory? This question can be considered in the light of Dodwell's criticism, and also with reference to the critical comments by the mathematician C. P. Bruter and the psychologist T. M. Caelli at the same meeting.

TABLE 6.2.
Visual Constancies Versus the Corresponding Lie Transformation Groups

Perceptual Invariance	Lie Transformation Group	Lie Derivative (s)*	Invariant trajectories
A) *Shape constancy*	A) *Affine group*		
a) Location in the field of view	Horizontal and Vertical translation group	$L_X = \dfrac{\partial}{\partial x},\ L_Y = \dfrac{\partial}{\partial y}$	
b) (Form memory, "object constancy")	Time translations	$L_t = \dfrac{\partial}{\partial t}$	
c) Orientation	Rotation group	$L_R = -y\,\dfrac{\partial}{\partial x} + x\,\dfrac{\partial}{\partial y}$	
d) Binocular vision	Pseudo-Euclidean (hyperbolic) rotations	$L_b = y\,\dfrac{\partial}{\partial x} + x\,\dfrac{\partial}{\partial y}$	
B) (Efferent binocular perception)	B) (Hyperbolic rotations in plane-time)	$L_B = x\,\dfrac{\partial}{\partial x} - y\,\dfrac{\partial}{\partial y}$ $L_{B_1} = t\,\dfrac{\partial}{\partial t} - x\,\dfrac{\partial}{\partial x}$ $L_{B_2} = t\,\dfrac{\partial}{\partial t} - y\,\dfrac{\partial}{\partial y}$	
C) Size constancy	C) Dilation group	$L_S = x\,\dfrac{\partial}{\partial x} + y\,\dfrac{\partial}{\partial y}$	
D) Motion invariance	D) Lorentz group of order 2	$L_m = -L_R$ $L_{m_1} = ct\,\dfrac{\partial}{\partial y} + x\,\dfrac{\partial}{\partial (ct)}$ $L_{m_2} = ct\,\dfrac{\partial}{\partial y} + y\,\dfrac{\partial}{\partial (ct)}$	
E) (Cyclopean, or egocentred perception)	E) Rotation group in plane-time	$L_m = -L_0'$ $L_{m_1} = x\,\dfrac{\partial}{\partial (ct)} - ct\,\dfrac{\partial}{\partial x}$ $L_{m_2} = y\,\dfrac{\partial}{\partial (ct)} - ct\,\dfrac{\partial}{\partial y}$	

*x = horizontal distance from the perceptual centre ,
y = vertical distance from the centre of perception ;
t = time measured from observer's present in cortical (neuropschological) units ;
c = maximum flow velocity of cortical signals.

From Hoffman (1971)

The basic idea in Hoffman's theory may, according to the participants in the seminar, be condensed to the following statements (without using his actual expressions):

1. The most relevant description of perceptual processes can be found in the topological treatment of mathematical vector fields.
2. The reason for this extraordinary correspondence between a mathematical model and perceptual reality is given in the morphological structure of vertebrate visual cerebral tissues.

To put it another way, familiar perceptual data such as illusions or constancy phenomena may best be analyzed and described in terms of differential Lie-algebra, yet the neurophysiological basis for the fitness of this mathematical calculation is involved in the structure of the net of visual pathways.

During the two seminar days at Marseilles, it became clear that the first of these statements could be almost generally accepted, whereas the second one was met with severe criticism.

Consider the development of the statements. After carefully observing and analyzing the relational invariances involved in geometric illusions and in constancy phenomena, Hoffman (1977) discovered that they correspond to geometrical formulations in that a certain group of equations can be found (the Lie group), the descriptive character of which is a definite orbit (trajectory). The structure of these trajectories is surprisingly similar to the morphological structure of certain neurons. As Bruter puts it: "Geometry is formed by the same trajectory defined both by vector fields, which are physical, and Lie groups, which are abstract" (1977, p. 187).

Caelli (1977), on the other hand has summarized Hoffman's propositions in the following table (Table 6.2). According to him, there is no difficulty involved in the four first-mentioned cases of correspondence (A: a to d). They are reflected in statement No. 1 in Hoffman's research program. On the other hand, the following propositions included in Table 6.2 (marked B to D) are most controversial. Caelli points out that the traditional interpretation of constancies also includes recognition under noncontinuous, even nonparametric, transformations. Therefore, the "affine groups" as listed in Table 6.2 do not cover all instances of the term constancy as understood by perceptionists. "For example, the recognition of Fig. 6.4 (a) as equivalent to Fig. 6.4 (b) cannot be explained in terms of the restricted domain of Hoffman's constancies. Even the topologies of shape 2 in Fig. 6.4 are different, let alone their invariant Lie transformation groups" (Caelli, 1977, p. 198).

In my opinion, Caelli, however, is missing the point in this part of his criticism. I would rather agree with Hoffman on what is essential in the perceptual theory of constancies. I myself (1966, 1977) have looked upon these important events as evident proofs of the *relational invariances* included in the object

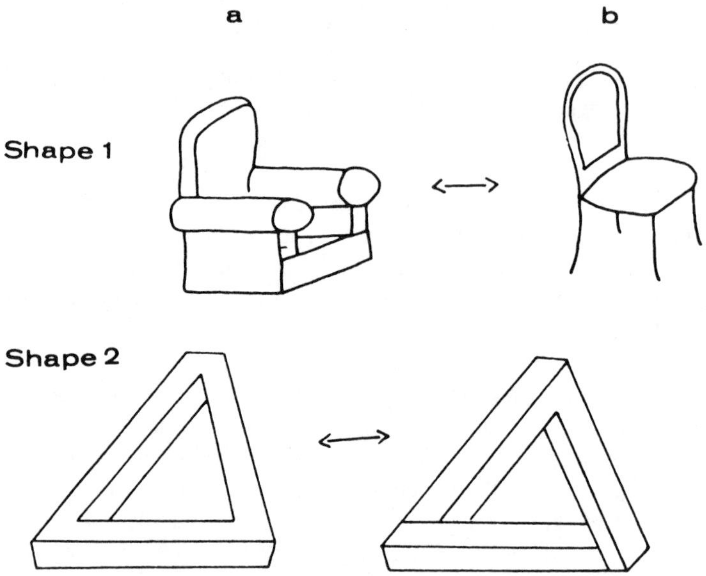

FIG. 6.4. Figures (a) and (b) appear globally equivalent but there is no one Lie transformation group which carries one into the other. (From Caelli, 1977. Reprinted by permission from Cahiers de Psychologie, 1977, *20*, 198.)

perception conditions. In terms of modern terminology, therefore, the meaning of "constancy" cannot be transferred (e.g., to recognition of "class-belonging-ness" or restricted to what is "permanent" or "transgredient" in objects; see von Fieandt & Moustgaard 1977, pp. 392–398).

The valuable paper by Caelli (1977) contains a number of critical comments and interesting remarks which cannot all be touched upon in this article. Let us, therefore, point out some of his most essential objections. Hoffman confines himself to those applications of "Lie algebra" which are listed in Table 6.2. A kind of analogy or even an isomorphism is claimed to exist between the "bodies" of the Lie mathematical equations (e.g., the orbits or trajectories) and some types of cortical neurons. However, topologically speaking we do not have enough evidence to assert that *pattern perception* should be reflected in the *morphology* of a certain type of single cell in the CNS.

Meanwhile, we shall turn back to the six criteria for a good theory enumerated by Dodwell. What is the outcome of his evaluation? Compared with Caelli and Bruter, his is more favorable. To him the LTG/NP theory meets criterion 1, "forms of coding and computing actually occur within the visual nervous system" (Dodwell 1977b, p. 197). There is also no doubt concerning criterion 2; the model allows a prediction of novel illusions and aftereffects.

As to the validity of criterion 3, the model has been applied to a wide range of psychological phenomena. Certainly LTG/NP shows great originality as required by criterion 4 and has the power of simplicity required for criterion 5. What is most important, the model even meets the last criterion: It fits with the view that neural processing underlies pattern perception behavior.

On the other hand, Dodwell also has serious objections to Hoffman's work:

1. First: the interpretation of the calculus, the elements, the Lie operators, cannot be achieved by psychologists.
2. LTG/NP attempts to go from the model as *interpretation* to the model as *reality*.
3. What experimental proof do we have that the individual cells of the visual cortex can, in fact, compute functions of the type attributed to them by the Hoffman model?

Bruter, the mathematician, evidently comes up with the sharpest criticism. He argues that Poincaré was well acquainted with Lie algebra, whereas Hoffman lacks sufficient understanding of the ontogeny and phylogeny of the sensory motor system. We miss an appropriate neurophysiological explanation. The trajectory of an ellipse as we meet in everyday life might originate in innumerable ways. Is there any sense in applying the same Lie group transformation to so many different occasions? The metrics in Hoffman's mathematical works are also deplorably similar to the Euclidean metrics of elementary threshold measurements. Hoffman's main idea presupposes a connection between *form* and *function*. However, can an *external morphological structure* (the cell body) act as an equivalent to what *forms an internal function?* To substitute neuronal integration for a mathematical one looks like a rather crude type of coordination.

Hoffman's model seems on one hand to be related to the well-known attempts of Gestaltists, and on the other hand to Dodwell as an advocate of modern neurophysiology. They both strive for isomorphic explanations as descriptions of important invariances in perceptual events. The Lie transformation model must so far be taken as an algorithm only; it does not serve as a unitary model of explanation. Wisely, it has been limited to deal with some basic features of pattern perception. Therefore, it has no statistical relevance. This is not necessarily a weakness. Some decades ago Lewin (1936) gave an excellent example of a mathematical theory whose application was completely *dynamic* (i.e., lacked any statistical relevance). It was a strong theory because it was satisfied with a conceptual framework at the psychological level exclusively, with no ambitions to reductionism.

CONCLUSIONS

To compare the models presented in retrospect looks like a rather hopeless task because of the differences in their approaches and their diverging ways of argumentation. There are, in fact, at least three types of precautions which have to be taken into account in the discussion of interdisciplinary mathematical descriptions of perceptual events. The construction of models meets with the obstacles of: (1) interdisciplinary barriers and a certain lag in intercommunication, (2) diverging levels of mathematical description, and (3) a false overemphasis on reductionism.

precautions which have to be taken into account in the discussion of inter-disciplinary mathematical descriptions of perceptual events. The construction of models meets with the obstacles of: (1) interdisclipinary barriers and a certain lag in intercommunication, (2) diverging levels of mathematical description, and (3) a false overemphasis on reductionism.

Let us have a closer look at each of them:

(1) Differences in conceptual framework and terminological semantics often seem to be enormous even between closely related fields of research. A theory—even if constructed by an expert scientist—which looks universal and acceptable, usually fails to take into account all the detailed results revealed by specialists, especially the most recent ones. Progress within the fields of biological research has been extraordinarily rapid, and a certain lag is always to be found in neighboring fields when they are trying to incorporate new scientific achievements. Therefore, parallel biotheoretical models are always likely to prevail.

(2) The mathematical description concerned with pattern perception has circulated on the *elementary metric level* (e.g., where threshold measurements are concerned); on the *statistical level,* which is characteristic of the system theory and the signal detection theory; and last, but not least, on the *topological level,* represented by Lewin's theory of vector fields and by Hoffman's model. There has been much confusion in discussions of theoretical models because these levels have not been kept sufficiently apart. Probably we shall never reach theories which are truly universal or which have complete world view compatibility because of the different explanatory tasks of the various models concerned.

(3) A false enthusiasm for "universal models" is also rooted in the popularity of reductionism. During Lewin's lifetime there had been serious efforts to go "outside the limits of psychology" in searching for organic counterparts of "needs," "goals," "drives," and so forth. It was to Lewin's credit that he emphasized the value of a topological vector theory regardless of the possibility of reaching reductionistic explanations for his mathematical formulations. In my opinion, Hoffman's model—if mathematically valid—has a psychological explanatory value quite independent of whether or not the "geometric orbits or trajectories" can be given a detailed neurophysiological interpretation.

REFERENCES

Barlow, H. B. Visual experience and cortical development. *Nature,* 1975, *258,* 199–204.

Bertalanffy, L. v. The theory of open systems in physics and biology. *Science,* 1950, *111,* 23–29.

Blakemore, C., & Campbell, F. W. On the existence of neurones in the human visual system selectively sensitive to the orientation and size of retinal images. *Journal of Physiology,* 1969, *203,* 237–260.

Boycott, B. B. Aspects of the comparative anatomy and physiology of the vertebrate retina. In R.

Bellairs & E. G. Gray (Eds.): *Essays on the nervous system: A Festschrift for Professor J. Z. Young.* Oxford: Clarendon Press, 1974.

Bruter, C. P. On Hoffman's work. *Cahiers de Psychologie,* 1977, *20,* 183–195.

Caelli, T. M. Criticisms of the LTG/NP theory of perceptual psychology. *Cahiers de Psychologie,* 1977, *20,* 197–204.

Campbell, F. W., & Robson, J. Application of Fourier Analysis to the visibility of gratings. *Journal of Physiology,* 1968, *197,* 551–566.

De Valois, R. L. Contribution of different lateral geniculate cell types to visual behavior. *Vision Research Supplement,* 1971, No *3,* 383–396.

Dodwell, P. C. *Visual pattern recognition,* New York: Holt, Rinehart & Winston, 1970.

Dodwell, P. C. Space perception and pattern recognition. *Cahiers de Psychologie,* 1977, *20,* 91–105. (a)

Dodwell, P. C. Criteria for a neuropsychological theory of perception. *Cahiers de Psychologie,* 1977, *20,* 175–182. (b)

Fieandt, K. von *The world of perception.* Homewood, Ill.: Dorsey Press, 1966.

Fieandt, K. von & Moustgaard, I. K. *The perceptual world.* London: Academic Press, 1977.

Hebb, D. O. *The organization of behavior.* New York: John Wiley & Sons, 1949.

Hensel, H. *Allgemeine Sinnesphysiologie: Hautsinne, Geschmack, Geruch.* Heidelberg: Springer, 1966.

Hoffman, W. C. An informal historical description (with bibliography) of the "L.T.G./N.P." (Paper presented before the International Seminar on "Lie Transformation group model for perceptual and cognitive psychology." The seminar met in Marseille, July 13, 1976 on the occasion of Prof. Hoffman's sabbatical year in France.) *Cahiers de Psychologie,* 1977, *20,* 135–174.

Hubel, D. H., & Wiesel, T. N. Receptive fields, binocular interaction and functional architecture in the cat's visual cortex. *Journal of Physiology,* 1962, *160,* 106–154.

Hubel, D. H., & Wiesel, T. N. Receptive fields and functional architecture in two nonstriate visual areas (18 and 19) of the cat. *Journal of Neurophysiology,* 1965, *28,* 994–1002.

Husserl, E. *Logische Untersuchungen* I-II. 4–5. Aufl. Tübingen: Max Niemeyer Verlag, 1968.

Keidel, W. D. Grundprinzipien der akustischen und taktilen Informationsverarbeitung. *Ergebnisse der Biologie,* 1961, *24,* 213–246.

Köhler, W. *Die physischen Gestalten in Ruhe und im stationären Zustand.* Erlangen: Verlag der Philosophischen Akademie, 1924.

Köhler, W. *Gestalt Psychology.* New York: Liveright Publishing Corp., 1929.

Kohler, I. Über Aufbau und Wandlungen der Wahrnehmungswelt. Insbesondere über 'bedingte Empfindungen.' *Österreichische Akademie der Wissenschaften, Philosophisch-historische Klasse;* Sitzungsberichte, 227. Band, 1. Abhandlung. Wien: Rohrer, 1951.

Kohler, I. Past, present and future of the recombination procedure. *Perception,* 1974, *3,* 515–524.

Kohonen, T. *Associative memory.* Heidelberg: Springer, 1977.

Kohonen, T., Lehtiö, P., & Oja, E. Storage and processing of information in distributed associative memory systems. Report *A 402,* Helsinki University of Technology, Dept. of Technical Physics, 1979.

Lehtiö, P., & Kohonen, T. Associative memory and pattern recognition. *Medical Biology,* 1978, *56,* 110–116.

Lewin, K. *Principles of topological psychology.* New York & London: McGraw-Hill, 1936.

Marr, D., & Poggio, T. *A theory of human stereo vision.* M.I.T. A.I. Lab. Memo *451,* 1977.

Reenpää, Y. *Aufbau der Allgemeinen Sinnesphysiologie.* Frankfurt a.M.: Vittorio Klostermann, 1959.

Reenpää, Y. Theorie des Sinneswahrnehmens. *Annales Academiae Scientiarum Fennicae.* A V (Medica) 1961, *78.*

Shannon, C. E., & Weaver, W. *The mathematical theory of communication*. Urbana: University of Illinois Press, 1949.

Weizsäcker, C. F. von Zum Weltbild der Physik. 6.Aufl., Zürich, 1954.

Wiener, N. *Cybernetics, or control and communication in the animal and the machine*. Cambridge, Mass.: MIT-Press, 1961 (2 ed.).

7
The Internal Representation of Solid Shape and Visual Exploration

J. J. Koenderink
Department of Medical and Physiological Physics
State University of Utrecht
Utrecht, The Netherlands

ABSTRACT

A basic fact of vision is that all opaque, solid objects, seen from any vantage point, have visible and invisible parts. Any model of solid shape that is tailored to vision must at least be able to predict which surface patches go in or out of sight when the observer moves with respect to the object. Modern mathematics is able to provide a complete inventory of qualitatively different solid shapes and provides the means to describe all visual events when the observer makes exploratory movements. The structures revealed by such analysis must form the backbone of any useful (for sensorimotor coordination) model of shape. They also form a basis for any psychophysical research on solid shape perception.

Curiously, little is known about human capabilities with regard to the perception of *solid* shape as compared to that of *flat* shape. I distinguish here between the perception of depth or slant, stereo vision in short, and the perception of *shape*. This is partly a result of the lack of available stimulus generators.[1] One may compare sculpture with drawing, cinema, or television. But it is also a fact that scientists and laymen alike are very unsure when it comes to a really useful description of the stimulus in the three-dimensional case.

I do not mean simple things like cubes or spheres but, for example, a torso. The most basic facts of morphology are completely outside the scope of the

---

[1] See Gibson (1979) about this problem. Gibson relied on the good sense of an artist to procure his stimuli. He certainly did not know how to quantify stimulus differences.

sculptor or the visual scientist, even if they have been known for decades or centuries. How then can we even hope to interpret a psychophysical response?

There is no reason why this situation should not be remedied: Modern mathematical methods enable us to make general statements about solid shape in a form suitable for practical use. These disciplines are: differential geometry, differential topology, and "catastrophe theory." Instead of mere case studies for simple shapes these methods yield general facts for complicated shapes. In my opinion, for the scientist interested in solid shape perception, these methods are the necessary instruments to handle the stimulus description. For instance, stimulus complexity or the amount of difference between two views of the same object may be quantified. Perhaps a simile may help: The fact that the angle sum for a plane triangle is 180° teaches us nothing about the shape of the earth, yet who would attempt to practice geodesy without such knowledge?

In this chapter I consider only the most basic fact of vision: interposition, the fact that I can see only part of the surface of any object from a given position.[2] How the visibility of any surface patch changes as I alter my vantage point as a function of global solid shape must be the backbone of any expectations I may have about a shape. Thus, there is nothing ad hoc about the present theory: It treats the topological structure of visibility and invisibility, a mathematically uniquely defined problem. If you want to build a psychophysical theory of shape along these lines the question is not *if* the structure of visibility versus invisibility is of any relevance, but how much of the available structure is actually effective.

To give an example: If the theory developed in this chapter is applied to a coin, you obtain the result that you can only see one side at a time with one eye and that you have to turn it over to see the other side. Whereas this may seem trivial, it is difficult to doubt that these facts must be of great importance for any understanding of the perception of coins. Applied to more complicated shapes you obtain results that look horribly complicated. But that is just because complicated objects have more "sides," and these sides are related in more complicated ways. It may be that a perceiver takes only part of the available structure into account. If so, his knowledge of the object must be incomplete. It is the task of psychophysics to find out about such things. The present theory just presents a

---

[2]The importance of this fact is clear from its role in fiction and folklore. Nowadays, we have the "X-ray vision" of superman, and medieval man had similar dreams. Bartholomew Rimbertus, quoted in Baxandall (1972): "An intervening object does not impede the vision of the blessed. . . . If Christ, even though himself in heaven after his ascension, saw his mother still on earth and at prayer in her chamber, clearly distance and the interposition of a wall does not hinder their vision. The same is true when an object's face is turned away from the viewer so that an opaque body intervenes. . . . Christ could see the face of his mother prostrate on the ground . . . as if he were looking directly at her face. It is clear that the blessed can see the front of an object from the back, the face through the back of the head" (p. 104).

complete description of the available "sides." This seems a necessary starting point for the quantification of psychophysical facts. Because the theory also considers such manipulations as "turning the coin," it is a dynamic theory, or a theory of multiple vantage points.

Thus, in the spirit of Ivo Kohler (1953), I consider the perception of solid shape to be intimately related with active, explorative, manipulative, and orientational motor behavior of the perceiver. Many others have proposed such ideas, Gibson (1966) perhaps most incisively.

I introduce the matter through a trivial example: the cube. Then, I generalize to arbitrary although smooth solid shapes, like the human body for instance. I only note results: Anyone desiring deeper insight will have to consult the technical mathematical papers (see for instance C. McCrory, 1980).

THE CASE OF THE CUBE

A cube (Fig. 7.1) is a volume bounded with 6 flat facets a, $\bar{a}$, b, $\bar{b}$, c, $\bar{c}$ (chosen such that a is opposite to $\bar{a}$, etc.). The facets meet in 12 edges (e.g. the edge $[bc]$), the edges in 8 vertices (e.g. the vertex $[\bar{a}b\bar{c}]$). I can never see more than 3 facets simultaneously. From a given vantage point, I describe the *aspect* obtained by noting the visible facets, e.g. the aspect $\{a, b, c\}$. When I traverse a smooth *orbit* in the *ambient space* of the cube, the aspect is subject to sudden changes, a facet being *created* or *annihilated* at a time. I call such changes *events*. The example (Fig. 7.2) shows an *event train:* annihilation of c, of b, then creation of $\bar{c}$, of $\bar{b}$. This event train transforms aspect $\{a, b, c\}$ into aspect $\{a, \bar{b}, \bar{c}\}$. Exploration of different orbits reveals many different event trains that transform $\{a, b, c\}$ into $\{a, \bar{b}, \bar{c}\}$. What are the possible event trains, and how are they connected with the orbits?

By prolongation of the planes of the facets through all ambient space, you obtain a *parcellation* into 26 cells, meeting each other in 48 common boundaries. Clearly the aspect cannot change when you stay inside a cell, but it changes when you cross a boundary and you get a well-defined event. Only aspects for cells with a common boundary are connected with an event. The connectivity is explicitly shown in the *visual potential* or *aspect graph* of the cube (Fig. 7.3, the event train of Fig. 7.2 is indicated). The visual potential concisely summarizes all possible event trains.

The visual potential (not to be confused with the VECP) of the cube is a model of the cube seen from all sides at once: Any possible motor action results in a predictable chain of events; any event train specifies an equivalence class of space orbits. Thus, the visual potential is the basic structure that underlies any sensorimotor knowledge of the cube, and permits both the interpretation of the optic array as well as egocentric orientation with respect to the cube. Note that it

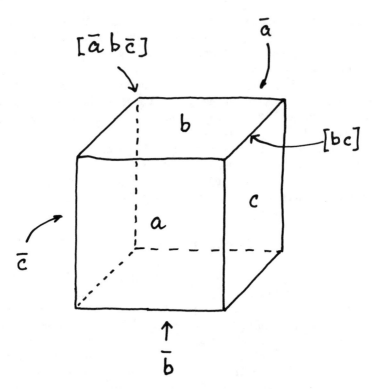

FIG. 7.1. A cube with facets a, ā, b, ƀ, c, c̄ and edges [bc] (the boundary between facets b and c) etc. and vertices [āƀc̄] (the common point of facets ā, b and c̄) etc.

In this figure the facets a, b and c are visible (towards the observer); ā, ƀ and c̄ invisible (at the hindside). The edges [ac̄], [bc̄], [bā], [cā], [cƀ] and [aƀ] form the rim.

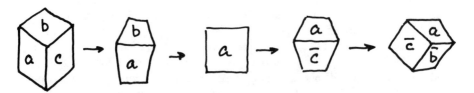

FIG. 7.2. A possible event train when the observer traverses the ambient space of the cube, or turns the cube in his hands.

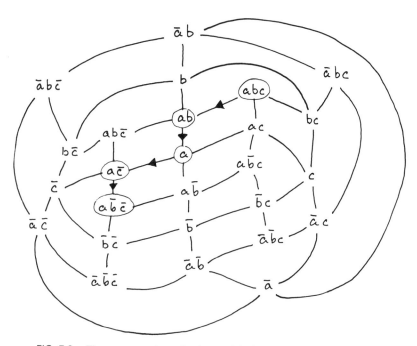

FIG. 7.3.   The aspect graph or visual potential of the cube. The event train of
Fig. 7.2 is indicated. Every node of the graph is a possible aspect, every edge a
possible event, every edge progression a possible event train. In this graph *all
possible event trains* are concisely bundled in a simple structure.

is a *flat graph;* i.e., it can be drawn on paper without edge crossings. Thus, you
need not have a little three-dimensional cube in the head (cf. the models discussed by Arnheim, 1956) in order to know a cube: The little cube in the head
may well be a flat data structure.

SMOOTH SHAPES

Preliminary Notions

Smooth shapes are bounded volumes without sharp edges or points. Think of the
human torso as a general smooth shape. From any vantage point you see only
part of the surface of the body. The boundary of the visible part is called the *rim*.
The rim consists of a family of nested, closed, smooth curves on the surface. All
visual directions that end on the object are bounded by a conical surface: the
contour. One often describes the contour with the curve obtained when the visual
directions are projected on a sphere surrounding the observer. The contour may

FIG. 7.4.   Pablo Picasso: Nu couché, 1920.

consist of several disconnected parts, it may form a closed loop, or end on another part of the contour or even just vanish at some point. It often helps to think of the object as made out of "tinted air": Then you can see the back side and the contour is seen to be made up from a family of nested, closed curves. But these curves are not smooth and may mutually and self-intersect.

The draftsman's impression of the object on paper is often bounded by *an outline*. In Fig. 7.4, a nude by Picasso, 1920, examples can be seen of convex and concave arcs, inflections of the outline, ending contours, T-junctions, disconnected pieces of the outline. Even for "realistic" drawings there are many characteristic differences between contour and outline. Their study reveals interesting idiosyncrasies in the shape perception of artists (Koenderink & van Doorn, in press). In this chapter I treat contour and rim exclusively.

In any *real* situation nothing much happens when I perturb the orbit of the vantage point or the shape of the object by an infinitesimal amount. Such situations are called *generic*. The assumption of genericity does not limit generality, but forbids many extremely unlikely situations (such as cannot occur in practice because infinite precision would be needed to set them up) that lead to mathematical monstrosities. I assume genericity here to obtain general and simple mathematical properties, without treating the technical side of genericity here. The interested reader may consult Thom's book (1972).

TYPES OF SURFACE PATCHES

If you are interested in the rim, you must consider visual directions that graze along the surface, are *tangent to* the surface at a given point. All such directions that graze the surface at one point span a plane: the *tangent plane* at that point. Only if the visual direction lies completely *outside* the surface you can see the rim. Hence you must consider whether the tangent plane cuts the object or not. There are but few generic possibilities. They are:

—The tangent plane lies completely on one side of the surface. Then the surface curves in the same sense in all directions, it is *isoclastic*. If the plane lies on the outside the patch is *convex* (like the outside of an egg-shell; Fig. 7.5a), if inside it is *concave* (like the inside of an egg-shell).
—The tangent plane lies partly inside, partly outside the object and cuts an hourglass-shaped region out of the object. Then the surface curves with different sense in different directions; it is *anticlastic*. (The shape of the patch is saddle-like Fig. 7.5b.)
—The tangent plane lies partly inside, partly outside the surface. The surface curves only in a single direction, is *monoclastic* or cylinder-like (like the outside of a column, or the inside of a reed, Fig. 7.6; in the mathematical literature one speaks of elliptic, hyperbolic and parabolic points instead of iso-, anti-, and monoclastic points).

The iso- and anticlastic points fill regions on the surface, divided by curves on which the monoclastic points lie (Fig. 7.6a; α anticlastic, β isoclastic, the dotted curve a curve of monoclastic points). Certain monoclastic points hold a special place: Those where the cylinder-axis is directed along the curve of monoclastic points (Fig. 7.6b: α anticlastic, β isoclastic, the dotted curve normal monoclastic points, the indicated point a special one). Such points indicate the beginning of a ridge or a furrow of the surface relief, therefore I call them "*pedal-points.*" (One speaks of "Gaussian cusps" in the mathematical literature.)

This is the inventory of all generic surface patches. Attempts to construct such

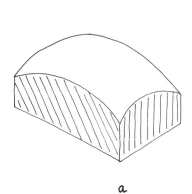

a

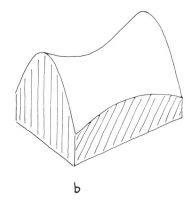

b

FIG. 7.5a.   A convex, isoclastic patch.   FIG. 7.5b.   An anticlastic patch.

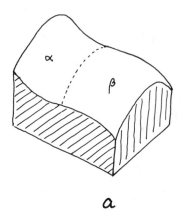
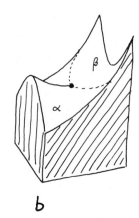

FIG. 7.6a.   Patch α is anticlastic, patch β isoclastic and convex. Their common boundary is a line of monoclastic (cylinder-like) points.

FIG. 7.6b.   Patch α is anticlastic, patch β isoclastic and concave. The common boundary is again a line of monoclastic points. The indicated point on this boundary is an isolated "pedal point." At this pedal point the cylinder axis is parallel to the line of monoclastic points.

inventories have been made often by artistic theorists (e.g. Alberti in the 15th, Kurt Badt in the 20th century with many in between) and experimental psychologists (e.g. Arnheim, 1956; Gibson, 1979) with rather incomplete results.[3] Even the basic dichotomy iso/anti-clastic has been missed by the scientists a century and a half after Gauss's famous investigation (Gauss, 1872). (Consult, for instance, the book of Hilbert & Cohn-Vossen 1932.) The remarks of a geometer (Felix Klein) on the importance of this division for visual perception and esthet-

---

[3]Alberti writes in his treatise "Della Pittura" (1435/1976): "We now have to treat of other qualities which rest like a skin over all the surface of the plane. These are divided into three sorts. Some planes are flat, others are hollowed out, and others are swollen outward and are spherical. To these a fourth may be added which is composed of any two of the above. The flat plane is that which a straight ruler will touch in every part if drawn over it. The surface of water is very similar to this. The spherical plane is similar to the exterior of a sphere. We say the sphere is a round body, continuous in every part; any part on the extremity of that body is equidistant from its centre. The hollowed plane is within and under the outermost extremities of the spherical plane as in the interior of an egg-shell. The compound plane is in one part flat and in another hollowed or spherical like those on the interior of reeds or on the exterior of columns" (p. 45).

Kurt Badt writes in "Wesen der Plastik" (1963): "Diese hat drei Grundmöglichkeiten: Ebenen, konvexe und konkave Krümmungen. Von den dreien ist—als Zeichen und Ausdruck der anschaulich hervorbrechenden Lebenskraft—nur das Konvex dem Wesen nach plastisch" (p. 144).

Arnheim (1956) is of the same opinion, whereas Gibson (1979 p. 35) writes: "A *curved convexity* is a curved surface tending to enclose a substance"; "A *curved concavity* is a curved surface tending to enclose the medium"; and implies completeness.

ics have largely been forgotten[4] (Fig. 7.7, the Apollo of Belvedere with curves of monoclastic points as drawn by Klein). In artistic *practice*, the anticlastic patches are often treated as a mere "ground," a kind of "glue" that holds the isoclastic ("thinglike"), plastic parts together. (In many styles of sculpture the anticlastic parts dwindle to merely V-shaped grooves.)

It is easy to sketch qualitatively the contours that result from the basic surface patches (Fig. 7.8).

—A concavity is never visible at the contour.

—A convexity yields a convex arc (Fig. 7.8b, the stippled area is the background).

—An anticlastic patch is either invisible or yields a concave arc (Fig. 7.8a).

—A monoclastic patch is either invisible or yields an inflection of the contour (Fig. 7.8c).

—A pedal point is either invisible or yields a flat (zero curvature) contour (Fig. 7.8d).

Complications occur when the visual direction is along the edge of the hourglass-shaped area of an anticlastic point (Fig. 7.9: The hatched area is where the tangent plane is inside the object). Visual direction α yields a concave contour; for direction γ the point is not visible; for direction β the point is visible but nevertheless the visual direction enters the object. In this case the rim is directed *along* the visual direction and the contour *ends*. Figures 7.10 and 7.11 make this more clear. In Fig. 7.10 α is the rim, β the contour. The occluded part of the contour is the broken line. In Fig. 7.11, lines of equal distance from the eye are drawn, in the hatched part the object is cut away for clarity, the stippled area is the background. If the object were of tinted air, the contour would display a *cusp*. The direction β, in Fig. 7.9, is an important special direction, associated with the surface patch. At any anticlastic patch there are two such *asymptotic*

---

[4]The story is told in a footnote in D. Hilbert and S. Cohn-Vossen's "Anschauliche Geometrie" (1932/1952).

"Die parabolischen Kurven sind von F. Klein zu einer eigenartigen Untersuchung herangezogen worden. Er nahm an, dass die künstlerische Schönheit eines Gesichts ihren Grund in gewissen mathematischen Beziehunger hätte, und ließ deshalb auf dem Apollo von Belvedere, dessen Gesichtszüge uns einen besonders hohen Grad von klassischer Schönheit wiedergeben, die sämtlichen parabolischen Kurven einzeichnen. Diese Kurven besaßen aber weder eine besonders einfache Gestalt, noch ließ sich ein allgemeines Gesetz ausfindig machen, dem sie gehorchten" (p. 174).

(The parabolic curves were the object of a singular study of F. Klein. He started from the hypothesis that the artistic beauty of a face is based on certain mathematical relations, and therefore had all parabolic curves drawn on the Apollo of Belvedere whose countenance displays an especially high degree of classical beauty. However, these curves did not possess a particularly simple shape, nor was it possible to find a general rule which governed them.)

FIG. 7.7. The bust of the Apollo of Belvedere with curves of monoclastic points as drawn by Felix Klein. The bust is now at Göttingen University. (This figure is a tracing of the photograph printed in Hilbert and Cohn-Vossen, 1932.)

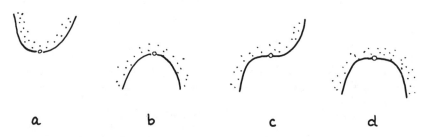

a   b   c   d

FIG. 7.8a. Contour of anticlastic patch.

FIG. 7.8b. Contour of convex patch.

FIG. 7.8c. Contour at monoclastic point.

FIG. 7.8d. Contour at pedal point. The apparent curvature vanishes at the pedal point.

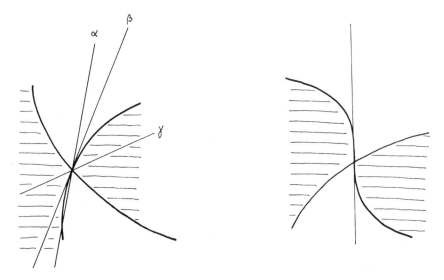

FIG. 7.9. If you cut an anticlastic patch with a tangent plane at one of its points you obtain an hourglass-shaped area of points where the tangent plane is *inside* the object (hatched area). Thus, the straight line γ runs wholly inside the object and cannot correspond to a visual ray. Line α touches the patch at one isolated point and runs inside the object from another point. Line β enters the object at the same point where it touches it. This direction (β) corresponds to the case depicted in Fig. 7.10. If one of the boundaries of the hourglass-shaped areas has an inflection at the constriction, you can have a visual ray that just goes through. Such a point is a "flecnodal point." The "see through" condition is illustrated in Fig. 7.11b.

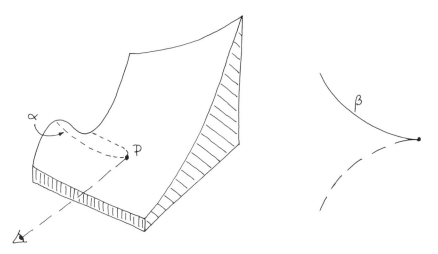

FIG. 7.10. In the qualitative sketch of the visual situation, the indicated line of sight corresponds to β in Fig. 7.9. The line of sight grazes the patch at P and at the same point enters the object. Curve α is the rim. In the visual field the rim α appears as the contour β. It has a cusped singularity of which only one branch is visible.

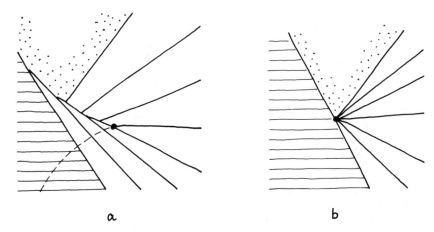

a   b

FIG. 7.11a.   The visual field in the case of Fig. 7.10. The stippled area is the background; the hatched area is a cut through the object. The drawn lines are curves of equal distance to the eye. Their envelope is the cusped contour of Fig. 7.10.

FIG. 7.11b.   Similar to Fig. 7.11a, except that the special case of a flecnodal point is depicted. In this case you can "see through"; the cusped contour degenerates into a point.

directions. Only when the side of the hourglass-shaped area has an inflection, you can "see through" (Figs. 7.9, 7.11b). Such points are called *flecnodal points*. They lie on flecnodal curves; curves that run from pedal point to pedal point through anticlastic areas, or form closed loops inside these areas.

EVENTS AND THE PARCELLATION OF AMBIENT SPACE

Basically, there are only five generic visual events possible (Fig. 7.12). They are:

—The contour develops a pair of inflections (Fig. 7.12 α).
—A concave arc develops a pair of cusps (Fig. 7.12 β).
—A bell-shaped closed loop is created (Fig. 7.12 γ).
—Two arcs meet and part again as two "beaks" (Fig. 7.12 δ).
—A beak-shaped contour splits off a "bell" (Fig. 7.12 ε).

Fig. 7.12 is drawn for an object composed of tinted air. For opaque objects part of the contour may be occluded (e.g. at a cusp visibility *always* alters). This may happen in different ways, so that the basic five types may occur in different variants.

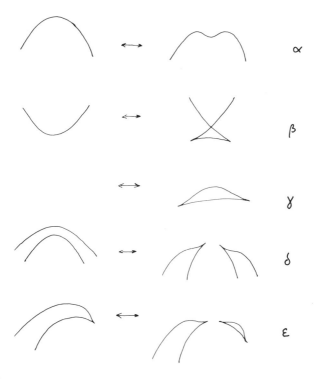

FIG. 7.12.   The generic visual events associated with the contour.
α. creation or annihilation of a pair of inflections.
β. creation or annihilation of a pair of cusps.
γ. creation or annihilation of a bell-shaped closed loop.
δ. creation or annihilation of a pair of cusps with a change in connectivity.
ε. split-off or capture of a bell-shaped closed loop by a beak-shaped cusped contour.

These events occur, just as with the cube, when the vantage point crosses certain well-defined surfaces in the ambient space. These surfaces bound cells. Thus, we have again a parcellation of ambient space into cells, such that a single aspect is obtained for all positions of the eye within a cell. Despite the fact that few visual scientists seem to know about their existence, these surfaces are basic entities for the vision of solid shape. They govern all changes of the contour for exploratory movements of the eye. There exist three types.

—Tangent planes of pedal points. When you cross these planes, two inflections are created or annihilated (Fig. 7.12 α).
—The surface generated by the asymptotic directions of the inflections at flecnodal points. When you cross these surfaces a pair of cusps is created or annihilated (Fig. 7.12 β).

—The surface generated by the cylinder axes of monoclastic points. When you cross these surfaces, one of the events concerning beaks and bells (Figs. 7.12 γ, δ, ε) occurs.

These surfaces mesh into each other because they all contain the cylinder axes of the pedal points. They may intersect mutually or intersect themselves. In this way fantastically shaped parcellations divide ambient space of even very simple objects. I give an example later on.

T-JUNCTIONS

When the sun goes down, and part of its disc is obscured by the horizon, there are two visual directions that are tangent to both the earth and the sun. I call them *bitangent rays*. For any object you can find such bitangent rays by means of the following simple device (at least in principle, but certain theoretical difficulties are easily overcome). Place the object on a plane table. Then you can have three distinct occurrences:

—The object rests stable on three points: You have found a tritangent plane;
—The object can be rolled in a single direction: It rests on two points and these define a bitangent ray;
—The object can be rolled in all directions (as with an egg).

Only the second case interests us here. When you roll the object along, you generate a continuous series of bitangent rays. Together they span a surface, built from straight lines, that touches the object along two curves: the *bitangent surface*. Sometimes you can roll the object a complete turn: then the bitangent surface is a complete (generalized) cone. It will be clear that the bitangent surface can be rolled out flat into a plane. Such surfaces are technically called "developables." Such a developable in general does not have a single vertex, but instead contracts into at least two distinct curved arcs, so that at least five distinct cells are formed (Fig. 7.13). The aspect seen from a cell may display 0, 2, or 4 "T-junctions" (Guzmán, 1969). Such T-junctions (or crossed contours) are important visual cues as to radial order (the before/behind order; different from depth).

It may happen that you cannot roll the object a full turn around, but that the two curves with which the bitangent surface touches the object run together and end. If they do, then it is at a pedal point. Figure 7.14 shows a furrow in an otherwise ovoid shape. The area of isoclastic points (I) is divided from that of anticlastic points (A) by the broken curve. The pedal point is *f*. (There is another one "behind the hill." A few bitangents are indicated.) The cylinder axis of the

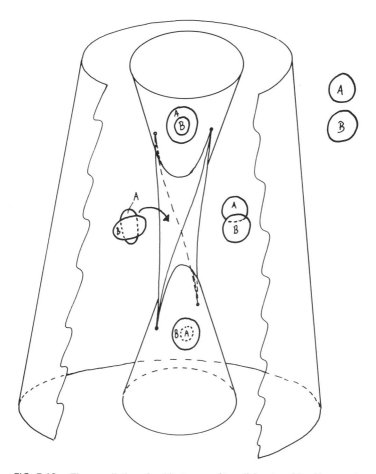

FIG. 7.13.   The parcellation of ambient space of two disjunct ovoids with respect to the creation or annihilation of *T*-junctions. There are five distinct cells. The aspects obtained by vantage points in the different cells are schematically indicated. The typical possibilities are: *A* and *B* juxtaposed; *B* occludes *A;* the projection of *B* is contained in the projection of *A;* a *T*-junction pair; two *T*-junction pairs.

For the outer conical surface the ovoids are both on one side of the conical surface; for the inner cone they are on different sides. (These cones correspond to the boundaries of the umbra and penumbra of solar eclipses by the moon, as shown in many elementary optics textbooks.)

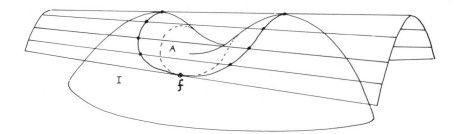

FIG. 7.14. The bitangent developable surface for a furrow-shaped patch. The broken curve is a curve of monoclastic points; A is an anticlastic, I an isoclastic area. The point f is a pedal point.

pedal point is a final (degenerated) bitangent ray. With this ray the bitangent surface is attached to the surface of cylinder axes of the monoclastic curve through the pedal point. Figure 7.15 summarizes the situation. When you cross α the aspect changes from $a \rightarrow b$, when you cross β from $b \rightarrow c$, when you cross γ (the tangent plane of the pedal point) from $a \rightarrow d$. (p is the curve where the bitangent surface touches the object, q the monoclastic curve, Ω the cylinder-axis of the pedal point.)

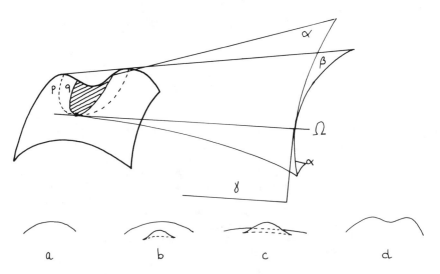

FIG. 7.15. Typical geometry at a pedal point. The bitangent developable surface β touches the patch at the broken curve p; the developable surface of monoclastic cylinder axes α touches the patch at the curve of monoclastic points q (the hatched area is a patch of anticlastic points). The tangent plane γ at the pedal point meets α and β along the cylinder line of the pedal point Ω. These surfaces delimit four cells. For vantage points in these cells you obtain the aspects a, b, c, d.

AN EXAMPLE

Perhaps the simplest (non-trivial) example is a tomato shape: an ovoid with a furrow (technically: an ovoid with an isolated, singly connected, anticlastic patch with two pedal points). The cells at great distance from the object are due to the flecnodal curve (Fig. 7.16, drawn with broken curves), the cylinder axes (drawn with full curves; α and β), the bitangent surface (γ) and the tangent planes at the pedal points (drawn with stippled curves). At the other side of the object this structure is duplicated. Note that this parcellation is tightly connected with the object: If I rotate the object, the whole structure rotates with it; just remember that *visually* I cannot sample the object, but only the parcellation. *My idea of the object can in a sense be understood as my response to the parcellation which I can sample directly through exploratory movement.*

The visual potential is given in Fig. 7.17: It is incomplete since I left out the left-hand side and the structure close by the object. Moreover, if you consider the

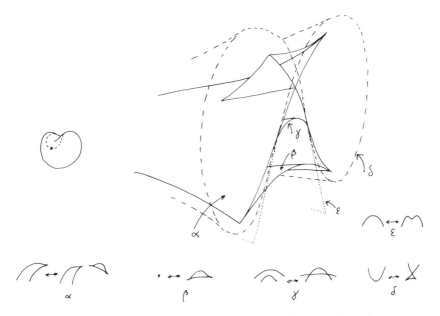

FIG. 7.16.   Part of the parcellation of ambient space of a tomato shape shows how complicated things can get even for simple shapes.

The surfaces delimiting the cells are:

α, β: developable surface formed by cylinder axes of monoclastic points.

γ   : developable surface formed by bitangent rays.

δ   : surface formed by ''see through'' rays of flecnodal points.

ε   : tangent planes at pedal points.

When the vantage point crosses one of the surfaces α, β, γ, δ, or ε the event denoted with the same symbol occurs.

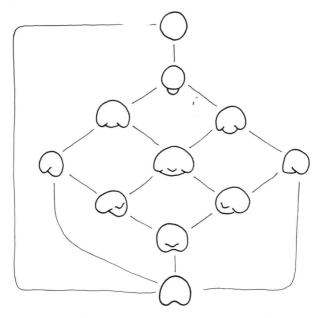

FIG. 7.17.   Aspect graph (a visual potential) for the parcellation shown in Fig. 7.16.

object as composed of tinted air several distinct aspects, not drawn here, are introduced. Even so, the more important features stand out clearly. Note how complicated the structure turns out to be even for such an exceedingly simple shape.

This example is of more than passing interest because furrows in otherwise globular patches (egg-shaped parts) are extremely common in biological shapes. By way of an example I offer a tracing of a drawing by Annibale Caracci with a few of such instances indicated. Several more can be found (Fig. 7.18).

For a somewhat more complicated shape than the tomato—a statuette by Giambologna (also called Giovanni Bologna)[5], made to be appreciated from multiple vantage points, I have estimated the total number of distinct aspects to exceed 100,000. No one can hope to know all aspects of such a piece. Yet the

[5]Giovanni Bologna: Astronomy, signed, C. 1573, Gilt bronze, 39 cm. Vienna: Kunsthistorisches Museum.

In real life one certainly does not sample all possible aspects of such a statuette (e.g. extreme ''close-ups,'' views from below, above, etc.); most people sample global structure first before descending to ''details.'' That we are often satisfied with a poor understanding of shape is clear from the fact that many people easily accept even very mediocre copies of the Venus de Milo, for example, as satisfactory. Yet, when seen juxtaposed, we easily spot and can describe differences in detailed shape of original and copy.

FIG. 7.18.   Annibale   Caracci:
Nude. Red chalk. 37.5 × 22.8 cm
Royal Library, Windsor.
(Tracing).

situation is not as hopeless as that: Many aspects can be grouped into modular subunits of the visual potential, e.g. the "furrow in globularity" occurs many times over, just as in Caracci's drawing. In such a way the complexity can be much reduced. The search for such modular subunits is both a problem for geometry and for experimental psychology. Each subunit would correspond to a "canonical surface undulation" (e.g. a furrow). A complete inventory from the mathematical standpoint can be made. The sculptor's jargon may provide a first approximation to a psychologically valid inventory.

CONCLUSIONS

In a way the present method provides a manner to describe the "proximal stimulus": just what is obtained when the eye is moved through ambient space. The method also provides a metric and measures of *visual complexity* (Koenderink & van Doorn, 1979) of shape: The "distance" between different aspects can be measured along the shortest route in the visual potential and the size of the visual potential can be defined as the longest "shortest route" between any two aspects. Such an idea can easily be checked in the laboratory: Shepard and Metzler's (1971) paradigm, for instance, provides a way to check the metric.

These methods, of course, describe the maximum available structure: It is up to visual psychophysics to determine the amount of structure actually sampled by human observers. The example of Giambologna's statuette already indicates that we can at most hope to find a very coarse-grained version of the visual potential in the mind. The readiness with which most people accept even very mediocre copies of pieces of sculpture as reasonable or even good substitutes for the original artifacts illustrates this point.

REFERENCES

Alberti, L. B. [Della Pittura]. Trans. by J. R. Spencer: *On painting*. Westport, Conn.: Greenwood Press, 1976.

Arnheim, R. *Art and visual perception*. London: Faber & Faber, 1956.

Badt, K. *Wesen der Plastik*. Köln: Du Mont, 1963.

Baxandall, M. *Painting and experience in fifteenth century Italy*. London-Oxford-New York: Oxford University Press, 1972.

Gauss, C. F. *Disquisitiones generales circa superficies curvas 1872. General investigations of curved surfaces*. New York: Raven Press, 1965.

Gibson, J. J. *The senses considered as perceptual systems*. Boston: Houghton Mifflin, 1966.

Gibson, J. J. *The ecological approach to visual perception*. Boston: Houghton Mifflin, 1979.

Guzmán, A. Decomposition of a visual scene into three-dimensioned bodies. In A. Grasselli (Ed.), *Automatic interpretation and classification of images*. New York: Academic Press, 1969.

Hilbert, D., & Cohn-Vossen, S. *Anschauliche Geometrie*. Berlin: Julius Springer, 1932. (*Geometry and the imagination*. New York: Chelsea Publishing Co., 1952.)

Koenderink, J. J., & Doorn, A. J. van The internal representation of solid shape with respect to vision. *Biological Cybernetics*, 1979, *32*, 211–216.

Koenderink, J. J., & Doorn, A. J. van The shape of smooth objects and the way contours end. Perception, in press.

Kohler, I. Umgewöhnung im Wahrnehmungsbereich. *Die Pyramide*, 1953, *3*, 92–96, 109–113.

McCrory, C. *Profiles of surfaces*. Coventry: University of Warwick, 1980.

Shepard, R. N., & Metzler, J. Mental rotation of three-dimensional objects. *Science*, 1971, *171*, 701–703.

Thom, R. *Stabilité structurelle et morphogénèse*. Reading, Mass.: W. A. Benjamin Mc., 1972.

8 Object, Percept, Concept, Word

Ernst L. Moerk
California State University, Fresno

ABSTRACT

The recent controversies dealing with conceptual and semantic development of young children are briefly summarized and conceptually evaluated. The bipolar dimensions generally employed to describe these developments, ranging from a "perceptual" to a "functional" pole or from a "static" to a "dynamic" one are shown as being conceptually deficient in that those terms denote sets and subsets of experience and not diametrically opposed conceptualizations. Additionally, the question concerning the primacy versus secondary nature of specific experiences is reopened and factually explored. Neurological findings, nonverbal behavior, and early vocabulary development are utilized to describe the early course of perceptual/conceptual development. The neurological evidence suggests three sequential systems, beginning with the so-called "secondary visual system," progressing to the "primary visual system" and finally involving also the intrinsic areas of the brain. Non-communicative evidence from human and non-human realms indicates again a triple division into an early distinction of merely "good" and "bad" aspects, later finer differentiation of perceptual details, and finally the exploration and memory storage of utilitarian relationships between objects or actions and objects. Parallel phenomena in the microgenetic formation of percepts and concepts are briefly noted. In surveying communicative and verbal evidence, nonverbal, connotative, and denotative aspects are considered. A basic and early evaluative/connotative aspect is found universally. Whereas some controversy exists as to clearly differentiable stages of verbal development, a preponderance of nouns before the common appearance of verbs and expressions of relationships is found quite generally. A selection of early-employed nouns, as found in a wide variety of diary studies, is analyzed. It persuasively indicates that stable visual features pro-

143

vided the basis for the generalization of these words. This general triple sequence of first affective, then objective, and last utilitarian categorizations is related to ecological principles.

During the last decade, developmental psychologists have first turned to semantic studies (Bloom, 1970; Schlesinger, 1971) and then to the analysis of the cognitive bases of language (McNamara, 1972; Moerk, 1973), in their attempts to understand language acquisition and performance. With this emphasis upon preverbal conceptual development, renewed attention has been paid to the continuity of the processes and the developmental trends that result in language mastery. Bloom (1973) set an example in exploring the gradual developments during the one-word stage and the gradual transition from one-word utterances to successive single-word utterances and finally to two-word utterances. Her valuable discussion of the continuity between ''concepts, words, and sentences'' (1973, pp. 113–141) influenced the present study. Nelson (1974) joined this endeavor in a theoretical analysis and became one of the most active researchers in this field (Nelson, 1976, 1979; Nelson, Rescorla, Gruendel, & Benedict (1978). Her results and even more her interpretations of the results are however often in sharp contrast to the careful and broad-ranging studies of other authors, such as Anglin (1977), Clark (1973, 1977), Gruendel (1977), and many others.

A basic controversy has therefore arisen between one group of investigators, such as Anglin and E. Clark, who see simple perceptual processes as the most important bases of concept formation and later vocabulary, and Nelson and some of her students on the other hand, who propose a ''functional explanation'' of concept formation. Whereas a partial revision and improvement of the latter's formulation is found in Nelson et al. (1978) and Nelson (1979), a more thorough reevaluation of the contrasting viewpoints seems to be required. Since the logical bases as well as the interpretations of factual evidence pertaining to neurological, perceptual, cognitive, and vocabulary development are controversial, both will be considered. In this wide range of content areas, not even the specialists are always in agreement whether to accept specific findings as valid or how to conceptualize them. A definitive resolution of all the controversies can therefore not yet be expected. It is however hoped that the perspectives suggested, both in regard to the logical reevaluations and the attempted integration of research areas, will prove fruitful even if specific points need to be improved upon in subsequent research. Before the major topics are explored, the terms of the title will be briefly analyzed to clearly define and delimitate the area of discussion.

The Object.   The term *object* is introduced in the title for two purposes: First to alert the reader that the following discussion of perceptual and conceptual development is mainly restricted to only a small part of the field, namely the perception and conceptualization of objects, involving their spatial relations, the relations between their features, to a small extent their movements, and the possible effects of their movements. The perception and conceptualization of actions, their goals and effects, and of many other physical and logical relationships are excluded. Similarly the perception of the self and the self-concept are not touched upon.

The second function of the term *object* is more epistemological. It serves to indicate that the present analysis is based upon a Gestalt and Gibsonian point of view that assumes that the perceptual system has evolved to immediately perceive wholes, things, or at least figure-ground contrasts. The term *object* as employed here does however not need to involve tangibility and graspability. It will even be seen and argued in the course of the discussion that this experience of graspability is conspicuously absent in the case of many early concepts of infants, such as that of the moon, of ducks swimming in a lake, etc. Bower's research (1966, 1971) has shown too that Gestalt qualities of virtual objects suffice to elicit object-adequate responses in the very young infant.

The Percept.   Though the term perception is employed ubiquitously, it is difficult to find a definition which is generally agreed upon. In the present context, the terms *perception* and *percept* are contrasted with those of *conceptualization* and *concept*. With this contrast, the aspect of information reception is emphasized in the former terms. In contrast to mere sensation, the central processing of the incoming information and the resulting complex organizations and configurations are stressed with the terms *perception* and *percept*.

The Concept.   With concepts and conceptualizations the emphasis shifts to information contributed from memory, to new structures that might be produced through internal processing of inputs from many channels, in short to complex interrelationships between informational structures. Sensory input is not a necessary condition anymore for concepts to be activated, and in this manner concepts are clearly different from percepts. Since constructive processes are involved in both perceptions and conceptualizations, many partial overlaps between both exist.

The Word.   For the present purposes and in accordance with common terminology, the term *word* will be employed for sound complexes that are relatively stable in their acoustic quality and their patterns of use. Resemblance in acoustic quality to the words of the input language, while being very common, is not an absolute necessity in the case of infants. As specified above, only labels that refer to objects will be studied in the present context, so that the terms *label* and *word* can be used interchangeably.

After the terminology has been sufficiently clarified to assure effective communication, the four goals can be broached successively.

A CONCEPTUAL REEVALUATION

The first goal is still largely conceptual/terminological, pertaining to the terms and dichotomies commonly encountered in the description of conceptual and semantic development. Since E. Clark's early study (Clark, 1973) and Nelson's (1974) first counterproposal, the controversy has mostly been formulated as dealing with a dipolar dimension of "perceptual vs. functional" factors that predominate in the formation of the core meaning of concepts and words. Nelson (1974) employed also the dichotomy "static vs. dynamic" and in one of her recent articles she has changed this to a dichotomy of "form vs. function" (Nelson, 1979). Since the "perceptual-functional" dichotomy is encountered predominantly and is employed by Nelson more or less synonymously with the other terminologies, it will mainly be considered. The other dichotomies will be briefly dealt with toward the end of this section to be contrasted with the main one.

Whereas the term perception was defined before, for the understanding of the dichotomy to be evaluated, some historical considerations are in order. The emphasis upon perception is encountered in Post-Renaissance time in John Locke's theory on human understanding and more generally in the writings of the English empiricists. Whereas the term perception involves all sensory organs and the stimuli received through them, Locke's emphasis upon "ideas" (in the Greek meaning of the term, i.e., visual images) have led him, Berkeley, and many later philosophers to view vision as the most typical or even most important mode of perception. This emphasis is still encountered in the publications of Eve Clark (1973, 1977), who strongly stresses the impact of visual perception upon early concept formation and word meanings, and in the counterproposals of Nelson (1974, 1979).

The term *functional* has had a wider range of meanings and wider ramifications. Since Darwin's functional conceptualization of evolution, the idea became prominent in the social sciences, especially in anthropology (Malinowski, Radcliffe-Brown) and psychology. In the latter field it acquired many shades of meaning. The Würzburg school (Külpe; Bühler) emphasized the dynamic aspects of psychological processes, whereas the Chicago school (Dewey, Angell) stressed the principle of adjustment, i.e., the consequences of behavior, an emphasis that survived the Chicago school in behaviorism. The breadth and vagueness of this concept is also reflected in the definition of Nelson (1974), who has made herself the spokesperson for functionalism in conceptual development and semantics. She defines functional aspects as "actions and the results of actions, whether these are caused by the child himself or by others . . ." (Nelson, 1974, p. 279), and contrasts this pole of her dichotomy with the perceptual pole, which is not defined but exemplified through visual features.

In the meantime, many authors and even Nelson herself (Nelson, 1979) have recognized that this dichotomy is untenable. Most obviously, the spontaneous movement of objects is perceived through the sensory organs and is therefore a subset of the perceptual pole, indeed. Furthermore, children could not know about the results caused by themselves and by others if they did not receive information about these effects through their sensory organs and their perceptual processes. Nelson's propounded polarity of ''perceptual vs. functional'' conceptualizations has consequently revealed itself as being rather a relationship of one large set of perceptual processes that can be subdivided into several subsets. Which subdivision is optimal will be explored presently. Before this can be done, the two other formulations frequently encountered in the literature need to be, even if only briefly, evaluated. These are the proposed dichotomies consisting of either a ''static and a dynamic'' pole or representing ''form vs. function.'' Only very few of the problems that pertain to these dichotomies can be suggested. The main problem seems to be a confounding of levels of explanation. The terms *static* and *form* must be meant to refer to an objective external world, almost in the sense of a naive realism at least in the Gibsonian sense (Henle, 1974). A characterization as *static* can certainly not refer to the psychological aspect of the experience. This aspect is highly ''dynamic'' as research on visual scanning (Maurer & Salapatek, 1976; Salapatek, 1975) has shown. The tactual scanning by blind persons is almost self-evident for anybody who ever observed the exploration of a new object by a blind person. That the processes that lead from perceptual scanning to the conceptualization of a specific object are ''dynamic,'' i.e., they are ''processes,'' has been demonstrated convincingly by research on the central processes of perception (e.g., Carterette & Friedman, 1978). The outcome of these complex processes is then the percept of an object having a specific form (e.g., Metzger, 1974).

On the other hand, the terms *dynamic* and *function* pertain fully to the psychological level, if they are employed in the sense usual in the social sciences, that is as signifying insights into cause-effect or utilitarian relationships. For example, in the often quoted definition given by children: ''a chair is to sit on,'' both the chair and the sitting are quite ''static,'' if ''static'' is taken as meaning the absence of objective real-world motion. Nevertheless this definition is taken as a typical instance of ''functional explanations.'' Employing the traditional meanings of the terms, a confounding of levels of explanation is therefore encountered across the two poles of the proposed dimension. Employing Nelson's definition as quoted above, which includes external movement and the results of actions under the ''functional pole'' the two levels are confounded within the meaning of one and the same term. It will therefore be the task of the present and future analyses to unequivocally define the level of explanation for which suggested explanatory principles are proposed to apply. If the same or similar explanatory principles apply at various levels of explanation, this can be taken as support for the fruitfulness of the proposed conceptualization. Such an attempt will be presented shortly.

But before this can be done a related but different problem has to be briefly touched upon, since it is commonly encountered in contemporary controversies about concept formation. This is the question, whether the dimensions, however formulated, impinge upon the processes of concept formation in a temporal sequence or whether they influence it only to different degrees. Nelson employed in her major theoretical article (Nelson, 1974) the terms *primary* versus *secondary* in describing the impact of functional and perceptual aspects upon concept formation, respectively. The examples she provides suggest almost exclusively a temporal sequence. The argument employed by her, that the child develops a "functional core concept," is neutral in respect to temporal order or order of importance. The terms *primary* and *secondary* can certainly be employed in both senses. E. Clark in describing her "semantic feature hypothesis" (CLark, 1973, p. 72 ff) proposes a very clear temporal sequence so that "the first semantic features . . . are liable to be derived from the encoding of his percepts . . ." and that children later restructure their concepts on the basis of further experience. In contrast to Nelson's theoretical proposal, a factual study performed by her (Nelson, 1973) showed that children classified objects first on the basis of their visual features. Only after this classification conflicted with their expectations about the uses the furnished objects could be put to, did they tend to prefer a classification based upon possible uses of the objects. Accordingly, Nelson concluded that "function (what it does and what can be done with it) is *ultimately* defining" (Nelson, 1979, p. 52, my emphasis). Nelson employs in these papers the two terms *primary* and *ultimately* as if they were synonymous for the description of the putative impact of her "functional aspects." The Latin roots of these terms, i.e., *primus* and *ultimus,* are obviously diametrically contrasting in their meaning. When the terms are employed as synonymous, it is therefore difficult indeed to surmise what their intended meaning might be.

Since however, as shown above, the dimensions that influence concept formation are ill-defined in themselves, it is premature to speculate about the order of their impact. If the dimensions can be clearly defined on various levels of explanation, the pertinent evidence might also provide insights into their temporal order or the importance of their impact. The discussion turns therefore to the evaluation of factual evidence at various levels of analysis.

EVIDENCE ON THE DEVELOPMENT OF PERCEPTION, CONCEPTUALIZATION, AND LANGUAGE

Five possible levels appear to exist: that of the external world, that of the neurological basis for the perception of the external world, that of perception, that of concepts, and finally the verbal level. The level of the external world belongs to the subdisciplines of physics and is too remote from the psychological level to be included. Evidence pertaining both to perceptual processing and conceptual synthesis is provided on the nonverbal level through the behavior of the organisms. The available research does not always differentiate those two levels; they will therefore be collapsed in the following discussion. This leaves three levels for the analysis of the principles that guide the organism in dealings with the environment: the neurological level, the perceptual/conceptual level as demonstrated in nonverbal behavior, and the linguistic level as demonstrated in verbal behavior. These three levels will be dealt with successively.

(a) The Neurological Evidence. Since the pathbreaking discussions of Trevarthen (1968) and Schneider (1969), studies have accumulated that strongly suggest the existence of at least two predominant pathways from sensory organs to the centers that process the incoming information. The research has almost exclusively concentrated on visual perception and the evidence to be referred to will therefore have to pertain mostly to visual experience. Salapatek (1975) and Uttal (1978) have recently provided well-balanced critical reviews of the research and the controversies in this area. These two summaries were employed predominantly for the following discussion. However, important critical and confirmatory data were also taken from the recent monograph on "Neuronal mechanisms in visual perception" (Pöppel, Held, & Dowling (1977) and from many other sources.

For visual perception, one of the pathways which contains the majority of optic tract fibers (Brown, 1975) leads from the fovea and macula of the retina to the lateral geniculate nucleus and then to the striate and peristriate areas of the cortex (areas 17, 18, 19). This is the main or "primary visual pathway." A "secondary pathway," containing by far fewer optic tract fibers and receiving its stimuli mainly from the peripheral areas of the retina, reaches first the superior colliculus, mainly the surface layers of it, and continues then over the pulvinar to the circumstriate areas of the cortex. Bronson (1974, Fig. 1) gives a good diagrammatic presentation of these two pathways. Though being commonly labeled "secondary" in the human being and other higher animals, this pathway is primary in an evolutionary perspective, since lower level animals without a well-developed cortex process all visual stimuli over this pathway (Ebbeson, 1970). As Bronson (1974) has argued, this pathway seems to become functional first in the course of ontogenesis. It certainly is primary in a microgenetic sense, since the colliculus, after receiving stimuli from the peripheral areas of the retina, induces eye movements which allow the organism to focus upon the stimuli and to analyze them in more detail. This brief description of the functioning of the two pathways and of their sequential action suggests already the functional division existing between them. It is summarized in considerable detail by Bronson (1974), Salapatek (1975), and Uttal (1978). The collicular pathway is more involved in establishing the orientation of an object vis-à-vis the organism, its general localization in space, and probably also its movement, and a preliminary impression of its overall shape. Uttal aptly characterized the function of the superior colliculus: "The superior colliculus in mammals appears to act as an initial early warning system that acquires visual stimuli and contributes to the orientation of the animal . . ." (Uttal, 1978, p. 308). In contrast, the "primary pathway" originates in the fovea and the somewhat larger area of the macula where the cones are more slender and most densely packed (Salapatek, 1975, p. 154, Fig. 3.4 provides a clear graphical presentation) making possible fine discriminations of stimulus patterns. It ends in the striate cortex, which accordingly serves fine-grained form perception, analyzing much more specifically size, shape, orientation, and direction of movement.

This division into two perceptual systems has been described specifically for the visual system since most research has been concentrated on it. Gordon (1972) and Dräger and Hubel (1975) report however that a very similar subdivision holds for several of the other senses. Whereas the main information arising from them is channeled to the cortex, a secondary pathway leads to the superior colliculus and specifically to the deeper layers of it. For all these senses the information in the superior colliculus seems to be topographically organized (Gordon, 1972). The various layers of this neural structure seem to fulfill therefore a general orientation function, whether the information comes from the eyes, the ears, or some other sensory organs. The superior colliculus, being part of the mid-brain, has extensive connections with many parts of the limbic system (Uttal, 1978) and also with the ascending reticular system (Cohen, DeLoache, & Strauss, 1979; McCleary & Moore, 1965). As widely recognized, the limbic system and the reticular formation represent the affective-evaluating and energizing centers of the brain, respectively. The collicular early warning system as Uttal has described it fulfills consequently the function not only to attract attention to possibly important stimuli, but also to relay information to activate the organism for a response to the environmental events. It leads in Zajonc's (1979) terminology to "hot cognition." The "primary sensory pathways" ending in the cortex lead in contrast to "cold cognition," which is much finer, more differentiated, and also more complex.

The above described two systems do however not yet account for the third type of perceptions and cognitions, that of cause-effect relationships, i.e., the utilitarian kind that has generally been labeled "functional." The understanding of cause-effect relationships, that is operant relationships, involves quite obviously learning of the temporal contiguities that exist between perceptual events and it involves therewith necessarily time-binding. The question as to the neurological bases of learning is certainly not yet fully solved. Yet Pribram has presented (Pribram, 1954) and summarized (Pribram, 1960) impressive evidence that the areas mainly responsible for these higher processes are what had been called the "association areas" and what are now labeled following Pribram's suggestion "intrinsic areas." Pribram (1954) has demonstrated that two major regions exist that fall under this category: the inferotemporal sector that is specifically related to visual learning, and the anterofrontal sector that is most important for time-binding. Utall's (1978) survey over the more recent research shows that no basic reconceptualizations of the functional localizations are required.

In conclusion, it can be asserted with considerable confidence that three major neurological systems can be differentiated that handle incoming information and contribute to concept formation. For the best explored visual sense they are: The first and more primitive is the pathway leading from the peripheral retina to the superior colliculus, and over the pulvinar to the cortical areas with independent processing of the incoming information in the superior colliculus. The second leads from the macula and fovea to the lateral geniculate body and to the primary visual area in the cortex. Finally a third system shares the preliminary path with the second system but continues from the primary sensory areas to the association or intrinsic areas where cross-modal associations and conceptual structures are established over shorter and longer time intervals.

Having differentiated these three systems, the question remains if the neurological evidence suggests any answers for the controversial question as to which of these systems might be "primary" or "secondary" in concept formation. When considering first the temporal meaning of *primary* and *secondary* the answer is clear. It is well known since Flechsig (1927), it has been explored in a more sophisticated manner by Conel (e.g. Conel, 1939a, 1939b), and has been recently summarized by Tanner (1970) that the brain stem including the superior colliculus develops earliest and becomes functional to a large degree before birth. The primary sensory areas develop somewhat later but become functional soon after birth. The association or intrinsic areas develop even more slowly, at least during the first 2 years of life. Bronson (1974) has summarized in more detail these neurological developments and has related them to the behavioral findings in the field of visual perception. Considering the microgenetic establishment of a percept and concept, the sequence is the same: The object in question has to be first noticed through peripheral vision that is processed in the superior colliculus before it can be focused upon in the fovea and analyzed in the primary visual area. To discover many or even all utilitarian aspects of an object, prolonged experience with this object is required. It is therefore logically necessary that the utilitarian or "functional" aspects of an object are incorporated relatively late into a conceptualization of it.[1]

Having concluded from the neurological structures of the perceptual systems and their maturation that three types of information processing exist, the quite similar argument of Altman (1978) and the wide range of evidence he presents for "three levels of mentation" can serve a valuable supporting function. Though he employs different terminologies in speaking of "pathic mentation," "iconic mentation," and "noetic mentation," his conceptual approach and even

---

[1]Considering the other meaning of primary and secondary, that is order of importance, it would appear to depend upon whether a specific object can be and is used as an instrument by a specific child. Some objects, like the moon, might almost never lend themselves to such a use, while others, such as a spoon, are "primarily" considered from this point of reference. Experimental research is needed to answer this question.

more his neurological argument are in close agreement with the above discussed evidence. It is well known that J. Bruner has formalized a similar trichotomy of the mental functions in describing "enactive, iconic, and symbolic representations." Bruner's argument and evidence pertains however predominantly to the behavioral realm and belongs therefore more to the following section. That nonexperimental behavioral and introspective evidence led Plato and Aristotle to similar conceptualizations of layers of personality is well enough known, since this system has been propagated by many European psychologists (Lersch, 1951; Remplein, 1962) until the recent present.

(b) Nonverbal Behavioral Evidence.   Almost one and a half centuries of neurological research have established agreed-upon categories of neurological structures and it was therefore easy to follow this established taxonomy in the description of those structures underlying percept and concept development. Though behavioral observations are as old as mankind, a behavioral taxonomy that is equally accepted as the neurological one does not exist. With the exception of the subset of reflexes, no other subsets of behavior have been generally delimited. For the present discussion this entails a shift in the emphasis of the presentation. Instead of dwelling intensively upon the categorizations of behavior and adding temporal/developmental considerations only briefly toward the end, the order of emphasis is reversed. Developmental and microgenetic aspects are predominantly discussed and their possible implications for behavioral categorizations are only briefly alluded to.

One type of behavior that appears very early in the course of development and that probably falls also into a special category is the expression of emotions. Bridges' (1932) reports, which have not substantially been improved upon in the intervening years, suggest that infants show already at the age of 2 months a differentiation between distress and delight in their behaviors, i.e., infants make global value judgments of "good vs. bad." Similarly, the defensive reactions to apparently approaching objects as found in the studies of Bower (e.g. Bower, 1966) suggest an evaluative response combined with a differentiation of an activity dimension. The latter is also exemplified in the neonate's tracking of visual objects, which, though jerky and irregular, is exhibited quite consistently as demonstrated by Dayton and Jones (1964).

Concentrating upon research on perceptual and cognitive development, the intensively explored Piagetian system deserves to be considered first. Piaget proposed as a first stage of development a "stage of reflexes," which already by its label and even more through its description suggests behavioral patterns that are clearly distinct from the later appearing ones. It is of great import for the present analysis that Piaget's stage of reflexes corresponds in its time interval quite closely to the period for which Bronson (1974) argued that the "secondary visual system" predominates almost exclusively. Piaget's stage of "primary circular reactions" (1–4 months) coincides with the period during which the "primary perceptual system" gradually takes over the functions of information processing. According to Piaget, the child's schemas begin to undergo some alterations as a function of experience; reflex "seeing" changes to active accommodatory "looking" at stationary objects and to smooth tracking when the objects move. Infants react with a smile to familiar objects and soon show the first signs of "recognitory assimilation" but do not yet have, at least according to Piaget, an "object concept" which involves the integration of several sensory modalities. Only in stage 3, the stage of "secondary circular reactions" (4–8 months) can be found the first signs of temporal integrations of causes and effects. Secondary circular reactions are defined as acts intended to maintain an interesting sensory event just produced, i.e., they cement the tie between a certain behavior and an outcome. With this come the first steps toward intentionality and the conceptualization of means, the sensorimotor analogues of classes and relations, and acts of representation as demonstrated in "motor recognition." All these preliminary beginnings reach a more accomplished level in stage 4, "the coordination of secondary schemas and their application to new situations" (8–12 months). With this goal-directedness and the first appearance of object permanence, time-binding is shown in two behavioral realms of the infant.

It is well enough known that Piaget's hypotheses have been investigated for over a quarter of a century by many researchers and that they have generally been confirmed, with only minor revisions concerning the exact temporal appearance of traces of new accomplishments. Therefore, Piaget's system would lend itself easily to a justification of a threefold distinction of perceptual and conceptual development into: (a) a pre-cognitive stage of reflexes; (b) a period of perceptual analysis and recognition; and (c) a period of temporal integration of experiences, which involves complex conceptual relationships.

There are however several troublesome exceptions to such a facile use of Piaget's system. First come to mind Bower's (1966, 1971, 1972) studies on early evidence for an object concept. He could show that infants only a few days old produce defensive behavior in reaction to an apparently approaching object on a direct-hit path. In another experiment of his, infants around 2 weeks old provided evidence that they expected a seen object to have tactile consequences, i.e., substance (Bower, Broughton, & Moore, 1970). In a similar vein, Wertheimer (1961) has demonstrated that newborns can already coordinate auditory and visual space a few minutes after birth. Both these types of behavior demonstrate intermodal functioning which according to Piaget should not be exhibited so early. Bower argued therefore "that in man there is a primitive unity of senses" (Bower, 1971, p. 32). Research with visual evoked responses (Berg & Berg, 1979; Maurer, 1975) indicates that during the neonatal period the primary sensory areas are quite immature in their response potential, and anatomical evidence shows that the association areas are not yet myelinated and generally not functioning (Tanner, 1970). Taken together, these findings make it highly plausible that the behavior demonstrated by Bower and Wertheimer has to be based upon a more primitive system. Since the superior colliculus represents an early maturing neurological structure in which such a primitive unity of sensory systems has been demonstrated, it is probable that it is involved in the processing of the pertinent incoming information.

Space limitations do not permit the discussion of the complexities that arise for a taxonomy of behavior due to the fact that logically similar behaviors that both entail intermodal functioning are grouped into two different classes because of anatomical and developmental considerations. Gesell's (1946) concept of "reciprocal interweaving" and Piaget's "vertical décalage" were partly designed to deal with these complexities. For the present purposes, the note of caution suggested by Bower's findings suggests a further search for evidence external to Piaget's school.

Such a very active area of research, which can in no way be treated adequately in the present context, is the area of neonate and infant learning with all its controversies and contradictory reports as summarized by Brackbill and Koltsova (1967), Stevenson (1972), and Sameroff and Cavanaugh (1979). In spite of the diversity of the findings and interpretations, it has become increasingly evident that neonates can be conditioned, though it may remain controversial whether they show only operant conditioning (Sameroff, 1971), mainly classical conditioning (Brackbill & Koltsova, 1967), or both (Stevenson, 1972). Much comparative research as briefly summarized by Munn (1965) has shown that lower level animals with little or no cortex can be conditioned too. Conditioning and learning involve some time-binding, which seems in man to be localized in the anterofrontal sector of the cortex. Since this area of the cortex does not yet function in the neonate and is nonexistent in some lower level animals, a conceptual and factual problem exists that needs intensive exploration. Since this cannot be done in the present context, only preliminary hypotheses can be proposed.

The following three sequential developmental steps in concept development are suggested by the above discussed areas of research: In a stage of precognitive functioning which extends approximately through Piaget's "stage of reflexes," i.e., the first 1 to 2 months of life, global-diffuse affective differentiations are made along dimensions of "good versus bad," and "active versus passive." Such simple differentations could also form the basis for the early forms of conditioning, whereby in these early forms the effect of some behavior would only be noticed in the form of the affect resulting from it and not in the form of an external consequence. During a second period, which lasts most of the remainder of the first year of life, much finer perceptual differentations are made leading to the articulation of features of the environment and the recognition of objects. Finally, around the first birthday, the first evidence of cause-effect understanding and real time-binding is encountered, which results in conceptualizations of utilitarian or "functional" relationships.

Considering the microgenetic aspect of concept formation, a somewhat lengthy quote from the field of comparative research (Weisler & McCall, 1976) can specify the general principles involved:

> There seems to be considerable similarity—even sterotypy—in the general form of behavior across situations, specimens of a species, and species. For example the sequence tends to be: (a) alerting or the recruiting of attention to the new stimulus situation, (b) distance-receptor scanning or examination of the situation in which the organism may perambulate the environment or manipulate the object to explore it more completely, and (c) active physical interaction apparently for the purpose of discerning what will happen as a consequence of the organism's interactions with the object or situation. There is a tendency toward invariance in this sequence, though the length of time devoted to each phase may vary and components *b* and *c* may alternate. (p. 493)

The mechanisms described here as prevailing across species and specimens within the species are also well known from observations of infants and children. Component *a* reflects most closely Kagan's (1966, 1970) involuntary attention-evoking mechanisms; they can be acoustic as well as visual; infants respond to movement and change as well as contrast. All these descriptions are in close accord with what was summarized above about the functioning of the "secondary perceptual system" generally and the superior colliculus specifically. The more superficial layers of the superior colliculus contain the cells responsible for the optical aspects of this orienting and attending, whereas the deeper layers fulfill the same functions for acoustic and somatic stimuli, especially moving sound sources and light touch (Gordon, 1972). Component *b* comes closest to what has often been termed *perceptual,* but it is certainly not static nor solely visual. Distance-receptor scanning and examination in the case of vision involves foveal focusing and cortical analysis. The organism's perambulation through the environment involves movement of the visual image on the retina and the need for saccadic eye movements to refocus the object in question. If the object in question is moving, the visual focus will follow the moving object. This movement or the lack of it will be only one aspect of the object concept to be developed, i.e., whether the object in question will be preliminarily classified as animate or inanimate. Whether the object is a source of sounds or not will also influence this classification. Finally, the object's movement or immobility will profoundly influence step three in the perceptual process. How the exploring organism interacts with the object is a function of the spontaneous movement of the object and its reactions to the explorer's interaction with it. This component *c* comes therefore closest to the *functional* aspect as the term is generally employed in the social sciences but not in the full sense Nelson uses it. It has been labeled "utilitarian" or "effective" in the present discussion since it involves the sensory feedback that results from the organism's actions and therefore information about cause-effect relationships. Out of physical necessity it has to come after the object is noticed and at least partly analyzed so that a first attempt at handling it can be made. Active physical interaction also takes considerably more time than mere noticing or sensory inspection and analysis. Finally, for most objects there are definite maxima of information that can be extracted by mere sensory inspection. For the utilitarian properties of objects, the limitations lie mainly in the ingenuity of the experimenter as studies of problem solving and technical progress have shown.

Weisler and McCall make it clear that the three steps described by them are generally in an antecedent-consequent relationship; as suggested above, this relationship is one of necesssary but not sufficient antecedents. Many stimuli impinge upon the visual periphery but are not analyzed in detail though they have been noticed. Furthermore, many objects might be visually analyzed but they are not actively experimented with so that little or no evidence about their functional relationships could be accumulated. This later fact certainly applies for a large portion of human experiences encompassing most of the stable environmental aspects. This necessary but not sufficient antecedent-consequent relationship implies logically also differential frequencies with which the various experiences impinge upon the perceptual system. Stimuli from a particular object will arrive most frequently in the peripheral retina and be relayed from there to the superior colliculus. They will be less frequently focused upon and analyzed in the primary sensory areas. Intensive and active exploration of the object in question and the processing of the resulting information in the intrinsic portions of the brain will be least frequent. If frequency has any impact upon importance for concept formation, then these differential frequencies should be considered in theories about concept formation and the meanings underlying verbal labels. For example, infants will have had for a long time vague impressions of the furniture in their home before they study specific pieces of the furniture in detail and long before they know for certain all the possible functions of each furniture item. The adult similarly may have enjoyed the refreshing green and cool shade of a particular group of trees on the way to work without being aware of specific features of these trees. In this last instance, experimentation that leads to utilitarian feedback-based knowledge is probably never established.

Two further topics of microgenesis need brief exploration to evaluate the above arguments. They are the processes observed in response to tachistoscopic exposures of stimuli and the findings on first impression formation. The research tool of microgenetic experiments was propagized by H. Werner (Werner, 1957). Werner and Kaplan (1963) give a description of microgenetic processes that is so appropriate to the present topic that it deserves to be quoted in part: The microgenetic "process is essentially an orderly, sequential one. It begins with a phase in which meanings are felt or suffered rather than cognitively apprehended. The earliest representations are presumed to be of an affective-sensory-motor nature, (they serve only) to establish global outlines of the experience. . . ,'' they are followed by differentiation and articulation and finally "the experience is shaped more and more for communication to others" (Werner & Kaplan, 1963, p. 242). The parallels between these formulations and the descriptions given above for the three-step processes in percept and concept formation are striking indeed, though Werner and Kaplan specify more the symbolic aspect of the third step. This last step will be of importance for the next section of this essay. More experimental research on microgenesis was recently summarized by Zajonc (1979). He quoted findings that even after one-millisecond exposures, when the subjects could neither recognize nor identify stimuli, clear effects of these stimuli in the emotional domain as far as liking versus disliking is concerned could be demonstrated. These findings and many others he quotes show again that emotional-evaluative reactions come before there is any conscious processing of the incoming information in the brain.

Finally, there are the broad areas of impression formation, attitude formation, and general preference judgements. They too are briefly surveyed by Zajonc and they illustrate the same principle: Emotional reactions arise before enough physical features are processed to justify these evaluations. The latter are often not even dependent upon specific physical features. It is also widely known that these first impressions are very resistant to change and they can be permanent even if they conflict with consciously accessible insights and utilitarian considerations. It is not clear from these brief and somewhat undifferentiated remarks whether the available evidence suggests a dipolar division between "hot and cold cognition" as Zajonc suggests, or if a triple differentiation between affective, feature-dependent, and utilitarian categorization is suggested. The evidence seems to support, however, at the least a differentiation between affective brainstem processing on the one hand and various aspects of cognitive cortical processing on the other.

(c) Communicative and Verbal Evidence.   It is presupposed in the following discussion that during infancy concepts are generally established first, that labels are attached to them later, and that therefore the latter can provide at least partial evidence for the former. The following analysis will only deal with this course of development, which according to the present understanding of infant development is predominant during this age period. Common sense considerations as well as diary reports suggest however that the opposite sequence might become quite frequent during the later stages of early childhood. Toward the end of the preschool years children often ask "What's a . . .?" in reaction to an unknown vocabulary item. In this case and even more in school when new words are introduced in a planned manner, Brown's remark applies that "the word functions as a lure to cognition" (Brown, 1956, p. 278). The perceptual and conceptual processes that are involved in the development of those concepts that are

established as a consequence of a newly introduced word for which no concept existed may be very different from those involved in early preverbal concept formation. They deserve therefore a separate discussion.

Well-established, though not well-defined, categories exist for the description of major categories of meaning and the following discussion will adopt these categorizations. Meaning is generally subdivided into connotation and denotation, the latter being again differentiated into two subsets: word-meaning and sentence-meaning. The main emphasis will be placed in accordance with the present topic upon word-meaning, and specifically on the meaning of nouns. The topics of connotation and sentence-meaning are however highly relevant for the understanding of the development of meaning and they need to be dealt with even if only in passing.

Evidence of connotational or affective meaning is found in paralinguistic phenomena, such as the voice qualities of pitch, intensity, extent, etc.; partly in nonverbal vocalizations that can accompany verbalizations, such as laughing, crying; in the studies on auditory-visual synesthesia as predominantly explored by H. Werner (cf. Werner, 1940, 1955); and of course in the Semantic Differential that was employed so widely by Osgood (Osgood, May, & Miron, 1975; Osgood, Suci, & Tannenbaum, 1957). It would take a separate treatise to deal with all these topics satisfactorily. They can therefore be only briefly summarized.

Affective vocal expressions are certainly produced by the infant before the first words; they are also comprehended before language is comprehended. Elkonin (1971) has summarized some of the pertinent Russian evidence and Moerk (1977) has done this for studies in the West. Research on paralinguistic phenomena in adult speech and their relationships to emotional states has been surveyed by Mahl and Schulze (1964). In many of the pertinent studies including those on synesthesia, two major aspects of connotative meaning have been described: an aspect of evaluation in the good-bad dimension, and an aspect of excitement/quiescence. These two aspects are obviously in close accord with Osgood's "evaluation" and "activity" dimension and also with two of W. Wundt's three dimensions of feeling: "pleasantness/unpleasantness" and "excitement/quiescence." Whether Osgood's third factor, "potency," and Wundt's third dimension of feelings, "strain/relaxation," is also reflected in vocal connotative behavior would need to be explored in a more intensive analysis.

Considering the wide range of evidence accumulated in these fields the following conclusions seem warranted. There exists a primitive aspect of affective meaning that develops very early and before linguistic meaning in the narrow sense. It is more predominant during the years of childhood as most often reported in the studies on synesthesia and is based upon an undifferentiated unity of senses that Werner described as the "syncretic character of primitive organization" (H. Werner, 1940, p. 59 ff). These dimensions of meaning are retained throughout adulthood, they are closely tied to denotative word meanings, and they appear quite universally across cultures as shown in the wide-ranging research of Osgood (esp. Osgood et al., 1975). That these meaning dimensions exhibit striking resemblances to the functions attributed to the superior colliculus does not need emphasizing. The continuity between preverbal emotional expressions, their comprehension, the synesthetic conceptual structures and the connotative structures of words is close enough to suggest a stable meaning system consisting of two or three dimensions.

Proceeding to the level of words a brief retrospect might help to put the recent controversies in perspective. The latter represent namely a replay of very similar argumentations encountered throughout the last century. Meumann (1908) reacted to preceding overly rationalistic interpretations of early word meaning by overemphasizing the emotional-volitional aspect of early words. Stern and Stern (1907) as well as Delacroix (1924) presented a more balanced interpretation of the early meanings of the child, emphasizing both ''functional'' and ''perceptual'' aspects. Lewis however (1951, 1957) stressed again heavily ''functionalist'' interpretations. As Nelson (1974) has shown, this was followed by predominantly rationalist approaches to concept formation. Nelson repeated somewhat in her own writings this vacillation between emphases. First (Nelson, 1973, 1974, 1977) she emphasized ''the primacy of functional aspects,'' later (Nelson et al., 1978) her position was considerably more balanced when she conceded that ''the naming evidence . . . has not revealed a uniform structure of preferred or more reliable identifying features. . . .'' (Nelson et al., 1978, p. 962). When she described in one of her last publications the influence of ''functional'' aspects as applying ''ultimately'' (Nelson, 1979, p. 52), she has, at least implicitly, arrived at a position opposite her original one.

If the analyses presented in the preceding sections are accepted, they suggest an explanation why developmental psycholinguists could not reach an agreement on the question as to which features influence early word use. It was argued above that at the beginning of word use infants have developed far enough to employ any or several of the various types of features for their concept formation. Which of them they actually employ would depend to a large degree upon the object in question, i.e., whether it has utilitarian value or whether it attracts attention only through some of its features that can be analyzed through simple observation. The principles underlying concept formation might therefore be more complex than often assumed and motivational and ecological aspects might influence the formation of many or most concepts. Conclusions as to ''the most important principle'' might therefore easily reflect more the preconceived notions of individual investigators and not the actual functioning of children. Contradictory conclusions would consequently be expected.

Awareness of object-dependent, situational, and individual influences does not however necessarily negate general overall trends. If earlier developmental sequences are repeated at later levels, as often suggested with concepts such as ''the law of recapitulation'' or ''vertical décalage,'' then both general trends and motivated exceptions could be expected. It was argued in the preceding sections that concepts often are formed in a triple-step process: An affective reaction is followed by concentration upon the objective features of the object of attention, which in turn can be, but need not be, followed by an exploration of its utilitarian properties. An almost identical triple-step sequence appears to exist in language development. The affective aspect of it was discussed in the immediately preceding section. Stern and Stern (1907) have concluded that the first stage in vocabulary use is a "noun stage." This conclusion is generally confirmed by a wide range of vocabulary evidence, though the expected exceptions exist. The next two stages in language that the Sterns differentiated are a "verb stage" and a "relations stage." The "relations stage" was intended to describe more-word constructions that either include characteristics of objects or relations between objects. It falls therefore predominantly outside the realm of the present discussion and partly pertains, at least in respect to the emphasis upon relations between objects, to the third step, the utilitarian/"functional"/effective level. The situation is especially interesting in regard to the "verb stage." Verbs express by definition a relationship whether they are accompanied by their arguments or not. When infants employ verbs they demonstrate thereby that they have conceptually begun to handle relationships. As long as they omit the arguments of the verbs in their one-word utterances, they also demonstrate that they have not yet mastered the linguistic tools to fully express their conceptualizations. They will therefore be forced for communicative purposes to convey their conceptually more sophisticated intentions by means of single verbs or nouns, with the choice being dependent upon the communicational requirements in the specific context (Greenfield & Smith, 1976). The observing developmental psycholinguist will then have ample opportunity to record nouns which are employed in contexts that suggest "functional" emphasis or relational verbs without a specification of their relations. Only in the case of more-word sentences can infants convey their conceptualizations more completely on the verbal level and neither they nor their observers need to confound conceptual diffuseness with linguistic deficits in expressing them. Since the problem of sentence formation has been omitted from the present discussion in order to remain within the space limitations, only the one-word utterances and more specifically nouns need to be considered.

The information pertinent to this question is overwhelmingly large, going back to the diary recordings of over one hundred years ago. It cannot be surveyed here. Valuable summaries have recently been provided by E. Clark (1973, 1977) for some of the older data, by Anglin (1977) pertaining mainly to experimental evidence, and by Gruendel (1977) who employed observational methods in her data collection. Clark's data persuaded her to become the spokesperson for the so-called "perceptual" position. Anglin (1977) reported that only five out of 236 instances in the diary literature suggest an overextension due to "functional" or feedback-based similarity. Bowerman (1978) who studied her own two children, reported that there was only a handful of examples of overextension of words to new objects purely on the basis of similar function in the absence of shared perceptual features, and these occurred relatively late. Even Gruendel (1977), though coming from Nelson's school, had to report a predominance of "form" as the criterion for word choice together with clear instances of a progression from reliance upon "form" to later emphasis upon "functions." A few examples from a wide variety of sources will demonstrate more clearly the principles children employ in their word use.

As the onomatopoetic sound patterns of several of these words suggest, the words presented in Table 8.1 are some of the earliest produced by the children of the authors mentioned. In their variety, their differences, and similarities they provide impressive hints as to how these children had shaped their concepts underlying these words: The moon (mooi) is obviously removed from the child's active experimentation and nevertheless it appears quite often in the early vocabulary. As the overextensions suggest in the present case, the visual feature of a somewhat rounded pattern and nothing else was the basis of this concept. In respect to the watch (ga), it is improbable that the child was permitted to do much experimenting, which at this early age still may consist of shaking, throwing, banging, and so forth. Again the roundness of the form seems to have been the main feature defining this concept. Mauthner's child, who generalized the label for dog (wauwau) to chickens might have relied upon spontaneous movement plus possibly some restrictive features for his concept of "animal" or "domestic animal." It is barely probable that he had much feedback-based experience with the chicken. When Lewis's child overgeneralized the label for a cat (tee), he neglected very obviously any utilitarian aspects he might have observed probably in favor of the visual feature of four-leggedness. Only knowledge about his nonverbal experiences could show whether he touched the fur of all these animals. It appears quite improbable. In contrast to the above two overgeneralizations which appear quite "reasonable" even for an adult, Stern's child must have relied exclusively upon some Gestalt qualities of his percepts when he included pictures and his shadow in the concept labeled *bebau*, the child's equivalent for "dog." Certainly this concept could not have been feedback-based either and even mobility versus a lack of it was irrelevant in its formation. Taine's child followed a similar principle by including in the range of the word *bebe* pictures, small statues, and live children.

The last two examples can also serve to draw attention to an argument forcefully made by Anglin (1978) that the range of a label may not reflect the differentiation of the child's conceptual domain. Even adults would be prone to label a statue of a child "a child." Whereas adults might do this in the interest of minimal effort, the child might be forced to do it because the more complex means to express the message exactly are not yet in his repertoire. This argument of Anglin's raises an important methodological caveat whose implications need to be briefly considered: It certainly means that the conceptual domain might be more finely differentiated than the verbal one. If it is, however, assumed that the

TABLE 8.1

Examples of Concepts of Young Children That Suggest the Principles Underlying Their Formation

Author	Sound Pattern	Basic Meaning	Extended Meaning
Chamberlain & Chamberlain (1904)	mooi	moon	cakes, round marks on windows, writing on the windows, writing on paper, round things in books, tooling in books, faces, postmarks, the letter O
Lindner (1882)	ga	watch	compass, everything similar to a watch
Mauthner (1901)	wauwau	dog	chicken
Lewis (1951)	tee	cat	small dog, cow, horse
Stern and Stern (1907)	bebau	dog	most animals, his own shadow, pictures
Taine (1877)	bebe	picture of baby	all small statues, all children
Stern and Stern (1907)	ball	ball	everything round such as a ball of wool, printed circular forms
Stern and Stern (1907)	psi	flowers	leaves, tree, fruit from trees
Sander cited in Stern and Stern (1907)	peite	branches for whipping	trees
Scupin and Scupin (1907)	tiktak	watch	kitchen scales, pills, round holes

child's word choice is cognitively based and not arbitrary, it follows that some intensional similarities persuaded the child to form a set large enough to justify the application of the same label to all its members. In Rosch's (1975) terminology, dogs and babies might have represented the prototypes for the set, respectively, but the other items must have been located somewhere along a gradient of similarity to elicit a common label.

The word and concept for ball (ball) which Stern's child had adopted can serve as a forceful example against Nelson's (1973, 1974) arguments concerning a "functional core concept" for the word *ball*. The child probably had sufficient opportunities to become familiar with the functions of a ball. Nevertheless, it is clear that "functional aspects" influenced the concept formation neither "primarily" nor "ultimately" since the term was generalized to a round ball of wool (which does not bounce) and printed circular forms (which do not move). The label of Stern's child, *psi,* suggests an underlying concept "plant," though any encounters the child might have had with leaves, trees, and their fruits certainly would have resulted in very diverse feedback-based experiences. Similarly, the children of Sander and Scubin in their application of their terms *peite* and *tiktak,* respectively, demonstrated a supreme disregard for any utilitarian or feedback-based aspects.

Whereas selected examples cannot prove a hypothesis, they can provide devastating counterevidence against a hypothesis that postulates that they should not be found. Such examples can and do also suggest the impact of predominant principles resulting in general trends. They suggest that young children disregard functional aspects in their use of nouns and that they rely upon objective environmental features when employing and generalizing nouns. Their attempts to master functional relationships, while already beginning during their second year of life, appear to be reflected in their language behavior only after the beginning of more-word sentences. It is a task mainly for the preschool years, but it remains a challenge throughout life.

CONCLUSION

It has been argued that a "perceptual-functional" dichotomy as formulated and retained during the last centuries is untenable on logical grounds. All information obtained from the environment has to be received through the senses and processed by the perceptual systems. It is therefore without exception "perceptual". Utilitarian feedback-based aspects are only a subset of perceptual information. Neurological, perceptual/conceptual, and linguistic evidences suggests a triple differentiation of concept-shaping factors that results in affective-, objective-, and utilitarian-effective categorizations. Developmentally as well as microgenetically these three types of processing appear sequentially so that the antecedents are necessary but not sufficient for the consequent processes to happen. This antecedent-consequent relationship entails differential frequencies of processing which in turn should have some impact upon concept-formation, - storage, and -retrieval. The earlier a skill/faculty is acquired, the clearer these sequential developments can be seen. They are quite obvious in emotional and reflexive behavior and they could be demonstrated clearly in perception. Whereas the evidence was more complex for conceptualizations and vocabulary, since a fully functional nervous system allows exceptions to these trends in response to environmental variations, the same general principles could be discerned unmistakably.

REFERENCES

Altman, J. Three levels of mentation and the hierarchic organization of the human brain. In G. A. Miller & E. Lenneberg (Eds.), *Psychology and biology of language and thought. Essays in honor of Eric Lenneberg.* New York: Academic Press, 1978.

Anglin, J. M. *Word, object, and conceptual development.* New York: Norton, 1977.

Anglin, J. M. From reference to meaning. *Child Development,* 1978, *49,* 969–976.

Berg, W. K., & Berg, K. M. Psychophysiological development in infancy: state, sensory function, and attention. In J. D. Osofsky (Ed.), *Handbook of infant development.* New York: John Wiley & Sons, 1979.

Bloom, L. *Language development: Form and function in emerging grammars.* Cambridge, Mass.: MIT Press, 1970.

Bloom, L. *One word at a time.* The Hague: Mouton, 1973.

Bower, T. G. R. The visual world of infants. *Scientific American,* 1966, *215,* 80–92.

Bower, T. G. R. The object in the world of the infant. *Scientific American,* 1971, *225,* 30–38.

Bower, T. G. R. Object perception in infants. *Perception,* 1972, *1,* 15–30.

Bower, T. G. R., Broughton, J. M., & Moore, M. K. Demonstration of intention in the reaching behavior of neonate humans. *Nature,* 1970, *228,* 679–680.

Bowerman, M. The acquisition of word meaning: An investigation of some current conflicts. In N. Waterson & C. Snow (Eds.), *Development of communication: social and pragmatic factors in language acquisition.* New York: John Wiley, 1978.

Brackbill, Y., & Koltsova, M. M. Conditioning and learning. In Y. Brackbill (Ed.), *Infancy and early childhood.* New York: The Free Press, 1967.

Bridges, Katherine M. B. Emotional development in early infancy. *Child Development,* 1932, *3,* 324–341.

Bronson, G. W. The postnatal growth of visual capacity. *Child Development,* 1974, *45,* 873–890.

Brown, R. Language and categories. In J. S. Bruner, J. J. Goodnow, & G. A. Austin (Eds.), *A study of thinking.* New York: John Wiley & Sons, 1956.

Brown, T. S. General biology of sensory systems. In B. Scharf (Ed.), *Experimental sensory psychology.* Glenview, Ill.: Scott, Foresman, 1975.

Carterette, E. C., & Friedman, M. P. (Eds.) *Handbook of perception* (Vol. 9). New York: Academic Press, 1978.

Chamberlain, A. F., & Chamberlain, J. C. Studies of a child. *Pedagogical Seminary,* 1904, *11,* 264–291.

Clark, E. V. What's in a word? On the child's acquisition of semantics in his first language. In T. E. Moore (Ed.), *Cognitive development and the acquisition of language.* New York: Academic Press, 1973.

Clark, E. Universal categories: on the semantics of classifiers and children's early word meanings.

In A. Juilland (Ed.), *Linguistic studies offered to Joseph Greenberg on the occasion of his sixtieth birthday*. Saratoga, Calif.: Anma Libri, 1977.

Cohen, L. B., DeLoache, J. S., & Strauss, M. S. Infant visual perception. In J. D. Osofsky (Ed.), *Handbook of infant development*. New York: John Wiley & Sons, 1979.

Conel, J. L. *The postnatal development of the human cerebral cortex. I: Cortex of the newborn*. Cambridge, Mass.: Harvard University Press, 1939. (a)

Conel, J. L. *The postnatal development of the human cerebral cortex. VI: Cortex of the twenty-four-month infant*. Cambridge, Mass.: Harvard University Press, 1939. (b)

Dayton, G. O. Jr., & Jones, M. H. Analysis of characteristics of fixation reflexes in infants by use of direct current electrooculography. *Neurology*, 1964, *14*, 1152–1156.

Delacroix, H. *Le language et la pensee*. Paris: Alcan, 1924.

Dräger, U. C., & Hubel, D. H. Responses to visual stimulation and relationship between visual, auditory, and somatosensory inputs in mouse superior colliculus. *Journal of Neurophysiology*, 1975, *38*, 690–713.

Ebbesson, S. O. E. On the organization of central visual pathways in vertebrates. *Brain, Behavior and Evolution*, 1970, *3*, 178–194.

Elkonin, D. B. Development of speech. In A. V. Zaporozhets & D. B. Elkonin (Eds.), *The psychology of preschool children*. Cambridge, Mass.: MIT Press, 1971.

Flechsig, P. *Meine myelogenetische Hirnlehre mit biographischer Einleitung*. Berlin: Springer, 1927.

Gesell, A. The ontogenesis of infant behavior. In L. Carmichael (Ed.), *Manual of child psychology*, (2nd ed.). New York: John Wiley & Sons, 1946.

Gordon, B. The superior colliculus of the brain. *Scientific American*, 1972, *227*, 72–83.

Greenfield, P. M., & Smith, J. *The structure of communication in early language development*. New York: Academic Press, 1976.

Gruendel, J. M. Referential extension in early language development. *Child Development*, 1977, *48*, 1567–1576.

Henle, M. On naive realism. In R. B. MacLeod & H. L. Pick, Jr. (Eds.), *Perception. Essays in honor of James J. Gibson*. Ithaca, N.Y.: Cornell University Press, 1974.

Kagan, J. Developmental studies in reflection and analysis. In A. H. Kidd & J. L. Rivoire (Eds.), *Perceptual development in children*. New York: International Universities Press, 1966.

Kagan, J. Attention and psychological change in the young child. *Science*, 1970, *170*, 826–832.

Lersch, P. *Der Aufbau der Person*. München: Ernst Reinhardt Verlag, 1951.

Lewis, M. M. *Infant speech*. New York: The Humanities Press, Inc., 1951.

Lewis, M. M. *How children learn to speak*. London: George G. Harrap, 1957.

Lindner, G. Beobachtungen und Bemerkungen über die Entwicklung der Sprache des Kindes. *Kosmos*, 1882, *6*, 321–342, 430–441.

Mahl, G. F., & Schulze, G. Psychological research in the extralinguistic area. In T. A. Sebeok, A. S. Hayes, & M. C. Bateson (Eds.), *Approaches to semiotics*. The Hague: Mouton, 1964.

Maurer, D. Infant visual perception: Methods of study. In L. B. Cohen & P. Salapatek (Eds.), *Infant perception: From sensation to cognition* (Vol. 1), *Basic visual processes*. New York: Academic Press, 1975.

Maurer, D., & Salapatek, P. Developmental changes in the scanning of faces by young infants. *Child Development*, 1976, *47*, 523–527.

Mauthner, F. *Beiträge zu einer Kritik der Sprache*. Stuttgart: Cotta, 1901.

McCleary, R. A., & Moore, R. Y. *Subcortical mechanisms of behavior*. New York: Basic Books, 1965.

McNamara, J. Cognitive basis of language learning in infants. *Psychological Review*, 1972, *79*, 1–13.

Metzger, W. Can the subject create his world? In R. B. MacLeod & H. L. Pick, Jr. (Eds.), *Perception. Essays in Honor of James J. Gibson*. Ithaca, N.Y.: Cornell University Press, 1974.

Meumann, E. *Die Entwicklung der ersten Wortbedeutungen beim Kinde.* Leipzig: Engelmann, 1908.

Moerk, E. L. Specific cognitive antecedents of structures and functions involved in language acquisition. *Child Study Journal,* 1973, *3,* 77–90.

Moerk, E. L. *Pragmatic and semantic aspects of early language development.* Baltimore: University Park Press, 1977.

Munn, N. L. *The evolution and growth of human behavior.* Boston: Houghton Mifflin, 1965.

Nelson, K. Some evidence for the cognitive primacy of categorization and its functional basis. *Merrill-Palmer Quarterly,* 1973, *19,* 21–39.

Nelson, K. Concept, word, and sentence: Interrelations in acquisition and development. *Psychological Review,* 1974, *81,* 267–285.

Nelson, K. Some attributes of adjectives used by young children. *Cognition,* 1976, *4,* 13–30.

Nelson, K. The conceptual basis of naming. In J. McNamara (Ed.), *Language learning and thought.* New York: Academic Press, 1977.

Nelson, K. Explorations in the development of a functional semantic system. In W. A. Collins (Ed.), *Children's language and communication. The Minnesota Symposia on Child Psychology* (Vol. 12). Hillsdale, N.J.: Lawrence Erlbaum Assoc., 1979.

Nelson, K., Rescorla, L., Gruendel, J., & Benedict, H. Early lexicons: What do they mean? *Child Development,* 1978, *49,* 960–968.

Osgood, C. E., May, W. H., & Miron, M. S. *Cross-cultural universals of affective meaning.* Urbana: University of Illinois Press, 1975.

Osgood, C. E., Suci, G. J., & Tannenbaum, P. *The measurement of meaning.* Urbana, Ill.: University of Illinois Press, 1957.

Pöppel, E., Held, R., & Dowling, J. E. (Eds.). Neuronal mechanisms in visual perception. *Neurosciences Research Program Bulletin,* 1977, *15,* 315–553.

Pribram, K. H. Toward a science of neuropsychology (method and data). In R. A. Patton (Ed.), *Current trends in psychology and the behavioral sciences.* Pittsburgh: University of Pittsburgh Press, 1954.

Pribram, K. H. A review of theory in physiological psychology. In P. R. Farnsworth & Q. McNemar (Eds.), *Annual review of psychology* (Vol. 11). Palo Alto, Calif.: Annual Reviews, 1960.

Remplein, H. *Die seelische Entwicklung des Menschen im Kindes- und Jugendalter.* München: Ernst Reinhardt Verlag, 1962.

Rosch, E. Universals and cultural specifics in human categorization. In R. Brislin, S. Bochner, & W. Lonner (Eds.), *Cross-cultural perspectives on learning.* New York: Halsted, 1975.

Salapatek, P. Pattern perception in early infancy. In L. B. Cohen & P. Salapatek (Eds.), *Infant perception: From sensation to cognition* (Vol. 1). *Basic visual processes.* New York: Academic Press, 1975.

Sameroff, A. J. Can conditioned responses be established in the newborn infant? *Developmental Psychology,* 1971, *5,* 1–12.

Sameroff, A. J., & Cavanaugh, P. J. Learning in infancy: A developmental perspective. In Joy D. Osofsky (Ed.), *Handbook of infant development.* New York: John Wiley & Sons, 1979.

Schlesinger, I. M. Production of utterances and language acquisition. In D. I. Slobin (Ed.), *The ontogenesis of grammar: A theoretical symposium.* New York: Academic Press, 1971.

Schneider, G. E. Two visual systems. *Science,* 1969, *163,* 895–902.

Scupin, E., & Scupin, G. *Bubis erste Kindheit.* Leipzig: Grieben, 1907.

Stern, C., & Stern, W. *Die Kindersprache.* Leipzig: Barth, 1907.

Stevenson, H. W. *Children's learning.* New York: Appleton-Century-Crofts, 1972.

Taine, H. Acquisition of language by children. *Mind,* 1877, *2,* 252–259.

Tanner, J. M. Physical growth. In P. H. Mussen (Ed.), *Carmichael's manual of child psychology* (3rd ed). New York: John Wiley & Sons, 1970.

Trevarthen, C. B. Two mechanisms of vision in primates. *Psychologische Forschung,* 1968, *31,* 299–337.

Uttal, W. R. *The psychobiology of mind.* Hillsdale, N.J.: Lawrence Erlbaum Assoc., 1978.

Weisler, A., & McCall, R. B. Exploration and play: Resume and redirection. *American Psychologist,* 1976, *31,* 492–508.

Werner, H. *Comparative psychology of mental development.* New York: International Universities Press, 1940.

Werner, H. (Ed.) *On expressive language.* Worcester, Mass.: Clark University Press, 1955.

Werner, H. The concept of development from a comparative and organismic point of view. In D. B. Harris (Ed.), *The concept of development.* Minneapolis, Minn.: University of Minnesota Press, 1957.

Werner, H., & Kaplan, B. *Symbol formation.* New York: John Wiley & Sons, 1963.

Wertheimer, M. Psycho-motor coordination of auditory-visual space at birth. *Science,* 1961, *134,* 1692.

Zajonc, R. B. *Feeling and thinking: Preferences need no inferences.* Paper presented at the annual meeting of the American Psychological Association, New York, September 1979.

9 Towards an Algebraic Theory of the Spectacles Experiment

John C. Hay
University of Wisconsin-Milwaukee

ABSTRACT

The algebraic theory of permutations is used to construct a model of the distorting spectacles experiment. This model is used to explain the relationship between the movement distortions and the stationary distortions of spectacles, and the adaptations to those distortions. It is shown that stationary distortion can occur without movement distortion, while movement adaptation can occur without stationary adaptation.

Helmholtz (1962, 1977, pp. 1–26) inaugurated the distorting-spectacles experiment in the context of his research in mathematics as well as in perception, but Kohler (1953) is among the few of his psychological successors who have considered the link between the experimental paradigm and mathematics. Welch's (1978) intensive review of a century's research on the spectacles paradigm makes no mention of the mathematical link. Yet the paradigm of rearranging a set of sensory inputs finds a remarkably close-fitting model in the algebraic theory of permutations, and it seems possible that that model may offer insights into the meaning of the research findings.

In this study we test the usefulness of the algebraic model by applying it to one of the most striking effects of distorting spectacles: the way in which spectacles distort movements when first put on, and the way in which their prolonged wearing induces adaptations to those movements. These movement distortions and their adaptations may be exemplified by a subject's protocol in Kohler's (1964) book:

First day of wearing prism spectacles: "I am particularly impressed by the move-ments observable in the visual field and accompanying bodily motion. They are even more striking than the curvatures."

Tenth day of wearing prism spectacles: "The sensations of movement have become less pronounced. I am hardly aware of them now. . . . yesterday, while I was *not* wearing the spectacles, I noticed a slight displacement of the wall in front of me while moving my head up and down, the direction of the displacement being opposite to the one occurring with the spectacles." (protocol of Professor Erismann, p. 62 in Kohler, 1964)

Certain movement adaptations, e.g. those involved in position constancy (Welch, 1978), seem to be among the largest adaptations induced by spectacles, while some theorists have proposed that movement adaptation leads the way for other types of adaptation (Festinger, Burnham, Ono, & Bamber, 1967; Held, 1961; Taylor, 1962).

Prior to introducing the algebraic model, it is necessary to make a clear formulation of the concepts of movement distortion, other spectacles distortions, and adaptation to them. The following definitions will be used:

Stationary distortion is a transformation of a stationary sensory input from the environment. Spectacles do this by refracting or reflecting the light traveling from the environment to the eye. Putting on the spectacles, while holding other conditions constant, replaces one stationary sensory input with another.

Movement distortion is a transformation of the sequence of sensory inputs. The type of movement to be emphasized in the present analysis is that accom-panying motor actions by the spectacles wearer: what von Holst (1954) and Held (1961) call *reafference*. Putting on the spectacles, while holding other conditions constant, replaces one sensory sequence during motor action with another senso-ry sequence.

Stationary adaptation is the condition in which the response to a distorted sensory input is the same as the response to the original sensory input, before putting on the spectacles. An example would be judging the curvature produced by prism spectacles as straight (Welch, 1978).

Movement adaptation is the condition in which the response to a distorted sensory sequence becomes the same as the response to the original sensory sequence, before putting on the spectacles. Two types of movement adaptation are subsumed in our analysis. The first type involves response to an actual sensory sequence, as when the subject in the above protocol ceases to notice the distorted visual movements that accompany his body movements. The second type involves response to a desired sensory sequence, as when the subject sees his hand in one location and a target in a second location: this sensory input specifies a desired subsequent sensory input (hand in second location), and the subject selects a response to realize that sensory sequence. In both these types of movement adaptation, the same response must be made to the distorted sensory sequence as was previously made to the original, undistorted sensory sequence.

With these definitions two basic questions may be formulated to test the usefulness of the algebraic model. *Question 1:* What is the relation between stationary distortion and movement distortion? *Question 2:* What is the relation between stationary adaptation and movement adaptation?

The algebraic model is developed here only so far as is necessary to answer these two questions. The model makes a minimum of psychological assumptions. This is a merit, inasmuch as the questions are then answered in a widely applicable fashion. It also means that the answers are in rather abstract form, and further interpretation of the model will be needed to apply them to specific experiments.

We begin by presenting the structure of the algebraic model, merely listing its few psychological assumptions. A subsequent section attempts to justify the psychological assumptions.

The full apparatus of the mathematical theory is not presented, since while basic it is very elementary and can be found in most standard textbooks on abstract algebra. References to such textbooks are provided.

THE ALGEBRA OF PERMUTATIONS AS A MODEL FOR THE DISTORTING SPECTACLES EXPERIMENT

We first assume that the sensory system has a finite number of discrete states. We denote the set of all these states by the capital letter Σ, and individual sensory states by lower case letters σ (cf. Bobrow & Arbib, 1974; Taylor, 1962).

We assume, second, that putting on a pair of spectacles produces a one-to-one rearrangement of these sensory states so that, for example, σ_1 is replaced by σ_2, σ_2 by σ_1, σ_3 by σ_3, and so forth. Such a one-to-one rearrangement of a finite set is called a *permutation* (MacLane & Birkhoff, 1979, p. 68 et seq.). Let the permutation produced by the spectacles be denoted by d. Then the stationary distortion produced by the spectacles can be formulated thus:

Stationary Distortion Formula: $\sigma^* = d(\sigma)$

We note the following algebraic properties of permutations: A permutation may be regarded as a set of (σ, σ) pairs, one pair for each member of Σ. Two permutations may be *multiplied* to form a third: $c = ab$. Some, but not all, permutations *commute* with one another, so that $ab = ba$. Leaving the elements of Σ unchanged is a permutation, the *identity* permutation. Every permutation has a unique *inverse:* the inverse of a being denoted by a^{-1}.

The third and final assumption is that movements can also be represented as permutations of Σ. For example, if the subject turns his head up, the sensory state σ_1 before the head movement is replaced by the sensory state σ_2 after the head movement. The permutation produced by a movement will be denoted by m.

From just these three assumptions we may deduce the relationship between stationary distortions and movement distortions, the answer to our first question. The answer lies in the concept of *conjugation* of a permutation m by a permutation d (MacLane & Birkhoff, 1979, p. 70):

Movement Distortion Formula: $m* = dmd^{-1}$

Notice the difference between the Stationary Distortion Formula and the Movement Distortion Formula: the d term enters the latter twice. The significance of the difference can be developed in terms of the following two theorems. To express the theorems we employ the following definitions:

C = the set of all permutations that commute with m, excluding the identity permutation.

N = the set of all permutations that do not commute with m.

nC = the set C multiplied by a member of N

Theorem I. If the spectacles distortion d *is a member of* C, *then it produces stationary distortions without any movement distortion.*
    Proof: Since C does not contain the identity permutation, the Stationary Distortion Formula gives us the inequality:

$\sigma* \neq \sigma$

From the commutation property of C, the Movement Distortion Formula gives us the equality:

$m* = dmd^{-1} = mdd^{-1} = m$

Theorem II. If two spectacles have their distortions d_1 *and* d_2 *unequal, but both members of the set* nC, *then the two spectacles produce different stationary distortions, but the same movement distortion.*
    Proof: If d_1 and d_2 are unequal but both members of nC then for two members of C, c_1 and c_2, the following is true:

$d_1 = nc_1$

$d_2 = nc_2$

$c_1 \neq c_2$

The Stationary Distortion Formula now gives unequal distortions:

$$d_1(\sigma) = nc_1(\sigma) \neq nc_2(\sigma) = d_2(\sigma)$$

The Movement Distortion Formula, in contrast, gives equal distortions:

$$d_1 m d_1^{-1} = nc_1 m c_1^{-1} n^{-1} = nmc_1 c_1^{-1} n^{-1} = nmn^{-1}$$

$$d_2 m d_2^{-1} = nc_2 m c_2^{-1} n^{-1} = nmc_2 c_2^{-1} n^{-1} = nmn^{-1}$$

JUSTIFICATION OF THE ASSUMPTIONS MADE BY THE ALGEBRAIC MODEL

The first assumption, that the sensory system can be represented by a finite set of states, is of the same kind that is used in treating general information-processing systems (Bobrow & Arbib, 1974). In fact, the analysis does not depend on the finiteness of the set, but would be the same if transformations of an infinite set were substituted for permutations (MacLane & Birkhoff, 1979).

It should be noted that the concept of a sensory state lumps together the visual system with all the other sensory systems of the body and, for the present analysis, no segregation by modality is assumed. It might be claimed that spectacles can only transform the visual parts of sensory states. However, in fact spectacles may also be construed as transforming postures of the body, as when prism spectacles impose a new combination of eye and hand positions during fixation of the gaze on the hand (cf. Kohler, 1964, p. 38). Thus the prism spectacles alter the proprioceptive part of the sensory state associated with gazing at the hand.

The second assumption, that spectacles distortions can be represented by permutations of S, is equivalent to the assumption that the spectacles do not destroy sensory information. It means that, with or without spectacles, there is the same number of possible sensory states and, if there is a nonuniform frequency distribution of those states, that distribution will apply to the permuted states (cf. Attneave, 1959). Certain physical spectacles may violate this assumption, wherever it can be shown that they exclude certain sensory states. For example, a pair of concave lenses outside the accomodation power of the eyes would exclude sensory states caused by sharp illumination gradients on the retina (cf. Gibson, 1964). Spectacles that cause chromatic aberration, such as prism spectacles, do not necessarily violate the present assumption. It is true that white lines on the retina are transformed into spectrums, but the spectacles should also transform the reverse spectrums into white lines, and this feature is in fact used in measuring adaptation to chromatic aberration (Hay, Pick, & Rosser, 1963).

A special aspect of the second assumption involves the effects of eye movement, and the *situational* effects of spectacles described by Kohler (1964). If the spectacles are fixed to the head, as is usually the case, moving the eyes may cause the light to the fovea to traverse a different optical medium. Thus a foveal input which was normally the same for two eye postures is replaced by two different foveal inputs. However, the present model does not segregate the visual system from the sensory system as a whole (see preceding discussion of the first assumption) and in so doing is consistent with the approach advocated by Gibson (1966). The sensory states for two different eye positions are different; hence the fact that the spectacles may assign different new sensory states to them is consistent with the one-to-one assumption of the model.

The third and final assumption, that movements can also be represented as permutations, would seem justified by the following considerations. A movement, or any change, can be time-sliced as finely as desired into successive states of the moving, or changing, system. Each state after the first can be represented as the result of a permutation applied to the first state.

PSYCHOLOGICAL IMPLICATIONS OF THE ALGEBRAIC MODEL

Theorem I provides a direct answer to Question 1: What is the relation between stationary distortions and movement distortions? *The answer is that movement distortions imply stationary distortions, but not the other way around. Stationary distortions may occur, without movement distortion, if the permutation caused by the spectacles commutes with the movement.*

Theorem II provides an indirect answer to Question 2: What is the relation between stationary adaptation and movement adaptation? *The answer is the converse of the first: stationary adaptation implies movement adaptation, but not the other way around.* This answer depends on indirect reasoning, since it involves the concepts of stationary and movement adaptation, about which the algebraic model makes no assumptions. We argue as follows: Suppose a subject has completely adapted to a pair of spectacles whose distortion comes from the set nC of Theorem II. This means he responds to the movement distortion, m^*, in the same way he previously responded to m, and that he responds to the stationary distortion, σ^*, in the same way he previously responded to σ. Now let him switch to a second pair of spectacles, also drawn from the set nC of Theorem II. By that theorem, the new m^* will be the same as before, hence his response to it must be the same; however, the new σ^* will be different, hence his response to it may be different. The subject may thus have movement adaptation to the new pair of spectacles, but not stationary adaptation to them. (See the definition of the adaptations.) On the other hand, let him switch to a third pair of spectacles, not drawn from the set nC of Theorem II. The new m^* will now be different from the first, as will the new σ^*; his responses to both may therefore be different: he may have neither movement adaptation nor stationary adaptation. We have now exhausted the set of possible spectacle distortions (nC and not-nC), so we have shown that movement adaptation may exist without stationary adaptation, but not the other way around.

REFERENCES

Attneave, F. S. *Applications of information theory to psychology*. New York: Holt, 1959.

Bobrow, L. S., & Arbib, M. A. *Discrete mathematics: Applied algebra for computer and information science*. Philadelphia: Saunders, 1974.

Festinger, L., Burnham, C. A., Ono, H., & Bamber, D. Efference and the conscious experience of perception. *Journal of Experimental Psychology*, 1967, *74*, (4, Whole No. 637), 1–36.

Gibson, J. J. Introduction to *Kohler, 1964*.

Gibson, J. J. *The senses considered as perceptual systems*. Boston: Houghton-Mifflin, 1966.

Hay, J. C., Pick, H. L., Jr., & Rosser, E. Adaptation to chromatic aberration in the human visual system. *Science*, 1963, *141*, 167–169.

Held, R. M. Exposure-history as a factor in maintaining stability of perception and coordination. *Journal of Nervous and Mental Diseases*, 1961, *132*, 26–32.

Helmholtz, H. von *Treatise on physiological optics*. New York: Dover, 1962.

Helmholtz, H. von On the origin and significance of the axioms of geometry, in his *Epistemological writings*. Dordrecht: Reidel, 1977.

Holst, E. von Relations between the central nervous system and the peripheral organs. *British Journal of Animal Behavior*, 1954, *2*, 89–94.

Kohler, I. Fundamental remarks about the geometry of sensory spaces. *Wiener Zeitschrift für Philosophie, Psychologie und Pädagogik*, 1953, *4*, 225–232.

Kohler, I. The formation and transformation of the perceptual world. *Psychological Issues*, 1964, *3*, (4), Monograph 12. New York: International Universities Press.

MacLane, S., & Birkhoff, G. *Algebra* (2nd ed.). New York: Macmillian, 1979.

Taylor, J. G. *The behavioral basis of perception*. New Haven: Yale, 1962.

Welch, R. B. *Perceptual modification: Adapting to altered sensory environments*. New York: Academic Press, 1978.

10 Subject Variables in Perception and Their Control

G. A. Lienert
School of Education
University Erlangen-Nürnberg
Nürnberg, West Germany

ABSTRACT

Starting from the notion that organismic or subject variables (like age and sex of Ss) may not be interpreted conclusively in factorial designs, it is proposed to replace the traditional two-variable paradigm (involving dependent and independent variables only) by a three-variable paradigm where independent variables are subdivided into randomized treatment variables and nonrandomizable subject variables. In terms of the three-variable paradigm, ANOVA models are specified in such a way as to allow for conclusive evaluation and interpretation of factorial designs, including subject variables. The numerical procedure is exemplified by an example from Ivo Kohler's perceptual research.

INTRODUCTION

In analysis of variance (ANOVA) designs, there are often two types of independent variables included: (1) *randomized treatment variables* (treatment factors) and (2) *nonrandomizable organismic or subject variables* (block factors). While main effects from treatment factors may be interpreted conclusively, *main effects* from organismic or *subject factors* may *not* since they may be confounded with other organismic or subject variables (Fischer, 1978, p. 142). For example, female subjects (Ss) may not do as well as male subjects in a speed performance test because they have higher neuroticism scores than male Ss. Sex is confounded with neuroticism such that poor test performance may not conclusively be attributed to sex as the organismic or subject variable under study.

What holds true for main effects of organismic variables holds similarly true for their *interaction effects:* If a tranquilizer treatment were found to be more effective in preventing anxiety in females than in males, this effect may be due to females' higher neuroticism scores as well as to their sex. Thus, interaction between a treatment (like tranquilizer versus placebo) and a subject variable (like sex) is not to be interpreted conclusively as a *differential treatment effect* (or treatment-subject interaction effect) due to sex differences.

Paradigms in Psychological Experimentation

The *conclusivity argument* against including subject variables in factorial designs is intrinsically based on the traditional *two-variable paradigm* of R. A. Fisher. This two-variable paradigm may be represented by a two-dimensional scheme with rows being combinations of independent factors and columns being classes of the dependent (or outcome) variable (e.g., grouped performance scores). Within such a two-variable paradigm the rows of the two-dimensional contingency table are made up of treatment-subject factor combinations (e.g., tranquilizer-placebo and male-female combinations) if an organismic factor has been introduced in addition to a treatment factor. Randomized treatment factors and the nonrandomizable subject factor form one variable, the independent variable "treatment-subject" combinations within the two-variable paradigm, whereas the other dimension is made up from the dependent variable.

If, however, for conclusivity argumentation, nonrandomizable independent subject variables are to be separated from randomized independent treatment variables, the two-variable paradigm has to be expanded to become a *three-variable paradigm* which requires a three-dimensional schematic representation: The independent randomized treatment variable (e.g., tranquilizer or placebo assigned by coin-tossing to a sample of N Ss) may form the two rows of a *contingency cube;* the dependent outcome variable (e.g., good or poor performance) may form the two columns of the cube and the independent nonrandomizable subject variables (e.g., male or female Ss) may form the two layers (or strata) of the contingency cube. Thus, in general, the treatment variables form the *length,* the subject variables the *width,* and the outcome variables the *height* of a three-dimensional contingency cube in a three-variable paradigm of psychological experimentation.

By replacing the traditional two-variable paradigm by a three-variable paradigm, the classical *ANOVA evaluation* of experimental designs must be suitably changed in a way to overcome the conclusivity argument. The paradigms are compared considering a hypothetical experiment which could have been performed at the Psychology Department of Innsbruck University.

A Prism Experiment a la Kohler

Ivo Kohler, in his habilitation monograph (Kohler, 1951) studied the factors which favor the *rectification of visual perceptions* distorted by prisms. The degree of rectification (or re-adaption) of distorted perceptions was measured goniometrically as the dependent outcome variable (X). The two types of independent variables, two treatment variables and one subject variable, were defined and operationalized as follows:

1. Treatment variables:
    A = the *duration* distorting prisms worn by a S ($A1$=short, $A2$=long) where long duration was expected to be more favorable to rectification than short duration, implying rectification to be a Gibson-type sensory-adaptation effect (see Day, 1969).
    B = the distortion *intensity* of the prisms worn by a S ($B1$=weak, $B2$=strong) where weak glasses were expected to be more favorable than strong glasses.
2. Subject variable:
    C = *Age of S*s which was either low ($C1$=children) or medium ($C2$=adults) according to the design described below.

The two treatment factors (duration, distortion) and the one subject factor with two modalities pro factor define a $2 \times 2 \times 2 - factorial\ design$. This design was realized by randomly dividing a group of 40 children into $2 \times 2 = 4$ subgroups and randomly assigning the four subgroups to the $2 \times 2 = 4$ treatment combinations ($A1B1$, $A1B2$, $A2B1$ and $A2B2$). The same procedure was applied to a group of 40 adults.

TABLE 10.1
Rectification Scores X in a 2×2×2-Factorial Design

				Treatment Factors				
		A1					*A2*	
	B1			*B2*		*B1*		*B2*
					Subject Variables			
	C1	*C2*	*C1*	*C2*	*C1*	*C2*	*C1*	*C2*
	76	36	43	37	94	74	67	67
	66	45	75	22	85	74	64	60
	43	47	66	22	80	64	70	54
	62	23	46	25	81	86	65	51
	65	43	56	11	80	68	60	49
	43	43	62	27	80	72	55	38
	42	54	51	23	69	62	57	55
	60	45	63	24	80	64	66	56
	78	41	52	25	63	78	79	68
	66	40	50	31	58	61	80	58
$\bar{X}$	60	42	56	25	77	70	66	56

TABLE 10.2
Table 10.1 Data Evaluated by 3-Factorial Model (1) ANOVA

Source	SS	df	MS	F
A	9309.6	1	9309.6	105.07*
B	2656.5	1	2656.5	29.98*
C	5695.3	1	5695.3	64.28*
A × B	27.6	1	27.6	0.31
A × C	1336.6	1	1336.6	15.09*
B × C	374.1	1	374.1	4.22
A × B × C	108.1	1	108.1	1.22
Error-1	6378.1	72	88.6	—
Total	25886.0	79	—	—

The *rectification performance* X of the total sample of $N=80$ Ss is given in Table 10.1 for the 2×2 groups of children, C1, or adults, C2, where data are from Edwards (1968, Table 13.1). According to the traditional two-variable paradigm considering the dependent variable (rectification) as a stochastic function of three independent variables (duration, distortion, sex), Table 10.1 was evaluated as a randomized groups design by a *three-factorial ANOVA* in Table 10.1 for $\alpha = .01$.

From Table 10.1 in combination with their $2\times2\times2$ bottom row averages, *we may conclude that* (1) long-worn prisms favor rectification better than do shortly-worn prisms, (2) weak prisms favor rectification better than do strong prisms, (3) children rectify better than adults. Besides the three significant *main effects,* there is only one significant *interaction effect* in Table 10.2: The $A\times C$ interaction indicates that (4) children's vision rectifies after a short duration nearly as well ($60/2+56/2=58$) as after a long duration ($77/2+66/2=62$) whereas adults rectify after a short duration much more poorly ($42/2+25/2=44$). Thus, the duration of wearing prism glasses as a main effect A is modified by its interaction effect with age, $A\times C$.

Classical Evaluations by the Two-Variable Paradigm

1. The prism glasses experiment in Table 10.1 was evaluated in Table 10.2 by the *three-factors ANOVA* Model 1.

$$X_{ijkm} = \alpha_i + \beta_j + \gamma_k + \alpha_i\,\beta_j + \alpha_i\,\gamma_k + \beta_j\,\gamma_k + \epsilon_{ijkm} \qquad (1)$$

Note that the *classical three-factorial Model 1* does *not* distinguish between the treatment factors A and B with parameters α and β on one side and the subject factor C with parameter γ on the other side. Model 1 allows for interpreting the

TABLE 10.3
Table 10.1 Data Evaluated by 2-Factorial Model (2) ANOVA

Source	SS	df	MS	F
A	9309.6	1	9309.6	50.93*
B	2656.5	1	2656.5	14.53*
A × B	27.6	1	27.6	0.15
C	5695.3	1		
A × C	1336.6	1		
B × C	374.1	1		
A × B × C	108.1	1		
Error-1	6378.1	72		
Error-2	13892.2	76	182.8	—
Total	25886.0	79	—	—

main and interaction effect of the subject factor C (age of Ss) in the same way as for main and interaction effects of the two treatment factors contrary to previous conclusivity argumentation.

2. However, a ANOVA evaluation of Table 10.1 data will become conclusive by assuming that the *subject variable is ineffective*, i.e., has neither main nor interaction effects. Under this assumption the subject factor is *eliminated* by pooling measurements X over $C1$ and $C2$ in Table 10.1 and evaluating them by the *two-factorial* Model 2.

TABLE 10.4
Table 10.1 Data Evaluated by Separation Model (3) ANOVA

Source	SS	df	MS	F
A	9309.6	1	9309.6	85.18*
B	2656.5	1	2656.5	24.30*
A × B	27.6	1	27.6	0.25
C	5695.3	1	—	—
A × C	1536.6	1		
B × C	374.1	1		
A × B × C	108.1	1		
Error-1	6378.1	72		
Error-3	8196.9	75	109.3	—
Total	25886.0	79	—	—

TABLE 10.5
Table 10.1 Data Evaluated by Separation of Model (4) ANOVA

Source	SS	df	MS	F
a) A (C1)	1795.6	1	1795.6	20.27*
B (C1)	518.4	1	518.4	5.85
A × B (C1)	122.5	1	122.5	1.38
Error-C1	4123.4	36	114.5	—
Total-C1	6559.9	39	—	—
b) A (C2)	8850.7	1	8850.7	99.92*
B (C2)	2512.2	1	2512.2	28.36*
A × B (C2)	13.3	1	13.3	.15
Error-C2	2254.7	36	62.6	—
Total-C2	13630.8	39	—	—
c) Error-4	6378.1	72	88.58	Error (C1 + C2)
Total-4	20190.7	78		Total (C1 + C2)
C	5695.3	1	—	—
Total-1	25886.0	79		Total-4 + C

$$X_{ijm} = \alpha_i + \beta_j + \alpha_i \beta_j + \epsilon_{ijm} \qquad (2)$$

Table 10.3 gives the ANOVA of Table 10.1 data under Model 2 assumptions. The evaluation of the subject factors *elimination Model* 2 in Table 10.3 leads to significant main effects for duration of prism-wearing (A) and distortion intensity (B) despite the fact that the error-variance "error-2" is substantially larger than "error-1" in Table 10.2 as a result of including the variance components (C, A×C, B×C, A×B×C) of the subject's factor age (C).

Models of ANOVA which do not eliminate the subject factors variance but do, at least partially, control for them are discussed in the following section.

Subject Variables Control by Alignment

If the subject variable age (C) is considered to have *only a main effect* but no interaction effect and if it is *separated* from the treatment effects (A and B), Model 3 may be used for ANOVA evaluation.

$$X_{ijkm} = \alpha_i + \beta_j + \alpha_i\beta_j + \gamma_k + \epsilon_{ijkm} \qquad (3)$$

Following Model 3, Table 10.7 data are suitably evaluated in Table 10.4. Since Model 3 is considered as a three-variable model including two treatment factors and one subject factor, only treatment main effects and their interaction may be tested in Table 10.4, since testing against subject main effects, though compatible with Model 3 can not be interpreted conclusively.

In Model 3, age is supposed to have a main effect on rectification only. If it has an interaction effect beyond its main effect within Model 1 the treatment tests in Table 10.4 are conservative, though less conservative than in Table 10.3 compared to Table 10.2 evaluation. The reason for this is that treatment × subject factor interactions enter the error variance in Model 3 called "error-3" in Table 10.4.

Subject variables following Model 3 have been called control variables by Bredenkamp (1980, p. 81). The model itself may be called an *alignment model* since the result of Table 10.4 ANOVA may also be achieved by aligning (or making equal) the two age groups $C1$ and $C2$ for their rectification performances, e.g. by adding $D = \bar{X}_m$ (male) $- \bar{X}_f$ (female) to every one of the 40 female rectifications in Table 10.1. (See Lehmann, 1975, p. 138–140 for alignment procedures.)

Note that the alignment Model 3 is valid if the two age groups differ only in their location parameters γ which are included in Model 3. If the two age groups differ also in their treatments × age interactions, then Model 3 has to be replaced by the model to follow.

Subject Variables Control by Separation

If the subject variable "age" is supposed to *interact* with at least one of the two treatments (duration, distortion), the two levels $C1$ and $C2$ of the age-variable should be separated from each other and evaluated by the *separation Model 4*.

$$X_{ijkm} = \alpha_i(\gamma_k) + \beta_j(\gamma_k) + \alpha_{ij}(\gamma_k) + \gamma_k + \epsilon_{ijkm} \tag{4}$$

TABLE 10.6
Calculating Sums of Squares for Model (4) ANOVA Evaluation

a) Correction term (C1)	$= (601 + 564 + 770 + 663)^2/40$	$= 2598^2/40$
Total (C_1)	$= 76^2 + 66^2 + \ldots + 79^2 + 80^2 - 2598^2/40$	$= 6559,9$
Between (C_1)	$= 601^2/10 + 564^2/10 + \ldots - 2598^2/40$	$= 2436,5$
A (C_1)	$= (601 + 564)^2/20 + (770 + 663)^2 - 2598^2/40$	$= 1795,6$
B (C_1)	$= (601 + 770)^2/20 + (564 + 663)^2/20 - 2598^2/40 =$	$518,4$
AB (C_1)	$= 2436,5 - 1795,6 - 518,4$	$= 122,5$
Error (C_1)	$= 6559,9 - 2436,5$	$= 4123,4$

b) Correction term (C_2)	$= (417 + 247 + 703 + 556)^2/40$	$= 1923^2/40$
Total (C_2)	$= 36^2 + 45^2 + \ldots + 68^2 + 58^2 - 1923^2/40$	$= 13630,8$
Between (C_2)	$= 417^2/10 + 247^2/10 + \ldots - 1923^2/40$	$= 11376,1$
A (C_2)	$= (417 + 247)^2/20 + (703 + 556)^2/20 - 1923^2/40$	$= 8850,6$
B (C_2)	$= (417 + 703)^2/20 + (247 + 556)^2/20 - 1923^2/40$	$= 2512,2$
AB (C_2)	$= 11376,1 - 8850,6 - 2512,2$	$= 13,3$
Error (C_2)	$= 13630,8 - 11376,1$	$= 2254,7$

TABLE 10.6

Model 1	→	Model 4
A + AC	→	A (C1) + A (C2)
B + BC	→	B (C1) + B (C2)
AB + ABC	→	AB (C1) + AB (C2)

Model 4 is *conditional* on the two levels of the subject variable age (indexed by k) and allows for (non-testable) main effects of age thus including Model 3.

Model 4 is evaluated by the ANOVA shown in Table 10.5 where the error-variance "error-4" is the pooled within-cells error of both age groups (as is error-1) under the assumption that the error-variances of both age groups are *homogeneous*.

Table 10.6 sums of squares (SS) may not be derived from Table 10.2 (as in Models 2 and 3) but must be derived from Table 10.7. As may be checked from comparing the *sums of squares* in Table 10.5 from Table 10.6 with those of Table 10.2, their sources are related as in Table 10.6. The above relations have been pointed out to the author by Bredenkamp (1981).

Note that the *separation model* 4 requires the error-variances of $C1$ and $C2$ to be homogeneous. If this homogeneity requirement is not met, the two error-terms should be separated in Model 4 by replacing ϵ_{ijkm} by ϵ_{ijm} (γ_k) in Model 5.

$$X_{ijkm} = \alpha_i(\gamma_k) + \beta_j(\gamma_k) + a_i\beta_j(\gamma_k) + \gamma_k + \epsilon_{ijm}(\gamma_k) \tag{5}$$

The inhomogenity-considering separation Model 5 requires each of the two age groups to be evaluated separately according to Model 2. Model 5 might be called a *perfectly* separating model as opposed to Model 4 which is an *imperfectly* separating model of the three-variable paradigm type.

Model 4 evaluation following the three-variable paradigm will be discussed below in relation to the Model 1 evaluation as representing the two-variable paradigm.

Comparison of Results from Rivaling Models

Comparing the Model 4 results in Table 10.5 with the Model 1 results from Table 10.2 leads to the following *conclusions:*

1. Treatment A (duration of wearing prismic glasses) can be interpreted as a *general main effect* since, according to model 4, treatment A was shown to be significant in *both* age groups. The same result may be derived from model 1 in Table 10.2 (significant main effect of A). Thus, prolonged wearing of distorting glasses favors rectification irrespective of subject's chronological age.

2. Treatment B (intensity of prismic distortion) can be, unlike treatment A, interpreted as a *differential main effect* of B since B is significantly effective only in adults, not in children as concluded from Model 4 in Table 10.5. Contrary to Model 4, Model 1 allows treatment B to be interpreted as a general treatment effect since $B \times C$ is not significant at the .01 level of significance. Thus, the two models disagree whether weak prisms are generally or differentially more effective in rectifying distorted perceptions.

3. Interaction between the two treatments (A and B) may not be concluded either from the Model 4 evaluation in Table 10.5 or from the Model 1 evaluation in Table 10.2 because of lack of significance. Thus, there is neither a general nor a differential interaction between duration of wearing glasses and degree of distortion of perceptions in rectification performance. The same conclusion may be derived from Model 1 evaluation in Table 10.2

General and Differential Effects Defined by Separation Model Analysis

From the three-variable paradigm Model 4, main and interaction effects of treatment variables A and B have been defined as general or differential effects above by the following decision rule:

1. An effect like the main effect of A in Table 10.5, is defined as a *general effect* if it is significant in either level of the subject variable (age groups).

2. On the other hand, an effect like an interaction effect $A \times B$ is defined as a *differential effect* if it is significant in at least 1 or at most K-1 levels of a subject variable with K levels. Thus, general and differential treatment effects are *uniquely defined* within the *three*-variable paradigm ANOVA evaluation. Remember that the alternative *two*-variable Model 1 does not allow for defining main and interaction effects disjunctively: In Table 10.2, treatment A has a main effect as well as an interaction $A \times C$ effect. Identifying main effect with general effects and treatment interactions with differential effects, treatment A would have a differential effect as well as a general effect, i.e., a *compound* rather than a *simple* treatment effect.

Comparing the *two notions* of general and differential effects corresponding to the two models, it is evident that Model 4 is more restrictive in defining general effects and more liberal in defining differential effects than is Model 1 which is in favor of what might be called "differential"—rather than general experimental psychology experimentation. In addition as already mentioned, Model 4 from three-variable paradigm is defining general and differential and no treatment effects as three mutually exclusive events where "no effect" is defined to exist if there is no treatment effect at any of the K levels of the subject variable.

METHODOLOGICAL CONCLUSIONS

The psychological experiment was introduced by Wilhelm Wundt as a means of detecting general *relation* between independent (manipulated) and dependent (or observed) variables, called "laws" of psychological functioning. Although McKeen Cattell, in Wundt's laboratory, had also tried to derive such relationships in a *differential perspective,* experimental psychology has persisted in looking for general laws from the *two*-variable paradigm in which subject variables are treated as modifiers rather than as stratifiers.

If the *three*-variable paradigm is recognized as a methodological means of overcoming difficulties in conclusively interpreting modified treatment effects (or treatment × subjects interactions), its models allow for detecting general *as well as* differential relationships between treatment and outcome variables. Thus, differential psychology may, possibly, become in the same way an experimental (rather than a correlational) science in the future as general psychology has been in the past.

Thus defined, *experimental differential psychology* may be established by replacing the traditional two-variables paradigm with the proposed three-variables paradigm in evaluating factorial experiments using subject variables besides treatment variables: If age of *S*s was shown to be such a variable in Ivo Kohler's prism experiments, then visual perception as a main area of general psychology today may also become a differential psychology topic in the future.

REFERENCES

Bredenkamp, J. *Theorie und Planung psychologischer Experimente.* Darmstadt: Steinkopff, 1980.

Bredenkamp, J. *Personal communication,* June 16, 1981.

Edwards, A. L. *Experimental design in psychological research.* New York: Holt, Rinehart and Winston, 1968 (3rd ed.).

Day, R. H. *Human perception.* New York: Wiley, 1969.

Fischer, G. H. Experiment. In Th, Herrmann, P. R. Hofstätter, H. P. Huber, & F. E. Weinert (Hrsg.), *Handbuch der psychologischen Grundbegriffe.* München: Kösel, 1978.

Kohler, I. Über Aufbau und Wandlungen der Wahrnehmungswelt. Insbesondere über 'bedingte Empfindungen'. *Österreichische Akademie der Wissenschaften, Philosophisch-historische Klasse; Sitzungsberichte,* 227 Band, 1. Abhandlung. Wien: Rohrer, 1951.

Lehmann, E. L. *Nonparametric statistical methods based on ranks.* New York: McGraw-Hill, 1975.

SPACE PERCEPTION AND BODY ORIENTATION

11 Size Constancy as a Function of Fixation Distance and Retinal Disparity

Manfred Ritter
University of Marburg
West Germany

ABSTRACT

When looking at a visual scene one normally fixates an object and at the same time perceives objects that are closer to or farther from the fixation point. The size of these indirectly seen objects can be perceived veridically only if the visual system processes the following three variables: retinal image size, absolute or fixation distance, and relative distance, i.e., the distance between the point of fixation and any other point lying in front of, or behind it. In the case of binocular vision the relative distances of indirectly seen objects can be determined by processing fixation distance and retinal disparity. An investigation was carried out to determine how perceived distance and perceived size of stereoscopically presented stimuli depend upon fixation distance and retinal disparity. The data revealed that there exists a single functional relation between perceived distance and perceived size which is independent of the fixation distance. This indicates that size scaling in visual perception presumably takes place at the stage of stimulus processing necessary for stereopsis or at a higher level.

INTRODUCTION

Perceived size of objects is directly related to their distance from the observer. If one looks at an object from different distances, its perceived size remains fairly constant, whereas the size of its retinal image changes. This is true at least if the object is fairly close to the observer. This phenomenon is called ''size constancy,'' and has been thoroughly investigated experimentally (e.g. Epstein, 1977; Holway & Boring, 1941). It is explained by assuming that the visual system ascertains the perceived size of an object by jointly processing the two variables ''retinal image size'' and ''observation distance'' (Bischof, 1966).

Up to now, investigations of size constancy have been based on situations in which perception of size was determined only for objects which were looked at directly, i.e., foveally. This approach does not take into account the fact that in normal vision the observer also sees other, peripheral, objects that are closer to or farther from the fixation point. These objects form images with different retinal disparities, depending on their distance from the fixation point. The size of these indirectly seen objects can be perceived veridically only if the visual system processes retinal disparity as well as retinal image size and observation distance.

There is an additional reason for expecting this kind of stimulus processing: As a rule, spatial perception comprises a succession of stimulus samples (Foley & Richards, 1972; Ritter, 1979 b). Each of these samples contains the information received during a single fixation period of about 250 msec. In the course of observation, the same object can thus be seen directly at first, and then in the following fixation period, indirectly, with resultant retinal disparity. In both cases, optimal evaluation of the stimuli must lead to the same perceived size, even if the determination of distance is based in one case on fixation distance alone and in the other case both on fixation distance and retinal disparity. The following study examines this problem by determining the perceived size of simple geometric forms as a function of fixation distance and retinal disparity.

THE PROBLEM

Figure 11.1 schematically shows the stimulus conditions under investigation. An observer looks at a fixation point F at a fixation distance $D,$ and simultaneously sees an object O that is at a distance d from the fixation point. In the following a distance d is called a relative distance, since it designates a distance between some object and the particular fixation plane and not a distance directly between some object and the eyes of the observer. This latter one is named an absolute or egocentric distance as opposed to a relative distance.

Object O with its physical size S forms a retinal image with size $s;$ this follows, in simplified form, from the relation:

$$s = c \cdot \frac{S}{D \pm d}, \tag{1}$$

where c is a constant representing the scaling factor for the retinal image. The relative distance d of object O from the fixation point causes a retinal disparity γ in the magnitude of:

$$\gamma = \frac{i}{2} \cdot \frac{d}{D^2} \ (\text{rad}). \tag{2}$$

(This relation is valid only if the eye position is symmetrical and if D is considerably larger than d and i.)

From equations (1) and (2), the size s of the retinal image is as follows:

$$s = c \cdot \frac{S}{D \pm \dfrac{2\gamma D^2}{i}}. \tag{3}$$

If the physical size S of the object O is to be perceived veridically, the influence of the fixation distance D and the relative distance d on the retinal image size s must be compensated for by stimulus processing. For this case the visual system first has to determine the fixation distance D and, via retinal disparity γ, the relative distance d of the object O from the fixation point F. From these values, $D \pm d$, the distance from O to the observer, can be derived. In a further step, the variable $D \pm d$ must be multiplied by the variable s (size of the

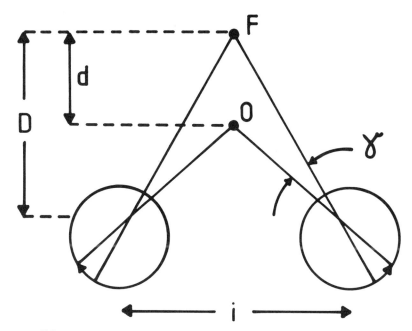

FIG. 11.1. Schematic presentation of the stimulus conditions. An observer looks at a point F having a distance D, and simultaneously sees an object O which is at a distance, d, in front of the fixation plane; i designates the interocular distance, and γ the retinal disparity with which O is imaged on the two retinae.

retinal image). This kind of compensatory stimulus processing ensures that sizes are perceived veridically. From this point of view, size constancy as previously investigated was only a special case in which the object (standard stimulus) always lay in the same frontoparallel plane as the fixation point.

The following experiment was intended to examine how the perceived relative distance and the perceived size of simple stereoscopic stimuli are dependent upon retinal disparity and fixation distance. (The first part of the experiment repeats part of an earlier study [Ritter, 1979a].) It was expected that both perceptual variables would be dependent upon fixation distance and retinal disparity, in accordance with the stimulus analysis given above.

In a subsequent analysis it was ascertained to what extent the perceived size is dependent upon the perceived distance from the stimuli, using a single functional relation. In this case it was expected that for identical perceived-distance values obtained with varying combinations of fixation distance and retinal disparity, identical values would be obtained for perceived size.

METHOD

Subjects.   The subjects were eight students whose visual and stereoscopic acuities were first tested with the Roda test (Rodenstock, Munich). No abnormalities were found.

Experimental Setup and Stimuli.   The experimental arrangement is shown schematically in Fig. 11.2. Each subject looked through polarizing filters, a half-silvered mirror, and a rectangular mask at a projection screen with a visual angle of 40×12 deg. The screen was uniformly illuminated by a projector (background luminance: 30 cd/m^2). The other projectors provided the fixation mark and the stereoscopic stimuli (luminance: 150 cd/m^2). The subject saw the stimuli directly in front of him at eye level. On a track lying obliquely to the subject's line of sight, there was a small circular target that could be moved and its position read off. The image of this target was superimposed onto the main direction of stimulus presentation by means of the beam splitter. The target had a diameter of about .5 deg, and served as a comparison stimulus in measuring the perceived distance. A chin rest was used to minimize head movements.

A disc served as a comparison stimulus for the determination of size; its diameter could be altered by means of an iris diaphragm (.4 to 8.2 deg). The disc was at eye level to the right of the subject and in order to adjust the size, the subject had to swivel his chair to the right. A chin rest was again used. The subject could gradually increase or reduce the diameter of the iris diaphragm by pressing two keys controlling an electric motor. The diameter of the iris diaphragm was measured by a potentiometer and displayed on a digital voltmeter. The distance from the disc to the eye of the subject was 32 cm.

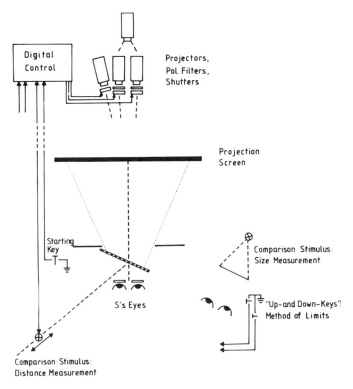

FIG. 11.2.   Schematic presentation of the experimental set-up.

Four different stimuli were thus used: the fixation mark, the stereoscopic stimuli, and one comparison stimulus each for determining the perceived distance and size (cf. Fig. 11.3). The fixation mark was rectangular (.75 × 3.5 deg). In the middle of its lower edge there was a triangular slot that was to be fixated by the subject. The stereoscopic stimuli were round, with a diameter of 1.5 deg.

The stimuli were presented as follows: After an acoustic signal, the fixation mark appeared for 2 sec. During the last 150 msec of this period, the stereoscopic stimuli were added. In distance-measuring trials, the 2-sec comparison stimulus was presented 1 sec later. In size-measuring trials, the comparison stimulus was presented from the same point of time onward, without limitation, until the subject had determined the size. The sequence and duration of the stimuli were controlled by digital modules of the Marburg system (Kalveram, 1975).

Independent Variables.   The fixation distance was either 90 or 120 cm. Retinal disparity was changed in six steps: Two of the steps −40 and −20 min of arc, were uncrossed disparities (i.e., the stereoscopic stimulus was seen behind

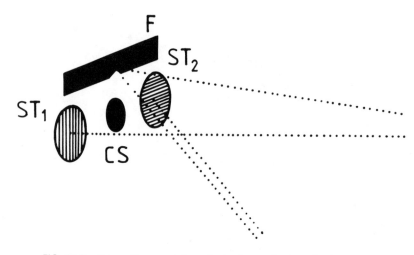

FIG. 11.3. Schematic presentation of stimulus application: fixation mark *F*, stereoscopic stimuli *ST*₁ and *ST*₂, and comparison stimulus *CS*. The horizontal and vertical hatching of the stereoscopic stimuli indicates the plane of polarization of the light used for the stimulus.

the fixation plane); one step was zero disparity (i.e., the stereoscopic stimulus was seen in the fixation plane); and three steps 20, 40 and 60 min of arc, were crossed disparities (i.e., the stereoscopic stimulus was seen in front of the fixation plane). When the fixation distance was 120 cm, the -40 min-of-arc value was omitted, since preliminary tests had shown that certain of the subjects could no longer fuse these stimuli into one image.

Subjects' Tasks and Dependent Variables. The subjects had two tasks: (a) For the determination of distance, they had to look at the fixation stimulus and remember the spatial location of the brief, additional stereoscopic stimulus. Following this, the comparison stimulus was presented and its position changed in accordance with instructions from the subjects, until its perceived position matched the position of the previously perceived stereoscopic stimulus. The stimuli were repeated until the subject was satisfied with the comparison. (b) The size of the stereoscopic stimuli was then determined. The stimuli were presented again. The subject had only to remember the size of the stimulus and then to turn to the comparison stimulus and change the diameter of the latter until its perceived size matched that of the stereoscopic stimulus. Each subject was free to repeat this procedure as often as desired.

The series of measurements for perceived distance and perceived size were each repeated twice using the method of limits. The mean diameter which the subject had adjusted by means of the iris diaphragm served as the measurement of perceived size. The measurement of perceived distance was ascertained from the mean position of the comparison stimulus in the following way: In a previous study (Ritter, 1979 a) based on ratio-estimation methods, it was shown that the positional values D thus obtained (at least for distances between 40 and 200 cm) corresponded to the perceived distance D' only after the linear transformation $D' = -6.76 + .87\,D$. Therefore, the measured positions were converted by means of this transformation.

RESULTS

As Fig. 11.4 shows, the perceived relative distance increases with an increase in retinal disparity; this is true for both the crossed and the uncrossed disparities. If the fixation distance is greater, this increase will likewise be greater. If retinal disparity is varied over a wider range of values than was the case in the present experiment, the result will be an inverse U-shaped relation between perceived distance, d, and retinal disparity for both the crossed and uncrossed disparities

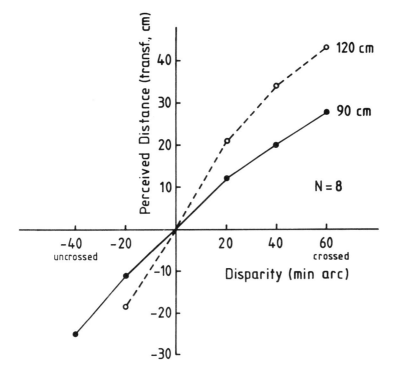

FIG. 11.4.   Perceived relative distance of the stereoscopic stimuli as a function of retinal disparity at two fixation distances; mean values from eight subjects. The perceived relative distance was calculated from the values set by the subject, following a function given by Ritter (1979 a).

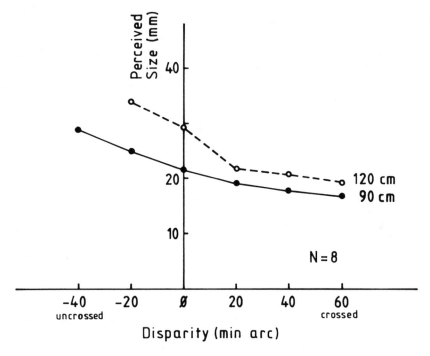

FIG. 11.5. Perceived size of the stereoscopic stimuli as a function of retinal
disparity at two fixation distances; mean values from eight subjects.

(Richards, 1975; Ritter, 1979 a). Thus, Fig. 11.4 contains only a small section of
the total relation. An analysis of variance showed that the perceived relative
distance, d, is dependent upon the fixation distance and upon retinal disparity. In
addition to the main effects, i.e., fixation distance and retinal disparity, the
interaction between these factors was also significant [$F(3,21) = 54.0; p < .01$].

Figure 11.5 shows that the perceived size of a stereoscopic stimulus increases
with an increase in its uncrossed retinal disparity and decreases with an increase
in its crossed retinal disparity. If size-constancy processes are in effect, this
dependency can be expected when the retinal stimulus is kept constant and its
distance from the observer is varied. This dependency is more pronounced for
the larger of the two fixation distances. An analysis of variance revealed that the
interaction between fixation distance and retinal disparity was significant:
[$F(4,28) = 7.3; p < .01$]. For zero disparity, the size of the stimulus was
underestimated only slightly at both fixation distances (90 cm: 2.3 cm expected
vs. 2.2 cm observed; 120 cm: 3.1 cm expected vs. 2.9 cm observed). The
experimental values are thus only slightly lower than can be expected with
complete size constancy.

The results presented in Fig. 11.4 and Fig. 11.5 can also be used to examine whether the perceived size is dependent upon the perceived distance in accordance with a single function, regardless of which fixation distance and which retinal disparity were used by the visual system in ascertaining the perceived distance. Figure 11.6 shows how the perceived size depends upon the perceived distance. The measurement values obtained in the experiment as shown in Fig. 11.4 were converted to perceived relative distances (related to the particular fixation distance). In Fig. 11.6 they are presented as perceived distances between observer and stimulus. All the values obtained can be described by a simple linear function. The coefficient of determination, r^2, is .99 with $df = 9$.

DISCUSSION

The data show that size constancy may also apply to the perception of objects which are not being looked at directly at the moment the stimulus is presented, since they are either in front of or behind the fixation plane. For the determination of perceived distance, which is required for size constancy, the visual

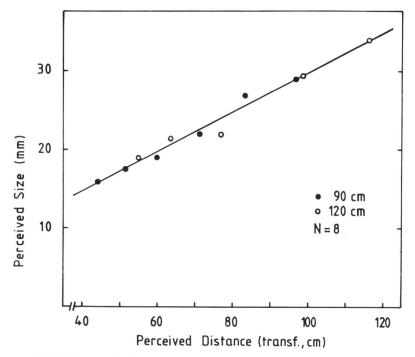

FIG. 11.6. Perceived size of the stereoscopic stimuli as a function of their perceived distance.

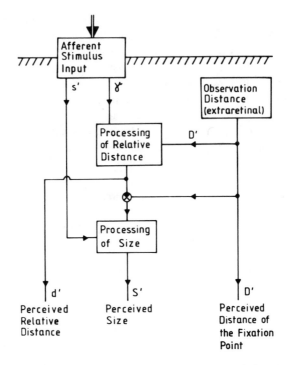

FIG. 11.7.   Tentative scheme of stimulus processing on which size constancy is based.

system thus evaluates both the fixation distance as well as a combination of fixation distance and retinal disparity.

The relation between perceived size and perceived distance can be described by a single function. This is also true of measurements derived from perceived distances that result from various combinations of fixation distance and retinal disparity. This result is to be expected if it is assumed that an important function of perception consists in constructing a veridical, internal representation of the external environment. For the proper perception of size, the size of the retinal image as well as the observational distance must be taken into account in evaluating the stimulus. Thus, it can be assumed that, as a rule, all the distance variables available in a given situation will be processed. Such a multi-stimulus processing of various distance informations can only be effective if the determinations of distance based on these variables are compatible.

It was found that the variation of retinal disparity and fixation distance led to a change in perceived size. This was to be expected in accordance with the principle of size constancy. From this, it can easily be assumed that the evaluation of retinal disparity is the first stage in the evaluation process that finally leads to size constancy. Figure 11.7 shows schematically how the successive evaluation processes may take place. Afferent visual stimulus input results in a variable, s', corresponding to the size of the retinal image and in a variable, γ', corresponding to retinal disparity. In the next step, the distance, d', of an object relative to the fixation point is determined from the calculation of γ' and D'. D', for example, can be obtained from the convergence position of the two eyes. The difference between, or the sum of, D' and d' provides the distance value which is required for converting retinal size, s', to perceived size S'.

It has not yet been tested whether such a model reflects the functional relations among the individual variables. Recent investigations of the neurophysiological localization of evaluation processes on which size constancy is based assume that the integration of retinal form information and distance information takes place at a relatively high processing stage in the visual cortex.

The model presented here agrees with this assumption. Blakemore, Garner, and Sweet (1970) showed that there was excellent size constancy for the perception of bar width or spatial frequency of a sinusoidal grating. Two gratings presented at different distances look similar in respect to their spatial frequency if the actual width, not the angular width, of their stripes is the same. After looking at a high-contrast sinusoidal grating the maximum adaptation of a test grating, presented at a different distance, occurred at the same angular spatial frequency as that of the adapting pattern. The authors locate the neuronal processes which cause this adaptation in the primary visual cortex on the basis of neurophysiological findings. From this, they concluded that the processing for size constancy can take place only at later stages than the primary visual cortex. Indeed, lesion experiments performed by Ungerleider, Ganz, and Pribram (1977) showed that the prestriate visual cortex can be considered to be the processing stage at which information on form and distance are integrated. It was not clear whether the inferotemporal cortext plays a modifying part in this process. All in all, these results contradict the hypothesis advanced by Richards (1970) that the distance-dependent calibration required for size constancy takes place earlier, in the lateral geniculate nucleus or in the primary visual cortex. Likewise, there is no confirmation of the hypotheses of Gross (1973) that the integration of form and space information required for size constancy takes place only in the inferotemporal cortex.

ACKNOWLEDGMENT

The author wishes to thank Mr. F. Herbertz for performing the experiment.

REFERENCES

Bischof, N. Psychophysik der Raumwahrnehmung. In W. Metzger (Ed.), *Handbuch der Psychologie, Allgemeine Psychologie* (Bd I/1). *Wahrnehmung und Bewußtsein* . Göttingen: Hogrefe Verlag, 1966.

Blakemore, C., Garner, E. T., & Sweet, J. A. The site of size constancy. *Perception,* 1970, *1,* 111–119.

Epstein, W. (Ed.) *Stability and constancy in visual perception: Mechanisms and processes.* New York: Wiley, 1977.

Foley, J. M., & Richards, W. Effects of voluntary eye movements and convergence on the binocular appreciation of depth. *Perception & Psychophysics,* 1972, *226,* 725–749.

Gross, Ch. G. Inferotemporal cortex and vision. In E. Stellar & J. M. Sprague (Eds.), *Progress in Physiological Psychology* (Vol. 5). New York: Academic Press, 1973.

Holway, A. H., & Boring, E. Determinants of apparent size with distance variant. *American Journal of Psychology,* 1941, *54,* 21–37.

Kalveram, K. Th. Das Marburger System. 1. Teil. Das Digital-System. *Berichte aus dem Institut für Psychologie der Philipps-Universität Marburg,* Nr. 44, 1975.

Richards, W. Oculomotor effects upon binocular rivalry. *Psychologische Forschung,* 1970, *33,* 136–154.

Richards, W. Visual space perception. In E. C. Carterette & M. Friedman (Eds.), *Handbook of Perception* (Vol. 5). *Seeing.* New York: Academic Press, 1975.

Ritter, M. Perception of depth: Processing of simple positional disparity as a function of viewing distance. *Perception & Psychophysics,* 1979, *25,* 209–214. (a)

Ritter, M. Stereoskopische Raumwahrnehmung des Menschen: Untersuchungsstand und offene Fragen. *Psychologische Beiträge,* 1979, *21,* 563–588. (b)

Ungerleider, L. G., Ganz, L., & Pribram, K. H. Size constancy in rhesus monkeys. Effects of pulvinar, prestriate and inferotemporal lesions. *Experimental Brain Research,* 1977, *27,* 251–269.

12 The Breakdown of Size Constancy Under Stroboscopic Illumination

Bernice E. Rogowitz
I.B.M. Thomas J. Watson Research Center
Yorktown Heights, New York

ABSTRACT

Under *size constancy* the perceived size of an object does not change as we approach it, despite large changes in the size of that object's retinal image. The experiments in this chapter demonstrate a breakdown of size constancy under stroboscopic illumination. This effect is a tuned function of strobe frequency. In the vicinity of 8 Hz, objects appear to loom dramatically as we approach them and shrink as we back away. The magnitude of the effect also depends on the spatial frequency of the target, and perhaps more important, on whether the pattern stimulates the peripheral retina. If only the central retina is stimulated by the pattern, or if there is no relative motion between the observer and the pattern, the looming effect disappears and size constancy is regained.

Classically, size constancy is described as a spatial phenomenon. The visual system takes note of various spatial dimensions, does trigonometry, and arrives at an estimate of the object's size. As the observer moves toward an object, the corresponding increase in that object's angular subtense is "corrected for" by the correlated decrease in perceived distance, and as a result, the apparent size of the object remains unchanged (Helmholtz, 1890; Holway & Boring, 1941).

Size constancy does not hold, however, when this experiment is repeated under stroboscopic illumination. Over a large range of temporal frequencies, objects increase in apparent size with each approaching step and decrease with each step backwards. They "loom" and "shrink" instead of maintaining a constant size.

The first observations of this effect were purely subjective. As I moved toward and away from a geometric picture on the wall, it seemed to expand and contract under the stroboscopic light. I called in my colleagues, and we soon discovered that the spatial pattern need not be periodic; other people's faces, for example, provided a curious and frightening stimulus. We also found that this dramatic distortion was most pronounced at about 8 Hz, and that the effect was strong whether the subject moved toward the pattern or the pattern moved toward the subject.

I have now studied this "looming" effect more systematically, explicitly varying both spatial and temporal parameters. Three points emerge from these studies. First, stroboscopic illumination, per se, does not seem to disrupt size constancy. Either the observer must move toward the pattern or the pattern toward the observer. Second, perceived loom is a broadly tuned function of strobe frequency. Third, the looming effect depends on the retinal location stimulated. When a small-diameter pattern is presented to the fovea, size constancy obtains. That same stimulus, presented peripherally, looms. It is as if the visual mechanisms of the central and peripheral retina operate differently upon the same retinal (proximal) information.

STIMULUS MATERIALS

In the following experiments, black and white checkerboards were viewed binocularly under constant and stroboscopic illumination. Checkerboards had either 1, 2, 4, or 8 checks to the inch. The fundamental frequency of a checkerboard with N checks to the inch, viewed at a distance of D inches falls at $\sqrt{2} \cdot N/2 \cdot D/57$ cycles per degree (cpd) and is oriented diagonally. At 57 inches, 1 inch on the pattern subtends 1 degree of visual angle. At this distance, the four checkerboards have fundamental Fourier components at .7, 1.4, 2.8, and 5.6 cpd, respectively. Spatial frequency scales with distance; halving the distance, for example, halves the spatial frequency.

Constant illumination was provided by overhead fluorescent lamps which directed 404.4 Lux onto the surface of the checkerboards. Stroboscopic illumination was provided by a Strobotac Stroboscope which was pointed to a spot two feet above the illuminated pattern from a distance of ten feet. Pulse duration was 250 microseconds and the time average illumination delivered to the patterns was 2.2, 4.4, 7.1, 2.7, and 4.9 Lux for 2, 4, 8, 16, and 32 Hz strobe rates, respectively.

EXPERIMENT 1

The first experiment tested whether the breakdown in size constancy could be attributed to some general disruption in size estimation under stroboscopic illumination. In this experiment, two observers judged the apparent size of 1, 2, and 4 check/inch checkerboards from three viewing distances (28.5, 57, and 114 inches; 72, 144, and 288 cm). These judgments were made under constant illumination and under 2, 4, 8, 16, and 32 Hz stroboscopic illumination.

In each case, the observer varied the check size of a comparison checkerboard until it matched the apparent check size of the target checkerboard. These judgments were made while seated at a small desk directly facing the target checkerboard. On the desk was a light table whose near surface was 14.25 inches from the observers' eyes. Over the light table, but behind an 8-inch by 6-inch rectangular aperture passed a ribbon of eleven computer-drawn comparison checkerboards. Three of the comparison checkerboards were identical in check size to the three target patterns. The rest were distributed equally in 0.1 log unit steps about them, with two between each target size and two at each extreme. On each trial of the experiment, one of the three 8-inch diameter target checkerboards was presented, and the subject advanced the checkerboard ribbon until the comparison checks matched the perceived size of the target checks. Since the comparison checkerboards were back-lit, each stroboscopically-illuminated target was matched to a constantly illuminated comparison. (The luminance of the white and dark checks was 9.2 and 1.1 Ft-L, respectively.)

These data are shown in Fig. 12.1. In each panel, the check size chosen to match each target is plotted for the three targets at each of the three viewing distances. Each point represents the mean of five estimates. The number within each panel indicates the temporal frequency of stroboscopic illumination under which the judgments were made.

The diagonal lines show the prediction of size constancy, where the observer matches the target checkerboard with a comparison checkerboard of identically sized checks, regardless of viewing distance. In size constancy, the match is based on the actual size of the checks, that is, on the 'distal' stimulus. The data fall quite consistently on this diagonal line, suggesting the reliance on distal information both under constant and under stroboscopic illumination. These data also show that the proximal stimulus, the size of the retinal image, does not determine the judgment of perceived size under these conditions. Were this the case, the data would have fallen on lines parallel to the diagonal indicated, displaced vertically in proportion to the ratio of the target and comparison stimuli's distances. For example, at a viewing distance of 28.5 inches, twice the distance to the ribbon of comparison checkerboards, all targets would be matched to a comparison having twice the number of checks per inch as the target. Quite clearly, however, this distance term is unnecessary; the number of checks to the inch in target and matching pattern is always equal. When neither the observer nor the pattern moves, the match is based upon the distal stimulus. Moreover, check size is neither overestimated at near distances nor underestimated at far distances. It is not likely, therefore, that looming occurs because size judgments are biased under stroboscopic illumination. This result is consistent with Leibowitz, Chinetti, & Sidowski (1956) and Harvey & Leibowitz (1967) who

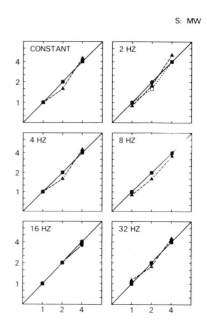

FIG. 12.1. Judgments of check size at three distances under constant and stroboscopic illumination. Stroboscopic illumination, per se, does not produce misjudgments of size.

have demonstrated size constancy under similar viewing conditions with short exposure durations (on the order of microseconds).

EXPERIMENT 2

The next experiment measured the magnitude of the looming effect while the distance between observer and target was varied dynamically. The target was presented at eye-level and the observer used a rocking motion to move toward and away from it. He rocked forward to a position 28.5 inches from the target, and back to a position 57 inches from the target at the rate of 0.5 Hz (1 second per direction) in time to a metronome. These are the two nearest distances studied in the static, size-estimation experiment. As in the previous experiment, the target was an 8-inch diameter disc checkerboard viewed under constant or stroboscopic illumination. Checkerboards were presented one at a time, with check size (spatial frequency) and strobe frequency varied randomly from trial to trial, with five observations per condition.

On each trial the subject judged whether or not the checks seemed to grow larger as he approached and to shrink as he receded, and rated the degree of looming with respect to the perceived loom of a standard. The standard, or reference, pattern was a checkerboard of 2 checks/inch, viewed under 8 Hz

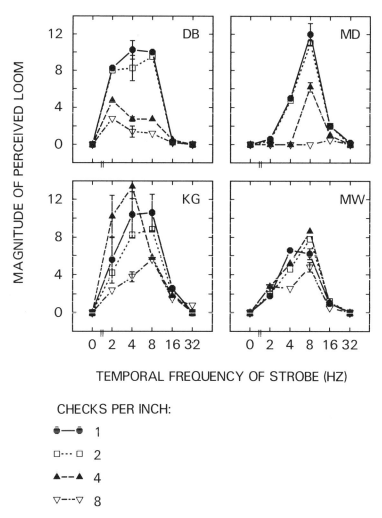

CHECKS PER INCH:

●—● 1

□··· □ 2

▲--▲ 4

▽---▽ 8

FIG. 12.2.   Perceived loom of an 8-inch diameter checkerboard viewed centrally. Perceived loom is a tuned function of temporal frequency, and is less robust for high spatial-frequency checkerboards.

illumination. This pattern had been identified during pilot investigations as providing a strong looming effect. The degree to which this pattern was perceived to loom was assigned the number 10, and the subject was instructed to rate all other patterns with respect to this standard according to an interval scale. This pattern was shown to the subject roughly every ten minutes to help him maintain a consistent scale throughout the experiment.

The data for four subjects are shown in Fig. 12.2. Here, the estimate of perceived loom is plotted as a function of temporal frequency. The curves within each graph show how these estimates vary with check size. Under constant illumination (0 Hz), no looming is observed. Perceived size remains constant despite a factor of two change in distance. The movement of the observer, per se, thus, cannot be held responsible for whatever looming might occur under stroboscopic illumination.

When a rocking motion is added, however, checkerboard patterns loom under stroboscopic illumination. For all subjects, the looming effect is a tuned function of temporal frequency. The effect is maximal between 4 and 8 Hz, and falls off for lower and higher temporal frequencies. This function is relatively flat for the subjects in the left-hand column and sharply peaked at 8 Hz for the other two subjects. Full bandwidth at half amplitude varies between two and three octaves.

For all subjects, the magnitude of the looming effect is greatly diminished for the highest spatial-frequency pattern (8 ck/in). This is not, however, a very high frequency checkerboard. Its fundamental Fourier components vary between 3 and 6 cpd during the rocking procedure, suggesting that looming may be a low spatial frequency phenomenon. In fact, two of the subjects show a marked decrease in perceived loom for a checkerboard of half that spatial frequency.

FURTHER EXPERIMENTS

Under constant illumination and under stroboscopic illumination, each linear step taken toward an object causes the area of that object's retinal projection to expand as the square. Under constant illumination, the expansion of the proximal stimulus is not sufficient to produce the perception of looming. Viewing the expansion stroboscopically, however, produces looming. Since constant illumination provides us with continuous samples from this accelerating function while stroboscopic illumination provides us with discrete samples, it may be that size constancy requires a smooth transition from increment to increment in the proximal stimulus.

This characterization, however, is not adequate. When the same stroboscopically illuminated expanding pattern is viewed through a reduction tube, the looming effect is significantly reduced and often eliminated. In this case the retinal image expands in discrete, sampled steps, yet size constancy is preserved. The following experiments were designed to explore why stroboscopically illuminated patterns do not loom when the observer rocks to and fro, viewing the patterns through a hand-held reduction tube.

Several possibilities were considered. One effect of a reduction tube is to eliminate distance cues. Since size constancy is known to be impaired when distance cues are reduced (e.g., Holway & Boring, 1941; Ono, 1966), and the tube produces a dramatic *recovery* of size constancy, it seems unlikely that size constancy is regained because distance cues are reduced.

The main effect of the reduction tube is to fix the angular subtense of the distal stimulus. In this case, the tube's quarter-inch diameter stopped the field of view down to 4 deg of visual angle. Another effect is to change the distribution of foveal and peripheral excitation. While the 8-inch checkerboard, viewed freely without the tube, projects onto peripheral as well as central regions of the retina, that same target, viewed through the reduction tube, stimulates only the central retina. An additional effect of the reduction tube is to eliminate peripheral exposure to the stroboscopic illumination. Under free viewing conditions, the stroboscopic illumination stimulates the periphery, but with the reduction tube, the visual world is dark, but for the area of the central retina seen through the tube.

Thus, the reduction in apparent looming experienced when the stroboscopically illuminated checkerboard is viewed through a reduction tube could be attributed to (1) the reduction in the effective size of the target, (2) the reduction in peripheral regions stimulated by the strobed checkerboard, or (3) the reduction in non-patterned peripheral stimulation. To distinguish between these possibilities, perceived loom was compared when the large, 8-inch diameter checkerboard is viewed either directly or through a 4-deg reduction tube, and under two conditions where the area of the target is reduced not by a reduction tube, but by a reduction in target size. In one case, a 2-inch diameter checkerboard was viewed foveally; in the second, that same target was viewed peripherally. Both targets subtended 4 degrees at 28.5 inches and 2 degrees at 57 inches.[1] The rocking motion was always normal to the center of the target.

The amount of loom predicted depends upon the mechanisms involved. (1) If the effect is wholly determined by the area of the retina stimulated by the strobed pattern, then the two 2-inch targets should loom as little as the target viewed through the reduction tube, both should loom less than the 8-inch target, and there should be no difference between foveal and peripheral viewing. (2) If the effect requires the patterned stimulation of the peripheral retina, then the small

[1]In the peripheral condition, the fixation dot was placed 12 inches from the center of the target, and thus both the area of the target's retinal projection and its eccentricity changed as the subject rocked between the two distances. Data produced by this method, however, did not differ from those collected when this possibly confounding variable was corrected for by fixing the fixation point and moving the target to and from the observer. A series of experiments is planned in which the target is moved toward the observer, and the size, spatial frequency, and eccentricity of the target are varied.

peripheral target should loom as much as the 8-inch target, since both stimulate the periphery, and the small foveal target should loom as little as the target seen through the reduction tube. (3) If the only condition necessary for looming is stroboscopic illumination in the periphery, then all targets should loom, unless viewed through a reduction tube.

The data for these experiments are shown in Fig. 12.3. In all cases, perceived loom is plotted as a function of temporal frequency. The three columns show data for the three subjects; the three rows show data for checkerboards having 1,

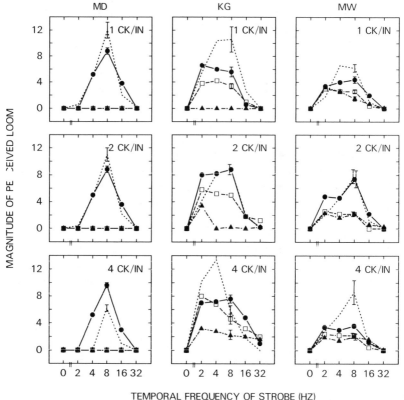

FIG. 12.3.   The dependence of perceived loom on peripheral stimulation. Perceived loom is greatest for patterns which stimulate the peripheral retina, and is greatly reduced for patterns falling only on the central retina.

2, and 4 checks per inch, respectively. These data were collected, as before, in a randomized design, with the magnitude of the looming effect referenced to the loom perceived with the standard checkerboard (2 checks per inch, illuminated at 8 Hz).

The dotted lines without symbols show the data from Experiment 2, where the target was an 8-inch diameter checkerboard viewed without a reduction tube. Perceived loom is strong in the mid-range of temporal frequencies. Notice that while the various experimental manipulations affect the magnitude of the looming effect, none produces systematic changes in the shape of this temporal tuning curve. It is also remarkable that for all conditions, no looming occurs under constant illumination (0 Hz). The effect of the reduction tube is shown in closed triangles. For all target frequencies and for all subjects, the looming effect is greatly reduced, and in many cases, disappears when the field of view is limited to 4 degrees. A similar reduction is seen when the foveal 2-inch target is examined (open squares). For two subjects, this target looms no more than the target seen through the reduction tube. For the third (KG), the small foveal target looms less than the 8-inch target, but more than the target seen through the reduction tube. For this subject, unpatterned stroboscopic light to the periphery is sufficient to disrupt size constancy for a small, centrally fixated target. Closed circles show the effect of viewing this same 2-inch diameter pattern with the peripheral retina. Viewed peripherally, the small target produces a *large* looming effect. In fact, the peripheral target often appears to loom as much or more than the 8-inch pattern, despite its smaller subtense. For two of the three subjects, then, looming occurs only when the peripheral retina is stimulated by a succession of patterns increasing discretely in size. For all subjects, the magnitude of the looming effect is greatest when the target projects onto the peripheral retina.

DISCUSSION

The looming and shrinking effects of stroboscopic illumination on the perception of spatial patterns are extremely robust, and can be demonstrated over a large range of spatial and temporal frequencies. When the pattern is either large enough or eccentric enough to stimulate the peripheral retina, the magnitude of the perceived loom is a tuned function of temporal frequency.

It is not the stroboscopic illumination, per se, which produces this breakdown in size constancy. At a fixed distance, size judgments are based on the distal stimulus for intermittent as well as constant illumination. Neither does relative motion, by itself, introduce a departure from size constancy, although such an effect has been reported by von Holst & Mittelstaedt (1950) and by Gregory & Ross (1964, for receding motions only). Together, however, these two temporal modulations produce a pattern of excitation which is interpreted by the periphery as a change in object size. The foveal and peripheral systems, however, apparently differ in how they interpret this succession of changing retinal images. In the periphery the object looms; in the fovea it maintains a constant size.

What mechanisms underlie this looming effect? One candidate mechanism is the oculomotor cues. Various experimental studies have supported von Holst & Mittelstaedt's (1950, 1955) proposal that accommodation and convergence are important in size constancy (Heinemann, Tulving, & Nachmias, 1959; Leibowitz, & Moore, 1966; Leibowitz, Shina, & Hennessy, 1972). Basically, these studies show that for distances less than a meter, the perceived size of an object depends upon these cues. When accommodation and convergence are artificially altered via lenses, it is the "equivalent distance" not the real distance which controls perceived size. Since these cues are important to size constancy at distances which include our near viewing condition, and since Harvey & Leibowitz (1967) have shown a failure of these cues for short duration presentations at short distances, it is possible that the looming reported here might owe to a disruption of oculomotor cues. The data from Experiment 1, however, show no breakdown of size constancy under stroboscopic illumination when viewing distance is static, even for distances well within the reported range (1 meter). Since stroboscopic illumination exerts no noticeable effect on oculomotor cues in the static case, it is unlikely to be responsible for the large looming effects observed in the later experiments. Furthermore, although perceived loom is greater at near distances, it can be easily perceived at distances outside the range in which these oculomotor cues are critical for size constancy. Still, it would be interesting to measure accommodation dynamically while the observer makes judgments of perceived loom under stroboscopic illumination, and particularly interesting to compare these measurements at distances within and beyond a meter.

Regan and Beverley (1978) have provided evidence for looming detectors in the human visual system. Their stimulus is a square whose edges move in and out sinusoidally, producing a square whose size is modulated. They find that adapting to such a stimulus produces a selective threshold elevation for a similar square of changing size. The magnitude of the effect is a tuned function of the adapting pattern's oscillation frequency (Beverley & Regan, 1980), suggesting the operation of tuned channels for changing size. Since the range of temporal frequencies over which this effect occurs includes 0.5 Hz, the size-oscillation frequency induced by the rocking of our observers in the above experiments, changing-size channels could be involved in the looming effects reported here. In our experimental situation, however, perceived size did not appear to change under constant illumination as in the Regan and Beverley studies. Furthermore, even under stroboscopic illumination, little or no looming was observed with the small foveal target which subtended an area similar to the proposed receptive field size of the changing-size mechanism, 1.5 deg (Beverley & Regan, 1979).

The *optical expansion pattern* (Gibson, 1950; Johansson, 1958) presents another avenue of inquiry. In the above experiments, the retinal projection of the checkerboard pattern increases radially with each approaching step, and the displacement (velocity) of the image increases with eccentricity. Under constant illumination, however, no looming was observed, and thus it is not the geometric transformation of the image, per se, which produces looming. Under stroboscopic illumination, the observer sees snapshots of this continuous acceleration. Size constancy breaks down in the presence of large stroboscopic displacements of the proximal stimulus in the peripheral retina.

Certain aspects of the data are consistent with a model where size constancy is mediated by sustained channels, and breaks down when the activity of the sustained channels is inhibited by the response of transient mechanisms. For example, the largest looming effects occur between 4 and 8 Hz, a range well-matched to the temporal sensitivity of transient mechanisms (Kulikowski & Tolhurst, 1973). The largest effects are observed when the peripheral retina is stimulated, consistent with the increasing distribution of transient mechanisms with eccentricity (Fukuda & Stone, 1974). Furthermore, the magnitude of the looming effect is greatly reduced for high spatial frequency checkerboards (see Figure 12.2), which is consistent with Kulikowski and Tolhurst's (1973) finding that the spatial sensitivity of transient channels peaks at the low spatial frequency end of the spectrum and falls off quite sharply with increases in spatial frequency. This last correspondence, however, is not correct in detail, since the sensitivity of the transient channel is rather flat over the range of spatial frequencies used here. However, since the looming effect decreases with spatial frequency for the large target (which presumably stimulates both sustained and transient mechanisms) but remains constant for the small peripheral target (which presumably stimulates mainly transient mechanisms), it may be that the magnitude of the effect depends on the ratio of transient to sustained activity. In this context, the effect of stroboscopic illumination may be to increase the contribution of transient mechanisms, which in turn produce a greater inhibition of the sustained, size-constancy mediating mechanisms. Another possibility is that the transient channels contribute to looming directly. Were this the case, however, we would expect transient mechanisms and Regan and Beverley style loom detectors to interact. This does not seem to be the case. Adapting to flicker does not affect the threshold for detecting a square oscillating in size (Regan & Beverley, 1978).

Another possible mechanism involves the utilization of distance cues. Holway and Boring (1941) have shown that size judgments are based on the distal stimulus when distance cues are available, and rely on angular subtense when distance information is degraded. Since under static conditions size judgments are based on the distal stimulus, it is unlikely that distance cues are disrupted. Under certain dynamic conditions objects loom, suggesting a possible degradation of distance cues. Were this the case, we might also expect distortions in the apparent velocity of an approaching target, and in fact, the velocity of optically expanding two-dimensional patterns can be overestimated under stroboscopic illumination (Aiba, 1977). Several questions remain unanswered, however, such as why the periphery should be less capable than the fovea to utilize distance cues under these conditions, and why cues which are available in the static case become degraded when movement is introduced.

Approaching a pattern under stroboscopic illumination can change its appearance dramatically, causing its size to expand perceptually with every approaching step. This looming effect, however, requires both stroboscopic illumination and changes in the size of the image projected to the peripheral retina. Looming is not observed when the size of the retinal image is changed continuously, and is not observed when only the central retina is stimulated. This effect, thus, both highlights the importance of temporal information in the processing of suprathreshold spatial patterns and identifies a situation where the same proximal stimulus is interpreted differently by fovea and periphery. The breakdown of size constancy is rather like a perceptual illusion, important not because it demonstrates a flaw in our perceptual systems, but because it provides us a special opportunity for exploring the mechanisms of perception.

REFERENCES

Aiba, T. S. Perceived velocity of radial motion in stroboscopic illumination. *Psychologia (Symposium)*, 1977, *20*, 180–189.

Beverley, K. I., & D. Regan Visual perception of changing size: The effect of object size. *Vision Research*, 1979, *19*, 1093–1104.

Beverley, K. I., & D. Regan Temporal selectivity of changing-size channels. *Journal of the Optical Society of America*, 1980, *70*, 1375–1377.

Gibson, J. J. *The Perception of the Visual World*. Boston: Houghton and Mifflin, 1950.

Fukuda, Y., & J. Stone Retinal distribution and central projections of Y- X- and W-cells of the cat's retina. *Journal of Neurophysiology*, 1974, *37*, 749–772.

Gregory, R. L., & H. E. Ross Visual constancy during movement I: Effect of S's forward and backward movement on size constancy. *Perceptual and Motor Skills*, 1964, *18*, 3–8.

Harvey, L., & H. W. Leibowitz Effects of exposure duration, cue reduction, and temporary monocularity on size matching at short distances. *Journal of the Optical Society of America* 1967, *57*, 249–253.

Heinemann, E. G., E. Tulving, & J. Nachmias The effect of oculomotor adjustments on apparent size. *American Journal of Psychology* 1959, *72*, 43–45.

Helmholtz, H. von *A Treatise on Physiological Optics, Volume 3*. J. P. C. Southall (Ed. and Translator). New York: Dover, 1962.

von Holst, E., & H. Mittelstaedt Das Reafferenzprinzip. *Die Naturwissenschaften*, 1950, *37*, 464–476.

von Holst, E., & H. Mittelstaedt Ist der Einfluß der Akkommodation auf die gesehene Dinggröße ein "reflektorischer" Vorgang? *Die Naturwissenschaften*, 1955, *42*, 445–446.

Holway, A. F., & E. G. Boring Determinants of apparent visual size with distance variant. *American Journal of Psychology*, 1941, *54*, 21–37.

Johansson, G. Rigidity, stability and motion in perceptual space. *Acta Psychologica*, 1958, *14*, 359–370.

Kulikowski, J. J., & D. Tolhurst Psychophysical evidence for sustained and transient neurones in human vision. *Journal of Physiology*, 1973, *232*, 149–162.

Leibowitz, H. W., P. Chinetti, & P. Sidowski Exposure duration as a variable in perceptual constancy. *Science*, 1956, *123*, 668–669.

Leibowitz, H. W., & D. Moore Role of changes in accommodation and convergence in the perception of size. *Journal of the Optical Society of America*, 1966, *56*, 1120–1123.

Leibowitz, H. W., K. Shina, & H. R. Hennessy Oculomotor adjustments and size constancy. *Perception & Psychophysics*, 1972, *12*, 497–500.

Ono, H. Distal and proximal size under reduced and non-reduced viewing conditions. *American Journal of Psychology*, 1966, *79*, 234–241.

Regan, D., & K. I. Beverley Looming detectors in the human visual pathway. *Vision Research*, 1978, *18*, 415–421.

13 Psychophysics of Visual Flow Patterns and Motion in Depth

David Regan
Kenneth I. Beverley
Department of Physiology/Biophysics and Department of
Ophthalmology, Dalhousie University
Halifax, Nova Scotia, Canada

ABSTRACT

This chapter briefly discusses the following topics: (a) How a moving observer might visually judge his or her direction of self-motion. It is argued that differences in the rate of change of magnification across the retinal image may be important in some special situations where the focus of the expanding flow pattern may be of little significance. (b) Visual sensitivity to changing size. We propose that the visual pathway contains a functional subunit that is selectively sensitive to changing size. (c) The stereoscopic perception of moving stimuli. Evidence is reported in support of our proposal that, in addition to the classical stereoscopic subsystem for relative position in depth, the visual pathway contains a second stereoscopic subsystem sensitive to the direction of motion in depth. (d) The relative effectiveness of a monocular and a binocular cue for motion-in-depth sensation. This depends on the object's width and speed and the inspection duration, but hardly at all on the viewing distance. (e) Attempts to extrapolate laboratory models of vision to the description of real-world skilled performance.

1. INTRODUCTION

This chapter briefly discusses some restricted investigations of a broad topic namely the psychophysical and physiological aspects of the visual processing of motion information. Throughout these studies a persistent attempt has been made to bring together psychophysical studies in man with single-unit studies in animal. It is probably overoptimistic to expect more than very partial successes in this direction. We report here some partial correlations and some less so.

The sections below discuss the observer's self-motion through the external world as well as the motion of external objects relative to the observer. The material reviewed here can be listed under the following four headings: (a) a discussion of how a moving observer might visually perceive his direction of self-motion (Section 2); (b) visual sensitivity to changing-size (Section 3); (c) stereoscopic perception of moving stimuli (Section 4); (d) a comparison of changing-size and changing-disparity as stimuli for motion-in-depth sensation (Section 5); (e) attempts to extrapolate laboratory models of vision to the description of real-world skilled visual performance (Section 6).

For reasons of space, this chapter is mainly restricted to research carried out in our laboratory, and contains only a minimal review of the extensive literature in this area.

2. VISUAL STIMULI GENERATED BY SELF-MOTION

Flow Patterns Caused by an Observer's Motion through a Fixed Outside World

Gibson proposed that humans and animals can visually judge their direction of self-motion by utilizing visual flow patterns caused by self-motion (Gibson, 1950, p. 128 and 1958, p. 187), and this proposal has been cited widely (e.g. Johnston, White, & Cumming, 1973; Warren, 1976). Subsequently, several authors have theoretically analyzed flow fields at a quantitative mathematical level (e.g. Gordon, 1965; Koenderink & van Doorn, 1976; Nakayama & Loomis, 1974; Prazdny, 1980).

It is sometimes assumed that when an observer is moving forward the retinal image contains an expanding flow pattern, and the local center of the expanding flow pattern coincides with the observer's destination.[1] Figure 13.1, however, provides a particular illustration that the retinal image flow pattern can be strongly affected by the direction of gaze. Although previously noted (Koenderink & van Doorn, 1976; Richards, 1975), this point often seems to have been ignored in studies of visually guided locomotion. One consequence is that it is not correct to assume that the center of focus of the retinal image expanding flow pattern during forward motion necessarily corresponds to the observer's destination. For example, in the specific case illustrated in Fig. 13.1, this assumption is invalid if the observer looks at some point in the external world other than the point

---

[1]Gibson's later writings on expanding flow patterns were couched in terms of the "optic array" rather than the retinal image. The "optic array" is defined so that it does not depend on eye movements. This concept has been critically discussed elsewhere (Boynton, 1974; Gibson, 1974).

FIG. 13.1 Photographic illustrations of expanding flow patterns similar to the flow patterns in the retinal image of an observer moving through the external world. **A** is a single exposure. Multiple exposure **B** was taken with a camera moving towards the head while pointing directly at the head. Multiple exposure **C** was taken with a camera moving towards the head while pointing to one side (arrowed dot). Clearly, the center of the expanding flow pattern did not coincide with the direction of motion, but with the direction of the camera's "gaze." From Regan & Beverley, *Science,* 1982, *215,* 194–195.

FIG. 13.1C

towards which he is moving. If an observer is moving towards a vertical plane as in Fig. 13.1 and looks at a point other than his destination, the eye must continuously rotate, thus imposing an overall translational velocity on the image. The point of gaze in the image must, of course, remain stationary on the fovea, but it might seem reasonable to suppose that the destination remains the center of expansion, merely drifting away from the fovea as a result of the translational velocity. However, although this may sometimes be the case it is not necessarily so. With some geometries of the outside world and directions of gaze the focus is displaced from the destination. In other cases the flow pattern's focus is destroyed rather than being displaced. In the specific case of Fig. 13.1, the flow pattern's center is displaced away from the direction of motion and coincides with the direction of gaze (Regan & Beverley, 1982). Our main point here is that the center of the expanding retinal flow pattern does not in general coincide with the observer's destination unless the observer looks directly at his destination or maintains his gaze at a fixed angle relative to his destination.[2]

Whether or not observers can use the location of the flow pattern's focus to

---

[2]If, in an automobile traveling the way it is pointing, an observer maintains his gaze at some fixed angle relative to the interior of the automobile, the center of expansion coincides with his destination and is merely displaced across the retina, since the direction of gaze is maintained at a constant angle relative to the direction of motion. This is a trivial case, since the observer has prior knowledge of his direction of motion.

accurately judge the direction of self-motion is an empirical rather than a theoretical question. Nakayama and Loomis (1974) have suggested that for some tasks, the visual system might be able to discount an overall translation velocity of the retinal image. In order to check this point experimentally for flow patterns we measured subjects' ability to judge the position of the center of expansion when translational velocities were imposed on the image (Regan & Beverley, 1982).

First, we carried out an unrealistic experiment. We measured a subject's ability to judge the location of the expanding flow pattern when no overall translational velocity was superimposed on the pattern. Our pattern was a sine-wave grating displayed on the CRT screen, and a fixed reference mark was provided at the center of the screen. In Experiment 1 subjects were asked to judge whether the center of expansion was to the left or right of the mark, and in successive trials the center of expansion was located different distances to the left and right of the mark. This task was performed accurately, with a threshold of about 0.5° for the spatial frequencies tested (.5–3 c/deg). This experiment was unrealistic because subjects could judge the location of the expansion pattern merely by noting whether the pattern was flowing leftwards or rightwards past the stationary fixation mark. Subsequently, in Experiment 2 we mimicked real-world conditions more closely by adding on overall translational velocity to the pattern to ensure that the pattern was always stationary at the fixation mark (i.e. on the fovea), wherever the center of expansion was located. Findings were quite different. Subjects were now unable to judge the location of the center of expansion. A previous report by Llewellyn (1971) came to a similar conclusion. His subjects were unable to locate the expansion center of a dot pattern with a mean error of less than 5°–7°. His conditions more nearly resembled our Experiment 1 than Experiment 2, but he did not supply a reference mark on the screen. Furthermore, his stimulus pattern was two-dimensional whereas ours was one-dimensional.

Having discounted the expansion pattern center as a useful aid in our experimental conditions, we searched for some feature of the transforming retinal image that could, at least in some situations, indicate the direction of self-motion whatever the direction of gaze. One candidate is the local rate of change of magnification. For some (but not all) visual environments, when an observer moves through the external world the rate of change of magnification is greater at the retinal image of the point towards which he is moving than at neighboring points in the retinal image.[3] As compared with the location of the center of the

---

[3]It is easily shown that when moving in a straight line at right angles to a plane surface, the maximum rate of change of magnification coincides with the point of impact on the plane. Given without proof in Regan and Beverley (1982) is that for inclined trajectories, the maximum falls at a point half way between the point of impact and the closest point on the plane. (Perhaps this could guide visual corrections to self-motion). A formal proof of this relationship appeared while that article was in process of publication (Koenderink & van Doorn, 1981).

expanding flow pattern, it is easy to see that the location of the maximum rate of change of magnification within the retinal image has the geometrical advantage that it is independent of the point on the target at which the subject is looking. We investigated experimentally whether subjects can accurately judge the position of a local maximum in the rate of change of magnification independently of the point on the target at which the subject is looking.

As an external object we used a sinewave grating for simplicity and because visual responses to such gratings have been much studied. This visual situation roughly corresponded to approaching an extended line of vertical fence posts, these posts appearing somewhat blurred. In our experiments the observer did not move. Instead we mimicked the spatial transformations of the retinal image caused by self-motion by geometrically distorting the image of the sinewave grating presented to the observer. The rationale of this experiment was to optically dissociate two aspects of the retinal image, namely the expanding flow pattern and nonuniformity in the rate of change of magnification. The motion of the pattern consisted of two components, one being an expansion and one an overall translational motion.

The instantaneous velocity at any point in the pattern $V(s)$ was first made a power function of distance s across the pattern. Then a uniform translational speed was added to render stationary the pattern at the center of the screen (the point of gaze). An expansion pattern for which the rate of change of magnification was uniform across the pattern had $n = 1$. An expansion pattern for which the rate of change of magnification was slightly greater at one point in the pattern than elsewhere had $n = .5$. An expansion pattern for which the rate of change of magnification was considerably greater at the arrow than elsewhere had $n = 0.3$. In different stimulus presentations the point of maximum rate of magnification occurred at the center of the screen or at varying distances to left and right of center, but the pattern at the center of the screen was always stationary. The field size was $16°$ vertical $\times$ $20°$ horizontal. The method of constant stimuli was used to find thresholds.

Subjects fixated on the stationary center of the screen and a fixation mark on the glass screen was provided. This mimicked the situation when a moving observer looks steadily at some fixed point in the outside world that is not necessarily his destination.[4] The grating pattern contained a vertical black bar, created by blanking one whole grating cycle. This provided a reference mark on the pattern, and mimicked a fixed reference mark in the outside world. In different presentations, the point of maximum rate of change of magnification was located either on the bar or at four different distances to the left or to the right of the black bar, and the black bar was located either at the center of the screen or at one of four different distances to the left or to the right of the center of the

---

[4]However, our experiments leave the loophole that in the real world, observers generate their own eye or head rotations. We are currently carrying out experiments to cover this point.

screen. The nine different positions of the bar mimicked nine different directions of gaze relative to a fixed reference object in the outside world (i.e., the black bar) and the nine different locations of the local maximum rate of magnification mimicked nine different directions of self-motion for each direction of gaze. The rate of change of magnification was equivalent to the forward view from an automobile traveling at 55 km/hr directly at a wall 76 m away.

Consider first the results for expansion patterns whose rate of change of magnification was uniform ($n = 1.0$) or near-uniform ($n = .9$) over the whole visual field. When $n = 1.0$ the subject's task was to judge whether the center of the flow pattern was to the left or right of the black bar. As already mentioned, with $n = 1.0$ subjects could not do the task at all. With $n = 0.9$ subjects either still could not do the task at all or were only able to judge direction to a very poor accuracy of about $5°–8°$ (Fig. 13.2A and 13.2B). Note that all these visual stimuli for $n = 1.0$ and $n = .9$ contained an expanding flow pattern with a clear center of expansion. These findings indicate that subjects could not disregard an overall translational velocity of the retinal image when locating the center of expansion of the flow pattern, at least in our experimental conditions.

Subjects performed quite differently for expansion patterns for which the rate of change of magnification was moderately greater at one point than elsewhere (curves marked $n = .8$ and $.7$ in Fig. 13.2A and 13.2B). With $n < 1$ the stimulus contained a local maximum in the rate of change of magnification and the subject's task was to judge whether this local maximum was to the left or right of the black bar. For the stimuli with $n = 0.8$ and 0.7 our subject's accuracy in the psychophysical task was roughly $1.0°$. When the rate of change of magnification was markedly greater at one point than elsewhere ($n = 0.5$ and 0.3 in Fig. 13.2A and 13.2B), a subject's accuracy was better than $.5°$. All these stimuli contained a clear center of expansion of the velocity flow pattern, but in view of our results for $n = 1.0$ we assume that subjects were not using the location of the center of flow pattern expansion to carry out the task. Instead, we suppose that subjects used the location of the maximum rate of change of magnification. Figure 13.2C and 13.2D show the progressive decay in directional judgment as exponent n increased to unity. We interpret Fig. 13.2 as indicating that subjects are very sensitive to changing geometric distortion of the retinal image even in the presence of translational motion. In our experiment, as in real-world scenes, the location on the retinal image of the maximum rate of change of magnification was not generally affected by the direction of gaze, even though the center of expansion may shift across the retinal image as the direction of gaze alters.

The ability to disregard translational velocity seems to be task-dependent. A translational velocity degrades differential velocity discrimination (Nakayama, 1981), but has little effect on vernier acuity (Westheimer & McKee, 1975).

We found experimentally that, in our specific conditions, retinal image translation exerted quite different effects on visual sensitivity to flow patterns and on

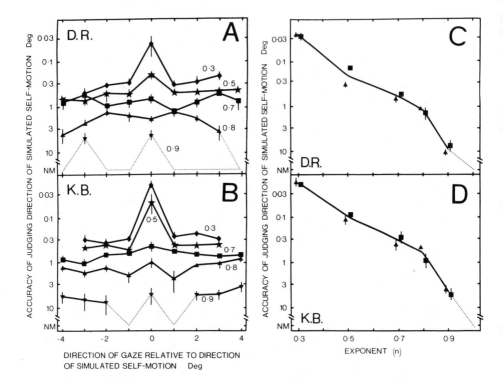

FIG. 13.2.   A and B - Subjects were not able to disentangle the direction of gaze from the direction of self-motion when the rate of change of spatial frequency was uniform over the pattern ($n = 1.0$), and could hardly perform the task for $n = 0.9$, but when the rate of change of magnification was appreciably greater along the direction of simulated self-motion, subjects were able to judge the direction of simulated self-motion almost independently of the direction of gaze ($n = .8$, $n = .7$). For $n = .5$ and $n = .3$ subjects were somewhat more accurate when looking approximately along the direction of simulated self-motion. The rate of expansion in all cases was equivalent to impact with the target 5 sec after onset of stimulation. Initial spatial frequency was 5 c/deg. Field size was 16° vertical and 20° horizontal, mean luminance 30 cd/m² and viewing was monocular. C and D were measured in a separate experiment with subjects looking approximately along the direction of motion. From Regan & Beverley, *Science*, 1982, *215*, 194–195.

visual sensitivity to the location of the maximum rate of magnification in the retinal image. Although these experimental findings are not necessarily consequent on the following point, it is worth noting that the focus of expansion on the retinal image may be affected by retinal image translation produced when the observer looks at some point other than his destination (Fig. 13.1), whereas the location on the retinal image of the maximum rate of magnification is not affected by eye movements. Gibson (1950) drew attention to the fact that (to paraphrase), from a moving observer's point of view, the visual scene undergoes continuous spatial deformation in the sense that the rate of magnification is spatially nonuniform, and in addition the scene contains a pattern of flow. One implication of our experiments is that retinal image translation has different effects on visual sensitivity to these two consequences of self-motion. (In particular, translation affects visual sensitivity to the flow pattern not to the pattern of spatial deformation.)

Extrapolating our laboratory results to real-world situations we proposed that, contrary to Gibson's proposal, subjects might not generally be capable of using the center of the expanding flow pattern to accurately judge the direction of self-motion[4,5] (Regan & Beverley, 1982). Special exceptions include: (1) the case where a vehicle is known to be traveling along a straight line with no yaw or pitch so that the moving observer can hold his eye fixed in the vehicle's coordinates, and in addition static aiming marks are provided; (2) where the moving observer fixates a distance reference object such as a star or distant horizon. Our experimental findings also suggest that, in some situations, a local maximum in the rate of change of magnification might provide an indication that subjects could use in judging the direction of self-motion. Furthermore, the human visual system is very sensitive to this indication. On the other hand, this visual indication is likely to be of value in only some external world geometries.

The Same Physiological Activity that Accounts for Specific Sensitivity to Changing-Size may also be Involved in Visual Judgements of the Direction of Self-Motion.

It may not be necessary to postulate an ad hoc neural mechanism to account for subjects' ability to judge where, on the retinal image, magnification is changing most rapidly. There is experimental evidence that the human visual system processes changing-size information from a local retinal area almost independently of all other visual parameters so far investigated (see next Section). The test stimuli used to establish this conclusion consisted, for the most part, of those shown in Fig. 13.3, namely "antiphase" and "inphase" oscillations of a square's (or a rectangle's) edges. Therefore, in order to test whether specific sensitivity to changing-size might be involved in the judgments of Fig. 13.2, we

---

[5]W. Richards (1975) has shown that the retinal flow pattern is asymmetric when the direction of gaze differs from the direction of motion. Symmetry might well provide a cue to the direction of self-motion, but it seems unlikely that accuracy would be better than $10°–20°$ even with a wide field of view.

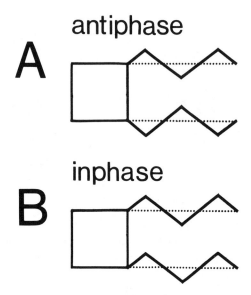

FIG. 13.3.   Antiphase (changing-size) and inphase oscillations of the test square's edges. The oscillation of only one pair of edges is shown. Inphase oscillations caused the square to oscillate bodily along a diagonal.

used these same (Fig. 13.3) test stimuli previously used in the changing-size experiments.

Figure 13.4 illustrates our experiment. Subjects fixated on the mark M throughout the experiment. The fixation mark M did not necessarily coincide with the focus of the pattern. At 5-sec intervals the direction of flow of the pattern was reversed, so that the line segments first lengthened and moved at constant speed radially away from the focus of the pattern, and then shortened and moved back towards the focus. Before and after the 10-min adaptation period the radial pattern was not present. It was replaced by a test square whose edges oscillated either in antiphase (changing-size) or inphase. The test square was located at a variable distance X from the fixation mark (M) (Fig. 13.4A). Baseline thresholds were measured after adapting to a static pattern (Fig. 13.4B). Postadaptation thresholds were measured after adapting to a pattern that alternately expanded and contracted. Thus, the only difference between baseline and adapted conditions was the presence of radial motion. (There was no motion aftereffect since opposite directions of adapting motion were counterbalanced.)

Figure 13.4C shows that antiphase (changing-size) thresholds were most elevated at the retinal location previously occupied by the focus of the pattern. An explanation for this observation in terms of simple motion sensitivity is rejected by the finding that inphase threshold elevations were much smaller than anti-phase threshold elevations, and showed no maximum near the flow pattern's focus (Regan & Beverley, 1979a; Regan, Beverley, & Cynader, 1979).

The data of Fig. 13.4 can be understood if we assume that physiological activities selectively sensitive to changing-size occur within the visual pathway (see next Section for evidence), and that selective activity of this type is stronger near the focus of the radial flow pattern than at other points. Since the rate of change of magnification is considerably greater near the focus of the Fig. 13.4 flow pattern than elsewhere on the pattern, this line of argument leads to the idea that the same selective physiological activity that can explain the changing-size experiments below can also explain subjects' ability to identify the region in a flow pattern where magnification is changing most rapidly.

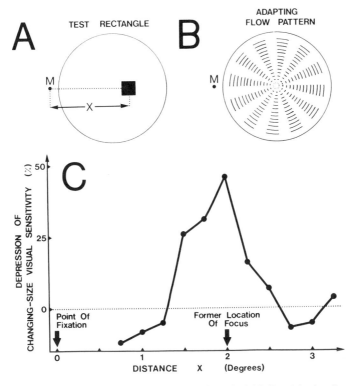

FIG. 13.4.   A - Test square. Fixation point is marked M. B - Adapting flow pattern. C - Threshold elevations for antiphase (changing-size) test square versus position of test square following exposure to adapting flow pattern. From Regan, Beverley, & Cynader, *Scientific American*, 1979, *241*, 136–151.

3. EVIDENCE FOR THE PROPOSAL THAT
PHYSIOLOGICAL RESPONSES TO CHANGING-SIZE
ARE LARGELY INDEPENDENT OF OTHER VISUAL
PARAMETERS

Psychophysical Studies

Figure 13.5 shows experimental evidence rejecting the trivial explanation that the processing of changing-size information can be explained entirely in terms of responses to motion. Subjects viewed a pair of bright squares on a dimmer background. We used the two stimulus oscillations shown in Fig. 13.3, namely inphase oscillations and antiphase oscillations. Subjects first measured the smallest oscillation amplitude that could just be detected for an inphase test oscillation

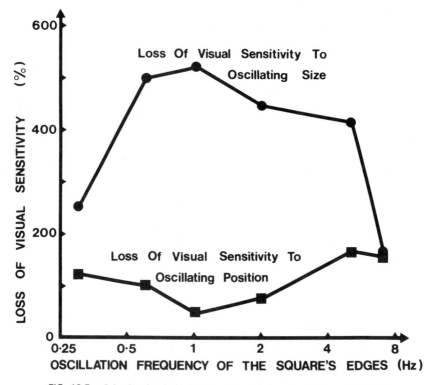

FIG. 13.5.   Selective threshold elevations for changing size. The two test stimuli are shown in Figure 13.4. Ordinates plot loss of visual sensitivity to oscillation caused by inspecting a strong 2-Hz size oscillation. Changing-size sensitivity fell considerably, but sensitivity to oscillating position was little affected. Note that the only difference between the two test stimuli is in the relationship between the motion of opposite edges of the square.

and for an antiphase test oscillation. Then they inspected a strong antiphase oscillation for 20 min and measured the two thresholds again. The antiphase threshold was much elevated, but the inphase threshold was comparatively little affected. When the experiment was repeated with an inphase adapting oscillation, threshold elevations were small for both test stimuli (Regan & Beverley, 1978).

This differential effect was still observed when the adapting stimulus was a bright square on a dark ground and the test stimulus was a dark square on a bright ground. Furthermore, flickering the square's intensity produced no appreciable threshold elevations. Therefore, we can discount changes of light flux or luminance as explanations for the differential threshold elevation of Fig. 13.5.

A weakness of these early experiments is that they were limited to two directions of motion, namely motion along a line through the eye (i.e., antiphase oscillations) and motion parallel to the frontoparallel plane (i.e., inphase oscillations), as illustrated in Fig. 13.6A and B. A more recent experiment extended the conclusions to a range of adapting trajectories. The rationale of this later experiment is illustrated in Fig. 13.6C. On separate days, subjects adapted to 11 different trajectories. Each adapting oscillation had the same velocity along a line through the eye, i.e., the same antiphase component, but each adapting oscillation had a different velocity parallel to the frontoparallel plane (i.e., a different inphase component of oscillation). If the human visual pathway does indeed respond to the antiphase component, and responds in a way that is unaffected by the inphase component, then all 11 adapting oscillations should produce the same threshold elevation for the antiphase test stimulus.

Figure 13.6D shows that this prediction was upheld to an accuracy of at least about ±5% over a very wise span trajectories. (The abscissa plots inphase motion components ranging from zero to ±8 times the amplitude of the antiphase motion component [Regan & Beverley, 1980].)

Figure 13.7 illustrates a proposed explanation for the experimental findings described above. According to this explanation the visual pathway functions as though it contained filters. A particular filter passes only a specific type of information. In Fig. 13.7 the only possible output of the motion filters is velocity information. We suppose that the two motion filters shown receive input from opposite edges of our stimulus square. We suppose that the outputs of these two motion filters neurally represent the velocities of the stimulus square's opposite edges. The two motion filters feed the changing-size filter. The output of the changing-size filter neurally represents the difference between its two velocity inputs, i.e., the quantity $x - y$ shown in Fig. 13.7. Thus, if the stimulus square is expanding such that each edge moves at a speed of 3 deg/sec and opposite edges move in opposite directions, then the output of the changing-size filter will represent 6 deg/sec, and if the square is moving bodily while expanding so that one edge moves at 51 deg/sec and the opposite edge moves at 45 deg/sec *n the same direction*, then the output of the changing-size filter again represents 6 deg/ sec [since $3 - (-3) = 6$ and $51 - 45 = 6$]. Since the antiphase threshold elevations of Fig. 13.6 do not vary by more than about $\pm 5\%$, the subtraction $\mathbf{x} - \mathbf{y}$ in Fig. 13.7 is required to maintain better than $\pm 5\%$ accuracy while the magnitude of $\mathbf{x}$ and $\mathbf{y}$ vary by up to $8(\mathbf{x} - \mathbf{y})$.

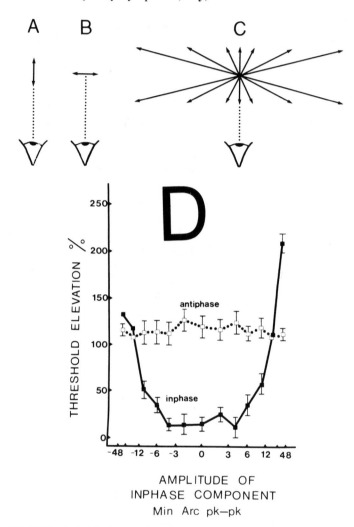

FIG. 13.6.   Left side shows trajectories that would produce antiphase (A) and inphase (B) oscillations. C shows experimental rationale. All adapting trajectories had the same antiphase oscillation component of 6 min arc peak to peak, but different amplitudes of inphase component were added. D - Threshold elevations produced by adapting to the 11 trajectories in A. Antiphase test oscillations are dotted while the continuous line plots inphase test oscillations.

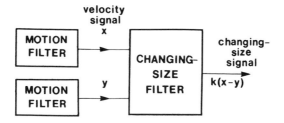

FIG. 13.7.   Psychophysical model to account for threshold evaluations caused by adaptation to changing-size and moving stimuli (Fig. 13.5 and 13.6). The motion filters may overlap, but their regions of maximum sensititivy are some distance apart in the visual field. The output of the changing-size filter is closely related to the time to collision with an external object. From Regan & Beverley, *Journal of the Optical Society of America*, 1980, *70*, 1289–1296.

The computation of $(x-y)$ is an important property of the (hypothetical) changing-size filters (Fig. 13.7) since it explains why, in Fig. 13.6, anti-phase threshold elevations were experimentally independent of frontal plane motion (i.e., of inphase oscillations). We suppose that the selective adaptation of Figs. 13.5 and 13.6 is due to stimulus-induced modification of the changing-size filter. The absence of threshold elevation following exposure to flicker we attribute to the nature of selective filtering, i.e. rejection of all but one type of input.

Single-unit Studies

Although all 101 units studied by Regan and Cynader (1979) in area 18 of cat visual cortex responded to changing-size, these authors applied a fourfold criterion to select units that responded *selectively* to changing size. These control experiments eliminated all but one of these 101 units by showing that they were responding to changes in light flux or to motion of a single edge rather than to changing size. There was, however, evidence that a considerable proportion of units slightly, but systematically, emphasized changing-size information, so that population behavior might in principle be capable of signaling changing size even though no systematic preference was evident in simple spike counts of individual neurons.

4. STEREOSCOPIC VISUAL SENSITIVITY TO MOTION IN DEPTH

Psychophysical Studies

When there is relative motion in depth between an observer's head and an external object, both the left and right retinal images will, in general, move

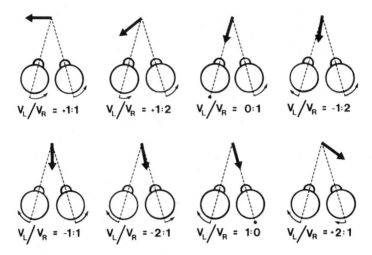

FIG. 13.8.   The ratio between the velocities of the left (V_L) and right (V_R) retinal images provides an unambiguous cue to the direction of motion in depth. Positive values of V_L/V_R mean that the retinal images move in the same direction, while negative values indicate opposed motion.

across the retinae. Figure 13.8 illustrates that the relative velocity (V_L/V_R) of the left and right retinal images has a fixed relation to the direction of the object's motion in depth (Beverley & Regan, 1973). Whether the human visual system utilizes this geometrical fact is the question that triggered several experimental studies described in this section.

The first experimental study showed that visual sensitivity to motion in depth was depressed after inspecting an image that oscillated in depth, though visual

FIG. 13.9.   Evidence that the human visual system contains four subsystems each tuned to a different direction of motion in depth. Threshold elevations for detecting stereoscopic motion in depth caused by adapting to 13 different values of V_L/V_R. These 13 different values of V_L/V_R can be regarded as 13 different directions of motion in depth. Threshold elevations were separately measured for up to 13 different test trajectories for each of the 13 adapting trajectories. **A** shows that all three different adapting trajectories directed to the left of the head produced the same threshold elevations, and the same threshold elevations were produced by all three different adapting trajectories directed to the right of the head. **B** shows that all three different adapting trajectories directed between the nose and the right eye produced the same threshold elevations, and the same threshold elevations were produced by all three different adapting trajectories directed to the right of the head. **C** shows that an adapting trajectory passing directly through the nose elevated thresholds over a narrow range of trajectories passing through the head. The threshold elevations produced by the 13 different adapting trajectories can be explained in terms of only four mechanisms tuned to V_L/V_R as shown in Fig. 13.10. From Beverley & Regan, *Journal of Physiology*, 1973, *235*, 17–29.

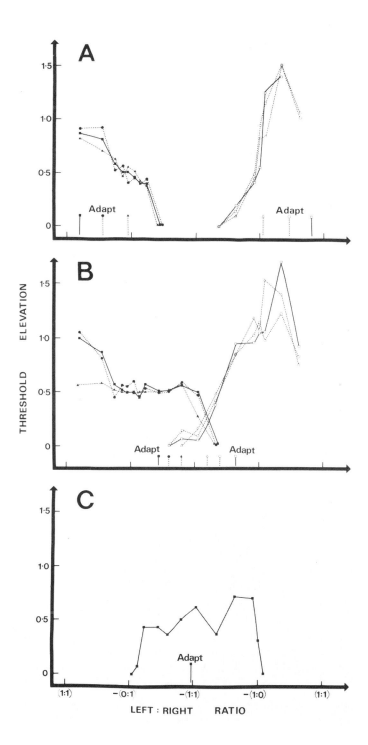

sensitivity to motion in the frontal plane was comparatively little affected. An important experimental point is that for a given adapting trajectory visual sensitivity was depressed for only a restricted range of test directions of motion in depth. However, it was not necessarily the case that the greatest loss of sensitivity was along the adapting trajectory. In particular, 13 experiments in which we adapted to 13 different trajectories produced only five clearly different shapes of threshold elevation curve (Fig. 13.9A, B, C).

Our proposed explanation for the above experimental findings on stereo motion again uses the concept of psychophysical filters, so that our model has the same general format as the Fig. 13.7 model already discussed. We proposed that the visual pathway functions as though it contains filters that give an output only when the velocity ratio V_R/V_R lies within a limited range of values. As illustrated in Fig. 13.8, selective sensitivity to the ratio V_L/V_R means that the filters will be

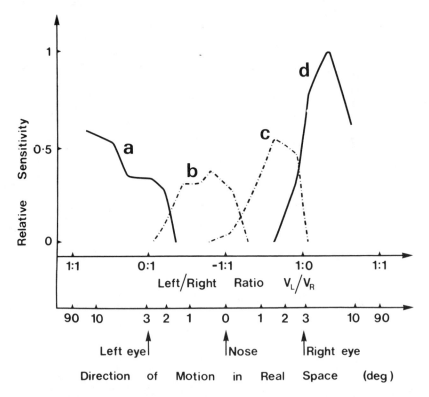

FIG. 13.10.   Sensitivity curves for stereoscopic motion filters in the human visual system. These filters are selectively tuned to the ratio V_L/V_R. Values of V_L/V_R are plotted as abscissae, with corresponding directions in space indicated. Note that the narrow cone of directions passing between the eyes is exaggerated in this plot, so that the two center filters are very sharply selective to the direction of motion in depth.

selectively tuned to the direction of motion in depth, and this is indicated on the lower abscissa in Fig. 13.10. Plotted in this way it is evident that our two hypothetical filters tuned to opposed motion in the left and right eyes are very sharply selective, responding to a range of directions of only about 2° (b and c). These two filters respond to objects moving along trajectories that pass between the eyes. In contrast, the two hypothetical filters tuned to the same direction of motion in the left and right eyes respond to a comparatively broad range of directions of motion in depths (a and d).

We suppose that the selective adaptation of Fig. 13.9 is due to stimulus-induced modification of the V_L/V_R filters.

Although the subsystems set out in Fig. 13.10 can account for threshold elevation data, they cannot explain why discrimination of different direction of motion in depth (roughly 0.2°) is about 10 times more acute than the narrowest of the filter bandwidths (Regan, Beverley, & Cynader, 1978). A proposed explanation is that the filter outputs interact, much as the outputs of cone mechanisms have been suggested to interact so as to enhance color discrimination (Beverley & Regan, 1975).

Richards and Regan (1973) reported evidence that there is separate visual processing of stereoscopic position in depth and of stereo motion in depth. They found subjects whose visual field contained regions that were "blind" to disparity, yet were sensitive to motion in depth, while other regions of the visual field were blind to motion in depth, yet sensitive to disparity.

Single-unit Studies

Single neurons that were selectively sensitive to the ratio between left and right retinal image velocities have been found in visual cortex of anaesthetized cat (Cynader & Regan, 1978; Regan & Cynader, 1982) and in areas 17 and 18 of awake, visually active monkey (Poggio & Talbot, 1981). In effect, these neurons were tuned to the direction of motion in depth.[6] There were corresponding neurons in cat visual cortex for all the psychophysical motion-in-depth filters in man proposed on the basis of the Figs. 13.9 and 13.10 data. Some of the most sharply tuned neurons fired best to binocular stimulation when the retinal images moved in opposite directions, and thus responded to a range of directions spanning no more than 1° to 2°. Some of these neurons maintained their directional tuning over at least a fourfold range of speeds (Fig. 13.11A). This finding is difficult to explain in terms of velocity tuning of monocular responses (Regan & Cynader, 1982). A second class of neurons fired best for trajectories that missed the head. These were tuned to a broader range of directions than the "hitting the

---

[6]Note that these motion-in-depth neurons are not adequately described as being selectively sensitive to the rate of change of disparity, i.e., to the difference between the left and right image velocities (Regan & Cynader, 1982).

head'' class of neurons. Some of the neurons in these two classes maintained their tuning to motion in depth over a range of disparities as large as 12° (Cynader & Regan, 1982). In such neurons, tuning to the direction of motion in depth cannot easily be explained as a trivial consequence of choosing a specific static disparity. Other neurons of this type systematically changed their tuning as a function of disparity, for example, favoring motion towards the frontoparallel plane whether the object were nearer or farther than the frontoparallel plane.

A third class of neurons showed strong interocular facilitation (up to 100-fold) when motion was accurately parallel to the frontoparallel plane (Fig. 13.11B). Thus, this class of neurons also can be regarded as being very selective to the direction of motion in depth. This third class of neurons was comparatively sharply tuned to disparity, i.e., to position in depth. In this they differed from many neurons in the first two classes. This third class probably corresponds to the well-known binocular disparity-sensitive units (Barlow, Blakemore, & Pettigrew, 1967; Hubel & Wiesel, 1970; Pettigrew, Nikara, & Bishop, 1968).

We should note that, although the firing of a neuron such as that shown in Fig. 13.11A strongly emphasized the direction of motion in depth, we found no neuron whose firing might be said to provide an unequivocal representation of the direction of motion in depth. For example, the firing of the Fig. 13.11A neuron was affected not only by the V_L/V_R ratio, but also by the orientation, contrast, and luminance of the stimulus bar.

5. TWO STIMULI FOR MOTION-IN-DEPTH: COMPARATIVE EFFECTIVENESS OF CHANGING-DISPARITY AND CHANGING-SIZE

When an object moves directly toward the head, the two retinal images move away from each other and also grow larger. By itself, opposed motion of the two retinal images can generate a sensation of motion in depth. By itself, changing-size has long been known to be capable of generating a sensation of motion in

---

FIG. 13.11.   Spikes recorded from single neurons in cat visual cortex (plotted radially) as a function of the direction of motion in depth (plotted as azimuthal angle). A - This unit maintains its very selective tuning to the direction of motion in depth over a 4:1 speed range. Note that firing is almost restricted to a range of directions little wider than 1°. This directional tuning is achieved by interocular inhibition as shown by the arrows. B - This unit fired appreciably only when the target moved closely parallel to the frontoparallel plane in a left-right direction and when vision was binocular. Closed circles show firing when the two eyes were stimulated separately and open circles show firing when binocular vision was used. The dotted area indicates the very strong interocular facilitation observed for binocular vision. From Regan & Cynader, *Investigative Ophthalmology & Visual Science*, 1982, *22*, 535–550.

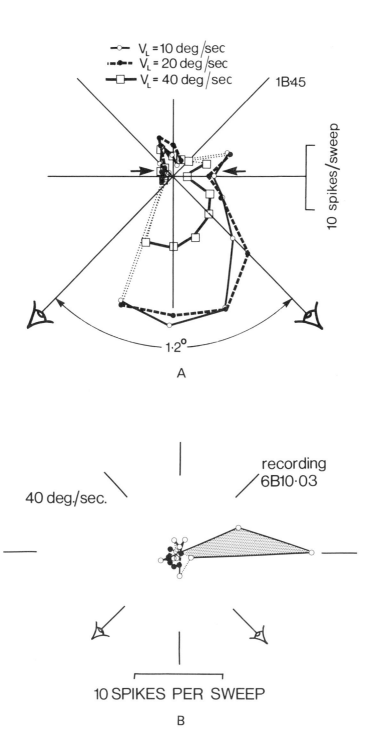

A

B

depth[7] (Wheatstone, 1852). In the real visual world both stimuli are generally present at the same time, and the situation is almost always as described above, but in order to measure the relative effectiveness of the two inputs as stimuli for motion in depth we created artificial electronically generated targets in which the two motion-in-depth stimuli were antagonistic; for example, as a target came closer it grew smaller. (In these experiments disparty was changed while binocular convergence was carefully held constant, using nonious lines to monitor convergence. The experiments were repeated for several fixed values of binocular convergence, showing that the angle of convergence had little effect on results.)

Subjects viewed a square whose size changed at a fixed rate, so that the square appeared to move in depth. The rate of change of disparity was then adjusted by the subject so as to exactly cancel the impression of motion in depth produced by the fixed rate of change of size. In this way it was possible to show that the relative effectiveness of the changing-disparity inputs was increased by faster speeds, narrower targets, and longer inspection times, but was not appreciably affected by the viewing distance (Regan & Beverley, 1979b).

6. CORRELATIONS BETWEEN SIMULATOR AND AIRCRAFT FLYING PERFORMANCE AND VISUAL TEST RESULTS

To what extent the theoretical ideas outlined above provide an adequate description of visual function in real-world visual environments is not yet established, and moreover is the subject of some controversy, hence this disgression.

It will be evident that the experimental approach described above shares a rationale with those who use simple laboratory stimuli, often at threshold levels, with the aim of uncovering elementary functional subunits of the visual pathway.[8,9] Our version of these subunits is typified by hypothetical information-

---

[7]Poincaré (1913) pointed out that when retinal image magnification is changing (i.e., size is changing but shape is constant), quite different explanations are geometrically possible: The object might be physically changing size, or the object might be moving in depth and, of course, combinations of the two cannot be distinguished using only the information contained in a single two-dimensional retinal image. Several different explanations have been proposed for how the brain resolves this ambiguity (Poincaré, 1913; von Fieandt & Gibson, 1959; Johansson, 1964). Our own suggestion is that the visual pathway is biased to produce a "safest guess" perception (Beverley & Regan, 1979).

[8]It is straightforward to show that $T = (\frac{\dot{\theta}}{\theta})^{-1}$ where T is time to collision, $(\frac{\dot{\theta}}{\theta})^{-1}$ is fractional rate of change of angular size, $\dot{\theta}$ is object's rate of change of angular size and θ is object's instantaneous angular size. Lee and his colleagues have discussed rate of change of size and its relation to "time to collision" in their studies of locomotion and how automobile drivers judge when to slow and brake (Lee, 1976, 1980; Lee & Lishman, 1977).

[9]If they are to easily predict visual function in a complex visual environment, these subunits should function approximately independently. However, it is not required that a given subunit should be linear.

processing filters as, for example, in Fig. 13.7. This is not everyone's approach to vision research, and we should emphasize that it is not self-evident that functional subunits (even granted that they do exist at near-threshold levels) would continue to exist and operate reasonably independently when the visual environment was complex and stimulus levels were well above threshold. Nevertheless, this question is open to experimental test. In principle, we can experimentally find how adequate a description of real-world motion and depth perception is provided by theoretical models such as that outlined in Fig. 13.7 and proposed above for V_L/V_R sensitivity. Indeed, the intent to explore how adequately laboratory-based models can describe visual function in complex, real-world visual environments was an important factor in undertaking our earliest laboratory experiments.

We now describe ongoing experiments in which the results of visual tests on pilots were compared with flying performance on a flight simulator (A-10 aircraft) and with aircraft flying grades (T-38 jet trainer).

It may well be true that in most flying situations the limits to a pilot's performance are set by his cognitive skills developed by prior training and experience. Nevertheless, flying situations may exist for which his flying performance comes up against the limited sensitivity or discrimination of his visual sensory system. For example, the importance of seeing one's adversary before he sees you was a byword 65 years ago among pilots high above the Western Front. If we assume then, that in some situations flying performance is limited by visual sensory factors, we might expect that flying tasks could be found for which a pilot's performance could be predicted on the basis of visual tests. However, this expectation has not yet been fulfilled. Reports of strong correlations between flying performance and visual test results have so far been sparse (Semple, Hennessy, Sanders, Cross, & McCauley, 1980).

As a working hypothesis we assumed that in flying conditions, motion information is processed by the filters such as those illustrated in Fig. 13.7. In this context an important property of the hypothetical filters is that they reject all but one type of information. For example, an ideal changing-size filter (Fig. 13.7) is supposed to receive negligible "cross talk" from stimulus motion in the frontal plane. Thus, if filter A were important in flying task B, then visual test results involving filter A would correlate with performance in task B, while if filter C were important in flying task D, then visual test results involving filter C would correlate with performance in task D (Kruk, Regan, Beverley, & Longridge, 1981; Regan, 1982).

More speculatively, the ability of humans to acquire eye-hand coordination skills that generalize to a variety of visual environments might be explained in part if an early stage of physiological processing is to split retinal image information into a number of orthogonal elements by means of information-processing filters specific, for example, to changing-size, stereo motion, spatial frequency, and color. If, for example, learning how to catch a ball can be regarded as a process of establishing one or more "hard wired" ways of processing the outputs of certain visual filters, then the skill would transfer from a simple visual environment to a complex visual environment, because the absence of overlap and of "cross talk" between filters would render the initial channel analysis more or less indifferent to scene complexity (Regan, 1982; Regan & Beverley, 1980).

Conversely, either too much "cross talk" or too much overlap between filters might cause flying performance in a complex visual situation to fall below flying performance in a simple visual situation. In order to test this suggestion, we designed a tracking device that assesses a subject's ability to use his changing-size channels in conditions where appreciable cross talk with motion channels is possible (Regan & Beverley, 1980). A further aim of the 13 visual measures collected from pilots by Kruk et al. (1981, 1982) was to assess the specific visual sensitivities that seemed likely to be involved in the various flying tasks. Flying tasks included formation flight, low-level flight, and restricted visibility landing. Visual tests comprised superthreshold velocity discrimination of a radially expanding flow pattern, manual tracking of both changing size (i.e. motion in depth) and motion in the frontal plane, motion thresholds and contrast thresholds for a moving square and a static sinewave grating.

Landing and formation flight performance correlated with both manual tracking and expanding flow pattern test results. Pilots who were better able to discriminate different rates of expansion of the expanding flow pattern performed better on the low-level flight task. Aircraft flying grades for student pilots correlated with expanding flow pattern test results and with manual tracking of changing-size (Kruk et al., 1981, 1982).

In a recent follow-up study using telemetry-tracked fighter aircraft, correlations were found between flying performance in low-level flight and in air-to-air combat, and visual test results with manual tracking and the expanding flow pattern (Kruk, Regan & Beverley, unpublished data).

ACKNOWLEDGMENTS

We thank the following for illuminating comments and discussions: Drs. M. Cynader, D. van Essen, J. Hochberg, L. Kaufman, J. A. Movshon, W. Richards and K. Stevens. This research is currently supported by the NSERC of Canada and sponsored by the Air Force Office of Scientific Research, Air Force Systems Command USAF, under Grant AFOSR–78–3711. Previous support (1964–75) was received from the MRC of Great Britain.

REFERENCES

Barlow, H., Blakemore, C. B., & Pettigrew, J. D. The neural mechanism of binocular depth discrimination. *Journal of Physiology*, 1967, *193*, 327–342.

Beverley, K. I., & Regan, D. Evidence for the existence of neural mechanisms selectively sensitive to the direction of movement in space. *Journal of Physiology*, 1973, *235*, 17–29.

Beverley, K. I., & Regan, D. The relation between discrimination and sensitivity in the perception of motion in depth. *Journal of Physiology*, 1975, *249*, 387–398.

Beverley, K. I., & Regan, D. Separable aftereffects of changing-size and motion in depth: different neural mechanisms? *Vision Research*, 1979, *19*, 727–732.

Boynton, R. M. The visual system: Environmental information. In C. Carterette and M. P. Friedman (Eds.), *Handbook of Perception*, Vol. 1. New York: Academic Press, 1974, pp. 285–307.

Cynader, M., & Regan, D. Neurones in cat parastriate cortex sensitive to the direction of motion in three-dimensional space. *Journal of Physiology*, 1978, *274*, 549–569.

Cynader, M., & Regan, D. Neurons in cat visual cortex tuned to the direction of motion in depth: effect of positional disparity. *Vision Research*, 1982, *22*, 967–982.

Fieandt, K. von & Gibson, J. J. The sensitivity of the eye to two kinds of continuous transformation of a shadow pattern. *Journal of Experimental Psychology*, 1959, *57*, 344–347.

Gibson, J. J. Motion picture testing and research. Army Air Force Report, #7, Ad–651, 1947.

Gibson, J. J. *The perception of the visual world*. Boston: Houghton Mifflin, 1950.

Gibson, J. J. Visually controlled locomotion and visual orientation in animals. *British Journal of Psychology*, 1958, *49*, 182–194.

Gibson, J. J. A note on ecological optics. In E. C. Carterette and M. P. Friedman (Eds.), *Handbook of Perception*, Vol. 1, New York: Academic Press, 1974, pp. 309–312.

Gordon, D. A. Static and dynamic fields in human space perception. *Journal of the Optical Society of America*, 1965, *55*, 1296–1303.

Hubel, D. H., & Wiesel, T. N. Cells sensitive to binocular depth in area 18 of macaque monkey cortex. *Nature (Lond.)*, 1970, *225*, 41–42.

Johansson, G. Perception of motion and changing form. *Scandinavian Journal of Psychology*, 1964, *5*, 181–207.

Johnston, I. R., White, G. R., & Cumming, R. W. The role of optical expansion patterns in locomotor control. *American Journal of Psychology*, 1973, *86*, 311–324.

Koenderink, J. J., & van Doorn, A. J. Local structure of movement parallax of the plane. *Journal of the Optical Society of America*, 1976, *66*, 717–723.

Koenderink, J. J., & van Doorn, A. J. Exterospecific component of the motion parallax field. *Journal of the Optical Society of America*, 1981, *71*, 953–957.

Kruk, R., Regan, D., Beverley, K. I., & Longridge, T. Correlations between visual test results and flying performance on the Advanced Simulator for Pilot Training (ASPT). *Aviation, Space & Environmental Medicine*, 1981, *52*, 455–460.

Kruk, R., Regan, D., Beverley, K. I., & Longridge, T. Flying performance on the Advanced Simulator for Pilot Training (ASPT). *Human Factors*, 1982. In press.

Lee, D. N. A theory of visual control of braking based on information about time to collision. *Perception*, 1976, *15*, 437–459.

Lee, D. N. The optic flow field: the foundation of vision. *Philosophical Transactions of the Royal Society, London*, 1980, *290*, 169–179.

Lee, D. N., & Lishman, R. Visual control of locomotion. *Scandinavian Journal of Psychology* 1977, *18*, 224–230.

Llewellyn, K. R. Visual guidance of locomotion. *Journal of Experimental Psychology*, 1971, *91*, 245–261.

Nakayama, K. Differential motion hyperacuity under conditions of common image motion. *Vision Research*, 1981, *21*, 1475–1482.

Nakayama, K., & Loomis, J. M. Optical velocity patterns, velocity sensitive neurons and space perception: a hypothesis. *Perception*, 1974, *63*, 80–87.

Pettigrew, J. D., Nikara, T., & Bishop, P. O. Binocular interaction on single units in cat striate cortex: simultaneous stimulation by single moving slits with receptive fields in correspondence. *Experimental Brain Research*, 1968, *6*, 391–416.

Poggio, G. F., & Talbot, W. H. Mechanisms of static and dynamic stereopsis in foveal cortex of rhesus monkey. *Journal of Physiology*, 1981, *315*, 469–492.

Poincaré, H. *The value of science*. New York: Science Press, 1913.

Prazdny, K. Egomotion and relative depth map for optical flow. *Biological Cybernetics*, 1980, *36*, 87–102.

Regan, D. The concept of visual information channeling: its relevance to ophthalmology and to the performance of skilled tasks involving eye-limb coordination. *Psychological Review*, 1982, *89*, 407–444.

Regan, D., & Beverley, K. I. Looming detectors in the human visual pathway. *Vision Research*, 1978, *18*, 415–421.

Regan, D., & Beverley, K. I. Visually-guided locomotion: psychophysical evidence for a neural mechanism sensitive to flow patterns. *Science*, 1979, *205*, 311–313. (a)

Regan, D., & Beverley, K. I. Binocular and monocular stimuli for motion-in-depth: changing-disparity and changing-size inputs feed the same motion-in-depth stage. *Vision Research*, 1979, *19*, 1331–1342. (b)

Regan, D., & Beverley, K. I. Visual responses to changing size and to sideways motion for different directions of motion in depth: linearization of visual responses. *Journal of the Optical Society of America*, 1980, *70*, 1289–1296.

Regan, D., & Beverley, K. I. How do we avoid confounding the direction we are looking with the direction we are moving? *Science*, 1982, *215*, 194–195.

Regan, D., Beverley, K. I., & Cynader, M. Stereoscopic depth channels for position and for motion. In S. J. Cool & E. L. Smith (Eds.), *Frontiers in visual science*. New York: Springer-Verlag, 1978.

Regan, D., Beverley, K. I., & Cynader, M. The visual perception of motion in depth. *Scientific American*, 1979, *241*, 136–151.

Regan, D., & Cynader, M. Neurons in area 18 of cat visual cortex selectively sensitive to changing size: nonlinear interactions between responses to two edges. *Vision Research*, 1979, *19*, 699–711.

Regan, D., & Cynader, M. Neurons in cat visual cortex tuned to the direction of motion in depth: effect of stimulus speed. *Investigative Ophthalmology & Visual Science*, 1982, *22*, 535–550.

Richards, W. Visual space perception. In C. Carterette and M. P. Friedman (Eds.), *Handbook of perception* (Vol. 5). New York: Academic Press, 1975.

Richards, W., & Regan, D. A stereo field map with implications for disparity processing. *Investigative Ophthalmology*, 1973, *12*, 904–909.

Semple, C. A., Hennessy, R. T., Sanders, M. S., Cross, B. K., & McCauley, M. E. *Aircrew training device fidelity features (final report)*. Canyon Research Group, Inc., 1980, CRG-TR-3041B, ASD/AFHRL Wright Patterson AFB, Ohio.

Warren, R. The perception of egomotion. *Journal of Experimental Psychology*, 1976, *2*, 448–456.

Westheimer, G., & McKee, S. P. Visual acuity in the presence of retinal image motion. *Journal of the Optical Society of America*, 1975, *65*, 847–850.

Wheatstone, C. Contributions to the physiology of vision. II. *Philosophical Transactions of the Royal Society*, 1852, *142*, 1–18.

14

Die zeitabhängige Veränderung der schwerkraftbezogenen subjektiven Raumrichtung beim Menschen

Silvia Lechner-Steinleitner
Max-Planck-Institut für Verhaltensphysiologie
Seewiesen, West Germany

ABSTRACT

The subjective vertical (SV, the angle ß between a subjective vertical line and the medial plane of the head) exhibits a distinct time-dependency, when measured over several minutes. To show this, data from different experiments are presented. Subjects were tested in different head-to-trunk-pitch and head-to-trunk-roll postures. They were tilted to the side from either a standing or a prone position, into positions of different angles of clockwise or counterclockwise rotation (i.e., lateral tilt). Other variables were the magnitude and time of preceding tilt; interfering stimuli, such as a background field of parallel lines placed to the left or right of the luminous reference line; and, in experiments carried out under water, the influence of the somatoreceptor system. In addition, the auditory subjective vertical was also measured, by estimating when the direction of a sound was vertical.

Under all experimental conditions the amount of change of the subjective vertical in time depends on the degree of lateral tilt. With a tilt of 30° and 45°, there is a significant increase of ß in time, whereas a significant decrease of ß occurs at tilts of 90°, 120°, 135° and 150° (Figs. 14.1, 14.2). The effect of the background field and the hysteresis effect (i.e., the ß-difference between clockwise and counterclockwise attainment of position) are superimposed on these time dependent changes. Findings indicate that the time which is spent in the pre-tilt position magnifies the hysteresis effect of the subjective vertical (Fig. 14.3). The comparison between the visual and the auditory subjective vertical reveals similarities. The time course of the auditory subjective vertical shows a significant increase at a body tilt of 30°, as does the corresponding curve of the visual subjective vertical (Fig. 14.4).

The results are discussed on the basis of the hypothesis that the influence of the statolith organs decreases with increasing body tilt. This amplifies the effect of interfering stimuli (e.g., somatoreceptor input and optical reference). Adaptation of the somatoreceptors is assumed to account for the temporal change of the subjective vertical. Furthermore, it is supposed that the aftereffects and hysteresis differences in the perception of position and of the subjective vertical also depend on the adapting processes in the somatoreceptor system which interact with the labyrinthine posture-receptors. But the possibility that a central mechanism processing statolithic information is also involved cannot be ruled out.

ZUSAMMENFASSUNG

Es werden Versuche beschrieben, in denen die subjektive Vertikale in Abhängigkeit von der Körperlage über einen Zeitraum von mehreren Minuten untersucht wurde. Weitere Variablen der Experimente waren die Kopf-zu-Rumpf-Stellung, die Rumpfdrehachse (Seitwärtsneigung aus aufrechter und liegender Position), die Stellungsänderung in und gegen den Uhrzeigersinn, ein zusätzlich gebotenes Streifenfeld links oder rechts der vertikal einzustellenden Linie, die Einstellung einer Schallquelle zur subjektiven Vertikalen und die Änderung des Somatorezeptoreneinflusses durch Messung der Vertikalen unter Wasser. Bei allen oben genannten Versuchsbedingungen zeigte die subjektive Vertikale (gemessen als Winkel ß zwischen der Kopfhochachse der Versuchsperson und der eingestellten Leuchtlinie) eine deutliche Zeitabhängigkeit, deren Ausmaß vor allem von der Größe der Seitwärtsneigung abhing. Der Effekt des Streifenfeldes und die aus der Richtung der Stellungsänderung resultierenden Unterschiede (Hysteresis) überlagerten sich diesem Zeitgang.

Es wird versucht, die Veränderung der subjektiven Vertikalen in der Zeit auf eine adaptive Veränderung der Somatorezeptorenmeldung zurückzuführen. Auf Grund der Ergebnisse kann aber nicht ausgeschlossen werden, daß möglicherweise auch zentrale Mechanismen in der Verrechnung der Statolitheninformation beteiligt sind.

EINLEITUNG

Die Raumwahrnehmung des Menschen und die Vertikalenkonstanz, d.h. das Konstantbleiben der visuellen Umwelt trotz Neigung des Kopfes zur Schwerkraft, sind das Ergebnis einer vielschichtigen Interaktion verschiedener sensorischer Systeme: Rezeptoren im Innenohr (Statolithenorgane) messen die Stellung des Kopfes relativ zur Schwerkraft. Haut-, Lage- und Gelenkrezeptoren (Somatorezeptoren) registrieren die Rumpf- und Gliedmaßenstellung, das Auge bezieht die Struktur der optischen Umwelt mit ein, wobei im Normalfall eine größere Anzahl parallel gerichteter Konturen und Formen die optische Vertikale anzeigt. Die aus diesen Eingängen berechnete Information über die Orientierung des Körpers und der Körperglieder im Raum und zueinander ermöglicht es, die räumlichen Veränderungen der Bewegungen zu überprüfen und das Verhalten im und zum Raum zu ordnen. Versuche zeigten, daß die Gewichtung der

Meldungen aus den einzelnen Sinnessystemen abhängig ist sowohl von der Stellung der Versuchsperson zur Schwerkraft (Brown, 1961; Graybiel & Clark, 1962; Quix & Eijsvogel, 1929), als auch von der Größe und Helligkeit des visuellen Feldes und der darin enthaltenen Strukturen (Bischof & Scheerer, 1970; Kleint, 1936; Nyborg, 1972; Wade, 1969). Die Effektivität der Statolithenorgane als Lagemelder nimmt mit zunehmender Körperneigung ab, während gleichzeitig andere Sinnessysteme an Einfluß gewinnen (Dichgans, Brandt, & Held, 1975; Lechner-Steinleitner, 1978; Schöne, 1975; Schöne & Udo de Haes, 1971; Young, Oman, & Dichgans, 1975).

Aus Experimenten kann geschlossen werden, daß die Utriculi die entscheidenden Statolithenorgane sind, und als rezeptoradäquater Reiz muß die Scherung angesehen werden (vgl. Guedry, 1974, S.3–154). Die Scherungskräfte (F), die auf den Utriculus wirken, sind gleich dem Produkt aus der Feldstärke (G) und dem Sinus des Winkels zwischen Schwerkraftrichtung und Kopfhochachse (F = G · sin α). Da die Schwerkraft durch Zentrifugieren in Richtung und Größe verändert wird, werden dadurch auch die Scherung und die von dieser abhängigen Lagesignale der Utriculi beeinflußt. Während danach die Statolithensignale der Scherung folgen, hängt die Somatorezeptorenreizung ausschließlich vom Grad der Körperneigung ab. Bei einer Seitwärtsneigung von 30° und einer durch Zentrifugieren erhöhten G-Zahl von 1.73 signalisieren beispielsweise die Statolithenorgane 60°, während die Somatorezeptoren nur 30° anzeigen. Die Ergebnisse solcher Zentrifugenversuche lassen auf eine Mittelung der Statolithen- und Somatorezeptorenmeldungen schließen (Lechner-Steinleitner, Schöne, & Wade, 1979).

Die subjektive Vertikale (SV), definiert durch die Richtung einer Leuchtlinie, die die Versuchsperson im Dunkeln lotrecht zu stellen versucht, hängt auch von der Vorneigung ab (Schöne & Lechner-Steinleitner, 1978) und der Zeit, die die Versuchsperson in dieser Vorneigung verbracht hat (Lechner-Steinleitner & Schöne, 1978, S.326–331). Auch die Reproduzierbarkeit der subjektiven Vertikalen ist eine Funktion der Körperneigung: die Streuungen sind in aufrechter Stellung am kleinsten und nehmen mit zunehmender Seitwärtsneigung zu. Damit verbunden ist die Zeitabhängigkeit der subjektiven Vertikalen, d.h. eine mehr oder minder starke Veränderung der wahrgenommenen Vertikalen innerhalb einer mehrminütigen Versuchsdauer. Solche Änderungen in der Wahrnehmung trotz gleichbleibender Reizsituation wurden bei Trocken- und Unterwasserversuchen festgestellt und sollen nun zusammenfassend beschrieben werden.

METHODIK

Die wahrgenommene Vertikale wurde relativ zur Versuchsperson und nicht relativ zur Schwerkraft gemessen, d.h. das Einstellen der Leuchtlinie wurde als eine Reaktion der Versuchsperson auf die Reizung der verschiedenen Sinnesorgane betrachtet. Registriert wurde als abhängige Variable der Winkel ß zwischen der Kopfhochachse der Versuchsperson und der eingestellten Leuchtlinie (Correia,

Hixson, & Niven, 1965; Schöne, 1962). Wenn also mit zunehmender Kopfneigung die Linie richtig eingestellt werden soll, so bedeutet dies eine dementsprechende Gegendrehung der Leuchtlinie.

ERGEBNISSE

A. Die Veränderung der subjektiven Vertikalen in der Zeit bei Trockenversuchen

1. Zeitgänge der subjektiven Vertikalen bei veränderter Kopf-zu-Rumpfneigung

Schöne und Udo de Haes (1968) untersuchten den Einfluß der Kopf-zu-Rumpfstellung auf die Richtung der wahrgenommenen Vertikalen. Die Versuchsperson lag im Dunkeln in einem um die Längsachse drehbaren Bett, den Kopf so weit hochgenommen, daß sich die Maculae der Utriculi in etwa horizon-

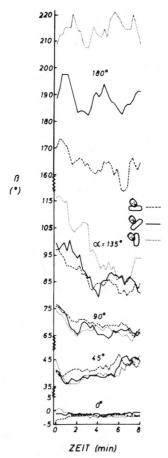

FIG. 14.1. Subjective vertical (ß, angle between a subjective vertical line and the medial plane of the head) as a function of time (min) at five different head positions (α) and three head-to-trunk postures. Curves are averaged across five subjects and two 8-min tests per condition. (From Schöne & Udo de Haes, 1968. Reprinted by permission from *Zeitschrift für vergleichende Physiologie*, 1968, *60*, 442.)

taler Lage befanden. Der Kopf konnte bei fester Lage des Rumpfes zur Seite gedreht werden. Bei Stellungen des Kopfes zur Schwerkraft von 0°, 45°, 90°, 135° und 180° wurden je drei Rumpflagen gemessen (Winkel Kopf zu Rumpf von 0°, 45° zur linken und 45° zur rechten Seite). Die Richtung der subjektiven Vertikalen zeigte bei einer Versuchsdauer von 8 Minuten eine deutliche Zeitabhängigkeit, nämlich eine in der Zeit annähernd konstante Einstellrichtung bei 0° und 180° (mit starken Schwankungen bei 180°), einen nach einem Anfangsabfall wieder größer werdenden Einstellwinkel bei 45° und einen in der Zeit kleiner werdenden Einstellwinkel bei 90° und 135° (Fig. 14.1).

2. Zeitgänge der subjektiven Vertikalen bei Seitwärtsneigung aus stehender und liegender Ausgangsstellung

Ähnliche Zeitkurven wurden bei 19 Versuchspersonen gefunden, die in einem Mehrachsendrehbett von aufrechtstehender und liegender Stellung in 6 Seitwärtslagen (0° bis 150°) gebracht wurden. Die Orientierung des Kopfes im Raum war bei den zwei unterschiedlichen Ausgangsstellungen dieselbe (Steinleitner, 1975; Lechner-Steinleitner, 1978). Signifikant ansteigende Werte fanden sich bei Einstellungen über 8 Minuten bei einer Seitwärtsneigung von 30°, signifikant abfallende bei 90°, 120° und 150° (Fig. 14.2). Bei einer weiteren Untersuchung des Bereiches zwischen 60° und 90° zeigte sich, daß zwischen 70° und 80° der Anstieg des Einstellwinkels in einen Abfall übergeht.

3. Zeitgänge der subjektiven Vertikalen bei Streifenfeldwirkung

Die Versuchsperson sieht bei diesen Experimenten im Dunkeln zusätzlich zum Leuchtstrich ein Feld mit dünnen parallelen Linien im Hintergrund, das in einem bestimmten Winkel (entweder 15° nach links oder 15° nach rechts geneigt) zur Leuchtlinie fixiert ist. Feld und Linie werden als Ganzes gedreht, um zu gewährleisten, daß der Einfluß dieser optischen Vertikalen in allen Seitwärtsneigungen derselbe ist. Die subjektive Vertikale wird in Richtung Streifenfeld abgelenkt, die Einstellungen bilden eine Art Kompromiß zwischen der Schwerkraftvertikalen und der Hauptrichtung des Streifenfeldes (optische Vertikale) (Schöne & Udo de Haes, 1971; Lechner-Steinleitner & Schöne, 1980). Die Größe des Streifenfeldeinflusses ist abhängig von der Körperneigung und von der Zeit, er nimmt besonders in Körperlagen über 90° im Laufe der Versuchsdauer deutlich zu.

4. Hysteresisphänomene

Die subjektive Vertikale zeigt sich von der vorangegangenen Körperneigung abhängig, das heißt, die Richtung der Neigungsänderung spielt eine Rolle

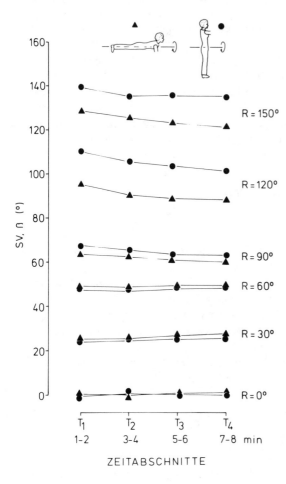

FIG. 14.2. Subjective vertical (ß) as a function of time at six different side tilts (R). Subjects were tilted to the side from either a prone (triangles) or a standing (dots) position. T_1, T_2, T_3, T_4 represent 2-min sections of the 8-min test. Data are averaged across 19 subjects and three tests per condition. (From Lechner-Steinleitner, 1978. Reprinted by permission from *Psychological Research*, 1978, *40*, 70.)

(Lechner-Steinleitner & Schöne, 1978; Schöne & Lechner-Steinleitner, 1978; Lechner-Steinleitner & Schöne, 1980). Wenn eine Versuchsperson nach einer längerdauernden Rechtsneigung in die aufrechte Stellung zurückgedreht wird, glaubt sie bereits aufrecht zu stehen, wenn sie in Wirklichkeit noch 10°–15° nach rechts geneigt ist. Wird sie dann in die objektive Lotrechte weitergedreht, so nimmt sie eine Linksneigung wahr und verstellt die Leuchtlinie nach rechts. Dieses Hysteresisphänomen kann man in allen Stellungen beobachten. Es ist umso stärker, je länger die Versuchsperson in der Vorneigung verbracht hat und klingt im Laufe der Versuchszeit ab, die Kurven nähern sich an (Fig. 14.3).

5. Der Zeitgang der auditiven subjektiven Vertikalen

Als Indikator für die wahrgenommene Lotrechte wurde eine Schallquelle verwendet, die im Bogen um die Versuchsperson herumgeführt und nach ihren

FIG. 14.3. Subjective vertical (ß) in end-tilt positions of 0° (two lower curves), 60° (third curve from below) and 120° (upper curve) as a function of time (= Neigungszeit). The end-tilts (= Neigg.) were preceded by pre-tilt positions (= Vorngg.). These were: for 0° of end-tilt, 30° left and right (lowest curve) and 60° left and right (second curve from below); for 60° of end-tilt, 30° and 90°, and for 120° of end-tilt, 90° and 150°. The time of pre-tilt was either 1 min (left curves) or 8 min (right curves). The dashed curves refer to pre-tilt left of end-tilt (0°) or smaller than end-tilt (60°, 120°), the dotted curves to pre-tilt right of end-tilt (0°) or larger than end-tilt (60°, 120°). Curves are averaged across four subjects (0°/30° left and right), six subjects (0°/60° left and right; 60°/30° and 90°) or five subjects (120°/90° and 150°) and three 2-min tests per condition. (From Lechner-Steinleitner & Schöne, 1978. Reprinted by permission from "Hysteresis in orientation to the vertical [the effect of time of preceding tilt on the subjective vertical]" in *Vestibular mechanism in health and disease*, J. D. Hood, Ed. Copyright 1978 by Academic Press Inc., London, Ltd.)

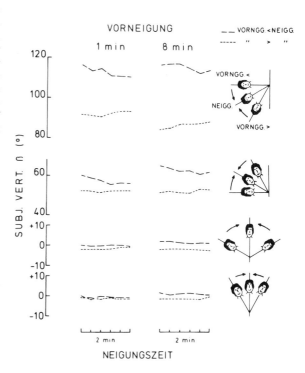

Anweisungen in eine Position gebracht wurde, die sie als senkrecht über ihrem Kopf befindlich wahrnahm (Lechner-Steinleitner, Schöne, & Steinleitner, 1981). Neben ähnlichen Abweichungen von der objektiven Vertikalen, wie sie kennzeichnend für die visuelle subjektive Vertikale sind, zeigte sich auch hierbei derselbe Zeitverlauf (Fig. 14.4).

B. Die Veränderung der subjektiven Vertikalen in der Zeit bei Unterwasserversuchen

Unter Wasser wird im Gegensatz zu vergleichbaren Versuchen im Trockenen eine der Informationsquellen über die Stellung des Körpers im Raum, nämlich die Meldung aus den Somatorezeptoren, abgeschwächt. Dadurch sollte auch die Wechselwirkung von Statolithen- und Somatorezeptorensystem beeinflußt werden. Eine in einem Wasserbassin aufgebaute Versuchsanordnung erlaubte es,

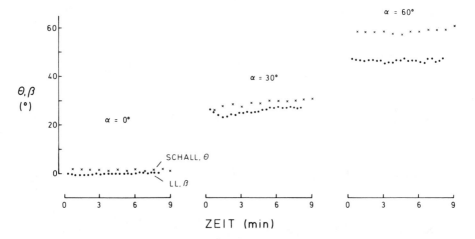

FIG. 14.4. Time course of the auditory subjective vertical (Schall, θ) and the visual subjective vertical (LL, ß) measured at three different side tilts (α). Visual subjective vertical: 19 subjects, three 8-min tests per condition; auditory subjective vertical: 10 subjects, four 9-min tests per condition. (From Lechner-Steinleitner, Schöne & Steinleitner, 1981. Reprinted by permission from *Acta Otolaryngolica*, 1981, *92*, 73.)

bei einer Kopfstellung von 0° den *Einfluß der relativen Rumpflagen* (Winkel Kopf zu Rumpf 0°, 45° zur linken und 45° zur rechten Seite) auf Größe und Zeitverlauf der subjektiven Vertikalen auch unter Wasser zu untersuchen (Schöne & Udo de Haes, 1967 unpubl.). Die Ergebnisse zeigten eine deutliche Abschwächung der im Trockenversuch gefundenen zeitlichen Veränderung des Einstellwinkels in den ersten zwei Minuten.

Eine andere experimentelle Serie unter Wasser untersuchte den *Hysteresiseffekt* in einem Neigungsbereich von 0° bis 180°. Sie ergab, daß dieser im Vergleich zum Trockenversuch in den Stellungen bis 90° etwas kleiner, über 90° jedoch größer ist (Lechner-Steinleitner & Schöne, 1980).

Der *Streifenfeldeffekt* ist unter Wasser für die Körperlagen von 90° bis 180° größer als an Land, nimmt aber im Laufe der zweiminütigen Versuchsdauer kaum mehr zu (Lechner-Steinleitner & Schöne, 1980).

DISKUSSION

Bei den Kopf-gegen-Rumpf-Drehungsversuchen (A 1) fanden sich trotz gleicher Stellung des Kopfes im Raum bei den verschiedenen Rumpflagen unterschiedliche Einstellwinkel, besonders in den Lagebereichen jenseits von 90°. Diese Unterschiede in der Wahrnehmung der Vertikalen wurden auf die Auswertung der Rumpflagemeldung zurückgeführt und ihr zeitliches Abklingen als

Adaptation der entsprechenden Rumpfrezeptoren gedeutet. Diese Interpretation wurde durch Unterwasserversuche (B) gestützt: in der 0°-Stellung des Kopfes ist der Anfangsunterschied zwischen Rumpf-links- und Rumpf-rechts-Stellung stark abgeschwächt. Verhaltens- und elektrophysiologische Experimente (Lowenstein & Roberts, 1949; v. Holst, 1950) legten die Annahme nahe, daß der Statolithenapparat adaptationsfrei meldet. Daher wurde die bei Körperneigungen über 90° auftretende Verkleinerung des Einstellwinkels in der Zeit von Schöne und Udo de Haes (1968) erstmals mit der Zeitabhängigkeit des Somatorezeptoren-einflusses in Verbindung gebracht. Die Tatsache, daß sich Änderungen in der Zeit in Seitwärtsneigungen über 90° besonders ausgeprägt fanden, wurde darauf zurückgeführt, daß in diesen Stellungen der Einfluß der Statolithenorgane auf die subjektive Vertikale schwächer ist, dementsprechend die Wirksamkeit der Somatorezeptoren des Rumpfes zunimmt und deren Adaptation sich somit stärker auswirken kann.

Der Streifenfeldeffekt (A 3) vergrößert sich im Trockenversuch im Laufe der zweiminütigen Versuchsdauer besonders bei Körperneigungen über 90° in einem beträchtlichen Ausmaß, wogegen seine Zunahme im Unterwasserversuch gering ist. Die Tatsache, daß das Streifenfeld im Trockenversuch im Laufe des Experimentes immer wirksamer wird, kann eine Folge des in der Zeit geringer werdenden Einflusses des Somatorezeptoren-Systems sein. Unter Wasser ist die Wirkung der kutanen Mechanorezeptoren abgeschwächt, das konkurrierende visuelle Signal kann sich schon von Beginn an stärker durchsetzen, aber der Streifenfeldeffekt zeigt dann kaum mehr eine Zunahme in der Zeit.

Der Hysteresis der subjektiven Vertikalen vergleichbare Einflüsse der Vorneigung des Kopfes wurden als Nacheffekte beschrieben (Day & Wade, 1966; Wade, 1968). Nach einer längerandauernden Kopfneigung in die aufrechte Lage gebracht, wurde der Kopf als leicht in die Gegenrichtung gekippt empfunden. Ähnliche Befunde finden sich auch bei Clark und Graybiel (1964): die Versuchspersonen, die sich nach einer seitlichen Körperneigung von 2 Minuten selbst wieder in die aufrechte Lage zurückdrehen sollten, hielten an, noch ehe sie die Vertikale erreicht hatten. Dieses Verhalten war bei Labyrinthdefekten stärker ausgeprägt. Das stützt die Deutung, die Hysteresiseffekte der subjektiven Vertikalen und ihr Abklingen in der Zeit auf Anpassungsprozesse im Somatorezeptoren-System zurückzuführen (Lechner-Steinleitner & Schöne, 1978; Schöne & Lechner-Steinleitner, 1978). Die Hypothese beruht auf der Annahme, daß bereits während der Vorneigung ein Teil der lageanzeigenden Somatorezeptoren adaptiert und beim Weiterdrehen in eine neue Stellung daher nur mehr abgeschwächt meldet. Die frisch gereizten (also noch nicht adaptierten) Rezeptorengruppen bewirken, daß die Positionssignale eine schon weiter fortgeschrittene Neigung anzeigen, als von der Versuchsperson wirklich erreicht wird. Von einer Körperlinksneigung auf 0° gedreht, dominieren die neu gereizten Somatorezeptoren der rechten Körperseite, da die der linken bereits durch die Vorneigung adaptiert sind. Das Somatorezeptoren-System als Ganzes zeigt daher in 0° eine Rechtsneigung an. Dieser Hysteresiseffekt wird im Laufe der Versuchszeit durch Adaptation der neu beteiligten Somatorezeptoren abgeschwächt (A 4).

Da das Hysteresisphänomen im Unterwasserversuch (B) nicht in der erwarteten Weise abgeschwächt wurde, kann nicht ausgeschlossen werden, daß auch Anpassungsvorgänge im Bereich des Statolithenapparates zu den Ergebnissen der Zeituntersuchungen beigetragen haben. Dessen periphere Neurone zeigen phasisch-tonische Charakteristika, d.h. man mißt bis zu 30 Sekunden eine anfängliche Zunahme der Frequenz, gefolgt von einer stetigen Entladungsrate, solange das Tier in der Stellung gehalten wird (Lowenstein & Roberts, 1949), beziehungsweise während der gesamten Dauer der Linearbeschleunigung in der Zentrifuge (Fernandez & Goldberg, 1976). Da auch die vestibulären Neurone zweiter Ordnung nicht adaptieren (Adrian, 1943; Fujita, Rosenberg, & Segundo, 1968; Schoen, 1957), scheidet höchstwahrscheinlich das periphere vestibuläre System als Ursache für die Zeitabhängigkeit der subjektiven Vertikalen aus. Eine Schwellenerhöhung bei der Wahrnehmung der Eigenbewegung nach längerandauerndem Hin- und Herschwingen in einer Parallelschaukel wurde als Hinweis dafür angesehen, daß auch die Statolithenorgane als Quelle der Lagesignale ermüden (Parker, Gulledge, Tubbs, & Littlefield, 1978; Parker, Wood, Gulledge, & Goodrich, 1979). Eine Beteiligung der Somatorezeptoren war aber dabei nicht völlig auszuschließen. Sollte wirklich der Statolithenapparat an der Veränderung der subjektiven Vertikalen in der Zeit mitwirken, so sind eher zentrale Mechanismen daran beteiligt. Man müßte Anpassungsvorgänge annehmen, ähnlich denen, die unter der Bezeichnung ''habituation'' der vermutlich zentralen Gewöhnung an Bogengangsreize zugrundegelegt worden sind (Collins, 1974, S. 369–383).

Die Vermutung, daß die zeitlichen Veränderungen der subjektiven Vertikalen mit einem nachlassenden Empfinden der Lage des Körpers im Raum in einem direkten Zusammenhang stehen, wurde immer wieder durch verbale Aussagen der Versuchspersonen bestätigt: besonders in Stellungen über 90° wurden sie nach 1 bis 3 Minuten unsicher über ihre Orientierung im Raum. Das ging in manchen Fällen einher mit einem plötzlichen Abfall des Einstellwinkels um 50° bis 100° (Steinleitner, 1975). Ein anderer Hinweis darauf, daß die Adaptation der Somatorezeptoren Veränderungen der subjektiven Vertikalen in der Zeit verursacht, liegt in folgender Beobachtung. Spannt eine Versuchsperson in 120° Seitenlage nach 3 bis 4 Minuten Versuchszeit vor Einstellen der Leuchtlinie kurz die Muskeln an, sodaß der Körper gegen die Befestigungen und die Auflagefläche gedrückt wird und die Versuchsperson dadurch ''frische'' Information aus dem Somatorezeptoren-System erhält, so wird das Absinken der Werte gestoppt. Der Einstellwinkel steigt um 20° bis 30° nach oben, fällt aber von dort bei weiteren Einstellungen wieder ab (Lechner-Steinleitner, unpubl.).

Unterschiedliche Seitwärtslagen werden in den oben beschriebenen Versuchsanordnungen von den kutanen Mechanorezeptoren angezeigt, von denen wiederum nur die Pinkus-Iggo-Rezeptoren und die Merkelzellen in den Epithelzapfen der Epidermis in einem für die Fragestellung bedeutsamen Zeitraum adaptieren. Diese Intensitätsdetektoren, die Stärke, Eindruckstiefe und Dauer eines mechanischen Hautreizes messen, adaptieren von allen Mechanorezeptoren der Haut am langsamsten. Die Meissner-Körperchen, Geschwindigkeitsdetektoren, deren Impulsrate von der Eindrucksgeschwindigkeit abhängig ist, adaptieren bereits nach 50 bis 500 Millisekunden, noch schneller die Pacini-Körperchen, deren adäquater Reiz die Beschleunigung der Hautverschiebung ist (Andres & v. Düring, 1973, S. 3–28). Die sensorischen Endungen in den Ligamenten der Wirbeltiergelenke, Rezeptoren vom Golgi-Typ, adaptieren ebenfalls langsam und können, unbeeinflußt von Spannungsänderungen in den Muskeln, exakt die Stellung des Gelenkes anzeigen (Skoglund, 1973, S. 111–136). Diese Rezeptoren in den Gelenken werden zwar bei stehender und liegender Ausgangsstellung sowie bei den Kopf-zu-Rumpf-Drehversuchen unterschiedlich gereizt, liefern aber über einen Bereich von 0° bis 360° Seitwärtsneigung und auch unter Wasser mehr oder minder gleichbleibende Werte.

Die Annahme, daß diese zeitlichen Änderungen auf eine Veränderung im Informationsfluß aus den Somatorezeptoren zurückzuführen sei, kann auch zum Verständnis der Befunde über den zeitabhängigen Anstieg (bei Seitwärtsneigungen bis ungefähr 70°) beziehungsweise Abfall des Einstellwinkels (bei Seitwärtsneigungen über 80°) beitragen (A 2). Durch diesen Anstieg und Abfall nähern sich die Meßwerte den theoretischen, aus der alleinigen Wirkung der Statolithenorgane errechneten Werten an (Steinleitner, 1975; Lechner-Steinleitner, 1978). Es wäre denkbar, daß die Somatorezeptoren bei Körperneigungen von 0° bis etwa 70° kleinere Neigungswinkel anzeigen als der Statolithenapparat und daß der Einstellwinkel mit der Adaptation der Somatorezeptoren auf ein der Scherung proportionales Niveau ansteigt. Bei Seitwärtsneigungen größer 80° würden die Somatorezeptoren zu Beginn des Versuches größere Winkel anzeigen als die Statorezeptoren. Durch Adaptation der Somatorezeptoren würde der Einstellwinkel mit der Zeit kleiner werden und sich wiederum Werten nähern, die durch die alleinige Meldung der Statolithen zustande kämen. Die Meßwerte bei 70° und 80° Seitwärtsneigung, die keine nennenswerte Veränderung in der Zeit aufweisen, würden eine Versuchssituation aufzeigen, in der Statolitheninformation und Somatorezeptorenmeldung übereinstimmen. Diese Hypothese würde auch erklären, warum bei den unterschiedlichen Versuchsbedingungen die Richtung des Zeitverlaufes der subjektiven Vertikalen vor allem von der Größe der Seitwärtsneigung abhängt.

ACKNOWLEDGMENTS

Die in diesem Artikel beschriebenen Experimente wurden teils am Max-Planck-Institut für Verhaltensphysiologie, Seewiesen, teils im Psychologischen Institut der Universität Innsbruck durchgeführt. Ich danke Herrn Prof. Dr. H. Schöne, MPIV Seewiesen, für die

Durchsicht des Manuskriptes und für die Zusammenarbeit der letzten acht Jahre und Herrn Prof. Dr. Ivo Kohler für das Interesse, das er meiner Arbeit immer entgegengebracht hat, und für die Überlassung des Versuchsraumes. Danken möchte ich auch der Max-Planck-Gesellschaft für die Unterstützung der Versuchsprojekte und Frau Renate Alton für das Anfertigen der Zeichnungen.

REFERENCES

Adrian, E. D. Discharges from the vestibular receptors in the cat. *Journal of Physiology*, 1943, *101*, 389–407.

Andres, K. H., & von Düring, M. Morphology of cutaneous receptors. In A. Iggo (Ed.), *Handbook of sensory physiology* (Vol. 2), *Somatosensory system*. Berlin, Heidelberg, New York: Springer-Verlag, 1973.

Bischof, N., & Scheerer, E. Systemanalyse der optisch-vestibulären Interaktion bei der Wahrnehmung der Vertikalen. *Psychologische Forschung*, 1970, *34*, 99–181.

Brown, J. L. Orientation to the vertical during water immersion. *Aerospace Medicine*, 1961, *32*, 209–217.

Clark, B., & Graybiel, A. Perception of the postural vertical following prolonged bodily tilt in normals and subjects with labyrinthine defects. *Acta Oto-laryngologica*, 1964, *58*, 143–148.

Collins, E. Habituation of vestibular responses and visual stimulation. In H. H. Kornhuber (Ed.), *Handbook of sensory physiology* (Vol. VI/2), *Vestibular system*. Berlin, Heidelberg, New York: Springer-Verlag, 1974.

Correia, M. J., Hixson, W. C., & Niven, J. I. *Otolith shear and the visual perception of force direction: discrepancies and a proposed solution* (Nami-951. NASA Order R-93). Pensacola, Fla.: Naval Aerospace Medical Institute, 1965.

Day, R. H., & Wade, N. J. Visual spatial after-effect from prolonged head tilt. *Science* 1966, *154*, 1201–1202.

Dichgans, J., Brandt, Th., & Held, R. The role of vision in gravitational orientation. *Fortschritte der Zoologie*, 1975, *23*, 255–263.

Fernandez, C., & Goldberg, J. M. Physiology of peripheral neurons innervating otolith organs of the squirrel monkey. I. Response to static tilts and to long-duration centrifugal force. *Journal of Neurophysiology*, 1976, *39*, 970–984.

Fujita, Y., Rosenberg, J., & Segundo, J. P. Activity of cells in the lateral vestibular nucleus as a function of head position. *Journal of Physiology*, 1968, *196*, 1–18.

Graybiel, A., & Clark, B. Perception of the horizontal or vertical with head upright, on the side, and inverted under static conditions, and during exposure to centripetal force. *Aerospace Medicine*, 1962, *33*, 147–155.

Guedry, F. E. Psychophysics of vestibular sensation. In H. H. Kornhuber (Ed.), *Handbook of sensory physiology* (Vol. VI/2), *Vestibular system*. Berlin, Heidelberg, New York: Springer-Verlag, 1974.

Holst, E. von Die Arbeitsweise des Statolithenorganes bei Fischen. *Zeitschrift für vergleichende Physiologie*, 1950, *32*, 60–120.

Kleint, H. Versuche über die Wahrnehmung. *Zeitschrift für Psychologie*, 1936, *138*, 1–34.

Lechner-Steinleitner, S. Interaction of labyrinthine and somatoreceptor inputs as determinants of the subjective vertical. *Psychological Research*, 1978, *40*, 65–76.

Lechner-Steinleitner, S., & Schöne, H. Hysterisis in orientation to the vertical (the effect of time of preceding tilt on the subjective vertical). In J. D. Hood (Ed.), *Vestibular mechanism in health and disease*. London, New York: Academic Press, 1978.

Lechner-Steinleitner, S., & Schöne, H. The subjective vertical under "dry" and "wet" conditions at clockwise and counterclockwise changed positions and the effect of a parallel-lined background field. *Psychological Research*, 1980, *41*, 305–317.

Lechner-Steinleitner, S., Schöne, H., & Steinleitner, A. The auditory subjective vertical as a function of body tilt. *Acta Oto-laryngologica*, 1981, *92*, 71–74.

Lechner-Steinleitner, S., Schöne, H., & Wade, N. J. Perception of the visual vertical: Utricular and somatosensory contributions. *Psychological Research*, 1979, *40*, 407–414.

Lowenstein, O., & Roberts, T. D. M. The equilibrium function of the otolith organs of the thornback ray (Raja clavata). *Journal of Physiology*, 1949, *110*, 392–415.

Nyborg, H. Light intensity and perception of the vertical. *Scandinavian Journal of Psychology*, 1972, *13*, 314–326.

Parker, D. E., Gulledge, W. L., Tubbs, R. L., & Littlefield, V. M. A temporary threshold shift for self motion detection following sustained, oscillating linear acceleration. *Perception & Psychophysics*, 1978, *23*, 461–467.

Parker, D. E., Wood, D. L., Gulledge, W. L., & Goodrich, R. L. Self-motion magnitude estimation during linear oscillation: Changes with head orientation and following fatigue. *Aviation, Space and Environmental Medicine*, 1979, *11*, 1112–1121.

Quix, F. H., & Eijsvogel, M. H. Experimente über die Funktion des Otolithenapparates beim Menschen. *Zeitschrift der Hals-Nasen-Ohren-Heilkunde*, 1929, *23*, 68–96.

Schoen, L. Mikroableitungen einzelner zentraler Vestibularisneurone von Knochenfischen bei Statolithenreizen. *Zeitschrift für vergleichende Physiologie*, 1957, *39*, 399–417.

Schöne, H. Über den Einfluß der Schwerkraft auf die Augenrollung und die Wahrnehmung der Lage im Raum. *Zeitschrift für vergleichende Physiologie*, 1962, *46*, 57–87.

Schöne, H. The "weight" of the gravity organ's signal in the control of perceptual and reflex type orientation at different body positions. *Fortschritte der Zoologie*, 1975, *23*, 274–283.

Schöne, H., & Lechner-Steinleitner, S. The effect of preceding tilt on the perceived vertical. *Acta Oto-laryngologica*, 1978, *85*, 68–73.

Schöne, H., & Udo de Haes, H. *Das Zeitverhalten der subjektiven Vertikalen; ein Versuch zur Differenzierung zwischen Kopf-, Hals- und Rumpfeinflüssen.* Unveröffentl. Bericht MPIV Seewiesen, 1967.

Schöne, H., & Udo de Haes, H. Perception of gravity vertical as a function of head and trunk position. *Zeitschrift für vergleichende Physiologie*, 1968, *60*, 440–444.

Schöne, H., & Udo de Haes, H. *Space orientation in humans with special reference to the interaction of vestibular, somaesthetic and visual inputs.* Biokybernetik III, Material. 2. Internationales Symposium für Biokybernetik, Fischer Jena, 1971, 172–191.

Skoglund, S. Joint receptors and kinesthesis. In A. Iggo (Ed.), *Handbook of sensory physiology.* (Vol. 2), *Somatosensory system.* Berlin, Heidelberg, New York: Springer Verlag, 1973.

Steinleitner, S. *Untersuchungen zum Einfluß der Somatorezeptoren auf die Wahrnehmung der Vertikalen im Dunkelraum.* Dissertation, Universität Innsbruck, 1975.

Wade, N. J. Visual orientation during and after lateral head, body and trunk tilt. *Perception & Psychophysics*, 1968, *3*, 215–219.

Wade, N. J. The effect of stimulus line variation on visual orientation with head upright and tilted. *Australian Journal of Psychology*, 1969, *21*, 177–185

Young, L. R., Oman, C. M., & Dichgans, J. M. Influence of head orientation on visually induced pitch and roll sensation. *Aviation, Space and Environmental Medicine*, 1975, *3*, 264–268.

To supplement Chapters 14 and 15, we present here a picture that shows Professor Kohler seemingly defying gravity. In this picture, the Professor is "sitting" on a chair fastened to the ceiling of his laboratory while his dog is looking up to him in excitement. Even more bewildered is the student who after taking off his inverting goggles seems to wonder whether to believe his own eyes. This is just one example of Professor Kohler's indomitable spirit that prompted him to try his laboratory findings in everyday life: while skiing, motorcycling, swimming, even fencing.

The Editors

15 Körperlageregelung des Menschen bei elektrischer Reizung des Vestibularsystems

A. Hajos
W. Kirchner
Fachbereich Psychologie
der Justus Liebig Universität
Gießen, West Germany

ABSTRACT

Body control has been studied in two experiments. In both experiments electrical current (100–500 μA) was applied as system input; body position relating orientation to gravity was considered as the dependent variable (system output).

In the first experiment step signals (100–350 μA, 100–700 mS) were given. The unit step response was defined.

In the second experiment a sinusoidal current was applied. On the basis of the registrated data a linear approximation of control systems and the time constant of the transfer function were defined.

EINLEITUNG

Die Wirkung des elektrischen Stromes auf die verschiedenen Sinnessysteme ist mindestens seit J. Müller (1826) bekannt. Kohler beschreibt einen eindrucksvollen Demonstrationsversuch (1968, pp. 57–114), bei dem die Wirkung des elektrischen Stromes auf die Körperlageregelung nachgewiesen werden kann. Zu meiner Studienzeit pflegte Kohler diesen Demonstrationsversuch, der nicht nur in prägnanter Weise dem Hörer Kenntnisse über den Lagesinn vermittelte, sondern in der Regel auch allgemeine Erheiterung hervorrief, in mehreren Varianten durchzuführen.

Der Versuchsperson wurden zwei Wäscheklammern, die mit Zellstoff überzogen und mit Kochsalzlösung getränkt waren, an die Ohrläppchen geklemmt. Diese "Elektroden" wurden dann an ein "Zaubergerät" angeschlossen, das in einer Zigarrenkiste (ein damals beliebtes Experimentiergehäuse) verborgen war. In dieser Kiste befand sich eine Batterie, ein regelbarer Vorwiderstand, der in Serie zur Vp geschaltet war, und ein Schalter. Mit dem Gerät war es möglich, die Vp über die Ohrläppchenstrecke mit unterschiedlichen Stromstärken und vorwählbarer Strom-Flußrichtung zu reizen. Um labil zu stehen, sollte die Vp die Füße hintereinander stellen. Zuerst wurde bei geöffneten Augen ermittelt, welche Stromstärken von der Vp noch akzeptiert wurden. Dann wurde die Vp aufgefordert, ihre Augen zu schließen und ruhig zu stehen. Nach Einschalten des Stromes wurde die seitliche Körperlageabweichung deutlich, was Kohler natürlich vorher den Hörern signalisierte. Auch bei vorangehender Warnung der Vp: "Achtung! Links" wich die Vp deutlich nach links ab, gelegentlich war sogar ein Seitenschritt zur Aufrechterhaltung der Körperposition notwendig.

Eine Variante dieser Demonstration destand darin, der Vp eine links-rechts-Umkehrbrille aufzusetzen. So lange die Vp unter der Brille die Augen geschlossen hielt, konnte sie ihre Standposition einigermaßen kontrollieren; öffnete die Vp jedoch die Augen, so war deutlich, daß die Lageregelung des Körpers auch ohne elektrische Reizung erheblichen Störungen unterliegt: die retinale Information war auf das Gesamtsystem der Körperlageregelung durch die Umkehrbrille positiv rückgekoppelt. Wurde nun die gemeinsame Wirkung, links-rechts Umkehrbrille und elektrische Reizung demonstriert, so erreichte die Erheiterung ihren Höhepunkt: unter diesen kombinierten Bedingungen "bestand" keine Vp die Prüfung. Kohler ließ schließlich die Vp mit geschlossenen Augen im Hörsaal herumgehen und steuerte die Gehrichtung der Vp durch den elektrischen Strom.

Die im folgenden beschriebenen Experimente zur Körperlageregelung wurden in den Jahren 1970 bis 1974 durchgeführt. Mit Ausnahme eines Teilergebnisses (Sattel, 1976) blieben sie bisher unveröffentlicht. Ein Teil der Ergebnisse wurde in den Diplomarbeiten der Herren Heuser (1974). Zebralla (1974) und Rau (1975) beschrieben. Zur Durchführung dieser Experimente gab die eben beschriebene Demonstration von Kohler den Anstoß, und es gibt keinen geeigneteren Anlaß als diese Festschrift, die Experimente zusammenfassend zu beschreiben. Neben einigen Teil- bzw. Zusatzfragen, wie z.B. nach der Konditionierbarkeit der Körperlagereaktion, oder nach der Alkoholwirkung auf die Körperlagereaktion bei elektrischer Reizung, war es das Hauptanliegen dieser Experimente, die Kohlersche Demonstration in eine experimentelle Anordnung zu zwingen und den Zusammenhang zwischen der verabreichten elektrischen Stromstärke und der Körperlagereaktion quantitativ zu beschreiben.

FRAGESTELLUNG UND EINIGE PROBLEME DER METHODE

Die Fragestellung der Experimente ergibt sich aus einer Systemdefinition. Der elektrische Strom als Funktion der Zeit $I(t)$ und die in lateraler Richtung registrierte Körperlage $K(t)$ werden als Systemumfang definiert. $I(t)$ ist Eingang, $K(t)$ ist Ausgang des Systems. Die Frage ist: durch welche Struktur bzw. Transformationsregel ist der Zusammenhang zwischen $I(t)$ und $K(t)$ beschreibbar? Die Aufgabe besteht also darin, eine Übertragungsfunktion $F(I,K)$ möglichst einfacher Form quantitativ zu beschreiben.

Natürliche Reize für das System der Körperlageregelung sind IST-Abweichungen der Körperlage von einem "willentlichen" Soll-Wert. Für die Experimente wurde per Instruktion von den Vpn eine aufrechte, gerade Körperhaltung mit "Kopf geradeaus" gefordert. Die Ist-Abweichung $K(t)$ kann mit einfachen Mitteln registriert werden, ihre Ursachen bedürfen jedoch einer zusätzlichen Analyse, weil in $K(t)$ die Einflüsse verschiedener Variablen enthalten sein können, z.b. vestibulärer, visueller oder propriozeptiver Art. Zur Ausschaltung visueller Informationen trugen die Vpn bei den Experimenten (mit Ausnahme einer Serie, siehe später) eine Abschlußbrille und sollten zusätzlich die Augenlider schließen.

Die Variable $K(t)$ kann auch ohne elektrische Reizung registriert und einer Analyse unterworfen werden (Dichgans & Brandt, 1978; dort weitere Literatur). Man transformiert $K(t)$ nach Fourier und betrachtet die in der Funktion enthaltenen Anteile verschiedener Harmonischen, bzw. den Verlauf des Autoleistungsspektrums. Die Experimente können unter verschiedenen Bedingungen, z.B. bei geschlossenen oder geöffneten Augen, bei bewegtem optischem Muster, bei kinästhetischer Vorreizung usw. durchgeführt werden. Vergleicht man die jeweiligen Autoleistungsspektren, so können Aussagen über das Gesamtsystem der Körperlageregelung formuliert werden. Man kann spektrale Komponenten, oder zumindest deren Amplitudengewichte visuellen, propriozeptiven und vestibulären Eingangskanälen zuordnen.

Eine Ist-Abweichung $K(t)$ von der aufrechten Körperlage erreicht man mit verschiedenen Methoden. Beliebt sind bewegte optische Muster. Die nächstliegende physikalistische Maßnahme bestünde darin, den Boden unter der Vp plötzlich oder allmählich, z.B. nach sinusförmigem Verlauf, zu kippen. $K(t)$ würde einen für die Kippung charakteristischen Zeitverlauf annehmen und könnte dann als Funktion der Bodenbewegung betrachtet werden. In einem solchen Fall wirken die stützmotorischen Reflexe als ein Kaskadenregelsystem der Kippung entgegen, sofern das Vestibularsystem intakt ist (Kornhuber, 1974). Der Einfluß der Kippung wird durch die stützmotorischen Reflexe größtenteils behoben, sodaß in $K(t)$ nur eine Restgröße, als Fehler der stützmotorischen Reflexe, angezeigt wird. Will man den Einfluß des Vestibularsystems untersuchen, dann muß eine Reizgröße gesucht werden, die primär auf das Vestibularsystem wirkt, günstigenfalls sogar auf das periphere Rezeptorsystem, und zwar möglicherweise allein auf dieses.

Inwiefern der elektrische Strom diese Bedingungen erfüllt, ist zunächst eine Frage. Vieles spricht dafür, daß eine schwache elektrische Reizung, an den Ohrläppchen ansetzend, nur peripher wirkt, obwohl eine zentrale Wirkung kaum mit Sicherheit auszuschließen ist. Auch ist es zunächst eine Frage, ob der elektrische Strom auf die Bogengänge, auf die Maculaorgane oder auf beide bzw. auf die neuronalen Strukturen dieser Organe wirkt. Dohlmann (1929) konnte zeigen, daß die entsprechende Wirkung des elektrischen Stromes ausbleibt, wenn die Vestibularganglien nicht intakt sind. Ebenso bleibt eine Wirkung aus, wenn der Vestibularnerv durchtrennt ist (Blonder & Davis, 1936; Devito, Brusa & Arduini, 1955; Spiegel & Scala, 1943.) Die Ergebnisse von Jung, Kornhuber und Da Fonseca (1963) zeigen, daß bei Katzen u.a. stromrichtungsspezifische Erregungen im Vestibularcortex bei elektrischer Reizung des peripheren Vestibularorgans registriert werden können. Die stromrichtungsspezifische Antwort corticaler Neurone war bei einer Stromstärke von 100 Mikroampere peripherer Reizung eindeutig. Die Ergebnisse schließen eine diffuse Stromwirkung auf corticale Neurone bei obiger Reizstärke aus. Erst bei einer Stromstärke um 1 Milliampere werden die neuronalen Antworten unspezifisch für die Stromrichtung.

Es ist bewiesen, daß Menschen bei elektrischer Reizung an den Ohrläppchen zur Anode hin schwanken. Ein Gegenbeispiel ist nicht bekannt und trat auch bei unseren Experimenten nicht auf. Diese Tatsache, die noch zu beschreibende spezifische Wirkung des elektrischen Stromes auf die Körperlage, sowie die neurophysiologischen Ergebnisse mögen die Annahme rechtfertigen, daß der elektrische Strom nicht einen diffusen, sondern einen peripher-spezifischen Reizeinfluß ausübt.

Schon in der frühen Psychophysik wurde der elektrische Strom als allgemeiner Reiz bezeichnet, im Gegensatz zu spezifischen, den Sinnesorganen adäquaten Reizen. Dennoch stellt der elektrische Reiz einen unnatürlichen Eingriff dar. Im Falle der Vestibularreizung mit elektrischem Strom gesellt sich zu der Unnatürlichkeit ein Folgeproblem. Reizt man das Auge, das Ohr, die Zunge oder die Haut mit elektrischen Strömen, so stellen sich Sinneserlebnisse ein, die sich gewöhnlich auch bei Reizung dieser Organe mit Licht, Schall, bestimmten chemischen Stoffen, mechanischer Vibration usw. einstellen (Monjé, 1936; Purkinje, 1825; Schwarz, 1940 u.a.). Ein Zweifel daran, daß der elektrische Strom in diesen Fällen spezifisch wirkt, ist kaum aufrecht zu erhalten, sich andernfalls bei Reizung des Auges auch Klänge, Geruch, Geschmack usw. einstellen müßten. Dies ist nur bei hohen Stromstärken der Fall. Das Problem der elektrischen Reizung des Vestibularsystems besteht nun darin, daß es hier eine entsprechende Sinnesqualität, wie Farben, Formen, Klänge usw. nicht gibt. Der Erlebnisbereich möge mit den Worten eines zwölfjährigen Jungen (siehe die Experimente mit Sinusreizung weiter unten) beschrieben werden: ''Mir wird schwindlig, es tanzt mich so.'' Im übrigen sind die Erlebnisberichte der Vpn kläglich, es wird eine ''Unsicherheit,'' ''Falltendenz'' des Stehens aus ''unerklärlichen Gründen'' empfunden. Von einer Drehbewegung oder einer empfundenen Beschleunigung usw. berichtete keine der Vpn, auch nicht von Licht, Geräuschen o.ä.. Ganz offensichtlich bewirkt die elektrische Reizung an der Ohrläppchenstrecke eine Reizung des Sensors, welcher die Schwerkraftrichtung für die Soll-Lage des Körpers meldet. Sie wirkt auf eine der Stützmotorik übergeordnete Reglerinstanz. Sattel (1976) fand bei elektrischer Reizung mit gleicher Methode keinen Unterschied der $K(t)$, wenn er die Standposition der Vpn von voreinander gestellten Füßen bis zur breitesten, noch natürlichen Stemmposition variierte.

Ob nun der elektrische Strom allein an den Rezeptoren, an den Vestibularganglien oder an anderen neuronalen Strukturen wirkt, ist eine anatomisch-physiologisch wichtige Frage, für die vorliegende Untersuchung ist die spezifische Wirkung der Beeinflussung der Soll-Lage durch elektrischen Strom von Interesse. Zusätzlich wäre es eine Überlegung wert, ob und inwiefern der elektrische Strom unnatürlicher ist als eine kalorische Reizung, eine Reizung durch Rotationsmuster, Kippaggregate und sonstige Beschleunigungsgeräte.

EXPERIMENT I

Vpn vertragen bei gut leitenden Elektroden ohne besonderen Schmerz Ströme bis zu 500 μA und noch darüber. Wir wählten Stromstärken $I(t)$ im Bereich zwischen 100 und 350 μA. Durch den elektrischen Strom sollten Körperlagereaktionen induziert werden, die dem natürlichen Regelbereich des Systems entsprechen und bei denen eine periphere Wirkung (siehe vorher zitierte Experimente von Jung et al., pp. 207–240) noch annehmbar ist. Es wurden bei diesem Experiment rechteckförmige Stromreize verabreicht. Die Dauer des Stromflusses (τ) wurde in sieben Stufen variiert: von 100 ms in Intervallen von 100 ms bis 700 ms. Die Stromstärken wurden ebenfalls in sieben Stufen (122, 140, 149, 222, 245, 293, 350 μA) variiert. Dies ergab eine $7 \times 7 = 49$ Versuchsmatrix, bei Berücksichtigung der Stromflußrichtung (Anode rechts: Rechtsreizung, Anode links: Linksreizung) 98 Felder, die als Reizvolumen pro Vp verwendet wurden. Die genannten Stromstärken ergaben sich durch drei Vorwiderstände, die von einem Hewlett-Packard, DOS III-System geschaltet wurden. Die Reizrichtung wurde regelmäßig alterniert, Stromstärken und Reizdauer erfolgten nach Zufallsreihe, jedoch so, daß die Produktsummen I · t über den Versuch etwa ausgeglichen waren. Der Versuch dauerte rund eine Stunde. Die Reizungen erfolgten in einem Abstand von rund 25 Sekunden, während $K(t)$ über die Gesamtzeit mit einer Tastrate von 40 Messungen/Sekunde registriert wurde (1024 Meßwerte für 25 Sekunden).

Die $K(t)$ wurde wie folgt gemessen: Die Vp trug einen einer alten Ritterrüstung ähnlichen Brustpanzer aus Aluminium. In der Höhe des 3.-4. Brustwirbels wurde eine Schnur eingehängt, die, über ein Potentiometer gewickelt, zu einem Gewicht von 130 g führte. Die seitliche Abweichung des Brustmittelbereiches wurde durch die Schleifenspannung des Potentiometers linear auf eine Analogrechnerschaltung, von dieser auf einen 80 kHz-ADC übertragen und auf dem Plattenspeicher des Rechensystems abgespeichert. Die Linearität der

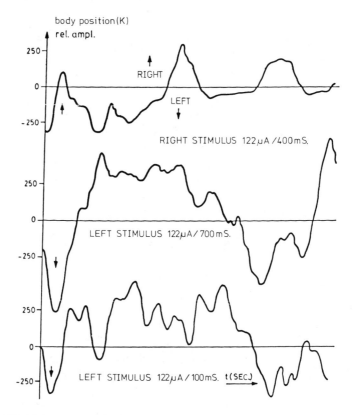

FIG. 15.1.   Course of the body position (K) during brief electrical stimulation.
Abscissa: time (25 sec.). Ordinate: body position relative to the gravitational
direction. Stimulus was applied at time zero. Upper curve: positive electrode right;
lower curves: positive left. Arrows indicate the polarity of the stimulus current.
The responses do not exceed (spontaneous) body sway.

Übertragung war besser als .5 Prozent und die Empfindlichkeit betrug rund
2 mV/0.1 Millimeter Körperauslenkung für einen Schwankungsbereich von
± 5 cm. Die mechanische Trägheit der Registrieranlage beschränkte den
übertragenen Frequenzbereich von $K(t)$ von 0 bis 12 Hz (siehe auch Tastrate).

An dem Versuch nahmen 20 Vpn im Alter zwischen 18 und 38 Jahren teil,
größtenteils Studierende, je zur Hälfte weiblich und männlich.

Die Analyse des Datenmaterials ergab, daß es keinen festen Nullpunkt von
$K(t)$ gibt. Die Vpn balancierten in einem Bereich von +10 mm, manchmal sogar
darüber. Es erscheint daher angebrachter von Körperschwankung statt von Körperlage zu sprechen. Die Daten mußten nun auf einen digital berechneten Nullpunkt bezogen werden. Abbildung 15.1 zeigt drei Reaktionen einer Vp,
stellvertretend für $N = 1960$ ähnliche. Aus dem Verlauf der $K(t)$-Funktionen

erkennt man, daß alle *K*-Funktionen kurz nach Applikation des Reizes eine Körperauslenkung in die Reizrichtung (Anode) zeigen. Ähnliche Änderungen entdeckt man jedoch auch an anderen Stellen der Funktionen, ohne daß dort ein elektrischer Reiz wirksam war, manche sind sogar, als spontane Regelabweichungen, wesentlich größer. Eine genaue Potentialform von $K(t)$, die die spontanen Schwankungen von den elektrisch bedingten trennt und nur letztere zeigt, kann durch eine Zeitmittelwertfunktion dargestellt werden.

Zunächst abstrahierten wir von den Parametern des Versuchs (Stromstärke, Reizdauer und Stromrichtung) und berechneten die Zeitmittelwerte, wobei die "Linksreaktionen" sinngemäß invertiert wurden. Abbildung 15.2 zeigt den Verlauf des Zeitmittelwertes ("Average") für 20 Vpn und je 98 Reaktionen für die Registrierdauer von 25 Sekunden ($N = 1960$, $M = 1024$).

An der Ordinate ist das relative Maß der Schleifenspannung des Potentiometers aufgetragen, dem Ordinatenbereich von 200 entspricht eine horizontale Körperlageabweichung vom Nullpunkt von ca. 2 cm.

Nach der Applikation des elektrischen Stromes erfolgt nach einer Totzeit von rd. ⅓ Sekunde eine Auslenkung zur Richtung der Anode. Eine maximale Aus-

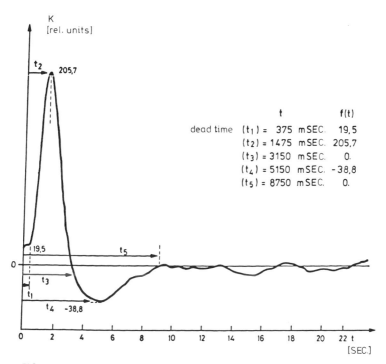

FIG. 15.2.   Time-average of a total of 1660 responses from 20 *S*s. Latency (dead time) is .3 to .4 sec. The time intervals t_i ($i = 1$–5) increases. Abscissa: time (sec.); Ordinate: body position (relative units).

lenkung wird erst 1.5 Sekunden nach Reizbeginn erreicht. Danach wird die Auslenkung geringer und schlägt etwa fünf Sekunden nach Reizbeginn in eine Untersteuerung um. Im weiteren ist der Verlauf der Funktion, bedingt durch den Anteil der spontanen Schwankungen kaum mehr erkennbar, er läßt sich aber als ein Auspendeln eines speziellen Pendels interpretieren. Die Amplitude ist (exponentiell) gedämpft, die Teilperioden verlängern sich linear. Dies ist ein Verlauf, den man bei einem Pendel erreicht, wenn außer einer Amplitudendämpfung zusätzlich die Pendelschnur linear verlängert wird. In diesem Sinne läßt sich von einer zusätzlichen Frequenzdämpfung sprechen. Dies erkennt man deutlich, wenn man die Teilzeiten, Totzeit, Maximum, Nulldurchgang, Minimum, Nulldurchgang als Funktion der Registrierzeit aufträgt. Der Offset von rund 2 mm zu Beginn der Funktion zeigt, daß in den 25 Sekunden die Reaktion entweder nicht voll abgeklungen ist, oder aber, daß es sich um ein System ohne vollständigen Nullausgleich handelt.

In weiteren Auswerteschritten wurde kontrolliert, ob im Laufe des Experimentes eine Änderung der Körperlagereaktion auf den elektrischen Strom erfolgt ist. Die Auswertung der ersten sieben Reaktionen, der 50. bis 56. und der letzten sieben Reaktionen, also von der 92. bis zur 98., ergab, über alle 20 Vpn, eine gute Übereinstimmung, womit Ermüdung, Habituation, Elektrodenpolarisation usw. ausgeschlossen werden konnten und Reaktionen aus den verschiedenen Abschnitten des Versuchs zusammengefaßt werden dürften.

Zur Kontrolle wurde die Stichprobe von 20 Vpn halbiert und der Gesamtverlauf des Zeitmittelwertes von je 10 Vpn korreliert. Die Korrelation betrug nur .72, was anzeigt, daß 10–15 Prozent der Varianz in den Zeitmittelwertkurven nicht durch den elektrischen Strom bedingt oder individuellen Ursprungs ist. Eine zusätzliche Analyse zeigte, daß die Totzeiten intraindividuell bei allen Reizbedingungen so gut wie konstant sind, interindividuell jedoch eine erhebliche Varianz zeigen. Dies spricht gegen die Berechnung und eine Interpretation der Form der Zeitmittelwerte aus den Daten verschiedener Vpn. Auf die Berechnung von Systemkennwerten wurde daher verzichtet. Die Korrelation der mittleren Reaktionen bei Links-und Rechtsreizung ergab bei den ersten 10 Vpn ein $r = -.987$ und bei den zweiten 10 Vpn ein $r = -.983$. Dies bestätigt die Interpretation der Totzeiten und zeigt zusätzlich, daß im System eine gute Symmetrie der Reaktionen bei Links-und Rechtsreizung gegeben ist. In dieser Interpretation fügen sich die praktisch identischen mittleren Maximalwerte (mit Vorzeichensymmetrie) der Links-und Rechtsreaktionen gut ein. Die Stromflußrichtung bestimmt die Richtung der Körperlagereaktion, beeinflußt aber nicht deren Ausmaß. Aus diesem Grund erschien uns möglich, die Minima und Maxima der Zeitmittelwerte als Funktion der Stromstärke und Reizdauer gemeinsam zu analysieren. Die Ergebnisse lassen erkennen, daß bei einer Reizdauer bis etwa 400 ms das Amplitudenmaximum der mittleren Reaktion eine lineare Funktion des Produktes aus Stromstärke und Reizdauer ist. Oberhalb von

500 ms Reizdauer sind die Maxima niedriger als es nach dem Stromstärke-Reizdauer-Produkt zu fordern wäre. Etwa bis 400 ms Reizdauer integriert das System über die Stromstärke mit guter Linearität, so daß Stromstärke und Reizdauer arbiträre Größen sind (analog dem Bloch' schen Gesetz im Bereich des Sehens).

EXPERIMENT II

Der Versuch unterschied sich von Versuch I darin, daß der elektrische Reiz nicht aus Stromstößen, sondern aus kontinuierlich andauernder, sinusförmiger Stromreizung bestand. Es wurde eine impedanzunabhängige Strompumpe (R_f-Zweig eines Operationsverstärkers als Vp-Strecke) verwendet, was einen spannungsgesteuerten Stromdurchfluß und damit sinusförmige Stromreizung erlaubte.

Dieser Versuch wurde zunächst mit 5 Vpn durchgeführt. Es schloß sich eine Kontrollserie (Rau, 1975) mit weiteren 5 Vpn an. Schließlich wurden noch 5 Kinder im Alter zwischen 11 und 15 Jahren untersucht.

In einem Vorversuch mit 2 Vpn wurden 12 verschiedene Reizamplituden zwischen 100 und 460 Mikroampere und fünf Frequenzen zwischen .1 und .7 Hz verwendet. Bei den einzelnen Frequenzen war die Reaktionsamplitude der Reizamplitude proportional, so daß eine Linearität des Übertragungsverhaltens im genannten Strom-Frequenzbereich angenommen werden konnte. Unterhalb .3 Hz zeigte sich bei den Amplituden der Reizantwort keine wesentliche Änderung, der kritische Frequenzbereich (Dämpfungsbereich) lag oberhalb .3 Hz. Daher wurde der Hauptversuch mit 14 verschiedenen Reizfrequenzen von .1 Hz bis 1.0 Hz und mit zwei Stromstärken, zur Kontrolle der Linearität, durchgeführt. Der Stromverlauf war sinusförmig und hatte bei den Amplitudenmaxima bzw. Minima 180 (-180) und 250 (-250) μA. Die verwendeten Frequenzen wurden in etwa logarithmischen Abständen gewählt.

Die vierzehn Frequenzen und beide Stromstärken wurden in zufälliger Reihenfolge appliziert mit bei 15–30 Sekunden Pause zwischen den Reizblöcken. Jeder der 28 Reizblöcke dauerte 24 Perioden lang. Der Rechner überlas die ersten vier Perioden. $K(t)$ wurde ab der 5. Periode registriert. Die Tastrate für $K(t)$, wie auch die Generierung der Sinusfunktion, die die Reizstromstärke steuerte, hielten wir proportional der Periodendauer, so daß pro Periode in allen Frequenzen stets 400 Meßwerte von $K(t)$ registriert wurden. Hieraus ergibt sich, daß die Daten in relativer Zeit organisiert waren. Die anderen Bedingungen entsprachen Experiment I: geschlossene Augen, voreinander gestellte Füße, Kopf geradeaus und aufrechte, gerade Körperhaltung.

Nach Durchführung der ersten Versuchsserie mit 5 Vpn standen uns pro Vp je 400 Meßwerte von $K(t)$ pro Periode, 20 Perioden pro Frequenz, 14 verschiedene

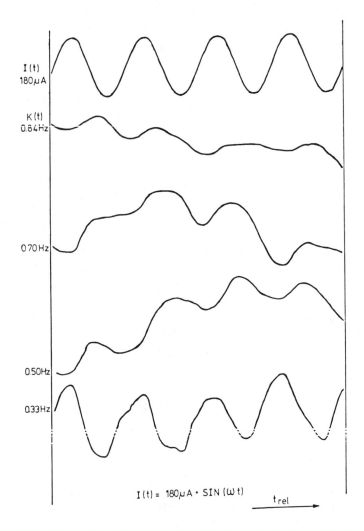

FIG. 15.3. Body position during sinusoidal electrical stimulation. Abscissa: time, related to period duration. Ordinate: current (upper curve) and body position (K) relative to the vertical (all other curves, relative units). The four lower curves are scaled at different current modulation frequencies and show that the relative amplitude of the response to electrical current decreases with increasing frequency.

Frequenzen bei 2 verschiedenen Amplituden zur Verfügung. Ziel der Auswertung war es, aus den $K(t)$- Funktionen zuverlässige Schätzungen für die Übertragungsfunktion zu erhalten.

Abbildung 15.3 zeigt zunächst ein Beispiel der registrierten $K(t)$-Funktionen bei 4 der 14 Frequenzen (Abszisse t-relativ, $T/400$ Sek.). In der oberen Reihe ist der Stromverlauf dargestellt. Aus dem Verlauf der $K(t)$-Funktionen ist ersichtlich, daß wir uns bei einer Reizstromstärke von 180 bis 250 μA an der Grenze der spontanen Körperschwankungen bewegten.

Im ersten Schritt der Datenreduktion wurden wiederum, wie bei Experiment I, spontane von elektrisch induzierten Körperschwankungen getrennt. Dazu wurde eine Perioden-Mittelwert-Funktion aus den 20 Perioden, getrennt für jede Vp, berechnet. Ein Beispiel der pro Frequenz und Stromstärke berechneten Zeitmittelwerte einer Versuchsperson zeigt Abbildung 15.4.

Berücksichtigt man, daß diese Mittelwertfunktionen nur aus zwanzig Perioden berechnet wurden, so ist die Annäherung an einen sinusförmigen Verlauf relativ gut. Die Mittelwertfunktionen wurden durch Nullsetzen der Summe der Funktionswerte symmetriert. Dann wurde die Summe der Beträge der Funktionswerte berechnet. Diese diente als Amplitudenschätzung. Die Abbildungen 15.5a bis 15.5c zeigen die Amplitudengänge von je fünf Vpn. 15.5a von Erwachsenen bei 180, 15.5b bei 250 Mikroampere Stromstärke, 15.5c von 5 Kindern bei 180 Mikroampere Reizstrom. Die Abbildungen 15.5a und 15.5b stammen von denselben Erwachsenen und aus dem gleichen Versuch. Die Variation der individuellen Frequenzgänge ist erheblich und dürfte von der Körpergröße, Trainiertheit usw. mit abhängig sein. Bei den Kindern unterscheidet sich der Amplitudengang eines Mädchens (mit Rechtecken markiert) im oberen Frequenzbereich deutlich von den anderen. Das Mädchen besuchte, wie sich herausstellte, seit sechs Jahren eine Ballettschule. Sicher geht ein Teil der interindividuellen Varianz der Amplitudengänge auf Reihenfolgeeffekte zurück. Die zufällige Aufeinanderfolge der verschiedenen Frequenzen und Amplituden scheint die Varianz zu erhöhen.

Berechnet man jeweils die mittleren Amplitudengänge der fünf Vpn, so erhält man die Schätzungen der mittleren Amplitudengänge, die in Abbildung 15.6 dargestellt sind und erstaunlich übereinstimmen. Der Amplitudengang der Kinder ist mit denen der Erwachsenen nahezu identisch, die Verläufe der Erwachsenen stimmen bei 180μA und 250 μA-Reizstrom gut überein.

Letzteres bestätigt die Ergebnisse der Vorversuche hinsichtlich linearer Beziehungen zwischen Reiz-und $K(t)$-Amplituden. Aus einer geschätzten Asymptote der Amplitudengänge ergibt sich ein Proportionalitätsfaktor von .2 Millimeter Körperabweichung pro μA Reizstrom. Dieser Proportionalitätsfaktor gilt zwischen 100 und 500 μA. Unterhalb dieser Stromstärke wird es schwierig sein, eine Entscheidung herbeizuführen (vgl. Nashner & Wolfson, 1974). Anzeichen einer Schwelle fanden wir nicht.

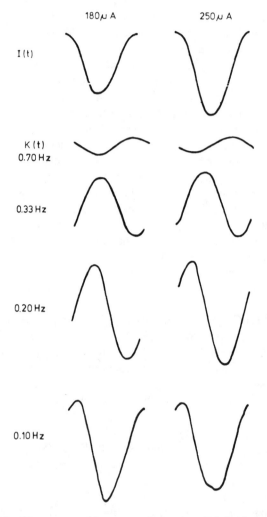

FIG. 15.4.   Time-average of the response during sinusoidal electrical stimulation
with two different currents (180μA, 250μA). The average increases with current
intensity and decreases with frequency.

Durch den Versuch I wurde nahegelegt, daß es sich bei dem System nicht um
ein Phasenminimumsystem handeln kann. Daher war es notwendig, die
Phasengänge zu untersuchen. Die Schätzungen der Phasenverschiebungen φ
wurde mit Hilfe der Kreuzkorrelierten zwischen dem Reizverlauf und der $K(t)$-
Funktion ermittelt. In den Abbildungen 15.7a und 15.7b sind die Phasengänge
der fünf Erwachsenen bei 180 und 250 μA Reizstrom dargestellt. Bei den
Phasengängen zeigt sich eine überraschend geringe interindividuelle Variation.

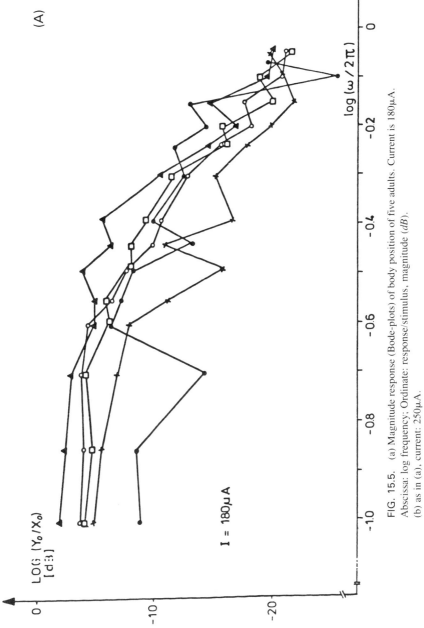

FIG. 15.5. (a) Magnitude response (Bode-plots) of body position of five adults. Current is 180μA. Abscissa: log frequency; Ordinate: response/stimulus. magnitude (*dB*).
(b) as in (a), current: 250μA.
(c) as in (a). Ss were five children (11–15 years).

267

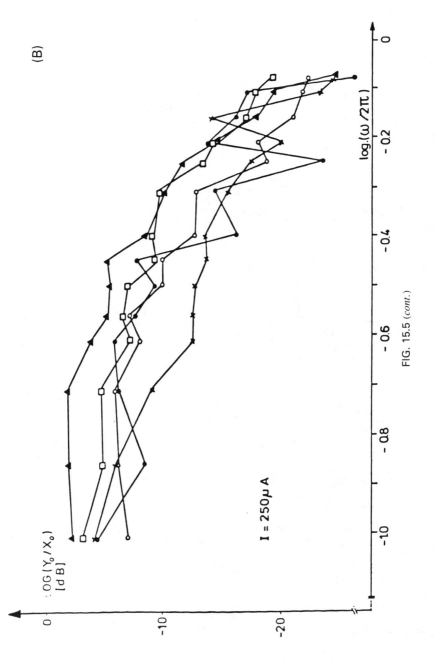

FIG. 15.5 (cont.)

(B)

$LOG(Y_o/X_o)$
[d B]

$I = 250\mu A$

$\log.(\omega/2\pi)$

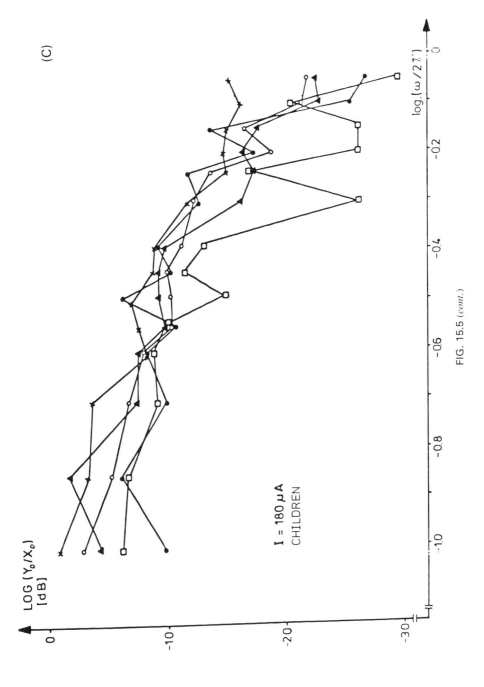

(C)

LOG (Y_0/X_0)
[dB]

$I = 180 \, \mu A$
CHILDREN

$\log_{10}(\omega/2\pi)$

FIG. 15.5 (cont.)

269

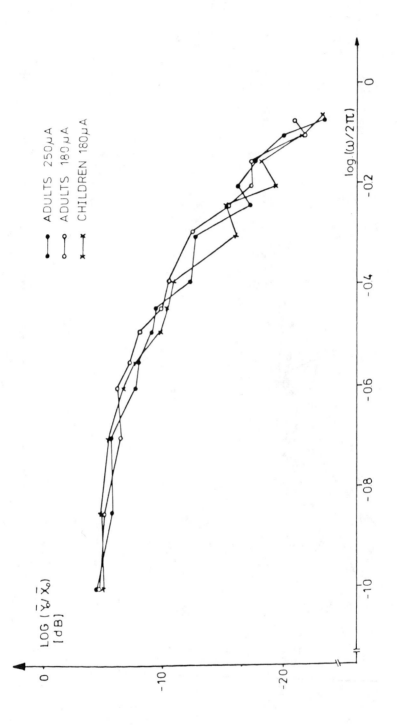

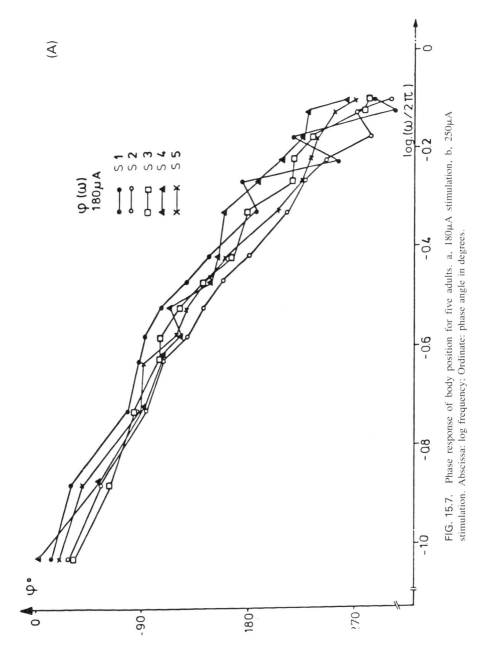

FIG. 15.7. Phase response of body position for five adults. a, 180μA stimulation, b, 250μA stimulation. Abscissa: log frequency; Ordinate: phase angle in degrees.

271

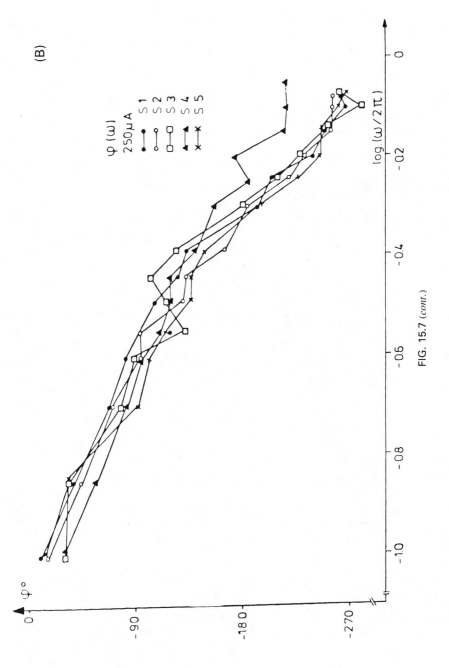

FIG. 15.7 (cont.)

Abbildung 15.8a zeigt die mittleren Phasengänge der fünf Erwachsenen bei 180 und 250 µA Reizstrom.

Über eine Dekade der Reizfrequenz geht der Phasenwinkel φ von nahe Null Grad bis 270 Grad in Richtung Nachhalt. Mit den bisher dargestellten Ergebnissen, dem mittleren Amplituden-und Phasengang, ist die Beschreibung einer Übertragungsfunktion möglich, die eine relativ einfache Struktur haben wird. Hierzu sollen die Abbildungen 15.8a und 15.8b dienen.

Die Abb. 15.8a und 15.8b zeigen, daß die Übertragungsfunktion durch ein Totzeitglied und einen Tiefpaß zweiter Ordnung beschrieben werden kann. Aus dem Versuch I läßt sich die Totzeit auf 330 bis 390 ms schätzen. Wie die Annäherungsrechnung ergibt, trifft eine Totzeit von 360 ms gut zu. Berechnet man die Phasenverschiebung eines Totzeitgliedes mit einer Zeitkonstanten von 360 ms und zieht man diese von den empirischen Phasengängen ab, so reduziert sich die Rest-Phasenverschiebung in der Weise, wie es in Abbildung 15.8a durch die ausgefüllten Punkte gezeigt ist. Die eingezeichnete mittlere Kurve schmiegt sich asymptotisch an die 180° Abszissenparallele an und zeigt den typischen Phasengang eines Tiefpasses zweiter Ordnung.

Die Berechnung der beiden Zeitkonstanten des Tiefpaßgliedes ergibt für T_1 = .97 und T_2 = .49 Sekunden, bei einer kritischen Frequenz von .32 Hz und einem Dämpfungsgrad von .99. Die Übertragungsfunktion einer Ersatzschaltung lautet:

$$F(p) = \frac{5 \cdot e^{-p \cdot .36}}{.97p + .49^2 \cdot p^2}$$

oder als Differenzen-Differentialgleichung des Systems:

$$.24 \frac{d^2X}{dt^2} + .99 \frac{dX}{dt} + 5X(t) = Y(t + .36)$$

wobei X die Reizstromstärke in µA und Y die Körperauslenkung in mm bedeuten.

Das Experiment II wurde von Rau (1975) im Rahmen seiner Diplomarbeit unter gleichen Bedingungen mit weiteren fünf Vpn wiederholt. Die Konstanten des Tiefpaßgliedes waren: T_1 = 1.06 und T_2 = .53 Sekunden. Die kritische Frequenz betrug .30 Hz bei einem Dämpfungsgrad von 1.00. Aus dem Vergleich der beiden Serien kann gefolgert werden, daß die Zeitkonstanten nicht wesentlich von 1 Sekunde und .25 Sekunden-Quadrat abweichen und die kritische Frequenz nahe bei .3 Hz liegt, mit einem Dämpfungskoeffizienten von rund 1.0. Die mittlere Totzeit liegt in beiden Fällen bei 360 ms.

In einem zweiten Versuch (Rau, 1975) betrachteten die Vpn während der elektrischen Reizung ein Streifenmuster. Das Streifenmuster hatte lotrechte schwarz-weiße Streifen mit einem Sehwinkel von 12° und 40 Streifenperioden. Die Leuchtdichte betrug rund 3 cd/m^2, das Leuchtdichteverhältnis war 1:50.

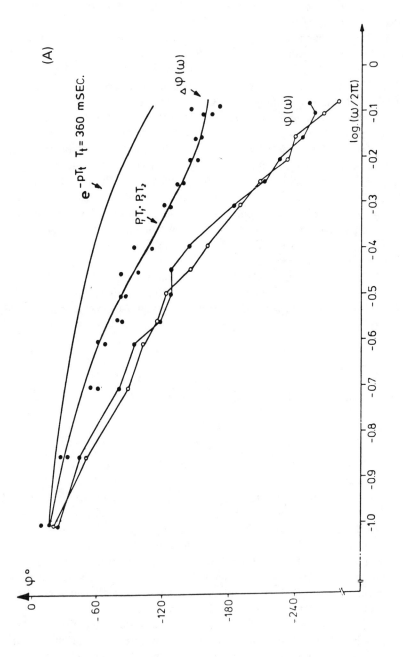

(A)

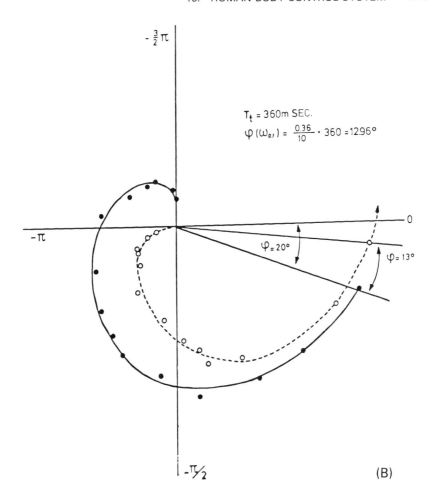

$T_t = 360m$ SEC.

$\varphi(\omega_{ot}) = \dfrac{0.36}{10} \cdot 360 = 12.96°$

$\varphi = 20°$

$\varphi = 13°$

(B)

FIG. 15.8.   Analysis of the phase response of the body position control system.

a Abscissa: log frequency; Ordinate: phase angle. The two lower curves are the means of the data in Fig. 15.7. The middle curve represents the calculated phase shift of a second order low-pass filter. The upper curve represents the phase response of the dead time component. The subtraction of these theoretical values from the data in the lower curve results in values that fit a second order low-pass filter (filled dots).

b Equivalent to a by the method of polar diagram, showing amplitudes (polar vector) as well as phase (polar angle). The filled dots represent the amplitudes and phase angles of the body position. The open dots represent the values after subtraction of the 360 ms dead time. The dotted line is a good approximation to the polar diagram of a second order low-pass filter with a critical frequency of .3 Hz and a damping factor of 1.0.

Das Ergebnis dieses Versuches zeigte, daß die spontanen Schwankungen des Körpers wesentlich geringer waren als bei geschlossenen Augen. An der Wirkung der elektrischen Reizung änderte sich kaum Wesentliches. Die Zeitkonstanten des Tiefpaßgliedes betrugen: $T_1 = 1.12$ und $T_2 = .54$ Sekunden, sie lagen also ein wenig höher als bei den vorigen Versuchen. Die kritische Frequenz war .29, der Dämpfungskoeffizient lag bei 1.04, wiederum ein wenig höher als bei den Versuchen mit geschlossenen Augen. Die Proportionalitätskonstante war um 5 Prozent niedriger als bei den beiden früheren Serien. Zwar weisen alle Abweichungen der Konstanten in Richtung einer stabilisierenden Wirkung des visuellen Kanals hin, die Abweichungen sind jedoch gering.

In weiteren Experimenten wurde ein visueller Bewegungsreiz eingeführt und die Körperlagereaktion sowohl nach der bisherigen Methode als auch über Oberflächenpotentiale myographisch an der Beinmuskulatur registriert. Als visueller Bewegungsreiz diente ein vertikales Streifenmuster von 120° Sehwinkel, welches sich sinusförmig mit .3 Hz in der Frontalebene hin und her bewegt. Bei willkürlichen Bewegungen des Körpers im Rhythmus des optischen Musters, konnten die über die Muskelpotentiale registrierten Körperbewegungen mit geringem Phasenunterschied beschrieben werden. Eine periodische Wirkung des optischen Musters auf die Körperlagereaktion blieb bei allen 21 Vpn aus, unabhängig davon, ob die Vpn einen Punkt fixierten oder den Streifen mit ihrem Blick folgten. Es ergab sich auch kein Zusammenhang zwischen dem optokinetischen Nystagmus (Elektrookulogramm) und der Körperschwankung, wenn die Vpn dem bewegten Muster mit den Augen folgten.

DISKUSSION

Überdenkt man alle diese Ergebnisse, so bleibt als einfachste Lösung die Annahme, daß die elektrische Reizung—zumindest bei schwachen Strömen im unteren Mikroamperebereich—eine neurophysiologische Signalkomponente moduliert, welche für die primäre Meldung über die Schwerkraftrichtung zuständig ist. Diese Signalkomponente könnte die Ruhe- bzw. Dauerentladung der Maculaorgane sein. Wenn diese Annahme zutrifft, so ist die beschrieben Übertragungsfunktion eine Schätzung der Regelstruktur des Reglers, welcher das Gesamtsystem mit Information über die Schwerkraftrichtung versorgt. Der Regler lernt nicht, d.h. er adaptiert nicht, obwohl er durch ca. hundert Stromstöße regelmäßig links-rechts gereizt wird. Zudem bleibt die Körperlagereaktion auf den elektrischen Strom bei der Einführung eines stabilisierenden optischen Signals praktisch unverändert. Die Stromreizung setzt sich trotz visueller Bezugsinformation durch. Ist obige Annahme richtig, so ist der Regler auch an der Bestimmung der Lotrechten beteiligt, die Grundlage für die Vertikalenwahrnehmung ist. Schwankt diese mit dem Bezugsystem des Reglers, so kann das Streifenmuster keine stabilisierende Wirkung auf die durch den elektrischen

Strom induzierte Körperlage, sondern nur auf spontane Körperschwankungen haben.

In diese Richtung weist auch das Ergebnis von Sattel (1976). Durch die elektrische Reizung wird nicht etwa die Körperlage labil, sondern die den Sollwert bestimmende Information wird verändert und die Stützmotorik reagiert darauf, unabhängig von der Größe der Stützfläche.

Bei der visuellen Kontrolle der Körperlage haben optische Reize dann eine Wirkung, wenn sie die Änderung eines visuellen Schwerkraftgradienten melden, bzw. wenn sie eine Änderung der Richtung von Konturen oder Bildelementen relativ zu Netzhautkoordinaten signalisieren. Eine links-rechts-Umkehrbrille invertiert nicht nur die Bewegungsrichtung, sondern sie verändert auch die Entzerrungskennlinien für die Vertikale im peripheren visuellen Bereich. Nicht die Verschiebung von Konturen und Formdetails an der Retina, sondern ein Neigungsgradient (Bildrotation) scheint die Informationsquelle für den visuellen Ast der Körperstabilisation zu sein. Daher ist es verständlich, daß insbesondere eine periphere visuelle Reizung wirksam ist (vgl. Dichgans & Brandt, 1978). Der visuelle Ast der Körperlageregelung hat die Funktion eines Verstärkungsfaktors im Gesamtregler, woraus ein Vorhalt für die Regelung gebildet werden kann. Der visuelle Signalbereich ist, wie die Brillenversuche zeigen, lernfähig und bildet ein durch ständige Eichung abgesichertes Frühwarnsystem. Die nicht selten auftretende Übelkeit bei Umkehrbrillenversuchen findet hierdurch ihre natürliche Erklärung, ebenso die zähe Adaptation an die störenden Effekte von Prismen-und Umkehrbrillen bei scheinbaren Schwankungen des Horizontes.

Kurz nach Durchführung der Versuche ist uns die Arbeit von Nashner und Wolfson (1974) bekannt geworden. Die dort angegebene Regelstruktur stimmt weitgehend mit der unseren überein. Ein Unterschied ergibt sich darin, daß wir oberhalb der Frequenz von 100 mHz keine Vorhalteeigenschaften fanden. Ein D-Glied ist nach unseren Ergebnissen nicht notwendig. Im übrigen sollte man beim Versuch, die Übertragungsfunktion aus stark verrauschten Gewichts- und Übertragungsfunktionen bestimmen zu wollen, sehr vorsichtig sein, insbesondere bei Nicht-Phasenminimum-Systemen. Bemerkenswert ist, daß die gefundene Struktur, verglichen mit anderen motorischen Regelstrukturen, sehr träge ist.

Die Zeitkonstanten waren für uns überraschend, obwohl sie durch die Beobachtung nachvollziehbar sind. Die manuelle Regelstruktur des Menschen, die im übrigen beim geübten Operator und stochastischen Eingangsgrößen die gleiche Form aufweist wie die der Körperlageregulation, hat wesentlich kleinere Zeitkonstanten. Dies gilt auch für die Augenfolgebewegung. Der Hinweis auf die große Masse des Körpers hat dann eine Bedeutung, wenn man bedenkt, daß es kräftesparender ist, in einem relativ breiten Bereich langsam zu schwanken als in einem kleineren Bereich schnell.

Zum Abschluß soll noch darauf hingewiesen werden, daß das hier beschriebene Regelsystem die Körperlage zwar reguliert, sie aber nicht bestimmt. In diesem Sinne wurde der Ausdruck ''mitdefiniert'' verwendet. Dieses Regelsystem ist ein Folgeregler für jede gewollte bzw. gewünschte Lage. Daher greifen suggestive Einflüsse wahrscheinlich in die Führungsgröße dieses Regelsystems und nicht in das Regelsystem selbst ein (De Rivera, 1959 u.a.; Eysenck & Furneaux, 1954).

SUMMARY

Two body control experiments were performed with electrical stimulation of blindfolded Ss. The question was: Which transferfunction describes the behavior of the body control feedback system? The variables of the feedback system are the electrical current, $I(t)$ (system input) and the lateral deviation of body position relative to the verical, $K(t)$ (system output).

During the first experiment, brief electrical stimulation was applied to the vestibular system of 20 Ss. The current intensity varied between 100μA and 350μA in seven steps. The duration of the stimulus also varied in seven steps between 100 ms and 700 ms. This gave a 7 × 7 design, which, in conjunction with the current direction (left or right), resulted in 98 stimulus conditions which were presented in a random order.

Figure 15.1 shows that the current intensities used cause responses which do not exceed spontaneous body sway. The current induced responses can be separated from the spontaneous body sway by applying time-average techniques.

The average over 20 Ss is in Figure 15.2. The system is quasi-linear with a dead time of 340–380 ms. The amplitude of the first maximum, attained after about 1.5 sec, is linearly dependent on the product of current and stimulus duration (up to 350μA and 500 ms).

In the second experiment current intensity was sinusoidally modulated. There were two stimulus amplitudes 180 or 250μA. The period duration T varied from 1 sec to 10 sec in fourteen steps. Ss were five adults and five children. The stimulus intensity for the children was always 180μA.

Figure 15.3 gives examples of body position, $K(t)$, for frequencies of .7, .5 and .33 Hz. With increasing AC-frequency (decreasing period duration) the response amplitude decreases. The current-induced response was again separated from the spontaneous body sway by time-averaging.

Figure 15.4 shows the time-averages for one subject for frequencies ranging from .7 to .1 Hz. The amplitude of the variation of body position was calculated from the absolute value of the average integral.

Figure 15.5 shows the relationship between response amplitude and stimulus modulation frequency for each subject: BODE plots of five Ss each, adults with 180μA (a) and 250μA (b), children with 180μA (c).

Figure 15.6 shows the mean of the data presented in Figures 15.5a–c. Phase angle was calculated by cross-correlation of body position, $K(t)$ and current intensity, $I(t)$.

Figure 15.7 shows the adults' phase response for the two current intensities of 180μA (a) and 250μA (b). Figures 15.8a, and b. show the phase plots. The transfer function was divided into two parts: a dead time component with a time lag of 360 ms and a second order low-pass filter with time constants of .25 s^2 and about 1.0 s. The repetition of the experiment with another group of five Ss showed that the constants varied by no more than 5%.

In other experiments, where the Ss fixated black and white vertical bars or had their feet in different positions, the same results were obtained.

Our results agree with those of Nashner and Wolfson (1974). The transfer function describing body control is essentially the same as that describing a man-machine interactive system with stochastic inputs.

The results indicate that the electric current affected that part of the system structure, which determines the gravitational direction. No adaptation was found.

The results indicate that the signals of gravitational vertical was be affected by electrical stimulation of the vestibular system. No adaptation was found.

REFERENCES

Blonder, E. J., & Davis L. The galvanic falling reaction in patients with verified intracranial neoplasms. *Journal of the American Medical Association,* 1936, *107,* 411–412.

Devito, R.v., Brusa, A., & Arduini, S. Cerebellar and vestibular influences on Deitersian units. *Journal of Neurophysiology,* 1955, *19,* 241–253.

Dichgans, J., & Brandt, T. Visual-vestibular interaction: Effects on self-motion perception and postural control. In R. Held, M. Leibowitz, & H. L. Teuber (Eds.), *Handbook of sensory physiology* (Vol. 8), *Perception.* Berlin: Springer, 1978.

Dohlman, G. Experimentelle Untersuchungen über die galvanische Vestibularis-Reaktion. *Acta otorhinolaryngologica,* 1929, Suppl. *8,* 48.

Eysenck, H. J., & Furneaux, W. D. Primary and secondary suggestibility. *Journal of experimental Psychology,* 1945, *35,* 485–503.

Heuser, H. P. *Galvanische Reizung des Vestibular-Apparates. Eine empirische Untersuchung über Körperschwankungen.* Diplomarbeit, FB Psychologie, Gießen, 1974.

Jung, R., Kornhuber, H. H., & Da Fonseca, J. S. Multi-sensory convergence on cortical neurons, neuronal effects of visual, acoustic and vestibular stimuli in the superior convolutions of the cat's cortex. In G. Moruzzi, A. Fessard, & H. H. Jasper (Eds), *Brain Mechanisms* (Vol. 1). *Progress in Brain Research.* Amsterdam: Elsevier, 1963.

Kohler, I. Wahrnehmung, In R. Meili & H. Rohracher (Hrsg.), *Lehrbuch der experimentellen Psychologie* (2. Auflage). Bern und Stuttgart: Huber, 1968.

Kornhuber, H. H. The vestibular system and the general motor system. In H. H. Kornhuber (Ed.), *Handbook of sensory physiology (Vol. 6/2), Vestibular system.* Berlin: Springer, 1974.

Monjé, M. Über die Wirkung von Wechselströmen verschiedener Frequenz auf die Hautsensibilität, *Zeitschrift für Sinnesphysiologie,* 1936, *122,* p. 57.

Müller, J. Zur vergleichenden Physiologie des Gesichtssinnes, Leipzig, *1826.*

Nashner, L. M., & Wolfson, P. Influence of head position and proprioceptive cues on short latency postural reflexes evoked by galvanic stimulation of the human labyrinth. *Brain Research,* 1974, *67,* 256–268.

Purkinje, J. E. *Beobachtungen und Versuche zur Physiologie der Sinne* (2.Bd). G. Reimer: Berlin, 1825.

Rau, E. *Lageregelung bei elektrischer Reizung mit Einbeziehung des visuellen Einganges unter systemanalytischen Gesichtspunkten.* Diplomarbeit, FB Psychologie, Gießen, 1975.

Rivera, J. de *The postural sway test and its correlations* (Rep. No. 3). U.S. Navy, Pensacola, 1959.

Sattel, L. Laterale Körperschwankungen bei galvanischer Reizung des Vestibularapparates bei verschiedenen Standbreiten. *Psychologische Beiträge,* 1976, *18,* 105–116.

Schwarz, F. Quantitative Untersuchungen über die optische Wirkung sinusförmiger Wechselströme. *Zeitschrift für Sinnesphysiologie,* 1940, *69,* 1–26.

Spiegel, E. A., & Scala, N. P. Response of the labyrinthine apparatus to electrical stimulation. *Archives of Otolaryngology,* 1943, *38,* 131–138.

Zebralla, J. *Körper-und Lageregulationsprozesse unter dem besonderen Einfluß von Alkohol.* Diplomarbeit, FB Psychologie, Gießen, 1974.

16 Some Efferent and Somatosensory Influences on Body Orientation and Oculomotor Control

James R. Lackner
Paul DiZio
Department of Psychology
Brandeis University
Waltham, Massachusetts

ABSTRACT

In recent physiological and related psychophysical studies, similarities have been found between the response properties of individual vestibular nuclei neurons and certain characteristics of visually induced apparent self-motion. These findings have led to the development of linear sensory-convergence models of body orientation. In the present chapter, we demonstrate that illusory self-rotation and compensatory nystagmus can be elicited in seated, stationary subjects (a) by somatosensory stimulation of the soles of the restrained feet, (b) by pedaling a motor-driven platform and (c) by pedaling a free-moving platform. These observations extend the range of afferent patterns that influence apparent orientation and indicate that efferent inputs are also involved. In fact, the motor figure-ground reversals produced the most intense illusions and compensatory nystagmuses. The pattern of our results is inconsistent with single-neuron sensory convergence models of orientation. Instead, our findings make it clear that the ongoing, perceived orientation of the body is determined on the basis of computations involving multiple sensory and motor patterns conveying information about the configuration of the entire body. One consequence of these computations is a lability in the representation of the apparent position of the parts of the body in relation to each other and of the body in relation to its environment.

INTRODUCTION

The perception of body orientation is dependent on multiple sources of afferent and efferent information concerning the spatial configuration of the body and its relation to its surroundings. Such information is necessary in order to preserve an accurate distinction between those changes in sensory and motor activity contingent on self-motion and those contingent on motion of the world. Stable maintenance of this distinction provides an essential background for the ongoing control of normal body movement and posture. The range of sensory and motor inputs that influence orientation and the intricate ways in which they interact in determining apparent orientation is only beginning to be understood. It is our intent, here, to describe some of the known interactions implicating the visual, vestibular, auditory, and proprioceptive systems along with some new experimental data which underscore the great complexity of the computations involved in determining apparent orientation. Ivo Kohler in his studies of sensory rearrangement was one of the first scientists to appreciate and to illuminate this complexity.

Situations in which the distinction between self-motion and motion of the world breaks down provide insight into the nature and organization of the processes responsible for the normal maintenance of sensory and postural integrity. The visual induction of illusory self-motion represents one such instance with a long history of investigation (Helmholtz, 1962; Mach, 1886/1962). Indeed, recently with the discovery of neurons within the vestibular nuclei of various animals that receive both vestibular and visual projections, there has been renewed interest in visually induced self-motion (Allum, Graf, Dichgans, & Schmidt, 1976; Azzena, Azzena, & Marini, 1974; Daunton & Thomsen, 1979; Dichgans, Schmidt, & Graf, 1973; Duensing & Schaefer, 1958, 1959; Henn, Young & Finley, 1974; Keller & Precht, 1978, 1979; Waespe & Henn, 1977 a,b). Dichgans and Brandt and Berthoz and their collaborators have examined systematically the temporal, spatial, and intensity factors affecting the latency and strength of visually induced self-motion (Berthoz, Pavard, & Young, 1975; Brandt, Dichgans, & Büchele, 1974; Brandt, Dichgans, & König, 1973; Brandt, Wist, & Dichgans, 1975; Dichgans & Brandt, 1972, pp. 327–338, 1974, pp. 123–129, 1978, pp. 755–804; Dichgans, Held, Young, & Brandt, 1972; Held, Dichgans, & Bauer, 1975; Young, Dichgans, Murphy, & Brandt) From these psychophysical studies and related electrophysiological experiments, similarities have been found between the response properties of visually and vestibularly driven neurons in the vestibular nuclei and the latency and strength of visually driven apparent self-motion.

Illusory body motion can also be induced by a variety of forms of sensory stimulation other than visual. For example, both illusory self-rotation and compensatory nystagmus can be elicited by rotating sound fields (Dodge, 1923; Lackner, 1977). Auditorily induced illusory self-motion is more difficult to elicit than visually induced self-motion, is generally experienced much less compellingly, and is not experienced by everyone (Lackner, 1977; Marme-Karelse & Bles, 1977).

Brandt, Büchele and Arnold (1977) have been able to evoke apparent self-motion and nystagmus by having stationary subjects place their arm against the inside wall of a moving drum. Such subjects tend to perceive their moving arm as stationary and their stationary body as turning in the direction opposite the arm displacement. By contrast, when subjects extend their arms sideways and let the palms of their hands be stimulated by the moving drum, they neither exhibit nystagmus nor experience illusory motion of their body. In related experiments, Bles (1979, 1981 pp. 47–61), Bles and Kapteyn (1977), and Kapteyn and Bles (1977) have demonstrated that blindfolded subjects walking in place on the floor of a rotating drum experience "apparent stepping around." That is, the subjects report forward motion of their bodies even though they maintain a constant position on the rotating treadmill. Bles and Kapteyn (1977) indicate that none of their subjects could distinguish apparent stepping around from real stepping around, and that during both types of stepping similar compensatory nystagmuses appeared.

Brandt, Büchele, and Arnold (1977) attribute the induction of illusory self-rotation and nystagmus by passive arm movements to a somatosensory-vestibular convergence in which somatosensory joint afferents come together with vestibular afferents in the "central vestibular system." Bles and Kapteyn (1977) argue that in addition to joint receptor afferents, receptors in muscles and tendons participate in the induction of apparent stepping ahead, i.e., that a central proprioceptive-vestibular convergence is the origin of the perceived forward motion.

In this context, it should be noted that many other recent studies have also stressed the importance of muscle spindle receptors in contributing to limb position sense (Goodwin, McCloskey, & Matthews, 1972a,b; McCloskey, 1978). The importance of spindle information in the control and appreciation of human posture is best exemplified by vibratory myesthetic illusions. Vibration of a skeletal muscle with a hand-held physiotherapy vibrator elicits a reflex contraction of that muscle, a "tonic vibration reflex" (Hagbarth & Eklund, 1966). In the dark, if the motion of a limb moving under the action of a tonic vibration is resisted, then movement of the limb in the opposite direction will be experienced because the abnormally high spindle discharge level which results, both of spindle primaries and secondaries, is interpreted as muscle stretch and is attributed to motion of the limb controlled by the muscle (Goodwin, McCloskey, & Matthews, 1972a,b). If illusory motion is induced in limbs related to stance, then apparent motion of the entire body will result. For instance, vibration bilaterally of a standing, restrained subject's quadriceps muscles will make him feel as if he is falling continuously backwards. Such apparent motion is treated centrally as if it were true motion of the body. Thus, if a stationary target light is visible in the otherwise dark experimental chamber, the subject will see it as moving, keeping pace with his own apparent motion but leading him slightly. When a target light is not present, the subject often exhibits a nystagmus compensatory for the direction of his apparent self-motion (Lackner & Levine, 1979). Using appropriate patterns of muscle vibration it is possible to elicit nearly any direction of experienced body motion in a stationary person.

The relation between vibration-induced illusions of body motion and visual localization is in fact bidirectional, underscoring the complexity of the underlying processes. For example, if a subject's forearm is restrained and his biceps muscle is vibrated, he will experience illusory extension of the forearm. If a target light is attached to his index finger and the procedure is repeated, he will see the stationary target light move in keeping with the apparent motion of his stationary arm (Lackner & Levine, 1978). However, the magnitude of the illusory arm motion will be less than when the target light is absent. This indicates that just as aberrant information about arm position is affecting visual direction, so too is information about visual direction influencing the registration of arm position (Levine & Lackner, 1979). While the subject is perceiving visual motion, his eyes remain steadily fixating the stationary target. Because the subject's head and body are also stationary, and perceived as stationary, and the retinal stimulus is not moving, it seems likely that at some central level the eyes are interpreted as being in motion. Otherwise, the subject should not experience visual motion. In fact, subjects often report feeling their eyes move in the direction of the illusory target motion (Levine & Lackner, 1979).

Another line of experimentation suggests that under certain circumstances, touch and pressure stimulation of the body surface can induce illusory body motion. Z-axis recumbent rotation or "barbeque spit" rotation is often used as a way of exploring the response properties of the otolith organs which are known to be sensitive to linear acceleration (Benson & Bodin, 1966; Correia & Guedry, 1966; Guedry, 1965). Investigators thought that when a blindfolded subject lying horizontal is rotated at constant angular velocity about his long body axis, his perceived body motion and patterns of eye movements must reflect the response properties of his otolith organs—which are sensitive to linear acceleration and which are continually reoriented relative to the gravitational force vector (Guedry, 1974, pp. 3–154). Lackner and Graybiel (1978a,b, 1979) have demonstrated, however, that at rotational velocities above approximately 8–12 rpm a subject's sense of orientation and nystagmoid eye movements are in fact being determined by the patterns of support touch and pressure cues provided by the experimental apparatus as the subject turns. Through modifying the touch and pressure cues on his body, a subject can dramatically influence both his apparent orientation and his patterns of eye movements even though the ongoing position of his head and trunk remain constant (Lackner, 1978, 1981, 143–173; Lackner & Graybiel, 1978a,b). Moreover, in the free fall phase of parabolic flight where there are no touch and pressure cues acting on the body of a subject undergoing constant velocity barbeque spit rotation (because he is weightless and there are no contact forces of support), the subject may lose all sense of rotation. Most subjects, in fact, retain awareness only of the relative configuration of their body and have no feeling of their position in relation to the aircraft (Lackner & Graybiel, 1979).

Together the experiments that have been described emphasize the wide range of sensory inputs that influence human spatial orientation and that affect the interpretation and perceptual attributions of self-motion and world-motion. It is clear that visual, auditory, proprioceptive and kinesthetic, touch and pressure, and vestibular servation are involved. Their contributions may be present in complicated combinations and often their actions are not unidirectional as shown by bidirectional interactions between illusory changes in arm position elicited by muscle vibration and changes in visual localization associated with a target light attached to the hand.

Recently, Lackner and Mather (1981) have further illustrated the complexity of these processes by showing that perception of one's willed movements is also influenced by visual and kinesthetic factors. Oculomotor tracking of one's un-seen hand in total darkness is possible but quite poor (Jordan, 1970; Mather & Lackner, 1980a,b,c; Steinbach, 1969). However, if a vivid positive afterimage of the arm, virtually indistinguishable in appearance from the real arm, is pro-duced and projected by voluntary eye movements onto the sensed position of the arm in darkness, tracking accuracy is greatly enhanced both for active and passive limb movements (Jordan, 1970); but, as Lackner and Mather (1981) found, in a very curious way. The subject's eyes follow smoothly the changing position of his arm but move through a considerably smaller angular extent. Many subjects experience the vivid afterimage arm as being their real arm and perceive their real arm as undergoing the seen motion of the afterimage arm. Motion of the afterimage arm is dependent on the angular extent of the eye movement which is less than that of the actual arm motion. Consequently, in passive movement trials, subjects feel their arm is being moved through the seen trajectory of the afterimage arm even though their arm is describing twice that arc. In the active movement trials, subjects perceive themselves as voluntarily moving their arms through a trajectory corresponding to that of the seen motion of the afterimage arm even though in fact they are moving their arm voluntarily through a much larger trajectory. This observation means that "sense of will" or effort is not dependent solely on monitoring efferent commands to move a limb and proprioceptive feedback resulting from the movement. Instead it is clear that under some circumstances afferent and efferent information about the configura-tion of the rest of the body, including eye position, can influence the apparent effort involved in moving the limbs.

It appears, therefore, that there is a great lability in the representation both of the ongoing position of the body and of the willed movements of the body. This means that centrally the division between sensory and motor events is indistinct. The appreciation and representation of each type of event are subject to correla-tion and influence from other spatial mechanisms of the body.

The present studies were directed to further exploring the spatial constancy mechanisms related to sensory and postural stability especially with regard to motor and somatosensory aspects. The findings show that powerful illusions of self-rotation and compensatory nystagmuses can be elicited in seated, stationary subjects (a) by stimulation of the soles of the feet, (b) by actively moving the feet in time with a rotating platform, and (c) by actively displacing the platform by pushing with the feet.

METHOD

Subjects.   Eight undergraduate students participated voluntarily. They were without sensory or motor anomalies that could have influenced the experimental findings.

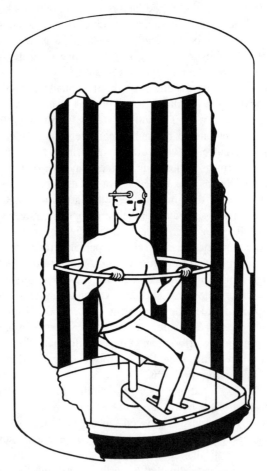

FIG. 16.1.   Illustration of the experimental apparatus. The subject is in position for the hands-and-feet subcondition of Condition A which involved somatosensory stimulation of the soles of the feet and palms of the hands.

Apparatus.   The subjects were seated within a large optokinetic drum on a chair mounted on a circular platform. The chair, the drum, and the platform could be moved independently and controlled in any desired configuration. Figure 16.1 illustrates the apparatus. For the present experiment, the optokinetic drum was always stationary and totally dark, except when the subject's eye position was being calibrated; the subject's chair remained stationary throughout all experimental manipulations. The chair was equipped with a head-holder with four adjustable rods tipped with rubber flanges; when tightened these rods held the subject's head firmly in position. A horizontal plate could be attached to the shaft of the chair 4 in above the level of the platform. Two narrow slits in this plate allowed the subject to place his feet on the surface of the platform while preventing any lateral motion of his feet. In trials not involving passive tactile stimulation of the feet, the plate was removed. The platform itself could be driven by a variable speed motor or could be allowed to freewheel so that the subject could move it with his feet. A tachometer geared to the platform provided a velocity signal that was recorded on one channel of a Grass model 7b polygraph.

Horizontal eye position was monitored using conventional d.c. electrooculography. Eye position was displayed on a polygraph channel adjacent to the tachometer record of platform velocity.

Subjective Reports.   Prior to each condition subjects were instructed to report during the experiment whether they were experiencing self-motion, and, if so, how much they were displacing by pressing a marker button each time they felt 360° of rotation. They also reported whether the platform seemed to be stationary or moving, and, if moving, how fast and how far over time. At the end of each condition they were asked to rank order the velocity of apparent rotation, if any, during each subcondition; and at the end of the experiment they were asked to rank order the velocity of apparent rotation during the hands-and-feet subcondition of each condition.

An intercom system allowed the experimenter and subject to communicate with one another. A two-channel tape recorder was used to record these communications and a timing signal allowed synchronization of the magnetic tape record with the polygraph displaying the subject's eye position and the tachometer indication of platform velocity.

Procedure.   Three experimental conditions were run in a single experimental session; the order of conditions was counterbalanced across individual subjects. The conditions involved (a) tactile stimulation of the soles of the restrained feet, (b) actively moving the feet in keeping with the motion of the motor-driven platform, (c) actively moving the freewheeling platform by pushing with the feet. Each condition included a period during which the subject also received passive tactile stimulation of the palms of his hands by a circular railing rigidly attached to the revolving platform, or voluntarily moved his hands in keeping with the motion of the railing.

Condition A began with three horizontal calibration lights visible on the wall of the drum; the drum was moved until the center light was reported to be straight ahead. After eye position was calibrated, the lights were turned off, and the subject was asked to continue looking straight ahead where the center light had been visible. The subject then held his feet above the surface of the platform while it was accelerated to a constant clockwise angular velocity of 3.8 rpm. The subject held his feet above the plate for the next 30 sec and reported any sensations of rotation he might be experiencing. He was then instructed over the intercom system to lower his stockinged feet through the slits in the plate and to let them make contact with the platform. For the next 60 sec he reported on any motion he was experiencing. All instructions and reports were tape recorded. He was then told to hold his hands in front of him so that he could feel the circular rail attached to the platform move against the palms of his hands. The subject did this in such a fashion that his hands were stationary while the turning circular rail stimulated his palms. During the next 60 sec, the subject reported on any self-motion or changes in self-motion that he was experiencing. The subject was then instructed to return his hands to his lap and to continue reporting. After 60 sec elapsed, he was told to lift his feet from the platform and for the next 2 minutes the subject reported on his experiences of motion.

The first and last parts of Condition B were like those of Condition A; the subject's feet were above the platform and he reported on experiences of motion. In the experimental portions of the condition, the subject pedaled with his legs keeping pace with the motion of the platform which was driven at a constant velocity of 3.8 rpm. The subject's "pedaling" did not affect the motion of the platform. After 60 sec of pedaling, the subject voluntarily moved his hands in keeping with the motion of the moving railing repositioning them as necessary for the next 60 sec; during the final 60 sec of pedaling the subject returned his hands to his lap.

Condition C was identical to Condition B, except that the platform was freewheeling and moved by the subject's pedaling action. Because of this, there were periods of platform acceleration and deceleration associated with the subject's pushing with his feet and hands in the middle section of the condition, and then repositioning for the next pushes. The experimenter for the first few seconds of the condition helped the subject attain an approximately 3.8 rpm velocity of the platform by telling him to slow down or speed up his pedaling as necessary.

RESULTS

In all three experimental conditions, most subjects experienced illusory self-rotation (ISR) in the direction opposite platform displacement and exhibited patterns of compensatory nystagmus appropriate for their direction of apparent self-motion. Because of important differences across conditions, each condition is described separately.

Condition A.   None of the subjects experienced self-motion or exhibited nystagmus prior to lowering their feet to make contact with the moving platform. After contact was established, six of the eight subjects experienced ISR in addition to platform rotation after latencies varying from 11 to 77.5 sec. Five of the subjects experienced a dissociation between their apparent velocity and the extent of their apparent change in position, with the illusory displacement always being too small in relation to velocity of apparent motion. Five people felt ISR with only their feet in contact with the moving platform; one person did not feel ISR until her palms were stimulated as well by being placed in contact with the railing. When the five subjects, who had already begun to feel ISR with only stimulation of the feet, placed their hands on the circular railing so that they were receiving somatosensory stimulation both of the soles of their feet and the palms of their hands, this invariably augmented, within 0–8 sec, the strength of their ISR. They felt that their angular velocity had increased and that the degree to which they were changing position had also increased. For four subjects, when the hands were placed on the rail, there was a dissociation between the apparent velocities and positions of the upper and lower parts of the body during the few seconds before ISR had changed to the overall higher rate. In these cases the feet and lower body would seem displaced further to the left and rotating at a higher velocity than the hands and upper body. Within 0–8 sec after removing their hands from the railing subjects felt that they had slowed down and also were not displacing as much. Dissociation of the upper and lower parts of the body also occurred at this time with the lower body again feeling displaced further to the left and faster than the upper part. At the end of the stimulation portion of the condition when the subjects lifted their feet from the surface of the platform, if they had not felt stopped even before lifting their feet, they felt stopped either immediately or after 3 s of leftward illusory after-rotation. In three cases, subjects experienced an aftereffect of slow rotation to the right after all motion to the left had ceased.

Recordings of horizontal eye position indicated that five subjects had compensatory, fast phase left, nystagmus. During stimulation four subjects experienced ISR and exhibited a compensatory nystagmus, while two subjects experienced ISR without compensatory nystagmus. One other subject exhibited a small compensatory nystagmus but had no sense of ISR. For the four cases with both ISR and nystagmus, ISR always occurred before the onset of nystagmus. See Table 16.1 for the temporal pattern of occurrence of ISR and nystagmus.

Analysis of the nystagmus records showed that the nature of the compensatory eye movements is dependent on the velocity of the subject's ISR. In the subcondition where the hands and feet received stimulation simultaneously, the subject

TABLE 16.1
Onset and Offset of Illusory Self-Rotation (ISR) and Nystagmus
(NYS) Elicited by Somatosensory Stimulation of the Soles of the
Feet and by Pedaling the Motor-Driven and the Free-Wheeling
Platform

Measurement	Subject	Feet Restrained Platform Driven		Feet Following Platform Driven		Feet Pushing Platform Free	
		ISR	NYS	ISR	NYS	ISR	NYS
Onset latency	SC	23	43.5	13.5	25	6	4.5
(sec)	MO	—[a]	—	63	92	34	80
	DG	—	79	19	85	38	23
	JB	15.5	77.5	14	27	20	22
	HL	77	—	24	10	58	28
	RM	21	71	6.5	13.5	0	23
	RF	26	61	15	24	21	62.5
	AN	11	—	19.5	9	26.5	34
Offset latency	SC	0[b]	−60	0	−14	3	12
(sec)	MO	—	—	0	12	3.5	16
	DG	—	−28	0	22	4	30
	JB	0/12[c]	−53	2	7	0	1
	HL	0/30	—	0/8.5	2.5	8	6
	RM	0/62	39	0/61	0	8.5	17
	RF	3	−8.5	0/70	−48	9.5	25.5
	AN	−60	—	16	32.5	8	10.5

[a]A missing score means illusory self-rotation or nystagmus did not occur.

[b]A "zero" entry means illusory self-rotation or nystagmus ceased as soon as stimulation ended; a negative entry indicates that illusory self-rotation or nystagmus ceased during the stimulation period; a positive entry indicates that leftward illusory self-rotation or nystagmus persisted into the post-stimulation period.

[c]The number after the slash indicates how long rightward illusory self-rotation was experienced; the number before the slash indicates the duration of leftward illusory self-rotation during the post-stimulation period.

always reported that the velocity of ISR was faster than with the feet alone. Correspondingly, the eyes exhibited a nystagmoid pattern of movement prior to the hands-and-feet subcondition only once, and after the end of the hands-and-feet subcondition only once; by contrast, nystagmus appeared a total of five times during the hands-and-feet subcondition. In the two separate instances of nystagmus occurring during stimulation of the feet alone, the slow phase velocity and amplitude were less by nearly one half than when the hands were also in contact with the moving railing. It appears, therefore, that a faster velocity of ISR is associated with a higher velocity and amplitude compensatory nystagmus. This will become even more apparent in the subsequent conditions.

Condition B.   Until they lowered their feet onto the surface of the turning platform, subjects did not experience self-rotation nor exhibit nystagmoid eye movements. After they began pedaling with their feet in keeping with the platform's motion, all subjects reported smooth compelling illusory self-rotation, with latencies of 6.5 to 63 sec. When the subjects repositioned their feet to the opposite side to resume moving them in keeping with the platform's motion, they tended to feel as if they had slowed down slightly when their feet were momentarily off the platform. As in Condition A, all subjects experienced a dissociation between the velocity of their experienced self-rotation and their extent of rotary displacement, with the latter being less than appropriate for the velocity experienced. All subjects reported strong self-motion but nevertheless also perceived the platform as turning to some extent. When the subjects placed their hands on the surface of the railing, pushing it in a way similar to that of the feet, their illusory self-rotation was enhanced within 0 to 7.5 sec, and it often felt as if the platform and railing were stationary while only they rotated. Taking their hands from the railing restored the prior pattern within 0 to 5.5 sec. Some subjects, as in Condition A, experienced their feet and lower body as moving faster and being displaced more to the left than their upper body and hands during the time immediately after placing the hands on the railing and after removing them from the railing. When subjects raised their feet away from the platform surface their sensations of illusory self-rotation to the left persisted for varying periods ranging from 0 to 16 sec. Three subjects experienced slow rotation to the right, after the initial rotation to the left.

The nystagmus records showed that all subjects exhibited compensatory nystagmus from 14 sec before to 66 sec after reporting illusory self-motion; two of these subjects did not exhibit nystagmus until placing their hands on the railing. At the end of the condition, when the subjects lifted their feet from the moving platform, ISR stopped before nystagmus in all cases except one where both stopped immediately.

Nystagmus intensity was closely related to the velocity of the subject's experienced self-rotation. The reported illusion velocity was greatest in the condition where both hands and feet were used and the percentage of time exhibiting nystagmus, the slow phase velocity, and the nystagmus frequency were greatest; the fast phase amplitude was greater in the hands-and-feet subcondition than in the initial subcondition with feet alone, but less than the subsequent subcondition with feet alone. Table 16.2 contains these data.

The eye movement data are summarized in Table 16.3.

Condition C.   No self-motion was experienced nor nystagmus present until subjects began pedaling the platform with their feet. The illusory self-rotation in this condition was much more compelling in character than that elicited in Conditions A and B. Those subjects who had experienced visually induced ISR

TABLE 16.2
Properties of Nystagmus Elicited in Individual Subjects by
Somatosensory Stimulation of the Soles of the Feet and by Pedaling
the Motor-Driven and the Freewheeling Platform

		Feet Restrained Platform Driven			*Feet Following Platform Driven*			*Feet Pushing Platform Free*		
Measure	*Subject*	*Feet Only*	*Feet & Hands*	*Feet Only*	*Feet Only*	*Feet & Hands*	*Feet Only*	*Feet Only*	*Feet & Hands*	*Feet Only*
Slow phase	SC	1.7	4.4	—	4.2	9.8	6.4	3.7	10.9	8.6
velocity	MO	—	—	—	—	5.6	3.7	—	12.1	7.6
(°/sec)	DG	—	4.7	—	—	8.5	3.9	4.2	6.9	3.1
	JB	—	3.1	—	2.1	4.8	5.4	1.9	10.0	—
	HL	—	—	—	3.2	4.0	3.2	2.3	3.2	3.8
	RM	—	1.6	—	2.7	5.6	—	3.4	5.1	—
	RE	—	1.9	1.8	1.6	4.7	3.0	—	6.6	5.3
	AN	—	—	—	3.8	9.2	—	7.3	6.5	—
Nystagmus	SC	.5	1.0	—	.7	1.1	1.1	.9	1.5	.8
frequency	MO	—	—	—	—	.8	.7	—	1.1	1.3
(beats/sec)	DG	—	.8	—	—	1.3	.7	1.2	1.1	.6
	JB	—	.7	—	1.0	2.0	1.6	.9	2.0	—
	HL	—	—	—	1.8	1.5	1.3	1.1	1.8	1.2
	RM	—	.4	—	1.1	1.1	—	.7	1.1	—
	RF	—	.4	.8	.4	1.4	.6	—	1.9	1.7
	AN	—	—	—	.8	.9	—	1.0	1.1	
Percent of trial	SC	9.4	64.3	0	23.1	46.7	35.8	25.3	63.9	40.0
nystagmus	MO	0	0	0	0	55.7	9.1	0	70.9	17.8
present	DG	0	22.2	0	0	85.3	80.4	15.5	67.3	86.8
	JB	0	5.2	0	8.3	34.5	9.6	53.3	33.9	0
	HL	0	0	0	5.3	40.7	27.1	6.6	56.1	4.2
	RM	0	8.2	0	4.9	66.1	0	6.3	30.4	0
	RF	0	22.6	6.2	40.5	15.5	9.0	0	50.0	41.8
	AN	0	0	0	16.9	30.7	0	5.4	10.4	0
Fast phase	SC	3.8	6.6	—	8.1	10.9	10.4	6.0	10.4	12.1
amplitude	MO	—	—	—	—	7.8	3.6	—	12.5	8.1
(degrees)	DG	—	6.3	—	—	7.6	8.0	4.8	7.0	5.9
	JB	—	6.4	—	3.0	3.0	3.0	2.0	8.5	—
	HL	—	—	—	2.2	3.2	2.6	.8	1.8	3.7
	RM	—	11.9	—	3.3	5.3	—	7.0	5.6	—
	RF	—	3.2	3.1	4.1	5.0	15.6	—	3.6	3.7
	AN	—	—	—	5.3	9.9	—	7.9	6.3	—

TABLE 16.3
Average Properties of Nystagmus Elicited by Somatosensory
Stimulation of the Soles of the Feet and by Pedaling
the Motor Driven and the Free Wheeling Platform

Measure		Feet Restrained Platform Driven			Feet Following Platform Driven			Feet Pushing Platform Free		
		Feet Only	Feet & Hands	Feet Only	Feet Only	Feet & Hands	Feet Only	Feet Only	Feet & Hands	Feet Only
Slow phase	N*	1	5	1	6	8	6	6	8	9
velocity	$\bar{X}$	1.7	3.2	1.8	2.9	6.5	4.3	3.8	7.7	5.7
(°/sec)	SD	—	1.4	—	1.0	2.3	1.3	1.9	3.0	2.3
Nystagmus	N	1	5	1	6	8	6	6	8	5
frequency	$\bar{X}$	.5	.7	.8	.9	1.2	1.0	1.0	1.4	1.2
(beats/sec)	SD	—	.2	—	.4	.3	.4	.1	.4	.4
Percent of trial	N	8	8	8	8	8	8	8	8	8
nystagmus	$\bar{X}$	1.2	15.3	0.7	12.3	46.9	21.3	14.1	47.8	23.8
present	SD	3.4	21.8	2.2	13.9	21.9	26.9	17.9	21.1	30.8
Fast phase	N	1	5	1	6	8	6	6	8	5
amplitude	$\bar{X}$	3.9	6.9	3.1	4.4	6.6	7.2	4.8	7.0	6.7
(degree)	SD	—	3.1	—	2.1	2.9	5.2	2.8	3.5	3.5

*N = number of subjects in the different sub-conditions exhibiting nystagmus (maximum possible entry is 8); $\bar{X}$ = mean; SD = standard deviation.

in an optokinetic drum reported that the illusory motion caused by pedaling the platform was much stronger and more compelling. When subjects pushed the platform to the right with their feet, giving it an impulse before repositioning their feet to the left to push again, it felt as if their bodies were given an *acceleration* to the left, like being accelerated by a spring released after being compressed. Subjects felt that they were still turning as they repositioned their feet and pushed again. The velocity of ISR was calculated by using marks on the polygraph record made when subjects pressed an event marker at the end of several successive perceived revolutions of their bodies. (Only five subjects could do this, but they gave consistent ratings for repeated revolutions.) The highest velocity was reported in this condition—17.1 rpm; the highest in Condition B was 9.0 rpm; the highest in Condition A was 6.5 rpm. The experienced displacements were also much more in keeping with the experienced velocities compared to Conditions A and B. Pushing the railing with the hands, in addition to pushing with the feet, augmented the illusion and gave rise to a temporary dissociation of the upper and lower parts of the body as in the previous conditions. When subjects ceased pedaling the platform they continued to experience self-motion for periods ranging from 0 to 9.5 sec. No subject experienced an aftereffect of slow drift to the right as in Conditions A and B.

The eye movement recordings showed that nearly coincident with the induction of illusory self-rotation, a powerful compensatory nystagmus appeared; five subjects experienced ISR first, three exhibited nystagmus first. Nystagmus appeared from 30 sec before to 46 sec after the onset of ISR. Both ISR and nystagmus persisted until the end of the condition; once the feet were lifted from the platform seven subjects felt they had stopped rotating before nystagmus disappeared.

Inspection of the nystagmus records showed that just as subjects experienced the most compelling illusions in this condition, the nystagmus intensity was also most intense. For all three subconditions—feet alone prior, hands and feet, feet alone post—the mean measures for percent duration of nystagmus, nystagmus frequency, slow phase velocity, and fast phase amplitude were as high as or higher than the values for the same subconditions of Condition A and B, except that fast phase amplitude in the hands-and-feet subcondition of Condition B was greater by .5 degrees than in the same subcondition of Condition C. However, analysis of the nystagmus measures between similar subconditions using separate one-tailed t-tests (for unequal n where necessary) to acknowledge individual and inter-individual variability showed that means in Condition C were significantly greater than those in Condition A for slow phase velocity, nystagmus frequency, and percent duration of nystagmus in the hands and feet subcondition; the only significant difference between Conditions C and B was that fast phase amplitude in the initial feet only subcondition of Condition C was greater.

Figure 16.2 presents representative eye records from each of the three experimental conditions for an individual subject.

DISCUSSION

Compelling illusions of self-rotation and compensatory nystagmus were elicited by somatosensory stimulation of the soles of the feet, by active following of the motion of a turning platform with the feet, and by pedaling the freewheeling platform with the feet. These findings extend the range of sensory signals known to elicit apparent self-rotation and prove that motor signals can be involved as

---

FIG. 16.2. Polygraph records for a single subject of platform velocity (upper traces) and horizontal eye position (lower traces) during (A) somatosensory stimulation of the soles of the restrained feet, (B) active following of the motor-driven platform with the feet, and (C) pedaling of the freewheeling platform with the feet. The first record of each condition presents eye movements during the initial part of the condition involving only the feet at a time when the subject was reporting strong illusory self-rotation. The second record shows eye movements when the hands were brought into play as well (arrow); the portion of the record after the break illustrates the period involving both hands and feet when the subject was reporting strong illusory self-rotation.

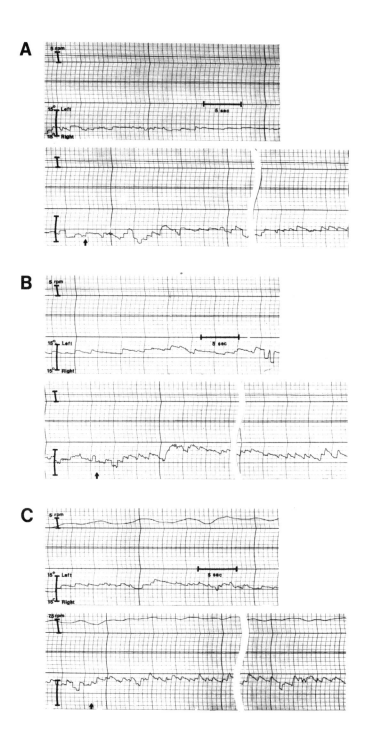

well. In fact, of our three experimental conditions, the two involving voluntary pedaling of the platform produced the most compelling and powerful illusions. This asymmetry underscores the fact mentioned earlier that the spatial constancy mechanisms involved in the attribution of self-motion and world motion also influence the perception of sense of effort and the results of that effort (see also Lackner & Mather, 1981). We think it likely on the basis of our Conditions B and C that the phenomenon of apparent stepping around reported by Bles and Kapteyn (1977) also represents, at least in part, a motor figure-ground reversal of the type we have described rather than a proprioceptive-vestibular convergence of some form.

In our three experimental conditions, it was always the case that the more compelling the apparent self-rotation the more intense the associated compensatory nystagmus. The latency to induction of illusory self-rotation was also similar across our three conditions; nevertheless, it took nearly twice as long for nystagmus to become manifest in Condition A compared to the active pedaling Conditions, B and C. This asymmetry may be due to the weaker illusions of self-rotation experienced in Condition A. Here it should be noted, however, that in Condition A nystagmus virtually always followed reports of self-rotation, whereas in Conditions B and C nystagmus occasionally appeared before self-rotation was reported. This latter pattern is also characteristic of situations involving actual acceleration of the body (Clark & Stewart, 1962; Graybiel, Clark, MacCorquodale, & Hupp, 1946; Graybiel & Hupp, 1946) and may reflect the different control processes involved, one "reflexive", the other judgmental.

Illusions of self-rotation and nystagmus persisted to some extent into the post-stimulation period in all three conditions, but most strongly in Conditions B and C. The after-nystagmus was always of the same sign as the per-stimulation nystagmus, but the direction of illusory self-rotation tended to reverse a few seconds into the post-stimulation periods of Conditions A and B, but not of Condition C which involved pedalling the freewheeling platform. This asymmetry may be related to the much stronger per-stimulation nystagmuses and illusory self-rotations elicited in the latter condition. Illusions of self-movement and nystagmus (optokinetic after-nystagmus) also continue after optokinetic stimulation is ended and like the aftereffects described here are initially of the same sign as the primary effects elicited (Brandt, Dichgans, & Büchele, 1974). Moreover, in the present study, the nystagmic "Schlagfeld" was also displaced (approximately 5 to 8°) in the direction of the fast phase side as occurs with optokinetic stimulation and with arthrokinetic stimulation of the arm to induce apparent self-rotation (Brandt, Büchele, & Arnold, 1977). These similarities, and related findings using muscle vibration (Lackner & Levine, 1979), rotating sound fields (Lackner, 1977) and apparent stepping around (Bles, 1979, 1981, pp. 47–81; Bles & Kapteyn, 1977) to elicit apparent self-rotation, suggest that regardless of the mode of access, sensory or motor, the representation of body motion and postural compensation for represented body motion are governed by the same general principles. Inputs from the semicircular canals are dependent on the response and adaptation properties of the peripheral end organs as well as the level of activity in efferent vestibular fibers and hence may represent a partial exception to this generalization by embodying additional complexity. Nevertheless, the patterns that have been described indicate that orientation is determined by multimodal computations involving virtually all sensory and motor systems of the body providing exteroceptive and proprioceptive messages. Such complexity makes it extremely unlikely that hypotheses invoking the existence of simple convergences of vestibular and visual or vestibular and somatosensory inputs on single neurons can be of much explanatory value in understanding spatial orientation. Such hypotheses do not adequately represent the behavioral complexity involved in orientation and hence represent an inappropriate level of conceptual analysis.

This latter point becomes clear through a consideration of what happened in our three experimental conditions when the hands as well as feet were involved. Within 0 to 8 sec from the time subjects began moving the railing with their hands or allowed their palms to be passively stimulated by the railing, they reported changes in the motion they were experiencing. The illusion of rotation not only became more compelling but the upper and lower parts of the body seemed to be rotating at different speeds. After a brief period, the torso seemed to increase in speed until the entire body had the same subjective velocity. Such an initial perceptual dissociation of the torso and the lower part of the body constitutes a physically impossible body configuration but more importantly it points to a lability of representation of the parts of the body in relation to one another of a form not understandable in terms of sensory convergences on single neurons in the vestibular nuclei.[1]

In summary, the present findings emphasize the multimodal aspects of the mechanisms responsible for the relative assignment of self-motion and world-motion; they also forcefully implicate efferent signals in the evocation of illusory self-motion. Clearly signals from virtually all modalities conveying proprioceptive and exteroceptive information participate in this process. It is equally apparent, however, that this process is not simply one of convergence or confluence but that analysis and computation concerning and related to the ongoing configuration of the entire body is taking place as well. Nowhere is this more obvious than in the recent demonstration that terrestrial sensory-motor control is dynamically calibrated to a 1-g background force level (Lackner & Graybiel, 1981). During exposure to 2-g force levels in the high force phases of parabolic flight maneuvers in a Boeing KC-135 aircraft, subjects experience illusory motion of the aircraft and of their bodies when moving about. These illusory motions arise

---

[1]Such physically impossible perceptual dissociations of body parts are also characteristic of somatosensory aftereffects (Lackner & Graybiel, 1977) and of the illusory limb motion induced by muscle vibration.

from alterations in the normal relationships between patterns of efferent innervation, muscle spindle activity, and body movement. The failure of the body to move in the fashion appropriate for a given pattern of muscle activation results in abnormal patterns of muscle spindle activity which leads to misinterpretations of limb position and of the stability of the substrate of body support (see also Lackner & Levine, 1979). This means that efferent commands to the musculature are monitored and their expected consequences are compared with the actually resulting patterns of proprioceptive activity and body motion. Such monitoring necessarily takes into account the ongoing configuration of the entire body and whether loads are being carried which would alter the demand characteristics associated with movement; otherwise illusory, body and substrate motion would be experienced when we carry heavy loads. An analogous form of monitoring is known to occur in oculomotor control (cf. Teuber, 1960, pp. 1595–1668; von Holst, 1954) and in the production and reception of speech (Lackner, 1974; Lackner & Tuller, 1979, pp. 281–294).

The observations we have described considerably complicate the task of identifying and understanding the neuronal mechanisms responsible for human spatial orientation and movement control because they extend the range of systems involved and the analyses being performed. In particular, they make it increasingly unlikely that simple analyses of converging afferent or afferent and corollary discharge inputs on particular neuronal populations will be of direct, understandable, functional significance beyond the periphery.

ACKNOWLEDGMENT

The research described was supported by NASA Contract NAS 9–15147.

REFERENCES

Allum, J. H. J., Graf, W., Dichgans, J., & Schmidt, C. L. Visual-vestibular interactions in the vestibular nuclei of the goldfish. *Experimental Brain Research,* 1976, *26,* 463–485.

Azzena, G. B., Azzena, M. T., & Marini, R. Optokinetic nystagmus and the vestibular nuclei. *Experimental Neurology,* 1974, *42,* 158–168.

Benson, A., & Bodin, M. Interaction of linear and angular accelerations on vestibular receptors in man. *Aerospace Medical,* 1966, *37,* 144–154.

Berthoz, A., Pavard, B., & Young, L. R. Perception of linear horizontal self-motion induced by peripheral vision (linearvection). Basic characteristics and visual-vestibular interactions. *Experimental Brain Research,* 1975, *23,* 471–489.

Bles, W. *Sensory interactions and human posture.* Thesis, Urije University, Amsterdam, 1979.

Bles, W. Stepping around: Circular vection and Coriolis effects. In J. Long & A. Baddeley (Eds)., *Attention and Performance IX.* Hillsdale, N.J.: Lawrence Erlbaum Associates, 1981.

Bles, W., & Kapteyn, T. (1977) Circular vection and human posture: I. Does the proprioceptive system play a role? *Agressologie,* 1977, *18,* 325–328.

Brandt, Th., Büchele, W., & Arnold, F. Arthrokinetic nystagmus and ego-motion sensation. *Experimental Brain Research*, 1977, *30*, 331–338.

Brandt, Th., Dichgans, J., & Büchele, W. Motion habituation: Inverted self-motion perception and optokinetic after-nystagmus. *Experimental Brain Research*, 1974, *21*, 337–352.

Brandt, Th., Dichgans, J., & König, E. Differential effects of central versus peripheral vision on egocentric and exocentric motion perception. *Experimental Brain Research*, 1973, *16*, 476–491.

Brandt, Th., Wist, E. R., & Dichgans, J. Foreground and background in dynamic spatial orientation. *Perception & Psychophysics*, 1975, *17*, 497–503.

Clark, B., & Stewart, J. P. Perception of angular acceleration about the yaw axis of a flight simulator. *Aerospace Medicine*, 1962, *33*, 1426–1432.

Correia, M. J., & Guedry, F. E. Modification of vestibular responses as a function of rate of rotation about an earth-horizontal axis. *Acta Otolaryngologica* (Stockholm), 1966, *62*, 297–308.

Daunton, N., & Thomsen, D. Visual modulation of otolith-dependent units in cat vestibular nuclei. *Experimental Brain Research*, 1979, *37*, 173–176.

Dichgans, J., & Brandt, Th. Visual-vestibular interaction and motion perception. In J. Dichgans & E. Bizzi (Eds.), *Cerebral control of eye movements and motion perception*. Basel, New York: S. Karger, 1972.

Dichgans, J., & Brandt, Th. The psychophysics of visually induced perception of self-motion and tilt. In F. O. Schmitt & F. G. Worden (Editors-in-Chief) *The neurosciences: Third study program*. Cambridge, Mass.: MIT Press, 1974.

Dichgans, J., & Brandt, Th. Visual-vestibular interaction: Effects on self-motion perception and postural control. In R. Held, H. Leibowitz, & H.-L. Teuber (Eds.), *Handbook of sensory physiology* (Vol. 8), *Perception*. Berlin-New York: Springer-Verlag, 1978.

Dichgans, J., Held, R., Young, L. R., & Brandt, Th. Moving visual scenes influence the apparent direction of gravity. *Science*, 1972, *178*, 1217–1219.

Dichgans, J., Schmidt, C. L., & Graf, W. Visual input improves the speedometer function of the vestibular nuclei in the goldfish. *Experimental Brain Research*, 1973, *18*, 319–322.

Dodge, R. Thresholds of rotation. *Journal of Experimental Psychology* 1923, *6*, 107–137.

Duensing, F., & Schaefer, K.-P. Die Aktivität einzelner Neurone im Bereich der Vestibulariskerne bei Horizontalbeschleunigung unter besonderer Berücksichtigung des vestibulären Nystagmus. *Archiv für Psychiatrie und Nervenkrankheiten*, 1958, *198*, 225–252.

Duensing, F., & Schaefer, K.-P. Uber die Konvergenz verschiedener Afferenzen auf einzelne Neurone des Vestibulariskerngebiets. *Archiv für Psychiatrie und Nervenkrankheiten*, 1959, *199*, 345–371.

Goodwin, G. M., McCloskey, D. I., & Matthews, P. B. C. Proprioceptive illusions induced by muscle vibration: Contribution to perception by muscle spindles? *Science*, 1972, *175*, 1382–1384. (a)

Goodwin, G., McCloskey, D. I., & Matthews, P. B. C. The contribution of muscle afferents to kinaesthesia shown by vibration-induced illusions of movement and by the effects of paralysing joint afferents. *Brain*, 1972, *95*, 705–748. (b)

Graybiel, A., Clark, B., MacCorquodale, K., & Hupp, D. I. The role of vestibular nystagmus in the perception of a moving target in the dark. *American Journal Psychology*, 1946, *59*, 259–266.

Graybiel, A., & Hupp, D. I. The oculogyral illusion, a form of apparent motion which may be observed following stimulation of the semicircular canals. *The Journal of Aviation Medicine*, 1946, *43*, 3–27.

Guedry, F. E. Orientation of the rotation axis relative to gravity: Its influence on nystagmus and the sensation of rotation. *Acta Otolaryngologica* (Stockholm), 1965, *60*, 30–48.

Guedry, F. E. Psychophysics of vestibular sensation. In H. H. Kornhuber (Ed.), *Handbook of sensory physiology* (Vol. VI/2), *Vestibular System*. Berlin: Springer-Verlag, 1974.

Hagbarth, K.-E., & Eklund, G. Motor effects of vibratory muscle stimuli in man. In R. Granit (Ed.), *Muscular afferents and motor control*. Stockholm: Almqvist & Wiksell, 1966.

Held, R., Dichgans, J., & Bauer, J. Characteristics of moving visual scenes influencing spatial orientation. *Vision Research*, 1975, *15*, 367–365.

Helmholtz, H. von *Physiological optics* (Translated from the third German edition). New York: Dover, 1962.

Henn, V., Young, L. R., & Finley, C. Vestibular nucleus units in alert monkeys are also influenced by moving visual fields. *Brain Research*, 1974, *71*, 144–149.

Holst, E. von Relations between the central nervous system and the peripheral organs. *British Journal of Animal Behavior*, 1954, *2*, 89–94.

Jordan, S. Ocular pursuit as a function of visual and proprioceptive stimulation. *Vision Research*, 1970, *10*, 775–780.

Kapteyn T. S., & Bles W. Circular vection and human posture: III. Relation between the reactions to various stimuli. *Agressologie*, 1977, *18*, 335–339.

Keller, E. L., & Precht, W. Persistence of visual response in vestibular nucleus neurons in cerebellectomized cat. *Experimental Brain Research*, 1978, *32*, 591–594.

Keller, E. L., & Precht, W. Visual-vestibular responses in vestibular nucleus neurons in intact and cerebellectomized alert cat. *Neuroscience*, 1979, *4*, 1599–1613.

Lackner, J. R. Speech production: Evidence for corollary-discharge stabilization of perceptual mechanisms. *Perceptual and Motor Skills*, 1974, *39*, 899–902.

Lackner, J. R. Induction of illusory self-rotation and nystagmus by a rotating sound field. *Aviation, Space, and Environmental Medicine*, 1977, *48*, 129–131.

Lackner, J. R. Some mechanisms underlying sensory and postural stability in man. In R. Held, H. W. Leibowitz, & H.-L. Teuber, (Eds.), *Handbook of sensory physiology* (Vol. 8), *Perception*. Berlin: Springer-Verlag, 1978.

Lackner, J. R. Some aspects of sensory-motor control and adaptation in man. In R. D. Walk & H. L. Pick (Eds.), *Intersensory perception and sensory integration*. New York: Plenum, 1981.

Lackner, J. R., & Graybiel, A. Somatosensory motion after-effect following Earth-horizontal rotation about the Z-axis: A new illusion. *Aviation, Space, and Environmental Medicine*, 1977, *48*, 501–502.

Lackner, J. R., & Graybiel, A. Postural illusions experienced during Z-axis recumbent rotation and their dependence on somato-sensory stimulation of the body surface. *Aviation, Space, and Environmental Medicine*, 1978, *49*, 484–488. (a)

Lackner, J. R., & Graybiel, A. Some influences of touch and pressure cues on human spatial orientation. *Aviation, Space, and Environmental Medicine*, 1978, *49*, 798–804. (b)

Lackner, J. R., & Graybiel, A. Parabolic flight: Loss of sense of orientation. *Science*, 1979, *206*, 1105–1108.

Lackner, J. R., & Graybiel, A. Illusions of visual, postural and aircraft motion elicited by deep knee bends in the increased gravitoinertial force phase of parabolic flight: Evidence for dynamic calibration of sensory-motor control to Earth-gravity force levels. *Experimental Brain Research*, 1981, *44*, 312–316.

Lackner, J. R., & Levine, M. Visual direction depends on the operation of spatial constancy mechanisms: The oculobrachial illusion. *Neuroscience Letters*, 1978, *7*, 207–212.

Lackner, J. R., & Levine, M. Changes in apparent body orientation and sensory localization induced by vibration of postural mechanisms: Vibratory myesthetic illusions. *Aviation, Space, and Environmental Medicine*, 1979, *50*, 346–354.

Lackner, J. R., & Mather, J. A. Eye-hand tracking using afterimages: Evidence that sense of effort is dependent on spatial constancy mechanisms. *Experimental Brain Research*, 1981, *44*, 138–142.

Lackner, J. R., & Tuller, B. Role of efference monitoring in the detection of self-produced speech errors. In E. Walker, & W. Cooper (Eds.), *Sentence processing*. Hillsdale, N.J.: Lawrence Erlbaum Associates, 1979.

Levine, M., & Lackner, J. R. Some sensory and motor factors affecting the control and appreciation of eye and limb position. *Experimental Brain Research*, 1979, *36*, 275–283.

Mach, E. *The analysis of sensations*. English translation, New York: Dover, 1962. (Originally published, 1886.)

Marme-Karelse, A., & Bles, W. Circular vection and human posture II. Does the auditory system play a role? *Agressologie*, 1977, *18*, 329–333.

Mather, J. A., & Lackner, J. R. Visual tracking of active and passive movements of the hand. *Quarterly Journal of Experimental Psychology*, 1980, *32*, 307–316. (a)

Mather, J. A., & Lackner, J. R. Adaptation to displaced vision with active and passive limb movements: Effect of movement frequency and predictability. *Quarterly Journal of Experimental Psychology*, 1980, *32*, 317–324. (b)

Mather, J. A., & Lackner, J. R. Multiple sensory cues enhance the accuracy of pursuit eye movements. *Aviation, Space, and Environmental Medicine*, 1980, *51*, 586–589. (c)

McCloskey, D. I. Kinesthetic sensibility. *Physiological Reviews* 1978, *58*, 763–820.

Steinbach, M. J. Eye tracking of self-moved targets: The role of efference. *Journal of Experimental Psychology*, 1969, *82*, 366–376.

Teuber, H.-L. Perception. In J. Field, H. Magoun, & V. Hall (Eds.), *Handbook of physiology: Section I, Neurophysiology*, (Vol. 3). Washington, D.C.: American Physiological Society, 1960.

Waespe, W., & Henn, V. Neuronal activity in the vestibular nuclei of the alert monkey during vestibular and optokinetic stimulation. *Experimental Brain Research*, 1977, *27*, 523–538. (a)

Waespe, W., & Henn, V. Vestibular nuclei activity during optokinetic after-nystagmus (OKAN) in the alert monkey. *Experimental Brain Research*, 1977, *37*, 337–347. (b)

Young, L. R., Dichgans, J., Murphy, R., & Brandt, Th. Interaction of optokinetic and vestibular stimuli in motion perception. *Acta Otolaryngologica*, 1973, *76*, 24–31.

17

Dissociations Between Perceptual and Oculomotor Effects Induced by Rotating Visual Displays

Ronald A. Finke
Michail Pankratov
Richard Held
Massachusetts Institute of Technology

ABSTRACT

When a large visual display is observed rotating about the line of sight, it induces the sensation that the body is tilted, accompanied by an induced torsional rotation of the eyes in the opposite direction. We present three sources of experimental evidence showing that the magnitude of apparent bodily tilt can vary independently of the magnitude of the induced ocular torsion. Whereas visually induced tilt increases when observers perceive themselves to be rotating, increases when the head is tilted off the vertical, and is just as large when the rotating field stimulates central regions of the retina as when it stimulates peripheral regions, visually induced torsion increases when observers perceive themselves to be stationary, does not change when the head is tilted off the vertical, and is larger when the rotating field stimulates central regions of the retina than when it stimulates peripheral regions. These findings suggest that mechanisms underlying visually induced changes in perceived bodily orientation may be dissociated from mechanisms underlying visually induced changes in eye position.

In this chapter we bring together the findings of several recent experiments that we conducted on the perceptual and oculomotor effects of observing rotating visual displays, which demonstrate that changes in the magnitude of these two types of effects do not always correspond. We investigated, specifically, the perceptual and oculomotor effects induced when a person watches a large display of visual noise rotating about the line of sight. When this rotating display is

303

observed from the upright position, one has the sensation that the body is rotating continuously in the opposite direction (termed *roll vection*) together with the sensation that the body is tilted off the vertical, also in the opposite direction. The magnitude of the apparent bodily tilt increases when the rotating field is first observed, but soon reaches a limiting value of about 10–15 deg as nonvisual sources of information about bodily orientation conflict with and constrain the illusion. As a rule, the induced sensations of bodily rotation and tilt increase as the angular velocity of the display increases (up to about 30 deg/sec) and as the size of the display increases (Held, Dichgans, & Bauer, 1975).

One can measure the induced sensation of bodily tilt visually, by having the observer adjust a small bar that is centrally fixated until it appears perfectly horizontal or vertical. However, this illusion is not merely a visual effect, for the perceived direction of gravity is also changed. This has been shown by studies in which the apparent tilt of a fixation bar was found to correspond with changes in posture and bodily orientation that were also induced by the same rotating display (Dichgans, Brandt, & Held, 1974; Dichgans, Held, Young, & Brandt, 1972).

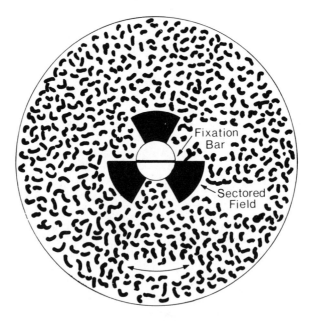

ROTATING DISPLAY FIELD

FIG. 17.1.   The visual display viewed in experiments on state reversals of apparent bodily rotation. The display subtended a visual angle of 122 degrees and was rotated at an angular velocity of 40 degrees/second. The three opaque sectors and the fixation bar remained stationary with respect to the observer as the display was rotated.

In addition to sensations of apparent bodily rotation and tilt, the rotating visual display induces a small rotation of the eyes (termed *torsion*) in the same direction as the display (and hence, in the direction opposite the apparent rotation and tilt). Like visually induced tilt, visually induced torsion increases as the display is first observed but eventually achieves a steady angular displacement, most likely as a result of mechanical constraints on how far the eye can rotate. At one time it was thought that the magnitude of the induced bodily tilt could be accounted for entirely by the magnitude of the visually induced torsion (Hughes, Brecher, & Fishkin, 1972), but recent studies have shown that the induced tilt can be considerably larger than the induced torsion. In particular, whereas visually induced tilt can be as large as 30 deg in some individuals, visually induced torsion seldom exceeds 4 or 5 degrees (Dichgans et al., 1972; Merker & Held, 1981). Much larger amounts of eye torsion can be produced, however, when the head is actually tilted (see Cohen, 1971) or when people are given special training in controlling eye rotation (see Balliet & Nakayama, 1978).

In the following three sections, we present evidence that changes in sensations of visually induced tilt may occur independently of changes in visually induced torsion. This evidence will come from (a) studies on reversals of sensations of apparent bodily rotation, (b) studies on interactions between the visually induced effects and head tilt, and (c) studies comparing effects induced by the selective stimulation of central and peripheral regions of the retina.

EVIDENCE FROM STUDIES ON REVERSALS OF SENSATIONS OF APPARENT BODILY ROTATION

Held et al. (1975) noted that following prolonged viewing of a rotating visual display the sensation of apparent bodily rotation, which is normally continuous, would cease abruptly for brief periods of time. When this occurred the visual display appeared to rotate more rapidly and observers perceived themselves to be stationary. This condition or ''state'' in which apparent bodily motion was absent would then alternate periodically with that in which observers had the sensation that they were rotating. Held et al. also noted that sensations of bodily tilt induced during the state of apparent bodily rotation were larger than those induced during the state of no apparent bodily rotation. In a recent study (Finke & Held, 1978), we measured and compared visually induced tilt and torsion occurring in each of these states.

The method and procedure used in the first experiment of this study is described in some detail, since experiments we report later in this chapter involve similar methods and procedures. The visual display (shown in Fig. 17.1) consisted of a large circular field of visual noise that subtended a visual angle of 122 deg, and was rotated at an angular velocity of 40 deg/sec. Six male and six female observers watched this rotating display while sitting in the upright position and made judgments of tilt and torsion by adjusting a small black bar about which the field rotated. The bar was mounted on a white circular background that subtended a central visual angle of 16 deg. To make judgments of visually induced bodily tilt, the observers aligned the fixation bar until it appeared horizontal with respect to the apparent direction of gravity both before and during rotation of the display. To measure visually induced torsion, a bar-shaped afterimage was first produced using a strobe flash and observers then aligned the fixation bar with the afterimage. These judgments were also made both before and during field rotation. Vertical head position was secured using a biteplate.

After the observers practiced making judgments of tilt and torsion the experimenter described the states of apparent and no apparent bodily rotation (designated as "State 1" and "State 2," respectively), and how these states alternate during prolonged viewing of the rotating field. They were then asked to make judgments of tilt and torsion induced in each state. For each type of judgment, five settings were averaged together for both clockwise and counterclockwise directions of field rotation.

To facilitate the perception of state reversals, three stationary, opaque sectors were mounted on a clear plexiglass screen in front of the rotating display and

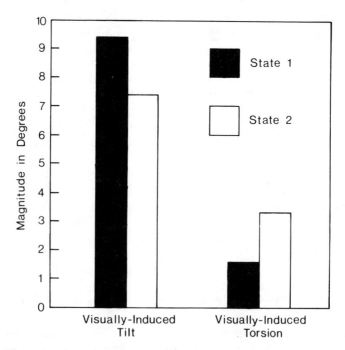

FIG. 17.2.   Mean visually induced tilt and torsion obtained in states of apparent (State 1) and no apparent (State 2) bodily rotation. Measures for induced tilt and torsion are averaged across 12 subjects. Data are from Finke and Held (1978).

were positioned so that they were centered about the small central field contain-ing the fixation bar. These sectors appeared to rotate with the observer in the state of apparent bodily rotation and appeared stationary in the state of no apparent bodily rotation. The alignment of these sectors is also shown in Fig. 17.1[1].

Figure 17.2 presents the mean tilt and torsion obtained in each state, averaged across directions of field rotation. We found, as expected, that visually induced tilt was larger in each of the states than visually induced torsion and that the mean tilt induced in State 1 was larger than that induced in State 2. However, the mean torsion induced in State 1 was *smaller* than that induced in State 2. These results were shown consistently by each observer. Moreover, the magnitude of the changes in induced tilt was uncorrelated with those of induced torsion across reversals of the two states. The failure to find equivalent variations in the magni-tude of visually induced tilt and torsion across state reversals provided our first source of evidence that changes in these two effects can be induced inde-pendently.

EVIDENCE FROM STUDIES ON INTERACTIONS BETWEEN VISUALLY INDUCED EFFECTS AND HEAD TILT

As noted previously, when one observes a rotating visual display while sitting in the upright position the magnitude of visually induced tilt seldom exceeds 10–15 deg. In this section, we first present evidence that constraints on the magnitude of visually induced tilt result largely from competing information about orienta-tion provided by the otoliths, which are receptors sensitive to inertial forces due to linear acceleration in general and to gravity in particular. We then present evidence that the otoliths do not constrain the magnitude of visually induced torsion.

It is known that the accuracy with which one can perceive the direction of gravity decreases as the head becomes tilted off the vertical. For small angles of head tilt this loss of accuracy is known as the *Müller effect;* for large angles of head tilt it is known as the *Aubert effect* (e.g., see Howard & Templeton, 1966). Several studies have recently shown that these effects may be explained by the fact that the otoliths decrease in sensitivity with increasing head tilt (e.g., see Young, 1974). This would lead one to predict that both the magnitude of and variation in visually induced tilt should increase with head tilt, since constraints on induced tilt imposed by the otoliths would be reduced.

---

[1]Having stationary features in the visual field is not necessary for producing state reversals of sensations of apparent bodily rotation. We have observed that these reversals occur even when no stationary features are positioned in front of the rotating visual display.

These predictions were confirmed in studies by Dichgans, Diener, and Brandt (1974) and by Young, Oman, and Dichgans (1975). In addition, other studies have shown that the effects of head tilt on visually induced tilt are more pronounced when the head is tilted in the direction opposite field rotation than when it is tilted in the same direction (Dichgans, Brandt, & Held, 1974; Dichgans, Diener & Brandt, 1974). It thus appeared that visually induced tilt is constrained at least to some extent by competing information about the direction of gravity provided by the otoliths.

With regard to these findings, we considered whether the decrease in otolith efficiency with increasing head tilt would also influence the magnitude of visually induced torsion. In three experiments, we used the same general procedure described in the previous section to obtain judgments of visually induced tilt and torsion under conditions of varying head position.

In the first experiment (Merker & Held, 1981), six male observers made judgments of tilt and torsion first with the head in the upright position, and then with the head tilted to positions of 15, 30, and 45 deg off the vertical. These angular displacements of head position were produced by rotating the biteboard assembly about the center of the visual display. The display was similar to that shown in Fig. 17.1, except that it subtended a visual angle of 130 deg and was rotated at an angular velocity of 20 deg/sec. Also, the central target field subtended 30 deg of visual angle and was not surrounded by the three stationary opaque sectors. Levels of head tilt and the direction of field rotation were randomized across subjects. In this first experiment, no distinction was made between the states of apparent and no apparent bodily rotation.

The results are presented in Fig. 17.3. The top half of the figure shows that the amount of visually induced tilt increased with increasing head tilt and that this effect was greatest when head tilt and field rotation were in opposite directions. These results so far replicated the findings of the studies discussed above. However, in marked contrast to these results, the lower half of the figure shows that the amount of visually induced torsion was the same for all angles of head tilt. Moreover, we found that while the variation in the magnitude of visually induced tilt increased with increasing head tilt, the variation in the magnitude of torsion remained constant. These findings suggest that competing information about orientation provided by the otoliths, which evidently constrains visually induced tilt, does not influence visually induced torsion.

In the second experiment, we investigated how head tilt might interact with variations in visually induced tilt and torsion produced by state reversals of apparent bodily rotation. Ten of the 12 observers who participated in the previous experiment on state reversals served as paid volunteers. Measures of tilt and torsion were taken in States 1 and 2, respectively, for the upright position and for positions of head tilt 30 deg clockwise and counterclockwise off the vertical. The visual display, which included the three stationary sectors, was identical to that shown in Fig. 17.1.

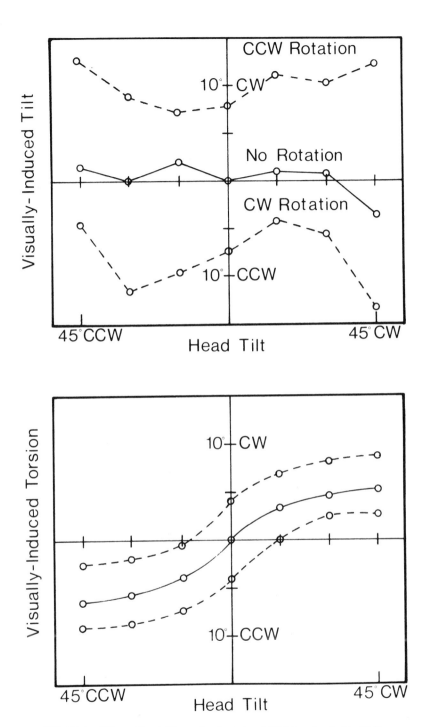

FIG. 17.3. Effect of head tilt on visually induced tilt (above) and visually induced torsion (below). Each measure is averaged across six subjects. Data are from Merker and Held (1981). Reprinted by permission from *Vision Research*, 1981, *21*, 543–547.

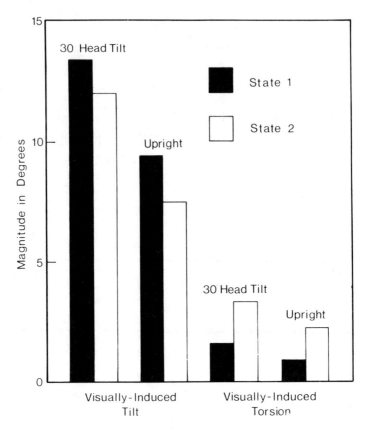

FIG. 17.4.   Effects of head tilt and state reversals of apparent (State 1) and no apparent (State 2) bodily rotation on visually induced tilt and torsion ($N = 10$).

The results for induced tilt and torsion, averaged across directions of field rotation and head tilt, are shown in Fig. 17.4. In agreement with the findings reported above, the mean visually induced tilt was significantly larger when the head was tilted than when the head was in the upright position (correlated-t = 7.81, $df = 9$, $p < .001$), while the mean visually induced torsion was not statistically different for all head positions. Changes in the magnitude of induced tilt and torsion resulting from state reversals were also the same for all head positions. These results provide additional evidence that the magnitude of visually induced tilt, but not that of visually induced torsion, is constrained by the otoliths. They suggest further that the effects of state reversal on visually induced tilt and torsion reported previously for the upright position (Finke & Held, 1978, Experiment 1) can be generalized to other head positions as well.

We then investigated the case in which otolith constraints on visually induced effects are minimized, repeating the state reversal experiment in the supine position (Finke & Held, 1978, Experiment 2). Six of the 10 subjects who partici-pated in the two previous state-reversal experiments viewed the same rotating visual field, this time while lying on their backs. Measures of torsion were taken in each state, as before, while measures of induced "tilt" were taken with respect to the observer's head position, since induced sensations of bodily rota-tion would now occur in the plane perpendicular to the direction of gravity.

The results of this experiment extended the previous findings. The average amount of tilt induced in each state did not differ significantly from baseline measures taken without field rotation, even though each of the observers reported experiencing the usual state reversals of apparent bodily rotation. The observers did, however, show significant amounts of visually induced torsion in the two states. In addition, the average torsion in each state was statistically identical to that which had been obtained when the same observers had viewed the rotating field from the upright position (cf. Fig. 17.2). Again, visually induced torsion appears to be generated independently of head position.

These findings therefore provide a second source of evidence that the magni-tude of visually induced tilt can vary independently of the magnitude of visually induced torsion: Only the former is influenced by changes in head position and corresponding changes in the sensitivity of the otoliths.

EVIDENCE FROM STUDIES COMPARING EFFECTS INDUCED BY STIMULATION OF CENTRAL AND PERIPHERAL REGIONS OF THE RETINA

Several studies have shown that sensations of apparent bodily rotation about the axis of the head (termed *circularvection*) are induced more effectively by stim-ulating peripheral regions of the retina than by stimulating central regions (e.g., Brandt, Dichgans, & König, 1973; Brandt, Wist, & Dichgans, 1975). A similar result has also been found for sensations of apparent bodily acceleration induced by laterally moving visual displays (Berthoz, Pavard, & Young, 1975; Les-tienne, Soechting, & Berthoz, 1977). The opposite result has been obtained for opto-kinetic nystagmus, however, which is elicited more effectively by stimula-tion of central regions of the retina (e.g., Brandt et al., 1973).

In their investigation of visually induced tilt, Held et al. (1975) found that when central and peripheral regions of the rotating visual display were equated for solid angle of exposure, the peripheral regions were slightly more effective in inducing apparent bodily tilt than the central regions. In the following three experiments, we explored the possibility that visually induced torsion, like opto-kinetic nystagmus, is induced more effectively by central stimulation.

In the first experiment, three practiced observers gave judgments of tilt and torsion while viewing rotating displays restricted to central and peripheral re-gions of their visual field. Central and peripheral masks were used to control how

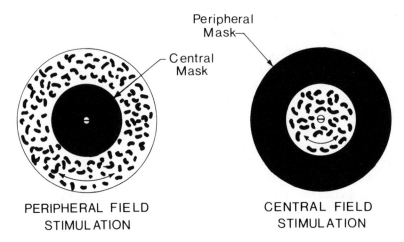

FIG. 17.5.   Examples of central and peripheral masks used in experiments on selective stimulation of central and peripheral regions of the retina. The unmasked rotating display subtended a visual angle of 100 deg.

much of the rotating field was displayed. An example of a central mask is presented in the left half of Fig. 17.5, and an example of the corresponding peripheral field mask is presented in the right half of the figure.

Each observer viewed the rotating display from the upright position using his right eye. Five central and five peripheral masks were each mounted on a clear plexiglass screen that was positioned between the observer and the rotating display. When no masks were used, the display extended to 100 deg of visual angle.

The five peripheral masks, which exposed only central regions of the rotating display, were centered about the observer's line of sight and exposed areas that were 81, 59, 38, 19, and 5% of the total solid angle for the unmasked display field. When these masks were used the fixation bar was mounted on a clear plexiglass support so that the most central region of the rotating field would also be exposed.

The five central masks, which exposed only peripheral regions of the rotating field, were also centered about the observer's line of sight. These masks were of complementary diameter to the peripheral masks, and thus exposed 95, 81, 62, 41, and 19% of the total solid angle for the unmasked display field. Small viewing holes were made in the centers of the central masks so that the observers could see and adjust the fixation bar without seeing any other part of the central region of the rotating field. In this case the fixation bar was mounted on an opaque, white background.

Again, five measures were taken of induced tilt and torsion for each direction of field rotation. The display was rotated at an angular velocity of 28 deg/sec, and judgments were made only when the observers were in State 1. The order of masking conditions was randomized across subjects and the direction of field rotation was counterbalanced.

When the unmasked visual display was viewed, the mean visually induced tilt was 9.7 deg, ranging from 6.6 to 15.2 deg. The mean visually induced torsion was 3.4 deg, ranging from 2.1 to 5.0 deg. These results correspond to those we obtained in our earlier experiments on judging tilt and torsion in the upright position.

The results for the masking conditions are presented in Fig. 17.6, which shows the rate at which the size of each effect increased with increasing stimulation from the central and peripheral regions of the display. Although visually induced tilt was elicited equally well by stimulation from central and peripheral regions (shown in the left half of the figure), visually induced torsion was elicited much more effectively by stimulating central regions (shown in the right half of the figure). These two effects were demonstrated consistently by each of the three observers. It is worth noting that the maximum effect for torsion could be elicited when only 59% of the central field was exposed, and that 41% of this effect could be elicited when just 5% of the central field was exposed. By comparison, exposing 5% of the central field resulted in only 6% of the maximum effect for visually induced tilt. Of further interest, we found that for both induced tilt and torsion, contributions from complementary central and pe-

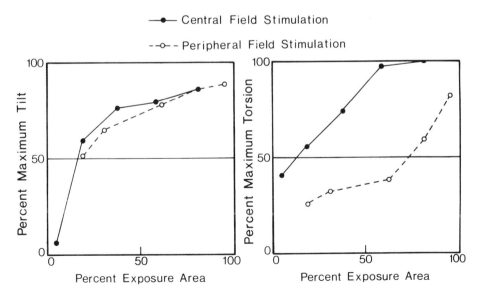

FIG. 17.6. Percentage of maximum effect for visually induced tilt and torsion elicited by increasing stimulation of central and peripheral regions of the retina ($N = 3$).

ripheral exposure regions were not additive, for their sum exceeded the magnitude of effects induced by the unmasked rotating display.

We then conducted a second experiment using the same three observers and two additional masking conditions, to investigate how much torsion could be induced by very small central regions of stimulation. Masks were constructed that exposed only 2.2% and .2% of the central area of the rotating display. In all other regards the experimental procedure was the same. The results showed that even for the smallest central exposure of .2%, 26% of the maximum effect for torsion was obtained.

To demonstrate that the central field advantage for visually induced torsion was reliable, we next tested six naive observers using similar procedures. These subjects viewed, in separate conditions, non-overlapping central and peripheral regions of the visual display each consisting of 25% of the area for the unmasked field. The central and peripheral masks selected for this purpose were like those shown in Fig. 17.5. In this experiment, the state of observation (i.e., whether judgments were made in State 1 or State 2) was randomized.

The results confirmed our previous findings for practiced observers. The mean torsion of 5.8 deg induced by rotation restricted to the central field (87% of the maximum effect) was significantly larger than the mean torsion of 1.1 deg induced by rotation restricted to the peripheral visual field (correlated-$t = 3.02$, $df = 5$, $p < .05$).

Thus, the findings presented in this section provide a third source of evidence that changes in the magnitude of visually induced tilt do not always correspond with changes in the magnitude of visually induced torsion: Visually induced tilt is elicited about as well whether central or peripheral regions of the retina are stimulated, with perhaps a small advantage for peripheral stimulation, whereas visually induced torsion is elicited much more effectively when central regions of the retina are stimulated.

CONCLUSIONS

The major findings in this chapter may be summarized as follows: The amount of apparent bodily tilt induced when a visual display is observed rotating about the line of sight increases when accompanied by sensations of apparent bodily rotation and when the head is tilted off the vertical. Stimulation of central regions of the retina is approximately equivalent to stimulation of peripheral regions in eliciting the induced tilt. In contrast, the amount of visually induced torsion decreases when accompanied by sensations of apparent bodily rotation, is independent of head tilt, and is produced more effectively by stimulation of central regions of the retina.

We claim that these results provide convergent evidence that mechanisms underlying visually induced changes in perceived bodily orientation may be dissociated from mechanisms underlying visually induced changes in eye position. In addition, these results are in general support of recent proposals that dissociations exist among many different types of internal mechanisms in vision, especially among those mechanisms involved in the perception of orientation and identification (e.g., Held, 1970; Johnson, Leibowitz, Millodot, & Lamont, 1976; Schneider, 1969; Teuber, 1978).

Finally, we speculate on the possible neural basis for dissociations in mechanisms presumed to underlie the visually induced tilt and torsion. Wolfe and Held (1979) have recently demonstrated that although observers with normal vision show binocular summation for both tilt and torsion, stereoblind observers show binocular summation for induced torsion only. This result has been extended by Wolfe and Owens (1979), who showed that by inducing artificial anisometropia (a marked refractive difference between the two eyes) in people with normal vision, binocular summation could be eliminated in the case of visually induced tilt but not in the case of visually induced torsion. These findings suggest that visual influence upon the vestibular system, responsible for the induced tilt, may have a cortical origin, while visually induced torsion is likely to involve oculomotor processes mediated at subcortical levels of the visual system.

ACKNOWLEDGMENT

Preparation of this chapter was supported by NASA Grant NGL 22–009–308, NIH Grants EY–02621 and EY–01191, and a grant from the Sloan Foundation. We thank Herschel Leibowitz, Bob Post, Joe Bauer, and Joseph Thomas for helpful suggestions and Judy Romann for preparing the figures. Ronald Finke is now at the Department of Psychology, University of California, Davis, California 95616.

REFERENCES

Balliet, R., & Nakayama, K. Training of voluntary torsion. *Investigative Ophthalmology & Visual Science, 1978, 17,* 303–314.

Berthoz, A., Pavard, B., & Young, L. R. Perception of linear horizontal self-motion induced by peripheral vision (linear-vection): Basic characteristics and visual-vestibular interactions. *Experimental Brain Research, 1975, 23,* 471–489.

Brandt, Th., Dichgans, J., & König, E. Differential effects of central vs. peripheral vision on egocentric and exocentric motion perception. *Experimental Brain Research, 1973, 16,* 496–491.

Brandt, T., Wist, E. R., & Dichgans, J. Foreground and background in dynamic spatial orientation. *Perception & Psychophysics, 1975, 17,* 497–503.

Cohen, B. Vestibulo-ocular relations. In P. Bach y Rita, C. C. Collins, & J. E. Hyde (Eds.), *The control of eye movements.* New York: Academic Press, 1971.

Dichgans, J., Brandt, Th., & Held, R. The role of vision in gravitational orientation. In H. Schöne (Ed.), *Mechanisms of spatial perception and orientation as related to gravity.* Stuttgart: Fischer Verlag, 1974.

Dichgans, J., Diener, H. C., & Brandt, Th. Optokinetic-graviceptive interaction in different head positions. *Acta Otolaryngologica,* 1974, *78,* 391–398.

Dichgans, J., Held, R., Young, L. R., & Brandt, Th. Moving visual scenes influence the apparent direction of gravity. *Science,* 1972, *138,* 1217–1219.

Finke, R. A., & Held, R. State reversals of optically induced tilt and torsional eye movements. *Perception & Psychophysics,* 1978, *23,* 337–340.

Held, R. Two modes of processing spatially distributed visual stimulation. In F. O. Schmitt (Ed.), *The neurosciences: Second study program.* New York: Rockefeller University Press, 1970.

Held, R., Dichgans, J., & Bauer, J. Characteristics of moving visual scenes influencing spatial orientation. *Vision Research,* 1975, *15,* 357–365.

Howard, I. P., & Templeton, W. B. *Human spatial orientation.* New York: Wiley, 1966.

Hughes, P. C., Brecher, G. A., & Fishkin, S. M. Effects of rotating backgrounds upon the perception of verticality. *Perception & Psychophysics,* 1972, *11,* 135–138.

Johnson, C. A., Leibowitz, H. W., Millodot, M., & Lamont, A. Peripheral visual acuity and refractive error: Evidence for "two visual systems"? *Perception & Psychophysics,* 1976, *20,* 460–462.

Lestienne, F., Soechting, J., & Berthoz, A. Postural readjustments induced by linear motion of visual scenes. *Experimental Brain Research,* 1977, *28,* 363–384.

Merker, B., & Held, R. Eye torsion and the apparent horizon under head tilt and visual field rotation. *Vision Research,* 1981, *21,* 543–547.

Schneider, G. E. Two visual systems. *Science,* 1969, *163,* 895–902.

Teuber, H.-L. The brain and human behavior. In R. Held, H. W. Leibowitz, & H.-L. Teuber (Eds.), *Handbook of sensory physiology* (Vol. 8), *Perception.* New York: Springer Verlag, 1978.

Wolfe, J. M., & Held, R. Eye torsion and visual tilt are mediated by different binocular processes. *Vision Research,* 1979, *19,* 917–920.

Wolfe, J. M., & Owens, D. A. Evidence for separable binocular processes differentially affected by artifically induced anisometropia. *American Journal of Optometry and Physiological Optics,* 1979, *56,* 279–284.

Young, L. R. The role of the vestibular system in posture and movement. In V. B. Mountcastle (Ed.), *Medical physiology.* St. Louis: C. V. Mosby, 1974.

Young, L. R., Oman, C. M., & Dichgans, J. Influence of head orientation on visually-induced pitch and roll sensations. *Aviation, Space, and Environmental Medicine,* 1975, *46,* 264–268.

IV DIRECTIONAL ADAPTATION AND LEARNED REVERSAL

18 A Comparison of Intersensory Bias and Prism Adaptation

Robert B. Welch
University of Kansas

David H. Warren
University of California, Riverside

ABSTRACT

An assessment of the relationship between intersensory bias (visual bias of proprioception and proprioceptive bias of vision) and prism adaptation (negative aftereffect, proprioceptive shift, and visual shift) was provided by directly comparing the two phenomena under identical conditions. Three variables were manipulated: Strength of prismatic displacement, realism ("compellingness") of the visual-proprioceptive relationship, and the presence or absence of vibration of the prism-exposed limb.

Neither limb vibration nor prism strength affected either bias or adaptation. Degree of visual-proprioceptive compellingness, however, dramatically influenced the strength of intersensory bias (greater bias with high compellingness) but had no effect on any of the three aspects of prism adaptation.

It was concluded from this differential effect that bias and prism adaptation are, at least in some ways, qualitatively different phenomena. Future investigators of prism adaptation are alerted to the importance of taking account of the intersensory bias that is an inevitable concomitant of the situation within which adaptation occurs.

Viewing one's body through a prism has been found to have both immediate and long-term effects. The classic study of the immediate effects of prism exposure was by Hay, Pick, and Ikeda (1965). These investigators demonstrated that when the stationary hand is viewed through a 14-deg-displacing prism it is immediately felt to be located near its seen (optically displaced) position. Hay et al. referred to this "dominance," or bias, of vision over proprioception as "visual capture," a

319

term borrowed from Tastevin (1937). Subsequent studies (e.g., Pick, Warren, & Hay, 1969) have obtained visual bias of proprioception that has consistently amounted to 60–70% of the total visual-proprioceptive discrepancy. The occurrence of substantial visual bias suggests that under normal (i.e., non-discrepant) circumstances, when vision and proprioception are congruent in their specification of spatial location, it is vision that carries the greater weight in the perceptual experience. It is not the case, however, that the proprioceptive information is without influence. That is, not only is visual bias of proprioception usually less than 100%, but it is also commonly observed that proprioception biases the visual modality to the extent of 20–30% of the intersensory discrepancy (e.g., Pick et al., 1969; Warren & Pick, 1970). It should be noted, furthermore, that the *sum* of the two forms of intersensory bias typically approaches 100% of the total discrepancy, at least with prismatic displacements that do not exceed 11 deg and with a stimulus situation in which the subject has a direct view of his limb. Moreover, most subjects in this situation do not report a visual-proprioceptive conflict. One final point is that if the observer closes his eyes, bias dissipates in a matter of seconds (Hay et al., 1965).

Studies in which subjects are allowed to interact with the prism-displaced visual environment, or are otherwise provided with prolonged, salient exposure to the effects of the perceptual rearrangement, have revealed long-term perceptual modifications referred to as prism adaptation (Welch, 1978, Chapters 2 and 3). This form of adaptation seems to be acquired and lost much more gradually than intersensory bias. When it is assessed as the difference in eye-hand coordination between pre- and postexposure measures (in a compensating direction), the shift is called the "negative aftereffect." A number of studies have demonstrated further that the primary basis for the negative aftereffect is a temporary recalibration of felt limb position, the so-called "proprioceptive shift." Thus, Hamilton (1964) and Harris (1963) provided evidence that, at least under certain conditions of prism exposure, the negative aftereffect is the result of the subject coming to feel as if his hand is located where he has seen it through the prism. Harris (1963), for example, found that after removing the prism, the subject, with eyes closed, will position his hand off to one side when attempting to point straight ahead of his nose.[1] Another form of evidence for this type of adaptation is the fact that when asked to point to the felt position of his unseen index finger with his nonadapted other index finger, he will err in the same direction as the earlier prismatic displacement. In contrast to visual capture, the prism-adaptive proprioceptive shift persists for many minutes after the subject's vision is occluded (e.g., Choe & Welch, 1974).

It would seem that a rather close relation should exist between intersensory bias (particularly visual capture) and proprioceptive prism adaptation since both

---

[1]For certain types of prism exposure a change in the felt direction of gaze may also occur or may occur instead, leading to a prism-adaptive shift in apparent visual direction (e.g., Craske, 1967).

entail changes in felt limb position as a result of exposure to visual-propriocep-tive discrepancy. Indeed, a number of investigators (e.g., Easton & Moran, 1978; Epstein, 1975; Hay et al., 1965; Kelso, Cook, Olson, & Epstein, 1975) have proposed that the two phenomena are qualitatively the same and are pre-sumably based on the same processes. For example, Hay et al. (1965) concluded that ". . . visual capture is the more elementary phenomenon and . . . serves, when suitable auxiliary conditions are met, as the source of proprioceptive adap-tation" (Hay et al., 1965, p. 216).

The assumption of an intimate relation between visual capture and prism adaptation may be referred to as the "similarity hypothesis." Although widely expressed, in only one study (Welch, Widawski, Harrington, & Warren, 1979) has this notion been examined experimentally. In that investigation it was dem-onstrated that whereas active limb movement *increases* proprioceptive prism adaptation (as first observed by Held & Gottlieb, 1958), it *reduces* visual bias. Welch et al. therefore concluded that, contrary to the similarity hypothesis, visual capture and proprioceptive prism adaptation must, in some ways, be qualitatively different perceptual phenomena, since they react in opposite ways to the same experimental manipulation.

Nevertheless, the similarity hypothesis is so intuitively reasonable that we felt it deserved another test. To this end, several independent variables (to be de-scribed below) were manipulated and their effects on both bias and adaptation measured. The means used by Welch et al. to test the similarity hypothesis simply involved a direct comparison of intersensory bias and adaptation, each based on the total imposed intersensory discrepancy. Further consideration, how-ever, suggests what looks to be a more appropriate means of testing this hypoth-esis. In order to appreciate this alternative to the simpler test, it is necessary to understand our present conception of the nature of intersensory bias and adapta-tion and their relation to one another.

We take as a starting point the assumption that the presence of a discrepancy between two sensory modalities induces responses in the perceptual system that are aimed at resolving the discrepancy and thereby regaining a *unified* experi-ence. Two processes by which the perceptual system can react to intersensory discrepancy are bias and adaptation. Both of these processes cause perception to tend to agree with the assumption of a single distal event (the "assumption of unity," as it is referred to in a model of intersensory bias recently proposed by Welch and Warren, 1980). An important difference between the two processes is that intersensory bias operates much more quickly than does adaptation. Thus, the adaptive process does not have an opportunity to act upon the initial pris-matically induced visual-proprioceptive discrepancy, but rather comes into play only with respect to the discrepancy that remains after the fast-acting intersenso-ry bias has reached completion.

The present formulation leads, then, to the conclusion that in order to provide a valid test of the similarity hypothesis, adaptation must be represented as a percentage not of the prismatically induced visual-proprioceptive discrepancy, but of the registered discrepancy that is left after the sum of intersensory bias has been accounted for.

The three variables selected in the present study were limb vibration (versus no vibration), amount of imposed discrepancy (20 versus 30 diopters), and cognitive realism, or "compellingness" (low versus high). These variables are hypothesized to affect bias in the following ways. Vibrating the subject's hand was presumed to increase the salience of the proprioceptive information and thus decrease intersensory bias, by making the spatial discrepancy more evident. Increasing the imposed discrepancy should similarly decrease bias by making the discrepancy more evident. Increasing the compellingness of the visual-proprioceptive relation should increase bias by making the subject tend to regard the two sources of information as representing a single event (i.e., strengthening the assumption of unity).

If the similarity hypothesis is correct but the "traditional" means of testing it is used, then a condition that facilitates the production of intersensory bias should lead to an estimate of *reduced* adaptation, merely because there is relatively little of the initial visual-proprioceptive discrepancy left for the adaptive process to deal with. This outcome would lead the unwary investigator to conclude, incorrectly, that the similarity hypothesis had not been confirmed. If, on the other hand, the similarity hypothesis is true and the alternative means of assessing adaptation is used, then, indeed, one would expect to find a given independent variable having the same effect on adaptation as on bias.

METHOD

Design

The three independent variables were examined by means of a 2 (Vibration/No-Vibration) × 2 (Compelling/Non-Compelling) × 2 (20/30 prism diopter) between-groups design with 10 subjects per cell.

Subjects

Eighty male and female students at the University of Kansas served as subjects as part of a requirement for an introductory psychology course. All had normal or corrected vision, were right-handed, at least 5'2" tall (a requirement necessitated by the dimensions of the testing apparatus), and experimentally naive.

Measures

Visual bias of proprioception (visual capture), as well as proprioceptive bias of vision, were measured in the manner introduced by Pick et al. (1969) and used in nearly all subsequent research in this area. For these measures the subject sat in front of a table upon which rested a box-like arrangement with the open end facing the subject. A dental impression biteboard was used to maintain steady head position during the experiment. In order to determine the degree to which vision biased proprioception (and vice versa), four tasks were administered. The first is referred to as the proprioceptive control (P_c) measure and required that the subject point with his unseen right index finger at the unseen left index (target) finger. The target finger lay motionless on top of a horizontal occluding board, near its far edge, 11 or 17 deg to the left of center, depending upon the strength of the prismatic displacement to which the subject would later be exposed. Each of 12 pointing responses with the right hand was initiated from one of three wooden blocks which were located directly beneath the subject's chin on the surface of the near edge of the table and 15.5 cm to the left and right of this position. Each response involved reaching with the right hand under the occluding board (which was 30 cm above the table) and pointing with the index finger beneath the felt location of the left index finger. No feedback about the subject's performance was provided. Accuracy was measured by means of a metric ruler, attached to the backside of the far edge of the occluding board.

The second of the subject's tasks was to look through 11- or 17-deg (20 or 30 diopters, respectively) binocular rightward-displacing prism goggles and to point (12 times) with the right hand beneath the occluding board at a visual target in the otherwise dark testing room. Again, no feedback on accuracy was given. The visual target was located in the same position as the left index finger had been placed for the P_c measures, 11 or 17 deg to the left of center. Thus, because of the 11- or 17-deg rightward prismatic displacement, the visual target appeared to be directly in front of the subject's nose. As a consequence, the subject was never confronted with an asymmetrical visual display, thereby avoiding potential confounding perceptual or perceptual-motor effects (Howard, 1968). These, then, were the visual control (V_c) measures. Thus, the *difference* between the average P_c and average V_c response represents a measure of the effective prismatic displacement as experienced by the subject.

The third and fourth measures that were required for the calculation of intersensory bias entailed looking through the prism at the stationary left index finger as it lay motionless at the far edge of the topside of the occluding board, in the same location as for the P_c measures. During these prism-exposure trials, the subject was requested to point beneath the occluding board with his (unseen) right index finger either to where he *saw* his left index finger (on 12 trials) or to where he *felt* it (on 12 trials). These are referred to as the visual-exposure (V_e) and proprioceptive-exposure (P_e) measures, respectively. The index of the degree to which vision biased proprioception, symbolized $V(P)$, was the following:

$$V(P) = \frac{P_e - P_c}{V_c - P_c} \times 100.$$

The index of potential proprioceptive bias of vision, $P(V)$, was:

$$P(V) = \frac{V_e - V_c}{P_c - V_c} \times 100.$$

Thus, for example, if the subject, when asked during the prism-exposure trials to point with his (unseen) right index finger to where he felt his left index finger to be located (P_e measure), were to point to the same location as he had during the V_c trials, this would indicate that he felt his finger to be where he saw it and consequently the numerator and denominator differences would be identical, resulting in 100% $V(P)$. Conversely, pointing to the same location as during the P_c trials would indicate that vision had had no effect on felt limb position and, because the numerator would thus be zero, $V(P)$ would equal zero. Intermediate values would signify intermediate amounts of $V(P)$. Similar logic applies to the index of $P(V)$.

In addition to $V(P)$ and $P(V)$, potential adaptation to the prismatic distortion was assessed. Three measures were obtained, each of which is the difference between pre- and post-exposure responses. At the outset of the experiment (the baseline pre-exposure period) and immediately after each of four 1-min prism-exposure periods, the subject, with vision normal, was tested on his ability to (1) point at a centrally positioned visual target with the unseen left index finger (the finger seen during the prism-exposure period), (2) point to the unseen left index finger with the unseen right index finger (identical to the P_c measure), and (3) indicate when a point of light in the otherwise dark room appeared to be positioned straight ahead of his nose. A pre-post shift in the first measure (in a compensatory direction) represents a change in eye-hand coordination (negative aftereffect), in the second, a change in felt limb position (proprioceptive shift), and in the third, a change in visual localization, the last-mentioned referred to as the "visual shift."[2]

Procedure and Apparatus

After inducing partial dark adaptation (by means of an 8-min period during which the subject wore red-filter goggles) and training on the basic pointing response, 24 measures of the subject's accuracy in pointing at a visual target with each (unseen) hand were obtained. Half of these responses were made with the right hand and half with the left. The former were the V_c measures and the latter the pre-exposure measures for the potential prism-adaptive negative aftereffect. For half of the subjects the left- and right-handed pointing responses were blocked in the order: 6 right, 12 left, 6 right and for the other half the order was 6 left, 12 right, 6 left. For subjects in the Compelling condition (to be described below) the visual target was a rubber finger coated with fluorescein dye and illuminated by an ultraviolet (UV)

---

[2]It might be argued that to the extent that negative aftereffect and/or proprioceptive shift (assuming they occur) transfer from the exposed left hand to the right hand or that visual shift is induced, subsequent measures of intersensory bias will be contaminated. However, this criticism is unwarranted since the bias measures (P_c, V_c, P_e, and V_e) were obtained anew after each adaptation period, thereby taking into account cumulative adaptation and potential intermanual transfer.

light which was positioned above it. In order to facilitate viewing, the finger was placed at a 45-deg angle with respect to the in-out dimension. For subjects in the Non-Compelling condition (to be described below) the target was a 4.1-cm-diameter disc, also coated with fluorescein dye and illuminated by the UV light.

Next, 12 P_c measures were obtained in the manner described previously. During these measures the subject's left arm and hand lay out in front of his body upon an arm-shaped metal surface which rested on top of the occluding board. Although the subject's arm was horizontal, the hand was raised to approximately a 45-deg angle to afford the subject a good view of the index finger during those portions of the experiment in which he would be allowed to see it. In the No-Vibration condition the subject was told to relax the entire arm as completely as possible. In the Vibration condition he was to maintain a constant pressure on the metal surface while the latter was vibrated by means of an orbital sander to which it had been bolted. The entire arm, from finger tip to shoulder, was vibrated quite vigorously by the sander. During these measures of the subject's accuracy in pointing to his left index finger, a sliding panel was placed in front of his eyes to eliminate any possibility of seeing the target finger.

Next, 10 visual straight-ahead measures were obtained by having the subject turn 180 deg in his chair, place his head up against a pair of fixed, prismless welder's goggles, and turn a dial with his right hand which caused a small, red light-emitting diode to move from a far-left or a far-right position (five trials each) until it appeared to be straight ahead of his nose in the otherwise dark room.

For the prism-exposure measures (V_e and P_e), the subject wore a black cloth sleeve and glove over the left arm and hand (but not the index finger). For the Compelling condition, the index finger had been coated with fluorescein dye. In the Non-Compelling condition, a 4.1-cm-diameter circular disc had been attached to the subject's left index finger, an operation which the subject was made fully aware of. The disc was designed to be equal in area to the typical index finger. While the subject looked through his 11- or 17-deg rightward-displacing prisms, 12 V_e and 12 P_e measures were obtained, following the instructions that on these trials he was to do his best to point with his (unseen) right index finger either to where he *saw* his finger (disc), the V_e trials, or where he *felt* his finger, the P_e trials, and to ignore the other sensory modality. He was told specifically that the felt and seen positions of the finger might not be the same. For half of the subjects the order was 6 V_e, 12 P_e, 6 V_e and for half it was 6 P_e, 12 V_e, 6 P_e. Subjects in the No-Vibration condition made these responses with the left arm and hand in a relaxed position; subjects in the Vibration condition responded while the arm was being vibrated by the sander. The sliding panel was lowered between each response, allowing the subject to see the finger through the prism for only 3–4 sec per trial.

Immediately following the last of the prism-exposure measures a 1-min, prism-adaptation period was instituted, during which the subject viewed the stationary left index finger or the attached disc while his limb was vibrated or not. Immediately after this period, 6 measures of visual straight-ahead, 6 V_c measures, and 6 P_c measures were obtained, in that order. Next, 12 prism-exposure measures (6 V_e and 6 P_e) were taken, followed by a second 1-min, prism-adaptation period. The sequence was repeated for a total of four 1-min adaptation periods and series of postexposure measures.

To summarize, measures of $V(P)$ and $P(V)$ (according to the formulae presented earlier) were obtained in the initial baseline period and after each of the four prism-adaptation periods. Prism adaptation in terms of pre-post shifts in (1) eye-hand coordination (negative aftereffect), (2) felt limb position (proprioceptive shift), and (3) visual straight-ahead (visual shift) was also measured for each of the adaptation periods, in each case using as the pre-exposure scores the measures obtained during the initial baseline period. In accordance with traditional procedure, pre-exposure measures were not taken prior to each adaptation period since these measures most certainly would have been affected by previous adaptation, thereby obscuring the expected growth of adaptation over the course of the four periods.

RESULTS

The usual means of testing the similarity hypothesis is a comparison of intersensory bias with adaptation, each taking as its referent the total prismatically imposed discrepancy; the initial analyses were carried out in this fashion.

Figure 18.1 depicts the mean intersensory bias results (expressed as percentages) for the five measurement periods, presented separately for the Compelling and Non-Compelling conditions.

A Compelling/Non-Compelling × Vibration/No-Vibration × Prismatic Displacement (20/30 diopters) × Sex × Tests analysis of variance, with repeated measures on the last factor, was performed upon each of the measures of intersensory bias, $V(P)$, $P(V)$, and the *sum* of the two bias effects. The factor of sex was examined as an afterthought, as a result of some preliminary work suggesting possible sex differences in intersensory bias. "Tests" refers to the baseline (BL) and each of the four post-adaptation tests, for a total of five repetitions.[3]

For $V(P)$ and bias sum, the factor of Compellingness was highly significant, $F(1,64) = 15.39, p < .001$, and $F(1,64) = 9.42, p < .001$, bias being much greater in the Compelling condition (see Figs. 18.1-A and 18.1-C). There was,

---

[3]It will be noted in Fig. 18.1-A that the magnitude of $V(P)$ in the Compelling condition is, for the most part, substantially less than the 60–70% reported in most previous studies (e.g., Pick et al., 1969). The explanation for this relatively low value is almost certainly the fact that the dimly luminous index finger, while more compelling than the luminous disc, was nevertheless not as compelling as the traditional situation in which a normally illuminated finger or entire hand is viewed.

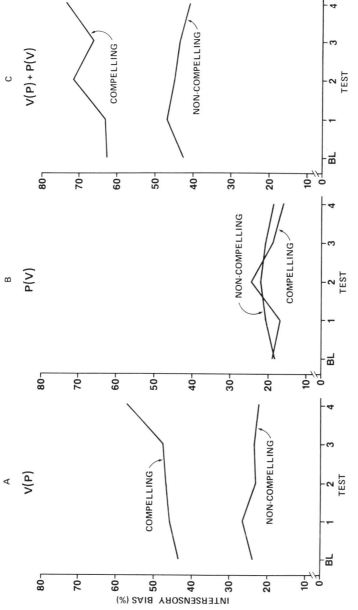

FIG. 18.1. Visual bias of proprioception [V(P)], proprioceptive bias of vision [P(V)], and bias sum [V(P) + P(V)] for Compelling and Non-Compelling conditions as a function of repeated tests. NOTE: BL = BASELINE MEASURE

327

however, no effect of this factor for $P(V)$, $F(1,64) < 1.0$ (Fig. 18.1-B). None of the other main effects or interactions was statistically significant for any of the three measures of intersensory bias.

In Figure 18.2 is presented the results for each of the three types of adaptation (taken as percentages of the total imposed discrepancy) for each of the four adaptation periods, presented separately for the 20- and 30-diopter conditions. It may be seen that both negative aftereffect and proprioceptive shift increased over successive adaptation periods, whereas visual shift revealed either little gain (30-diopter condition) or, inexplicably, a sharp decline (20-diopter condition).

A Compelling/Non-Compelling × Vibration/No-Vibration × Prismatic Displacement × Tests analysis of variance, with repeated measures on the last factor, was performed on each of the three indices of adaptation. "Tests" refers to each of the four adaptation periods (1–4).

Tests was a statistically significant factor for both negative aftereffect, $F(3,216) = 6.70$, $p < .001$, and proprioceptive shift, $F(3, 216) = 12.24$, $p < .001$, while Prismatic Displacement was significant only for proprioceptive shift, $F(1,72) = 4.66$, $p < .04$ (see Fig. 18.2-B). None of the other factors or interactions proved statistically significant for either of these types of adaptation. For the visual shift measure, the only significant effect was the quite unexpected Tests × Prismatic Displacement interaction, $F(3,216) = 3.66$, $p < .02$ (Fig. 18.2-C).

The results of the preceding analyses clearly fail to support the similarity hypothesis because the dramatic effect of compellingness on bias (visual bias and bias sum) was not paralleled by an effect on prism adaptation.

Due to the presumed complications of the accumulation of adaptation and resulting shift in baselines, further analyses were carried out in which only the first test of bias and the first test of adaptation were examined. Furthermore, it was felt that the most definitive comparison of the two prism phenomena would involve (1) the sum of bias and (2) the negative aftereffect. This seemed reasonable since the sum of $V(P)$ and $P(V)$ represents the maximum resolution of the intersensory discrepancy that the biasing mechanism has been able to produce, whereas the negative aftereffect is usually considered to be the equivalent of the algebraic sum of proprioceptive shift and visual shift, and thus represents the total resolution of the discrepancy of which the adaptation process is capable.

The bias sum for the first test was subjected to a Compelling/Non-Compelling × Vibration/No-Vibration × Prismatic Displacement analysis of variance. The compellingness factor proved to be highly significant, $F(1,79) = 7.06$, $p < .001$, the group means being 62.6 and 42.5% for Compelling and Non-Compelling conditions, respectively (see Fig. 18.1-C). None of the other main effects or interactions was significant.

Negative aftereffect (as a percentage) was subjected to the Compelling/Non-Compelling × Vibration/No-Vibration × Prismatic Displacement analysis of variance and revealed no significant main effects or interactions (see Fig. 18.2-A).

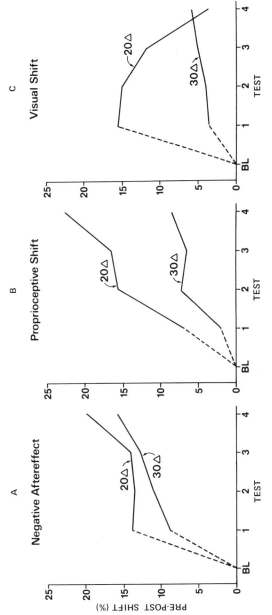

FIG. 18.2. Negative aftereffect, proprioceptive shift, and visual shift (as percentages of theoretical maximum) for 20- and 30-diopter prism conditions as a function of repeated tests. *NOTE:* BL = BASELINE MEASURE (ZERO, BY DEFINITION) △ = PRISM DIOPTER

Thus, it can be seen once again that whereas the factor of compellingness had a very strong influence on intersensory bias, no effect was obtained for adaptation. It may be concluded, then, that according to the traditional means of testing the similarity hypothesis, bias and adaptation are qualitatively different processes, just as Welch et al. (1979) had concluded from their study.

In order to examine the similarity hypothesis by means of the alternative ("refined") test described in the introduction, the negative aftereffect measure must be recalculated. Specifically, it is necessary first to subtract from the total imposed discrepancy (10.3 and 17.1 cm for 20- and 30-diopter conditions, respectively) the amount that was resolved by the bias sum and then to use this residual discrepancy as the devisor for the negative aftereffect. For example, if a particular subject in the 20-diopter condition obtained a bias sum of 50% (or .50) and a negative aftereffect of 2 cm, the adaptation percentage as calculated by the refined procedure would be:

$$2 \text{ cm}/[10.3 \text{ cm} - (.50 \cdot 10.3 \text{ cm})]$$
$$= 2 \text{ cm}/5.15 \text{ cm} = 39\%$$

By way of comparison, the traditional means of calculating percent adaptation, in which the initial bias is not taken into account, gives:

$$2 \text{ cm}/10.3 \text{ cm} = 19\%$$

Negative aftereffect, calculated in this new manner, was found in some cases to be excessively (and uninterpretably) large or small. As a consequence, a criterion was adopted in which scores that were greater than 150% or less than −50% were excluded from the analysis. Use of this criterion resulted in the loss of the data for 16 subjects. The eight group-means (along with their respective ns) are presented in Table 18.1.

According to a Compelling/Non-Compelling × Vibration/No-Vibration × Prismatic Displacement analysis of variance, none of the main effects or interactions was statistically significant.

In one final test of the similarity hypothesis, a Pearson product-moment correlation coefficient was calculated for the relationship between the group means of bias sum and the corresponding group means of the refined negative aftereffect percent. The result was an r of .33, which is not statistically significant ($p > .05$). Once again, the similarity hypothesis was not supported.

DISCUSSION

Even when evaluated by what we have argued is the more appropriate test, the similarity hypothesis was not supported by the present data. The differential effect of compellingness on bias and adaptation is in agreement with the results

TABLE 18.1
Negative Aftereffect as a Percentage of the Visual-Proprioceptive
Discrepancy Remaining after Removal of Bias Sum

	20Δ		30Δ	
Compellingness	*VIB*	*No-VIB*	*VIB*	*No-VIB*
Compelling	8	41	41	28
	(n = 6)	(n = 6)	(n = 9)	(n = 7)
Non-compelling	39	30	13	13
	(n = 8)	(n = 10)	(n = 10)	(n = 8)

of a study by Radeau and Bertelson (1977), in which degree of compellingness was found to have a marked effect on visual-auditory intersensory bias (''ventriloquism'') but not on visual-auditory adaptation.

Thus, it would appear that whereas the strength of the assumption of unity is integrally involved in intersensory bias, this is not the case for the process that underlies perceptual adaptation.[4] Why this should be so is unclear, since it seems reasonable to suppose in the case of prism adaptation that only if there is some belief that one's sources of visual and proprioceptive information are emanating from a single object would there be an effective discrepancy registered in the nervous system. Nevertheless, a study by Welch (1972) demonstrated that even when the subject believed that the finger that he saw displaced to one side of his own finger was the *experimenter's* (thereby presumably destroying the assumption of unity), a certain amount of prism adaptation occurred.

In any event, it may be concluded from the fact that compellingness affected bias but not adaptation that there is a qualitative difference between the two phenomena. The exact nature of this difference and its implications for the relationship between the processes of bias and adaptation remain to be clarified.

Unexpectedly, no effect of vibration was found in this study. This result contradicts the findings of a study by Kravitz and Wallach (1966) in which adaptation (negative aftereffect) for the stationary limb was enhanced by limb vibration. There are several differences between the present conditions and those of Kravitz and Wallach, including their use of longer exposure periods and of vertical rather than lateral prismatic displacement. It would certainly seem unwarranted to suggest that the present investigators failed to adequately stimulate the arm, since, as indicated previously, the limb was quite vigorously vibrated along its entire length.

---

[4]Support for the argument that degree of visual-proprioceptive compellingness is directly related to strength of the observer's assumption of unity comes from a follow-up study in which subjects used a 1-7 scale to rate the magnitude of their unity assumption in each of three situations of increasing compellingness, two of which were identical to those used in the present study. The results demonstrated clearly that as compellingness increased, so did the strength of the unity assumption as reported by the subject.

The variable of compellingness has largely been ignored in the designs of most intersensory research involving visual-proprioceptive discrepancies. This failure is likely to have led researchers to some incorrect conclusions. A notable example concerns the question of the degree to which the various spatial modalities (vision, proprioception, audition) operate as an integrative system. If it *is* such a system, then the demonstration by Pick et al. (1969) that vision strongly biases proprioception and proprioception moderately biases audition should lead to the expectation that vision will bias audition more than it does proprioception. In fact, Pick et al. found that vision biases audition much *less* than it biases proprioception. It is likely, however, that this apparent lack of transitivity among the three spatial modalities was the result of a failure to equate for intersensory compellingness.

Specifically, in the Pick et al. study, the visual-proprioceptive situation involved a view of the normally illuminated finger, whereas the visual-auditory situation consisted of seeing a stationary earplug speaker from which emanated a series of repetitive clicks. Clearly, the former situation is much more compelling (by the present definition) than is the latter. If precautions had been taken to equate the two situations on this variable, different results are likely to have been obtained. This expectation has found support in a recent study by Warren, Welch, and McCarthy (1981) in which it was demonstrated that when the visual-auditory relationship was highly compelling (a view of a human speaker's moving mouth and the sound of his synchronous voice), visual bias of audition was nearly 100%. This figure is substantially larger than the typical bias of vision over proprioception and therefore is congruent with the notion of transitivity among the spatial senses.

Although the overall conclusion regarding the relationship between intersensory bias and adaptation was not altered when the more refined procedure for assessing adaptation was used, the rationale for undertaking this alternative procedure should not be ignored. It is important that future investigators of prism adaptation take into consideration the fact that the same conditions that produce adaptation (i.e., exposure to the prismatically displaced limb) inevitably lead to bias, and because bias occurs very rapidly, it will almost certainly place a limit on the amount of adaptation that can subsequently occur. Indeed, to the extent that conditions favor substantial total bias, one should expect little adaptation. Thus, where it is possible, studies of adaptation would gain a much more accurate picture of the ways in which the perceptual system deals with imposed intersensory discrepancy by including measures of intersensory bias.

ACKNOWLEDGMENTS

This investigation was supported, in part, by a grant from the University of Kansas General Research Fund (No. 3426–0038). This article is based on a paper presented at the meeting of the Psychonomic Society, Phoenix, November, 1979. The authors wish to acknowledge Steven K. Latimer, Daniel L. Swagerty, and John S. Wait, of the University of Kansas, all of whom were involved in the testing of subjects and/or initial data reduction. Our special thanks go to Alex Ramirez, of the University of California, Riverside, for his advice and assistance in the statistical analyses. Requests for reprints should be sent to Robert B. Welch, Department of Psychology, University of Kansas, Lawrence, KS 66045.

REFERENCES

Choe, C. S., & Welch, R. B. Variables affecting the intermanual transfer and decay of prism adaptation. *Journal of Experimental Psychology,* 1974, *102,* 1076–1084.

Craske, B. Adaptation to prisms: Change in internally registered eye position. *British Journal of Psychology,* 1967, *58,* 329–335.

Easton, R. D., & Moran, P. W. A quantitative confirmation of visual capture of curvature. *The Journal of General Psychology,* 1978, *98,* 105–112.

Epstein, W. Recalibration by pairing: A process of perceptual learning. *Perception,* 1975, *4,* 59–72.

Hamilton, C. R. Intermanual transfer of adaptation to prisms. *American Journal of Psychology,* 1964, *77,* 457–462.

Harris, C. S. Adaptation to displaced vision: Visual, motor, or proprioceptive change? *Science,* 1963, *140,* 812–813.

Hay, J. C., Pick, H. L., Jr., & Ikeda, K. Visual capture produced by prism spectacles. *Psychonomic Science,* 1965, *2,* 215–216.

Held, R., & Gottlieb, N. Technique for studying adaptation to disarranged hand-eye coordination. *Perceptual and Motor Skills,* 1958, *8,* 83–86.

Howard, I. P. Displacing the optical array. In S. J. Freedman (Ed.), *The neuropsychology of spatially oriented behavior.* Homewood, Ill.: Dorsey, Press, 1968.

Kelso, J. A. S., Cook, E. Olson, M. E., & Epstein, W. Allocation of attention and the locus of adaptation to displaced vision. *Journal of Experimental Psychology: Human Perception and Performance,* 1975, *1,* 237–245.

Kravitz, J. H., & Wallach, H. Adaptation to displaced vision contingent upon vibrating stimulation. *Psychonomic Science,* 1966, *6,* 465–466.

Pick, H. L., Jr., Warren, D. H., & Hay, J. C. Sensory conflict in judgments of spatial direction. *Perception & Psychophysics,* 1969, *6,* 203–205.

Radeau, M., & Bertelson, P. Adaptation to auditory-visual discordance and ventriloquism in semi-realistic situations. *Perception & Psychophysics,* 1977, *22,* 137–146.

Tastevin, J. En partant de l'experience d'Aristote. *L'Encephale,* 1937, *1,* 57–84, 140–158.

Warren, D. H., & Pick, H. L., Jr. Intermodality relations in blind and sighted people. *Perception & Psychophysics,* 1970, *8,* 430–432.

Warren, D. H., Welch, R. B., & McCarthy, T. J. The role of visual-auditory "compellingness" in the ventriloquism effect: Implications for the transitivity among the spatial senses. *Perception & Psychophysics,* 1981, *30,* 557–564.

Welch, R. B. The effect of experienced limb identity upon adaptation to simulated displacement of the visual field. *Perception & Psychophysics,* 1972, *12,* 453–456.

Welch, R. B. *Perceptual modification: Adapting to altered sensory environments.* New York: Academic Press, 1978.

Welch, R. B., & Warren, D. H. Immediate perceptual response to intersensory discrepancy. *Psychological Bulletin,* 1980, *88,* 638–667.

Welch, R. B., Widawski, M. H., Harrington, J., & Warren, D. H. An examination of the relationship between visual capture and prism adaptation. *Perception & Psychophysics,* 1979, *25,* 126–132.

19 Perceptual Coding and Adaptations of the Oculomotor Systems

Sheldon M. Ebenholtz
University of Wisconsin-Madison

ABSTRACT

Plasticity in various oculomotor control systems is suggested as the basis for perceptual adaptation. A system of egocentric (head centered) angular coordinates patterned after Müller's K-system is proposed as the basis for the encoding of spatial orientation and distance in terms of the parameters of the oculomotor system responsible for the control of disjunctive and conjugate eye movements and their steady states.

Data are reported showing that adaptation to optical tilt produces a shift in apparent vertical and horizontal target orientation as well as in the direction of voluntary (self-directed) saccades, and in the direction of the vestibular ocular response (VOR). The VOR control system is suggested as underlying the adaptation of apparent egocentric target orientation.

INTRODUCTION

Professor Kohler's remarkable studies of adaptability in perception provoked and reinforced my own interest in this area of vision research, even as a graduate student. With funds from my first vision research grant I commissioned the construction of an optical device patterned after considerations in Helmholtz's Physiological Optics (1962, p. 60), which permitted rotation of the image around the line of sight, but with right-left reversals eliminated. I chose optical tilt as an important transformation because it seemed most unlikely to produce aftereffects that could readily be accounted for by changes in oculomotor posture, and hence, on the face of it, they might represent instances of true visual shift. To date, however, there is growing support to the effect that even tilt adaptation can be shown to arise from plasticity in oculomotor functioning, namely from changes in the direction of the vestibular-ocular reflex. Below, I offer arguments and describe the empirical evidence for the conclusion that there is a close and perhaps a causal association between the perception of visual orientation and oculomotor function, a position taken in general many times by Professor Kohler.

In the following work no attempt is made to assess competing theories based on an ''afference'' code such as Gibson's (1979) ecological approach. Neither does it address current attempts to resolve the question of the relative contributions of retinal and extraretinal eye position information to aspects of the perception of spatial orientation (Bridgeman & Stark, 1981; Matin, 1981; Shebilske, 1981).

OCULOMOTOR ENCODING OF SPATIAL ATTRIBUTES

The oculomotor basis for adaptation of apparent visual direction, eye-specific adaptation, and distance adaptation has been presented elsewhere (Ebenholtz, 1970a; 1974; 1981; Paap & Ebenholtz, 1976; 1977; Welch, 1978). These and other studies of apparent visual direction (Shebilske, 1981) serve to emphasize the important and sometimes unexpected role the oculomotor system plays in the encoding of spatial attributes of perception. In general terms, encoding the direction and distance of targets relative to an ego-center can be accomplished with the information provided by a three-dimensional polar coordinate system. Consider, for example, an egocentric (head centered) system such as Müller's (1916) K-system, but in angular coordinates (Linksz, 1952; Luneburg, 1947) as represented in Fig. 19.1. The angle Φ represents the target eccentricity or angular deviation from straight ahead in the left-right direction, while α represents the angular elevation relative to the horizon plane and γ is the convergence angle encoding distance from the ego center. These three angles are sufficient to locate a target in three-dimensional space near the coordinate center and to serve as coordinates for directed whole-body and manual movements. But how are these angles represented in the perceiving organism? The presence of independent oculomotor sub-systems controlling disjunctive or vergence eye movements and conjugate or version movements (Adler, 1965; Alpern, 1969) provides a likely solution. In fact, there is evidence that the horizontal component of the steady state aspect of disjunctive eye movements encodes distance (Ebenholtz, 1981; Ebenholtz & Fisher, 1982; Foley, 1975) whereas the steady states of vertical and horizontal conjugate eye movements encode vertical and horizontal angular displacements, respectively (Ebenholtz, 1976; 1978; Kohler, 1964; Park, 1969).

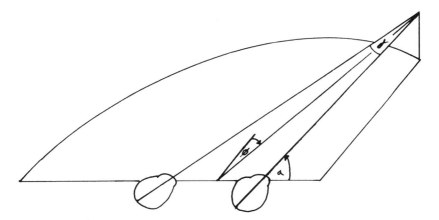

FIG. 19.1. A system of egocentric angular coordinates representing convergence distance (γ), elevation (α) and horizontal displacement (Φ).

Although the hypothesis of encoding egocentric orientation from signals derived from the oculomotor systems is not new (Berkeley, 1910; Bruell & Albee, 1955; Carr, 1935), only recently has a glimpse been provided of the underlying mechanisms. For example there is evidence for the encoding of saccades in the superior colliculus not according to a retinocentric code, but rather in terms of a spatial, headcentered egocentric coordinate system (Mays & Sparks, 1980a; 1980b). Furthermore, progress has been made in modeling the vergence control system (Krishnan & Stark, 1977; Schor, 1979) and in identifying the departure from the position of physiological rest (phoria) as a significant correlate of apparent distance (Ebenholtz, 1981; Ebenholtz & Fisher, 1982; Owens & Leibowitz, 1980, 1982).

In addition to the encoding of distance and egocentric angular orientation, oculomotor systems may also be used to encode orientation of the frontal plane itself. For this purpose it is necessary to consider the joint processing of retinal disparity and eye position information, as represented in Fig. 19.2. In this diagram it is assumed that the observer views the line target with illusory eye position information to the effect that the target, although fixated straight ahead, appears to the left at Φ degrees.[1] If the perception can be predicted from these geometrical considerations, then the line should be seen at θ deg from the frontal plane since only in this orientation will it project the identical pattern of binocular disparities as the frontal plane target that actually is fixated.

---

[1]A simple technique to produce an illusory eye position is to maintain a deviated ocular posture (e.g., a secondary position of gaze) for several minutes (Park, 1969) although other methods are available (Shebilske, 1981).

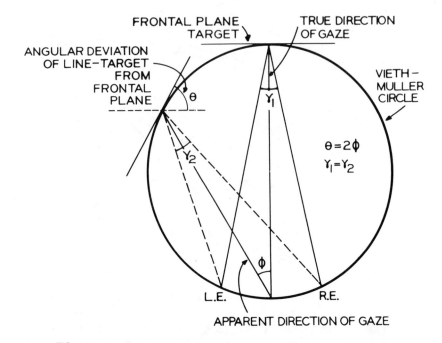

FIG. 19.2.   Fixation is straight ahead at the center of the frontal plane target but the apparent direction of gaze is assumed to be to the left at Φ deg. From "Further evidence for an orientation constancy based upon registration of ocular position." by S. M. Ebenholtz and K. R. Paap, *Psychological Research*, 1976, *38*, 395–409. Reprinted by permission of the publisher and the author.)

Another way of formulating this relation is to note the essential geometrical equivalence between a horizontal line target that is displaced left or right in the frontal plane, and one that is fixated straight ahead of the observer but rotated about a vertical axis (Ebenholtz & Paap, 1973). Since equivalent patterns of retinal disparity can be created in these two ways, if in the absence of other cues eye position information is inadequate to signal relative direction of gaze, one could not determine whether the target was straight ahead but rotated out of the frontal plane or in the frontal plane but laterally displaced. That displacement and rotation are indeed linked in this fashion can be immediately appreciated by viewing a horizontal line target through a pair of wedge prisms (Ebenholtz & Paap, 1976). Base right prisms will cause the line to appear rotated in depth with the right side away from the observer, while base left prisms produce the opposite rotation. Direct evidence for the role of the oculomotor system in these effects has been obtained without the potentially complicating factor of prismatic distortions by producing a bias in the oculomotor registration of lateral and vertical target-positions. In these instances illusory displacements were accom-

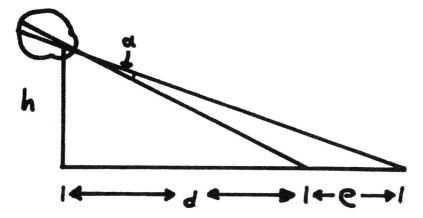

FIG. 19.3.   Linear element e at distance d and height h projects retinal angle α.

panied by illusory target rotations (Ebenholtz & Paap, 1973; 1976; Ebenholtz & Shebilske, 1973[2]).

Thus, by influencing apparent frontal plane orientation, eye position information also contributes to depth perception, but with no change required in binocular disparities.

One may derive additional spatial attributes based upon the oculomotor encoding of distance. Because of the constancies of size and depth (Wallach & Zuckerman, 1963) and their dependence on distance information, these spatial qualities may be modulated by variation in the magnitude of the distance signal.

An additional, particularly interesting example of the possible role of oculomotor encoding of spatial attributes appears to be that of distance constancy, a rarely investigated phenomenon (Baird, 1970; Gibson, 1979; Smith, 1958). In Fig. 19.3 the linear element e is viewed at distance d along the ground plane with the eye at height h. To a first approximation, assuming e is small relative to d, the retinal angle α produced by the element e can be represented as: $\alpha = h \cdot e / d^2$.

Thus, angle α is a function both of eye height and distance yet the perceived length of the element exhibits relatively good constancy with increasing distance (Smith, 1958). Such an accomplishment would be quite feasible, at least within a few meters (Leibowitz & Moore, 1966), if information concerning h and d were available. The encoding of distance by convergence, and eye height by ocular

---

[2]This type of encoding also plays a role in the E–effect with the observer at a backward pitch angle in the median plane (Ebenholtz, 1970b). Here the doll reflex (Ebenholtz & Shebilske, 1975; Shebilske & Fogelgren, 1977) causes an illusory target elevation with backward body tilt and a consequent illusory target rotation.

elevation angle seems to represent a likely solution, but direct tests of the role of these oculomotor systems in distance constancy are not available.

Although the several oculomotor systems can, in fact, encode and modulate such perceptual qualities as egocentric spatial orientation, frontal plane orientation, size, and even depth, there remains the important dimension of target orientation as represented within the frontal plane itself. This spatial attribute can be defined as an egocentric angular orientation relative to the mid-sagittal axis of the observer's head or as a retinal image at some angle relative to the vertical retinal meridian, and alternatively as a rotation of a line target around the line-of-sight axis. That egocentric target orientation is not dependent on a gravitational frame of reference has been demonstrated by, for example, Rock (1954) in paradigms in which supine observers adjust a luminous line target to parallel the sagittal axis of the head.[3] It is precisely with respect to egocentric target orientation which adapts and shifts after exposure to Dove prisms (Mack & Rock, 1968), that the question of the role of oculomotor control is now raised.

OCULOMOTOR PLASTICITY AND APPARENT TARGET ORIENTATION

Consider a locus of points on the retina that when visually stimulated registers as the egocentric vertical direction. This locus exhibits a good deal of plasticity as studies of tilt adaptation have shown (Ebenholtz, 1966). Furthermore, recent studies have established at least the plausibility of modeling egocentric target orientation as the controlled quantity or output in a negative feedback control system (Ebenholtz & Callan, 1980). The nominal input to such a system represented in Fig. 19.4 is the optical tilt imposed by the prism system, but what might the proximal or physiological input be? Recent electro-oculographic (EOG) studies of the effects of tilt adaptation on oculomotor performance suggest an answer. In one study (Callan & Ebenholtz, 1981), subjects adapted to a 30 deg clockwise (cw) tilt for 15 min by walking within a lighted hallway while viewing monocularly through a set of Dove prisms placed in tandem before the right eye. Adjusting a luminous line to the apparent egocentric vertical (6 to 12 o'clock) and horizontal (3 to 9 o'clock) resulted in significant pre- to post-exposure shifts of about 6 deg cw.[4] When the same subjects made self-directed vertical and horizontal saccades between the edges of a luminous outline circle, similar shifts in the direction of voluntary saccades were noted, averaging about

---

[3]A similar task requiring egocentric target orientation can also be performed in a near-zero gravity environment (Graybiel, Miller, Billingham, Waite, Berry, & Dietlein, 1967).

[4]Measures of adaptation were taken with the prism apparatus removed. Hence although all the reported shifts were adaptive when viewing was through prisms, they appeared as non-veridical distortions in the test conditions.

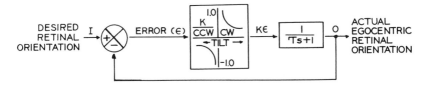

FIG. 19.4. A first-order control system model treating apparent egocentric orientation as a controlled quantity. κ represents gain, τ the time constant, and S is the Laplace operator. (From "Tilt adaptation as a feedback control process" by S. M. Ebenholtz and J. W. Callan, *Journal of Experimental Psychology: Human Perception and Performance*, 1980, *6*, 413–432. Copyright 1980 by the American Psychological Association. Reprinted by permission of the publisher and the author.)

3.4 deg cw. In a control condition in which subjects were exposed to a 0 deg tilt, no shifts were evident. Thus, tilt adaptation is associated with a systematic change in the egocentric direction of voluntary saccades.

But other eye movement systems are implicated as well. In a second EOG study (Callan & Ebenholtz, 1982), subjects were exposed to a 30 deg cw tilt for 20 min and adapted in excess of 3.0 deg cw as measured by the line-target settings. In addition, significant pre- to post-shifts in the direction of the horizontal vestibular ocular reflex (VOR) were found averaging 4.6 deg. In this task subjects had the head moved passively in the dark around a vertical axis, over a 30 deg amplitude and at a frequency of .25 Hz while performing mental arithmetic. Both the vertical and horizontal components of eye movement were recorded. All six subjects of this study exhibited a clockwise shift both in the horizontal VOR and in egocentric target orientation as though a Cartesian coordinate system controlling egocentric orientation had been rotated about its origin. Thus, the physiological basis for the control of egocentric target orientation may indeed reside in the control system governing the VOR (Wilson & Jones, 1979), and the directional plasticity of the VOR may underlie the adaptation of egocentric target orientation.[5]

CONCLUSIONS

1. Because of the association between spatial attributes of perception and the parameters of certain oculomotor systems, changes in the latter brought about by wearing lenses and prisms, or by other means, will necessarily also produce changes in the corresponding spatial attributes of perception.

---

[5]It is too early to tell whether or not the optokinetic stimulus that guides eye movements during prism exposure is the factor that underlies *both* the spatial adaptation and the altered VOR.

2. Although there is now a growing interest in the remarkable plasticity of the oculomotor control systems (Collewijn, Martins, & Steinman, 1981; Gonshor & Melville-Jones, 1976; Miles & Lisberger, 1981; Optican & Robinson, 1980; Robinson, 1975), a general appreciation of the important role these oculomotor processes play in space perception is lacking. The establishment of correspondence rules, relating changes in specific parameters of any given oculomotor control system with specific alterations in perception, would seem to be a most promising enterprise, viz., a mind-brain empiricism.

ACKNOWLEDGMENT

This research was supported in part by Grant EY02264 from the National Eye Institute.

REFERENCES

Adler, F. H. *Physiology of the eye: Clinical application*. Saint Louis: C. V. Mosby, 1965.

Alpern, M. Part I: Movements of the eyes. In H. Davson (Ed.), *The eye* (2nd ed. Vol. 3). *Muscular mechanisms*. New York: Academic Press, 1969.

Baird, J. C. *Psychophysical analysis of visual space*. New York: Pergamon Press, 1970.

Berkeley, G. *An essay towards a new theory of vision*. New York: E. P. Dutton and Co., Inc., 1910. (First published in 1709.)

Bridgeman, B., & Stark, L. Efferent copy and visual direction. *Investigative Ophthalmology and Visual Science Supplement*, 1981, *20*, 55.

Bruell, J. H., & Albee, G. W. Notes toward a motor theory of visual egocentric localization. *Psychological Review*, 1955, *62*, 391–400.

Callan, J. W., & Ebenholtz, S. M. Effects of tilt adaptation on the direction of voluntary saccades. *Perception*, 1981, *10*, 615–626.

Callan, J. W., & Ebenholtz, S. M. Directional changes in the vestibular ocular response as a result of adaptation to optical tilt. *Vision Research*, 1982, *22*, 37–42.

Carr, H. A. *An introduction to space perception*. New York: Longmans, Green & Co., 1935.

Collewijn, H., Martins, A. J., & Steinman, R. M. The time course of adaptation of human compensatory eye movements. In L. Maffei (Ed.), *Documenta Ophthalmologica Proceedings Series* (Vol. 30). The Hague: Dr. W. Junk, 1981.

Ebenholtz, S. M. Adaptation to a rotated visual field as a function of degree of optical tilt and exposure time. *Journal of Experimental Psychology*, 1966, *72*, 629–634.

Ebenholtz, S. M. On the relation between interocular transfer of adaptation and Hering's Law of Equal Innervation. *Psychological Review*, 1970, *77*, 343–347. (a)

Ebenholtz, S. M. Perception of the vertical with body tilt in the median plane. *Journal of Experimental Psychology*, 1970, *83*, 1–6. (b)

Ebenholtz, S. M. The possible role of eye-muscle potentiation in several forms of prism adaptation. *Perception*, 1974, *3*, 477–485.

Ebenholtz, S. M. Additivity of aftereffects of maintained head and eye rotations: An alternative to recalibration. *Perception & Psychophysics*, 1976, *19*, 113–116.

Ebenholtz, S. M. Aftereffects of sustained vertical divergence: Induced vertical phoria and illusory target height. *Perception*, 1978, *7*, 305–314.

Ebenholtz, S. M. Hysteresis effects in the vergence control system: Perceptual implications. In D. F.

Fisher, R. A. Monty, & J. W. Senders (Eds.), *Eye movements: Visual perception and cognition.* Hillsdale, N.J.: Lawrence Erlbaum Associates, 1981.

Ebenholtz, S. M., & Callan, J. W. Tilt adaptation as a feedback control process. *Journal of Experimental Psychology: Human Perception and Performance,* 1980, *6,* 413–432.

Ebenholtz, S. M., & Fisher, S. K. Distance adaptation depends upon plasticity in the oculomotor control system. *Perception & Psychophysics,* 1982, *31,* 551–560.

Ebenholtz, S. M., & Paap, K. R. The constancy of object orientation: Compensation for ocular rotation. *Perception & Psychophysics,* 1973, *14,* 458–470.

Ebenholtz, S. M., & Paap, K. R. Further evidence for an orientation constancy based upon registration of ocular position. *Psychological Research,* 1976, *38,* 395–409.

Ebenholtz, S. M., & Shebilske, W. Instructions and the A and E effects. *American Journal of Psychology,* 1973, *86,* 601–612.

Ebenholtz, S. M., & Shebilske, W. L. The doll reflex: Ocular counterrolling with head-body tilt in the median plane. *Vision Research,* 1975, *15,* 713–717.

Foley, J. M. Error in visually directed manual pointing. *Perception & Psychophysics,* 1975, *17,* 69–74.

Gibson, J. J. *The ecological approach to visual perception.* Boston: Houghton Mifflin, 1979.

Gonshor, A., & Melville-Jones, G. Short term changes in the human vestibulo-ocular reflex. *Journal of Physiology, London,* 1976, *226,* 361–379.

Graybiel, A., Miller, E. F., II, Billingham, J., Waite, R., Berry, C. A., & Dietlein, L. F. Vestibular experiments in Gemini flights V and VII. *Aerospace Medicine,* 1967, *38,* 360–370.

Helmholtz, H. *A treatise on physiological optics* (Vol. 3) (translated by J. P. C. Southall). New York: Dover, 1962. (First published by Voss, 1867.)

Kohler, I. The formation and transformation of the perceptual world. *Psychological Issues,* 1964, *3,* (4), Monograph 12. New York: International Universities Press.

Krishnan, V. V., & Stark, L. A heuristic model for the human vergence eye movement system. *IEEE Transactions on Biomedical Engineering,* 1977, BME–24, 44–49.

Leibowitz, H., & Moore, D. Role of changes in accommodation and convergence in the perception of size. *Journal of the Optical Society of America,* 1966, *56,* 1120–1123.

Linksz, A. *Physiology of the eye* (Vol. 2). *Vision.* New York: Grune & Stratton, 1952.

Luneburg, R. K. *Mathematical analysis of binocular vision.* Princeton, N.J.: Princeton University Press, 1947.

Mack, A., & Rock, I. A re-examination of the Stratton effect: Egocentric adaptation to a rotated visual image. *Perception & Psychophysics,* 1968, *4,* 57–62.

Matin, L. Suppression of the use of extraretinal eye position information (EEPI) for visual localization is normal in normally illuminated visual fields. *Investigative Ophthalmology and Visual Science Supplement,* 1981, *20,* 55.

Mays, L. E., & Sparks, D. L. Dissociation of visual and saccade-related responses in superior colliculus neurons. *Journal of Neurophysiology,* 1980, *43,* 207–232. (a)

Mays, L. E., & Sparks, D. L. Saccades are spatially, not retinocentrically, coded. *Science,* 1980, *208,* 1163–1165. (b)

Miles, F. A., & Lisberger, S. G. Plasticity in the vestibulo-ocular reflex: A new hypothesis. *Annual Review of Neuroscience,* 1981, *4,* 273–299.

Müller, G. E. Über das Aubertsche Phänomen. *Zeitschrift für Sinnesphysiologie,* 1916, *49,* 109–246.

Optican, L. M., & Robinson, D. A. Cerebellar-dependent adaptive control of the primate saccadic system. *Journal of Neurophysiology,* 1980, *44,* 1058–1076.

Owens, D. A., & Leibowitz, H. W. Accommodation, convergence, and distance perception in low illumination. *American Journal of Optometry and Physiological Optics,* 1980, *57,* 540–550.

Owens, D. A., & Leibowitz, H. W. Perceptual and motor consequences of tonic vergence. In C. M. Schor, & K. J. Ciuffreda (Eds.), *Basic and clinical aspects of binocular vergence eye movements.* Boston: Butterworths, 1982.

Paap, K. R., & Ebenholtz, S. M. Perceptual consequences of potentiation in the extraocular muscles: An alternative explanation for adaptation to wedge prisms. *Journal of Experimental Psychology: Human Perception and Performance*, 1976, *2*, 457–468.

Paap, K. R., & Ebenholtz, S. M. Concomitant direction and distance aftereffects of sustained convergence: A muscle potentiation explanation for eye specific adaptation. *Perception & Psychophysics*, 1977, *21*, 307–314.

Park, J. N. Displacement of apparent straight-ahead as an aftereffect of deviation of the eyes from normal position. *Perceptual and Motor Skills*, 1969, *28*, 591–597.

Robinson, D. A. How the oculomotor system repairs itself. *Investigative Ophthalmology*, 1975, *14*, 413–415.

Rock, I. The perception of the egocentric orientation of a line. *Journal of Experimental Psychology*, 1954, *48*, 367–374.

Schor, C. M. The relationship between fusional vergence eye movements and fixation disparity. *Vision Research*, 1979, *19*, 1359–1367.

Shebilske, W. L. Visual direction illusions in everyday situations: Implications for sensorimotor and ecological theories. In D. F. Fisher, R. A. Monty, & J. W. Senders (Eds.), *Eye movements: Cognitive and visual perception*. Hillsdale, N.J.: Lawrence Erlbaum Associates, 1981.

Shebilske, W. L., & Fogelgren, L. A. Eye position aftereffects of backwards head tilt manifested by illusory visual direction. *Perception & Psychophysics*, 1977, *21*, 77–82.

Smith, O. W. Distance constancy. *Journal of Experimental Psychology*, 1958, *55*, 388–389.

Wallach, H., & Zuckerman, C. The constancy of stereoscopic depth. *American Journal of Psychology*, 1963, *76*, 404–412.

Welch, R. B. *Perceptual modification: Adapting to altered sensory environments*. New York: Academic Press, 1978.

Wilson, V. J., & Melville-Jones, G. *Mammalian vestibular physiology*. New York: Plenum Press, 1979.

20

Direction-Specific Vergence Adaptation

David B. Henson
Department of Optometry
University of Wales Institute of
Science and Technology
Cardiff, UK

ABSTRACT

This Chapter describes the way in which the oculomotor system adapts to a step displacement of one eye's visual field. When visual experience after the displacement was confined to one direction of gaze, the subsequent adaptation was found to be direction specific, occurring maximally in the direction of gaze in which visual experience was gained.

If the two eyes are fixating a distance object and an ophthalmic prism is suddenly placed before one eye, then the subject momentarily sees a doubled image of the object. This doubled image provides a stimulus to the fusion mechanism which then initiates a vergence movement in order to re-establish single binocular vision. If now an occluder is placed before the eye looking through the prism, the eye behind the occluder is seen to gradually drift back to its former position (providing the subject is orthophoric). If, however, before the occluder is placed in front of the eye, the subject is allowed to fuse the target for a period of time, we find that on occlusion the eye no longer drifts all the way back (Henson & North, 1980). It is as though the resting position of the two eyes has been altered by the brief period of forced vergence. We also find that as the period of forced vergence is extended, the amount that the eye drifts back decreases.

This phenomenon, which we believe represents adaptation of the oculomotor systems vergence mechanism, has been noted by several researchers, including Alpern (1946), Ellerbrock (1950), Carter (1965), Ogle, Martens, and Dyer

(1967), and Schor (1979). It can be accurately measured with a Maddox rod[1] and tangent scale. When a Maddox rod is placed before one eye it distorts the vision to such an extent that a single point of light appears as a streak whose axis is at 90 deg to the axis of the rod. If a person with a Maddox rod before one eye binocularly views a single point of light, then they will see both the single point of light and a streak. The relative positions of the point and the streak will give a measure of the relative positions of the two eyes.

In our experiments, we force the eyes into an abnormal vergence position with a two-prism dioptre base up prism before the right eye. After 15 sec of forced vergence, we occlude the eye behind the prism with a photographic shutter and then place a Maddox rod with the axis vertical in front of it. After 15 sec of occlusion, during which time the eyes will have drifted back to their fusion-free position, we briefly open the shutter (.25 sec) and turn on a single distant light source. The type of light source used was a 6V tungsten filament bulb run on a 9V supply. The long axis of the filament subtended 2 min/arc at the eye. The subject sees, during the time the shutter is open, a spot of light and a streak. When the shutter closes, an illuminated vertical tangent scale appears which is centered on the distant light source. The subject is asked to report the position that the line took through the tangent scale. Trained observers can report the position of this line to within one eighth of a prism dioptre (4.3 min of arc). After recording the position, we repeat the process a further 13 times, each time giving the subject a further 15 sec of binocular visual experience through the prism followed by a further 15 sec of occlusion and a phoria measurement. The mean response of 8 subjects to 14 successive measurements taken in this way is given in Fig. 20.1. The curve drawn through the data is the best fitting (least squares) exponential of the form $y = P, \exp^{-Bx}$, where P equals the power of the prism in dioptres and B is a constant. This curve represents the rate at which the vergence system adapts to a step displacement of one eye.

An adaptive system, such as that shown in Fig. 20.1, is essential to the vergence mechanisms in order for it to keep approximately orthophoric throughout the normal life span. The growth of the eye during infancy, the changes in muscle structure with age, and the gradual enophthalmus[2] seen with age are just three factors which produce marked changes in the mechanics of eye movements to which the occulomotor system must adapt.

The types of changes I have just described could, only in exceptional cases, produce step displacements of the type we induced experimentally. It seems far more likely that the effects of these changes would be non-linear and would require different amounts of adaptation in different directions of gaze.

---

[1]A Maddox rod is a series of high-powered cylinders lying parallel to each other which produce a streak image of a spot source.

[2]Recession of the eyeball into the socket.

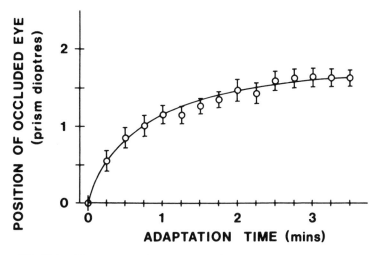

FIG. 20.1.   The mean rate of vergence adaptation and standard errors of eight subjects to a two-prism dioptre vertical displacement of the visual field to one eye. The ordinate is the position of the occluded eye relative to the non-occluded eye after 15 sec of occlusion. Zero on this scale means that the two eyes are pointing in exactly the same direction after one eye has been occluded for 15 sec.

The abscissa is the amount of binocular visual experience that the subjects have had through the two-prism dioptre base up lens before the RE.

If the adaptation I have just described in Fig. 20.1 is designed to deal with these types of changes, then it seems likely that it would occur primarily in the directions of gaze where binocular visual experience through the prism was gained. Put another way, if we restricted the binocular experience through the prism to one direction of gaze, then we would expect the adaptation to be maximal in that direction and occur either to a lesser extent or not at all in other directions.

We have investigated this by repeating the experiments just described in such a way that all the binocular visual experience was restricted to one visual direction. This was achieved by simply asking the subjects to maintain accurate fixation of a point on the chart during the 15-sec periods when the shutter was open. During the first part of the experiment, we recorded adaptation curves practically identical to those shown in Fig. 20.1. At the end of the adaptation period (after 3.5 min of binocular visual experience through the prism), we measured how much the subject had adapted in other positions of gaze.

The subject's head was controlled during this experiment with a dental impression and a forehead rest, both of which could be rotated around either a vertical or horizontal axis. A pointer was attached to the dental bite that indicated on an angular scale the exact position of the head. At the end of the adaptation period, the eye behind the prism was occluded and the subject asked to rotate his

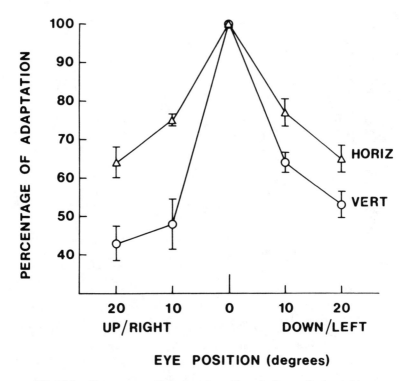

FIG. 20.2.   The mean spread of adaptation and standard errors for four subjects after 3.5 min of binocular visual experience through a two-prism dioptre base up prism before the right eye. All the binocular visual experience through the prism was obtained at the zero position on the abscissa.

head until the pointer had moved a given number of degrees on the scale. Throughout this procedure the subject's fixation was maintained at the same distant point. The relative position of the two eyes was then measured with the Maddox rod and tangent scale. By rotating the head in this way we have effectively moved the eyes to a new position in the orbit where no binocular visual experience through the prism has been gained. We then proceeded to measure the amount of adaptation that had occurred in a whole series of different positions along both the horizontal and vertical meridians. The mean result of four subjects is shown in Fig. 20.2. The y-axis of this figure gives the amount of adaptation that had occurred as a percentage of that measured along the direction in which binocular visual experience was given. The x-axis gives the position of the eyes. Zero represents the straight ahead position where the subjects gained binocular visual experience through the prism. It can be seen from Fig. 20.2 that when the eyes are turned away from the direction in which they had received the adapting stimulus, the amount of adaptation decreases. This result demonstrates that the adaptation mechanism is direction specific, adaptation occurring maximally in the direction of gaze in which visual experience was gained.

This experiment was conducted with the eyes at or close to the primary position during the period of binocular visual experience. We have repeated the experiment with the eyes positioned approximately 20 deg away from the primary position during the period of binocular visual experience in order to see if the same directional specificity exists. Our results are shown in Fig. 20.3. Again they demonstrate that adaptation was maximal in the direction of gaze in which binocular visual experience was gained.

To maintain a given eye position requires a specific amount of innervation to each of the 12 extra-ocular muscles. We can represent the oculomotor position maintenance system in the form of a two-dimensional map, the axes of which represent the horizontal and vertical meridians of the eye. At every point on the map there exists the innervational information required to maintain the eyes at that position in space. When the eyes are required to move, say 10 deg to the right, then the new position maintenance information is obtained by simply

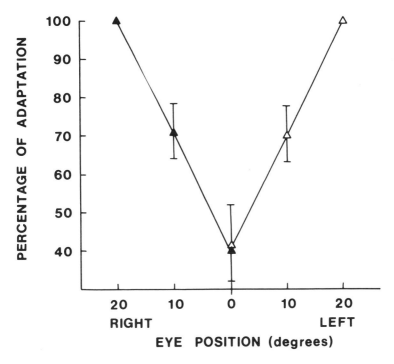

FIG. 20.3.   The mean spread of adaptation and standard errors for four subjects after 3.5 min of binocular visual experience through a two-prism dioptre base up prism before the right eye. All the binocular visual experience through the prism was obtained at either 20 deg to the right △ or 20 deg to the left ▲.

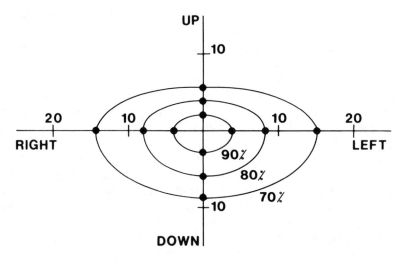

FIG. 20.4.   The results of Fig. 20.2 replotted on an eye position map. The
intersection of the ordinate and abscissa represents the primary position where all
binocular visual experience through the two-prism dioptre lens was obtained. The
numbers along the axes represent degrees from the primary position.
The lines drawn through the data connect points of equal adaptation.

moving, from the current position within the map, 10 deg to the right along the x
axis. Any further movements will be calculated from this new position.

The adaptation system just described can be viewed as being responsible for
updating the information contained within this map. If after moving to a new
position the visual system finds that a fusional movement is necessary in order to
maintain single binocular vision, then the output of this fusional effort operates
to modify the contents of the map at and around the eye position, where the
fusional stimulus existed. Schor (1979) has already proposed a model of the
adaptation system that is based upon the output of the fusion mechanism.

Figure 20.4 demonstrates from the results shown in Fig. 20.2, how the adaptation spreads across the map after a forced vergence has been maintained in the
primary position. At the very center of the map, the position where binocular
visual experience through the prism was gained, adaptation is maximal. As the
eyes move away from this position the amount of adaptation is seen to decrease.
The lines on this figure represent where the amount of adaptation has fallen to
90%, 80%, and 70% of that measured in the gaze direction where binocular
visual experience through the prism was gained. The results shown in Fig. 20.3
would suggest that similar adaptation pools exist across the whole motor map.
Thus, if the gaze direction during adaptation was fixed at some point on the map
other than the intersection of the axes, the resultant iso-adaptation lines would be
centered around this new point rather than the intersection of the axes as is shown
in Fig. 20.4.

REFERENCES

Alpern, M. The after-effect of lateral duction testing on subsequent phoria measurements. *American Journal of Optometry and Archives of American Academy of Optometry*, 1946, *23*, 442–447.

Carter, D. B. Fixation disparity and heterophoria following prolonged wearing of prism. *American Journal of Optometry and Archives of American Academy of Optometry*, 1965, *42*, 141–152.

Ellerbrock, V. J. Tonicity induced by fusional movements. *American Journal of Optometry and Archives of American Academy of Optometry*, 1950, *27*, 8–20.

Henson, D. B., & North, R. V. Adaptation to prism induced heterophoria. *American Journal of Optometry and Physiological Optics*, 1980, *57*, 129–137.

Ogle, K. N., Martens, T. G., & Dyer, J. A. *Oculomotor imbalance in binocular vision and fixation disparity*. London: Henry Kimpton, 1967.

Schor, C. M. The relationship between fusional vergence eye movements and fixation disparity. *Vision Research*, 1979, *19*, 1359–1367.

21 Learning in Space Perception

Hans Wallach
Swarthmore College

ABSTRACT

It is proposed that multiple stimulation is the rule in space and motion perception because potential cues become stimuli through simple learning that takes place when a potential cue occurs simultaneously with the perceptual variable it eventually comes to evoke. If such learning readily occurs, instances of previously unknown duplicating stimulation may yet be discovered. An experiment is cited that serves as an example; it demonstrated that the slope of the line of regard with which an object on the ground is seen serves as a cue for its distance from the eyes. Presumably, the slope of regard had often occurred while other stimulation caused perceptions of distance of objects on the ground and had become a stimulus for distance.

A similar kind of learning may be responsible for duplicating stimulation in stereoscopic depth perception, which consists in the differences in configuration in the two eyes that accompany retinal disparity. Because ordinarily such binocular configurational differences are inseparable from retinal disparities, their effectiveness was only recently discovered, and that was possible only because one kind of configurational difference is more effective than another kind. The greater effectiveness of one kind may result from more numerous learning opportunities.

Over the years it has become clear to some of us that simple associative learning plays a large part in space perception. Because most of the evidence for the pervasiveness of perceptual learning comes from demonstrations of perceptual adaptation, this topic is particularly fitting for a book honoring Ivo Kohler, for his experiments and his writing have had the largest share in focusing attention on perceptual adaptation. His showing how readily we adapt to reversed vision has made an enormous impression, and his description of the progress of adaptation to the swinging of the visual field that occurs when we turn the head while wearing left-right reversing prisms has aroused our interest in position constancy.

It would, of course, be best to demonstrate perceptual learning by studying perceptual development in infants, but that is a difficult task. So we mainly rely on the rapid adaptation or "Umlernen" that occurs in adults when they are exposed to unnatural viewing or listening conditions and infer that those perceptual functions that are easily altered are learned in the first place. In addition to the much studied adaptation to displaced visual direction, there is rapid partial adaptation to environmental motion dependent on head movements and to a tilted environment. Further, the relation between the *amount* of disparity and the *magnitude* of perceived depth can be rapidly altered by adapting subjects to a device that presents augmented disparities, and strong changes between oculomotor adjustments and perceived distance can be rapidly obtained.

Some of these adaptations take place only in the presence of veridical cues for the perceptual property that is affected by the adaptation. For adaptation in distance perception, for instance, appropriate spectacles alter the oculomotor adjustments so that convergence and accommodation are for distances that are, say, shorter than the objective distances (Wallach, Frey, & Bode, 1972). After the subject had walked with these spectacles for 20 minutes, distances given solely by these oculomotor cues were greatly overrated; adaptation had compensated for the effect of the spectacles in the amount of more than 50% of complete adaptation. Adaptation in this situation is possible because other distance cues, such as those provided by the perspective pattern with which the environmental space is given and by the image sizes of familiar objects, are unaltered. These veridical distance cues cause veridical distance perception, and a state of affairs results where the altered oculomotor adjustment are simultaneous with veridical perceived distances. The new combination of oculomotor adjustments with perceived distance gives rise to new connections between oculomotor cues and perceived distances that compete with the connections that were in use prior to adaptation. This probably accounts for partial adaptation.

A corresponding associative process may take place when oculomotor adjustments first become distance cues, provided that another viewing condition that varies with distance already causes distance perception. After convergence and accommodation have come into existence to provide fused binocular vision and sharp images, specific states of convergence and of accommodation occur repeatedly in simultaneity with specific perceived distances. If connections develop, oculomotor adjustments become distance cues. Cue acquisition and adaptation differ in one respect: In adaptation a relation between oculomotor adjustment and perceived distance already exists; specific states become connected in a different way. In cue acquisition, oculomotor adjustments and perceived distance are initially unrelated. It may be that the great frequency with which specific oculomotor adjustments occur with certain perceived distances accounts for the establishment of these novel connections, but I am inclined to believe that another factor plays a role here: Oculomotor adjustment and perceived distance covary, and this covariance becomes manifest when we move about. It may provide the signal for the initial contact between such heterogeneous events as convergence and perceived distance or, for that matter, between convergence and another distance cue such as image size of familiar objects, or covariance may operate directly in the formation of associations that operate in perception.

SLOPE OF REGARD AS A DISTANCE CUE

If it is true that simple learning will transform a viewing condition that happens to be covariant with a variable in space perception into a cue for that variable, it may be possible to discover previously unknown cues by simply looking for such viewing conditions. If the acquisition of cues in space perception is as simple as just outlined, a viewing condition that varies with, say, distance should be found to function as a distance cue. Wallach and O'Leary (1982) recently confirmed this prediction. They identified a viewing condition that varies with distance and demonstrated that it functions as a distance cue.

When we look at a point on the ground in front of us, the angle between the sloping line of regard and the horizontal varies roughly with the reciprocal of the distance of the point from the eyes. We demonstrated that his slope angle serves as a distance cue by using a condition in which the slope angle functioned non-veridically and by eliminating some other distance cues from the experimental conditions. The floor on which the target, a cardboard square, was displayed showed no texture and the subject observed monocularly. We used an analogue to a Galilean telescope that diminished, rather than increased, visual angles and that did so only in one dimension. The power of the slope was .7 and when it was oriented to minify in the horizontal dimension, objects seen through it looked too narrow by a factor of .7. When it was mounted with its optical axis horizontal and was turned to contract visual angles in the vertical dimension, it diminished the slope angle of the square on the floor by a factor of .7, in addition to making it look like a horizontal oblong, and increased the implicit distance of the target by the reciprocal of .7, that is, by a factor of 1.43. Instead of measuring the apparent distance of the cardboard square we obtained estimates of its dimensions. Because perceived size increases in proportion with perceived distance when, as was here the case, actual distance remains the same, size estimates are often used to measure perceived distance in situations such as ours. Size estimates made by adjusting the length of a small antenna rod were given with either orientation of the scope and with direct viewing. Estimates were obtained at two distances of the target, 6 m and 9 m. The target measured 28 × 28 cm.

When the scope contracted the horizontal dimension and left the slope of regard unaltered, mean height estimates were nearly the same as those made without the scope. The mean width estimates showed the optical effect of the scope; they averaged .67 of the mean height estimates. When the scope contracted the vertical dimension, mean height and width estimates, which were given by 12 subjects, were considerably larger than the mean width and height estimates that had been given by another group of 12 subjects when minification was horizontal. Mean height estimates were 55% larger and mean width estimates were greater by 56%, $[t(22) = 5.21$ and 5.97, respectively]. However, these values were not significantly different from the expected effect of the diminished slope angle, namely, of a size increase by 43%.

CONFIGURATIONAL CHANGE AS A STIMULUS IN MOTION PERCEPTION

That such a casual viewing condition as looking at a point on the ground in front serves as a distance cue shows how readily incidental conditions become cues or stimuli in space perception. As a result, multiple stimuli for the same perceptual variable should be the rule in space perception rather than the exception and that may well be the case. There are at least three classes of stimuli that cause perception of visual motion. Two concern the displacement of the moving object relative to the observer: displacement of its retinal image when the eyes are at rest and ocular pursuit when the eyes track the moving object. A third, configurational change, results from the displacement of the moving object relative to the stationary objects in the environment. Of the three, image displacement is probably the innate stimulus for visual motion; the other two were shown to be subject to perceptual adaptation and therefore are probably learned. Recently, Bacon and Wallach (1982) were able to change perceived motion directions that result from ocular pursuit by partially adapting subjects to a condition where the image displacement that normally takes place before the eyes take up pursuit is given a different direction from the motion that is given during pursuit. Previously, Wallach, Bacon and Schulman (1978) had altered the relation between configurational change and the perceived extent of motion by adaptation, a result that suggests that configurational change becomes a stimulus for motion through learning.

There is ample opportunity for such learning. In the large majority of instances where an object is seen to move, stationary objects are also visible or the moving object is seen against a patterned background. The resulting configurational change is given while either image displacement or ocular pursuit of the moving object cause the object's perceived motion. There is incessant simultaneity between configurational change and perceived motion, and the rate of configurational change varies with the physical velocity of the moving object and with the speed of its perceived motion. Eventually configurational change becomes a very potent stimulus for motion, under some conditions more potent than ocular pursuit. This is, for instance, the case in the perception of speed which is much more dependent on the rate of configurational change than on the rate of displacement relative to the viewer. This fact is implicit in Brown's (1931) experiments on the velocity-transposition phenomenon. Brown had subjects make speed matches when dots moved through apertures of different sizes. When the sizes of such "motion fields" were varied, with the shapes of the apertures and the proportion of dot and aperture size kept the same, perceived speeds were almost the same when physical velocities were increased in proportion to the size of the motion fields. At that point they were, of course, greatly different in absolute terms. This important discovery was largely disregarded in the last two decades, because Smith and Sherlock (1957) ascribed this effect to the rhythmic speed with which evenly spaced dots entered the aperture. They overlooked the fact that Brown repeated all his experiments with only a single dot visible at a time and obtained the same results. Brown did this with the expressed purpose of excluding an impression of rhythmic speed. At any rate, Brown's results mean that perceived speeds are not far from equal when the velocities measured in the scale of the motion fields are equal and, therefore, when the rates of configurational change are equal. Brown's numerical results show that the absolute velocities have little effect when the size ratios of the motion fields do not exceed 4:1. The absolute velocities are, of course, given by the stimulation that represents the rate of displacement relative to the viewer. That stimulation is here in conflict with the rate of configurational change, which proves to be much more effective.

The other fact that shows configurational change to be a potent stimulus for motion perception is induced motion. Because a relative displacement between an object and its surround almost always occurs when the object is actually moving and is perceived to move, this kind of configurational change becomes a stimulus for perceiving the object in motion. As a consequence, configurational change will tend to result in perceived motion of the object even when the object is actually at rest and the configurational change results from a motion of its surround. Although other cues represent the object as stationary, configurational change is here often dominant and causes the object to appear to move in the direction opposite to the direction of the actual motion of the surround.

BINOCULAR CONFIGURATIONAL DIFFERENCE IN STEREOSCOPIC VISION

That configurational change is an important stimulus for motion is, of course, widely recognized. That it has an analogue in stereoscopic vision is a new finding. When two points in the environment are at different distances from the

FIG. 21.1.   On the left are the retinal projections of two points in the median plane with the upper one farther from the eyes. The alignment of these points differs in the two eyes. On the right are the projections of two points in the horizontal plane with the right one farther. The distance between them differs on the two retinae.

eyes, their projections on the two retinae form different patterns because the eyes view the two points from slightly different directions. When the two points occupy the same horizontal plane, the distance between their retinal images differs in the two eyes, and when they occupy the same vertical plane, their alignment in the vertical dimension differs in the two eyes (Fig. 21.1).[1] These differences lead to the same kind of stereoscopic stimulus condition: When the eyes converge on one of the two points that are located at different depth, the images of the other point fall on non-corresponding places on the two retinae and that disparate location is the retinal disparity that causes the points to be perceived at different depth. Recently evidence has been mounting that the difference in configuration with which the points are given in the two eyes, the difference in distance and in alignment, also plays a role.

Wallach and Barton (1975) studied adaptation to spectacles that produced stereoscopic effects which resulted in perceived curvature of plane, frontal-parallel patterns. In the course of this work they observed that curvature in the vertical dimension was initially much more readily perceived than curvature in the horizontal dimension. The spectacles they used consisted essentially of 10-diopter wedge prisms, each mounted with the base vertical and toward the temples. Because the prisms were oppositely arranged, the shape distortion that they caused had opposite orientations on the two retinae and caused retinal disparities. One of the shape distortions occurs because light rays that traverse the prism coming from above or below the center of the visual field are slightly more displaced than center rays. It results in the well-known curvature of straight lines that are oriented parallel to the prism base. With the two prisms in opposite orientation, this displacement of environmental points above and below the center relative to the center point was to the left in the right eye and to the right in

_____

[1]These two basic forms of configurational differences occur together when two points at different depth occupy an oblique plane. Vertical alignment difference should not be confounded with vertical disparity, which does not give rise to stereoscopic depth experience. Only when all vertical distances are larger in one eye than in the other may a kind of depth be experienced that would result if all horizontal distances were larger in the other eye (induced effect).

the left eye and amounted to a sequence of vertical alignment differences in the two eyes. The resulting disparities caused straight vertical lines to be perceived with a concave curvature.

The other shape distortion caused by a wedge prism results from the fact that light rays that traverse the prism at different directions in the horizontal plane are displaced in different amounts. Those that pass the prism obliquely on the side of the prism base are less displaced than those that lie toward the prism apex. As a result, dots forming an evenly spaced horizontal row are seen as being slightly nearer each other where they are located toward the base of the prism and farther apart where they lie toward the apex side. Therefore a pair of horizontally arranged points to the right of center were seen by the right eye as having a slightly shorter distance between them than they had in the left eye. This horizontal difference caused a disparity that made the right one of the two points appear nearer than the left one. The corresponding difference between two points on the left of center was reversed along with the disparity: the left one of two points appeared nearer. The farther to the side the pair of points was located, the greater was the difference between them, and the greater was the resulting disparity. Together, these disparities caused a plane frontal pattern to be perceived with concave curvature with a vertical axis.

The two stereoscopic effects should add up to causing plane frontal patterns to appear spherically concave. While most subjects readily saw a cylindrical curvature with a horizontal axis, the curvature with the vertical axis was rarely reported. For this reason Wallach and Barton (1975) studied adaptation only to the former effect of their spectacles. Their observations suggested that disparities that result from differences in the vertical alignment of pairs of points in the two eyes (Fig. 21.1) are more effective in producing stereoscopic depth than disparities that result from differences in the horizontal distances within point pairs. It is this inference from Wallach and Barton's observation that I ultimately want to explain.

The notion that disparities that result from differences in the vertical alignment of pairs of points are especially effective was confirmed by a series of experiments performed by Wallach and Bacon (1976). They believed, correctly, that different alignments within the vertical dimension of pairs of points in the two eyes have an "added effectiveness" in stereovision. They considered such alignment difference to be another kind of disparity, quite different from the ordinary disparity that relates to non-corresponding locations of the images of individual points. They called this different kind of disparity transverse and demonstrated several effects of its added presence.

1. In stereoscopic tests depth was reported more rapidly when an alignment difference was present in the stereograms. Subjects were selected for stereovision by having them view a stereogram that yielded depth most readily: a smaller circle inside a larger one. For one eye, the two circles were concentrically arranged, and for the other eye the inner circle was displaced slightly to one side.

A   B

FIG. 21.2.   Two stereograms with different latencies.

When the pairs of circles were stereoscopically combined, they were seen as a truncated cone. In the subsequent experiment, two stereograms with disparities of equal magnitude were shown to the selected subjects (Fig. 21.2). In the left one of these stereograms the configurational difference that resulted in the disparity consisted in a difference in alignment in the vertical dimension and in the right stereogram the configurational difference consisted mainly in a distance difference in the horizontal dimension. The average latency with which depth was reported by 20 subjects was 7.2 sec in stereogram A where an alignment difference was foremost and 14.6 sec in stereogram B, a difference which was significant at the .01 level. Much larger latency differences were obtained when one of the random dot pattern stereograms created by Julesz was altered to eliminate alignment differences. In a stereogram where an inner square area is given with disparity in relation to the dot pattern frame that surrounds it and where an inner square area appears to float in front of a larger square area, alignment differences occur at the upper and lower edge of the inner square. They can be eliminated by removing the upper and lower part of the frame so that the upper and lower edge of the smaller square borders on a homogeneous area. This caused mean latency for reports of depth to increase from 18 sec for the full pattern to 45.8 sec for the reduced pattern.

   2. Wallach and Bacon (1976) reported two experiments in which retinal disparity was in conflict with other depth cues. They found that the presence of alignment differences changed the balance between the conflicting cues and strengthened the stereoscopic effect. An analogous result was recently reported by Gillam, Finlay and Flagg.[2] They used a meridional lens to produce a small magnification in the horizontal dimension in one eye, e.g., the right eye. The horizontal magnification that the lens produced in the right eye caused differences between horizontal distances in the two eyes, which resulted in a series of disparities. These optically produced disparities caused frontal patterns to appear turned into depth with the right side farther from the eyes than the left side. The frontal pattern used by the authors consisted of vertical and horizontal

---

[2]Gillam, Finlay and Flagg reported their experiment at the European Conference on Visual Perception, University of Sussex, Brighton, 1980.

rows of dots forming a square pattern. The configuration of this pattern served as a cue for its fronto-parallel orientation that conflicted with the lens-produced disparities that tended to give it a perceived slant. Conspicuous vertical alignment differences were introduced by replacing the lens with a half-lens that magnified only the upper half of the square pattern, while the lower half of the pattern was seen directly and was therefore given without disparities. The pattern of disparities thus corresponded to a scene where in the upper half a slanted surface was visible and a frontal surface in the lower half. Almost every pair of points one of which belonged to the upper and the other to the lower surface was given with an alignment difference; a pair of points that was seen vertically aligned by the left eye was seen with some tilt by the right eye. There was a further condition in which the part of the pattern previously seen below the half-lens was blocked out and was seen only with the other eye. Having the frontal pattern given only monocularly eliminated the binocular alignment differences.

There were actually two sets of lenses. One full and one half-lens magnified 5% and the other two lenses 8%. Two subjects gave estimates of the slants of the pattern or of the half-pattern by adjusting the slant of a monocularly observed test object by remote control. The half-lenses produced a larger perceived tilt of the square pattern than the full lenses. The half-lens with 5% magnification yielded 80% more depth than the full lens of equal power and in the case of the lens set with 8% magnification the corresponding difference was 90%. The slants measured in the condition where a half-lens was used but where alignment differences were absent, were about as large as in the full-lens condition. Thus, the added presence of alignment differences was quite effective in overcoming the conflicting effect of the square pattern and caused greater depth.

3. Finally, Wallach and Bacon showed that the presence in a stereogram of multiple alignment differences may increase perceived depth. They did this by obtaining depth estimates for the two-circle stereogram mentioned above and for a vertical line stereogram with identical main horizontal distance differences. Even more convincing are the results of an experiment by Bacon and Wallach which showed that increasing alignment differences alone caused an increase in perceived depth. They experimented with a simple stereogram, shown in Fig. 21.3 on the left. The difference in horizontal distance is obvious. The differences in the alignments of the ends of the vertical lines are at the tops indicated by the dashed lines. The alignment difference was made larger in the stereogram on the right by making the shorter line slightly longer in the right half-field than it was in the left half-field. The increase in the alignment differences made the mean perceived depth significantly larger as measured by estimation $[t(11) = 3.81]$ as well as by matching $[t(11) = 8.51]$.

I have introduced this report on the superior effectiveness of vertical alignment differences by claiming that it is an analogue in stereoscopic perception to the role that configurational change plays in motion perception. Just as configurational change is present in the vast majority of instances of objective motion,

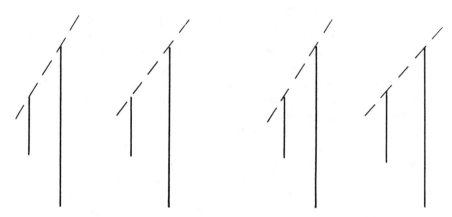

FIG. 21.3.   Two stereograms with the alignments of the upper ends of the vertical lines shown by dashed lines. The alignment difference is greater in the stereogram on the right.

configurational differences are always present in the projections on the two
retinae when depth between environmental objects is given by retinal disparity.
The claim that binocular configurational differences operate in stereovision along
with retinal disparity, however, does not explain the additional effectiveness of
vertical alignment differences. Horizontal distance differences in the two eyes
are also configurational differences. The question is why vertical alignment
differences are more effective than horizontal distance differences.

It is possible that vertical alignment differences are inherently effective, but I
prefer to assume that binocular configurational differences become stimuli for
stereoscopic depth perception through learning just as configurational changes
are acquired stimuli for motion perception.[3] There are ample occasions for such
learning. Configurational difference always accompanies retinal disparity and its
magnitude varies with the magnitude of the non-correspondence of image locations, a covariance that may be an important factor in associative perceptual
learning. If the contribution of configurational difference to stereovision is
learned, the superiority of vertical alignment differences may be due to better
learning opportunities. Alignment differences occur when patterned plane surfaces are viewed that are turned into depth about a horizontal axis, while horizontal distance differences occur on slanted vertical surfaces. Since the ground on
which we stand and walk belongs to the former, vertical alignment differences
are encountered and change in magnitude with great frequency.

---

[3]Whereas it has been shown that the effectiveness of configurational change in motion perception
can be altered by adaptation, an analogous demonstration concerning binocular configurational
difference seems unlikely.

CONCLUSION

Slope of regard being a distance cue and binocular configurational differences serving as stereoscopic cues are instances of multiple stimulation, a frequent occurrence in space perception.[4] But, along with the role that configurational change plays in motion perception, binocular configurational difference is of special interest. In both cases, multiple stimulation serves no purpose.[5] In motion perception, configurational change mediates the same information that either ocular pursuit or image displacement provide and is not needed, and binocular configurational difference duplicates retinal disparity exactly and provides no information that retinal disparity does not provide. If both of these duplicating stimuli come into operation only because they are easily learned, one wonders whether there are no further instances of duplicating stimulation to be discovered. That may be no easy task. Configurational change shows up as induced motion and results in Brown's (1931) velocity-transposition phenomenon, and the former led to its early discovery. The effect of binocular configurational difference, on the other hand, could be demonstrated only because one of its two basic forms, vertical alignment difference, happens to be more effective than its other basic form, horizontal distance difference.

REFERENCES

Bacon, J., & Wallach, H. Adaptation in motion perception: Alteration of motion evoked by ocular pursuit. *Perception & Psychophysics*, 1982, *31*, 251–255.

Brown, J. F. The visual perception of velocity. *Psychologische Forschung*, 1931, *14*, 199–232.

Smith, O. W., & Sherlock, L. A new explanation of the velocity-transposition phenomenon. *American Journal of Psychology*, 1957, *70*, 102–105.

Wallach, H., & Bacon, J. Two forms of retinal disparity. *Perception & Psychophysics*, 1976, *19*, 375–382.

Wallach, H., Bacon, J., & Schulman, P. Adaptation in motion perception: Alteration of induced motion. *Perception & Psychophysics*, 1978, *24*, 509–514.

Wallach, H., & Barton, W. Adaptation to optically produced curvature of frontal planes. *Perception & Psychophysics*, 1975, *18*, 21–25.

Wallach, H., Frey, K. J., & Bode, K. A. The nature of adaptation in distance perception based on oculomotor cues. *Perception & Psychophysics*, 1972, *11*, 110–116.

Wallach, H., & O'Leary, A. Slope of regard as a distance cue. *Perception & Psychophysics*, 1982, *31*, 145–148.

---

[4]In addition to slope of regard there are further distance cues, namely, accommodation and convergence, location on a pattern providing perspective depth, and image size of familiar objects.

[5]This is not so in the case of some of the cues for distance: Accommodation and convergence are needed for the perception of short distances whereas perspective cues serve for intermediate and large distances.

22 Through the Looking Glass: Rapid Adaptation to Right-Left Reversal of the Visual Field

Judith Rich Harris
New Providence, New Jersey

Charles S. Harris
Bell Laboratories
Murray Hill, New Jersey

ABSTRACT

Subjects adapted to right-left reversal of the visual field by looking through a stationary, monocular reversing prism. The dominant hand was viewed through the prism while the subject drew pictures and doodled. At first there was great difficulty in moving the pencil in the desired direction, but in a short time it was possible to draw normally again. Eight subjects each received four 15-minute exposures to reversal; they neither saw nor wrote any letters or numbers during this time. After each practice period vision was blocked off, and the subject wrote letters and numbers as the experimenter called them out. Many of these characters were written backwards, in ''mirror-writing.'' In addition, subjects sometimes wrote frontwards characters and *thought* they were backwards. These results are interpreted as indicative of a change in kinesthetic perception: After looking through the reversing prism at the moving hand, a left-to-right hand movement is perceived as right-to-left.

When Alice stepped through the Looking Glass she found a strange world, and had trouble adjusting to it. She would have had a great deal *more* trouble, though, if she had simply put on a pair of goggles that made everything look like its mirror image, reversing it right-for-left. Alice would have found that the stability of her visual world had vanished; every time she moved her head the visual field would stream by in front of her eyes. This instability would make her feel dizzy, and probably nauseated as well (Kottenhoff & Lindahl, 1960; Treisman, 1977). Should Alice decide to go to her medicine cabinet for something to quiet her stomach, she would find it difficult to walk from one room to another, because every time she saw that she was going to miss the doorway her corrections would take her farther in the wrong direction. When she eventually arrived at the medicine cabinet she would encounter additional problems in opening its door (which would now appear to be hinged on the wrong side) and in picking up the bottle of pills.

If Alice were as indefatigable as Kohler's subject (F. Grill) and Kohler himself, and persisted (as they did) in wearing the goggles despite the overwhelming difficulties involved, she would have found that these difficulties lessen after a time. We know from Kohler's reports (1951, 1953, 1964) that within a week or two she would be able to function well in walking and in reaching for things. The world would no longer stream past whenever she turned her head. Eventually she would even be able to read again, and things would begin to appear normal to her.

How does this adjustment come about? How does the adapted Alice, functioning normally after several weeks of wearing reversing goggles, differ from the bumping-into-walls Alice who had just put on the goggles?

One very important difference is this: The unadapted Alice sees her hand, for example, moving one way but feels it move in another. The adapted Alice sees and feels it moving in the same direction.

One possible interpretation of this change is that kinesthetic information about positions and movements of body parts is used to correct the visual misperceptions induced by the reversing prisms, and the result is a change in visual perception—a change that makes things look, through the prisms, the way they formerly looked without prisms. An alternative view (Harris, 1965) is that such adaptation consists, instead, of changes in the position sense—changes in the felt position of body parts (proprioceptive changes) and in the perception of motion of these parts (kinesthetic changes).

Kohler has described some of the extensive proprioceptive and kinesthetic changes that occur during various stages of adjustment to rearranged vision. For example, he reported that after a subject has worn reversing goggles for several days, "The kinesthetic sensations he experiences when he turns his head and moves his hands completely correspond to the reversed visual field" (1964, p. 153). Elsewhere, in discussing adaptation to inversion, he noted that "alterations in kinesthetic sensitivity are not infrequent; where they determine a person's *sense of orientation,* their role is of crucial importance" (p. 32).

Kohler's fascinating—and sometimes puzzling—observations inspired us to attempt to study adaptation to visual reversal under laboratory conditions. To do so, we simplified the situation and lessened the burden on the subject. Adaptation to the reversing goggles worn by Kohler's freely moving subjects was arduous and slow; Kohler reports that "some experiments had to be interrupted prematurely . . . when some subjects complained of dizziness or nausea, became depressed, or could not stand the pressure of the spectacles against the nose or ears'' (1964, p. 28). Our subjects, instead, look through an eyepiece rigidly attached to a supporting apparatus (so there is no vertiginous swinging of the visual world each time the head moves), and use monocular vision (so the reversal of stereoscopic depth cues is not a problem). Only one hand—the dominant hand—is seen through the reversing prism.

In our restricted situation, adjustment to reversed vision is rapid and relatively easy. When one first looks through the prism one sees the hand in reverse: the thumb is on the wrong side. If a pencil is put into this hand and one tries to draw a line between two points on a piece of paper, it is at first almost impossible. Every time one tries to move the pencil toward a given point the pencil veers in the opposite direction; the resulting zig-zag looks like a diagram of Brownian motion. After only a few minutes of practice, though, the task can be accomplished readily. Within an hour one is drawing about as well, while looking through the prism, as one formerly could without a prism.

Before we carried out the experiment reported here, we made some preliminary observations with a group of pilot subjects. We let these subjects adapt to reversal for a little while, and then told them to write a letter C while watching the hand through the prism. They drew a backwards C, which looked correct through the prism. We then told them to write another C, but this time to close their eyes in the middle of the act. At this early stage of adaptation, one of two things occurred. If the subject's pencil was moving fairly slowly it would change direction the instant the subject's eyes closed, and would trace out a backwards S—a surprise to the subject, who would expect to see a C. Or, if the pencil moved rapidly, the result would be a backwards C but the subject would still be surprised to see the letter because it had *felt* as though the pencil were moving in an S–curve. This phenomenon is called "visual capture." As long as the eyes are open the felt motion agrees with the seen motion, but the visual dominance ends the instant the eyes close.

With longer exposure, we have found, there is a change in kinesthesis that persists even after the eyes are closed. It is this phenomenon that the following experiment was designed to demonstrate. In the experiment reported here, the subjects wrote no letters or numbers during the time they were looking through the reversing prism—only afterwards, when they could not see what they were writing.

METHOD

Subjects

The subjects were eight right-handed graduate students at the University of Pennsylvania (four male, four female).

Apparatus

A reversing prism (a right-angle prism that acts as a total-reflecting mirror) was mounted in the right eyepiece of a stationary headrest in such a way that anything seen through the prism was reversed right-for-left. (The view through the left eyepiece was permanently blocked off.) The field of view through the prism consisted of the entire width, and almost the entire length, of a piece of standard white typing paper that was clamped to a stationary board. The board was fixed at an angle orthogonal to the line of sight through the prism, which was slanted downward so that the subject's head was inclined in the position normally assumed for reading or writing. The distance from the eye to the sheet of paper was also normal reading distance (approximately 45 cm).

Vision through the prism could be quickly occluded by sliding a metal plate into grooves in the eyepiece.

Procedure

Each subject participated in four sessions, given on four different days within a single week. Before the first session a pretest was given. The subjects sat with their heads against the headrest and the metal plate blocking off vision through the prism, and wrote letters and numbers on the sheet of paper as the experimenter called them out. The 10 characters were written in a vertical column. Since the subjects could not see what they were writing they had to judge how much to lower the pencil after each character was written so that the successive characters would not be superimposed. (Occasionally characters *were* superimposed, but they always remained legible.) Each test always consisted of the same seven letters (lower case *b, c, d, e, g, s,* and *z*) and three numbers (*2, 3,* and *7*); these were given in a different random order for each test. Three such tests were given to each subject before the first adaptation period.

The subjects spent each of the four 15-minute adaptation periods looking through the prism, while drawing and doodling on the piece of paper with a pencil held in the right hand. They were told that they could draw pictures or diagrams, play games of tic-tac-toe with themselves, or run the pencil at random over the paper; but they were cautioned never to write a letter or a number. They were also told to keep their left hand on their lap, out of view behind the board. The paper was changed whenever the subject requested it.

At the end of the 15 minutes a new piece of paper was inserted and the subject was instructed to draw a star at the top of the sheet. The metal plate was then dropped into the eyepiece in front of the prism and the posttest began at once, with the experimenter calling out each of the 10 letters and numbers as soon as the subject had finished writing the preceding one. Then the paper was changed, the metal plate was removed, the subject again viewed the right hand through the prism for several seconds while drawing three stars at the top of the paper, the metal plate was reinserted, and a second test of 10 characters was given. This was followed, in the same manner, by a third test. Thus, each subject wrote a total of 30 characters after each adaptation session, or 120 test characters in all.

Pilot work had taught us that looking only for letters and numbers written backwards might underestimate the actual amount of adaptation. We also wanted to know when a subject wrote a letter frontwards but *perceived* it as backwards. For this reason we explained to our subjects that in the posttest they might occasionally reverse a character as a result of the adaptation procedure, and that they should be sure to inform the experimenter if they noticed that they had done so.

RESULTS

Figure 22.1 shows some of the letters written by five different subjects after exposure to right-left reversal of the visual field. Of the eight subjects who

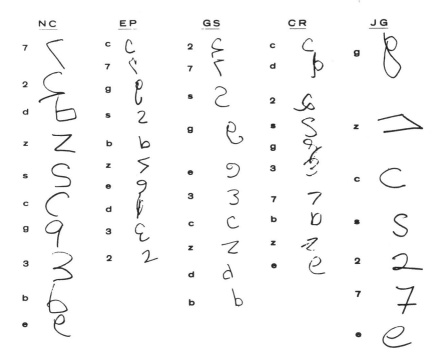

FIG. 22.1. Five subjects, who could not see what they were writing, produced these letters and numbers after exposure to right-left reversal of the visual field. The columns on the left show what these subjects were asked to write. Some of the characters that were written frontwards (NC's z, EP's c, and CR's c) were perceived as having been written backwards. Note that JG's z is partly reversed, partly frontwards.

participated in this experiment, seven wrote at least one backwards character in the posttests. None wrote any backwards letters or numbers in the pretest. Needless to say, this difference was significant [$t(7) = 3.4$, $p < .02$]. The median subject wrote a total of 12.6 backwards characters in the four posttests; the mean was 11.6 (standard error $= 3.4$). Overall, 10% of the posttest characters were written in reverse.

Every subject made at least one perceptual error after exposure to reversal. Two kinds of perceptual error were possible: A subject might write a character backwards and not realize that it was backwards (we call this error an "unnoticed reversal"), and a subject might write a character frontwards but *think* that it was backwards (a "false alarm").[1] Altogether there were 59 unnoticed reversals (a mean of 7.4 per subject) and 31 false alarms (a mean of 3.9).

The aftereffect was unstable, and the number of perceptual errors declined rapidly over time. Figure 22.2 shows the distribution of errors as a function of the number of letters written after vision was occluded (a rough measure of time since exposure). On the first character of a posttest the subjects made perceptual errors nearly 30% of the time, with about as many false alarms as unnoticed reversals. By the tenth letter there were seldom any errors; false alarms declined more rapidly than unnoticed reversals. This reflects the fact that an unnoticed reversal was followed by *another* unnoticed reversal 57% of the time, whereas 70% of false alarms were followed by non-reversed, errorless trials. *Noticed* reversals were also followed most often by a non-reversed character (75%). These differences in transitional probabilities were highly significant [$\chi^2(6) = 32.2$, $p < .005$].

Almost half (48%) of all backwards characters were written in the first of the three tests after the 15-minute exposure period [$\chi^2(2) = 10.7$, $p < .005$]. On the other hand, there was only a slight, nonsignificant tendency for more reversals to occur after the third and fourth experimental sessions (56%) than after the first and second (44%).

We wondered whether subjects were more likely to reverse "confusing" letters such as *s, z, b,* and *d,* than "easy" letters such as *g, c,* and *e.* The answer, as can be seen in Table 22.1, is that the probability of an *unnoticed* reversal was

---

[1]Scoring these errors was sometimes difficult. Occasionally subjects would say that they were not sure if a character had been written frontwards or backwards, or they would write a character and then say that they thought the character *before* that one had been written backwards. These cases were scored as one-half of a false alarm if the character was frontwards (this occurred eight times), or one-half of an unnoticed reversal if the letter was backwards (nine times). On the other hand there were a few occasions when the subject said only that a frontwards (or backwards) character "felt funny" or "peculiar" or "weird"; this was counted as no error (or as an unnoticed reversal).

In three cases subjects wrote characters that were partly reversed and partly frontwards, as subject JG's *z* in Figure 22.1. In all three of these cases the subject believed that the entire character had been written backwards; thus each of these cases was counted as one-half of a noticed reversal, one-half of a false alarm.

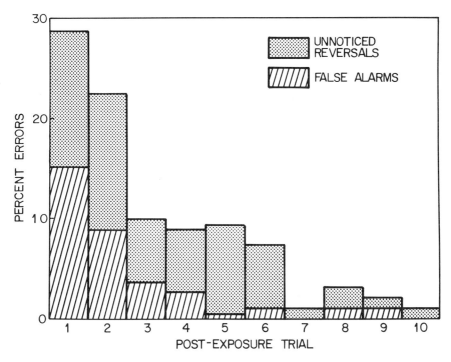

FIG. 22.2.   Perceptual errors as a function of the number of characters written after vision through the reversing prism was blocked off (a rough measure of time since exposure). Each of the eight subjects had 12 opportunities for an error on each of the 10 trials. ''Unnoticed reversals'' are characters written backwards that the subject thought were frontwards; ''false alarms'' are frontwards characters that the subject thought were backwards.

TABLE 22.1
Overall Posttest Results for Seven Letters and Three Numbers

	b	*c*	*d*	*e*	*g*	*s*	*z*	Mean Letter	*2*	*3*	*7*	Mean Number
Reversals												
Unnoticed	7	6	6	5	6	2	6	5.4	5	4	6	5.0
Noticed	4	—	.5	2	—	2	2.5	1.6	6	8.5	5	6.5
''Not sure''	—	1	1	—	—	1	2	.7	2	1	1	1.3
Total	11	7	7.5	7	6	5	10.5	7.7	13	13.5	12	12.8
Nonreversals												
False alarms	3	5	1	2	1	7	5	3.4	1	—	2	1.0
''Not sure''	—	1	1	—	1	4	—	1.0	—	—	1	.3

Note: The entries under the individual letters and numbers give the total number of occurrences of each type of response, out of the 96 opportunities (12 tests × 8 subjects) for each character.

about the same for all letters and numbers. There does appear to be a somewhat greater number of false alarms and of "not sure" responses for the letters *s* and *z;* however, there were not enough of these cases for proper statistical analysis. There *was* a significant difference, though, between letters and numbers: A number that was written in reverse was noticed 49% of the time, whereas a reversed letter was noticed only 19% of the time. This difference, whatever it means, was reliable [$\chi^2(2) = 10.7, p < .005$].

DISCUSSION

After a brief period of adaptation to visual reversal, our subjects wrote backwards letters and numbers. Did they do this because of some change in their vision, or in their visuo-motor coordination? No, because the characters were written in the *absence* of vision. Was it because they had learned new movement patterns during the adaptation period? No, because they had written no letters or numbers during adaptation, and the motions they made in drawing and doodling had as much in common with the motions of writing frontwards letters as with those of writing backwards letters.

It should be noted that writing backwards letters and numbers, which our subjects did with relatively little effort, is something that most people in the unadapted state cannot readily do. Many people can write in "mirror-writing" with their nondominant hand, particularly while writing normal letters with the dominant hand, but it is rare (especially in right-handed individuals) to be able to write backwards with the dominant hand (Corballis & Beale, 1976). Writing backwards goes *against* movement patterns that have been repeatedly practiced since childhood.

Even if a new movement pattern could have supplanted such a well-learned one so quickly, that would not account for these results: Our subjects not only wrote backwards characters—they also felt that they had written them frontwards, or they felt that frontwards characters were written backwards. When we showed the subjects what they had written they were usually quite amazed, and their amazement included not only reversed characters but frontwards ones as well ("I was *certain* I had written that *c* backwards!").

Perhaps the subjects, in the 15-minute adaptation period, developed new, reversed visual images of letters and numbers, and their posttest writing was directed by these new visual images. That hypothesis is unlikely for two reasons. First, they never saw any reversed letters or numbers during practice. Second, Kohler (1953, 1964) reports that in long-term adaptation to reversal, letters and numbers continued to look backwards when seen through the prisms long after other "errors" had disappeared.

There seems to be only one possible conclusion: During adaptation these subjects underwent a kinesthetic change, so that a left-right motion felt like a right-left motion.[2] This change removed the initial conflict between vision and kinesthesis, so the subjects were then able to direct the pencil without effort to wherever they wanted it to go. And this kinesthetic change sometimes persisted for a little while after vision was occluded.

This kind of kinesthetic change differs in a major way from the kind of change that has been proposed for adaptation to sideways-displacing prisms. Harris (1963, 1965) has presented evidence that a subject who sees one hand shifted to the right of where it really is comes to *feel* it in that location. After the prisms are removed the displacement of felt position declines steadily to zero. Such uniform decay is implausible for reversal: A perceived left-right motion is not likely to be felt as less and less of a motion and then as no motion at all before it is finally perceived (correctly) as a right-left motion. Instead, our observations suggest that it is more of an all-or-none effect. How fast a subject can go from one state to the other is demonstrated vividly by the partly backwards z of subject JG, shown in Fig. 22.1. This subject drew the top bar of the z frontwards, from left to right. His kinesthetic perception evidently switched at the instant he reached the first corner, and the down-slash and bottom bar are drawn backwards.

There is, however, one peculiar but possible intermediate state between "all" and "none," and this state may account for the times the subjects reported that they "weren't sure" whether a letter had been written correctly or in reverse. Occasionally subjects have told us that a given hand motion seemed to go *both* right-to-left and left-to-right.[3] The two kinesthetic states seem to be able to exist simultaneously, and sometimes are equal in strength. We can think of the process of adaptation to reversal as strengthening one of these states at the expense of the other.

Can we generalize from our simplified, restricted, short-term laboratory study to the much more complete adaptation that Kohler's subjects achieved after weeks of walking around with reversing goggles? We think so. Earlier we mentioned the experienced Alice, wearing reversing goggles but no longer bumping into doorways, and asked how this Alice differed from the first Alice, headed unsuccessfully for her medicine cabinet. Perhaps we can now answer this question in greater detail.

When the unadapted Alice looks down at her feet through the reversing prisms she sees her left foot on the right and her right foot on the left. When she commands her right foot to take a step, "it remains," in Kohler's words, "rooted to the ground, while the left one starts off" (1964, p. 150). She sees her right hand on her left side, but her position sense still tells her it is on her right so she uses it to reach for an object that appears to be on her right. Since the object

---

[2]Further discussion of possible alternative hypotheses, and reasons for questioning them, may be found in Harris (1965, 1980).

[3]This eerie sensation has also been experienced by both of the authors of this chapter, during informal exploratory work.

is really on her left, she misses. She sees her hand too far to the left of the object (it is really too far to the right) and she moves her hand farther to the right. It moves away from the object instead of toward it.

After two or three weeks of wearing prism goggles, Alice's proprioceptive and kinesthetic perceptions have come into line with her rearranged vision. When the adapted Alice looks down at her feet she still sees her right foot on the left, but now she also *feels* it on the left, so when she commands that foot to move it does move. Objects on her left are still seen on the right, but since that is where she feels her *left* hand to be she reaches with that hand. If she aims a little too far to the right she sees her hand to the left of the object, so she makes what looks and feels like a rightwards motion. Since it is really a leftwards motion it is successful, and the hand reaches its goal. The changed perception of the locations and motions of body parts has brought the proprioceptive and kinesthetic world into harmony with the visual world, and there are no problems in coordination. The visual world has regained its stability and no longer streams by when Alice moves her head, because now when she moves her head in one direction it feels as though it's moving in the other direction (toward the side from which objects are seen to enter her visual field).

Now Alice is able to use and respond to the verbal labels "left" and "right" correctly, as long as she understands these words to mean "nearer my left hand" and "nearer my right." Regardless of its felt location, the right hand still feels like a right (dominant) hand. Kohler describes what happens, at this stage of adaptation, when he tries to decide whether the right side of a diagram appears to be on the right or the left. "I see it to the right as long as I refer it to my hand. . . . Whether the corner of the figure is seen as right or left therefore depends entirely on whether I take my hand into account" (1964, p. 157). The hand is not taken into account when the judgment is made on a purely *visual* basis, relating it to pre-experimental visual memories. Then that corner of the diagram is still seen on the left side of the reversed visual field. This combination of unchanged vision and reversed kinesthesis helps us to understand many (though perhaps not all) of Kohler's detailed observations.[4]

Does vision ever change around, so that things seen through the reversing prisms look the way they did before the goggles were put on? We think not, and Kohler's reports lend support to this view. For example, Kohler's prisms produced a reversal of stereoscopic depth cues. Stereoscopic vision never adapted, it always "remains incorrect" (1964, p. 143). It is true that Kohler said that

---

[4]If a subject undergoes progressively more extensive kinesthetic and proprioceptive changes such as those we described, adaptive changes in motor behavior, visual-motor coordination, and verbal reports of visual perceptions follow naturally. There is no need to invoke additional changes within or between other sensory modalities, or between vision and kinesthesis or movements. (If one instead hypothesized that these other changes were primary, one would have to go on to postulate, ad hoc, additional changes within the kinesthetic sense.)

subject Grill, who wore the goggles without interruption for 37 days, "eventually achieved almost completely correct impressions, even where letters and numbers were involved" (p. 160), but this was apparently due to his growing familiarity with the backwards characters: "After much practice, 'mirror reading' became so well established and previous memories so secondary that even print looked all right, as long as attention was not too critical" (p. 160).

Lewis Carroll's Alice woke up to find that everything was back to normal—the Looking Glass world had all been a dream. *Our* Alice takes off the prism goggles and immediately finds herself bumping into walls again, and missing medicine bottles. The reversed kinesthetic and proprioceptive perceptions which we think are responsible for these aftereffects were demonstrated—in a small way—by our subjects (after as little as 15 minutes of exposure to reversal) when they wrote backwards letters and thought they were frontwards.

ACKNOWLEDGMENTS

This research was supported by National Science Foundation grant GB–3546 and was carried out while the authors were at the University of Pennsylvania. Some of the results were reported at the meeting of the Psychonomic Society, Chicago, October 1965.

REFERENCES

Corballis, M. C., & Beale, I. L. *The psychology of left and right.* Hillsdale, N.J.: Lawrence Erlbaum Associates, 1976.

Harris, C. S. Adaptation to displaced vision: Visual, motor, or proprioceptive change? *Science,* 1963, *140,* 812–813.

Harris, C. S. Perceptual adaptation to inverted, reversed, and displaced vision. *Psychological Review,* 1965, *72,* 419–444.

Harris, C. S. Insight or out of sight?: Two examples of perceptual plasticity in the human adult. In C. S. Harris (Ed.), *Visual coding and adaptability.* Hillsdale, N.J.: Lawrence Erlbaum Associates, 1980.

Kohler, I. Über Aufbau und Wandlungen der Wahrnehmungswelt. Insbesondere über 'bedingte Empfindungen'. *Österreichische Akademie der Wissenschaften, Philosophisch-historische Klasse; Sitzungsberichte,* 227. Band, 1. Abhandlung, Wien: Rohrer, 1951.

Kohler, I. Umgewöhnung im Wahrnehmungsbereich. *Die Pyramide,* 1953, *3,* 92–96, 109–113, 132–133.

Kohler, I. The formation and transformation of the perceptual world. *Psychological Issues,* 1964, *3(4),* Monograph 12. New York: International Universities Press.

Kottenhoff, H., & Lindahl, L. Laboratory studies in the psychology of motion-sickness. *Acta Psychologica,* 1960, *27,* 89–112.

Treisman, M. Motion sickness: An evolutionary hypothesis. *Science,* 1977, *197,* 493–495.

Tu tiefst ergriffen von Dölle's
eigenartigem Leben und Wirken
möchte ich anstelle eines Nachrufs

meine Hochschätzung mit
"den linken", d.h. der Hand-
schreiben, zum Ausdruck
bringen. (Ernst Kohler) vol. Prof.

An example of left-right mirror writing from Professor Kohler's own hand. The text is from a book dedicated to the eminent German psychologist Ernst August Dölle. (In: T. Herrmann, Ed., ''Dichotomie und Duplizität; Grundfragen psychologischer Erkenntnis,'' p. 248. H. Huber: Bern-Stuttgart-Wien, 1974).

The Editors

23

Spiegelschrift und Umkehrschrift bei Linkshändern und Rechtshändern: Ein Beitrag zum Balkentransfer und Umkehrlernen

Richard Jung
Clemens Fach
Abt. Neurophysiologie, Universität Freiburg
Freiburg i. Br., W-Germany

ABSTRACT

The writing of normal script, mirror script and inverted scripts with either hand is recorded in lefthanders and righthanders. Ten lefthanders writing with their right hand and 10 lefthanders writing with their left hand are compared to 10 righthanders writing with their right hand. Mirror script implies right-left reversal, and inverted script up-down reversal of writing.

When writing with their inexperienced hand, most subjects show a preference for mirror script. This facilitation of mirror script with the opposite hand is called "mirror script transfer," acquired by the writing of normal script with the experienced hand.

All lefthanders and many righthanders write mirror script faster with their left hand than with their right hand. The strongest mirror transfer occurs for the left hand of lefthanders who normally write with their right hand. This may be related to their predominant control of language by the right cerebral hemisphere. Since mirror writing with the opposite, inexperienced hand may be transferred via the corpus callosum, the mirror transfer from the left to the right cerebral hemisphere may contribute to the recognition of script. Lefthanders trained to write with their left hand have the weakest mirror transfer for their right hand, probably because language and writing are both coordinated by their right hemisphere.

Learning improves mirror and inverted scripts and often shortens the writing time for untrained scripts by one half within the first week of daily training. The slower the inexperienced script originally was, the greater the practice effect. A superior learning of mirror script versus inverted script by mirror-script transfer is not apparent from our results. The rapid learning of inverted script with practice is compared to Kohler's studies of learned responses to inverted vision.

377

Seit Anfang des 16. Jahrhunderts, als der linkshändige Leonardo seine Tagebücher in Spiegelschrift schrieb, ist bekannt, daß Linkshänder mit der linken Hand zur Spiegelschrift tendieren, wenn sie rechts schreiben gelernt haben. In früheren Jahrhunderten und in Deutschland bis zum letzten Jahrzehnt haben alle Linkshänder das Schreiben mit der rechten Hand gelernt. Erst neuerdings läßt man in den Schulen Linkshänder von Beginn an auch mit der linken Hand schreiben. Man kann daher *zwei Linkshändergruppen, rechtsschreibende und linksschreibende,* unterscheiden und vergleichen. Diese Arbeit behandelt das Schreibverhalten von Links- und Rechtshändern für Spiegel- und Umkehrschrift.

Die Tatsache, daß rechtsschreibende Linkshänder mit der linken Hand zur Spiegelschrift neigen, wurde mehrfach neu entdeckt (Orton, 1925; Pfeifer, 1919). Doch fehlen, abgesehen von einer Untersuchung der Handhaltung (Levy & Reid, 1978), bisher systematische Studien mit vergleichenden quantitativen Schreibproben von Normal- und Spiegelschrift bei Links- und Rechtshändern. Wir haben Untersuchungen mit Vergleichen von Spiegelschrift (horizontale Umkehr) und Umkehrschrift (vertikale Umkehr) begonnen und beschreiben im folgenden die ersten Ergebnisse. Wahrscheinlich wird die linkshändige Spiegelschrift durch Balkentransfer zwischen den beiden Großhirnhemisphären gebahnt, und die Ergebnisse können daher zum Verständnis des Balkentransfers beim Menschen beitragen. Darüber hinaus werden unsere Studien über vertikale Umkehrschrift mit Strattons (1897) und Kohlers (1951, 1961, 1964) klassischen Umkehrbrillenexperimenten verglichen.

METHODIK UND VERSUCHSPERSONEN

Als Standard-Testwort hatten die Versuchspersonen mit einem Bleistift das Wort ''Neurophysiologie'' abwechselnd mit der linken und rechten Hand in vier verschiedenen Schriftarten zu schreiben. Diese vier Schriftarten zeigt Abb. 23.1 am Übungsbeispiel ''Mama'':

1. a/b Normalschrift links/rechts (Mama)
2. c/d Spiegelschrift links/rechts (smaM)
3. e/f Umkehrschrift links/rechts (ewaW)
4. g/h Umkehrspiegelschrift links/rechts (Wgwg)

Die Schreibversuche begannen jeweils mit der schreibgeübten Hand, dann folgte die kontralaterale (schreibungeübte) Hand, also war die Reihenfolge bei Linkshändern a, b, c etc., bei Rechtshändern und rechtsschreibenden Linkshändern b, a, d, etc.

Für jede Schriftart wurde der Schreibdruck mit Hilfe einer Schreibwaage (Modifikation nach Enke 1930) und der Zeitbedarf mit einer Stoppuhr registriert. Die Schreibdruckkurven zeigen neben dem Schreibdruck auch das Schreibtempo.

Fehlerauswertung. Beim Vergleich der verschiedenen Schriftarten wurden die Schreibfehler an einzelnen Buchstaben nach folgenden vier Kriterien ausgezählt: (1) Seitenverkehrungen, (2) vertikale Umkehrungen, (3) Verunstaltungen der Buchstaben, (4) stärkere Abweichungen nach oben oder unten.

Versuchspersonen. Die Probanden waren junge weibliche und männliche Erwachsene (20 Linkshänder, 10 Rechtshänder). Sie waren vor den Versuchen 1–3 Jahrzehnte im Schreiben mit einer Hand geübt. Die Linkshänder wurden nach ihrer Schreibhand in rechtsschreibende und linksschreibende Linkshänder unterteilt. Damit ergaben sich *3 Gruppen von Probanden:*

Gruppe I: 10 rechtsschreibende Linkshänder schrieben seit dem ersten Schuljahr nur mit der rechten Hand, obwohl sie mit der linken andere Tätigkeiten (wie Zeichnen und Nähen) ausübten. Solche Linkshänder, die bereits geübt waren, mit der linken und rechten Hand Normalschrift zu schreiben und andere Geschicklichkeitshandlungen auszuführen, wurden als "Beidhänder" (Ambidexter) ausgesondert. Diese Ambidexter sind offenbar latente Linkshänder, da eine Anlage zur Beidhändigkeit zweifelhaft ist (Critchley, 1954).

Gruppe II: 10 linksschreibende Linkshänder hatten seit dem ersten Schuljahr mit der linken Hand schreiben gelernt und benutzten auch zum Zeichnen, Schrauben, Nähen und zu anderen Fertigkeiten die linke Hand.

Gruppe III: 10 rechtsschreibende Rechtshänder schrieben seit der Schulzeit nur rechts, nie links. Die sehr seltenen Rechtshänder, die nach Handverletzungen oder Amputationen mit der linken Hand schrieben, konnten noch nicht untersucht werden.

Das Durchschnittsalter war in allen Gruppen ähnlich: I: 23.9, II: 25.0, III: 27.5 Lebensjahre. Das Geschlechtsverhältnis Frauen/Männer war in I: 6/4, II: 7/3, III: 4/6. Unsere Linkshänder (Gruppe I und II) beteiligten sich in der Regel stärker an den Schreibversuchen und zeigten eine bessere Motivation als Rechtshänder (Gruppe III).

Schreibübungen. Die Erlernbarkeit der ungewohnten Spiegel-und Umkehrschriften wurde durch zweimal tägliche Wiederholung der Schreibaufgaben mit Zeitmessung nach einer Woche untersucht (Abb. 23.6 und 23.7).

ERGEBNISSE

Trotz individuell verschiedenen Schreibverhaltens waren Gruppenunterschiede im Schreibtempo deutlich zu erkennen. Außerdem zeigen die Schreibdruckkurven (Abb. 23.1 für "Mama" und Fig. 23.2 für "Neurophysiologie") qualitative und quantitative Verschiedenheiten des Normal-, Spiegel-, und Umkehrschreibens. Die Quantifizierung gelang am leichtesten durch die Schreibzeit des Standardwortes (Abb. 23.3).

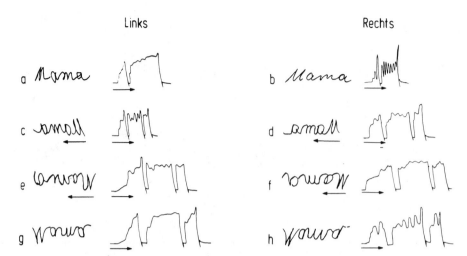

Links   Rechts

ABB. 23.1. *Der experimentelle Ablauf: Vier Schriftarten, mit der rechten oder linken Hand geschrieben und die entsprechenden Schreibdruckkurven.*

Als Übungswort sollten die Versuchspersonen "Mama" mit jeder Hand auf vier verschiedene Arten schreiben. Die Buchstaben verweisen auf: Normalschrift (a, b), Spiegelschrift (c, d), Umkehrschrift (e, f) und Umkehrspiegelschrift (g, h), jeweils für die linke und rechte Hand. Es wurde immer mit dem großen "M" begonnen. Die Abbildung zeigt die Schreibproben einer rechtsschreibenden Linkshänderin (B. S. ♀, 41 J.). Rechts neben jeder Schriftart sind die entsprechenden Schreibdruckkurven abgebildet. Schriftqualität und Schreibdruck zeigen charakteristische Unterschiede. Die Normalschrift, geschrieben mit der schreibgeübten rechten Hand (b), gelingt zügig mit rasch folgenden Auf- und Abstrichen und ausgeprägten Spitzen im Schreibdruck. Die ungewohnten Schriften rechts (d, f, h) und alle Schriften der linken Hand zeigen im Schreibdruck wenig modulierte Plateaus, wobei die Druckspitzen durch Wellen ersetzt sind. Pausen werden länger. Die Spiegelschrift der linken Hand ist die schnellste und beste aller ungeübten Schriften.

FIG. 23.1. The experimental procedure: Four modes of script written with the right or left hand and their corresponding writing-pressure recordings.

To introduce the subject to the test, he was requested to write a simple word, "Mama," in four different ways using either hand. Letters refer to normal (a, b), mirror (c, d), inverted (e, f) and inverted mirror script (g, h), for the left and right hand, respectively. Writing started always with the capital *M*. Depicted is the script of a lefthander trained to write with her right hand (B. S. ♀, age 41). To the right of each script is shown the corresponding recording of writing pressure. The quality of script and the writing pressure show characteristic differences. Normal script written with the experienced hand (b) is fluent and shows rapid sequences of steep spikes in the pressure curve. In contrast, the unfamiliar scripts of the right hand (d, f, h) and all scripts of the left hand (a, c, e, g) show less modulation, with smooth waves replacing the spikes. Pauses also become longer. Mirror writing with the left hand appears to be the best and fastest of all untrained scripts.

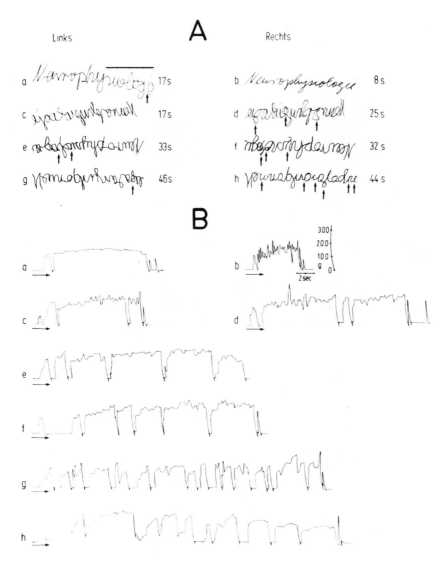

ABB. 23.2. *Schriftbilder (A) und Schreibdruckkurven (B) des links und rechts geschriebenen Testworts bei einer rechtsschreibenden Linkshänderin.* (B. S. ♀ 41 J.)

A "Neurophysiologie" wurde in vier Schreibarten geschrieben. Die beste Schriftqualität und die flüssigste Schrift haben die Normalschrift rechts (b) und die Spiegelschrift links (c). Die schreibgeübte rechte Hand schreibt Spiegelschrift (d) langsamer und schlechter als die schreibungeübte linke Hand. Die Schreibzeit (in Sek.) ist hinter den Schriften angegeben. Fehler (↑), die in den ungewohnten Schriften auftreten, sind meistens Buchstabenformen, die der Normalschrift ähneln.

(continued)

1. Schreibzeit

Eine Übersicht über die Zeitmessungen (Schreibzeiten des Testworts mit Mittel-wert (mean) und Standardabweichung (standard deviation)) bei den 3 Gruppen geben Tab. 23.1 und Abb. 23.3.

Normalschrift. Wie zu erwarten wird die Normalschrift bei allen Probanden jeweils mit der Schreibhand am schnellsten geschrieben, also bei Gruppe I und III rechts, bei Gruppe II links. Die Schreibzeiten sind im Durchschnitt bei den Rechtshändern kürzer als bei den Linkshändern der Gruppen I und II.

Dementsprechend benötigen alle Probanden mit der gegenseitigen Hand län-gere Schreibzeiten: Gruppe I und II benötigen kontralateral etwa die doppelte Zeit, Gruppe III braucht, entsprechend ihrer kürzeren Schreibzeit für geübte Normalschrift, etwa die dreifache Zeit.

Spiegelschrift. Fast alle Linkshänder und die meisten Rechtshänder schreiben die linksläufige Spiegelschrift mit der linken Hand schneller als mit der rechten. Wenn Spiegelschrift mit der schreibungeübten Hand geschrieben wird, zeigt sie bei den Gruppen I und III im Gegensatz zur Normalschrift im Durch-schnitt kürzere Schreibzeiten als mit der Schreibhand. Gruppe II zeigt dagegen kürzere durchschnittliche Schreibzeiten mit der Schreibhand und längere mit der schreibungeübten Hand. Nur 2 von 10 linksschreibenden Linkshändern und einer von 10 der rechtsschreibenden Linkshänder schrieben mit der rechten Hand schneller als mit der linken. Bei den Rechtshändern hatten 3 Probanden links längere oder gleich lange Schreibzeiten im Vergleich zur Schreibhand.

B Die Schreibdruckkurven geben Schreibfluß und Schreibgeschwindigkeit der verschiedenen Schriften wieder. Typisch ist die rasche Abfolge kurzer Druck-spitzen bei der geübten Normalschrift. Im Gegensatz dazu zeigen die ungeübten Schriften lange Druckplateaus mit Pausen, die den Schreibpausen entsprechen, z. B. nach Großbuchstaben oder vor dem i-Punkt.

FIG. 23.2.   Scripts and writing pressure recordings for a test word, written with either hand by a lefthander trained to write with her right hand (B. S. ♀, age 41). A ''Neurophysiologie'' is written in four different modes of script. The best writing quality and most fluent script is apparent in right normal script (*b*) and left mirror script (*c*). The right hand, trained in normal script, writes mirror script (*d*) more slowly and less well than the left hand, which is untrained. Writing time (in sec) is given behind the test word. Frequent errors (↑) occur in unfamiliar scripts and are mostly characterized by a change of the letter form towards that of normal script.

B The pressure curves reflect the fluency and speed of the trained normal script (*b*) by rapid sequences of short pressure spikes. In contrast, untrained scripts show long pressure plateaus with pauses. Intermittent zero pressure corresponds to writing pauses, for example, after the initial capital letter and before the ''i''-dot.

TAB. 23.1

Schreibzeiten des Testworts "Neurophysiologie" in Sekunden bei
den Gruppen I–III im ersten Schreibversuch

	Links		Rechts	
Schriftart	Mittelwert (sec)	Standard- abweichung	Mittelwert (sec)	Standard- abweichung
I: Rechtsschreibende Linkshänder (N = 10)				
Normalschrift	13.5	1.67	7.1	1.33
Spiegelschrift	18.7	2.66	24.9	2.96
Umkehrschrift	32.4	3.78	32.9	3.71
Umkehrspiegelschrift	37.2	4.21	37.0	3.64
II: Linksschreibende Linkshänder (N = 10)				
Normalschrift	7.6	1.79	13.0	2.07
Spiegelschrift	19.1	3.11	23.4	2.98
Umkehrschrift	25.8	2.59	28.3	2.95
Umkehrspiegelschrift	33.2	3.35	33.8	3.15
III: Rechtsschreibende Rechtshänder (N = 10)				
Normalschrift	18.3	2.20	6.5	1.34
Spiegelschrift	20.4	2.50	22.7	2.43
Umkehrschrift	25.5	2.75	26.4	2.74
Umkehrspiegelschrift	28.0	2.86	29.5	2.98

Umkehrschrift. Diese um 180° vertikal gedrehte Schrift kann ein dem
Schreibenden Gegenübersitzender (ebenso der Leser durch Drehen der Seite) als
Normalschrift lesen (Abb. 23.1 und Abb. 23.2, 4, 5; jeweils e und f). Sie wird
linksläufig von rechts nach links geschrieben wie die Spiegelschrift.

Alle Versuchspersonen empfinden die Umkehrschrift zunächst als schwierig,
die Schreibzeit ist entsprechend bei allen Versuchspersonen wesentlich länger als
bei Normal- und Spiegelschrift. Rechtshänder (Gruppe III) zeigen für Umkehrschrift durchschnittlich beiderseits etwas kürzere Schreibzeiten als Linkshänder (Gruppe I und II). Die Zeitunterschiede zwischen der Schreibhand und
der schreibungeübten Hand sind bei allen Gruppen sehr gering.

Umkehrspiegelschrift. Diese rechtsläufig geschriebene Schrift braucht bei
allen Versuchspersonen die längsten Schreibzeiten. Die Schreibzeit ist gegenüber der geübten Normalschrift bei allen Gruppen 4–5 fach verlängert. Die Gruppen zeigen keine Unterschiede zwischen der linken und rechten Hand. Die Gruppenunterschiede sind ähnlich der Umkehrschrift: Rechtshänder haben kürzere
Schreibzeiten als Linkshänder, die längsten Schreibzeiten zeigt wieder Gruppe I
(Tab. 23.1).

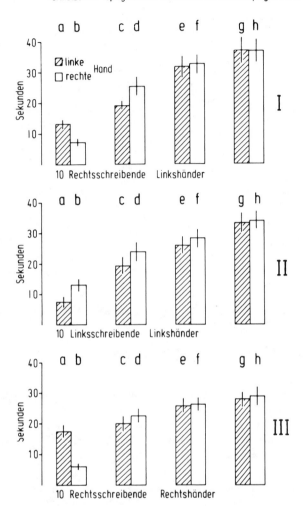

ABB. 23.3. *Durchschnittszeiten der vier Schriftarten für je zehn Versuchspersonen der drei Gruppen: Rechtsschreibende Linkshänder (I), linksschreibende Linkshänder (II) und Rechtshänder (III).*

Die Ordinate zeigt die durchschnittlichen Schreibzeiten, die für die vier verschiedenen Schriftarten benötigt wurde (Abszisse). Die Normalschrift, geschrieben mit der schreibgeübten Hand, ist bei allen Gruppen am schnellsten. Die Spiegelschrift wird mit der linken Hand schneller geschrieben als mit der rechten, selbst wenn die linke Hand schreibungeübt ist (Gruppe I und III). Dieser Spiegelschrifttransfer zur kontralateralen Hand ist bei rechtsschreibenden Linkshändern am deutlichsten. Die Umkehrschriften benötigen die längsten Schreibzeiten und zeigen keinen Unterschied zwischen rechter und linker Hand. Die Striche an den Durchschnittszeiten bezeichnen die Standardabweichungen.

2. Schreibdruckkurven und Schriftqualität

Schreibdruck.   Die Schreibdruckkurven lassen schon auf einen Blick die kürzeren Schreibzeiten und die stärkeren Druckunterschiede der geübten Normalschrift (Fig. 23.1b) gegenüber den ungewohnten Schriften (Abb. 23.1a und c–h) erkennen. Das Druckniveau auf der Schreibunterlage variiert zwischen 50g und 300g. Die Druckkurvenverläufe sind dagegen für jede Schriftart interindividuell ähnlich. Die Normalschrift der Schreibhand zeigt eine kurze Periode rasch aufeinanderfolgender steiler Druckspitzen der Auf-und Abstriche mit sehr kurzen Pausen des Drucks (z. B. nach einem Großbuchstaben oder vor einem i-Punkt). Dagegen haben die ungeübten Schriften fast immer längere und häufigere Pausen sowie längere Druckplateaus auf teils geringerem, teils höherem Druckniveau. Die Druckanstiege sind bei allen ungeübten Schriften im Vergleich zur geübten Normalschrift deutlich langsamer und wellenförmiger. Umkehrschrift und Umkehrspiegelschrift haben entsprechend ihren längeren Schreibzeiten links und rechts ähnliche langandauernde Druckplateaus und flachwellige Verläufe, doch sind die Druckanstiege gelegentlich bei der Schreibhand etwas steiler (Abb. 23.1h). Diese langen Druckkurven der Umkehrschriften werden hier nur für das kurze Übungswort ''Mama'' (Abb. 23.1 e–h) abgebildet. Für das Testwort ''Neurophysiologie'' gelten ähnliche Beobachtungen.

Schriftqualität.   Die ''Flüssigkeit'' und ''Güte'' der Schrift ist außer in den Schreibdruckkurven und Fehlerzahlen schwer quantitativ zu erfassen. Sie wird daher nur kurz eindrucksmäßig beschrieben. Auf einen Blick sieht man, daß die Normalschrift mit der Schreibhand jeweils ''besser'', ''flüssiger'' und lesbarer ist als die anderen Schriftarten. Charakteristische Beispiele mit Schreibdruckkurven des Testworts Neurophysiologie für Normal- und Spiegelschrift der drei Gruppen zeigen Abb. 23.2, 23.4 und 23.5.

Die Buchstaben a–h sind die Schriftarten, die in der Legende zu Abbildung 1 erklärt sind.

FIG. 23.3.   Average writing times of four kinds of script in three populations: lefthanders writing with the right hand (I), lefthanders writing with the left hand (II) and righthanders (III).
Mean duration (ordinate) as a measure of the speed of test-word writing is given for four different scripts (abscissa) in each group ($N = 10$). In all groups, normal script written with the trained hand is the fastest. Mirror script is written faster with the left hand than with the right, even when the left hand has no writing experience (Groups I and III). This mirror-script transfer towards the contralateral hand is most marked in lefthanders trained to write with their right hand. The up-down-inverted scripts need the longest time and show no difference between the right and left hand. Standard deviations are marked by vertical lines. Results for the left hand are represented by the hatched columns. Letters *a–h* refer to the designations explained in the legend to Fig. 23.1.

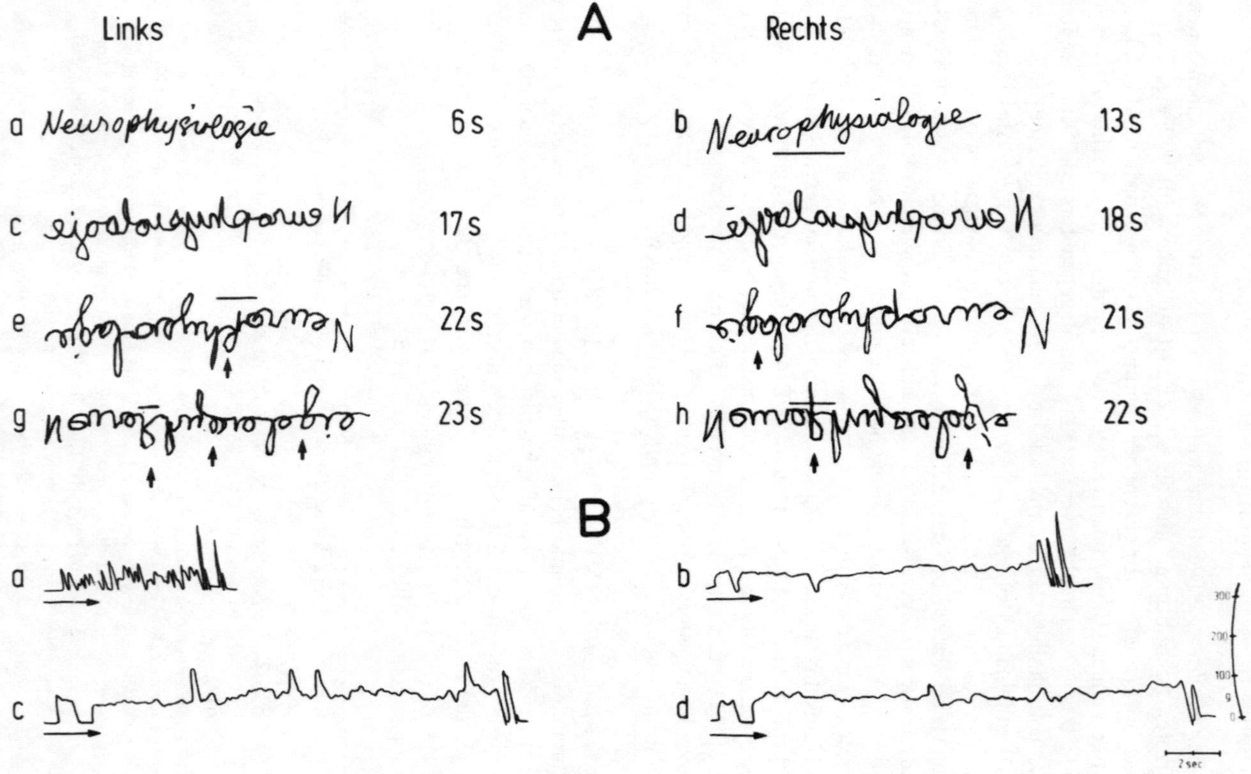

A

Links   Rechts

a Neurophysiologie   6 s   b Neurophysiologie   13 s

c Neurophysiologie   17 s   d Neurophysiologie   18 s

e Neurophysiologie   22 s   f Neurophysiologie   21 s

g Neurophysiologie   23 s   h Neurophysiologie   22 s

B

a   b

c   d

2 sec

386

3. Willensintention und subjektives Schreiberlebnis

Fragt man die Probanden nach ihrem Willens- und Müheaufwand und den Empfindungen beim Schreiben mit der rechten und linken Hand in verschiedenen Richtungen, so fällt allen Rechts- und Linkshändern die geübte Normalschrift am leichtesten und von den ungeübten Schriften die Umkehrspiegelschrift am schwersten.

Ein bemerkenswertes und deutliches Erleichterungserlebnis bei ungeübten Schriften schildern nur die rechtsschreibenden Linkshänder bei der Spiegelschrift links. Sie sagen meistens: "Die linke Spiegelschrift fällt mir von allen abweichenden Schreibaufgaben am leichtesten; nur die Normalschrift rechts ist noch leichter''. "Für die normale Schrift links muß ich mich mehr konzentrieren als für die Spiegelschrift links''.

ABB. 23.4.   *Schriftbild (A) und Schreibdruckkurven (B) einer linksschreibenden Linkshänderin (L. R. ♀ 25 Jahre)*

A) Die Schreibform der Normalschrift mit der linken Schreibhand ist flüssig und gerade, die anderen ungeübten Schriften zeigen geringere Schriftqualität und unsichere Zeilenführung. Das *Schreibtempo* ist für Normalschrift links (a) mit 6 sec rasch, sonst langsamer: Normalschrift rechts (b) hat doppelte Schreibzeit, alle anderen ungewohnten Schriften (c–h) brauchen die 4- bis 5-fache Schreibzeit gegenüber der Normalschrift links. Die *Spiegelschriften* (c, d) sind links und rechts zwar in Schriftbild und Schreibzeit ähnlich, aber die Schriftqualität ist mit der linken Hand besser und die Fehlerzahl (↑) geringer als mit der rechten. Die Umkehrschriften haben die meisten Fehler. Wie alle Probanden der Gruppe II begann die Probandin alle Schriftarten jeweils mit der linken Hand, also a vor b.
B) *Schreibdruckkurven* der Normal- und Spiegelschriften (a–d) desselben Testworts. Nur die schreibgeübte linke Hand zeigt bei Normalschrift (a) eine rasche und flüssige Abfolge steiler Auf- und Abstriche. Die rechte Hand (b) schreibt die Normalschrift länger mit wenig modulierten Druckplateaus und Druckspitzen nur für den i-Punkt. Die Spiegelschriften (c und d) sind noch langsamer und haben ein schwach moduliertes Druckniveau mit stumpfen Auf- und Abstrichen und wenigen Spitzen und steileren Abstrichen in der linken Spiegelschrift (c).

FIG. 23.4.   Scripts and writing pressure recordings of a lefthander trained to write with her left hand (L. R. ♀, age 25).
A Normal script with the trained left hand (a) is fluent and free of errors. The unfamiliar scripts (b–h) are of inferior quality and show errors of linearity (—) and spelling (↑). Most errors occur in inverted scripts. The writing time is shortest for left normal script (a) but doubles for the untrained right normal script (b). All other untrained scripts (c–h) are much slower and need three to four times the writing time required for the trained normal script. Mirror scripts (c, d) have about equal speed for the left and right hand.
B Recordings of writing pressure show fluent sequences of steep pressure spikes only for normal script written with the trained left hand (a). All other scripts, as well as the normal script written with the right hand (b), show less modulation, with plateaus and gradual pressure increases. Sharp spikes occur only for the ''i''-dot.

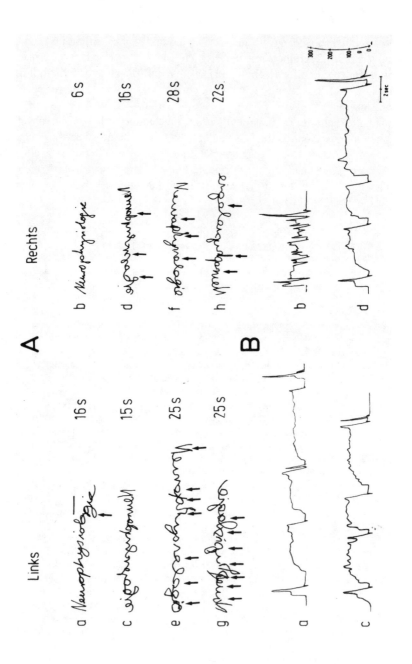

388

4. Lernversuche mit Schreibübungen

Da nur etwa die Hälfte der Versuchspersonen die Schreibübungen mit Spiegel- und Umkehrschrift durchführte, können wir nur vorläufige Ergebnisse der Lernversuche mitteilen. Die Lernwirkung wurde bei 9 Probanden (je 3 der Gruppen I–III) geprüft: über den Zeitraum einer Woche wurde das Testwort "Neurophysiologie" in allen Schriften täglich zweimal geschrieben. Ein Beispiel für fortschreitende Übung zeigt Abb. 23.6 bei einem rechtsschreibenden Linkshänder, der einmal besonders schnell, zum anderen besonders schön schreiben sollte. Abbildung 23.7 gibt eine Übersicht der Lerneffekte für Schreibzeiten und Fehler. Wegen der zu kleinen Stichprobe kann der Einfluß des Lernens noch nicht statistisch erfasst werden.

Schreibtempo. Die Schreibzeiten, die beim ersten Versuch für ungewohnte Schriften das Doppelte oder Dreifache der Normalschrift betrugen, verkürzten sich nach einer Woche Übung erheblich. Allgemein gilt: je langsamer die Schrift ohne Übung war, desto mehr beschleunigt sie sich durch Lernen. So zeigt Gruppe I die relativ stärkste Zeitverkürzung für Umkehrschriften, aber geringere Zeitverkürzung für die schon anfangs relativ rasche Spiegelschrift. Diese rechtsschreibenden Linkshänder schrieben Umkehr- und Umkehrspiegelschrift vor der Übung langsamer, nach der Übung schneller als andere Gruppen. In diesen

---

ABB. 23.5. *Schriftbilder (A) und Schreibdruckkurven (B) eines rechtsschreibenden Rechtshänders* (C. F. ♂ 22 Jahre)

A) Die Normalschrift ist rechts flüssig (b), aber links langsam und unsicher mit fast dreifacher Schreibzeit (a). Die Schriftqualität ist bei allen ungewohnten Schriften schlechter als für Buchstaben und Zeilenführung. Die Spiegel- und Umkehrschriften (c–h) brauchen links und rechts 3- bis 5-fache Schreibzeiten der Normal-schrift.

B) Die *Schreibdruckkurven* der Normalschrift rechts (b) haben die für flüssiges Schreiben typischen Abfolgen rascher spitzer Auf- und Abstriche. Die Normalschrift links (a) hat flache, wenig modulierte Druckplateaus mit einzelnen Pausen. Die Spiegelschriften (c u.d) haben ein etwas höheres Druckniveau als die Normalschrift mit langsameren Wellen. Steile Spitzen erscheinen nur beim N und i-Punkt. Links sind die Plateaus durch höhere langsame Wellen stärker moduliert (c).

FIG. 23.5. Scripts and writing pressure recordings of a righthander trained to write with his right hand (C.F. ♂, age 22).

A Normal script is fluent only with the right hand (b). The left hand (*a*) is almost three times slower and shows errors (– ↑). Mirror script and inverted scripts (*c–h*) are still slower for both hands and take three to five times longer to write than normal script with the trained hand. Also, there are many more errors.

B Recordings of writing pressure show typical fluent and steep sequence of pressure spikes only for the trained right hand. All other scripts have less modulated flat pressure plateaus with pauses.

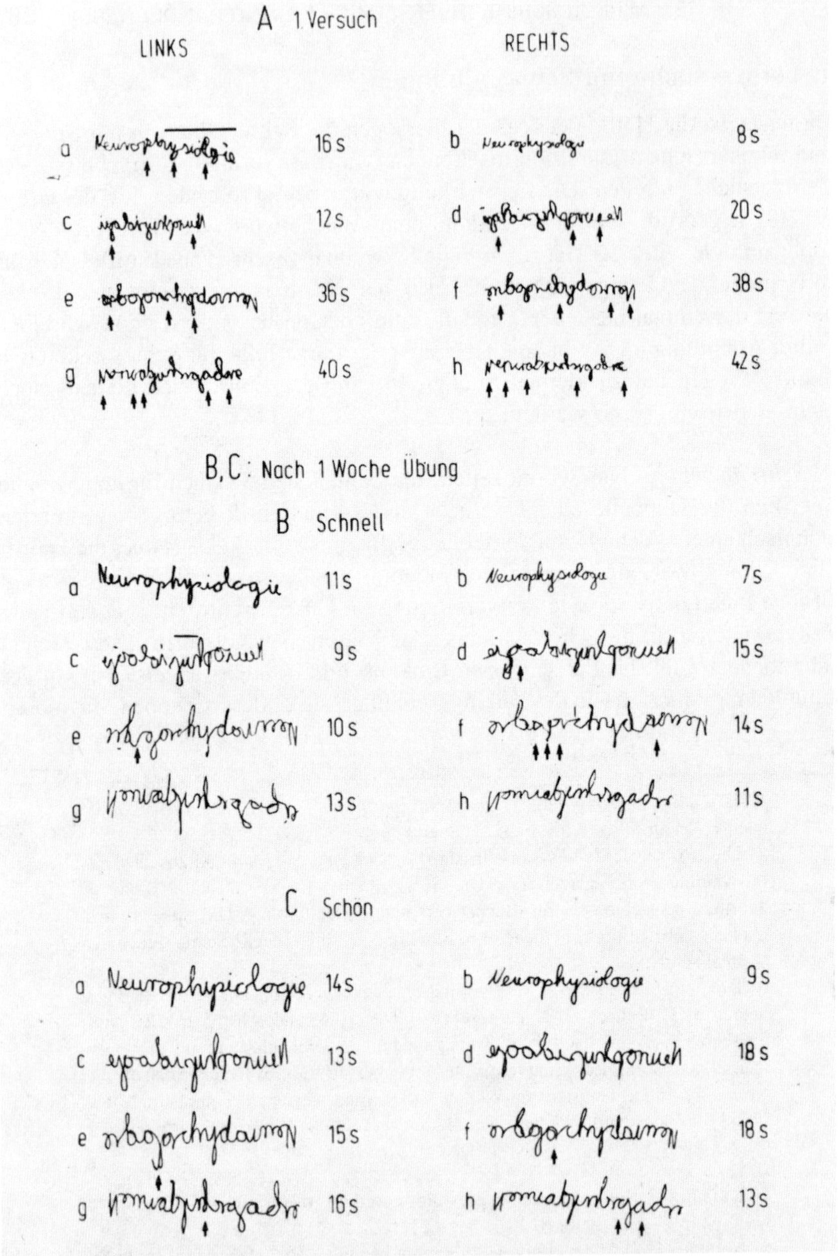

ABB. 23.6. *Übungseffekte der Schriften eines rechtsschreibenden Linkshänders: A vor und B, C nach Schreibübung* (F. D. ♂ 19 Jahre).

A) Beim 1. Versuch ist nur die geübte Normalschrift rechts flüssig, rasch und fehlerlos (b). Alle anderen Schriften sind ungeschickt und langsam mit schlechter Zeilenführung (—) und vielen Schreibfehlern (↑). Nur die linke Spiegelschrift (c) hat weniger Fehler und ist schneller als die anderen ungeübten Schriften, die für

Gruppen verkürzte sich die Schreibzeit der Spiegelschrift nur um etwa 60% oder weniger. Beide Umkehrschriften, die beim ersten Schreibversuch die längsten Zeiten hatten, wurden auch stärker in ihrer Schreibzeit verkürzt und näherten sich nach Übung denen der Spiegelschrift in allen Gruppen (Abb. 23.7).

Fehler.   Beim ersten Versuch machten alle drei Gruppen Schreibfehler bei der Buchstabenform in den Spiegelschriften und Umkehrschriften. Bei je drei Probanden der Gruppen I–III mit einwöchiger Schreibübung wurden die Fehler nach den obengenannten vier Kriterien (Seitenverkehrung, vertikale Umkehrung, Verunstaltung und Abweichung nach oben und unten) ausgezählt. Die Fehlerzahlen des ersten und letzten Schreibversuchs vor und nach Übung wurden verglichen. Abbildung 23.7 B zeigt die Fehlerzahlen der acht Schriften a–h vor und nach einwöchiger Übung. Linkshänder und Rechtshänder der Gruppen I–III machten bei den ungewohnten Schriften im ersten Schreibversuch zwischen 10 und 30 Fehler. Im Vergleich dazu war die Normalschrift der Schreibhand fast immer fehlerlos, die Normalschrift mit der schreibungewohnten Hand hatte höchstens 3 Fehler.

Umkehrschriften (e–h) bis zur 5-fachen Schreibzeit der Normalschrift verlangsamt sind.

B u.C) Nach 1 Woche täglicher Übung sind alle ungewohnten Schriften wesentlich schneller und besser geworden: *B)* Bei Instruktion ''*schnell*'' zu schreiben, erreicht Spiegelschrift links im Schreibtempo fast die Normal schrift rechts, aber ist, wie die Umkehrschriften in Form und Schriftqualität noch mangelhaft. *C)* Bei der Instruktion ''*schön*'' zu schreiben, ist das Schreibtempo zwar etwas langsamer als B, aber für Umkehrschrift viel schneller als in A. Die Fehler werden selten und die Schriftqualität ist auch für Spiegel- und Umkehrschriften viel besser.

FIG. 23.6.   Learned improvement of unfamiliar scripts in a lefthander trained to write with his right hand.

A, writing before, and *B, C* after 1 week of practice. Writing times are shown in seconds (F.D. ♂, age 19).

A In the first writing experiment only the right normal script (*b*) is fluent and free of errors. All other scripts are clumsy with unsteady linearity (—) and many errors (WA). The left hand mirror script (*c*) is faster and shows fewer errors than the other untrained scripts. Inverted scripts (e–h) are up to five times slower than trained normal script.

B and *C* After 7 days of training during which the test word was written twice daily the speed and quality of formerly untrained scripts are drastically improved. *B* With the instruction to *write quickly,* mirror script with the left hand (*c*) nearly reaches the writing time of right normal script (b) although writing quality and linearity (—) is still inferior. *C* With the instruction to *write well,* the writing times are somewhat longer than in B, but much shorter for inverted scripts than in A. Errors are rare and the quality of script is much better.

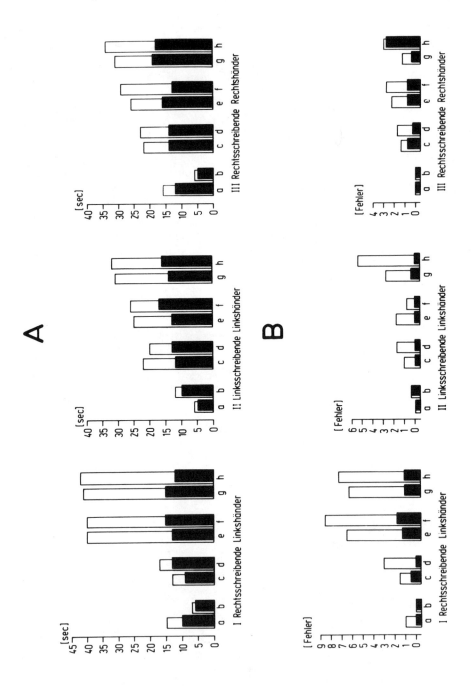

392

BESPRECHUNG DER ERGEBNISSE

Spiegelschrifttransfer bei Rechts- und Linkshändern. Rechtsschreibende Links- und Rechtshänder schreiben Spiegelschrift mit der schreibungeübten linken Hand leichter als mit der rechten Schreibhand. Wir nennen diese Spiegelschriftneigung der kontralateralen Hand *Spiegelschrifttransfer*, das heißt Transfer von der Schreibhand zur Gegenseite.

Vergleicht man unsere drei Gruppen (Abb. 23.3), so wird ein Befund deutlich: der Transfer für Spiegelschrift zur kontralateralen Hand ist bei den rechtsschreibenden Linkshändern (Gruppe I) am stärksten. Diese bessere Transferleistung der Gruppe I wird zusätzlich durch die Kriterien Fehlerzahl und rasches Lernen der Spiegelschrift links (Abb. 23.7) belegt. Auch Rechtshänder haben eine geringe Tendenz zur Spiegelschrift links, die sich in der kürzeren Schreibzeit der kontralateralen, linken Hand zeigt. Obwohl die rechte Hand schreibgeübt ist, wird die Spiegelschrift rechts langsamer und ungeschickter geschrieben als mit der schreibungeübten linken Hand.

Nur linksschreibende Linkshänder zeigen keinen Spiegelschrifttransfer zur

---

ABB. 23.7. *Übungseffekte für Schreibtempo und Fehlerzahl der vier Schriftarten.*

Durchschnittswerte von je drei repräsentativen Probanden der Gruppen I (rechtsschreibende Linkshänder), II (linksschreibende Linkshänder) und III (rechtsschreibende Rechtshänder). Die weißen Säulen zeigen die Werte vor, die schwarzen Säulen die Werte nach einwöchiger Übung.

A Die Schreibzeiten für die Spiegelschriften (c, d) und für die Umkehrschriften (e–h), die ursprünglich ungeschickt und langsam geschrieben wurden, sind bis zu 50% verringert. Gruppe I, die die längste Zeit benötigte, zeigt die größten Übungseffekte. Auffallend ist die Ähnlichkeit der Profile der schwarzen Säulen bei allen drei Gruppen.

B Die Fehlerzahlen zeigen ebenfalls die rasch erlernten Verbesserungen der Spiegel- und Umkehrschriften. Anfänglich zeigt Gruppe I viele Fehler bei den Umkehrschriften, nähert sich jedoch nach Übung den Gruppen II und III an.

FIG. 23.7. Learning effects on writing times and errors for four modes of script. Mean values of three representative subjects of Group I (lefthanders trained to write with their right hand), Group II (lefthanders trained to write with their left hand), and Group III (righthanders trained to write with their right hand) are shown before (white bars) and after (black bars) one week's practice.

A Writing time is reduced by as much as 50% for mirror scripts (c, d) and inverted scripts (e–h) where the original performance was clumsy and very slow. There is little reduction for normal script. Group I having had the longest writing times shows the greatest improvements after practice. Note the similar profile for the black columns in all three subject groups.

B The number of errors diminishes with the quick improvement of mirror and inverted scripts. Initially, Group I shows many errors for inverted scripts, but after training, closely approaches Groups II and III.

kontralateralen Hand. Sie schreiben alle Schriften mit der schreibgeübten, linken Hand besser und schneller als mit der rechten. Allerdings hatten einige dieser Probanden den Eindruck, die Spiegelschrift falle ihnen rechts leichter. Mangelnde Schreibgeschicklichkeit der gegenseitigen Hand kann den fehlenden Transfer des linksschreibenden Linkshänders nicht erklären, da die Umkehrschriften ebenso wie bei den übrigen Gruppen kaum Unterschiede des Schreibtempos zeigen. Auch der Rechtshänder ist links weniger schreibgeübt und schreibt doch Spiegelschrift schneller mit der linken als mit der rechten Hand (Abb. 23.3 c–d).

Spiegelschrifttransfer und Großhirndominanz.   Die ohne Schreibübung der kontralateralen Hand entstandene Tendenz zum spiegelförmigen Schreiben ist wahrscheinlich ein bewegungsspezifischer Spiegelbildtransfer von der Schreibhand zur Gegenseite, der auf einem automatischen Mitlernen spiegelbildlicher Bewegungen der gegenseitigen Hand beruht (Orton, 1925). Die erleichterte Spiegelschrift links bei allen rechtsschreibenden Probanden (Gruppe I, III) kann daher als Balkentransfer von der linken zur rechten Großhirnseite gedeutet werden, der mit der Schreibkoordination der rechten Hand erworben wurde. Die Schreibbewegungen der gegenseitigen Hand werden bei der Gruppe I wahrscheinlich von der sprachdominanten, bei den Gruppen II und III von der nichtsprachdominanten Großhirnhemisphäre gesteuert.

Schrift und Sprache.   Unsere Frage ist: kann die verschiedene Richtung und Stärke des Transfers einen funktionellen Sinn haben? Die Annahme, daß der Spiegelschrifttransfer vorwiegend eine Kommunikation zwischen den beiden Großhirnhemisphären über den Balken (callosal transfer im Sinne Sperrys, 1967) ist, impliziert Beziehungen zur Sprachdominanz. Eine seitenverschiedene Großhirnlokalisation von Sprache und Schreiben gibt es nur bei rechtsschreibenden Linkshändern (Gruppe I). Denn bei ihnen liegen die Sprachregionen meistens in der rechten Großhirnhemisphäre, während die sensomotorische Koordination für die schreibende Hand vom linken Großhirn gesteuert wird. Diese Linkshänder brauchen daher wahrscheinlich einen stärkeren Transfer zu ihrer sprachdominanten rechten Großhirnhälfte. Da die Seitenkoordination zwischen der rechten und linken Hand vorwiegend spiegelgerichtete Bewegungen betrifft, erscheint es verständlich, daß auch differenzierte Schreibmuster in Spiegelform zur kontralateralen Großhirnrinde transferiert werden. Dem rechten Großhirn werden dann die Schreibmuster, die das linke Großhirn steuert, als Spiegelmuster mitgeteilt. Als solche informieren sie auch die beim Linkshänder meist im rechten Großhirn gelegenen Sprachregionen. Insofern trägt wahrscheinlich der beim rechtsschreibenden Linkshänder besonders starke Spiegelschrifttransfer auch zum Sprachverständnis des Schriftbildes bei.

Bei den anderen beiden Gruppen, den rechtsschreibenden Rechtshändern und den linksschreibenden Linkshändern, ist offenbar Sprache und Schreiben in der gleichen Großhirnhäfte lokalisiert. Ein Balkentransfer zum kontralateralen nicht-sprachdominanten Großhirn ist daher beim Schreiben nicht unbedingt erforderlich. Warum der Spiegelschrifttransfer beim rechtsschreibenden Rechtshänder deutlicher als beim linksschreibenden Linkshänder ist, können wir allerdings noch nicht erklären. Man hätte eher das Umgekehrte erwartet, da bei Linkshändern die Sprachdominanz weniger konstant in der rechten Hemisphäre lokalisiert ist als bei Rechtshändern in der linken.

Natürlich war es nicht möglich, unsere gesunden linkshändigen Versuchspersonen durch die eingreifenden Testmethoden einer Carotisinjektion mit Barbituraten auf die Seitenlokalisation ihres Sprachzentrums hin zu testen. Doch darf man annehmen, daß bei beiden Gruppen von Linkshändern überwiegend die rechte Großhirnhemisphäre sprachdominant war. Erst eine Untersuchung größerer Populationen für die Spiegelschrift beider Hände wird zeigen, ob es noch spezielle Untergruppen gibt, bei denen ein mehr oder weniger ausgeprägter Spiegelschrifttransfer für Links- und Rechtsdominanz der Sprachfunktion spricht. Eine von uns beobachtete rechtsschreibende Linkshänderin, der die Spiegelschrift links besonders schwer fiel, könnte ein solcher Proband mit Sprachdominanz im linken Großhirn sein.

Rechts- und linksläufige Schrift.   Unsere europäischen Schriften sind alle rechtsläufig, d. h. die Zeile beginnt links und die Schrift läuft von der linken zur rechten Seite. Die Spiegelschrift ist dagegen linksläufig und wird umgekehrt von rechts nach links geschrieben. Damit ergibt sich die Frage, ob das raschere Schreiben der Spiegelschrift mit der linken Hand, das von der Schreibübung weitgehend unabhängig ist, mit der Linksläufigkeit zusammenhängt.

Der Einfluß der Links- und Rechtsläufigkeit der Schrift muß zunächst offen bleiben. Vielleicht werden entsprechende Untersuchungen mit linksläufigen semitischen Schriften (Arabisch, Hebräisch) weiterführen, die uns wegen Mangel an Probanden noch nicht möglich waren. Wir hoffen, später darüber berichten zu können.

Handinversion.   Viele linksschreibende Linkshänder schreiben mit umgekehrter Haltung der linken Hand, den Stift in Gegenrichtung von oben nach unten zum Schreiber hin gerichtet. Drei von 10 Probanden unserer Gruppe II verwendeten diese Inversion. Die von Levy und Reid (1978) angenommenen Beziehungen der Handinversion zur linkshirnigen Sprachlokalisation und der Schreibsteuerung durch die gleichseitige Hemisphäre haben sich nicht bestätigt (Herron, 1980). Die Handinversion erleichtert nur das linkshändige Schreiben. Auch Rechtshänder schreiben links besser mit umgekehrter Handhaltung und verwenden die Handinversion rechts für die Linksschraffur beim Zeichnen (Jung, 1977).

Spiegelsymmetrien. Die spiegelsymmetrische Anordnung von Normalschrift und Spiegelschrift mit von der Mitte divergierender Schreibrichtung entspricht dem Simmultantransfer des beidhändigen Schreibens. Diese in alten griechischen Vasen als ''Bustrophedon'' häufige Links-Rechtssymmetrie der Schrift und die umgekehrte Richtung von Profilzeichnungen der Links- und Rechtshänder (Hufschmidt, 1980) sind hier ebensowenig zu diskutieren wie die Charakteristika von Linkshänderzeichnungen (Jung, 1977). Orton's Hypothese spiegelartiger visueller Gedächtnisbilder in beiden Großhirnhälften (Orton, 1925), die er nach Untersuchung von Dyslexien aufstellte, trägt zur Erklärung der linkshändigen Spiegelschrift wenig bei. Spiegelschreiben ist vorwiegend motorischer Ausdruck gegenseitiger spiegelförmiger Bewegungskoordination und weniger optisch bedingt. Denn das kontralaterale Spiegelschreiben gelingt auch ohne visuelle Kontrolle, und ein gutes Lesen der Spiegelschrift wird von Linkshändern erst sekundär erworben, nachdem das Spiegelschreiben geübt wurde. Doch sind Wahrnehmung und Bewegung (Held, 1968) eng verbunden, und das Spiegelschreiben der linken Hand bei Linkshändern bahnt auch das Spiegellesen (Jung, 1981). Ob nur spiegelsymmetrische Bewegungen durch Transfer gebahnt oder auch gleichsinnige Bewegungen gehemmt werden, ist noch nicht geklärt.

Pfeifer postulierte schon 1919 nach Untersuchungen bei Hirnverletzten ein ''latentes Mitüben der anderen Hand'' für symmetrische spiegelbildliche Bewegungen und eine erworbene Hemmung gleichsinniger Bewegungen der kontralateralen Hand. Ein solcher Hemmungstransfer würde erklären, warum es meistens leichter ist, mit beiden Händen gleichzeitig in Normalschrift rechts und Spiegelschrift links zu schreiben als beiderseits in Normalschrift.

Schreibdruck, Schriftart und Übung

Merkwürdigerweise gibt es in der seit 50 Jahren sehr umfangreichen Literatur über die Schreibwaage (Enke, 1930; Grünewald, 1957) bisher keine vergleichende Untersuchung über das Rechts- und Linksschreiben. Beide Hände zeigen sehr eindrucksvolle Unterschiede, die der Schreibgeläufigkeit entsprechen. Die schreibgeübte Hand ist durch die rasche Abfolge der steilen Druckspitzen und ihre elegante Form von den schwerfälligen, langsam modulierten Druckformen der ungeübten Hand zu unterscheiden. Ähnlich schwerfällig, langsam und wenig moduliert schreibt auch die schreibgeübte Hand alle ungewohnten Schriften wie Spiegel- und Umkehrschrift (Abb. 23.1, 23.2, 23.4 und 23.5).

Rechtsschreibende Linkshänder können Schreibdruckbild und Schriftqualität der Spiegelschrift mit der schreibungeübten linken Hand nach kurzer Übung sehr verbessern, so daß die Spiegelschrift links zunehmend steilere und kürzere Druckspitzen gewinnt. Zwar erreichen sie nicht ganz die elegante Form der über Jahrzehnte geübten Normalschrift der Schreibhand. Die geübte Spiegelschrift der

Gruppe I wird jedoch der Normalschrift viel ähnlicher als bei den Gruppen II und III. Ob man durch längere Übung nicht nur Spiegelschriftbild und Tempo, sondern auch die Druckkurve der geübten Normalschrift angleichen kann, bleibt zunächst noch offen.

Umkehrsehen und Umkehrlernen. Unsere Lernversuche mit Spiegel- und Umkehrschrift haben manche Parallelen zu Kohlers Experimenten mit Umkehrbrillen und seitenverkehrenden Spiegelvorsätzen (Kohler, 1951, 1961). Die seit Stratton (1897) bekannte Erlernbarkeit des Umkehrsehens betrifft nicht nur kognitive, sondern auch sensomotorische Funktionen: Kohlers Versuchspersonen konnten mit der Umkehrbrille nach einwöchigem Lernen zielsicher greifen, sich auf Straßen zurechtfinden und sogar Ski laufen (Kohler, 1951, 1964). Die Möglichkeit des sensomotorischen Umkehrlernens von Spiegel- und Umkehrschriften konnten wir anhand von Schreibzeitverkürzung und Fehlerverminderung belegen (Abb. 23.7). Diese erlernten Umstellungen des Schriftbildes führten in einer Woche allerdings noch nicht zum fließenden Lesen der ungewohnten Schriften. Wahrnehmungsraum und Handlungsraum stimmen nicht immer ganz überein und können sich im Verhalten und Erleben gegenseitig beeinflussen.

Die Spiegelschrift ist mit der Rechts-Linksverkehrung, die Umkehrschrift mit der Oben-Untenumkehr der Spiegelexperimente Kohlers (1951, 1961) vergleichbar. Die von Kohler untersuchten Verkehrungen des Sehens waren auch mit einer allgemeinen Bewegungsumstellung der Zielmotorik verbunden. Die Spiegelschrift unterscheidet sich von Kohlers optischer Seitenverkehrung dadurch, daß sie nur erlernte Feinbewegungen einer Hand betrifft. Man kann annehmen, daß der erworbene Spiegelschrifttransfer von der Schreibhand zur gegenseitigen Hand mit einem latenten Lernen kontralateraler spiegelbildlicher Handmitbewegungen zusammenhängt. Aus dem Schulalltag ist bekannt, daß beim Schreibenlernen der Kinder Andeutungen leichter spiegelbildlicher Mitbewegungen auftreten. Solche unwillkürliche Mitbewegungen können allerdings nicht erklären, warum der Spiegelschrifttransfer bei rechtsschreibenden Linkshändern verstärkt ist. Im Anschluß an Kohlers Ergebnisse sind daher über mehrere Wochen dauernde Lernversuche mit Lesen von Spiegelschriften und Umkehrschriften geplant.

ZUSAMMENFASSUNG

Normale Schrift, Spiegelschrift und Umkehrschriften der rechten und linken Hand wurden bei rechtsschreibenden Linkshändern (Gruppe I), linksschreibenden Linkshändern (II) und Rechtshändern (III) verglichen und mit Schreibdruck und Zeitmessungen registriert.

Die meisten Versuchspersonen bevorzugen Spiegelschrift, wenn sie mit der schreibungeübten Hand schreiben. Diese Tendenz, mit der gegenseitigen Hand Spiegelschrift zu schreiben, nennen wir "Spiegelschrifttransfer". Er wird durch das Schreiben normaler Schrift mit der schreibgeübten Hand erworben.

Alle Linkshänder und viele Rechtshänder schreiben Spiegelschrift mit der linken Hand schneller als mit der rechten. Der deutlichste Spiegeltransfer zur linken Hand tritt bei rechtsschreibenden Linkshändern auf. Möglichweise hängst dies mit ihrer Sprachdominanz der rechten Hemisphäre zusammen. Wahrscheinlich kann der stärkere Spiegelschrifttransfer zur linken Hand bei rechtsschreibenden Linkshändern zum Sprachverständnis der Schrift beitragen, die vom nichtsprachdominanten Großhirn gesteuert wird.

Übung verbessert Spiegel- und Umkehrschreiben; nach einer Woche täglicher Übung sind die Schreibzeiten für ungewohnte Schriften häufig um die Hälfte reduziert. Die schnelle Erlernbarkeit von Umkehrschriften durch Übung wird mit Kohlers Ergebnissen über das Umkehrsehen verglichen.

ACKNOWLEDGMENT

Danksagung Für Hilfe bei den Schreibversuchen und Hinweise für Linkshändereigenschaften danken wir Frau B. Schramm, für Zeichnung und Reproduktion der Bilder Herrn J. Humburger.

REFERENCES

Critchley, M. Parietal syndroms in ambidextrous and left-handed subjects. *Zbl. Neurochir.*, 1954, *14*, 4–16.

Enke, W. Die Psychomotorik der Konstitutionstypen. *Z. angew. Psychol.*, 1930, *36*, 237–287.

Grünewald, G. Die Schreibdruckkurve. *Z. Menschenkunde*, 1957, *21*, 133–177.

Held, R. Dissociation of visual functions by deprivation and rearrangement. *Psychol. Forsch.*, 1968, *31*, 338–348.

Herron, J. Two hands, two brains, two sexes. In J. Herron, (Ed.), *Neuropsychology of left-handedness*. Pp. 233–260. New York, London: Academic Press, 1980.

Hufschmidt, H. J. Das Rechts-Links-Profil im kulturhistorischen Längsschnitt—Ein Dominanzproblem. *Arch. Psychiat. Nervenkr.*, 1980, *229*, 17–43.

Jung, R. Über Zeichnungen linkshändiger Künstler von Leonardo bis Klee: Linkshändermerkmale als Zuschreibungskriterien. In *Semper attentus. Beiträge für Heinz Götze* Pp. 189–218. Berlin, Heidelberg: Springer-Verlag, 1977.

Jung, R. Perception and action. In J. Szentagothai, M. Palkovits & I. Hamori (Eds.), *Advances physiol. Sci. 1: Regulatory functions of the CNS*. Pp. 17–36. Oxford: Pergamon Press, 1981.

Kohler, I. Über Aufbau und Wandlungen der Wahrnehmungswelt; insbesondere über "bedingte Empfindungen." Sitz.-Ber. Phil.-hist. Kl. Österr. Akad. Wiss. *227*, 1–118, Wien: Rohrer, 1951.

Kohler, I. Zentralnervöse Korrekturen in der Wahrnehmung. *Naturwiss.*, 1961, *48*, 259–264.

Kohler, I. The formation and transformation of the perceptual world. *Psychological Issues*, 1964, *3*(4), Monograph 12. New York: Int. Univ. Press Inc.

Levy, J., & Reid, M. L. Variation in cerebral organization as a function of handedness, hand posture in writing and sex. *J. Exp. Psychol.*, 1978, *107*, 119–144.

Orton, S. T. "Word blindness" in school children. *Arch. Neurol. Psychiat.*, 1925, *14*, 581–615.

Pfeifer, R. A. Beobachtungen an Rechts- und Linkshänderschrift von anscheinend weittragender Bedeutung. *Zsch. Neur. Psychiat.*, 1919, *45*, 301–315.

Sperry, R. W. Split-brain approach to learning problems. In G. C. Quarton, T. Melnechuk, & F. O. Schmitt (Eds.), *The neurosciences*. Pp. 714–722. New York: Rockefeller Univ. Press, 1967.

Stratton, G. M. Vision without inversion of the retinal image. *Psychol. Rev.*, 1897, *4*, 341–360, 463–481.

24 Richtungsspezifische Adaptation des Raum- und Bewegungshörens*

Walter H. Ehrenstein
Neurologische Universitätsklinik
Freiburg i.Br., West Germany

ABSTRACT

This study investigates whether acoustical aftereffects, analogous to the visual movement aftereffects, occur following exposure to moving sound. Subjects adapted for 2½ min to a sound source rotating in either a clockwise or counterclockwise direction. Following the adaptation period, subjects were asked to localize stationary sound sources in each of five positions: straight ahead, 10° and 20° to the left and right. No motion aftereffect was observed, however, adaptation caused an average displacement of 2° opposite to the direction of rotation. The results provide evidence for direction-specific auditory mechanisms in humans.

EINLEITUNG

Raum- und Bewegungswahrnehmung sind nicht auf einen Sinn beschränkt. Hör-, Seh- und Tasterlebnisse fügen sich alle zu einem gemeinsamen Sinnesraum zusammen und lassen sich selbst bei massiver Störung, z.B. durch Prismenbrillen (Kohler, 1951), nur vorübergehend voneinander trennen. Die Zusammenarbeit der Sinne legt die Vermutung nahe, daß sich zwischen den verschiedensten Sinnesleistungen Parallelen finden lassen, so z.B. vergleichbare Mechanismen der Adaptation (Kohler, 1966).

---

*Erste Ergebnisse wurden auf der 47. Tagung der Deutschen Physiologischen Gesellschaft in Regensburg, September 1976, mitgeteilt (*Pflügers Archiv 365,* R 49:195).

Bei der räumlichen Orientierung geht der akustische Fernsinn dem optischen in natürlicher Weise voran, wenn es sich um die Registrierung von Ereignissen außerhalb des Gesichtsfeldes handelt. Fast automatisch wenden wir den Kopf in die Richtung, aus der akustische Information ein Geschehen anzeigen, um so den Gesichtssinn zu "orientieren". Neben einer richtungsbezogenen Raumwahrnehmung vermittelt das Gehör auch die Wahrnehmung von Bewegung. Im Unterschied zum räumlichen Hören (Blauert, 1974) ist das Bewegungshören bisher jedoch kaum untersucht worden. Es finden sich lediglich einige frühe Arbeiten über akustische Scheinbewegung, bei der ähnlich der optischen Scheinbewegung ein Bewegungseindruck dadurch hervorgerufen wird, daß zwei räumlich getrennte Schallreize zeitlich nacheinander dargeboten werden (zur Literatur vgl. Briggs & Perrott, 1972). Erst in neuester Zeit sind reale Schallbewegung (Ehrenstein & Hellweg, 1976; Perrott & Musicant, 1977) sowie dichotisch simulierte Bewegungsverläufe (Altman & Viskov, 1977; Ehrenstein, 1977, 1978; Grantham & Wightman, 1977, 1978, 1979) näher untersucht worden.

In dieser Untersuchung sollte die Frage geklärt werden, ob bei Adaptation an gerichtete Schallbewegung akustische Nachwirkungen auftreten. Solche Nachwirkungen sind für das Sehen seit Aristoteles bekannt (Müller, 1826). Sie treten als Bewegungsnachbild, z.B. im Spiralnacheffekt, eindrucksvoll in Erscheinung. Blicken wir für einige Zeit auf eine sich drehende Spirale, so scheint sich diese, wenn sie plötzlich angehalten wird, in Gegenrichtung zu bewegen. Dieses Bewegungsnachbild kann mehrere Sekunden andauern. Neurophysiologisch werden die visuellen Bewegungsnachwirkungen durch die Existenz von Neuronen erklärt, die für eine bestimmte Bewegungsrichtung besonders empfindlich sind und während der Reizeinwirkung selektiv adaptieren. Nach Beendigung der Bewegungsreizung liegt die Aktivität der adaptierten Neurone unter der Spontanaktivität, so daß eine Scheinbewegung in Gegenrichtung auftritt (vgl. Ritter, Lücke, & Zihl, 1973; Sekuler, 1975; Sekuler, Pantle, & Levinson, 1978; Stadler & Kano, 1970).

Man sollte erwarten, daß bei akustischer Adaptation an die vorherrschende Bewegungsrichtung analog zum Sehen auch im Hören "Bewegungsnachbilder" auftreten. Seit Flügel (1920) ist bekannt, daß sich im Anschluß an gerichtete stationäre Beschallung die akustische Richtungseinstellung systematisch verschiebt. Wurde der Schall beispielsweise zuvor seitlich rechts dargeboten, so lokalisierte die Versuchsperson nachfolgend dargebotene Schallquellen stärker in die Gegenrichtung, also nach links verschoben. Der Effekt wurde von Flügel mit "lokaler Ermüdung" des zuvor stärker beschallten Ohres erklärt, also im wesentlichen als peripherer Adaptationsvorgang gedeutet. Weitere Untersuchungen (Krauskopf, 1954; Taylor, 1962) legen die Verwandtschaft dieses Nacheffekts zu den "figuralen Nachwirkungen" im Sinne von Köhler und Wallach (1944) nahe und sprechen gegen eine rein periphere Entstehung.

Aus den im Anschluß an stationäre Beschallung auftretenden Nachwirkungen lassen sich allerdings richtungsspezifisch adaptierbare Einheiten des menschlichen Hörsystems noch nicht zwingend ableiten. Wird der Schall stationär dargeboten, so ist die Adaptation an seitliche Schallrichtungen stets mit binaural ungleicher Einwirkung der Schallintensität verbunden. Das Hineinspielen rein intensitätsspezifischer Adaptation (Bray, Dirks, & Morgan, 1973) ist somit nicht auszuschließen. Richtungsspezifische Adaptation läßt sich erst dann nachweisen, wenn die Schallintensität während der Adaptationsphase für beide Ohren im zeitlichen Mittel gleich bleibt und nur die Schallrichtung variiert. Dies ist der Fall, wenn die Schallquelle nicht stationär bleibt, sondern den Hörer als Mittelpunkt im Uhr- oder Gegenuhrzeigersinn umkreist.

METHODIK

Abbildung 24.1 veranschaulicht schematisch die Versuchsanlage (Ehrenstein, 1977, 1981b). Über der Decke der Hörkammer ist ein Phasenmotor (M) an-

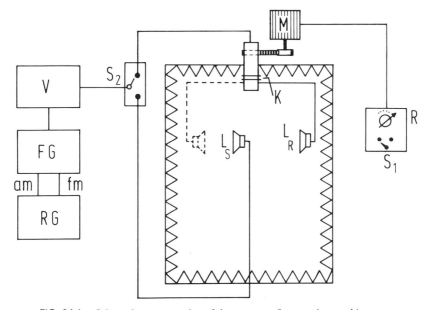

FIG. 24.1.   Schematic representation of the apparatus for exposing a subject to moving (rotating) or stationary sound (Ehrenstein, 1977).
A synchronous motor (*M*) is installed above the soundproof chamber and connected with the axis of rotation by a timing belt. The speed of rotation is adjusted continuously by turning a knob (*R*), the direction of rotation is alternated by a switch (*S₁*). The sound signal is produced by a noise-generator (*RG*), a function-generator (*FG*), and an amplifier (*V*). By means of a toggle switch (*S₂*), the sound signal can be alternatively directed to the rotating loudspeaker (*L_R*) or the stationary loudspeaker (*L_S*). The current flows through carbon rods that make contact (*K*) by sliding along a metallic ring. Sound exposure can be limited to sectors (semicircle, quarter-circle) by replacing the metallic ring by two partial rings, one from metal and the other from plastic.

gebracht, der über einen Zahnriemen mit der Drehachse der Schallrotation-sanlage verbunden ist. Über einen Regler (R) kann die Drehzahl des Motors stufenlos eingestellt werden, über einen Schalter (S₁) läßt sich die Drehrichtung umkehren. Das Schallsignal wird über Rausch-, Funktionsgenerator und Ver-stärker (RG, FG, V) erzeugt. Es kann über einen Kippschalter (S₂) wechselweise auf den rotierenden Lautsprecher (L$_R$) oder auf den stationären Lautsprecher (L$_S$) übertragen werden.

Insgesamt sind 8 radial im Abstand von 45° angeordnete Lautsprecher (L$_R$) in seitlicher Aufhängung angebracht. Die Stromzufuhr erfolgt über einen Schleifring, an dem gefederte Kohlestifte entlangfahren und so den Kontakt (K) herstellen. Durch Höhenverstellung des Kohlestifts läßt sich jeder Lautsprecher einzeln an- oder abschalten. Die Schalldarbietung kann außerdem auf ver-schiedene Sektoren (z.B. Halbkreis, Viertelkreis) dadurch begrenzt werden, daß der Metallring durch zwei Teilkreisringe (einer aus Metall, der andere aus Kunststoff) ersetzt wird.

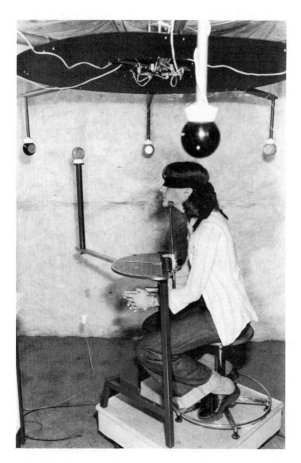

FIG. 24.2. Actual experimental situation.
A blindfolded subject, stabilized with a chin-rest, sits at a semi-circular desk from where the perceived direction of sound can be indicated. For this the subject uses a pistol-like grip whose pivot is beneath the desk. The position of the loudspeaker and the localization of the sound by the subject is read off a protractor mounted on the surface of the desk. On the ceiling is the rotary axis with loudspeakers suspended laterally.

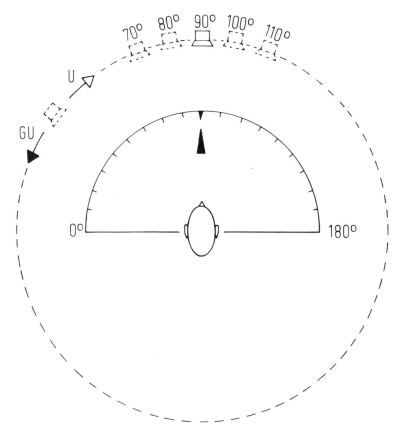

FIG. 24.3. Top view of the experimental set-up.
Subject sitting at a semi-circular desk adapts to a sound source moving clockwise
(*U*) or counterclockwise (*GU*) and subsequently indicates perceived direction of
sound coming from a stationary loudspeaker placed in one of five positions
(70–110°). Straight ahead equals 90°.

Die konkrete Versuchssituation veranschaulicht Abbildung 24.2. Die Versuchsperson (Vp) sitzt mit verbundenen Augen, den Kopf auf einer Kinnstütze geradeaus gerichtet, an einem halbkreisförmigen Pult, auf dessen Oberfläche ein Winkelmesser angebracht ist. Sie ist dabei so zentriert, daß der Mittelpunkt der Verbindungslinie beider Ohren mit der Drehachse zusammenfällt (s. Abb. 24.3). Durch beidhändiges Führen eines unter dem Pult an einem Drehpunkt befestigten pistolenartigen Griffes kann die Vp in die Richtung zeigen oder ''zielen'', aus der sie das Schallsignal hört. Die Richtungseinstellung wird durch einen mit dem Zeigegriff gekoppelten Zeiger auf dem Winkelmesser angezeigt. Der stationäre Lautsprecher (L_S in Abb. 24.1) ist auf einem unter dem Pult angebrachten Arm montiert und läßt sich auf einer halbkreisförmigen Bahn vor der Vp in jede gewünschte Stellung bringen. Dies wird von einem zweiten Zeiger auf dem gleichen Winkelmesser angezeigt. Dargebotene wie von der Vp eingestellte Schallrichtung lassen sich so auf einfache Weise anhand der Winkelmesseranzeigen ablesen und miteinander vergleichen.

VERSUCHSABLAUF

Voraussetzung für die Versuchsteilnahme war das positive Abschneiden in einem Hörtest. Mit Hilfe eines Standard-Hörprüfgeräts (PHONAK Selector A), wurde über 5 Frequenzstufen (0.5–6 kHz) für beide Ohren jeweils getrennt die Hörfähigkeit geprüft und jede Vp, bei der auf der untersten Intensitätsstufe (20 dB) Fehler auftraten, ausgeschieden.

In einer Einübphase wurde den Vpn Gelegenheit gegeben, sich mit der Zeigetechnik vertraut zu machen. Der Versuch bestand in einer Standardmessung (ohne Vorreiz), in der die psychophysische Null-Linie bestimmt wurde, und in einer Testmessung, die direkt im Anschluß an die Adaptationsphase (Vorreizung) erfolgte. Sowohl bei der Standard- wie auch bei der Testmessung hatte die Vp die Aufgabe, 5 verschiedene Lautsprecherpositionen je zweimal zu lokalisieren (Abb. 24.3). Die Lautsprecherpositionen wurden dabei in folgender Reihenfolge dargeboten:

I. 90°, 70°, 100°, 80°, 110°,

II. 90°, 110°, 80°, 100°, 70°.

Die Darbietungshälften I und II wechselten bei jedem Meßdurchgang in ihrer Reihenfolge ab. Der Lautsprecher befand sich in Kopfhöhe und war 1,15 m vom Mittelpunkt der Verbindungslinie beider Ohren entfernt. Der Schall wurde für 3 sec dargeboten und war in dieser Zeit zu orten. Zwischen den Darbietungen gab es eine Pause von 10 sec, in der der Versuchsleiter (Vl) das Ergebnis notierte und den Lautsprecher in die nächste Stellung brachte.

Während der Adaptationsphase wurde die Vp von einer Schallquelle (L_R in Abb. 24.1) umkreist. Die Drehgeschwindigkeit betrug 30°/sec, was einem Geschwindigkeitseindruck ''weder schnell noch langsam'' entsprach; die Adaptationsphase dauerte 2 ½ min. Als Schallsignal diente ein in Amplitude und Frequenz moduliertes Breitbandrauschen von 1 kHz Mittenfrequenz (Bandbreite ± .5 kHz; 2 dB). Der mittlere Schalldruck für den rotierenden Schall betrug 63 dB SPL, für den stationären 56 dB SPL (gemessen am Vp-Ort). Um zu vermeiden, daß sich die Nachwirkungen einer Schallbewegung im Uhrzeigersinn (U) mit denen einer Schallbewegung im Gegenuhrzeigersinn (GU) überlagern, fand das Experiment für jede Vp in zwei getrennten Versuchssitzungen statt. In der ersten Versuchssitzung wurde zunächst eine Standardmessung ohne Vorreiz (O_1) und eine Testmessung mit Vorreiz entweder in U oder GU vorgenommen; beide Messungen bestanden jeweils aus 10 Einzellokalisationen entsprechend der oben angegebenen Reihenfolge. In der zweiten Versuchssitzung folgte der Standardmessung (O_2) eine Testmessung mit umgekehrter Vorreizrichtung.

VORVERSUCHE

Der Richtungseindruck der Schallbewegung war am deutlichsten, wenn nur ein rotierender Lautsprecher angeschaltet war. Waren 4 oder 8 Lautsprecher zugleich eingeschaltet, so ergab sich bei längerer Darbietung und mittlerer Drehgeschwindigkeit (30°/sec) ein zunehmend diffuser werdender Richtungseindruck. Hierbei konnte es auch zu einem Richtungswechsel kommen, d.h. die anfangs gehörte Richtung kehrte sich um und wurde dann entgegengesetzt zur objektiven Drehrichtung wahrgenommen.

Um für die Adaptation eine Schallbewegung mit möglichst deutlichem Richtungseindruck zu erhalten, wurde als Vorreiz stets nur eine Schallquelle verwendet. Dabei wurde zunächst geprüft, ob im Anschluß an eine Schallbewegung eine stationär dargebotene Schallquelle analog zum visuellen Bewegungsnachbild in Gegenrichtung bewegt erscheint. Dies war niemals der Fall, selbst bei Adaptationszeiten bis zu 5 Minuten. Die Schallquelle schien höchstens ein wenig hin- und herzuschwanken. Wurden rotierender und stationärer Lautsprecher gleichzeitig dargeboten, so war dagegen manchmal ein leichtes Abwandern des stationären Lautsprechers entgegengesetzt zur Drehrichtung wahrzunehmen. Dieser Höreindruck bestand aber weniger in einer Gegenbewegung, sondern eher in einem kontrastierenden Abheben zwischen ruhendem und bewegtem Lautsprecher. Ein akustisches Gegenstück zu den optischen Bewegungsnachwirkungen wurde nicht beobachtet.

Die Hauptversuche zielten daher auf die Frage: Folgt auf Adaptation an gerichtete Schallbewegung statt anschaulicher Gegenbewegung eine entsprechende Verschiebung der akustischen Richtungseinstellung?

HAUPTVERSUCHE

I. Schallbewegung im Vollkreis

Während der Adaptationsphase wurde eine Schallbewegung im Vollkreis dargeboten (s. Versuchsablauf). Am Versuch nahmen 20 Vpn, Studenten im Alter von 20–25 Jahren teil. Abbildung 24.4 A zeigt die mittlere Richtungsverschiebung, bezogen auf die jeweilige Lautsprecherposition (Abszisse). Abweichungen von der tatsächlichen Schallrichtung sind auf der Ordinate in Winkelgraden angegeben: nach rechts ($+$), nach links ($-$).

Die Werte[1] für die Lokalisation ohne Vorreizung (O_1, O_2) sind einander sehr

---

[1]Jeder Punkt markiert den Mittelwert aus 40 Einzeleinstellungen (je 2 pro 20 Vpn). Da im vorliegenden Versuchsplan (Methode des Paarvergleichs bei korrelierenden Beobachtungspaaren) die interindividuelle Variation nicht zum Stichprobenfehler beiträgt (Lienert, 1955), wurde hier auf die Darstellung der Standardabweichungen verzichtet. Die Originaldaten und Standardabweichungen finden sich bei Ehrenstein (1977; Anhang).

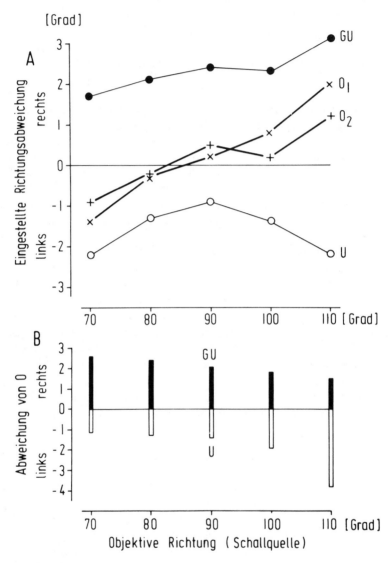

FIG. 24.4. Results obtained after 2.5 min exposure to full-circle sound motion.
A Difference between perceived and true direction of sound (ordinate) as a function of loudspeaker location (abscissa). Negative values on the ordinate refer to a shift to the left, positive values to the right. O_1, O_2: psychophysical zero-line, i.e., values obtained without adaptation. U, GU: values following exposure to clockwise (U) or counterclockwise (GU) sound motion. Twenty subjects, two settings each per condition.
B Deviation of U- and GU-values from the psychophysical zero-line ($O = O_1 + O_2 / 2$) plotted as a function of loudspeaker location.

ähnlich; eine Signifikanzprüfung (t-Test für Paardifferenzen) ergibt keine Signifikanz ($t = .28$; $p > .25$). Dies spricht für die Wiederholungszuverlässigkeit des Meßverfahrens (Reliabilität nach Spearman und Brown: $r_{tt} = .83$). Betrachten wir den Verlauf der O-Wert-Kurven, so fällt auf, daß die Lokalisation bei links (von geradeaus) dargebotenen Schallquellen nach links, bei rechts dargebotenen nach rechts verschoben ist. Die Kurvenverläufe für U and GU weichen deutlich voneinander ab, der Unterschied ist statistisch hochsignifikant ($t = 7.38$; $p < .001$). Dabei weichen die U-Werte durchweg negativ, die GU-Werte positiv von den O-Werten ab. Schallbewegung im Uhrzeigersinn bewirkt also eine Verschiebung nach links (GU), Schallbewegung im Gegenuhrzeigersinn eine Verschiebung nach rechts (U).

Bezieht man die adaptationsbedingte Richtungsverlagerung auf die gemessenen O-Werte als psychophysischer Null-Linie (Abb. 24.4 B), so ergibt sich eine klare Abhängigkeit der Stärke des Nacheffektes von der Lokalisationsrichtung. Für U ist die Abweichung am größten bei 110° (20° rechts) und am kleinsten bei 70° (20° links), für GU verhält es sich umgekehrt.

II. Schallbewegung im Halbkreis

Wie kommt es, daß richtungsspezifische Nachwirkungen auftreten, obwohl doch bei einer Schallbewegung im Vollkreis sich die Translationsrichtungen vertauschen, sobald der Lautsprecher vom vorderen in den hinteren Halbkreissektor übergeht? Eine von links nach rechts im Uhrzeigersinn kreisende Schallquelle bewegt sich hinten von rechts nach links. Es fragt sich also, wie der Nacheffekt trotz einander entgegengesetzter Richtungsinformationen aus hinterer und vorderer Halbkreisbewegung zustande kommt. Um diese Frage zu klären, wurde die Adaptation auf eine Schallbewegung im vorderen oder hinteren Halbkreis beschränkt.

a. Schallbewegung im vorderen Halbkreis

Versuchsanordnung und -ablauf sind bis auf die Beschränkung der Schallexposition auf den vorderen Halbkreis dieselben wie in Experiment I. Technisch wird dies dadurch erreicht, daß zwei Lautsprecher verwendet werden, von denen jeweils nur einer durch Kontakt mit dem vorderen Halbkreis (Metall) betätigt wird. Sobald der eine Lautsprecher aus dem vorderen in den hinteren Halbkreis (Kunststoff) übergeht, tritt der nächste an der gegenüberliegenden Seite neu in den Schallsektor ein. Auf diese Weise läuft die Schallbewegung ohne zeitliche Unterbrechung weiter. Durch nahezu nahtloses Anschließen der Teilkreisringe und zusätzliche Beschichtung der Oberfläche mit einem Kontaktspray konnten ''Knackgeräusche'' vermieden werden. Fünfzehn Vpn (Alter 15–28 J.) nahmen an dem Versuch teil.

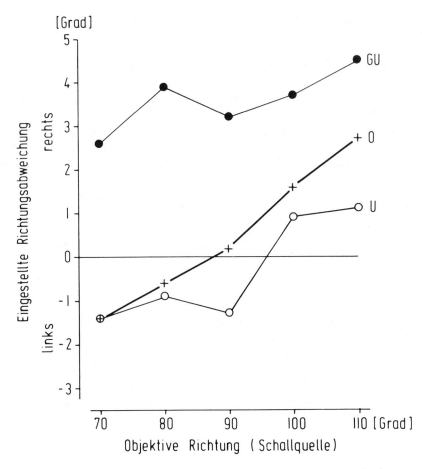

FIG. 24.5.   Results obtained after 2.5 min exposure to semi-circular motion in front of the subject (0–180°). Legend as in Fig. 24.4 A; 15 subjects, two settings each per condition.

Abbildung 24.5 zeigt die Ergebnisse (Mittelwerte aus 30 Einstellungen). Die O_1- und O_2-Werte unterscheiden sich nicht signifikant ($t = .58; p > .25$) und sind daher zu einem Mittelwert (O) zusammengefaßt. Dagegen weichen die Werte für U und GU stark voneinander ab ($t = 6.91; p < .001$). Beziehen wir die Kurven für U und GU auf die psychophysische Null-Linie (O), so finden wir wie schon in Experiment I Abweichungen, die für U negativ, für GU dagegen positiv sind. Allerdings ist die Richtungsverlagerung für U deutlich geringer als für GU. Eine derartige Asymmetrie war bei Vollkreis-Anordnung (Abb. 24.4) nicht aufgetreten. Die größte Abweichung für GU findet sich mit 4° bei 70°, die geringste mit 2° bei 110°. Die Abweichung für U erreicht bei 110° mit 2° ihren

Höchstwert. Ebenso wie bei der Vollkreis-Anordnung ist die räumliche Verteilung der Nacheffektstärken für U und GU jeweils entgegengesetzt.

b. Schallbewegung im hinteren Halbkreis

Bei Beschränkung der Adaptation auf eine Schallbewegung im hinteren Halbkreis ergibt sich für U eine Bewegung von rechts nach links, für GU eine von links nach rechts. Verglichen mit der Halbkreis-vorne-Anordnung sollten die Nacheffekte daher in Gegenrichtung von der Null-Linie (O) abweichen, nämlich nach rechts bei U und nach links bei GU.

In Abb 24.6 sind wiederum die Winkelgrad-Abweichungen der Lokalisationen als Funktion der Lautsprecherpositionen dargestellt. Die Werte für GU weichen nur bei Raumpositionen von 100° und 110° nach links, bei 70° und 80° jedoch paradoxerweise nach rechts ab. Auch für U erfüllt sich die Vorhersage nur bei 70° und bei 110°. Bei 90° unterscheiden sich beide Bedingungen weder von O noch voneinander. Da sich die Kurven für U und GU überkreuzen (80°,

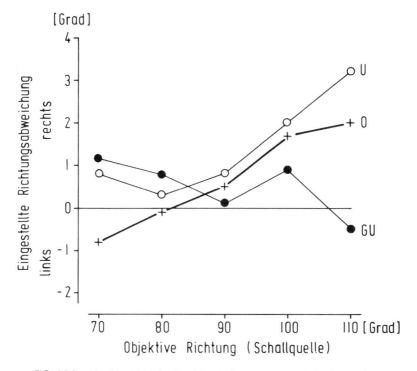

FIG. 24.6.   Results obtained after 2.5 min exposure to semi-circular motion behind the subject (180–360°). Legend as in Fig. 24.4 A; eight subjects, two settings each per condition.

TABLE 24.1

Comparison of localizations (in deg) obtained after exposure either to
full-circle sound-motion (*V*) or to semi-circular sound motion (*H*). *U:*
clockwise; *GU* : counterclockwise direction. *H*-values are the means of
adaptation to semi-circular motion in front and behind the subject.

| | | *Lautsprecherposition [Grad]* | | | | | *M* |
		70	80	90	100	110	90
Eingestellte Richtung [Grad]							
U	V	67.8	78.7	89.1	98.6	107.8	88.4
	H	69.7	79.7	89.8	101.5	112.2	90.6
GU	V	71.7	82.1	92.4	102.3	113.1	92.3
	H	72.0	82.4	91.7	102.3	112.0	92.1

70°), ergibt sich im Mittel kein Unterschied für die Kurvenverläufe von U und
GU (*t* = .61; *p* > .25).

c. Vergleich von Vollkreis- und Halbkreisanordnung

Vergleichen wir die Richtungsabweichungen aus dem Vollkreis-Experiment mit
den gemittelten Werten aus den beiden Halbkreis-Anordnungen (Tabelle 24.1),
so finden wir einander entsprechende Werte für GU, verschiedene Werte
hingegen für U. Bei Vollkreis-Bedingung liegen die U-Werte durchweg um
durchschnittlich 2.2° niedriger, was einem schwächeren Nacheffekt für die
Halbkreis-Bedingung entspricht.

Für eine im Uhrzeigersinn (U) kreisende Schallquelle läßt sich der
Richtungsnacheffekt mithin nicht durch Addition der Effekte aus vorderer und
hinterer Halbkreisbewegung herleiten.

III. Schallbewegung im Viertelkreis

Bei Schallbewegung in einem Viertelkreis-Sektor als Vorreiz trifft die Bedingung, daß beide Ohren während der Adaptationsphase im Mittel gleich intensiv beschallt werden, nicht mehr zu. In diesem Versuch wurde der vordere linke
Quadrant (0°–90°) gewählt und somit das linke Ohr stärker beschallt. Die anschließende Lokalisation sollte sich nach rechts, d.h. in Richtung auf das
weniger beschallte Ohr verlagern (Flügel, 1920). Diese Verlagerung käme also
zu der aus der Bewegungsrichtung abzuleitenden Verschiebung hinzu, die bei U
nach links, bei GU nach rechts zu erwarten wäre. Es wurden 4 Lautsprecher
benutzt, so daß sich zu jeder Zeit ein aktiver Lautsprecher im beschallten vor-

deren linken Quadranten befand. Die zu lokalisierenden Lautsprecher wurden in den Positionen 60°, 70°, 80°, 90°, 100° dargeboten, um Vorreiz- und Testreizdarbietung räumlich einander anzugleichen. O-Messungen wurden nur einmal vorgenommen. Zwölf Vpn (Alter 18–30 J.) nahmen an dem Versuch teil. Die mittleren Richtungseinstellungen für O, U und GU, bezogen auf die jeweils dargebotene Schallrichtung, zeigt Abbildung 24.7. Das Ergebnis ist überraschend. Entgegen der erwarteten Verschiebung nach rechts, zeigt sich eine Tendenz zur Verschiebung nach links, in Richtung auf das stärker beschallte Ohr. Der Nacheffekt für U tritt sehr deutlich für alle Schallrichtungen auf. Für

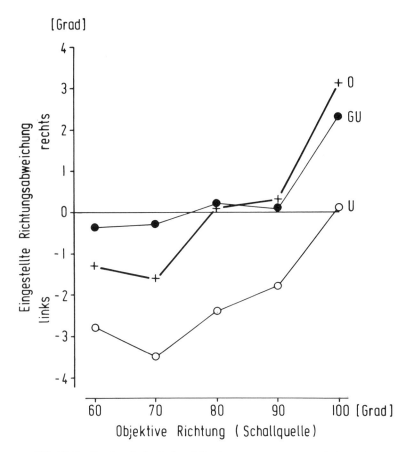

FIG. 24.7.   Results obtained after 2.5 min exposure to quarter-circle motion (frontal left quadrant: 0–90°). Legend as in Fig. 24.4 A; 12 subjects, two settings each per condition.

GU zeigt sich ein Nacheffekt nur in geringem Maße (bei Lautsprecherpositionen von 70° und 60°). Die Verläufe für U und GU unterschieden sich signifikant ($t = 3.55$; $p < .01$). Bezogen auf die Abweichungen von O findet sich wiederum ein relatives Maximum für U bei rechten, für GU bei linken Raumpositionen.

ERÖRTERUNG

Richtungsspezifische Nachwirkungen konnten in allen drei Adaptationsexperimenten (Vollkreis-, Halbkreis-, Viertelkreis-Anordnung) beobachtet werden. Im Unterschied zum Sehen tritt im Hören keine Gegenbewegung (Bewegungsnachbild) auf, sondern lediglich eine Verschiebung der stationären Lokalisation entgegengesetzt zur Richtung vorangegangener Schallbewegung. Weitere Versuche mit dichotischer Versuchsanordnung (Ehrenstein, 1977, 1978) ergaben ähnliche Richtungsverlagerungen. Man kann daher folgern, daß der Nacheffekt keine Besonderheit der Schalldarbietung im freien Feld darstellt.

Bei Adaptation an eine Schallbewegung im Vollkreis (Experiment I) erhalten wir bezogen auf die psychophysische Null-Linie (O-Werte) durchschnittliche Abweichungen von etwa 2° für U und GU. Für U ist die Abweichung umso größer, je weiter rechts sich die Schallquelle befindet, für GU verhält es sich umgekehrt. Es besteht also eine gegensinnige räumliche Anisotropie in der Stärke des Nacheffektes. Eine derartige systematische Zu- und Abnahme der Nacheffekstärken spricht deutlich gegen eine nur unspezifische Adaptation des Richtungshörens.

Bei einer Schallbewegung im Vollkreis (Experiment I) kehren sich die Translationsrichtungen um, sobald die Schallbewegung vom vorderen in den hinteren Halbkreissektor übergeht. Die sich hieraus ergebende Schwierigkeit für die Interpretation des richtungsabhängigen Nacheffektes läßt sich aber auflösen, wenn man zwischen vorderem und hinterem Hörfeld unterscheidet. Tatsächlich ergab ein Entfernungsschätz-Versuch (Ehrenstein, 1977; Versuch II.3), daß die Schallwirkung im hinteren Halbkreis weniger intensiv ist, als im vorderen. Die Ortslinie einer den Hörer umkreisenden Schallquelle erscheint in ihrer gehörten Entfernung nicht gleichabständig als Kreis, sondern birnenförmig, d.h. der Abstand ist hinten fast doppelt so groß wie vorne, nach links und rechts beträgt er etwa das 1 ½ fache des vorderen Abstandes. Dies könnte erklären, warum bei Beschränkung der Adaptation auf eine Schallbewegung im vorderen oder hinteren Halbkreis (Experiment II) nur für den vorderen ein deutlicher Nacheffekt auftrat.

Mittelt man die Nacheffektsbeträge für die beiden Halbkreis-Anordnungen und vergleicht sie mit denen für Vollkreis-Anordnung, so entsprechen sich beide Werte nur für Adaptation an Schallbewegung im Gegenuhrzeigersinn. Bei Adaptation im Uhrzeigersinn ergibt hingegen die Halbkreis-Anordnung einen um etwa

2° schwächeren Nacheffekt als bei Vollkreis-Anordnung. Adaptation an eine Bewegung von rechts nach links führt zu einem ausgeprägteren Nacheffekt als Adaptation in Gegenrichtung. Eine ähnliche Asymmetrie ergab sich bei stationärer Adaptation des Richtungshörens (Ehrenstein, 1981a). Dies weist möglicherweise auf eine unterschiedliche Beteiligung von linker und rechter Hemisphäre bei adaptiven Vorgängen hin.

Aus Experiment III (Schallbewegung im Viertelkreis) geht hervor, daß eine Richtungsverschiebung zum zuvor weniger beschallten Ohr (Flügel, 1920) nicht auftritt, wenn die Adaptation an eine bewegte, statt an eine ruhende Schallquelle erfolgt. Dies spricht dafür, daß die bei Bewegungsadaptation auftretenden Nachwirkungen sich funktionell von denen durch gerichtete stationäre Adaptation ausgelösten Nachwirkungen unterscheiden. Die in Experiment III aufgetretene Richtungsverlagerung zum stärker beschallten Ohr legt dabei sogar nahe, daß die Bewegungsadaptation die Richtungsnachwirkung der stationären Adaptation aktiv hemmt. Der Befund, daß für Schallbewegung im vorderen linken Quadranten der Nacheffekt für U wesentlich stärker ist als für GU, läßt sich vielleicht mit Hilfe des oben bereits angeführten Entfernungsschätz-Versuches (Ehrenstein, 1977) erklären. Aus ihm geht hervor, daß eine von links in den vorderen linken Quadranten eintretende Schallquelle bei ihrer Bewegung zur Mitte anschaulich ständig näher an den Hörer herankommt, während bei umgekehrter Bewegungsrichtung (GU) sich die Schallquelle ständig zu entfernen scheint. Eine sich anschaulich vom Hörer entfernende Schallbewegung scheint demnach einen geringeren Richtungsnacheffekt hervorzurufen als eine auf den Hörer anschaulich zukommende. Bei Zutreffen dieser Schlußfolgerung müßte bei einer Adaptation an eine auf den vorderen rechten Viertelkreis beschränkten Schallbewegung der Nacheffekt umgekehrt für GU stärker als für U ausfallen.

Unsere psychophysischen Befunde lassen sich leicht in einen Zusammenhang mit neurophysiologischen Untersuchungen bei der Katze bringen. Hier wurden im Colliculus inferior (Altman, 1968) und Corpus geniculatum mediale (Altman, Syka, & Shmigidina, 1970) Neurone gefunden, die selektiv auf die Richtung akustischer Bewegungsreize antworten. Entsprechende Neurone konnten Brugge, Dubrovsky, Aitkin, and Anderson (1969) sowie Sovijärvi und Hyvärinen (1974) auch in der Hörrinde der Katze nachweisen. Es fanden sich dabei neben kurzfristigen Initialentladungen (6–30 msec) auch relativ späte Entladungen (.5–4 sec), die von Altman et al. (1970) mit der Fixierung und Speicherung der Information im akustischen Kurzzeitgedächtnis in Verbindung gebracht werden. Es liegt nahe, bewegungs- und richtungsempfindliche Neurone auch im Hörsystem des Menschen anzunehmen. Die im Anschluß an Bewegungsvorreizung auftretenden Richtungsverlagerungen ließen sich demnach als Folge einer adaptationsbedingten Nullpunktverschiebung richtungsspezifischer Bewegungsdetektoren deuten. Offen bleibt dabei, warum im Unterschied zum Sehen im Hören kein ''Bewegungsnachbild'' auftritt. Die Adaptation der akustischen Richtungswahrnehmung könnte daher auch über disparitätsspezifische Neurone erfolgen, ähnlich denen, die für den stereoskopischen Tiefennacheffekt (Blakemore & Julesz, 1971; Köhler & Emery, 1947) verantwortlich gemacht werden (Mitchell & Baker, 1973).

Die Frage, ob die in unseren Untersuchungen aufgetretenen Nacheffekte eine Folge *bewegungs*-richtungsspezifischer Adaptation sind, oder lediglich auf Adaptation statischer (disparitäts-spezifischer) Richtungsdetektoren zurückgehen, läßt sich vorerst nicht entscheiden. Das Ausbleiben eines Bewegungsnacheffektes in den vorliegenden Versuchen spricht eher gegen die Existenz richtungsspezifischer Bewegungsdetektoren. Dagegen berichten Grantham und Wightman (1979) für dichotisch simulierte schnelle Bewegung von 200°/sec bei alternierender Adaptations-und Testreizdarbietung von 10 und 1 sec das Auftreten eines allerdings schwachen akustischen Bewegungsnacheffektes. Offen bleibt schließlich, ob Wechselwirkungen zwischen Bewegungsnachwirkungen und statischen ''figuralen'' Nachwirkungen bestehen, die den Einfluß von dynamischer Adaptation auf anschließende statische Änderungen der Raumund Richtungswahrnehmung erklären könnten (vgl. Köhler, 1965).

SUMMARY

In order to investigate whether direction-specific adaptation occurs in the human auditory system, an apparatus was designed which allowed exposure to moving and stationary sound sources (Fig. 24.1).

Subjects were adapted for 2.5 min to a sound source rotating either clockwise (C) or counterclockwise (CC) around the head at a constant speed of 30°/sec. Four different sectors of exposure were employed: full-circle (Exp. I), half-circle in front, half-circle behind (Exp. II), and quarter-circle in the frontal left quadrant (Exp. III). Following each exposure, subjects were asked to localize stationary sound sources in various directions: 10° and 20° to the left or right, and straight ahead (Figs. 24.2, 24.3).

Experiment I. Adaptation to a sound source traveling through a full-circle resulted in an average displacement of 2° in the opposite direction. For C-motion, the displacement was maximal for directions to the right of the subject's straight ahead; the reverse was found for CC-motion (Fig. 24.4).

Experiment II. To find out why full-circle rotation causes a directional shift, despite the reversal in the direction of translation as the sound moves from the front to the rear of the subject, adapation was tested for semi-circular motion alone. Exposure to semi-circular motion in front of the subject resulted in a stronger shift of localization for the CC-condition and a weaker shift for the C-condition (Fig. 24.5). No direction-specific shift was observed with semi-circular motion presented behind the subject (Fig. 24.6). If the sum of the aftereffects caused by semi-circular motion in front and behind is compared to the aftereffects caused by full-circle motion, equivalence is obtained for C-motion, but not for CC-motion (Table 24.1).

Experiment III. Exposure to sound-motion in the frontal left quadrant resulted in a strong leftward shift following C-motion, but in a weak shift to the right following CC-motion (Fig. 24.7). This result is surprising because based upon previous findings with stationary sound adaptation, one would have predicted a shift of localization towards the less intensely exposed, i.e., the right, ear. This discrepancy can, however, be interpreted by assuming that adaptation to stationary and to moving sound is processed by different mechanisms and that the motion-sensitive mechanism inhibits the "stationary" one. In addition, the change of apparent distance of the moving sound source may explain why C-motion caused a stronger aftereffect than CC-motion. It was observed in a distance-scaling-task that a sound moving from the left to straight ahead (C) appears to be approaching the subject, whereas for a sound moving from straight ahead to the left (CC), the source appears to move away and thus may be a less effective adapting stimulus.

In general, the results provide evidence for motion- and/or direction-specific auditory subsystems in man. Unlike the visual analog, adaptation to auditory motion does not result in a movement aftereffect, but rather causes a counter-directed shift of stationary localization.

ACKNOWLEDGMENTS

Die Versuche wurden als Teil der Doktorarbeit (1977) des Verfassers in der Abteilung Neurobiologie am Max-Planck-Institut für biophysikalische Chemie, Göttingen, durchgeführt. Ich danke Prof. O. Creutzfeldt für seine großzügige Förderung und Dr. F. C. Hellweg für seine Hilfe beim Aufbau des Labors. Das Manuskript entstand mit Unterstützung des SFB 70, Teilprojekt A6.

REFERENCES

Altman, J. A. Are there neurones detecting direction of sound source motion? *Experimental Neurology,* 1968, *22,* 13–25.

Altman, J. A., Syka, I., & Shmigidina, G. N. Neuronal activity in the medial geniculate body of the cat during monaural and binaural stimulation. *Experimental Brain Research,* 1970, *10,* 81–93.

Altman, J. A., & Viskov, O. V. Discrimination of perceived movement velocity for fused auditory image in dichotic stimulation. *Journal of the Acoustical Society of America,* 1977, *61,* 816–819.

Blakemore, C., & Julesz, B. Stereoscopic depth aftereffect produced without monocular cues. *Science,* 1971, *171,* 286–288.

Blauert, J. *Räumliches Hören.* Stuttgart: Hirzel, 1974.

Bray, D. A., Dirks, D. D., & Morgan, D. E. Perstimulatory loudness adaptation. *Journal of the Acoustical Society of America,* 1973, *53,* 1544–1548.

Briggs, R. M., & Perrott, D. R. Auditory apparent movement under dichotic listening conditions. *Journal of Experimental Psychology*, 1972, *92*, 83–91.

Brugge, J. F., Dubrovsky, N. A., Aitkin, L. M., & Anderson, D. J. Sensitivity of single neurons in auditory cortex of cat to binaural tonal stimulation; effects of varying interaural time and intensity. *Journal of Neurophysiology*, 1969, *32*, 1005–1024.

Ehrenstein, W. H. *Zur Psychophysik richtungsspezifischer Nachwirkungen der akustischen Bewegungswahrnehmung.* Dissertation, Math.-Nat. Fak., Universität Göttingen, 1977.

Ehrenstein, W. H. Direction-specific acoustical aftereffects. *Journal of the Acoustical Society of America*, 1978, *64*, S35:01. (Abstract)

Ehrenstein, W. H. Zur Frage Δt-spezifischer Adaptation des Richtungshörens. In W. Michaelis, (Hrsg.), *Bericht über den 32. Kongreß der Deutschen Gesellschaft für Psychologie in Zürich 1980*, Bd. *1*, 217–219. Göttingen: Hogrefe, 1981. (a)

Ehrenstein, W. H. Hinweise für den Aufbau eines Labors zur Untersuchung des Bewegungs- und Richtungshörens. In A. Schick (Hrsg.), *Akustik zwischen Physik und Psychologie*, Kap. *6.3*. Stuttgart: Klett-Cotta, 1981. (b)

Ehrenstein, W. H., & Hellweg, F. C. Richtungsspezifische akustische Nachwirkungen nach vorangegangener Schallrotation. *Pflügers Archiv*, 1976, *365*, R 49. (Abstract 195)

Flügel, J. C. On local fatigue in the auditory system. *British Journal of Psychology*, 1920, *11*, 105–134.

Grantham, W. D., & Wightman, F. L. Discrimination of a moving auditory "dot" from a stationary auditory "line." *Journal of the Acoustical Society of America*, 1977, *61*, S62:GG12. (Abstract)

Grantham, W. D., & Wightman, F. L. Detectability of varying interaural temporal differences. *Journal of the Acoustical Society of America*, 1978, *63*, 511–523.

Grantham, W. D., & Wightman, F. L. Auditory motion aftereffects. *Perception & Psychophysics*, 1979, *26*, 403–408.

Köhler, W. Movement aftereffects and figural aftereffects. *Perceptual and Motor Skills*, 1965, *20*, 591–592.

Köhler, W., & Emery, D. A. Figural aftereffects in the third dimension of visual space. *American Journal of Psychology*, 1947, *60*, 159–201.

Köhler, W., & Wallach, H. Figural after-effects. *Proceedings of the American Philosophical Society*, 1944, *88*, 269–357.

Kohler, I. Über Aufbau und Wandlungen der Wahrnehmungswelt. Insbesondere über 'bedingte Empfindungen'. *Österreichische Akademie der Wissenschaften, Philosophisch-historische Klasse; Sitzungsberichte*, 227. Band, 1. Abhandlung. Wien: Rohrer, 1951.

Kohler, I. Die Zusammenarbeit der Sinne und das allgemeine Adaptationsproblem. In W. Metzger (Hrsg.), *Handbuch der Psychologie*, I/1, Göttingen: Hogrefe Verlag, 1966.

Krauskopf, J. Figural after-effects in auditory space. *American Journal of Psychology*, 1954, *67*, 278–287.

Lienert, G. A. Kleingruppen-Versuchspläne als Präzisionsmittel im psychologischen Experiment. *Zeitschrift für Psychologie*, 1955, *158*, 121–147.

Mitchell, D. E., & Baker, A. G. Stereoscopic aftereffects: Evidence for disparity-specific neurons in the human visual system. *Vision Research*, 1973, *13*, 2273–2288.

Müller, J. *Über die phantastischen Gesichtserscheinungen. Mit einer physiologischen Urkunde des Aristoteles über den Traum.* Koblenz, 1826 (Neudruck: W. Fritsch, München 1967).

Perrott, D. R., & Musicant, A. D. Minimum auditory movement angle: Binaural localization of moving sound sources. *Journal of the Acoustical Society of America*, 1977, *62*, 1463–1466.

Ritter, M., Lücke, G., & Zihl, J. Selektive Analyse von Bewegungsrichtung und Geschwindigkeit in der visuellen Wahrnehmung des Menschen. *Psychologische Forschung*, 1973, *36*, 267–296.

Sekuler, R. Visual motion perception. In E. C. Carterette, & M. P. Friedman (Eds.), *Handbook of Perception*, (Vol. 5), *Seeing*. New York: Academic Press, 1975.

Sekuler, R., Pantle, A., & Levinson, E. Physiological basis of motion perception. In R. Held, H. W. Leibowitz, & H.-L. Teuber (Eds.), *Handbook of sensory physiology* (Vol. 8), *Perception*. Berlin: Springer, 1978.

Sovijärvi, A., & Hyvärinen, J. Auditory cortical neurons in the cat sensitive to the direction of sound source movment. *Brain Research*, 1974, *73*, 455–471.

Stadler, M., & Kano, C. Richtungsspezifische Bewegungsdetektion in der menschlichen Gesichtswahrnehmung? *Psychologische Beiträge*, 1970, *12*, 367–378.

Taylor, M. M. The distance paradox of the figural aftereffect in auditory localization. *Canadian Journal of Psychology*, 1962, *16*, 278–282.

25 Micro- and Macromelodies

Giovanni B. Vicario
Istituto di Psicologia
Università di Padova
Padova, Italia

ABSTRACT

Stumpf (1898) maintained that melodies played on micro- and macroscales (that is, on scales where the usual ratio between the frequencies limiting the octave is lessened or enlarged, being nevertheless divided in 12 tempered semitones) could preserve their tonal content rather well. Werner (1926) maintained a similar view, emphasizing the fact that even visual figures preserve their attributes when lessened or enlarged in visual space. An experiment conducted with six widely known melodies played on 12 special scales ranging from the proportional compression of the octave to one semitone, to the dilatation to the double octave, shows that the recognition of melodies rapidly drops under the 50% level when the compression reaches 40% of frequency, and the dilatation 30%. Trained subjects (undergraduate musicians) show a significant peak of 91% of recognition when the compression of the octave reaches seven semitones (i. e., the fifth, the most consonant interval except the octave itself). The experiment and the introspective reports of both trained and untrained subjects show that such a comparison between tonal and visual space is strongly dubious, and that factors not yet investigated may play a significant role in the *Erscheinungsweise* (mode of appearance) of the micro- and macromelodies. For instance, the use of unconventional intervals upsets the correct forming of the tonic (that is, the tonal frame of reference), supposedly preventing listeners from recognizing the original melody in its compressed or dilatated versions.

INTRODUCTION

This is a brief report on research carried out by Giuseppe Porzionato and me in the acoustical laboratory of our Institute. It is still unfinished, but I think that its theoretical premises and preliminary results may be of some interest for those who appreciate the auditory side of Professor Kohler's scientific work.

Micro- and macromelodies are terms coined by Werner (1926) in order to conceptualize a "Gedankenexperiment" devised by Stumpf (1898) upon suggestion by Brentano. These terms refer to melodies that are played on scales where the octave is not represented by the usual ratio (2:1), but by smaller ratios (e. g., the fifth: 3:2) and respectively greater ratios (e. g., the double octave: 4:1). These micro- and macrooctaves are still divided into 12 tempered micro- or macrosemitones that give rise to micro- and macroscales. A micromelody is a melody played on a microscale, so as to appear "compressed" in a smaller tonal space. A macromelody is a melody played on a macroscale, so as to appear "dilatated" on a larger tonal space. Of course, all the mutual frequency ratios between any two tones of the melodies are proportionally lessened or enlarged in their micro- or macroprojections.

At that time, Stumpf (1898) was engaged in explaining that the tonal effect of a melody is dependent on the relations among tones, rather than on their absolute frequency values. He wrote:

> Wenn es richtig ist . . . dass die tonale Wirkung einer Melodie wesentlich auf den Intervallen der darin aufeinanderfolgenden Töne, nicht auf der absoluten Tonhöhe beruht . . . dann müssten wir eine Melodie auch in verkleinertem oder vergrössertem Massstabe wiedergeben und verstehen können. . . Die Melodie müsste hierbei durchaus verständlich bleiben, und die Wirkung eine ähnliche sein wie bei einer verkleinerten oder vergrösserten Kopie eines schönen Gemäldes: etwas geht dabei wohl an Wirkung verloren, . . . aber das Wesentlichste, die Verhältnisse, bleibt ungeändert. Wir brauchen aber nicht zu sagen, dass eine so verkleinerte oder vergrösserte Melodie absolut sinnlos wäre: ein Zeichen, dass Abstand und Intervall zweierlei ist. (p. 69)

The Gedankenexperiment of Stumpf was taken up later by Werner (1926), who tried to demonstrate that a microsemitone, when repeated over and over, appears as a full semitone, making it possible to conclude that a microscale can be heard as a normal scale, and a micromelody as the original one. However, Werner was more interested in demonstrating the extreme plasticity of the auditory system (and the dependence of our tonal system on learning, adaptation, and cultural factors), rather than in comparing the auditory and visual modalities. Besides, he claimed, in a rather disconcerting way, that Stumpf and Brentano maintain that micro- and macromelodies are "sinnlos" (1926, p. 75). In a subsequent paper (1940) Werner became more aware of the theoretical relevance of the comparison between the two sense modalities, and posed the problem in a very interesting way. "An optical figure remains unchanged under two conditions: (a) when shifted along parallel lines, or (b) when reduced or enlarged in proportion. As to auditory forms, it is a well-known fact that a melody remains the same if moved up or down the scale. But the question now arises whether there is also a plasticity of hearing comparable to that of visual field, where a proportionate reduction in size leaves the Gestalt unaffected'' (1940, p. 149). On the other hand, Werner does not seem to take into account the strong criticism of Révész (1934), who denies, by means of detailed arguments, any true tonal existence to micro- and macromelodies.

Neither Stumpf nor Werner could bring to an experimental trial the excellent suggestion of Brentano, since they lacked the synthesizers and microcomputers which could promptly execute a melody in any thinkable micro- or macroprojection, or even produce any desired sequence of tones, in order to investigate the main problem: the suggested likeness between the auditory and visual field (on this topic, see also Julesz & Hirsh, 1972; Vicario, 1980, 1982). Of course, it is of no importance to demonstrate that Stumpf or Werner were wrong: We are simply curious to *hear* those micro- and macromelodies, and to ascertain whether Stumpf or Werner were right in suggesting a sort of isomorphism between the visual and auditory field.

SOME METHODOLOGICAL PROBLEMS

When we try to demonstrate that visual figures remain unchanged in spite of their proportional lessening or enlargement, we can make use of either senseless or significant patterns, such as geometrical shapes, pictures of real objects, human faces and so on. When we increase or decrease the scale of both classes of patterns and ask the subject for a description of what happened, we usually obtain this kind of answer: "It is the same thing, but enlarged (or lessened)." There is no problem about the sameness, and even the question about the intervening variation in size sounds trivial.

In the auditory field things go otherwise. When one listens to a melody, and then the experimenter makes him hear the same melody "compressed" into a fifth (that is, played on a scale where the fifth is representative of an octave with all its 12 semitones) or "stretched" on a tenth (that is, played on a scale where the tenth is representative of the octave with all its 12 semitones), the question about the intervening variation is anything but trivial. First, the subject does not grasp in what sense the two melodies (the normal and the projected one) should be the same: he just heard two clearly different things. Second, a tonally compressed melody appears in any way, but decreased in size. For high compression levels it may appear as "flattened", but in any case its "length" remains unchanged. A tonally dilatated melody appears in any way, but increased in size. For high dilatation levels it may appear as "broadened", but even in this case its length remains unchanged. The "optical figure" of Werner, when enlarged or lessened, changes in both height and length. Furthermore, nobody knows what kind of alteration is necessary in order to make a melody appear as "larger" or "smaller": Perhaps we must operate simultaneously on both tonal extension (by means of the micro- or macroprojection of the intervals) and duration (by means of a proportional reduction or augmentation of duration of all the tones and pauses) of the whole melody.

In any case, the state of the facts suggests the use of a rather cautious methodology. Making a subject listen to an unknown melody and then to its altered versions usually produces unreliable results. Untrained subjects are embarrassed by realizing what in the altered version is changed and what on the contrary is the same, assuming that the task is understood. Trained subjects (that is, students or graduates of a musical school) tend either (a) to emphasize the sameness, as they take the trial as a test of musical ability, or (b) to emphasize the dissimilarity, as they wish to demonstrate their skill in making subtle musical discriminations, and (c) to actually hear different melodies, especially when they are familiar with dodecaphonic theory and practice.

To sum up, the method of matching a melody (either known or unknown) with its altered versions seems rather doubtful. Therefore, we decided to resort to another method, that is to the recognition of well-known melodies in their altered versions. (On a variation of this method, see White, 1960.) In other words, we make the subject listen to the compressed or dilatated projection of a well-known theme, and then we ask him either to name or hum it. The guess is that when the subject is correct either in naming the original melody or in reproducing it vocally, we can assume that its tonal figure is unchanged in spite of its becoming "larger" or "smaller." In my opinion, this method produces less dubious results, even if it is not very suitable in encouraging subjects' introspective reports—a rather important thing, in the first moments of the research.

Subjects

There were 48 subjects of the experiment, divided into two groups: 24 musically untrained (all undergraduate students from the Psychological Institute), and 24 musically trained (all undergraduate students from the Conservatorio "C. Pollini" of Padua). We carefully ascertained that the untrained subjects were actually lacking in musical skill, and also had no hearing problems.

STIMULI AND APPARATUS

We selected from a large number of well-known melodies six themes (M1, M2, M3, M4, M5, M6) that are characterized by an even and as much as possible uniform "division," that is, by a succession of notes and pauses of equal duration. As a matter of fact, we know that the recognition of altered and distorted tunes is chiefly based on rhythm, that is, on the distribution of the duration of the notes within each bar (see, e. g., Deutsch, 1972; Dowling &

Hollombe, 1977; House, 1977; White, 1960). The selected melodies were the following:

  M1—Candlelight Waltz (popular British song), 9 bars, 28 notes, 25 sec in duration;

  M2—Adeste Fideles (popular Christmas song), 9 bars, 25 notes, 25 sec in duration;

  M3—Hymn to Joy (from the 9th Symphony of Beethoven), 8 bars, 30 notes, 17 sec in duration;

  M4—Shepherds' Song (from the 5th movement of Symphony no. 6 of Beethoven), 8 bars, 24 notes, 18 sec in duration;

  M5—God save the Queen (British national anthem), 14 bars, 41 notes, 35 sec in duration;

  M6—Eurovision signature tune (from the Te Deum of Charpentier), 9 bars, 38 notes, 17 sec in duration.

With some difficulty we reached a reasonable compromise between very familiar melodies and those without an easily recognizable rhythm. In fact, M6 has a very unusual division that makes it identifiable ''at a glance''. Nevertheless, we decided to insert it among the experimental items in order to ascertain its behavior.

We then calculated 12 scales, namely 6 microscales characterized by tonal compression, 1 normal scale and 5 macroscales characterized by tonal dilatation. In Tables 25.1 and 25.2 one can see the frequencies at which the tones of the melodies have been produced. In the right-hand column of Table 25.1 are the names of the notes (these names are ''real'' for the normal scale, and conventional for the micro- and macroscales). To the immediate left of this column are the frequencies of the normal tempered scale. In the remaining columns are the frequencies for every decreasing degree of compression (C6–C1). Table 25.2 presents the frequencies for every increasing degree of dilatation (D1–D5). The degree of compression and dilatation is summarized by the following:

1.	C6 = octave compressed into	1 semitone	(minor 2nd)
2.	C5	3 semitones	(minor 3rd)
3.	C4	5	(4th)
4.	C3	7	(5th)
5.	C2	9	(major 6th)
6.	C1	11	(major 7th)
7.	N = normal tempered scale	12	(octave)
8.	D1 = octave dilatated to	13	(minor 9th)
9.	D2	16	(major 10th)
10.	D3	19	(12th)
11.	D4	22	(minor 14th)
12.	D5	24	(double octave)

We played the six selected melodies (M1–M6) by means of an MOOG 8-channel synthesizer controlled by a ROLAND MC–8 microcomputer in all of the 12 above-mentioned degrees of compression and dilatation, obtaining 72 experimental items, which were recorded on tape. The following is the list of notes employed in playing the melodies:

M1: D_3, E_3, G_3, A_3, B_3, D_4, E_4;

M2: E_3, F_3 sharp, G_3sharp, A_3, B_3, C_4sharp, D_4;

M3: F_3, G_3, A_3, A_3sharp, C_4;

M4: C_3, D_3, E_3, F_3, G_3, A_3, A_3sharp, C_4;

M5: E_3, F_3, G_3, A_3, A_3sharp, C_4, D_4;

M6: C_3, F_3, G_3, A_3, A_3sharp, C_4.

TABLE 25.1

Frequency values of the notes of the microscales. C6 . . . C1 = decreasing degrees of tonal compression. Frequency values equal or near (at ± 1%) to the values of the normal tempered scale are underlined.

Microscales—Degrees of Compression							
C6	C5	C4	C3	C2	C1	N	
Into a minor 2nd 1 Semit.	Into a minor 3rd 3 Semit.	Into a 4th 5 Semit.	Into a 5th 7 Semit.	Into a Major 6th 9 Semit.	Into a Major 7th 11 Semit.	Normal Tempered Scale of 12 Semitones	Name of the Notes
421.3	386.4	354.3	324.9	297.9	273.2	261.6	C_3
423.4	392.0	362.9	336.0	311.1	288.1	277.2	C_3 sharp
425.4	397.4	371.8	347.6	324.9	303.7	293.7	D_3
427.5	403.5	380.8	395.5	339.3	320.2	311.1	D_3 sharp
429.5	409.4	390.1	371.8	354.3	337.7	329.6	E_3
431.6	415.3	399.6	384.5	370.0	356.0	349.2	F_3
433.7	421.3	409.4	397.7	386.8	375.4	370.0	F_3 sharp
435.8	427.4	419.3	411.3	403.5	395.8	392.0	G_3
437.9	433.7	429.5	425.4	421.3	417.3	415.3	G_3 sharp
440.0	440.0	440.0	440.0	440.0	440.0	440.0	A_3
442.1	446.4	450.7	455.1	459.5	463.9	466.2	A_3 sharp
444.3	452.9	461.7	470.7	479.8	489.2	493.9	B_3
446.4	459.5	472.9	486.8	501.1	515.7	523.3	C_4
448.6	466.2	484.5	503.5	523.6	543.8	554.4	C_4 sharp
450.7	472.9	496.3	520.7	546.4	573.4	587.3	D_4
452.9	479.8	508.4	538.6	570.6	604.5	622.3	D_4 sharp
455.1	486.8	520.7	557.0	595.9	637.4	659.3	E_4

TABLE 25.2

Frequency values of the notes of the macroscales. D1 . . . D5 = increasing degrees of tonal dilatation. Frequency values equal or near (at ± 1%) to the values of the normal tempered scale are underlined.

		Macroscales—Degrees of Dilatation				
	N	D1	D2	D3	D4	D5
Name of the Notes	Normal Tempered Scale of 12 Semitones	To a Minor 9th 13 Semit.	To a Major 10th 16 Semit.	To a 12th 19 Semit.	To a Minor 14th 22 Semit.	To a Double Octave 24 Semit.
C_3	261.6	250.5	<u>220.0</u>	193.9	169.6	<u>155.6</u>
C_3 sharp	277.2	266.7	237.6	211.7	188.6	<u>174.6</u>
D_3	293.7	283.9	256.6	<u>232.0</u>	<u>209.7</u>	<u>196.0</u>
D_3 sharp	311.1	302.8	<u>277.9</u>	254.2	<u>233.1</u>	<u>220.0</u>
E_3	329.6	321.8	299.4	<u>278.5</u>	<u>259.1</u>	<u>246.9</u>
F_3	349.2	342.6	323.3	305.2	288.1	<u>277.2</u>
F_3 sharp	370.0	364.7	<u>349.2</u>	334.4	320.2	<u>311.1</u>
G_3	392.0	<u>388.2</u>	377.2	<u>366.4</u>	356.0	<u>349.2</u>
G_3 sharp	415.3	<u>413.3</u>	407.4	401.5	<u>395.8</u>	<u>392.0</u>
A_3	440.0	<u>440.0</u>	<u>440.0</u>	<u>440.0</u>	<u>440.0</u>	<u>440.0</u>
A_3 sharp	466.2	<u>468.4</u>	475.2	482.1	<u>489.2</u>	493.9
B_3	493.9	<u>498.7</u>	513.3	<u>528.3</u>	543.8	<u>554.4</u>
C_4	523.3	530.9	<u>554.4</u>	578.9	604.5	<u>622.3</u>
C_4 sharp	554.4	565.1	598.7	634.4	672.1	<u>698.5</u>
D_4	587.3	601.6	646.7	<u>695.1</u>	747.1	<u>784.0</u>
D_4 sharp	622.2	640.5	<u>698.6</u>	761.7	<u>830.6</u>	<u>880.0</u>
E_4	654.3	681.8	754.4	<u>834.6</u>	<u>923.4</u>	<u>987.8</u>

The following 12 separate sequences of six different melodies each were used:

S 1: (M6–C1), (M1–C4), (M3–D2), (M2–C6), (M5–N), (M4–D4);

S 2: (M1–C1), (M3–C4), (M2–D2), (M5–C6), (M4–N), (M6–D4);

S 3: (M3–C1), (M2–C4), (M5–D2), (M4–C6), (M6–N), (M1–D4);

S 4: (M2–C1), (M5–C4), (M4–D2), (M6–C6), (M1–N), (M3–D4);

S 5: (M5–C1), (M4–C4), (M6–D2), (M1–C6), (M3–N), (M2–D4);

S 6: (M4–C1), (M6–C4), (M1–D2), (M3–C6), (M2–N), (M5–D4);

S 7: (M6–D1), (M1–C3), (M3–D3), (M2–C5), (M5–D5), (M4–C2);

S 8: (M1–D1), (M3–C3), (M2–D3), (M5–C5), (M4–D5), (M6–C2);

S 9: (M3–D1), (M2–C3), (M5–D3), (M4–C5), (M6–D5), (M1–C2);

S10: (M2–D1), (M5–C3), (M4–D3), (M6–C5), (M1–D5), (M3–C2);

S11: (M5–D1), (M4–C3), (M6–D3), (M1–C5), (M3–D5), (M2–C2);

S12: (M4–D1), (M6–C3), (M1–D3), (M3–C5), (M2–D5), (M5–C2).

The tone color was of pure sinusoidal waves; the speed of each melody was a mean of its most common performances.

PROCEDURE

At the beginning of the session, the subject was simply told that he had to recognize some altered melodies, and that the trial was not a test of hearing or musical ability.

The subject was seated in front of a hi-fi loudspeaker and was first invited to choose a comfortable sound intensity for the experimental melodies, by means of direct manipulation of the intensity of a 440 Hz tone. Then he was invited to listen carefully to the first melody. He was asked to name it. When the subject appeared to have recognized the melody, and yet to have forgotten the title of the tune, he was invited to hum it. When the subject did not recognize the altered melody, he was presented with the unaltered form. The aim of this was to ascertain whether the subject actually knew the unrecognized tune. We have therefore three kinds of outcomes from the trial: (+) recognition of an already known melody; (−) failure in attempt to recognize an already known melody; (o) unknown melody. With (+) or (−) outcomes the subject was asked to give a description of his feelings, especially if he was a trained musician. Afterwards, the other five melodies of the sequence were presented with the same procedure.

To sum up, each subject (untrained or trained) heard only the six melodies of a sequence given by chance. The two groups (24 trained and 24 untrained) heard all the 12 sequences.

At the end of the session, each subject was requested to describe his own general impressions. If the subject was trained, the experimenter explained the aim of the research and the underlying theory, taking note of the remarks of the musician.

RESULTS

The results of the experiment are represented in Table 25.3 (untrained subjects) and in Table 25.4 (trained subjects). A (+) means that the melody was named or hummed; a (−) means that the melody was known, but could not be recognized; an (o) means that the melody could not be recognized, because it was unknown.

Let us now summarize the results in order to answer the main question, the one arising from the statements of Stumpf (1898) and Werner (1926, 1940): Are auditory figures recognizable in their tonal projections, as visual figures are in their spatial projection?

At the moment the answer can be considered as tentative, since this chapter is nothing but a brief report on work still in progress. In particular, we are in need of a careful statistical analysis of the data that is not yet concluded. For instance,

TABLE 25.3
Results of the experiment for the 24 untrained subjects. M1:
Candlelight Waltz; M2: Adeste Fideles; M3: Hymn to Joy; M4:
Shepherds' Song; M5: God Save the Queen; M6: Eurovision
Signature Tune. C6: compression of the octave into 1 semitone; C5:
compression into 3 semitones; C4: into 5; C3: into 7; C2: into 9; C1:
into 11; N: normal scale; D1: dilatation of the octave to 13
semitones; D2: to 16; D3: to 19; D4: to 22; D5: to 24 (double
octave). (+): recognition of known melody; (−): failed recognition of
known melody; (○): unknown melody. Each subject is represented
by six judgments, in six random locations of the table.

		24 Untrained Subjects					
		Melodies					
		M1	*M2*	*M3*	*M4*	*M5*	*M6*
Compression	C6	− −	− −	− −	− −	− −	− −
	C5	− −	+ +	− −	+ ○	− −	+ −
	C4	− −	+ −	− ○	○ −	○ −	+ −
	C3	+ +	− −	− ○	− −	− +	+ +
	C2	+ +	− ○	○ +	+ +	− −	+ +
	C1	+ +	+ +	+ +	+ ○	○ +	+ +
Normal	N	+ +	+ ○	○ +	+ +	○ +	+ +
Dilatation	D1	+ +	○ +	+ +	+ ○	+ ○	+ +
	D2	+ −	+ ○	+ −	○ −	+ +	+ +
	D3	− +	− ○	− −	○ −	− ○	+ +
	D4	+ −	○ −	+ ○	○ −	○ −	− +
	D5	○ −	− −	+ −	− ○	○ −	+ −

we do not know whether the six melodies can be treated as items of comparable difficulty. A glance at Tables 25.3 and 25.4 reveals that the scores are rather similar, except perhaps for M1 (Candlelight Waltz) and M6 (Eurovision signature tune) which have been recognized in almost every projection—so as to confirm the widely shared point of view that distorted melodies are identified mostly by their rhythm.

Figure 25.1 shows the percentage of successful recognition of all six melodies (as a set of equivalent items) plotted against the percentage of compression into microscales or of dilatation on macroscales. The percentages of successful recognition are calculated as follows: number of successful recognitions/number of actually known melodies. For instance, in 12 untrained subjects, the 6 melodies compressed at level C2 yielded 7 successful recognitions on 10 real trials (2 melodies were not known to subjects, see Table 25.3); this corresponds to 70%. The percentages of compression are calculated as follows: $(R/12 \times 100)$, where R is the number of semitones of the interval at which the octave is reduced. For instance, the reduction to the 5th (7 semitones) = C3 = $(7/12 \times 100) = 41.7\%$.

TABLE 25.4
Results of the experiment for the 24 trained subjects.
(See also the caption of Table 25.3.)

| | | 24 Trained Subjects | | | | | |
| | | Melodies | | | | | |
		M1	*M2*	*M3*	*M4*	*M5*	*M6*
Compression	C6	− −	− −	− −	− −	− −	− +
	C5	+ +	− +	+ −	− +	+ +	+ +
	C4	+ −	− −	− −	− −	+ +	+ +
	C3	+ +	+ +	+ −	○ +	+ +	+ +
	C2	− +	+ −	+ +	+ −	○ +	+ +
	C1	+ +	+ +	+ +	+ +	+ +	+ +
Normal	N	+ +	+ +	+ +	+ +	+ +	+ +
Dilatation	D1	+ +	+ +	+ +	+ +	+ +	+ +
	D2	+ +	− +	− −	+ +	+ +	+ +
	D3	+ +	+ +	− −	− +	− ○	+ +
	D4	− +	+ −	− +	− −	− +	+ +
	D5	− +	+ −	+ −	○ +	− +	− +

The percentages of dilatation are calculated as follows: $(E \times 100)/(E + 12)$, where E is the number of semitones, exceeding the normal octave, to which the octave is expanded. For instance, the dilatation to the 12th (19 semitones) = $D3$ = $(7 \times 100)/(7 + 12) = 36.8\%$.

A simple statistical analysis of the data, performed with the chi square test, tells us two things. First, the performance of trained subjects is significantly better than the performance of untrained ones $(p < .01)$; second, the difference is likely due to the peak at $C3$ $(p = .042)$. The same analysis lets us guess that an increment in the number of trials (subjects) could make even the peaks of both curves at $C5$ significant. At a glance, the curve of untrained subjects resembles a normal curve.

Introspective Reports

The task did not create any difficulty either for trained or untrained subjects. The poorness of tone color of the experimental melodies was pointed out by almost all subjects (the melodies were played on pure tones), but just one trained subject felt that the task of recognition was affected by that poorness. We received no reports concerning aesthetics, emotions, and projective processes. When asked, both trained an untrained subjects reported that recognition had not been based upon particular cues, but on the perception of the whole melodies.

(a) As to the *Erscheinungsweise* (mode of appearance) of experimental melodies, only 6 trained subjects (out of 24) spontaneously made use of terms such as

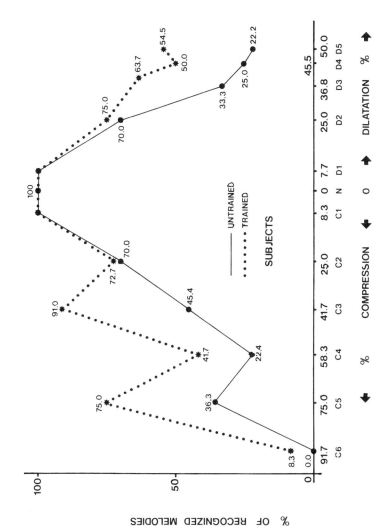

FIG. 25.1. Percentage of successful recognitions (ordinate) plotted against percentage of tonal compression (abscissa, on left) or of tonal dilatation (abscissa, on right). Zero point represents the normal projection, i. e., the usual tempered scale.

431

"compression" or "dilatation" in describing the mode of appearance of the melodies. Two other trained subjects erroneously spoke of "transposition" (that is, of transferring to a pitch other than the original one, without altering intervals) for the stimuli (M5–D1) and (M6–C1), i. e., for the smallest degrees of dilatation and compression. Untrained subjects mostly spoke of recognized experimental melodies as "mistuned" or "mangled." Sometimes they pointed out that single notes were wrong. Not one subject, trained or untrained, made use of terms such as "enlarged" or "lessened," or of like spatial expressions.

(b) As to the rôle of rhythm in making the recognition of experimental melodies easier, some trained subjects suggested that the melodies are recognized mostly by their rhythm, that is by the duration ratios among notes and pauses (which are obviously unaffected by tonal projection). One untrained subject ascribed to the rhythm the successful recognition of the stimulus (M6–C5): the Eurovision signature tune at a high compression level.

(c) Two trained and 11 untrained subjects spontaneously pointed out that experimental melodies seem artfully speeded up or slowed down. This unexpected report can perhaps be connected with the so-called acoustic kappa effect (see Cohen, Hansel, & Sylvester, 1954), according to which empty temporal intervals bounded by tones are underestimated when the tones are close in tonal space, and overestimated when the tones are far away. If such an effect takes place in our experimental melodies, compressed ones should be perceived as speeded up, and dilatated ones should be perceived as slowed down. In fact, trained subjects were consistent with the effect (M2–C5 and M4–C6 were judged as "faster," since they were "compressed"). However, untrained subjects behaved inconsistently. They judged speeded up three compressed melodies (M1–C6, M4–C2, M4–C6) and one dilatated (M3–D5), whereas they perceived as slowed down two dilatated melodies (M2–D2, M5–D5) and five compressed ones (M1–C3, M1–C5, M2–C3, M6–C4, M6–C5).

(d) Three trained subjects spontaneuosly reported that the intervals employed in the experimental melodies were not the correct ones, and stressed a sensation of changing tones during the performance of some items (M2–C2, M2–D4, M4–C2).

DISCUSSION

The main questions addressed in the present experiment are the following: (1) What support is there both for Gedankenexperiment of Brentano and Stumpf and for Werner's view on micro- and macromelodies? (2) How can the results of the experiment be explained, as a whole and in detail? (3) What contribution do the results make to the general issue of the comparison between visual and auditory perception?

1. With regard to the first question, Werner has been too trustful in considering auditory forms strictly comparable to visual ones. In fact, micro- and macroprojections of well-known melodies are fully recognizable just by slight shifts from the normal tempered scale, when micro- and macromelodies appear just as mistuned originals. Increasing compression and dilatation makes the percentage of recognition drop rather rapidly below 50% on either side, and the curve for untrained subjects is very close to being a normal curve. Untrained subjects are most apt to verify the comparison between tonal and visual space, since they are not biased by a practice based upon musical rather than barely auditory phenomena (consonances, dissonances, scales, harmonic tendency to the tonic, and so on). The curve for untrained subjects suggests an increasing inability to recognize well-known melodies with increasing transformation, even if projective, of the melodies themselves. Perhaps through careful removal of all rhythmic cues (presumably responsible for much of the recognition of the M1 and M6 micro- and macromelodies), the curve of untrained subjects would become smoother.

On the other hand, Brentano and Stumpf had a more realistic forecast of the results of their Gedankenexperiment. Stumpf says that ". . . the melody should therefore remain understandable . . . something of its value will be lost . . . but we cannot say that . . . it will be absolutely senseless" (1898, p. 69). The results of the experiment seem to fit rather well in Stumpf's view: Both trained and untrained subjects recognize micro- and macromelodies, but stress the loss of their tonal content.

2. Concerning the curve of trained subjects, the peaks on C3 and C5, as well as another probable peak at D5, are in some way not unexpected. We must point out that these three peaks correspond to the highest levels of consonance: the perfect fifth (C3), the minor third (C5), and the double octave (D5). It is reasonable to suppose that for trained subjects these highly consonant intervals could play the role of micro- and macrooctaves within which unusual intervals have more tonal content.

A correct interpretation of both curves needs many computations. I refer to the presence, in the micro- and the macromelodies actually heard, of intervals exactly or nearly reproducing the intervals of the normal tempered scale. For instance, in the D5 macroscale all the degrees are degrees of the normal scale (redoubled). In Tables 25.1 and 25.2 I underlined all those frequency values that are equal or near (at $\pm$ 1%) to the values of normal scale. A raw comparison between the number of the underlined frequencies in every micro- and macroscale and the percentage of successful recognition, shows no positive relation at all. For instance, C1 shares in common with N, five frequency values and scores 100% of hits, whereas C4 shares six frequency values and yet scores only 22.4% of hits for untrained and 41.7% for trained subjects; D1 shares in common with N, five frequency values and scores 100%, whereas D5 shares all the frequency values, and yet scores only 22.2% of untrained and 54.5% of trained subjects. Of course, such a comparison is not adequate, since we must take into account the notes actually played, and not the theoretical ones. In addition, it is more feasible to consider the intervals actually played, while succeeding each other, rather than a static frame of reference that can be credited for the trained subjects, and not for the untrained. If these computations too should not reveal any relation between the frequencies actually played and the percentages of successful recognitions, it would be hard to find an explanation of the results that was not the simple distribution of errors.

Another way of explaining the results is worth exploring. Some trained subjects, as well as some trained musicians who heard the experimental melodies, noticed that in employing unusual intervals succeeding each other, the tonic (i. e., the tonal frame of reference of every tonal object) keeps wandering in an irregular way (that is, in a way not allowed by harmonic rules), thus preventing the listener from having a satisfying tonal experience. Musicians report that the experimental melody starts on some tonic, then abruptly starts again on another tonic, then jumps to an "impossible modulation" and so on, leaving the listener disconcerted and deprived of the tonal sense of the preceding notes. If we had to find an instance of such an experience for the visual field, we should refer to that perception of the visual objects which is impaired by irregular and sudden displacements of the frame of reference. I rely very much on the exploration of this sort of changing-tonic effect, partly in order to solve the present problem of micro- and macromelodies, yet mostly in order to investigate the more challenging and unexplained phenomenon of the tonic itself.

3. As to the problem of a fruitful and positive comparison between tonal and visual space, I think that the results of the experiment show that such a comparison becomes more dubious every time.

First, let us remember that two kinds of space pertain to hearing: acoustic and tonal. Acoustic space as defined by the location of sound sources has three dimensions (up-down, left-right, and back-forth) and is point by point congruent with visual space. On the contrary, tonal space has only the up-down dimension, since we can speak of tones only in terms of "high" and "low." With some difficulty we could speak even of a back-forth dimension, since in music we have "voices" acting in front, and "accompaniments" that run behind melodic lines, like the ground behind visual figures. Of course, there is nothing in tonal space comparable to the left-right dimension, except perhaps the before/after temporal relation. I will not enumerate all the kinds of confusion that this comparison between left-right direction and before/after temporal direction can raise—and actually does. As to our problem, let me point out that visual objects, when enlarged or lessened, can vary in three dimensions, whereas tonal ones—like the melodies—can vary in just one dimension.

Second, let us remember that tonal space exhibits anisotropic features which seem to me unthinkable when applied to visual space. For all of them, let me consider the phenomenon of octave, which can be described by the fact that in doubling frequency we get the impression of being "higher" but yet "in the same place" (for a graphic representation of the phenomenon, see the cylinder of Révész, 1954). I cannot figure any anisotropy of visual space that can resemble this iterative structure of tonal space. Having lost their most important feature, i. e., the tonal content, I cannot figure any reason why micro- and macromelodies can resemble the original ones, or why they can be recognized by means of anything but their rhythm and the succession of ascending and descending intervals.

REFERENCES

Cohen, J., Hansel, C. E. M., & Sylvester, J. D. Interdependence of temporal and auditory judgments. *Nature,* 1954, *174,* 642–644.

Deutsch, D. Octave generalization and tune recognition. *Perception & Psychophysics,* 1972, *11,* 411–412.

Dowling, W. J., & Hollombe, A. W. The perception of melodies distorted by splitting into several octaves. *Perception & Psychophysics,* 1977, *21,* 60–64.

House, W. J. Octave generalization and the identification of distorted melodies. *Perception & Psychophysics,* 1977, *21,* 586–589.

Julesz, B., & Hirsh, I. J. Visual and auditory perception—an essay of comparison. In E. E. David, Jr. & P. B. Denes (Eds.), *Human communication: A unified view.* New York: McGraw-Hill, 1972.

Révész, G. "Tonsystem" jenseits des musikalischen Gebietes, musikalische "Mikrosysteme" und ihre Beziehung zu der musikalischen Akustik. *Zeitschrift für Psychologie,* 1934, *135,* 25–61.

Révész, G. *Introduction to the psychology of music.* Norman: University of Oklahoma Press, 1954.

Stumpf, C. Konsonanz und Dissonanz. In C. Stumpf (Ed.), *Beiträge zur Akustik und Musikwissenschaft* (Heft 1). Leipzig: Barth, 1898.

Vicario, G. B. Gottschaldt figures in hearing. *The Italian Journal of Psychology,* 1980, *7,* 197–202.

Vicario, G. B. Some observations in auditory field. In J. Beck (Ed.), *Representation and organization in perception.* Hillsdale, N.J.: Lawrence Erlbaum Associates, 1982.

Werner, H. Über Mikromelodik und Mikroharmonik. *Zeitschrift für Psychologie,* 1926, *98,* 74–89.

Werner, H. Musical "micro-scales" and "micro-melodies." *The Journal of Psychology,* 1940, *10,* 149–156.

White, B. W. Recognition of distorted melodies. *The American Journal of Psychology,* 1960, *73,* 100–107.

V INDUCTION BY BRIGHTNESS, COLOR, ORIENTATION, MOTION, AND DEPTH

26 The Role of Drifts and Saccades for the Preservation of Brightness Perception

H. J. M. Gerrits, H. P. W. Stassen and L. J. Th. O. van Erning
Department of Medical Physics and Biophysics
University of Nijmegen
Nijmegen, The Netherlands

ABSTRACT

A number of subjects observed squares of various sizes ($15' \times 15'$ up to $240' \times 240'$). They were instructed to keep their direction of gaze within the square. Their eye movements, being so restricted, were recorded, analyzed and separated into drift and saccadic components. These components were simulated and used to move a uniformly bright square in a stabilization set-up to investigate their contributions for generating or preserving the percept of brightness. The influence of the retinal eccentricity of the stimulus contours was also investigated.

When increasingly larger squares were observed, only the subject's mean saccade amplitudes increased, whereas drifts did not. Drift movements are effective in preserving vision only when stimulus contours are located in or near the foveal area. For larger stimuli saccades are needed as well. Intersubject differences and perceptual differences resulting from normal and simulated eye movements were also analyzed.

It is discussed how the small amplitude drifts and the larger amplitude saccades cooperate to preserve vision. The correlation of receptive (perceptive) field diameters and fading time constant, both increasing towards the periphery, are relevant for the understanding of the behavior of drifts and saccades in response to larger stimuli.

INTRODUCTION

Attempts made to prevent the image of a stimulus from shifting over the retina, i.e., to stabilize the image, have led to controversial conclusions. Some experimenters found that the stabilized images fade away in a faint residual brightness

(Barlow, 1963; Ditchburn & Pritchard, 1956; Gerrits, 1978; Gerrits, de Haan, & Vendrik, 1966; Yarbus, 1967), whereas others reported that the images come back in a few seconds or observed recurrent reappearances of lines or parts of lines (Evans & Piggins, 1963; Gerrits, 1979; Riggs, Ratliff, Cornsweet, & Cornsweet, 1953). Complete and permanent disappearances have also been described (Campbell & Robson, 1961).

One reason for these discrepancies is the lack of a method that ensures adequate stabilization of the image, i.e., a method in which the remaining de-stabilization is so small that it cannot be observed at all in any place of the visual field (Barlow, 1969).

Stabilization techniques were developed by researchers interested in the significance of physiological eye movements (Ditchburn & Ginsborg, 1953; Riggs et al., 1953) or those who wanted to study attention (Yarbus, 1967, p. 171). Ditchburn (1973) described the different methods used nowadays to obtain a stabilized image. All workers in this field agree that a percept disappears or, at least, deteriorates severely when the image is stabilized. This means that we only continue to see thanks to the continuous displacements of the image across the retina, resulting from eye and/or head movements. One way to investigate the importance of the various components of the natural eye movements is to de-stabilize a stabilized image with these components. In order to evaluate the reports on de-stabilization it should be kept in mind that the effects of de-stabilization depend critically on the location of the boundaries of the image on the retina.

Krauskopf (1957) and Ditchburn, Fender, and Mayne (1959) were the first experimenters to de-stabilize images. They investigated the effect of sinusoidal movements of a dark or bright line projected onto the fovea. Although eye movement components below 10 Hz seemed most important, the relative effectiveness of slow drifts and rapid jerks did not become clear. Ditchburn et al. (1959) stated that the drift movements, imitated by these oscillations, are by themselves inadequate to maintain the percept. Yarbus (1959) investigated the effect of unidirectional movement and described strong bright (on-effects) and dark (off-effects) comets evoked by this displacement. Riggs and Tulunay (1959) varied the amount of stabilization to allow for different image displacements across the retina. They presented a bipartite field inside an annulus and instructed the subject to fixate in the middle. They found that the fraction of time during which an image was seen (visibility time) increased with the contrast between stimulus and background if the degree of stabilization was held constant.

Campbell and Robson (1961), Barlow (1963) and Sharpe (1972) all found a decreasing effectiveness of regular, small amplitude, movements. That this "fatigue" was not observed by Krauskopf (1957) and Ditchburn et al. (1959) may be due to non-intended de-stabilization effects and the short observation times. Recent reports on the visibility time during which a moving line in the fovea is seen were published by Ditchburn and Drysdale (1977a, 1977b) and King-Smith and Riggs (1978). These experiments showed that saccades of 4.5' provided fairly good vision if they occurred more frequently than one per second. Even drifts and tremor appeared to be sufficient to maintain tolerably good vision of high contrast targets with sharp boundaries.

Tulunay-Keesey and Bennis (1979) investigated the effect of motion on the contrast sensitivity. These authors used spatial sinusoidal gratings as stimuli and one of their conclusions was that sensitivity can be lowered, primarily during long periods of fixation and image disappearance. Most of the reports mentioned before concern the visibility of lines or blood vessels (Drysdale, 1975). Nobody has raised the question of how the visual system manages to preserve the perception of the brightness or the darkness of larger stimuli. To investigate this question we provided our stabilization set-up with an optic fiber bundle (Gerrits & Vendrik, 1974 and Fig. 26.1 in this chapter) enabling us to de-stabilize a square of 4 by 4 degrees with different movement modes. Using sinusoidal or triangular movements (amplitude: 0–120' peak to peak; frequency: 0.5–3.0 Hz), a reasonable percept of the square was generated only for the large, non-physiological amplitudes of movement. It was, however, often observed that these movements caused habituation, especially for the smaller movement amplitudes. In contrast, imitated drift and saccadic signals generated from Gaussian and binary noise signals did not cause habituation effects. Moreover, the amplitudes of the noise signals needed to evoke the perception of a nearly homogeneous bright square were much smaller than those needed when sinusoidal or triangular signals were used. However, it proved impossible to generate exactly the same percept of the square as that observed during normal vision. Our conclusion was that in order to preserve the perception of uniform brightness, the movement of the square ought to be: (a) irregular, in order to prevent habituation; (b) continuous, in order to prevent fading. Only drifts possess these characteristics and therefore they seemed important to preserve perception in the foveal and parafoveal area. The discontinuous character of the saccadic movement seemed less suited for this purpose. The same conclusion about the importance of drifts was reached by Yarbus (1967).

In order to investigate the role of drifts and saccades in normal vision for the preservation of brightness and darkness perception in different retinal locations, we recorded and analyzed the eye movements made when larger stimuli were presented. Then we de-stabilized the image with the components of the recorded as well as artificially generated eye movements. The chapter starts, however, with the description of an experiment showing that the fading time constant, determining the time required for a local brightness- or darkness-activity to diminish a certain fraction, depends on the retinal eccentricity. This is essential for understanding how drifts and saccades preserve the continuous perception of brightness and darkness.

1. HOW DOES THE FADING TIME DEPEND ON THE RETINAL LOCATION OF A STIMULUS CONTOUR?

Method

Our method to stabilize images on the retina has been described previously (Gerrits & Vendrik, 1970a): A suction cap is used (Fig. 26.1a) which adheres to the eye of the supine subject by a small underpressure (max. 30 mm Hg = 4.10^3 Pa). The cap is heated to match the temperature of the subject's eye and to avoid condensation on the lens, which would obscure vision. The eye of the subject is

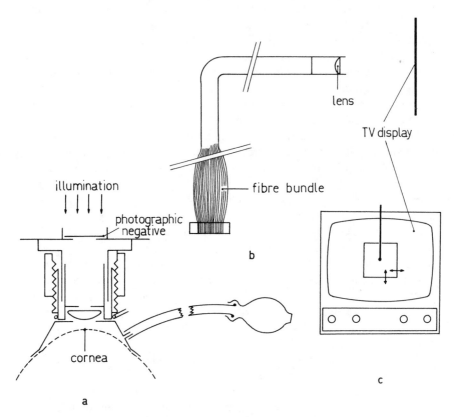

FIG. 26.1.   The suction cap, optic fiber bundle and TV display used in the stabilization set-up. (a) The subject focuses the stationary stimulus, a photographic negative, by adjusting the distance between object holder and lens. (b) The proximal end of the optic fiber bundle replaces the photographic negative when moving stimuli are to be presented. (c) The stimulus on the TV display. A bright square can be moved horizontally and vertically by artificial eye movements. The stationary disc is only observed when the stabilization is imperfect due to slippage of the suction cap.

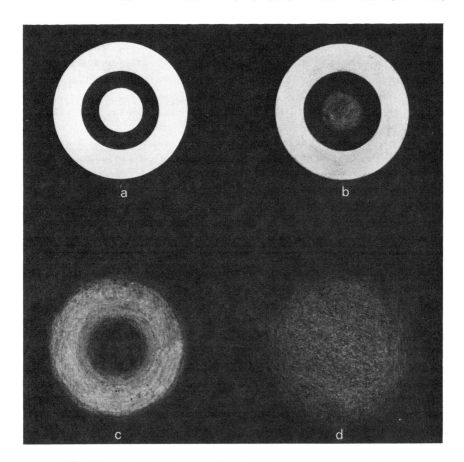

FIG. 26.2.   Activities closer to the fovea fade faster than activities further in the periphery. When an activity has disappeared it is filled in with the adjacent activity. (a) The stimulus consists of a bright disc (diameter 7°), surrounded by an equally bright annulus (inner diameter 12°, outer diameter 20°). Fixation is in the center of the bright disc. (b) The bright disc is the first to disappear and that area is filled in with the adjacent darkness-activity, resulting in a bright annulus around a uniform dark disc. (c) This darkness-activity disappears next. The homogeneous dark disc (see above) is filled in with brightness-activity from the bright annulus. (d) As soon as the dark homogeneous disc has disappeared completely a large homogeneous disc of diminishing brightness is observed which also finally disappears.

anaesthetized with novesine. The non-moving, photographic negative in the object holder is observed through a 50 diopter lens and an artificial pupil of 2 mm diameter. The field of vision is 20 degrees. Experiments to demonstrate that the foveal part of a line fades faster than the more peripheral parts (Gerrits, 1978), are very difficult because they demand an extremely high degree of stabilization.

The stimulus used here consisted of the disc and annulus shown in Fig. 26.2a. This stimulus, if fixated in the center of the disc, is much easier to stabilize because it presents no contours in the fovea. In this first experiment the subject is asked to give an accurate description of the perception of the stimulus after light-on.

Results

The results can be seen in the drawings made according to the subject's observations (Fig. 26.2b,c,d). The central parts situated closer to the fovea fade first and these faded areas are filled in with the darkness (Fig. 26.2c) or brightness (Fig. 26.2d) of the neighboring remaining part of the image. This property of the visual system is, in our opinion, important to understand the effects of the natural eye movements. The finding of West (1967) that the more peripheral parts disappear first may be attributed to imperfect stabilization. Small residual movements prevent fading in the fovea, but not in the periphery (Clarke, 1957; Clarke & Belcher, 1962; Neumeyer & Spillmann, 1977; Troxler, 1804).

2.   WHAT IS THE DISTRIBUTION OF NORMAL EYE MOVEMENTS FOR SQUARES OF DIFFERENT SIZES?

Method

In order to measure the eye movements of the subject looking at different stimuli, a modification of the method described by Robinson (1963) was adopted and built by Stassen (1980). In this set-up a small search coil, attached to the eye, moves in two perpendicularly oriented alternating electromagnetic fields driven at 30 kHz and 20 kHz for the horizontal and vertical direction, respectively. By selectively amplifying and measuring the voltages induced in the search coil by means of two lock-in amplifiers (Princeton Applied Research, model 128 A), eye movements can be accurately recorded. This search coil, designed by Collewijn, Mark, and Jansen (1975), embedded in a silicone rubber annulus, was sucked onto the sclera. The eye with the search coil was anaesthetized with novesine, the other eye was closed.

The frequency response of the system was flat from 0 Hz up to 220 Hz (-3dB) and the peak-to-peak value of the noise amounted to 18" in the 300' measuring range. As we wanted to record only the eye movements of the subject, not his head movements which also introduce voltages in the search coil, the subject's head was clamped in a suction pillow. It was found that errors due to head movements were reduced to about 3' maximal.

The eye-movement signals were recorded on tape by means of a 12-bit pulse-code modulation system (Kaiser, Munich), enabling five channels to be recorded simultaneously at a rate of 500 samples per second for each channel. The peak-to-peak noise level in the replayed signals measured about 20'. A digital computer (PDP 11/45) was used to analyze the recorded eye movements. The saccadic and intersaccadic components (drift and tremor) of the eye movements as well as the blink-associated eye movements were separated. Thereafter, the characteristics of the saccades, drifts, and tremor were calculated by determining the mean value and standard deviation of the amplitude-, frequency-, and velocity-distributions as well as the durations of the drifts (i.e., the intersaccadic intervals). A drift vector and a saccade vector were calculated from the horizontal and vertical drift and saccadic components. For further details concerning the recording and analysis see Stassen (1980).

Four subjects participated in the eye-movement recording experiments. Uniformly bright squares having a luminance of 5, 27 or 150 cd/m² and a contrast of 96% were presented on a TV display and the eye movements monitored. Squares ranged in size from 15' by 15' up to 240' by 240'. Subjects were instructed to fixate the surmised center of the square and, subsequently, to move their eyes in such a way around this center that a uniform perception of the square was obtained. Crossing the borders of the square was not allowed.

Results

Eye movements recorded during 180 sec are shown in Figs. 26.3 and 26.4 for an experienced subject (HS) and an inexperienced subject (JB). In general the eye movements increased in size with increasing dimensions of the square. Subject JB produced larger eye movements than subject HS observing a particular square size.

From the analysis of horizontal and vertical eye movement components, it was found that during the observation of small squares two to three saccades in rapid succession were made. The saccades did not show overshoots. The characteristics of the eye movements elicited by the smallest and the largest square can be found in Table 26.1 for three subjects. For all subjects the measured positions of the eye had approximately a bivariate normal distribution. Both the horizontal and vertical standard deviations increased about linearly with the length of the side of the square. The magnitude of the mean saccade vector increased with square size for subjects JB and GP by a factor of 5–6, for HS by a factor of 3. The magnitude of the mean drift vector increased much less if at all (HS). The change of the drift duration with square size was markedly different among the subjects.

The strategies followed by the subjects to produce the greater eye mobility required during the observation of increasingly larger squares were different:

–Subject JB produced larger saccades and drifts, with no systematic influence on the saccade rate;

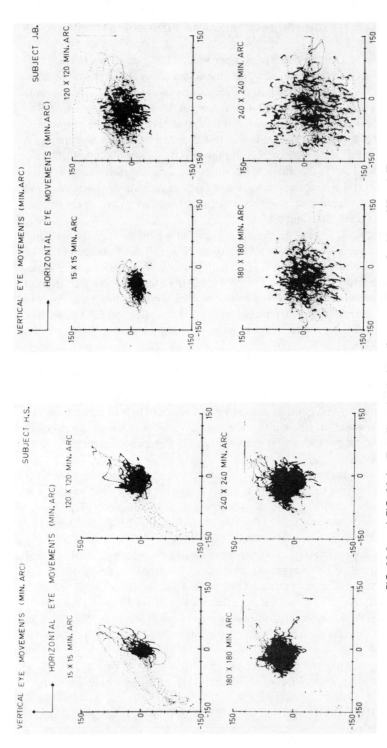

FIG. 26.3 and FIG. 26.4. Two-dimensional plots of eye movements of subjects HS and JB, recorded during 180 sec, as a function of square size. The subject's task was to move his eyes around the surmised center of the square, not outside the square, in such a way that a homogeneous image without brighter on- and darker off-borders was observed. (Note that because of DC- shifts the (0,0) position does not necessarily coincide with the center of the observed square.)

446

TABLE 26.1

	Subject HS		Subject GP		Subject JB	
Square size (min. arc)	15 × 15	240 × 240	15 × 15	240 × 240	15 × 15	240 × 240
Mean drift duration (seconds)	1.25	0.37	0.80	0.50	0.76	0.75
Mean saccade vector magnitude (min. arc)	8.6	25.6	13.7	80.5	18.8	94.5
Mean drift vector magnitude (min. arc)	9.2	8.6	5.9	7.2	7.9	13.9
Mean drift vector velocity (min. arc/sec)	20.3	38.2	16.4	22.9	16.6	25.3

—Subject HS produced only larger and more frequent saccades without any systematic influence on the drift vector magnitude;

—Subject GP produced mainly larger and more frequent saccades while his drift vector magnitude increased only slightly.

For all three subjects the mean drift vector velocity increased about equally during the observation of larger stimuli.

The following general conclusion can be drawn: A greater mobility of the eye is required to maintain the percept of brightness in larger squares. This greater mobility is mainly brought about by the saccades.

3. CAN A FADED PERCEPT BE RESTORED BY DE-STABILIZATION?

Method

In the stabilization set-up (Gerrits & Vendrik, 1974) a square was de-stabilized with either formerly recorded drifts or saccades or a combination of drifts and saccades. So we investigated the effectiveness of the eye movement components for the restoration of brightness and darkness. This was done by replacing the photographic negative (Fig. 26.1a) by the proximal end of a coherent optic fiber bundle directed to a color TV display on which the stimulus was presented (Fig. 26.1b). The thickest optic fiber bundle we used contained 160,000 individual fibers, each of 10 micron diameter, equaling 1.8′ in the visual field when a 50 diopter lens was used. The diameter of the visual field of this bundle was 13 deg. The stiff protecting mantle of the fiber bundle was removed over a length of 30 cm in order to allow the bundle to follow the subject's eye movements. These eye movements did not affect the position of the image on the subject's retina as long as the suction cap adhered well to his eye (Fig. 26.1a). The optic fiber bundle had, however, a small braking effect and, therefore could cause slippage.

To enable the subject to distinguish between a percept generated by a genuine stimulus movement or by an unwanted slippage of the suction cap, a small black disc at the end of a non-moving stalk was placed in front of the color TV display. This disc functioned as a control spot relative to the moving square (Fig. 26.1c) and enabled the center of the square to be projected onto the fovea before the onset of the movement of the square.

The stimulus was a uniform, bright square of 4 by 4 deg and its luminance (5 cd/m^2; 27 cd/m^2) was corrected for the loss of light occurring in the fiber bundle and at the artificial pupil present in the suction cap. After the subject reported the disappearance of the bright square, the experimenter started to move it on the screen. Two trained subjects (HG, HS) participating in these experiments were asked to describe their percepts.

(a) First, the previously recorded eye movements (section 2) were used to move the square over the retina. However, it proved impossible to determine the efficiency of the drifts or the saccades in this way as these eye movements were interrupted by the recorded blinks. These blinks drove the square off the screen of the TV display and thereafter presented the square as a new stimulus at the end of the blink movement. The blinks occurred three to seven times per minute. As their frequency spectrum overlapped with the spectrum of the other eye-movement components, they could not be removed by filtering.

(b) Because of this difficulty, an 8-sec section of the eye-movement record having no blinks was used in an endless loop. However, the resulting presentation of the square caused strong fluctuations in the generated percepts. These fluctuations correlated with the movement pattern. Moreover, the subjects soon recognized the recurrent sequence of the endless loop.

(c) Obviously, real eye movements could not be used to answer the question whether saccades or drifts or both were needed to preserve vision. Therefore, it was decided to imitate the drifts and saccades, their characteristics being determined from the computer analysis. Artificial drift signals were generated by low-pass filtering (0.1–3 Hz: -6 dB/oct; above 3 Hz: -12 dB/oct) and amplifying (15′–240′ peak to peak) Gaussian noise to match the specific drift properties of each subject. The saccades were imitated by a sequence of jumps with normally distributed amplitudes (0–300′ peak to peak). Constant saccade frequencies ranging from 1–5 jumps/sec were used. The combination of these artificial signals enabled the experimenter to move the stimulus with various combinations of drifts and saccades. When the subject indicated that the image had disappeared, the experimenter started to destabilize this image by the artificial drifts, artificial saccades, or both. It should be remembered that these signals showed the same amplitude distribution and frequency spectrum as the eye movements recorded when a subject observed the same square in the non-stabilized condition. To distinguish the different perceptual stages, the following scale was adopted:

0–Nothing at all, or only occasionally on- and off-borders while the rest of the stimulus remained as dark as the background.

2–A square with on- and off-borders and a very weak brightness in the center which is just detectable against the background.

4–A square with on- and off-borders and a weak brightness in the center which is clearly brighter than the background.

6–A square with on- and occasionally off-borders and a center brightness which is clearly lower than the on-borders.

8–A homogeneous, bright square with occasionally on-borders near the contours.

10–A homogeneous, bright square without any borders near the contours.

Uneven numbers were used to describe percepts in between the above described classes. Apart from these descriptions a row of drawings had been produced. Drawing 10 represented a homogeneous bright square of 100% brightness. In drawings 8, 6, 4 and 2 the center brightness was 85, 75, 60 and 30% of the center brightness of drawing 10. Also in these drawings on-borders were indicated.

The subjects were able to judge the quality of the percept during the experiment by comparing the brightness of the midpart of the square with that of the on-borders. Moreover, they refreshed their memory of the adopted scale by consulting the drawings before and after each experiment.

Results

As a result of the de-stabilization, the subject observed bright on-borders, dark off-borders (Gerrits & Vendrik, 1970b), and an inhomogeneous brightness in the center of the square. Bright on-borders were only generated at that location of the retina which was newly illuminated as a result of a stimulus movement. Dark off-borders arose where the illumination was switched off. Between these borders darkness and brightness were induced: darkness adjacent to the on-border and brightness adjacent to the off-border. The spreading of this induced brightness and darkness to the center of the square resulted in an inhomogeneous percept. The presence and strength of this brightness- and darkness-activity depended on the movement amplitude, the frequency and the location of the stimulus on the retina.

For both subjects (HG, HS) at least 20 to 30 sec of movement were needed before the midpart of the moving square had acquired its maximal brightness although it still fluctuated in time. Altogether it took 2 to 3 minutes of observation before they could decide on the quality of the percept. This time was needed both to average the fluctuating percept and to discard observations resulting from slippage of the suction cap (see Methods).

The outcome is given in Table 26.2. When the square was moved only with the imitated *drift signals*, subject HG classified the percept with scale number 6

TABLE 26.2

Subject	Stimulus Luminance cd/m²	Retinal Illumin. td$_{eff}$	Percept Qualification (Midpart Brightness in % of On-set)		
			Drifts Only	Saccades Only	Drifts + Saccades
HG	5	90	6 (75%)	7 (80%)	7 (80%)
	27	430	7 (80%)	7 (80%)	7–8 (80–85%)
HS	5	70	2–6 (30–75%)	7–8 (80–85%)	7–8 (80–85%)
	27	290	2–6 (30–75%)	7–8 (80–85%)	7–8 (80–85%)

and 7 for the darker (5 cd/m²) and brighter (27 cd/m²) square, respectively. In comparison, the classification by subject HS varied from 2 to 6. For both subjects the quality increased to 9 (90% of the brightness at on-set) if the artificial drift amplitude was increased to five times the level measured during the eye-movement recording (not shown in Table 26.2). When the square was moved with artificial *saccade signals,* the percept for subject HG was largely unchanged, whereas subject HS obtained better and less fluctuating percepts than with drift signals. When the artificial saccade amplitude was increased above the physiologically recorded values, the observed brightness also increased for both subjects. When the saccadic frequency was increased, the quality of the percept increased only slightly for subject HG, but considerably for subject HS in the 1 to 3 Hz range. Also with this type of movement the brightness values attributed to the percept fluctuated, mainly as a result of the noisy character of the movements. The combination of artificial drifts and artificial saccades did not improve the percept substantially.

It should be noted that the percept of the square, indicated by scale number 8 and the brightness observed in the midpart of the image (85%), is about equal to that perceived during the recording of the restricted eye movements. Remember that this restriction did not allow the subjects to obtain an optimal percept.

Discussion

From the fact that even an increase of the amplitudes of the artificial eye movements did not result in a normal percept we realized that in all these experiments the movements were started after the image had completely faded. Could it be that the normal eye movements do not *generate* but *preserve* the percept of brightness? A number of additional experiments showed that it made no difference whether the artificial eye movements were started at light-on or after complete fading of the image.

In normal vision the image deteriorates only if the subject stares at the stimulus by fixating a part of it, i.e., by pseudo-stabilization. By deterioration we mean the occurrence of on-borders and off-borders and/or the occurrence of brightness fluctuations in the square. A preliminary experiment showed that the image of a stationary, non-stabilized square of 4 by 4 deg did not fade or deteriorate if the subject was allowed to move his fovea at and across the contours, inside and outside the square, instead of only around the surmised center of the square (as in the previous experiment, section 2). Again the subject still limited the amplitudes of his saccades. He did not blink. The results of this experiment suggested that the distance between the fovea and a contour of the square is an important parameter in normal vision. Van Erning, in our group, started to investigate the influence of this distance on the perception.

4. IS THE REQUIRED IMAGE MOVEMENT DETERMINED BY RETINAL ECCENTRICITY OF THE CONTOURS?

Method

Four experiments were undertaken with LvE and HG serving as subjects. A homogeneous, bright square (4° by 4°, 63 cd/m²) and a fixation spot (10' by 10', 300 cd/m²) on a background of 6 cd/m² served as stimuli on a TV display. The square and the fixation spot could be moved independently. Each separate movement in the horizontal as well as in the vertical direction was controlled by an electrical signal. These signals were generated such that their combined action positioned either the fixation point at a constant distance from the contours of the stationary square or moved the contour of the square at a constant distance from the stationary fixation spot. An example of subsequent locations of the fixation spot, at a constant but adjustable distance D from the contours of the stationary square, is given in Fig. 26.5. The sequence of locations of the fixation spot on the "imaginary square" was chosen by a constantly running special purpose random generator. The sequence of the jumps displacing the square or the fixation spot was different in each trial of an experiment. Within an experiment the distance D was adjusted to 0.5°, 1°, 1.5° or 1.75° and the frequency was set at 0.5, 1, 1.5, 2 or 3 jumps per second. The task of the subject was to indicate *when* he detected any non-uniformity of the bright square. The time duration T_{hom} between the start of the movement and this moment was considered to reflect the effectiveness of the movement to preserve brightness.

In the first experiment the square jumped around and the subject had to fixate the stationary spot. His eye movements were monitored. In the second experiment the subjects had to follow the jumping fixation spot while the square was stationary. The eye movements were monitored again. From the records it was found that the subjects managed to follow the spot correctly only if the number of jumps did not exceed two per second. In the third experiment the subjects inspected the jumping homogeneous square through the stabilization set-up (Fig.

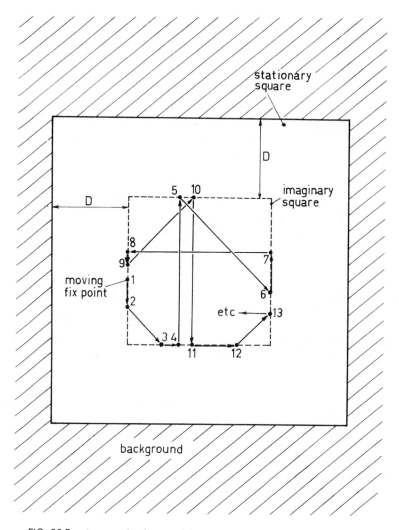

FIG. 26.5.   An example of a part of the movement sequence of the fixation spot on a stationary square of 4 by 4 deg. The subject had to follow the spot which remained at a fixed distance D from the nearest contour of the square. The reader can carry out the same experiment if he fixates the subsequent numbers in the figures.

26.1). The fixation spot, being stabilized, disappeared. Under all three conditions, the bright image deteriorated notwithstanding the movements imposed on it. We therefore decided to use a different sequence of jumps. In the fourth experiment, a certain sequence of jumps lasting maximally 64 sec) was presented again and again as an endless loop. The movement could be started each time from the same point in the sequence as well as from any other point. Experiments 1 and 2 were repeated with this "endless movement."

Results

During fixation, the image of a jumping square deteriorated after a few seconds, in other cases after tens of seconds, if the fovea remained 0.5 deg or more from the contours. Although the distance D was kept constant, the time duration T_{hom} fluctuated heavily within one session. When the square was stationary and the spot jumped, the subjects perceived the same deterioration and again T_{hom} fluctuated heavily. Also in the stabilized condition it was found that T_{hom} fluctuated.

In all these experiments the bright image deteriorated in spite of the movements imposed on it, sometimes sooner, sometimes later. Besides the question of why the movements of the square did not preserve the homogeneous image with any combination of the distance D and the frequency of jumping, the problem arose as to why the time duration T_{hom} fluctuated so much. It proved to be due to the different successions of jump amplitudes within each sequence. When the sequence was started at arbitrary points, i.e., datarecorder not triggered, the time duration T_{hom} fluctuated. However, when the movement was started a number of times from the same point in the sequence, i.e., datarecorder triggered, the duration time T_{hom} fluctuated much less. When another starting point was chosen by the experimenter, the repeated presentation of the movement resulted in a different, nearly constant time duration T_{hom}. If at each presentation the sequence of movements was started from the same point, the subjects were able to indicate *where* they observed changes within the original homogeneous image and *what aspect* of the percept had changed (brightness, borders). The outcomes proved that the character of the imposed movements caused the perceptual fluctuations. To demonstrate this relation the movement pattern was registered on line on an X-Y-recorder. The percept of the subject was so strongly related to the movements that the experimenter, watching the movement pattern, was able to tell the subject when and at what position within the image the subject had observed a deterioration, as he knew from experience that a number of small saccades followed by a larger one resulted in deterioration. A decrease of the distance D (fovea closer to the stimulus contours) resulted in a longer period of homogeneous perception (compare with the results of section 3).

DISCUSSION OF THE IMPORTANCE OF DRIFTS AND SACCADES

In the following we discuss the basic ideas about the cooperation of the drifts and saccades in preventing fading of brightness in uniform areas.

Receptive fields and their psychophysical analogs, perceptive fields (Jung &

Spillmann, 1970) are small near the fovea (Spillmann, 1971) but become increasingly larger towards the periphery (Kornhuber & Spillmann, 1964). Natural eye movements continuously activate the cells having these receptive fields by changing the amount of illumination. No movement means no change and this results in the gradual disappearance of the percept observed after the on-set of the illumination. A small movement of a contour located at a large retinal receptive field may insufficiently change the illumination within this field. In that case the image fades in spite of the eye movement. Thus, the effective movement amplitude is always closely related to the diameter of the receptive field at the location of the stimulus contour.

As a result it is understandable that it is extremely difficult to stabilize foveal images: Residual eye movements present with most stabilization methods are highly effective in the foveal area which has the smallest receptive fields but not in the periphery where receptive fields are larger.

Even if the eye movements suffice to move the contours of a large square adequately over the local receptive fields preventing fading there, receptive fields that are located in the center of the square receive a constant illumination. This part of the image could be considered as stabilized and should therefore disappear. What happens, however, is that these parts of the image are filled in with the brightness and eventually the color of the surrounding nonfading parts. An example of this behavior, as observed in a stabilization experiment, was shown in Fig. 26.2b,c,d. From this and several other stabilization experiments, it was found that the fading time constant, determining the time required for a local brightness- or darkness-activity to diminish a certain fraction, is much smaller in the fovea than in the periphery. An image in the fovea may fade fast, within a second, while the same image located in the far periphery may need seconds to disappear. Note, that this is not contrary to what is found in Troxler fading and the decrement of the fading time with the eccentricity of the stimulus contour, as observed by Neumeyer and Spillmann (1977). In both cases foveal fading is prevented by the fixational eye movements. Their observations have to be attributed to the decreasing effectiveness of residual eye movements with increasing eccentricity.

The increase of the receptive (and perceptive) field diameter and the increase of the fading time constant towards the periphery play an important role in the effectiveness of our eye movements, the continuous, small amplitude drifts, and the larger amplitude saccades.

Suppose we had only the drift movements to displace the image across the retina and the stimulus, i.e., a square was presented in such a way that its center fell upon the fovea. As the fovea moves around this center in accordance with the drift movements, the contours of the square move with the same amplitude. Whether these amplitudes are adequate to prevent the image from fading depends, of course, on the diameter of the receptive fields at the location of the contours. Large objects will fade, as is easily confirmed by fixating the surmised center of a large square.

In other words, the drifts are capable of preserving the perception of stimuli in and around the fovea but not of stimuli with contours far outside the fovea. What function have saccades in preserving vision of large squares?

Imagine the situation that the fovea is located in point 1 (see Fig. 26.6a) of a large square and drifts around that point. The part of the border denoted A-B is close to the fovea: The drift movement effectively changes the illumination of the receptive fields located there and activates the corresponding brightness-signalling cells (Jung, 1961). The local brightness-activity, mediated by these cells and resulting from the foveal stimulation, fades fairly fast but the continuous drift movements, activating new brightness-signalling cells and re-activating others, makes up for the short fading time. For the cells with larger receptive fields on the opposite side of the square (part C-D of the contour, Fig. 26.6a), the drift movement is insufficient. The corresponding brightness-activity begins to fade immediately after a saccade has ended, but here fading occurs more slowly. For another part of the contour, between E and F (Fig. 26.6a), the fading time of the corresponding brightness-activity lies in between those of the brightness-activities resulting from stimulation of areas A–B and C–D.

When a saccade is made, from point 1 to point 2 (see Fig. 26.6a), the square is repositioned with respect to the fovea, as shown in Fig. 26.6b, it will be seen that the fovea is now close to an adjacent border and activities are generated there by the drift movements. The slowly fading brightness-activity corresponding to the former border C–D is completely neutralized by darkness-activity (Gerrits & Vendrik, 1970a). This is indicated in the figure by "light-off." Adjacent to the part E–F of the former contour new activity is generated by the newly illuminated part (indicated by "light-on").

Thus, saccades are needed because with drifts alone we would be unable to preserve vision of large stimuli. But can we preserve vision with saccades only? The saccades activate large new parts of the retina by moving the eye. At the same time, however, they bring the fovea close to the borders of the stimulus. The brightness-activity originating from the foveal area will fade rapidly when the image is not moved in between the saccades. The drift is needed to prevent the fading of that part of the image located in and around the fovea. So we need both drifts and saccades for large stimuli.

It is therefore understandable why the amplitudes of the drift did not increase with the size of the square (section 2). All subjects increased their saccade amplitudes considerably, but their drift amplitudes increased only slightly as larger squares were presented. If one of the tasks of the saccades is to bring the fovea close to the contours of the stimulus, the saccade amplitude should indeed increase with square size. Once the fovea is displaced near a contour there is no need for the drift to increase its amplitude as the cells with small receptive fields present around the fovea are effectively activated as a result of the drift movement.

It proved impossible to preserve or to restore the original homogeneous bright percept of the square by moving the square with the artificial eye movements. A

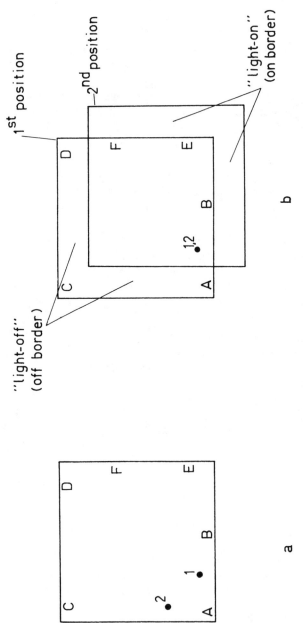

FIG. 26.6a. When the eye drifts around the fixation spot (1), the area A–B is effectively activated, area E–F less and area C–D the least. The brightness-activities in these peripheral areas fade, but slowly. Then the fovea jumps to the new position of the fixation spot (2).

FIG. 26.6b. The image is now displaced from position 1 to position 2. If the brightness-activity in area E–F has faded too far the brightness-activity in the newly illuminated part of the retina ("light-on") is stronger than that in area E–F and an on-border is reported. If the brightness-activity in area C–D has faded too far the darkness-activity in this darkened part of the retina ("light-off") is stronger than the residual brightness-activity and an off-border is reported in area C–D.

further analysis of the artificial and real eye movements to reveal differences, not encountered so far, is in progress.

Finally, we may remark that physically, in the stabilized condition, a moving stimulus is equivalent to a stationary stimulus seen by the moving eye. The experimental results over the last years have strengthened our belief in the equivalence of stimulus movement and eye movement for the perception of brightness and darkness. As for the perception of movement, the two conditions are different because in the latter case no movement of the stimulus is observed. Stevens, Emerson, Gerstein, Kallos, Neufeld, Nichols, & Rosenquist (1976) came to the same conclusion when they described the visual perceptions of three subjects paralyzed with curare.

ACKNOWLEDGMENTS

The students Jo Beelen, Gerard Peters and Peter Cox contributed considerably to the results. Cor van Kemenade and Arnold Brunekreeft solved the technical problems and assisted in the experiments. The authors are also grateful for the secretarial help of Janny Gerrits, Diny Piersma and Marianne de Leng.

REFERENCES

Barlow, H. B. Slippage of contact lenses and other artefacts in relation to fading and regeneration of supposedly stable retinal images. *Quarterly Journal of Experimental Psychology*, 1963, *15*, 36–51.

Barlow, H. B. Stabilized retinal images. In W. Reichardt (Ed.), *Proceedings of the International School of Physics Enrico Fermi, Course XLIII. Processing of optical data by organisms and machines*. Varenna, July 1968. New York: Academic Press, 1969.

Campbell, F. W., & Robson, J. G. A fresh approach to stabilized retinal images. *Journal of Physiology (London)*, 1961, *159*, 11P–12P.

Clarke, F. J. J. Rapid light adaptation of localised areas of the extra foveal retina. *Optica Acta*, 1957, *4*, 69–77.

Clarke, F. J. J., & Belcher, S. J. On the localization of Troxler's effect in the visual pathway. *Vision Research*, 1962, *2*, 53–68.

Collewijn, H., Mark, F. v.d., & Jansen, T. C. Precise recording of human eye movements. *Vision Research*, 1975, *15*, 447–450.

Ditchburn, R. W. *Eye-movements and visual perception*. Clarendon Press, Oxford: 1973.

Ditchburn, R. W., & Drysdale, A. E. The effect of retinal-image movements on vision. I. Step-movements and pulse-movements. *Proceedings of the Royal Society of London*, 1977, *B 197*, 131–144. (a)

Ditchburn, R. W., & Drysdale, A. E. The effect of retinal-image movements on vision. II. Oscillatory movements. *Proceedings of the Royal Society of London*, 1977, *B 197*, 385–406. (b)

Ditchburn, R. W., Fender, D. H., & Mayne, S. M. Vision with controlled movements of the retinal image. *Journal of Physiology (London)*, 1959, *145*, 98–107.

Ditchburn, R. W., & Ginsborg, B. L. Involuntary eye movements during fixation. *Journal of Physiology (London)*, 1953, *119*, 1–17.

Ditchburn, R. W., & Pritchard, R. M. Stabilized interference fringes on the retina. *Nature*, 1956, *177*, 434.

Drysdale, A. E. The visibility of retinal blood vessels. *Vision Research*, 1975, *15*, 813–818.

Evans, C. R., & Piggins, D. J. A comparison of the behaviour of geometrical shapes when viewed under conditions of steady fixation, and with apparatus for producing a stabilised retinal image. *The British Journal of Physiological Optics*, 1963, *20*, 1–13.

Gerrits, H. J. M. Differences in peripheral and foveal effects observed in stabilized vision. *Experimental Brain Research*, 1978, *32*, 225–244.

Gerrits, H. J. M. Apparent movements induced by stroboscopic illumination of stabilized images. *Experimental Brain Research*, 1979, *34*, 471–488.

Gerrits, H. J. M., Haan, B. de, & Vendrik, A. J. H. Experiments with retinal stabilized images. Relations between the observations and neural data. *Vision Research*, 1966, *6*, 427–440.

Gerrits, H. J. M., & Vendrik, A. J. H. Simultaneous contrast, filling-in process and information processing in man's visual system. *Experimental Brain Research*, 1970, *11*, 411–430. (a)

Gerrits, H. J. M., & Vendrik, A. J. H. Artificial movements of a stabilized image. *Vision Research*, 1970, *10*, 1443–1456. (b)

Gerrits, H. J. M., & Vendrik, A. J. H. The influence of stimulus movements on perception in parafoveal stabilized vision. *Vision Research*, 1974, *14*, 175–180.

Kornhuber, H. H. & Spillmann, L. Zur visuellen Feldorganisation beim Menschen: Die receptiven Felder im peripheren und zentralen Gesichtsfeld bei Simultankontrast, Flimmerfusion, Scheinbewegung und Blickfolgebewegung. *Pflügers Archiv für die gesamte Physiologie*, 1964, *279*R 5–6.

Jung, R. Korrelationen von Neuronentätigkeit und Sehen. In R. Jung & H. Kornhuber (Eds.), *The visual system: Neurophysiology and psychophysics*. Berlin: Springer-Verlag, 1961.

Jung, R., & Spillmann, L. Receptive field estimation and perceptual integration in human vision. In F. A. Young & D. B. Lindsley (Eds.), *Early experience and visual information processing in perceptual and reading disorders*. Washington D.C.: Proceedings of the National Academy of Sciences, 1970.

King-Smith, P. E., & Riggs, L. A. Visual sensitivity to controlled motion of a line or edge. *Vision Research*, 1978, *18*, 1509–1520.

Krauskopf, J. Effect of retinal image motion on contrast thresholds for maintaining vision. *Journal of the Optical Society of America*, 1957, *47*, 740–747.

Neumeyer, C. & Spillmann, L. Fading of steadily fixated large test fields in extra-foveal vision. *Pflügers Archiv European Journal of Physiology*, 1977, *368*, R 40.

Riggs, L. A., Ratliff, F., Cornsweet, J. C., & Cornsweet, T. N. The disappearance of steadily fixated visual test objects. *Journal of the Optical Society of America*, 1953, *43*, 495–501.

Riggs, L. A., & Tulunay, S. U. Visual effects of varying the extent of compensation for eye movements. *Journal of the Optical Society of America*, 1959, *49*, 741–745.

Robinson, D. A. A method of measuring eye movement using a scleral search coil in a magnetic field. *The Institute of Electrical and Electronics Engineers Transactions on Biomedical Electronics*, 1963, *10*, 137–145.

Sharpe, C. R. The visibility and fading of thin lines visualized by their controlled movement across the retina. *Journal of Physiology (London)*, 1972, *222*, 113–134.

Spillmann, L. Foveal perceptive fields in the human visual system measured with simultaneous contrast in grids and bars. *Pflügers Archiv European Journal of Physiology*, 1971, *326*, 281–299.

Stassen, H. P. W. *Measurements and analysis of eye movements and their role in the process of visual brightness perception*. Thesis, Catholic University, Nijmegen, The Netherlands, 1980.

Stevens, J. K., Emerson, R. C., Gerstein, G. L., Kallos, T., Neufeld, G. R., Nichols, C. W., & Rosenquist, A. C. Paralysis of the awake human: visual perceptions. *Vision Research*, 1976, *16*, 93–98.

Troxler, D. Über das Verschwinden gegebener Gegenstände innerhalb unseres Gesichsskreises. *Ophthalmologische Bibliothek* (Himly and Schmidt, Eds., Jena). *2*, 51–53 (1804).

Tulunay-Keesey, U., & Bennis, B. J. Effects of stimulus onset and image motion on contrast sensitivity. *Vision Research,* 1979, *19*, 767–774.

West, D. C. Brightness discrimination with a stabilised retinal image. *Vision Research,* 1967, *7*, 949–974.

Yarbus, A. L. The perception of images moving across the retina at a fixed speed. *Biophysics*, 1959, *4*, 70–80.

Yarbus, A. L. Eye movements and vision. (Translation editor, L. A. Riggs.) New York: Plenum Press, 1967.

27

Brightness Matching and Scaling of the Ehrenstein Illusion

Kenneth Fuld
Kathleen O'Donnell
University of New Hampshire

ABSTRACT

Brightness enhancement in the Ehrenstein illusion was measured using brightness matching and magnitude estimation. In one experiment, Ehrenstein patterns varied in number of constituent radial lines from 2 to 32. In another experiment, the size of the illusory area was varied from 9 to 34 min of visual angle. Increasing the number of lines resulted in increased brightness contrast. Over the restricted range of gap sizes investigated, the brightness effect was enhanced with increases of gap size. A receptive field model is proposed to accommodate these findings.

The standard version of the Ehrenstein brightness illusion (Ehrenstein, 1941, 1954) is produced by four black radial lines placed at right angles to each other on a white background. The lines do not intersect; instead the endpoints of the lines are equidistant from the potential point of intersection. In the resulting gap between the endpoints, an area of enhanced brightness appears relative to the area surrounding it. With white lines on a black background, the central area appears darker than the surround. When the lines are narrow, the area of brightness contrast is circumscribed by a subjective contour. Thicker lines produce an illusory square. Another illusion that has properties similar to those of the Ehrenstein illusion is the Kanizsa triangle (Kanizsa, 1974). This illusion has a triangular subjective contour, and the area within the contour appears to be brighter than the surround when the inducing pattern is of lower luminance than the background, and vice versa.

There are two general hypotheses accounting for the origin of these effects, one based on a neurophysiological mechanism and one suggesting a high-order,

461

cognitive process. According to the neurophysiological account (Brigner & Gallagher, 1974; Day & Jory, 1978; Frisby & Clatworthy, 1975; Jung & Spillmann, 1970; Spillmann, Fuld, & Gerrits, 1976), brightness and darkness information are extracted on the basis of receptive field organization. Although there are differences with regard to the proposed site along the visual pathway that mediates the brightness effect, the proponents of this hypothesis agree that receptive field organization in the primary visual pathway is the basis for the brightness illusion.

In general, the focus of attention for the cognitive hypothesis is on the subjective contour effect rather than the brightness effect (Bradley & Dumais, 1975; Coren, 1972; Coren & Theodor, 1975; Gregory, 1972; Kanizsa, 1974; Kennedy & Lee, 1976). The subjective contours are proposed to be a function of such cognitive factors as the processing of implicit depth cues and the Gestalt principles of closure and good continuation.

The effect of modifying certain parameters of the Kanizsa and Ehrenstein patterns on the resulting brightness contrast might allow for a better understanding of the origin of these illusions. Spillmann (1975), for example, has described how structural changes of the Ehrenstein pattern alter the magnitude of the brightness contrast effect. He found that increasing the width of the lines, introducing textured backgrounds, and increasing the number of radial lines each enhances the brightness contrast of the illusory area. These findings, corroborating the observations of Ehrenstein (1941, 1954), are generally consistent with a physiological account of the Ehrenstein illusion. This was a purely descriptive study, however, with no attempt made to quantify the perceived differences in brightness.

Dumais and Bradley (1976) determined the effect of level of illuminance and retinal image size of the illusory area on the apparent strength of the subjective contour in the Kanizsa triangle. They found that contour strength was inversely proportional to both the visual angle subtended by the illusory area and the illumination of the figure. This supported earlier observations of others (Coren, 1972; Ehrenstein, 1941, 1954; Kanizsa, 1974; Schumann, 1904). Although these investigators measured the relative strength of the subjective contour, their results may be generalized to the brightness contrast effect as well. There is evidence (Jory & Day, 1979) that the strength of the subjective contour correlates positively with the amount of contrast-induced brightness in these illusions. The smallest size of the illusory area, or gap, examined by Dumais and Bradley was 1.2 deg (corresponding to the side of an illusory equilateral triangle). The question arises as to what happens with smaller gap sizes. This would seem to be relevant to a hypothesis based on receptive field organization, since it is just such angles that correspond to assumed receptive field sizes in man.

The purpose of the study reported here was to expand on Dumais and Bradley's as well as Spillmann's findings by quantifying the effect of two structural changes of the Ehrenstein pattern on the resulting brightness contrast. Brightness differences were induced by varying the number of radial lines in the figure or varying the retinal image size of the illusory area for small visual angles. Brightness was assessed by both a matching and a scaling procedure.

EXPERIMENT 1

The aim of this experiment was to measure the brightness contrast produced by Ehrenstein patterns varying in number of radial lines.

Method

A two-channel projection system was used. Light for both channels was provided by a 45 W tungsten-halogen lamp. One channel projected the slide(s) of the Ehrenstein pattern onto a white screen, while the other projected a comparison stimulus onto the screen. The subject varied the intensity of the comparison stimulus by turning a neutral density wedge. The size of the comparison stimulus was regulated by use of an iris diaphragm serving as the field stop. A chin and forehead rest was employed to maintain the subject's position.

Four experimentally naive subjects were shown a series of slides with different numbers of radial black lines comprising the Ehrenstein pattern. There were five different stimulus slides with radial lines numbering 2, 4, 8, 16, 32. All radial lines were of a constant size (44 min in length and 2 min in width). The diameter of the gap within the inside endpoints of the lines was 20 min. The patterns were of high contrast.

There were two conditions in the experiment. In Condition 1 (magnitude estimation), the subjects were instructed to fixate a point midway between two Ehrenstein patterns. The center of each pattern was 1.0 deg away from the fixation point along the horizontal meridian. The pattern on the right, consisting of eight lines, served as the modulus, and the brightness of its gap was assigned a value of 10. The subjects were instructed to assign a value to the Ehrenstein pattern on the left representing the brightness of its gap compared to that of the modulus. The five stimuli were presented in a random order, five times each, during a single test session. There was no restriction on the length of time each stimulus was viewed. All observations were made binocularly and in a room illuminated only by light from the optical system. Background luminance was -0.42 log ft-L.

For Condition 2 (brightness matching) a round comparison field, the same size as the gap of each of the Ehrenstein patterns, was projected onto the screen, 1.0 deg to the right of the fixation point. The field was slightly defocused in order to match the appearance of the area of brightness enhancement. One of the five Ehrenstein patterns was projected to the left of fixation, 1.0 deg away. The subjects were instructed to fixate the fixation point and to adjust a knob controlling the wedge position until the comparison field was equal in brightness to the brightness of the gap in the illusion. Five matches were made for each pattern. Patterns were presented randomly. There was no limit on the length of observation time. Background luminance for this condition was −0.27 log ft-L.

For both Conditions 1 and 2, the subjects dark-adapted for 15 min at the beginning of each session.

Results

Figure 27.1a shows the individual data from the magnitude estimation task. Log estimated brightness is on the axis of ordinates, and number of lines is on the axis of abscissae. All subjects but A generally show an increase of brightness with number of lines. The mean values of the four subjects are plotted in Fig. 27.1b and show scaled brightness increasing with number of lines. The difference between the estimated brightness of a 2-line pattern and that of a 32-line pattern is 0.64 log unit. Most of the difference occurs from 2 to 8 lines.

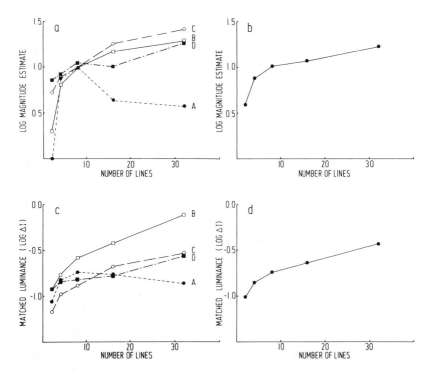

FIG. 27.1.   Brightness contrast in Ehrenstein patterns varying in number of radial lines: (a) magnitude estimation of brightness in the Ehrenstein illusion: individual subjects; (b) group mean magnitude estimates; (c) incremental luminance of a spot required to match the brightness in the Ehrenstein illusion: individual subjects; (d) group mean brightness matches.

Figure 27.1c shows the individual data for the brightness-matching condition. Matched luminance (logδI) is on the axis of ordinates and number of lines is on the axis of abscissae. Again, all but A show an increase of brightness as number of lines increases. The mean values of the four subjects (Fig. 27.1d) show the difference in brightness between the 2- and 32- line pattern to be 0.58 log unit.

EXPERIMENT 2

In this experiment, the effect of varying the gap size in the Ehrenstein pattern on the resulting brightness contrast was investigated.

Method

The same apparatus and two procedures were employed as those in Experiment I, except that instead of number of lines, gap size varied. Four different subjects were shown a series of slides in which the diameter of the gap of an 8-line Ehrenstein pattern was varied in visual angle. Five different visual angles were used (9, 16, 20, 26, and 34 min). The length and width of the constituent lines remained constant (44 and 2 min, respectively). The modulus in Condition 1 was an 8-line pattern with a gap size of 20 min. The comparison spot in Condition 2 was of constant size (20 min) for all stimulus presentations.

Results

The magnitude estimation results for individual subjects are plotted in Fig. 27.2a. Log estimated brightness is on the axis of ordinates, and gap size is on the axis of abscissae. There is close agreement among the curves, each showing an increase of brightness as gap size increases. The group mean data are shown in Fig. 27.2b. Over the range of gap sizes examined, the increase of brightness is 0.8 log unit. Results from the brightness matching task are shown in Fig. 27.2c (individual data) and 27.2d (group mean data). Matched luminance (logδI) is plotted as a function of gap size. Brightness assessed in this manner is shown to increase with increases of gap size. The total effect here is 0.23 log unit.

DISCUSSION

In Experiment I, both magnitude estimation and brightness matching showed an increasing, monotonic function when plotted against number of lines in the Ehrenstein pattern. Thus, the qualitative observation of Spillmann (1975) was confirmed.

In Experiment II, both magnitude estimation and brightness matching also yielded increasing, monotonic functions when plotted against size of the illusory

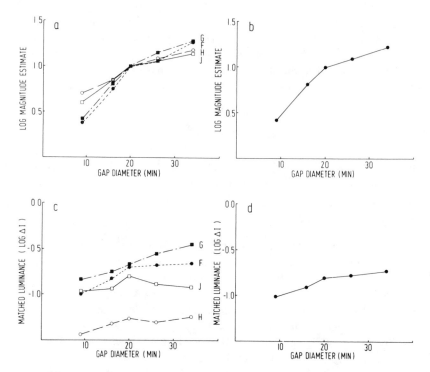

FIG. 27.2. Brightness contrast in Ehrenstein patterns varying in gap size: (a) magnitude estimation of brightness in the Ehrenstein illusion: individual subjects; (b) group mean magnitude estimates; (c) incremental luminance of a spot of constant size required to match the brightness in the Ehrenstein illusion: individual subjects; (d) group mean brightness matches.

gap. This is surprising in view of Dumais and Bradley's (1976) results and the qualitative observations of others (Coren, 1972; Ehrenstein, 1941, 1954; Kanizsa, 1974; Schumann, 1904; Spillmann, 1975) that the strength of the subjective contour and the brightness of the illusory area in such patterns *decrease* with increasing gap size. However, such findings have been based on patterns with gap sizes greater than those employed in the present study (or unspecified). It is likely, then, that the complete function of brightness versus gap size is inversely U-shaped, with a peak that has yet to be determined. (Larger gap sizes were not used in the present study because of limitations of the apparatus.)

The results reported here may be interpreted within the framework of the following receptive field model. According to this account, the Ehrenstein pattern produces maximal firing in cells whose receptive fields are elongated inhibitory regions surrounded by excitatory areas (e.g. hypercomplex cells). Presumably, each black line of the Ehrenstein pattern falls onto the inhibitory area of a receptive field, signaling darkness (Jung, 1973). This results in an overlap of the excitatory regions corresponding to the central gap of the Ehrenstein pattern and, thus, greater excitation (signaling brightness) is relayed for the gap than for the rest of the background. This is illustrated in Fig. 27.3.

The results from Experiment I are consistent with such a model. As the number of lines in a pattern increases, the number of receptive fields that overlap also increases. Hence, the brightness of the corresponding area should increase, which it does.

The results from Experiment II can also be accounted for by such a model. Consider again the pattern displayed in Fig. 27.3. A pattern with such a gap size might produce optimal brightness enhancement since there is maximal overlap of the excitatory surrounds without inhibition in any of the surrounds that would arise from the superimposition of the black lines. With a smaller gap size, each

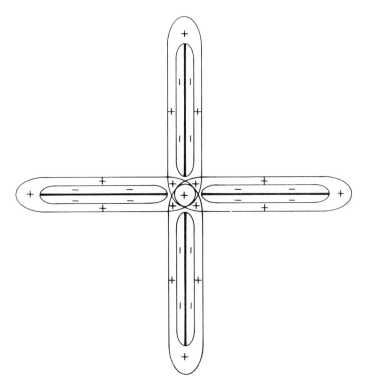

FIG. 27.3.   Proposed receptive field model to account for brightness contrast in the Ehrenstein illusion. The four lines of an Ehrenstein pattern maximally stimulate cells whose receptive fields are represented by the elliptically shaped figures. The receptive fields consist of an inhibitory center $(-)$ and an excitatory surround $(+)$. In the area corresponding to the gap of the Ehrenstein pattern, the excitatory surrounds overlap. The resulting summation is proposed to be responsible for the enhanced brightness seen in this region.

black line, in addition to falling onto the inhibitory center of a receptive field, would also fall onto portions of the excitatory surrounds of receptive fields of cells maximally stimulated by neighboring lines. This would reduce the overall level of excitation and thereby diminish the brightness enhancement. The smaller the gap size is, the more the black lines would encroach upon the excitatory surrounds and, therefore, the smaller the brightness contrast effect would be. This may be what was demonstrated by the results of Experiment II.

As mentioned earlier, it is almost certain that with relatively large gap sizes (greater than about 1.0 deg), the trend reverses. In this case, the *larger* the gap size is, the smaller the brightness contrast effect would be. This, too, can be accounted for by the proposed receptive field model. Here, as the lines recede from the point of potential intersection (i.e., the gap size increases), there would be less overlap of the excitatory surrounds. This would result in a reduction of brightness enhancement.

The proposed model in combination with the present data and those of Dumais and Bradley (1976) suggest receptive field sizes for this approximate retinal eccentricity that are at least consistent with electrophysiological determinations of those of monkey hypercomplex cells (Hubel & Wiesel, 1968). The data are also in accord with psychophysical estimates of such human cell receptive fields (Fuld, 1978). These values extend from roughly 0.5 to 1.0 deg in diameter.

While many observations concerning the effect of modifying the Ehrenstein pattern (and others similar to it) remain to be quantified, the qualitative accounts also lend themselves to such a receptive field explanation. For example, it has been reported (Kennedy, 1978; Spillmann, 1975) that if the lines of an Ehrenstein pattern are positioned such that they are no longer incident at 90 deg relative to the tangent of the gap, the brightness effect is reduced. With an incident angle of 0 deg, the effect is apparently abolished. This follows from the notion that with such a spatial configuration there is little if any overlap of receptive field excitatory surrounds.

REFERENCES

Bradley, D. R., & Dumais, S. T. Ambiguous cognitive contours. *Nature*, 1975, *257*, 582–584.

Brigner, W. L., & Gallagher, M. B. Subjective contour: apparent depth or simultaneous brightness contrast? *Perceptual and Motor Skills*, 1974, *38*, 1047–1053.

Coren, S. Subjective contours and apparent depth. *Psychological Review*, 1972, *79*, 359–367.

Coren, S., & Theodor, L. Subjective contour: the inadequacy of brightness contrast as an explanation. *Bulletin of the Psychonomic Society*, 1975, *6*, 87–89.

Day, R., & Jory, M. Subjective contours, visual acuity, and line contrast. In J. C. Armington, J. Krauskopf, & B. R. Wooten (Eds.), *Visual psychophysics and physiology*. New York: Academic Press, 1978.

Dumais, S. T., & Bradley, D. R. The effects of illumination level and retinal size on the apparent strength of subjective contours. *Perception & Psychophysics*, 1976, *19*, 339–345.

Ehrenstein, W. Ueber Abwandlungen der L. Hermannschen Helligkeitserscheinung. *Zeitschrift für Psychologie*, 1941, *150*, 83–91.

Ehrenstein, W. *Probleme der ganzheitspsychologischen Wahrnehmungslehre* (3. Aufl.). Leipzig: Barth, 1954.

Frisby, J. P., & Clatworthy, J. L. Illusory contours: curious cases of simultaneous brightness contrast? *Perception*, 1975, *4*, 349–357.

Fuld, K. A sensitization effect with rectilinear stimuli. *Vision Research*, 1978, *18*, 1045–1051.

Gregory, R. L. Cognitive contours. *Nature*, 1972, *238*, 51–52.

Hubel, D. H., & Wiesel, T. N. Receptive fields and functional architecture of monkey striate cortex. *Journal of Physiology* (London), 1968, *195*, 215–243.

Jory, M., & Day, R. The relationship between brightness contrast and illusory contours. *Perception*, 1979, *8*, 3–9.

Jung, R. Visual perception and neurophysiology. In R. Jung (Ed.), *Handbook of sensory physiology* (Vol. 7/3A), *Central visual information*. Berlin: Springer-Verlag, 1973.

Jung, R., & Spillmann, L. Receptive-field estimation and perceptual integration in human vision. In F. A. Young & D. B. Lindsley (Eds.), *Early experience and visual information processing in perceptual and reading disorders*. Washington, D.C.: National Academy of Sciences, 1970.

Kanizsa, G. Contours without gradients or cognitive contours? *Italian Journal of Psychology*, 1974, *1*, 93–113.

Kennedy, J. M. Illusory contours and the ends of lines. *Perception*, 1978, *7*, 605–607.

Kennedy, J. M., & Lee, H. A figure-density hypothesis and illusory contour brightness. *Perception*, 1976, *5*, 387–392.

Schumann, F. Einige Beobachtungen über die Zusammenfassung von Gesichtseindrücken zu Einheiten. *Psychologische Studien*, 1904, *1*, 1–32.

Spillmann, L. Perceptual modification of the Ehrenstein illusion. In S. Ertel, L. Kemmler, & M. Stadler (Eds.), *Gestalttheorie in der modernen Psychologie*. Darmstadt: Steinkopff, 1975.

Spillmann, L., Fuld, K., & Gerrits, H. J. M. Brightness contrast in the Ehrenstein illusion. *Vision Research*, 1976, *16*, 713–719.

28 The Effects of Successive Chromatic Contrast on Spectral Hue

B. R. Wooten
Brown University
Providence, R. I.

ABSTRACT

The effects of unique blue, green, and yellow pre-exposure fields on spectral hue have been determined. The observed changes in hue cannot be easily summarized. They are not completely consistent with a complementary-shift rule. Nor are all shifts in the direction of the adapting wavelength. Neither the von Kries Coefficient Law nor the Hering Opponent-Colors model accounts for all of the data. The two-process model of Hurvich and Jameson seems consistent with all of the effects of successive chromatic contrast on spectral hue.

INTRODUCTION

In 1672 Newton published his landmark paper establishing our understanding of the physical basis of color vision. In that paper he demonstrated, among other things, the fundamentals of light mixture, the difference between additive and subtractive color mixing, the circularity of perceptual color space, and that sunlight is composed of all wavelengths. These observations are still considered valid today. Thus, it does not significantly detract from Newton's place in the history of color to point out that he made one serious error: "To the same degree of Refrangibility ever belongs the same colour, and to the same colour ever belongs the same degree of Refrangibility."

We now know, of course, that Newton was wrong in asserting that wavelength and hue are immutably linked. A whole host of factors, in addition to

471

wavelength, determine a light's hue: Luminance, purity, retinal size and location, duration, and the color of adjacent stimuli come immediately to mind. One of the most potent factors influencing the hue-wavelength relation is the recent history of chromatic stimulation, i.e., the hue of what has preceded the stimulus on the same retinal locus. This variable is the topic of the present study.

The general class of phenomena in which the appearance of a portion of the visual field is altered by preceding stimulation was first systematically studied by Chevreul (1838). He coined the term successive contrast to refer to the subjective exaggeration of "real" differences in brightness and/or hue and/or saturation between two stimuli as a result of viewing one before the other. In referring only to changes in hue, I use the term *successive chromatic contrast*. If two different colored lights that fall on the same retinal locus are alternated, then each affects the hue of the other. To simplify the situation for experimental purposes, conditions are usually chosen so as to maximize the influence of one and minimize the influence of the other, e.g., the first stimulus (A) can be given a much longer duration than the second (B). I then refer to A as the *inducing stimulus* and B as the *test stimulus*. In describing the hue attributes, I use *inducing hue* in reference to A, *reacting hue* in reference to B seen without influence from A, *induced hue* in reference to the hue quality that is induced by A, and *resulting hue* in reference to B seen with the influence of A, i.e., reacting hue plus induced hue.

Hue is also affected by the chromaticity of adjacent stimuli, i.e., simultaneous chromatic contrast. The effects on hue of an adjacent stimulus are said to be similar to those of a comparable preceding stimulus. In most situations where simultaneous contrast is ostensibly being studied, however, voluntary and involuntary (fixational) eye movements and the effects of stray light permit the effects of successive contrast to become involved (Helmholtz, 1911; Walraven 1973). Furthermore, many studies that explicitly allow pre-exposure adaptation present the test field within an inducing field (Jameson & Hurvich, 1959). Thus, most studies that claim to be examining either successive or simultaneous chromatic contrast are in effect reflecting the combined action of both. While this confounding reflects the situation in everyday vision, it prevents a quantitative account of the underlying mechanisms of the separate effects. Hence, in this chapter I primarily consider only the studies that isolate the effects of successive chromatic contrast. Furthermore, I consider only the literature that deals with the changes in *hue* resulting from prior stimulation. That is, I do not consider such interesting variables as purity, luminance, stimulus dimensions, or temporal relations.

Because of the strength and pervasiveness of successive chromatic contrast effects, any theory of color vision which claims any degree of generality must deal with them. Indeed, there have been as many attempts to explain contrast as there have been color theories. Because of this, it is useful to consider chromatic contrast phenomena within the framework of the two historically most influential color theorists: Helmholtz and Hering. This approach is doubly fruitful since the issues considered by them are still alive today.

Helmholtz's (1911) account of successive chromatic contrast follows directly from his postulation of three receptors with overlapping, but nonidentical, spectral sensitivities. He argued that since colored lights stimulate the receptors to different degrees, they also fatigue or adapt the receptors to different degrees. Later, von Kries (1878, 1905) formalized and extended this concept and it is now generally known as the von Kries Coefficient Law. Within the framework of Helmholtz's model of hue, he argued that the resulting hue should be a perceptual mixture of the reacting hue and the complement of the inducing hue. For example, yellow (which results, according to Helmholtz, from equal stimulation of the red and green mechanisms) appears reddish-yellow after a green-inducing field because the green mechanism is strongly fatigued, thereby allowing the red mechanism to predominate.

While Helmholtz's theory of color vision was based primarily on the results of null or matching experiments, Hering's (1878) theory rested mainly on the direct psychological character of the sensations. Hering took as his starting point the conception that hue sensation can be analyzed into fundamental, mutually exclusive sensations: yellow as opposed to blue, and red as opposed to green. Hering felt it self-evident that one quality of a given pair can combine with either quality of each of the other pairs but that the two qualities of each pair are mutually destructive. For example, it is possible to combine the sensations green and yellow, or red and blue, but not green and red, or yellow and blue.

To account for the basic attributes of hue, Hering postulated that the visual system contains two substances: the blue-yellow-mediating and green-red-mediating substances. Moreover, the theory assumes that opposite processes, assimilative and dissimilative (A and D respectively), take place simultaneously in each substance. The resulting sensation is determined by the ratio of these opposite processes. Red and/or yellow result when the $A{:}D$ ratio is less than 1 in the appropriate substance(s); green and/or blue result when the ratio is greater than 1 in the appropriate substance(s). When the $A{:}D$ ratio is exactly 1 in the two substances, the sensation is devoid of hue. In the yellow-blue substance, light of about 400 to 500 nm results in $A{:}D > 1$ (blue), and light of about 500 to 700 nm results in $A{:}D < 1$ (yellow). In the green-red substance, 475 to 575 nm light causes $A{:}D > 1$ (green), and 575 to 700 nm light causes $A{:}D < 1$ (red). In addition, 400 to 475 nm light results in $A{:}D < 1$ in the green-red substance.

One additional postulate allows Hering to account for successive chromatic contrast : If the dissimilative process predominates during a period of light stimulation, the effectiveness of subsequent A stimuli is enhanced and vice versa. Thus, if the retina is exposed to light of 575 nm (pure yellow) for some interval of time, the blue component of any blue-green light which is subsequently directed to the same retinal region will be larger than normal, i.e., the blue-green light appears bluer. If the inducing light also had some red in it, e.g., 590 nm, then the green component of the reacting hue would also have been enhanced, causing a greener as well as bluer resulting hue. Similar arguments can be made for any inducing field-induced field combination. It is, therefore, clear that Hering's theory is compatible with the complementary rule for successive chromatic contrast because A and D stimuli result in a reciprocal temporal enhancement and because A and D stimuli are perfect perceptual complements.

Thus, both of the classical color theorists asserted the complementary rule, i.e., that the resulting hue is a perceptual mixture of the reacting and induced hues. The complementary rule, whether empirically correct or not, is consistent with Hering's theory. The rule is, however, not perfectly consistent with Helmholtz's model. Wooten (1970) has shown that while some hue shifts based upon Helmholtz's model do follow the complementary rule, many do not. For example, the rule predicts that a pure blue-inducing field should cause an orange-reacting hue to appear more yellow, blue's complement. But, when the Coefficient Law is actually applied in this situation, Helmholtz's model predicts that the resulting hue should be redder than the reacting hue. From such considerations, Wooten concluded that the complementary rule is not always consistent with Helmholtz's theory. (Both Helmholtz's and Hering's predictions are considered in detail with respect to observed hue shifts in the Discussion section.)

Quite apart from what resulting hues the theories of Helmholtz and Hering predict is the question of what hue changes are actually observed in successive chromatic contrast.

Most of the older reports (Aubert, 1865; Edridge-Green, 1891; Edridge-Green & Porter, 1914; Karwoski, 1929; Tschermak-Seysenegg, 1929), although disagreeing on particulars, indicate that the hue of the pre-exposure (inducing) field and the hue induced into a neutral test (induced) field are not exact mixture-complements. Edridge-Green (1891), for example, found that a blue-inducing field caused a yellow-reacting hue to become redder, a finding which is consistent with Helmholtz's theory but not with the complementary rule. Wilson and Brocklebank (1955), utilizing colored and achromatic paper discs, concluded that the induced hues resulting from violet, blue, and blue-green-inducing hues are displaced toward the longwave end of the spectrum relative to the mixture complements while the induced hues resulting from yellow-, orange- and red-inducing hues are shifted toward the shortwave end. More recently, Jacobs and Gaylord (1967) examined successive chromatic contrast utilizing the color-naming procedure of Boynton and Gordon (1965). They asked subjects to name the hues of monochromatic stimuli ranging from 440 to 650 nm. They used four inducing fields : a tungsten white, and three chromatic lights with dominant wavelengths of 646, 538, and 452 nm. The point of interest was the effect of the chromatic inducing fields, relative to the more-or-less white-inducing field, on the reacting hues. The results can be easily summarized : the derived compensatory wavelength shifts necessary to maintain constant hues (relative to the white condition) are generally towards the wavelength of the inducing fields. In terms of compensatory shifts, the complementary rule says that shifts should be towards the inducing wavelength if the reacting wavelength is located between the inducing wavelength and its complement, but away from the inducing wavelength otherwise. Thus, none of the older or newer studies is perfectly consistent with the complementary rule.

It appears, on the basis of the literature, that Hering's opponent scheme, as originally formulated, cannot explain the hue shifts observed in successive chromatic contrast since the complementary rule is not always correct. Direct tests of the von Kries Coefficient Law, however, have failed to verify Helmholtz's simple fatigue explanation (e.g. MacAdam, 1956; Wright, 1934). Specifically, the proportionality deduction from the Coefficient Law has been found to be false (Hurvich & Jameson, 1958, pp. 691–723).[1] These, and other considerations, led Hurvich and Jameson (1959, 1972, pp. 568–581) to formulate a two-process explanation. Basically, they propose a three-receptor stage with von Kries-type adaptation and an opponent stage that is a linear transformation of the receptor stage. Furthermore, they allow incremental, opponent (complementary) induction to occur at the opponent level. Hurvich and Jameson's model, then, has two stages of adaptation and encompasses aspects of both the Helmholtz-von Kries process and the Hering process. Thus, the relation between inducing, reacting, and resulting hues is complex in that both processes must be considered.

In recent years, there have been several studies that support the two-process model of Hurvich and Jameson (e.g. Larimer, 1981; Shevell, 1978; Walraven, 1976). None, however, consider a wide range of reacting hue conditions. The earlier studies, reviewed above, are pertinent but difficult to relate to the model because of poorly specified stimulus conditions or indeterminate perceptual states. The Jacobs and Gaylord (1967) study, for example, is technically sound, but arbitrary inducing wavelengths are used rather than perceptually simple ones. For example, their "green"inducing field was 538 nm for all subjects. Due to the known variability of unique green's spectral position, this wavelength is quite yellow for some subjects and almost perfectly green for others. The actual perceptual quality of 538 nm for the particular subjects used by Jacobs and Gaylord is, therefore, not known. Thus, it is impossible to relate the observed shifts in this experiment to the Hurvich and Jameson model.

One purpose of the present study is to measure the effects of pure successive chromatic contrast using inducing fields of known *hues,* i.e., hues determined for each subject. In this way, it is possible to determine the relations between

---

[2]The proportionality deduction states that an asymmetric metameric match, i.e., one in which the two fields are on patches of retina that are in different states of chromatic adaptation, should hold when the luminance of both sides is increased by the same amount.

inducing, reacting, and resulting hues, i.e., to ascertain the true hue shifts caused by successive chromatic contrast. The other purpose of the study is to evaluate the several models of successive contrast previously discussed by relating them to the observed hue shifts.

METHODS

Psychophysical Methods

The traditional procedure that could be applied to the problem of how hue is affected by chromatic contrast conditions is the matching method in which a comparison field is adjusted to match the appearance of the induced field. Ideally, the composition of the comparison field is adjustable to the extent that a perfect match can always be made. In practice, this is difficult to achieve, especially if a wide range of test and inducing wavelengths are used.

An alternative to the matching method is an absolute-judgment technique in which subjects are required to make responses that directly reflect their sensations of the test stimulus. Such techniques offer several advantages over the matching method for the study of chromatic contrast. One is that information is gained about the appearance of each visual stimulus rather than simply which physical stimuli match. Another advantage is that stimuli may be conveniently presented in brief and well-controlled flashes rather than in extended periods. This is an important consideration because hue varies as a function of stimulus duration (Kinney, 1965). Despite these two important advantages, the absolute-judgment techniques suffer one major drawback, namely, the problem of validity. With the matching method, it can safely be assumed, providing that perfect matches are possible, that every subject is acting as a null-detector. Absolute techniques, on the other hand, require the subjects to make abstractions about some aspect of their sensations. Boynton and Gordon (1965) have provided relevant data in a study in which they measured the Bezold-Brücke hue-shift using both a matching and an absolute-judgment technique. They found that the two procedures yielded similar data and that the absolute judgments were as reliable as the matches.

Given the many advantages of the absolute-judgment technique for the study of chromatic contrast, and given the evidence of Boynton and Gordon regarding its sensitivity and validity, it seems the appropriate tool to apply to the specific problems of my experiments. I used the continuous-judgment color-naming procedure described by Jameson and Hurvich (1959) and Werner and Wooten (1979). Basically, the subjects make percentage responses based upon the perceived ratio of red or green and yellow or blue in the total hue sensation. (The specific details are given in the next section.) The hue-scaling procedure of

Jameson and Hurvich appears to have all of the desirable features of Boynton's color-naming technique, yet it avoids the arbitrariness of assigning fixed point-values to the hue categories. It has the additional advantage of providing data which can be directly related to the opponent colors model.

In addition to the hue-scaling procedure, I adopted a method of constant stimuli in order to determine precisely the wavelength loci of unique (pure) blue, green, and yellow under the various adaptation conditions. The locus of unique yellow, for example, was determined by finding the wavelength which is as likely to be called greenish-yellow as it is to be called reddish yellow, i.e., the transition wavelength between red and green.

Optical System and Calibration

The optical system is described in detail by Wooten (1970). Briefly, it was a two-channel, Maxwellian-view system. Spectral light was provided by grating mono-chromators with nominal half-amplitude bandpasses of 10 nm. Broad-band blocking filters were used below 480 nm and above 600 nm to reduce the effects of stray light and second-order spectra. A non-Maxwellian-view channel pro-vided a fixation cross.

The retinal illuminance of the test channel with the monochromator set at 576 nm was determined by measuring, with a MacBeth illuminometer, the illumi-nance of a white test plate positioned in what was normally the retina's plane. The illuminance of the plate was converted to retinal illuminance using the method described by Westheimer (1966). With all filters removed, the 576 nm setting produced 150,000 photopic trolands.

The 24 monochromatic stimuli (430–660 nm) were equated by flicker-pho-tometric data using the 576 nm light, attenuated to 562 photopic trolands as the standard. The brightness of the inducing fields, provided by the other channel, was equated to the test fields by a direct-matching procedure. This was done for each subject since the unique-hue wavelengths were slightly different for the three subjects.

Procedures

Subjects were dark-adapted for 15 min prior to the beginning of the sessions. All three subjects had normal color vision as assessed by the American Optical pseudo-isochromatic plates. The subjects were instructed to trigger the stimuli with a hand-held switch. Fixation was aided by luminous cross-hairs which could be adjusted by the subjects in order to keep them dim but distinct. Subjects were allowed to repeat the stimuli as many times as they felt was necessary in order to feel confident about their judgments. Usually, one or two presentations were sufficient. A minimum inter-trial interval of 20 sec was employed.

The hue-scaling procedure, discussed earlier, is used in this experiment. Specifically, after each test flash, the subjects verbally reported what percentage of the total hue sensation was attributable to the red, green, yellow, and blue sensations. Subjects were instructed to arrive at the percentage response by first considering the ratio of the strengths of the constituent sensation. They were told, for example, that a hue which seems to be composed of equal strengths of blue and green should be described as "50% blue—50% green"; a hue which seems to be pure green should be described as "100% green"; a hue which seems to be composed of blue and green in the ratio of 3:1 should be called "75% blue—25% green." They were allowed to use the four hue names either singly or in pairs. Although restrictions were not placed on which hue names could be paired, none of the subjects ever used the blue-yellow or the red-green combinations. Each of the 24 test-wavelengths was presented four times in a given session, resulting in 96 trials per session. The trials were randomized. Only one pre-exposure condition was examined in any given session. Two sessions were run for each condition, giving a total of eight judgments per test-wavelength. One practice session was given for each subject prior to the beginning of the experiment.

The wavelength loci corresponding to the unique hues of blue, green, and yellow were precisely determined by a method of constant stimuli. These were first determined for each subject in the neutrally adapted condition. The resulting values were then used to define the monochromator settings for the unique blue, green, and yellow pre-exposure fields. In addition, unique hues were determined for the induced field in each chromatic contrast condition.

In each trial, the subjects first viewed the fixation cross, and when they felt that their fixation was accurate and stable, they initiated the stimulus sequence by closing a hand-held switch. The switch closure causes the fixation cross to be blocked and the 6° 20' inducing field to be exposed for from 2.5–5 sec, depending on the hue of the inducing field and the subject. Then, .7 sec after the termination of the pre-exposure field, the .3 sec test flash of 1° was presented.

The actual durations of the inducing fields were slightly different for the three subjects. For each subject, they were chosen so as to give selected hue shifts comparable to those found in an earlier experiment dealing with simultaneous chromatic contrast (Wooten, 1970). The values used for each subject in each adapting condition are shown in Table 28.1.

RESULTS

The hue judgments for the neutrally adapted (no inducing field) condition are shown for the three subjects in Fig. 28.1. The average percentage of red or green and yellow or blue is plotted as a function of wavelength with the zero-value at

TABLE 28.1
Durations of Inducing Fields

	Pre-expsoure Condition		
Subject	Unique-blue	Unique-green	Unique-yellow
BW	4.6 sec	3.1 sec	2.5 sec
SP	5.0 sec	3.0 sec	3.0 sec
OB	5.0 sec	3.2 sec	3.0 sec

the bottom of each graph for red-green and at the top for yellow-blue. The solid lines drawn through the data points represent best fitting curves based upon an informal fit by eye. The arrows indicate the unique hue determinations. The effects of unique-blue, -green, and -yellow-inducing fields are shown in Figs. 28.2, 28.3, and 28.4, respectively. Again, the loci of unique hues are indicated by the arrows. The dashed lines in Figs. 28.2, 28.3, and 28.4 are identical to the smooth lines drawn through the data in the neutrally adapted condition, that is, from Fig. 28.1. Unique-hue loci are tabulated in Table 28.2 for each subject and each pre-exposure condition.

The hue-scaling functions for the neutrally adapted condition (Fig. 28.1) show substantial agreement between the three subjects. The only large difference is found in the spectral region of 490–500 nm for SP who reported considerably higher percentages of green than did the other two subjects. The variance of the judgments is not shown, but is fairly uniform across wavelengths. The average standard deviation was about 7% for all subjects and all adaptation conditions. The hue-scaling functions shown in Fig. 28.1 are quite similar to those reported for three different subjects by Werner and Wooten (1979).

The effects of successive chromatic contrast on spectral hue can be seen in Figures 28.2, 28.3, and 28.4 by comparing the solid and dashed lines. The effects are fairly uniform across subjects. Unique-blue adaptation (Fig. 28.2) causes the reacting hues to become redder in the 430–460 and 570–660 nm regions, yellower in the 490–560 nm region, and greener in the 470–490 nm region. Unique yellow and green are shifted to shorter wavelengths while unique blue is unaffected. Unique-green adaptation (Fig. 28.3) causes the reacting hues to become redder in the 430–470 and 570–660 nm regions, bluer in the 480–490 nm region, and yellower in the 520–560 nm region. Unique blue is shifted to a longer wavelength, unique yellow is shifted to a shorter wavelength, and unique green is unaffected. Unique-yellow adaptation (Fig. 28.4) causes the reacting hues to become bluer in the 430–510 nm region, greener in the 530–570 nm region, and redder in the 580–660 nm region. Unique blue and green are shifted towards longer wavelengths, while unique yellow is unaffected. The theoretical implications of these effects are treated in the Discussion section.

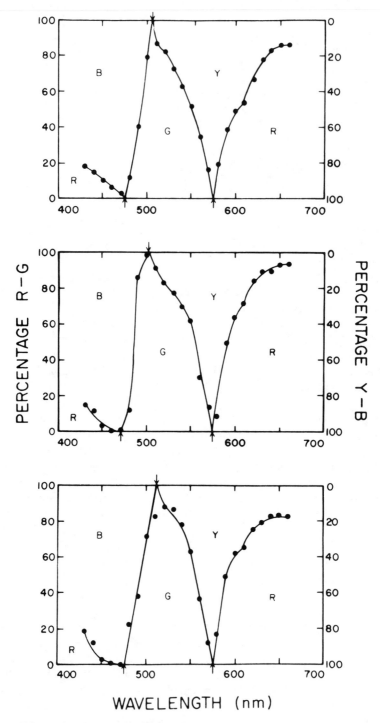

FIG. 28.1.   Average hue-judgments for the no-inducing-field condition. Arrows indicate unique hue loci. Top panel, subject BW; middle panel, subject SP; bottom panel, subject OB.

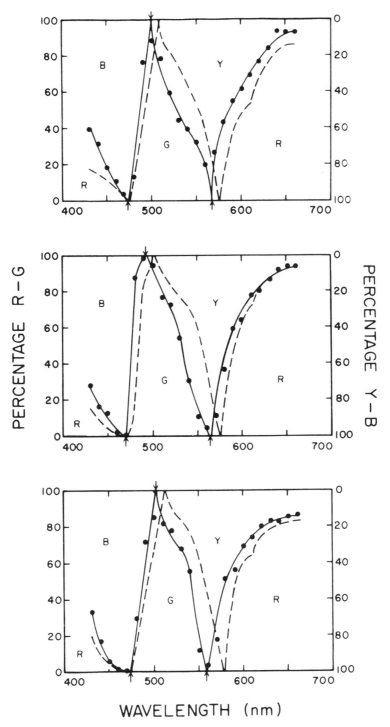

FIG. 28.2. Unique-blue pre-exposure condition. Details as for Fig. 28.1. Each subject's hue function from the neutral condition is indicated by the dashed lines.

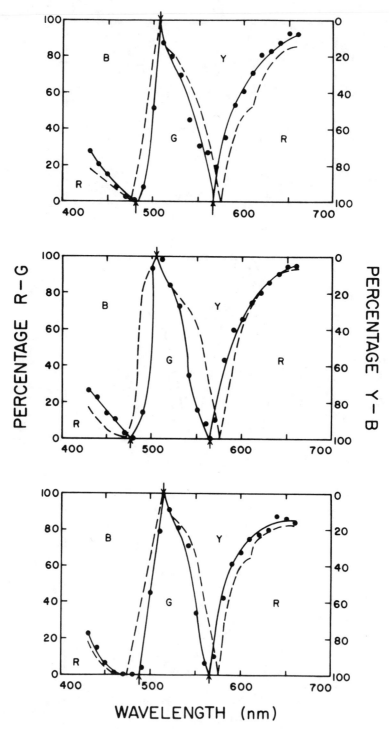

FIG. 28.3. Unique-green pre-exposure condition. Details as for Fig. 28.1 and Fig. 28.2.

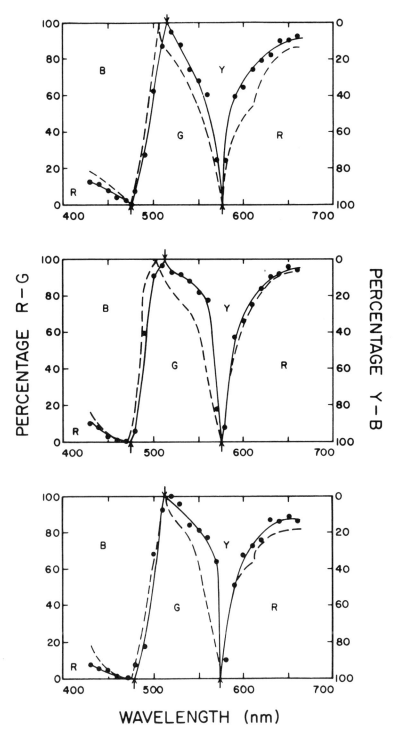

FIG. 28.4. Unique-yellow pre-exposure condition. Details as for Fig. 28.1 and Fig. 28.2.

483

TABLE 28.2
Unique-blue Loci

Subject	Pre-exposure Condition			
	No-Pre-exposure	Unique-blue	Unique-green	Unique-yellow
BW	474.5	475.0	481.0	477.5
	506.5	498.0	507.5	514.5
	576.0	565.5	567.0	575.0
SP	472.0	471.0	476.5	475.0
	503.0	491.5	504.0	511.0
	575.5	564.0	564.0	575.5
OB	474.0	474.5	488.0	478.0
	514.0	502.0	514.0	512.0
	575.5	559.0	564.0	574.0
		blue		
		green		
		yellow		

DISCUSSION

On The Impossibility of a Simple Shift-Rule

It would be desirable if, on the basis of the data shown in Figures 28.2, 28.3, and 28.4, a simple qualitative rule could be stated that summarizes the relations between the inducing, reacting, and resulting hues. Unfortunately, the results do not allow such a statement.

While Figures 28.2, 28.3, and 28.4 show the effects of successive chromatic contrast, it is more convenient to derive compensatory shifts (as defined previously) from them. I have done so on the basis of the smooth lines drawn through the data points and the derived values are shown in Fig. 28.5. In each of the three panels, which correspond to the chromatic inducing conditions, compensatory shifts for each subject (shown by the three types of symbols) are plotted on the axis of ordinates with minus values above and plus values below the axis of abscissas. (The lines drawn through the data are discussed in subsequent sections.)

In terms of compensatory shifts, the complementary rule can be stated as follows : The direction of the shift necessary to maintain a constant hue is toward the inducing wavelength except when the reacting wavelength is further away than the inducing wavelength's complement from the inducing wavelength, in which case the shift is away from the inducing wavelength. Figure 28.5 shows that the rule is obeyed for yellow- and green-inducing fields. For the blue-inducing field, however, the data do not support the rule for reacting wave-

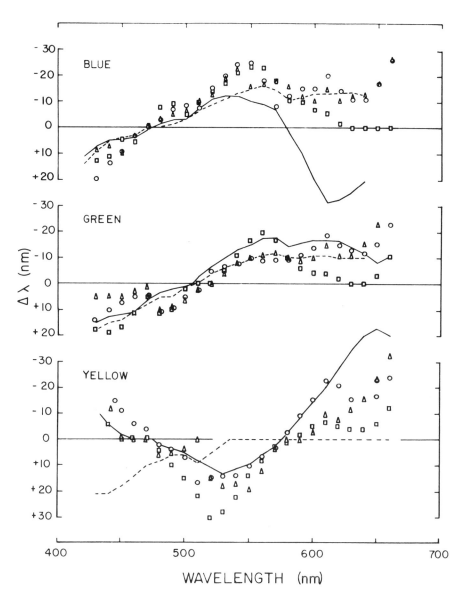

FIG. 28.5. Compensatory shifts for the blue, green, and yellow inducing hues (○-subject BW; □-subject SP; △-subject OB). The dashed line represents the predictions based upon a von Kries model. The solid line represents the predictions based upon a Hering-type opponent model.

485

lengths greater than about 570 nm. The rule states, for example, that a 610 nm reacting wavelength should shift away (positive compensatory shift) from the inducing wavelength. The data show that 610 nm actually shifts about 8 nm in the negative direction. Other reacting wavelengths greater than 570 nm show a similar shift. Thus, while the complementary rule holds for some inducing-reacting hues, it does not hold for all.

The set of compensatory shifts in Fig. 28.5 also allows an evaluation of a shift-rule that seems to summarize much of the literature reviewed in the Introduction and is advocated by Jacobs and Gaylord (1967), namely, that the compensatory shift is towards the inducing wavelength. The data of Fig. 28.5 are consistent with this rule for the blue- and green-inducing fields. The yellow adaptation, however, contradicts such a rule for reacting wavelengths in the 430 to 470 nm range.

The present data, taken as a whole, reject both of the commonly stated, general rules dealing with the effects of successive chromatic contrast on spectral hue. It seems unlikely that any simple, qualitative generalization can be formulated. The contrast effects apparently reflect complex processes that do not yield simple results. A more profitable approach might be to consider the quantitative predictions of specific models. This is done in the next two sections.

A von Kries Model

A central issue with respect to the effects of successive chromatic contrast on spectral hue is whether or not, or to what extent, the mechanism of selective receptor fatigue, as proposed by Helmholtz, can account for the observed hue shifts. As mentioned in the Introduction, tests of von Kries's elaboration of Helmholtz's proposal have failed to completely account for the data from experiments using metameric matching. Metameric matching, however, requires that the subjects equate the stimuli in all aspects, i.e., brightness and saturation as well as hue. The failure to confirm the von Kries Coefficient Law could, in principle, be due to complexities in the achromatic mechanism and/or interactions between the achromatic and chromatic mechanisms. My experiments involve only judgments of hue and, therefore, reflect solely activity of the chromatic systems. Thus, it is possible that the Coefficient Law is consistent with the present data.

In order to relate the Helmholtz-von Kries theory to the data on hue shifts, two things are necessary. First, one must assume a set of three relative spectral absorption curves in order to characterize the responsivity of the cone receptors. Second, one must define a set of equations relating receptoral activity to perceived hue. In other words, a model of hue perception is needed.

I have chosen Jameson's and Hurvich model (1968). While certain details of their theory may be debated, its essential elements (a three-receptor stage followed by an opponent stage,) are no longer questioned. The receptor stage is related to the opponent stage by two linear equations:

$$r_\lambda - g_\lambda = k_1 (a_1\alpha_\lambda + c_1\gamma_\lambda - b_1\beta_\lambda)$$

$$y_\lambda - b_\lambda = k_2 (b_2\beta_\lambda + c_2\gamma_\lambda - a_2\alpha_\lambda)$$

where r and g refer to red and green activity
y and b refer to yellow and blue activity
k_1 and k_2 are luminance-dependent constants
a, b and c are weighting constants
α, β, and γ are relative spectral absorption functions of the receptors.

The α, β, and γ functions are assumed to have peak sensitivities at 448, 528 and 567 nm respectively, to follow the shape dictated by Dartnall's nomogram (1953), and to be weighted by the average pre-retinal absorption values given by Wyszecki and Stiles (1967).

In the Hurvich and Jameson model, hue judgments are determined by the ratio of the chromatic activity in each channel to the total chromatic activity:

$$\% \text{ yellow or blue} = \frac{|y - b|_\lambda}{|y - b|_\lambda + |r - g|_\lambda} \cdot 100$$

$$\% \text{ red or green} = \frac{|r - g|_\lambda}{|y - b|_\lambda + |r - g|_\lambda} \cdot 100$$

By choosing appropriate values for the constants (k, a, b, and c), it is possible to generate a set of theoretical hue judgments that can be compared to the results of the neutral condition. These values are shown in Fig. 28.6 along with the predicted hue function. The open symbols are the average hue judgments for each of the three subjects. The theoretical hue function is in excellent agreement with the data for wavelengths greater than about 570 nm and for the region between unique blue and unique green. The most serious discrepancy is in the region between unique green and unique yellow where the data show less yellow (more green) than the theoretical function predicts. A systematic difference is also apparent at short wavelengths where the data indicate less red (more blue). A better fit of the theoretical predictions to the data could probably be attained by further manipulation of the receptor-weighting factors. Considering the tentative nature of the receptor functions, however, such an exercise does not seem worthwhile. Moreover, the purpose of deriving the theoretical hue functions in the present context is merely to "read out" the activity of the receptors so that comparisons can be made between the neutral state and the three states of chromatic adaptation with respect to hue.

$$y - b = 2.1 \, (.15 \, \beta + .04 \, Y - 1.0 \, \alpha)$$

$$r - g = 1.0 \, (.55 \, \alpha + .55 \, Y - 1.0 \, \beta)$$

assume 87% R at 660

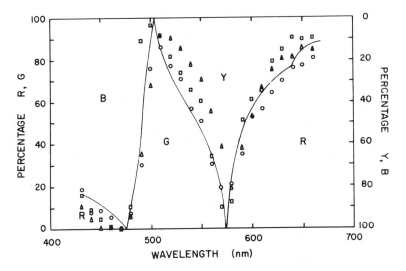

FIG. 28.6.   Average hue-responses of each subject (data points) for the no-inducing field condition. The smooth line represents predicted hue-responses based upon Hurvich and Jameson's model of hue. (○-BW, □-SP, △-OB).

Given a model relating receptors and hue, it is possible to calculate the effects of chromatic adaptation on spectral hue utilizing the von Kries Coefficient Law. To do so within the context of the Hurvich and Jameson hue model, it is only necessary to modify the weighting coefficients (*a, b,* and *c*) in accordance with von Kries's law, namely, reducing the weighting coefficients in proportion to the degree of receptor activation. Ideally, the exact relation between the degree of receptor activity and the magnitude of sensitivity reduction would be known. Unfortunately, it is not. However, it is possible to set the coefficients so that the compensatory shifts at two reacting wavelengths are satisfied and then examine the consequences at all other wavelengths. This procedure was followed for each of the three chromatic inducing conditions.

The theoretical hue function for the unique-blue adaptation was calculated by finding multiplicative constants for the α, β, and γ mechanisms that satisfy two experimental findings : (1) zero shift of the unique-blue locus, and (2) a −13 nm shift of the unique-yellow locus relation to the neutral condition. The values chosen were .61, .71, and .9 for α, β, and γ respectively. It should be emphasized that other values are possible and that these merely represent a degree of adaptation which is intermediate between the neutral state and the completely blue-adapted state. The resulting hue function is shown in Fig. 28.7a. For comparison, the hue function corresponding to the neutral state is also shown (dashed lines). Compensatory shifts were then calculated and are indicated by the dashed lines in Fig. 28.5. As can be seen, the theortical predictions are in perfect qualitative agreement and fair quantitative agreement with the observed compensatory shifts for the blue inducing field.

The theoretical hue function for unique-green adaptation was calculated by finding multiplicative constants which yielded values that agree with the data at two points : (1) zero shift in the locus of unique green, and (2) a -11 nm shift in the unique-yellow locus. The chosen values were .88, .70, and .85 for α, β and γ respectively. The resulting hue function is shown in Fig. 28.7b and the derived shifts are indicated by the dashed lines in the middle graph of Fig. 28.5. The predicted shifts are in good quantitative agreement with the data.

The theoretical hue function for unique-yellow adaptation was calculated by finding multiplicative constants that satisfied the following experimental results : (1) no shift in the unique-yellow locus, and (2) a $+7$ nm shift in the unique-green locus. A value of .6 was chosen for both β and γ. Since the sensitivity curve indicates that the α mechanism is insensitive to wavelengths in the unique-yellow region, a value of 1.0 was dictated for the corresponding multiplicative constant. The resulting hue function is shown in Fig. 28.7c. An obvious feature of this function is that it is identical to the neutrally adapted hue function for wavelengths greater than about 535 nm. This is a result of the lack of α-sensitivity in the unique-yellow region and the consequent necessity of choosing equal multiplicative constants (.6) for the β and γ mechanisms. This is a complicated point and should be explained in more detail. For the predicted compensatory shift of the unique-yellow locus to correspond to the data, that is, a zero shift, it is necessary for the r-g opponent-response function to be zero both before and after unique-yellow adaptation. The r-g activity is given by the following interaction equation :

$$r_\lambda - g_\lambda = 1.0 \, (.55\alpha_\lambda + .55\gamma_\lambda - 1.0\beta_\lambda)$$

But since $\alpha = 0$ in the spectral region corresponding to the unique-yellow locus the equation is reduced to

$$r_\lambda - g_\lambda = 1.0 \, (.55\gamma_\lambda - 1.0\beta_\lambda).$$

For the neutral state, the unique-yellow locus falls at 575 nm,

$$r_{575} - g_{575} = 0$$

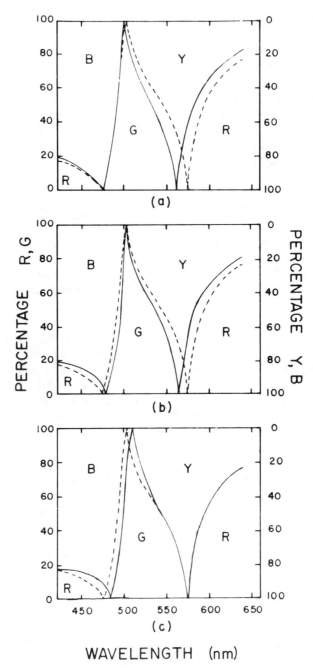

FIG. 28.7. Theoretical hue functions predicted from the von Krie Coefficient Law in combination with a non-adapting opponent stage. Dashed lines refer to neutral state of adaptation and are the same as in Fig. 28.6. Solid lines refer to (a) unique-blue, (b) unique-green, and (c) unique-yellow-inducing fields.

This means that in order to maintain r-$g = 0$ at 575 nm, it is necessary to choose identical multiplicative constants for the β and γ mechanisms. This, in turn, dictates that the hue of all wavelengths greater than 535 nm (where the sensitivity of α falls to zero) will be unaffected by the unique-yellow adaptation.

The derived compensatory shifts for unique-yellow adaptation are shown by the dashed lines in the bottom panel of Fig. 28.5. It is clear that there is virtually no agreement between data and prediction.

The evaluation of the Hurvich and Jameson hue model that had a von Kries-type adaptive stage as its *only* adaptive element is easily summarized: Compensatory shifts for blue and green adaptation are consistent with the model, but the data for yellow adaptation are inconsistent. The conclusion must be, as for metameric matching, that a von Kries mechanism *alone* cannot account for the effects of successive chromatic contrast on spectral hue. This conclusion, of course, does not rule out the possibility that such a mechanism may be part of a more complex adaptive process. (See Cicerone, Krantz, & Larimer, 1975.)

An Opponent Model

As discussed in the Introduction, Hering postulated a mechanism of successive chromatic contrast that involved only an opponent stage. For him, successive chromatic contrast was an incremental process involving the induction of opponent hues, for example, a unique-blue-inducing field would induce a fixed amount of yellow onto a reacting hue. Since such a model predicts that the complementary rule holds exactly and the present data show qualitatively that it does not, it can be concluded that pure opponent induction cannot account for all of the observed hue shifts. It is of interest, however, to make a quantitative evaluation of the model to see how badly and where in the spectrum it fails.

In the Hurvich and Jameson model just discussed, the opponent stage is essentially identical to Hering's model. It is possible, therefore, to test Hering's mechanism of successive chromatic contrast with the Hurvich and Jameson model by assuming that induction occurs only at the opponent level. This is done by simply adding a fixed amount of the inducing field's opponent response to the calculated r-g or y-b activity. Before the incremental activity is added, the chromatic activity must be calculated for the equal-luminance spectrum used in the experiment. The actual values used for the added increments were chosen to make the predicted compensatory shifts match the measured ones at certain wavelengths: for the unique-blue-inducing field, enough yellow-response was added to cause a compensatory shift of -10.5 nm at 520 nm; for the unique-green-inducing field, enough red-response was added to cause a compensatory shift of -13 nm at 540 nm; and for the unique-yellow condition, enough blue-response was added to cause a compensatory shift of $+10$ nm at 550 nm. The calculated hue functions are shown in Fig. 28.8. Calculated compensatory shifts are indicated by the solid lines in Fig. 28.5.

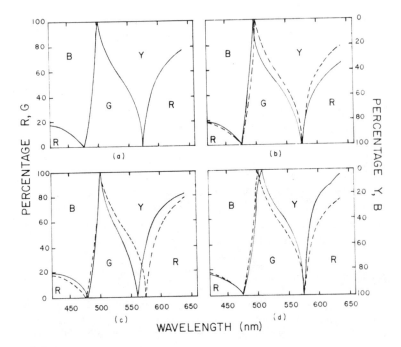

FIG. 28.8. Theoretical hue functions based upon opponent induction. (a) no-inducing field, (b) unique-blue-inducing field, (c) unique-green-inducing field, (d) unique-yellow-inducing field. Dashed lines in b, c, and d are same as solid line in a.

Agreement between the opponent model and the data is good for the unique-green condition, as can be seen by comparing the solid line and the data in the middle panel of Fig. 28.5. There is also good correspondence for the yellow condition (bottom panel) although the data are rather variable in the 620–660 nm region and the theory predicts somewhat larger shifts than those obtained. The only serious failure of the model occurs for the unique-blue condition (top panel) for wavelengths greater than about 540 nm. The theory predicts a zero shift at about 575 nm (the unique-yellow locus) and large positive shifts of the long-wave reacting wavelengths. The data, however, show sizable negative shifts over the entire longwave region.

Taken as a whole, the observed changes in hue resulting from chromatic adaptation do not support a mechanism that relies entirely on opponent induction.

CONCLUSIONS

Neither a pure opponent model nor a pure "fatigue" model accounts for all of the effects of successive chromatic contrast on spectral hue. The former fails primarily at the longwave end of the spectrum when a unique-blue-inducing field is employed; the latter fails entirely to account for the effects of a unique-yellow-inducing field. Both, however, are consistent with some of the data and this raises the possibility that both sensitivity changes and opponent induction are involved in the phenomenon.

Jameson and Hurvich (1959, 1972) have proposed a two-process model that allows multiplicative gain changes in the receptor systems and incremental induction in the opponent channels. Their model of chromatic contrast thus represents a hybrid of the Helmholtz-von Kries and Hering positions. It is consistent with a large body of data that seems to require both processes. A quantitative evaluation of their model will not be attempted here, but it is apparent from Fig. 28.5 that the model would provide a virtually perfect qualitative, and perhaps a good quantitative account of the observed shifts.

ACKNOWLEDGMENTS

This report is based upon data from a Ph.D. dissertation (Wooten, 1970; Brown University). The author wishes to thank Prof. L. A. Riggs for his advice and support and Prof. D. Yager for his enthusiastic interest in the experiments. The manuscript was written while the author held a Senior U.S. Scientist Award from the Alexander-von-Humboldt-Stiftung. The author wishes to thank Professors L. Spillmann and R. Jung of the Neurologische Universitätsklinik, Freiburg im Breisgau, B.R.D., for their gracious hospitality. Miss Peggy Leung assisted in the preparation of the manuscript. J. Walraven and A. Valberg provided helpful comments on an earlier draft.

REFERENCES

Aubert, H. *Physiologie der Netzhaut.* Breslau: Morgenstern, 1865.

Boynton, R. M., & Gordon, J. Bezold-Brücke hue shift measured by color-naming techniques. *Journal of the Optical Society of America,* 1965, *55,* 78–86.

Chevreul, M. E. The principles of harmony and contrast of colours and their applications to the arts. London: Bell 1838. (Originally published in 1838. Translation by C. Martel, 1899, 3rd ed.)

Cicerone, C. M., Krantz, D. H., & Larimer, J. Opponent-process additivity—III. Effect of moderate chromatic adaptation. *Vision Research,* 1975, *15,* 1125–1135.

Dartnall, H. J. A. The interpretation of spectral sensitivity curves. *British Medical Bulletin,* 1953, *9,* 24–30.

Edridge-Green, F. W. *Colour-blindness and colour-perception.* London: Kegan Paul, Trench, Trubner, 1891.

Edridge-Green, F. W., & Porter, A. W. Demonstration of the negative afterimages of spectral and compound colours of known composition. *Journal of Physiology, Proceedings of the Physiological Society,* 1914, *48,* January 24.

Helmholtz, H. L. F. von *Handbuch der physiologischen Optik* (3rd ed., 1st ed. 1866) W. Nagel, A. Gullstrand, & J. von Kries (Eds.). Hamburg and Leipzig: Voss, 1911.

Hering, E. *Grundzüge der Lehre vom Lichtsinne.* Vienna: Gerolds Sohn, 1878.

Hess, C. Über die Tonänderungen der Spektralfarben durch Ermüdung der Netzhaut mit homogenem Licht. *Archiv für Ophthalmologie,* 1880, *36,* 1–32.

Hurvich, L. M., & Jameson, D. Further development of a quantified opponent-colours theory. In *Visual problems of colour*. (Vol. 2) London: H.M. Stationary Office, 1958.

Jacobs, G. H., & Gaylord, H. A. Effects of chromatic adaptation on color naming. *Vision Research*, 1967, *7*, 645–653.

Jameson, D., & Hurvich, L. M. Perceived color and its dependence on focal, surrounding and preceding stimulus variables. *Journal of the Optical Society of America*, 1959, *49*, 890–898.

Jameson, D., & Hurvich, L. M. Opponent-response function related to measured cone photopigments. *Journal of the Optical Society of America*, 1968, *58*, 429–430.

Jameson, D., & Hurvich, L. M. Color adaptation: Sensitivity, contrast, afterimages. In D. Jameson & L. M. Hurvich (Eds.), Handbook of sensory physiology (Vol. VII/4). Berlin: Springer, 1972.

Karwoski, T. Variations toward purple in the visual afterimage. *American Journal of Psychology*, 1929, *41*, 625–636.

Kinney, J. A. S. Changes in appearance of colored stimuli with exposure time. *Journal of the Optical Society of America*, 1965, *55*, 738–739.

Kries, J. von Beitrag zur Physiologie der Gesichtsempfindungen. *Archiv für Anatomie und Physiologie*, 1878, *2*, 505–524.

Kries, J. von Die Gesichtsempfindungen. In W. Nagel (Ed.), Handbuch der Physiologie des Menschen (Vol. 3). Braunschweig: Vieweg, 1905.

Larimer, J. Red/green opponent colors equilibria measured on chromatic adapting fields: evidence for gain changes and restoring forces. *Vision Research*, 1981, *21*, 501–512.

MacAdam, D. L. Chromatic adaptation. *Journal of the Optical Society of America*, 1956, *46*, 500–513.

Newton, I. New theory about light and colours. *Philosophical Transactions of the Royal Society of London*, 1672, *80*, 3075–3087.

Shevell, S. K. The dual role of chromatic backgrounds in color perception. *Vision Research*, 1978, *18*, 1649–1661.

Tschermak-Seysenegg, A. Licht und Farbensinn. In *Handbuch der normalen und pathologischen Physiologie*. Berlin: Springer, 1929.

Walraven, J. Spatial characteristics of chromatic induction; the segregation of lateral effects from stray light artefacts. *Vision Research*, 1973, *13*, 1739–1753.

Walraven, J. Discounting the background—The missing link in the explanation of chromatic contrast. *Vision Research*, 1976, *16*, 289–295.

Werner, J. S., & Wooten, B. R. Opponent chromatic mechanisms: Relation to photopigments and hue naming. *Journal of the Optical Society of America*, 1979, *69*, 422–434.

Westheimer, G. The Maxwellian view. *Vision Research*, 1966, *6*, 669–682.

Wilson, M. H., & Brocklebank, R. W. Complementary hues of afterimages. *Journal of the Optical Society of America*, 1955, *45*, 293–299.

Wooten, B. R. *The effects of simultaneous and successive chromatic contrast on spectral hue.* Ph.D. Dissertation, Brown University, Providence, 1970.

Wright, W. D. The measurement and analysis of colour adaptation phenomena. *Proceedings of the Royal Society* (London), 1934, *B 115*, 49–87.

Wyszecki, G., & Stiles, W. S. Color science. New York: Wiley, 1967.

29

Änderung der Farbwahrnehmung bei gegensinniger Abfolge der Farbtöne im Farbenkreis[1]

Lothar Spillmann[2]
Christa Neumeyer[3]
Neurologische Universitätsklinik
Freiburg i.Br., West Germany

ABSTRACT

Twenty colored sectors were arranged on a disk in the sequence of the color circle. Colors were equidistant on the Munsell hue scale and had identical value and chroma notations. When the disks were rotated at approximately 7 revolutions/sec, the perceived hues varied with the direction of rotation. The temporal sequence purple, blue, green, yellow, red (counterclockwise rotation) elicited perception of blue-green and yellow-red, whereas the opposite sequence (clockwise rotation) led to the perception of red-purple and green. These colors were seen either as sectors or as diffuse patches without any clear demarcation between them. The difference in perceived hue is attributed to mutual inhibition between DeValois' opponent color processes at the level of the lateral geniculate nucleus.

ZUSAMMENFASSUNG

Zwanzig Farbtöne waren auf einer Kreisscheibe als Sektoren gemäß ihrer Reihenfolge im Farbenkreis angeordnet. Die Farben bestanden aus gleichabständigen Munsell-Papieren gleicher Helligkeit und Sättigung. Bei Drehung des

---

[1]Das hier beschriebene Phänomen wurde mehrfach in der Öffentlichkeit vorgestellt: ETP-Winterschool on "Mechanisms of Visual Perception", Zuoz 1974; Tagung der experimentell arbeitenden Psychologen, Gießen 1974; Fall-Meeting of the Optical Society of America, Boston 1975. Siehe auch Pflügers Arch. *347*, R58, Abstract 116 (1974).

[2]Mit Unterstützung des SFB 70, Teilprojekt A6.

[3]Jetzige Anschrift: Institut für Zoologie, Universität Mainz.

Farbenkreises mit etwa 7 Umdrehungen/sec wurde bei einer zeitlichen Abfolge der Farben purpur, blau, grün, gelb, rot, purpur nur das Farbenpaar blau-grün und gelb-rot wahrgenommen, bei der umgekehrten Folge dagegen nur das Farbenpaar rot-purpur und grün. Diese Erscheinung läßt sich vermutlich mit wechselseitiger Hemmung zwischen den von DeValois beschriebenen Gegenfarb-Neuronen erklären.

AUSGANGSBEOBACHTUNG

Zwei sich gegensinnig drehende Farbkreisel erzeugen unter geeigneten Bedingungen die jeweils komplementären Farbwahrnehmungen blau-grün und gelb-rot, sowie rot-purpur und grün. Die beiden verwendeten Farbkreisel bestanden aus je 20 subjektiv gleichabständigen Farbtönen (Munsell-Papiere 2.5/ und 7.5/), die in Sektoren von je 18° gemäß ihrer Reihenfolge im Farbenkreis auf einer weißen Pappscheibe aufgeklebt waren (Abb. 29.1). Die an den Rand geschriebenen Farbbezeichnungen geben die Anfangsbuchstaben der Farbtöne wieder. So steht beispielsweise RP für rot-purpur, G für grün und Y für gelb (yellow). Helligkeit und Sättigung der Farbpapiere waren gleich (Munsell −/6/6). Beide Scheiben waren identisch. Sie wurden mit gleicher Geschwindigkeit, jedoch in unterschiedlicher Richtung, gedreht. Dadurch ergab sich für den linksdrehenden Kreisel, bezogen auf einen Netzhautort, die zeitliche Abfolge der Farbtöne: purpur, purpur-blau, blau, blau-grün, grün, grün-gelb, gelb, gelb-rot, rot, rot-purpur und purpur. Für den rechtsdrehenden Kreisel war die Reihenfolge umgekehrt.

Versetzt man die beiden Kreisel langsam in Gegendrehung, so sieht man zunächst alle Farben des Farbenkreises. Die beiden Kreisel unterscheiden sich nicht. Mit steigender Drehzahl verschmelzen die Farben jedoch zu immer größeren Sektoren, und zwischen 3 und 8 Umdrehungen/sec treten nur noch zwei Farbpaare hervor. Diese sind für die beiden Kreisel deutlich verschieden. Auf dem linksdrehenden Kreisel überwiegt der Eindruck blau-grün und gelb-rot, auf dem rechtsdrehenden der Eindruck rot-purpur und grün. Die Farben sind räumlich nur wenig voneinander abgegrenzt, überlagern und durchdringen sich und wechseln beständig ihren Ort. Bei schneller Drehung der Scheiben gehen die Farben schließlich in ein gleichmäßiges Grau über.

FARBABGLEICH

Die Farbtonpaare auf den gegenläufig drehenden Kreiseln wurden mit Hilfe eines sukzessiven Farbvergleichs genauer bestimmt. Dazu wurden rechteckige, 7 × 10 cm große Proben der 20 verwendeten Munsell-Papiere auf einen weißen Karton geklebt, der unmittelbar unter den Kreiseln angebracht war. Aufgabe der Ver-

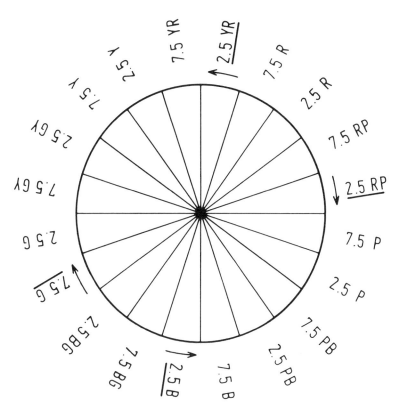

ABB. 29.1. Werden zwei sonst identische Farbkreisel von der dargestellten Art im Gegensinn gedreht, so beobachtet man bei Linksdrehung die Farbtöne blau-grün und gelb-rot mit den Munsell-Werten 2.5 B und 2.5 YR, bei Rechtsdrehung die Farbtöne rot-purpur und grün mit den Munsell-Werten 2.5 RP und 7.5 G. Bestimmend für den Farbunterschied ist die zeitliche Abfolge der Farbsektoren. Die Drehgeschwindigkeit war 7.3 Umdrehungen/sec. Die hierbei auf den Kreiseln wahrgenommenen Farbtöne wurden mittels eines sukzessiven Farbabgleichs mit 20 Munsell-Papieren, die den Sektorfarben entsprachen, bestimmt.

FIG. 29.1. Stimuli were two identical color disks of the kind shown by this schematic representation. Each consisted of twenty 18°-sectors of equal Munsell value and chroma (−/6/6), but different hue. Hue notations were as indicated. In the experiment, disks of 4.5° diameter were rotated in opposite directions, thus producing opposite sequences of stimulation. With counterclockwise rotation (ccw), the perceived colors matched Munsell hues 2.5 B and 2.5 YR, whereas with clockwise rotation (cw), the perceived colors matched 2.5 RP and 7.5 G. The speed of rotation was 7.3 revolutions/sec in both cases. All observations were made foveally and there was no time limit. However, hue differences were also seen at lower speeds, in extrafoveal vision, and at short exposure durations. Color deficient subjects usually failed to observe the effect.

suchsperson war es, durch rasches Hin-und Herblicken jeder der auf den Kreiseln beobachteten Farben eine der 20 Munsell-Farbstufen zuzuordnen. Dabei war die Schätzung von Zwischenwerten erlaubt. Als Beobachter dienten die beiden Autoren, beide normale Trichromaten.

Die Drehgeschwindigkeit betrug im Versuch 7.3 U/sec. Jeder Kreisel erschien unter einem Sehwinkel von 4.5°. Die Beobachtungsdauer war unbegrenzt. Zur Beleuchtung wurde eine gleichspannungsgespeiste Wolfram-Lampe (250 W) verwendet.

Unter diesen Beobachtungsbedingungen charakterisierten beide Beobachter die auf dem linksdrehenden Kreisel erscheinenden Farbtöne mit den Munsell-Werten 2.5 B und 2.5 YR, die auf dem rechtsdrehenden mit 2.5 RP und 7.5 G. Diese Werte sind zueinander komplementär. Sie wurden von mehreren Versuchspersonen bestätigt.

Randbedingungen

Ähnliche Ergebnisse erhält man, wenn die Kreisel aus großem Abstand (bis 0.5° Sehwinkel) gesehen, kurzfristig dargeboten (bis 50 msec) oder extrafoveal (bis 10° peripher) betrachtet werden. Dabei fiel auf, daß im peripheren Sehen die Sättigung der Farben bei gleichbleibendem Farbton zunahm. Farbfehlsichtige Beobachter berichteten keine oder nur geringe Unterschiede zwischen den beiden Kreiseln, doch fehlen systematische Beobachtungen.

ERGEBNISSE BEI TEILABDECKUNG DES FARBENKREISES

Welche Farben des Farbenkreises sind notwendig, um komplementäre Farbenpaare auftreten zu lassen und einen Unterschied zwischen Rechts- und Linksdrehung hervorzurufen? Um diese Frage zu prüfen, wurden beide Kreisel zunächst mit zwei gegenüberliegenden 90°-Sektoren ("Schmetterlingsfigur") aus grauem Munsell-Papier (N6) so abgedeckt, daß auf jedem Farbenkreis zwei gegenüberliegende Teilbereiche von je 5 Farbsektoren übrigblieben (Abb. 29.2a). Die grauen Abdeckungen drehten sich mit und wurden durch Verrücken um jeweils zwei Sektorbreiten in insgesamt 5 Stellungen dargeboten. Jede Stellung war auf beiden Kreiseln identisch. Die wahrgenommenen Farbtöne wurden, wie im ersten Versuch, von beiden Beobachtern mit Hilfe der Munsell-Farbstufen bestimmt. Jeder Vergleich wurde nur einmal durchgeführt, abweichende Antworten beider Versuchspersonen wurden gemittelt.

Ähnlich wie beim vollständigen Farbenkreis gaben die Beobachter jeweils 2 Farbantworten. Diese lagen stets in der Mitte der beiden Teilbereiche und waren komplementär. Die Farbangaben für Links- und Rechtsdrehung stimmten fast immer genau überein. Fünf zusammenhängende Farbsektoren reichen demnach nicht aus, um einen Farbtonunterschied zwischen den beiden Drehrichtungen hervorzurufen.

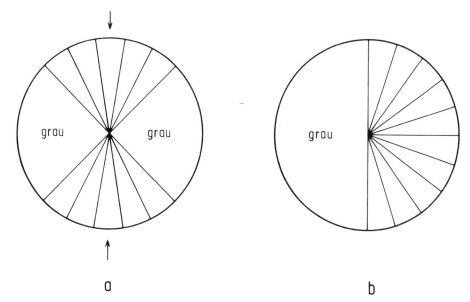

ABB. 29.2. (a) Bei Teilabdeckung des Farbenkreisels mit einer grauen (N6) Schmetterlingsfigur von 2 × 90° beobachtet man bei Links- und Rechtsdrehung die gleichen zwei Farbenpaare. Die wahrgenommenen Farben entsprechen dabei Sektoren, die in der Mitte der farbigen Teilbereiche liegen (Pfeile).

(b) Bei Abdeckung einer Hälfte des Farbenkreisels unterscheiden sich die wahrgenommenen Farben bei Links- und Rechtsdrehung beträchtlich. Von den zwei für jede Drehrichtung beobachteten Farbtönen entspricht der eine einem Sektor des farbigen Teilbereichs (''primäre'' Farbantwort), der andere, schwächere, einem Sektor unter der grauen Abdeckung (''induzierte'' Farbantwort). Die relative Lage der Farbantworten hängt von der Stellung der Abdeckung auf dem Kreisel ab.

FIG. 29.2. (a) No hue difference was perceived between ccw and cw-rotation, when each color disk was partially covered by a grey (N6), butterfly-shaped occluder exposing two segments of five color sectors each in juxtaposition. The occluder covered identical sections on each disk; by advancing it in two-sector steps, a total of 5 positions could be tested. Under all conditions, two hues corresponding to the middle sectors (arrows) were seen on each disk. Colors appeared less saturated than on the non-occluded disk (Fig. 29.1).

(b) A clear difference in hue was perceived between ccw and cw-rotation after each color disk was partially covered by a 180° grey occluder so that a train of 10 contiguous sectors remained visible. Here, two colors were again seen, one corresponding to the hue of a sector actually presented to the eye (''primary'' color response), the other, weaker one, corresponding to a sector covered by the grey occluder (''induced'' color response). The relative position of the two hues on the color circle varied with the position of the occluder. Ten such positions separated by two-sector steps were tested.

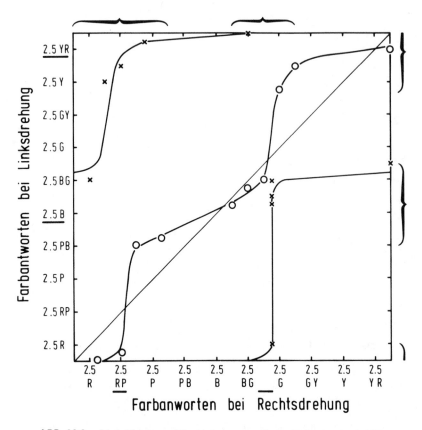

ABB. 29.3. Die bei Links- und Rechtsdrehung gegebenen Farbantworten bei 10 verschiedenen Stellungen der 180°-Abdeckung sind hier gegeneinander aufgetragen. Die Kreise beziehen sich auf primäre Farbantworten, die Kreuze auf induzierte Farbantworten. Die Diagonale gibt die Ortslinie gleicher Farbantworten für Links- und Rechtsdrehung an. Die Klammern bezeichnen Farbtonbereiche, innerhalb derer sich die Farbantworten zusammenfassen lassen. Die Mittelwerte dieser Antwortgruppen liegen bei 2.5 B und 2.5 YR für Linksdrehung und bei 2.5 RP und 7.5 G für Rechtsdrehung. Diese beiden Farbenpaare sind identisch mit denen, die auf dem nichtabgedeckten Vollkreis gesehen werden (Abb. 29.1). Die Ergebnisse sind Mittelwerte von 2 Versuchspersonen (LS und CN).

FIG. 29.3. Hue responses obtained with a semi-occluded color disk (Fig. 29.2b) are shown for 10 positions of the grey occluder. The responses for ccw-rotation (ordinate) are plotted against the responses for cw-rotation (abscissa). On both axes, Munsell 7.5 hue notations have been omitted for clarity; they belong halfway below or to the left of the corresponding 2.5 notations. Each data point refers to the responses elicited by a given occluder position. Circles represent primary color responses and crosses induced color responses (for definition see legend to Fig. 29.2). If the hues perceived on the two counterrotating disks had been the same or similar, data points would have fallen on or near the diagonal. This is found,

Anders verhielt es sich, wenn anstelle der grauen Schmetterlingsfigur von 2 ×
90° die Hälfte des Farbenkreises durch einen 180°-Sektor abgedeckt war. Hierbei
blieb auf jedem Farbkreisel ein Bereich von 10 Farbsektoren in zusammen-
hängender Folge übrig (Abb. 29.2b). Die graue Abdeckung wurde in 10 verschiedenen Stellungen relativ zum Farbenkreis in zufälliger Reihenfolge
dargeboten und die Munsell-Werte der dabei auftretenden Farbtöne bestimmt.

Wie schon vorher wurden auch in diesem Versuch bei jeder Drehrichtung 2
Farben beobachtet. Davon entsprach die eine einem Farbton, der im sichtbaren
Bereich vorkam (''primäre'' Farbantwort), die andere, schwächere, einem
Farbton, der durch den Grausektor verdeckt war und der mithin auf chromatische
Induktion durch einen Farbsektor zurückzuführen ist (''induzierte'' Farbantwort). Die Farbantworten bei Links- und Rechtsdrehung für die 10 verschiedenen Stellungen der Abdeckung sind in Abbildung 29.3 gegeneinander
aufgetragen. Wären bei Links- und Rechtsdrehung dieselben Farben aufgetreten,
so hätten sämtliche Farbantworten auf der Diagonalen durch den Ursprung liegen
müssen. Dies war jedoch nur für blau-grün und gelb-rot der Fall. Bei allen
anderen Paaren war ein deutlicher Unterschied zwischen den beiden Drehrichtungen zu beobachten, insbesondere für die induzierten Farbantworten. Die
kritische Zahl der für einen Farbunterschied erforderlichen (zusam-
menhängenden) Sektoren liegt demnach zwischen 5 und 10.

Die Verbindungslinien für primäre und induzierte Farbantworten (Kreise,
Kreuze) zeigen jeweils einen treppenförmigen Verlauf. Das heißt, die
wahrgenommenen Farben sind nicht gleichmäßig über den Farbenkreis verteilt,
sondern gruppieren sich um bestimmte Farbtöne. Bei Linksdrehung verteilen
sich alle Antworten auf die Farbtöne purpur-blau, blau and blau-grün, sowie auf
gelb, gelb-rot und rot, während bei Rechtsdrehung die Farbtöne rot, rot-purpur
und purpur, sowie blau-grün, grün und grün-gelb bevorzugt sind. Diese in Abbildung 29.3 durch Klammern gekennzeichneten Bereiche auf der rechten Ordinate und auf der oberen Abszisse sind zueinander etwa komplementär. Die
Mittelwerte für die einzelnen Bereiche entsprechen den Farben, die beim vollständigen Farbenkreis in Erscheinung getreten waren: 2.5 B und 2.5 YR für
Linksdrehung, sowie 2.5 RP und 7.5 G für Rechtsdrehung.

Bestimmt man die relative Lage der wahrgenommenen Farbtöne in jeder der

---

however, only for occluder positions eliciting primary color responses in the
blue-green and yellow-red ranges. For other positions, the perceived hues differed
considerably. *Example:* For (o), 2.5 PB on the ccw-rotating disk was correlated
with 7.5 P on the cw-rotating disk; and so was 2.5 Y with 7.5 RP for (x). Because
of their uneven distribution, color responses may be lumped together as indicated
by the brackets on the right and top axes. The mean values for data falling within
these brackets are 2.5 B and 2.5 YR for ccw-rotation, and 2.5 RP and 7.5 G for
cw-rotation (Munsell notations underlined). These are the same hues as perceived
on the non-occluded color disk shown in Fig. 29.1. Data are averages from two
subjects.

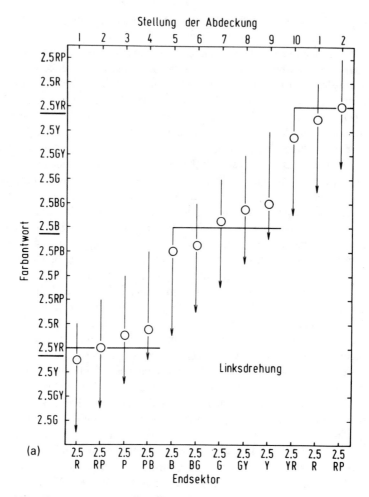

ABB. 29.4. Die primären Farbantworten sind für alle 10 Teilbereiche als Funktion der Farbe des jeweiligen Endsektors aufgetragen. Die bei den verschiedenen Stellungen der Abdeckung dargebotenen Teilbereiche sind durch Pfeile gekennzeichnet, wobei die Pfeilspitzen den Anfangssektor markieren und die Pfeilenden den Endsektor. Jeder Pfeil repräsentiert 10 Farbsektoren und entspricht einer Dauer von 68.5 msec. Kreise (in Abb. 29.4a) geben die Farbantworten bei Linksdrehung des Kreisels an, Dreiecke (Abb. 29.4b) die Farbantworten bei Rechtsdrehung. Die waagerechten Striche verdeutlichen die Lage der 4 ausgezeichneten Farbtöne: 2.5 B und 2.5 YR für Linksdrehung, sowie 2.5 RP und 7.5 G für Rechtsdrehung. Man beachte die Unstetigkeit in der Abfolge der Farbantworten, wenn einer dieser Farbtöne wegfällt und dafür der komplementäre hinzukommt. Siehe Beispiel im Text.

FIG. 29.4. Primary color responses obtained with the semi-occluded color disk (Fig. 29.2b) are plotted as a function of the color of the end sector, that is, the last sector in a train of ten. This is illustrated by a vertical arrow for each of 10 positions of the occluder (upper abscissa). The arrow head marks the beginning of

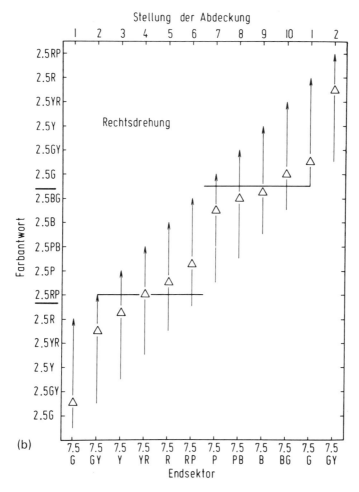

(b)

the train, the tail the end, and the length of the shaft the range of colors exposed (reading from bottom to top in Fig. 29.4a and from top to bottom in Fig. 29.4b). Each arrow represents 10 color sectors corresponding to a total duration of 68.5 msec. On the axis of ordinates, Munsell 7.5 hue notations (omitted) belong half-way below the corresponding 2.5 notations. Color responses for ccw-rotation are depicted by circles, and for cw-rotation by triangles. *Example:* In Fig. 29.4a, the first arrow indicates that the exposed segment of the color disk ranged from 7.5 G (first sector) to 2.5 R (last sector) and elicited the color response 7.5 YR (o). In Fig. 29.4b, the first arrow covers the same segment but in the opposite sequence. However, here the color elicited was 7.5 GY (△). Horizontal lines in Fig. 29.4a refer to the colors 2.5 B and 2.5 YR, in Fig. 4b to 2.5 RP and 7.5 G. These are the same as seen on the non-occluded disk (Fig. 29.1). On the semi-occluded disk, the perceived color depends greatly on which of these sectors is present in the exposed segment. *Example:* Going from occluder position 4 to 5 (in Fig. 29.4a), the perceived hue changes from red (5R) to purple-blue (2.5 PB). Here, sector 7.5 YR was omitted from the beginning of the train while sector 2.5 B was added at the end.

10 Stellungen der 180°-Abdeckung, so findet sich die Sonderrolle dieser beiden Farbenpaare wieder. In den Abbildungen 29.4a (für Linksdrehung) und 29.4b (für Rechtsdrehung) ist die Farbantwort (Kreise, Dreiecke) als Funktion des jeweiligen Endsektors aufgetragen. Damit ist derjenige Farbsektor gemeint, der in der zeitlichen Abfolge der 10 Farbsektoren zuletzt kommt, also unmittelbar vor der Grauabdeckung. Die senkrechten Pfeile bezeichnen den dargebotenen Ausschnitt des Farbkreisels bei den verschiedenen Stellungen der Abdeckung (obere Abszisse). Die Pfeilspitzen markieren dabei den Anfangssektor, also den Sektor, der unmittelbar auf die Grauabdeckung folgt. Bei Änderung der Drehrichtung von links nach rechts wird der bisherige Anfangssektor zum Endsektor und umgekehrt. Bedingt durch die Auswahl der Munsell-Farben hat der Endsektor im ersten Fall die Notation 2.5/ und im zweiten Fall 7.5/. Einem Teilbereich von 10 Farbsektoren entspricht eine Durchlaufzeit von 68.5 msec.

Die Lage des Sektors, dessen Farbton die gesehene Farbe bestimmt, ändert sich innerhalb des Teilbereiches mit der Stellung der Abdeckung. Und zwar verschiebt sich der wahrgenommene Farbton über 5 aufeinanderfolgende Stellungen hinweg fortlaufend von Farbtönen ähnlich dem Endsektor hin zu Farbtönen ähnlich dem Anfangssektor (Abb. 29.4a) oder umgekehrt (Abb. 29.4b). Bei der darauffolgenden Abdeckung kehrt die relative Lage des Farbtons wieder abrupt in Richtung des Ausgangspunktes zurück. Sprünge finden sich immer dann, wenn von zwei bestimmten Farbsektoren (2.5 B oder 2.5 YR für Linksdrehung, und 2.5 RP oder 7.5 G für Rechtsdrehung) der eine hinzukommt, während der andere wegfällt. Diese Farbtöne sind in der Abbildung durch waagerechte Linien gekennzeichnet. Beim Übergang von einer Linie zur anderen findet sich die beschriebene Unstetigkeit in der relativen Lage der Farbantworten.

So ändert sich beispielsweise beim Übergang von der 4. zur 5. Stellung der Abdeckung bei Linksdrehung (Abb. 29.4a) der wahrgenommene Farbton sprunghaft von rot (5 R) zu purpur-blau (2.5 PB), wobei die dazwischenliegenden Farbtöne rot-purpur und purpur ausgelassen werden. Hier war der vormalige Anfangssektor 7.5 YR weggefallen und der dazu komplementäre Endsektor 2.5 B neu hinzugekommen.

ERKLÄRUNGSVERSUCH

Von Professor R. DeValois, UC Berkeley, stammt der Vorschlag, unsere Ergebnisse mis Hilfe der von ihm untersuchten Gegenfarb-Neurone zu erklären. Bekanntlich unterscheidet De Valois im Corpus Geniculatum laterale des Rhesusaffen 4 Klassen von farbspezifischen Neuronen, die von dem Licht eines bestimmten Spektralbereichs erregt, von dem des dazu komplementären Bereichs dagegen gehemmt werden. Man bezeichnet diese Zelltypen mit $+B/-Y$, $+G/-R$, $+Y/-B$, $+R/-G$. Ihre Erregungsmaxima liegen bei 440, 500, 600 und 640 nm. Diese Zellen besitzen ihren Farbantagonismus auch bei Ganzfeldbelichtung (De-Valois, 1965).

		Linksdrehung	Rechtsdrehung

1 Reizfolge (P) - B - G - Y - R   R - Y - G - B - (P)

2 Erregungs -
verlauf im
CGL

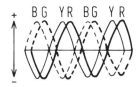 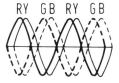

⊢———⊣
0.1 sec

3 Hemmung
zwischen
Farbprozessen

4 Wahrnehmung B - Y - B - Y   R - G - R - G

ABB. 29.5. Hypothetisches Schema zur Erklärung des wahrgenommenen Farb-unterschiedes bei Links- und Rechtsdrehung der Farbkreisel.
Zeile 1: Zeitliche Abfolge der Farbtöne auf jedem der beiden Farbkreisel, bezogen auf einen Netzhautort. Der Vereinfachung halber sind nur 5 Farben von 20 berücksichtigt.
Zeile 2: Zeitlicher Verlauf von Erregung und Hemmung in vier Klassen von Gegenfarb-Neuronen des Corpus Geniculatum laterale bei Reizung mit dem Far-benkreisel: (---) $+B/-Y$; (---) $+G/-R$; (—) $+Y/-B$; (—) $+R/-G$. Die Farbe purpur (P) ist vernachlässigt.
Zeile 3: Hypothetische Hemmwirkungen (Pfeile) zwischen den verschiedenen Gegenfarb-Neuronen.
Zeile 4: Resultierende Farbwahrnehmung.

FIG. 29.5. Schematic explanation of the perceived hue difference between ccw-rotation (left) and cw-rotation (right).
Row 1: Temporal sequence of colors as seen from a fixed point on the retina. For the sake of simplicity, only 5 colors out of 20 are considered.
Row 2: Hypothetical time course of excitation $(+)$ and inhibition $(-)$ in four classes of color-opponent cells in the lateral geniculate nucleus (after DeValois, 1965). Codes are as follows: (---) $+B/-Y$; (---) $+G/-R$; (—) $+Y/-B$; (—) $+R/-G$. Purple (P) has been omitted.
Row 3: Forward and backward masking (arrows) between color opponent cells are assumed to suppress two of the four color processes (see Discussion).
Row 4: Resulting color perception for ccw and cw-rotation. Predicted colors approximately match those actually seen.

Wir nehmen nun vereinfachend an, daß die Farben des Farbenkreises bei Drehung diese 4 Neuronentypen nacheinander reizen. Damit ergibt sich für ihre Erregung und Hemmung der in Abbildung 29.5, Zeile 2, gezeigte hypothetische Zeitverlauf bei der in Zeile 1 beschriebenen Sektorabfolge. Die linke Hälfte der Abbildung bezieht sich auf Linksdrehung, die rechte auf Rechtsdrehung. Wegen der ungleichmäßigen Verteilung der Erregungsmaxima über das Spektrum hin rücken die Kurvengipfel der Zelltypen $+B/-Y$ und $+G/-R$ zeitlich eng aneinander, ebenso die der Zelltypen $+Y/-B$ und $+R/-G$; für Links- und Rechtsdrehung allerdings in umgekehrter Folge. Wenn wir nun annehmen, daß innerhalb dieser beiden Gruppierungen der jeweils zuerst gereizte Zelltyp nach Art eines "forward masking" den kurz danach gereizten hemmt (wie mit den oberen Pfeilen in Zeile 3 verdeutlicht), so würden im wesentlichen nur die Aktivitäten zweier Zelltypen übrigbleiben, um die Wahrnehmung der zwei, in Zeile 4 aufgeführten Farbenpaare hervorzurufen.

Zur Erklärung der bei 180°-Abdeckung erhaltenen Ergebnisse sind jedoch zusätzliche Annahmen notwendig. Betrachten wir beispielsweise die Sektorfolge: BG, G, GY, Y, YR, die zur Wahrnehmung von 5Y (gelb) führte (Abb. 29.4a; zehnte Stellung der Abdeckung). Nach dem eben Gesagten sollte hier die Aktivierung der $+Y/-B$ Zellen die nachfolgende Erregung der $+R/-G$ Zellen hemmen und so eine Empfindung von rot unterdrücken. Außerdem sollte sich die Erregung der $+G/-R$ Zellen in der Wahrnehmung durch einen deutlichen Grünanteil auswirken, da diese Zellen wegen der geringen Reizung der $+B/-Y$ Zellen kaum gehemmt sein dürften. Letzteres ist jedoch nicht der Fall. Wir nehmen deshalb an, daß eine Erregung des $+Y/-B$ Zelltyps auch eine zeitlich vorher erfolgte Erregung des $+G/-R$ Zelltyps hemmen kann ("backward masking"). Dies ist zusammen mit anderen, auf die gleiche Weise erschlossenen, hemmenden Verbindungen in Zeile 4 mit den unteren Pfeilen gekennzeichnet. Alle hemmenden Wirkungen müssen wechselseitig angenommen werden, um auch die bei Rechtsdrehung gefundenen Effekte zu erklären.

Diese Betrachtungsweise vermag die meisten der beobachteten Farbwahrnehmungen auf den rotierenden Scheiben verständlich zu machen. Sie vernachlässigt jedoch neuere Befunde von Gouras und Zrenner (1979), wonach farbopponente Zellen nicht nur in sehr unterschiedlicher Zahl vorkommen, sondern auch ihre Gegenfarbeigenschaften bei kurzdauernden Reizen verlieren. Diese Beobachtung könnte vielleicht die Summation von Erregung erklären, die vermutlich für die bei $2 \times 90°$-Abdeckung erhaltenen Ergebnisse verantwortlich ist. Hier lagen die wahrgenommenen Farbtöne jeweils in der Mitte der dargebotenen 5 Farbsektoren. Noch zu klären ist ferner die Frage nach den zeitlichen Grenzen der Wechselwirkung; diese scheinen sich für Rückwärtshemmung über einen längeren Zeitraum zu erstrecken als für Vorwärtshemmung. In diesem Zusammenhang ist der Befund, daß der Farbunterschied zwischen den beiden Scheiben bis zu einer Darbietungszeit von etwa 50 msec zu sehen ist (entsprechend einem Durchlauf von 7 Sektoren), ein wichtiger Hinweis.

Eine direkte Beziehung unseres Phänomens zu den musterinduzierten Flickerfarben von Fechner und Benham erblicken wir nicht, da diese durch periodische
Leuchtdichteänderungen achromatischer Reize an benachbarten Netzhautstellen
hervorgerufen werden (von Campenhausen, 1968a). Auch ihre Erklärung mittels
phasenabhängiger lateraler Hemmung in der Netzhaut (von Campenhausen,
1968b) weist auf den andersartigen Charakter dieses Phänomens hin.

REFERENCES

Campenhausen, C. v. Über die Farben der Benhamschen Scheibe. *Zeitschrift für vergleichende Physiologie,* 1968, *60,* 351–374. (a)

Campenhausen, C. v. Über den Ursprungsort von musterinduzierten Flickerfarben im visuellen System des Menschen. *Zeitschrift für vergleichende Physiologie,* 1968, *61,* 355–360. (b)

DeValois, R. L. Analysis and coding of color vision in the primate visual system. *Cold Spring Harbor Symposium,* 1965, *30,* 567–579.

Gouras, P., & Zrenner, E. Enhancement of luminance flicker by color-opponent mechanisms. *Science,* 1979, *205,* 587–589.

30

Orientation-Specific Color Aftereffects and Simultaneous Color Contrast

C. F. Stromeyer III
Division of Applied Sciences
Harvard University
Cambridge, Massachusetts

ABSTRACT

Orientation-specific color aftereffects (McCollough effects) were shown to produce simultaneous color contrast: An aftereffect elicited by one test grating induced a contrast color on an adjacent test grating. Color contrast tended to be maximal when the spatial frequency of the test gratings were similar to each other; the relative orientation of the gratings, however, had little effect. Colored lights similar to the aftereffects induced colors similar to the colors induced by the aftereffects. The colors induced with the colored lights were likewise sensitive to the spatial frequency of gratings placed on the field and were not sensitive to grating orientation. These experiments suggest that color contrast may partly occur at a cortical level, on the assumption that the McCollough effect involves orientation-selective cortical mechanisms.

INTRODUCTION

The appearance of an area of given chromaticity may be modified by simultaneous stimulation of a neighboring area with light of a different chromaticity. The color of the area that is modified is shifted approximately toward the complement of the color that induces the change. This effect of simultaneous color contrast has been widely studied with spinning paper discs, colored shadows, and spot and surround configurations of colored lights (see reviews by Graham & Brown, 1965, and Jameson & Hurvich, 1972).

509

The present study examines simultaneous color contrast induced by the Mc-Collough effect, a color aftereffect that is specific to the orientation and spatial frequency of gratings of light and dark bars (see review, Stromeyer, 1978). McCollough (1965) discovered that prolonged viewing of black and white striped gratings in colored lights produced approximately complementary color aftereffects on neutral colored test gratings with orientations similar to the adaptation gratings. McCollough's work was inspired by the extensive pioneering work of Kohler (1951) on contingent aftereffects induced by wearing various types of spectacles that distorted spatial and color properties of the visual world. The contrast effect studied in the present chapter may be seen as follows. A test grating that is oriented to elicit no aftereffect is first presented alone. Next, test gratings that are oriented to elicit a color aftereffect are placed adjacent to the first test grating. The first test grating then appears tinted with the hue complementary to the aftereffect. This contrast effect is studied with a variety of adaptation and test conditions, and the influence of grating orientation and spatial frequency is examined. Initial demonstrations of the contrast effects have been reported elsewhere (Stromeyer, 1971).

These contrast effects clarify some perplexing findings on the McCollough effect. Second, they show that cortical mechanisms can induce color contrast, on the assumption that the McCollough effect is caused by adaptation of orientation-selective mechanisms in the cortex. Third, the effects demonstrate that color contrast is affected by the spatial frequency of gratings of light and dark bars.

METHODS

Observers.   The two observers had normal color vision according to the AO H-R-R Pseudoisochromatic Plates and the Farnsworth 100-Hue Test. The observers were experienced with the McCollough effect and the Munsell color system.

Procedure.   Color aftereffects were built up with vertical or horizontal square-wave gratings which were rear-projected on a ground glass screen by projectors with 500-watt incandescent bulbs. Without filters in the beams, the luminance of light and dark bars was 1900 and 45 cd/m^2, respectively. Kodak Wratten colored filters were placed in the projector beams. The characteristics of the filters for illuminant A, as specified by Kodak, are given in Table 30.1. While viewing the colored adapting gratings, the observer freely scanned the central area of the patterns. For the results shown in Figs. 30.3 and 30.4, the adapting gratings were 28° square from a viewing distance of 46 cm. For the results in Figs. 30.5, and 30.8, the gratings were 14° square, viewed from 92 cm.

After adapting to the colored gratings, the observer rested 10 min and then viewed a series of test patterns composed of gratings in various orientations. The patterns were constructed of white matte paper (High Surface Strathmore) and

TABLE 30.1
Wratten Adaptation Filters Used Throughout the Study, Specified for
Illuminant A

	Dominant λ (nm)	Excitation Purity (%)	Luminous Trans. (%)
Green #40	513	54	26
Magenta #31	513[c]	80	20
Blue #47a	478	92	3.4
Orange #106	596	96	43

[c]Denotes the complementary dominant wavelength on the CIE diagram.

matte black tape. The patterns were illuminated with a Macbeth daylight lamp, which has a correlated color temperature close to illuminant C.

Two forms of test patterns were used, as illustrated in Figs. 30.1 and 30.2. The pattern in Fig. 30.1 is a 3 × 3 checkerboard of alternating gratings. Each cell of the checkerboard was 4.8°, viewed from 180 cm. The luminance of the white areas of the pattern was 50 cd/m². Checkerboards of the following pairs of gratings were used: vertical and horizontal gratings (*v* and *h*); +45° and −45° gratings (+45° and −45°); vertical and +45° gratings (*v* and +45°); horizontal and −45° gratings (*h* and −45°); and checkerboards of alternating vertical grat-

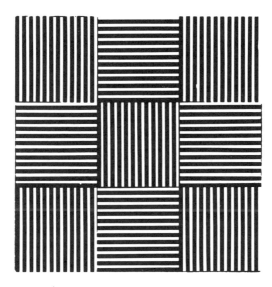

FIG. 30.1. One of the test patterns used in the first experiments. The test patterns consisted of checkerboards of gratings in alternate orientations, as described in text.

FIG. 30.2.   Form of test patterns used to examine the effects of spatial frequency and orientation selectivity on color induction. To examine the effect of spatial frequency the left and right vertical flanking gratings were held constant, and the spatial frequency of the center, +45° grating was varied. To examine the effect of orientation the left and right vertical flanking gratings were 5 c/deg, and the center grating, also of 5 c/deg, was varied in orientation.

ings (*v*) and uniform white squares or alternating horizontal gratings (*h*) and white squares. Given gratings of the checkerboards, e.g., vertical gratings, elicited the McCollough effect. The adjacent gratings, e.g. 45° gratings, appeared colored due to simultaneous color contrast. The observer matched the aftereffects and simultaneous contrast colors with a *Munsell Pocket Book* of matte colored chips. The book was placed at arm's length before the observer and illuminated with Macbeth daylight in the same manner as the test patterns. The *Munsell* system spans the hue circle in approximately equal apparent steps. For each hue, there are samples that vary in equal steps in lightness (Value) and color strength or saturation (Chroma). A designation 5*Y* 8/4, for example, means the sample is a pure yellow (not reddish or greenish) that is light (Value of 8) and of medium saturation (Chroma of 4). (See Wyszecki & Stiles, 1967, for details.)

Figure 30.2 shows the form of the test pattern used to study how color contrast is influenced by the orientation and spatial frequency of the test patterns. Each grating cell was 2.4°, from a viewing distance of 360 cm. The patterns were illuminated by Macbeth daylight, such that the white bars were 38 cd/m². The left and right gratings of the test pattern were held constant for a given session. They elicited the McCollough effect and, in turn, induced a simultaneous contrast color on the central grating, which was varied either in orientation or spatial frequency. The observer matched the color on the central grating by adjusting the intensity (with a neutral wedge) of a chromatic beam that illuminated a magnesium oxide disc 63' in dia, positioned 2.8° below the lower right corner of the test pattern. The beam came from a projector, fitted with a Wratten filter. The disc was also illuminated by the Macbeth lamp at a luminance of 38 cd/m². Each pattern was matched five times each session, in a random series. The saturation of the matches is arbitrarily expressed by the ratio of the luminance of the chromatic beam and Macbeth light falling on the disc.

I also attempted to mimic the induced colors using actual colored lights. The test patterns were illuminated with Macbeth daylight of 38 cd/m², as before. Light was then projected through Wratten filters (described later) on the left and right flanking gratings. The projectors had a variable aperture to control the intensity of the chromatic light. A second projector was used to cast light on the central grating component in order to equate its luminance with the flanking, colored gratings. This projector was fitted with Wratten 78b and 80a filters, which rendered its chromaticity close to Macbeth daylight.[1] The observer matched the color on the central grating as described above.

For some measurements, the flanking or central grating was replaced by a uniform white area (0 c/deg) that had the same luminance as the white bars of the gratings.

The parts of the test pattern that directly elicit a McCollough effect will often be referred to as the "inducing field" and the other parts of the pattern that appear colored due to simultaneous color contrast (induced by the McCollough effect) will be called the "test field."

RESULTS

Demonstration of Simultaneous Color Contrast
Induced by the McCollough Effect

In the first session, observers adapted to a vertical green grating (see Table 30.1) and horizontal magenta grating. In the second session, the adapting patterns were vertical blue and horizontal orange gratings. The two members of each pair of gratings were approximately complementary in color and thus the afterimage from one grating did not appreciably change the hue of the other grating. Before the second session, any remaining aftereffects were neutralized by readapting to the converse conditions of the first session (the adapting gratings were rotated 90°). In each session, the observer adapted 30 min, during which the gratings were interchanged every 10 sec. The adapting and test gratings were 2.5 cycle/degree.

Munsell matches of the aftereffects and the simultaneous contrast colors that they induce are shown in Table 30.2. The colors seen on the patterns containing only vertical (v) or only horizontal (h) gratings represent the aftereffects for each adaptation orientation, uninfluenced by color contrast. Each aftereffect is approximately the complement of the adaptation color. Gratings 45° removed from the adaptation orientation elicited no aftereffects: the +45° and −45° pattern was colorless. However, the 45° grating components of the v and +45° and the h and −45° patterns appeared colored, with the complements of the aftereffects seen on the vertical and horizontal gratings with which they are paired. These contrast

---

[1]Wratten filters 78b plus 80a convert illuminant A to an illuminant with a correlated color temperature similar to illuminant C (Macbeth daylight—6800°K), according to the mired nomograph (*Kodak Wratten Filters,* 1965, Eastman Kodak Co., Rochester, N.Y.).

TABLE 30.2
Munsell Matches of Colors Seen on Test Patterns, First Experiments.
Observers CS and (MW)-Matches for MW in Parentheses

Session 1: Adapt to v-green *and* h-magenta

Test Pattern		Color Matches	
v		10 RP 7/6	(2.5 R 7/6)
h		5 G 8/4	(2.5 G 8/6)
v and h	$\{ v$	10 RP 7/8	(5 R 7/8)
	$\ h$	5 G 8/4	(2.5 G 7/6)
+45° and −45°		white	(white)
v and +45°	$\{ v$	10 RP 7/6	(2.5 R 7/6)
	$\ +45°$	2.5 G 8/4	(2.5 G 8/4)
h and −45°	$\{ h$	5 G 8/4	(2.5 G 7/6)
	$\ -45°$	2.5 R 8/2	(2.5 R 8/2)

(*continued*)

colors induced on the 45° components are indicated in Munsell coordinates, Fig. 30.3. The origin of the vectors represents the aftereffects; the arrow tips, the contrast colors induced by the aftereffects.

The presence of a grating in the "test field" appears to be important for the color contrast effect, because both observers saw little color on the homogeneous white regions of the v and the h patterns. This effect is investigated later.

Control for Orientation Interactions

In the previous experiments, aftereffects were produced with vertical and horizontal adapting gratings of approximately complementary colors. The aftereffects, if broadly tuned for orientation, may approximately cancel at 45° (midway between vertical and horizontal). In this case, a small shift of the test grating from 45° may elicit a perceptible aftereffect. A vertical grating may cause a slight apparent angle expansion so as to shift the apparent angle of a 45° grating toward horizontal. This shift may cause the 45° grating to elicit the aftereffect associated with the horizontal test grating. Thus, the color seen on the 45° gratings (when paired with vertical gratings) may be a McCollough effect rather than a contrast color induced by the aftereffect elicited by the vertical grating. Studies by Gibson (1937) and Blakemore, Carpenter, and Georgeson (1970a) show that two lines separated by 45° are little affected by angle expansion; however, Bouma & Andriessen (1970) found an expansion effect as large as 10° between a vertical and 45° line. The following control experiments show that this effect does not account for the results.

In the first experiment, only a magenta aftereffect was built up; the aftereffect induced a green contrast color. The observer adapted 30 min to a horizontal

TABLE 30.2   *Continued*

Session 2: Adapt to v-*blue and* h-*orange*

Test Pattern		Color Matches	
v		7.5 YR 8/4	(2.5 Y 9/6*)
h		5 B 8/2	(2.5 B 8/4)
v and *h* { *v*		7.5 YR 8/6	(2.5 Y 8/8)
{ *h*		5 B 8/4	(2.5 B 7/6)
+45° and −45°		white	(white)
v and +45° { *v*		7.5 YR 8/6	(2.5 Y 8/8)
{ +45°		7.5 B 8/2	(2.5 B 7/4)
h and −45° { *h*		5 B 8/2	(2.5 B 7/6)
{ −45°		5 Y 9.5/5*	(2.5 Y 8/4)

*Extrapolated Munsell Value.

green grating alternating every 10 sec with a homogeneous magenta field (Wratten 31). The magenta field served to maintain the saturation of the green grating and neutralize the magenta afterimage of the green grating. Test patterns (Table 30.3, top) with vertical and 45° grating components, that is, the *v, v* and +45°, and +45° and −45° patterns, all appeared colorless. However, the vertical components of the *v* and *h* pattern appeared green; the magenta aftereffect on the horizontal components induced green on the verticals.

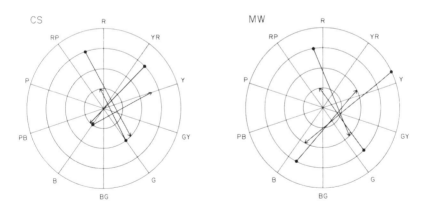

FIG. 30.3. The aftereffects and the contrast colors they induce shown in Munsell coordinates—first experiment. Table 30.2 describes adaptation conditions. The letters around the coordinates represent Munsell Hue, and each circle going outward from the center represents two steps of Munsell Chroma. The aftereffects seen on the vertical and horizontal grating components of the *v* and +45° pattern and the *h* and −45° pattern induced contrast colors on the 45° grating components. The origin of the vectors represent the aftereffects; the arrow tips, the colors induced by the aftereffects.

TABLE 30.3
Munsell Matches of Colors Seen on Test Patterns
Observers CS and (MW)

Adapt to h-green and Uniform Magenta Field

Test Pattern		Color Matches	
v		white	(white)
h		10 RP 7/6	(2.5 R 7/6)
v and *h* {	*v*	5 G 8/4	(5 G 8/4)
	h	10 RP 7/6	(2.5 R 7/8)
+45° and −45°		white	(white)
v and +45°		white	(white)

Adapt to 2.5 c/deg v-magenta and 10 c/deg v-green

Test Pattern		Color Matches
2.5 c/deg *v* and *h* {	*v*	7.5 G 8/4
	h	2.5 R 8/4
10 c/deg *v* and *h* {	*v*	10 RP 7/4
	h	5 G 8/4

In the second experiment green and magenta aftereffects were built up, each specific to a vertical grating of a given spatial frequency. Each aftereffect induced its own contrast color. Observer CS adapted 30 min to a 2.5 c/deg magenta vertical grating (15 sec exposure) alternating with a 10 c/deg green vertical grating (10 sec exposure). The aftereffects were viewed on the *v* and *h* test patterns (Fig. 30.1) composed either of 2.5 or 10 c/deg gratings. The 2.5 c/deg vertical test grating appeared green, whereas the 10 c/deg vertical grating appeared magenta. Each aftereffect induced its own contrast color on the adjacent horizontal gratings (Table 30.3, bottom).

In the third control experiment, vertical and horizontal adapting gratings were used which were not complementary in color, unlike the first experiment in this study. The adapting gratings were orange and green, which produced, respectively, blue and magenta aftereffects; each aftereffect induced its respective contrast color. All patterns were of 2.5 c/deg. The observers adapted 60 min to alternating 2-min periods of stimulation: to a vertical orange grating alternating every 10 sec with a homogeneous blue field, and, for the next 2 min, to a green horizontal grating alternating every 10 sec with a homogeneous magenta field. Two pairs of approximately complementary colors were used for adaptation, because direct alternation of the orange and green gratings would have modified the color of each grating in the direction of the afterimage of the other grating. The colors seen on the test patterns (Fig. 30.1) are described in Table 30.4. The *v* pattern appeared blue (adaptation to vertical-orange); the *h* pattern appeared

TABLE 30.4
Munsell Matches of Colors Seen on Test Patterns
Observers CS and (MW)

Adapt to Two Gratings of Non-complementary Colors: v-*orange Alternating with Uniform Blue Field and* h-*green Alternating with Uniform Magenta Field*

Test Pattern			Color Matches		
v			10 B 7/2		(5 B 7/4)
h			2.5 R 8/6		(2.5 R 7/8)
v and *h*	{	*v*	10 BG 7/4		(5 BG 6/4)
		h	5 R 7/8		(2.5 R 7/8)
+45° and −45°			white		(white)
v and +45°	{	*v*	10 B 7/4		(5 B 7/4)
		+45°	2.5 Y 8/6		(5 Y 9/6*)
h and −45°	{	*h*	10 RP 7/6	'	(2.5 R 7/8)
		−45°	2.5 G 8/4		(7.5 G 7/4)

*Extrapolated Munsell Value.

magenta (adaptation to horizontal-green). The *v* and +45° pattern appeared, respectively, blue and orange-yellow; the *h* and −45° pattern, magenta and green. Each aftereffect induced its complementary color, as may be seen in Fig. 30.4. The dotted lines represent the colors of the *v* and *h* pattern, which are respectively blue-green and red. The green addition to the blue aftereffect on the vertical components is induced by the magenta aftereffect on the horizontal components.

Color Contrast and Spatial Frequency

The contrast colors induced by the aftereffects appear to depend on the presence of a grating in the "test field." In the first experiment, little color was induced onto the homogeneous white cells of the *v* and the *h* checkerboard test patterns. In the following experiments the spatial frequency and orientation of the gratings are varied to determine how luminance modulated gratings affect color contrast.

The effect of spatial frequency was first examined. The observers adapted 30 min to a green vertical grating alternating every 10 sec with a magenta horizontal grating. One spatial frequency was used in a given session, either 2.5, 5, or 10 c/deg. The test patterns (Fig. 30.2) consisted of left and right, vertical gratings, which were maintained at the adapting spatial frequency, and a central, +45° grating that was varied in spatial frequency. The strength of the green contrast color seen on the central grating was matched by varying the intensity of a green beam falling on a small matching field placed below the pattern (see Methods). The saturation is expressed as the ratio of the luminance of the green beam and the Macbeth daylight (38 cd/m^2) falling on the small matching field. The green

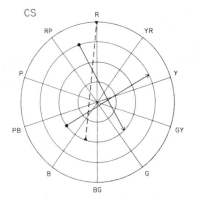 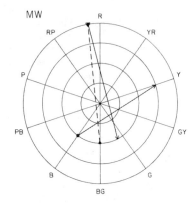

FIG. 30.4. The aftereffects and contrast colors they induce. The observer adapted to vertical and horizontal gratings of non-complementary colors, as described in Table 30.4. The aftereffects seen on the vertical and horizontal grating components of the v and $+45°$ pattern and the h and $-45°$ test pattern induced contrast colors on the $45°$ grating components. The origin of the vectors represents the aftereffects; the arrow tips, the colors induced by the aftereffects. Each aftereffect induced its complementary color. The triangles at the ends of the dotted lines indicate the aftereffects seen on the v and h test pattern—mutual color contrast between the aftereffects causes the colors to become approximately complementary.

beam was produced with a Wratten 55 green filter (dominant wavelength with illuminant A, 524 nm; excitation purity, 62%) for observer CS, and with a Wratten 65 filter (501 nm; 74%) for MW.

Any remaining aftereffects were then neutralized by adapting to the original condition with the gratings rotated 90°. The color contrast induction was then mimicked with colored lights. The test pattern was illuminated with Macbeth daylight so the white bars were 38 cd/m², as before. Magenta light was then projected on the left and right vertical flanking gratings so as to increase the illuminance of the light bars by an additional 1.3 cd/m². Light similar to Macbeth daylight (see Methods) was added to the central grating to equate the luminance of the gratings. The magenta light was produced with a Wratten 34a filter (574c nm; 92%) for observer CS and with a Wratten 32 filter (547c nm; 77%) for MW. The test patterns also included patterns in which the vertical flanking gratings were uniform fields (0 c/deg). The induced green on the central 45° gratings was matched as before.

The matches of the green color induced by the aftereffects and by the colored lights are shown in Fig. 30.5. The strength of the induced green varies with spatial frequency and tends to be maximal when the frequency of the vertical and +45° gratings match. The aftereffects and colored lights produce similar effects.

Figure 30.6 shows matches of the color induced on the central 45° grating as a function of its spatial frequency when the flanking fields were uniform (0 c/

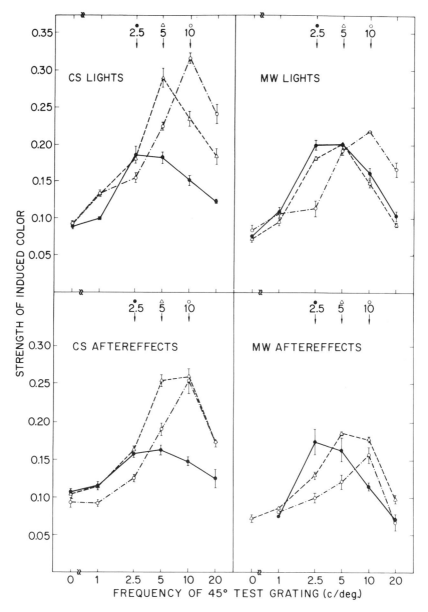

FIG. 30.5. Matches of induced green as a function of the relative spatial frequency of the test gratings. The vertical test gratings (Fig. 30.2) were made to appear magenta with aftereffects or colored lights, and the observer matched the induced green on the 45° center grating. The abscissa represents the spatial frequency of the +45° grating; the arrows, the frequency of the vertical gratings. In the case of the aftereffects, the arrows also indicate the spatial frequency of the adaptation gratings—the adaptation gratings and vertical test gratings matched in spatial frequency. The ordinate represents the strength of the induced green, expressed by the ratio of the luminance of the green and white lights that were mixed to match the induced green. The vertical lines indicate ±1 standard error of the mean ($n = 5$).

519

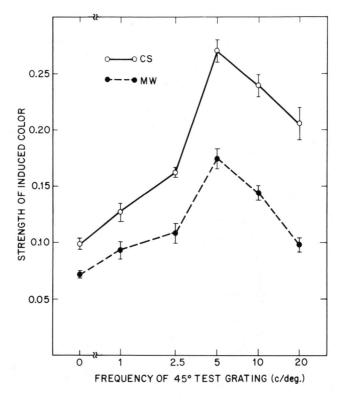

FIG. 30.6.   Matches of induced green on the +45° center grating when the side flanking fields were spatially uniform and illuminated with desaturated magenta *light* (see text). The abscissa represents the spatial frequency of the +45° center grating.

deg—Methods) and illuminated with magenta light, as described above. The induced green is weakest when the +45° grating is 0 c/deg and strongest when it is 5 c/deg.

Figure 30.7 shows that a yellow contrast color induced by blue light is also spatial-frequency selective. The vertical flanking gratings were illuminated with blue light (Wratten 47a) of 2.2 cd/m², as well as the Macbeth daylight. Other details on illumination of the patterns were identical to the previous experiment. The matching projector was fitted with a Wratten 8K2 yellow filter (581 nm; 84%) for CS and with a Wratten 9K3 filter (583 nm; 82%) for MW.

Color Contrast and Grating Orientation

The experiments of the previous section with green and magenta stimuli were repeated with the central test grating (Fig. 30.2) varied in orientation. The

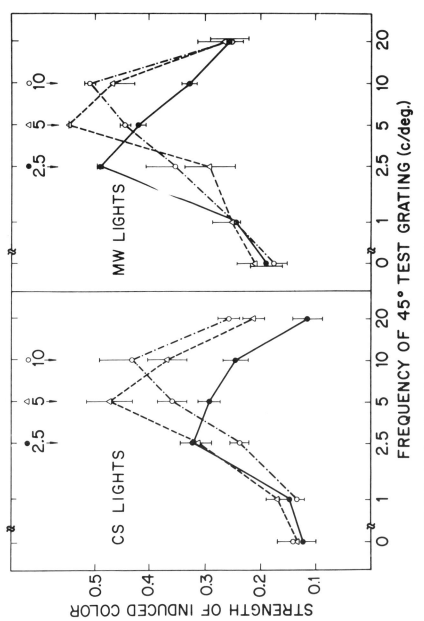

FIG. 30.7. Matches of induced yellow on the +45° center grating when the vertical side flanking gratings were illuminated with desaturated blue *light*. The abscissa represents the spatial frequency of the +45° grating; the arrows, the frequency of the vertical gratings. The ordinate represents the strength of the induced yellow, expressed as the ratio of the luminance of the yellow and white lights that were mixed to match the induced yellow.

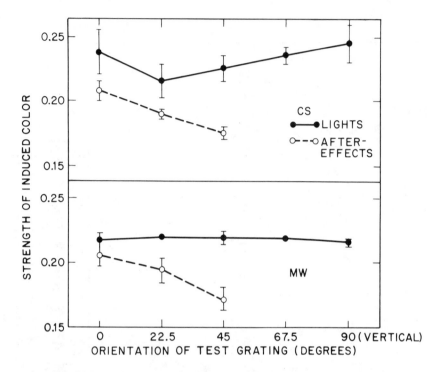

FIG. 30.8.   Matches of induced green as a function of the relative orientation of the test gratings. The vertical test gratings (Fig. 30.2) were made to appear magenta with *aftereffects* or *colored lights*, and the observer matched the induced green on the center grating. The abscissa represents the orientation of the center grating.

flanking gratings were vertical. All patterns were 5 c/deg. Figure 30.8 shows that the magenta *light* on the flanking gratings induces a green in the central grating which varies little with orientation of the center grating. A McCollough effect was produced by adapting 30 min to a 5 c/deg green vertical grating alternating every 10 sec with a uniform magenta field. The following colors were seen on the *center* test grating as it was varied in orientation. A vertical center grating appeared magenta due to the aftereffect. The 67.5° grating (22.5° from vertical) viewed in isolation appeared magenta, but in the presence of the flanking gratings it appeared neutral, presumably due to the green contrast color that was induced from the flanking gratings which appeared magenta. The 45°, 22.5° and 0° gratings appeared green (Fig. 30.8). The small variation of the induced green on these latter gratings may have been caused by an interaction of the induced green and magenta aftereffect on the center grating.

DISCUSSION

These experiments show that when a black and white test grating is made to appear colored, with either an aftereffect or colored light, a complementary color is induced onto adjacent gratings. Colored lights which were chosen to approximately match the aftereffects induced contrast colors similar to the colors induced by the aftereffects. These effects of simultaneous color contrast were sensitive to the spatial frequency of the test gratings but relatively insensitive to the grating orientation.

Spatial Frequency Effects

Color contrast was influenced in two ways by varying the spatial frequency of the test gratings.

Color contrast was generally strongest when the gratings within the "inducing" and "test" fields were of similar spatial frequency. Possibly, this effect may be due to a mechanism of lateral inhibition that is both color-specific and spatial frequency-specific.

A second effect of spatial frequency on color contrast was observed when a uniform inducing field was illuminated with colored light and the test field contained a grating whose frequency was varied. Saturation was maximal on test gratings of 5 c/deg and declined progressively at higher and lower frequencies. This variation of saturation with frequency describes a function similar to the contrast sensitivity functions for sinusoidal (Campbell & Green, 1965) and square-wave gratings (DePalma & Lowry, 1962), which also peak near 5 c/deg.

The variation in saturation with frequency might be related to the variation in the brightness modulation of the gratings. Bryngdahl (1966) showed that the brightness modulation of high-contrast sinusoidal gratings was always greater than the objective modulation. This brightness gain function was maximal for gratings of approximately 5 c/deg for a large range of contrast (measured up to 0.70 contrast). The spatial frequency of square-wave gratings also affects the Bezold-Brücke hue shift (presumably by an influence on brightness); however, the effect does not peak at 5 c/deg, but increases monotonically with frequency throughout the measured range of 2-12 c/deg (Van der Wildt & Bouman, 1968). The increase in induced color on gratings near 5 c/deg, observed in the present chapter, may be caused by an increase in brightness modulation. This suggestion is not necessarily inconsistent with the finding that color contrast becomes stronger as the luminance of the test field is lowered below the luminance of the inducing field; color contrast is maximal when the luminance of the test field is two or three times lower than the inducing field (Jameson & Hurvich, 1959; Kinney, 1962). The grating pattern in the test field may facilitate color contrast for two reasons. First, the high-contrast gratings reduced the mean spatial luminance of the test field by a factor of approximately two relative to the uniform white (0 c/deg) test field, since the white bars of the gratings and uniform white test field were equated in luminance. This factor, however, does not account for the stronger contrast colors seen on test gratings of 5 c/deg versus 20 c/deg. The second factor is that the mechanisms producing color contrast may be sensitive to the spatial luminance modulation of the test field, with peak sensitivity at approximately 5 c/deg.

Studies on the McCollough effect show that luminance contrast strongly affects the saturation of the aftereffects; the strength of the aftereffects increases with an increase in the contrast of both the adapting and test gratings (Ellis, 1977). Equi-luminance adapting gratings, e.g., gratings of alternating grey and green stripes, produce little if any aftereffects (Harris & Barkow, 1969; Stromeyer & Dawson, 1978). Hilz and Cavonius (1970) and Hilz, Huppmann, and Cavonius (1974) have also shown that introducing luminance contrast into chromatic gratings can strongly facilitate wavelength discrimination between adjacent bars of the grating patterns. These studies suggest that luminance and chromatic information are jointly processed.

Site of Color Contrast

The experiments suggest that cortical mechanisms can produce color contrast, on the assumption that the McCollough effect is caused by adaptation of orientation-selective mechanisms in the cortex. (This does not mean that color contrast may be an exclusively cortical effect.)

There are indeed two reasons for believing that the McCollough effect depends on cortical mechanisms. First, the effect is sensitive to line orientation (McCollough, 1965). In the cat and monkey, only cortical cells are strongly sensitive to orientation (Campbell, Cooper, & Enroth-Cugell, 1969; Hubel & Wiesel, 1968). Second, the McCollough effect can be varied by the Blakemore and Sutton apparent spatial frequency shift (Stromeyer, 1972), which is thought to be a cortical effect (Blakemore, Nachmias, & Sutton, 1970b).

Although color contrast might occur at a cortical level, it apparently occurs before the site of binocular interaction, for contrast is poor or absent with dichoptic stimulation (DeValois & Walraven, 1967; Hering, 1890; Land & Daw, 1962.) Studies of single cells in the monkey suggest that the lateral geniculate nucleus does not contain cells for color contrast (DeValois & Pease, 1971; Wiesel & Hubel, 1966); however, a few cells with the requisite properties (double-opponent cells) have been encountered in the cortex (Hubel & Wiesel, 1968).

Implications for Theories of Color Contrast

One theory of color contrast hypothesizes that there is lateral inhibiton that occurs within the three independent fundamentals mechanisms of trichromatic color vision (Alpern, 1964; Rollet, 1867; Young, 1807). In particular, stimulation of the short-, middle-, and long-wavelength sensitive cone pathways by the inducing field leads through lateral inhibition to reduced sensitivity of the same pathways that respond to the test field; this inhibition may be specific for each pathway acting independently (Alpern, 1964). Thus, for example, stronger stimulation of the long-wavelength cones by the inducing field causes a reduced sensitivity of the long-wavelength cones in the test field. Thus, a neutral test field will stimulate the short- and middle-wavelength cone pathways more than the long-wavelength pathways.

The above model has been described as a "sensitivity model" (Wooten, 1970), since only the sensitivity of independent cone pathways changes. However, there is evidence that a second color-opponent stage also operates (cf. Jameson & Hurvich, 1972; Shevell, 1978; Wooten, 1970), for the color appearance of a given spatial region cannot be predicted solely on the basis of the sensitivity model. This second, color-opponent stage induces a color change into the test field which is "opponent" to the activity in the inducing field. For example, if the opponent stage is stimulated in the red direction by the inducing field this induces the opponent hue, green, into the test field.

The present color contrast effects induced by the McCollough effect cannot readily be accounted for by the sensitivity model. The sensitivity model postulates differential stimulation or adaptation of the independent, distal cone pathways. These pathways are presumably in a neutral state when the observer sees the contrast colors in the present experiments. The contrast colors are induced by the McCollough effect which is orientation-selective and presumably occurs at the cortex. At present, there is no clear physiological evidence which shows that there are neural mechanisms at the cortex which receive inputs from single spectral classes of cones.

Implications for Studies on the McCollough Effect

In studying the McCollough effect, a distinction should be made between the aftereffect per se and contrast colors induced by the aftereffects. Failure to control for contrast colors may give rise to apparently complex results (Stromeyer, 1978). When a single aftereffect is viewed on adjacent test gratings of different orientations, a contrast color may be induced onto a grating which by itself appears achromatic. When two aftereffects of different hue are viewed on adjacent test gratings, the aftereffects may be modified by mutual color induction (as shown in Fig. 30.4). Moreover, successive color contrast (Stromeyer, 1969) can make a black and white adapting grating appear colored, which in turn may produce a McCollough aftereffect.

ACKNOWLEDGMENT

This work was supported in part by Grant EY–01808 (National Eye Institute).

REFERENCES

Alpern, M. Relation between brightness and color contrast. *Journal of the Optical Society of America*, 1964, *54*, 1491–1492.

Blakemore, C., Carpenter, R. H. S., & Georgeson, M. A. Lateral inhibition between orientation detectors in the human visual system. *Nature*, 1970, *228*, 37–39. (a)

Blakemore, C., Nachmias, J., & Sutton, P. The perceived spatial frequency shift: Evidence for frequency-selective neurones in the human brain. *Journal of Physiology*, 1970, *210*, 727–750. (b)

Bouma, H., & Andriessen, J. J. Induced changes in the perceived orientation of line segments. *Vision Research*, 1970, *10*, 333–349.

Bryngdahl, O. Characteristics of the visual system: Psychophysical measurements of the response to spatial sine-wave stimuli in the photopic region. *Journal of the Optical Society of America*, 1966, *56*, 811–821.

Campbell, F. W., Cooper, G. F., & Enroth-Cugell, C. The spatial sensitivity of the visual cells of the cat. *Journal of Physiology*, 1969, *203*, 223–235.

Campbell, F. W., & Green, D. Optical and retinal factors affecting visual resolution. *Journal of Physiology*, 1965, *181*, 576–593.

DePalma, J. J., & Lowry, E. M. Sine-wave response of the visual system: II. Sine-wave and square-wave contrast sensitivity. *Journal of the Optical Society of America*, 1962, *52*, 328–335.

DeValois, R. L., & Pease, P. L. Contours and contrast: responses of monkey lateral geniculate nucleus cells to luminance and color figures. *Science*, 1971, *171*, 694–696.

DeValois, R. L., & Walraven, J. Monocular and binocular aftereffects of chromatic adaptation. *Science*, 1967, *155*, 463–465.

Ellis, S. R. Orientation selectivity of the McCollough effect: Analysis by equivalent contrast transformation. *Perception & Psychophysics*, 1977, *22*, 539–544.

Gibson, J. J. Adaptation, after-effect, and contrast in the perception of tilted lines. II. Simultaneous contrast and the areal restriction of the after-effect. *Journal of Experimental Psychology*, 1937, *20*, 553–569.

Graham, C. H., & Brown, J. L. Color contrast and color appearances: brightness constancy and color constancy. In C. H. Graham (Ed.), *Vision and Visual Perception*, New York: John Wiley & Sons, 1965.

Harris, C. S., & Barkow, B. Color/white grids produce weaker orientation-specific color aftereffects than do color/black grids. *Psychonomic Science*, 1969, *17*, 123. (Abstract)

Hering, E. Beitrag zur Lehre vom Simultankontrast. *Zeitschrift für Psychologie und Physiologie der Sinnesorgane*, 1890, *1*, 18–28.

Hilz, R., & Cavonius, C. R. Wavelength discrimination measured with square-wave gratings. *Journal of the Optical Society of America*, 1970, *60*, 273–277.

Hilz, R., Huppmann, G., & Cavonius, C. R. Influence of luminance contrast on hue discrimination. *Journal of the Optical Society of America*, 1974, *64*, 763–766.

Hubel, D. H., & Wiesel, T. N. Receptive fields and functional architecture of monkey striate cortex. *Journal of Physiology*, 1968, *195*, 215–243.

Jameson, D., & Hurvich, L. M. Perceived color and its dependence on focal, surrounding, and preceding variables. *Journal of the Optical Society of America*, 1959, *49*, 890–898.

Jameson, D., & Hurvich, L. M. Color adaptation: sensitivity, contrast, after-images. In D. Jameson & L. M. Hurvich (Eds.), *Handbook of sensory physiology* (Vol. VII/4), *Visual psychophysics*. Berlin: Springer-Verlag, 1972.

Kinney, J. A. S. Factors affecting induced color. *Vision Research*, 1962, *2*, 503–525.

Kohler, I. Über Aufbau und Wandlungen der Wahrnehmungswelt. Insbesondere über 'bedingte Empfindungen.' *Österreichische Akademie der Wissenschaften, Philosophisch-historische Klasse; Sitzungsberichte*, 227. Band, 1. Abhandlung. Wien: Rohrer, 1951.

Land, E. H., & Daw, N. W. Binocular combination of projected images. *Science*, 1962, *138*, 589–590.

McCollough, C. Color adaptation of edge-detectors in the human visual system. *Science*, 1965, *149*, 1115–1116.

Rollett, A. Zur Physiologie der Contrastfarben. *Akademie der Wissenschaften, Mathematisch-naturwissenschaftliche Klasse; Sitzungsberichte*, 1867, *55*. Band, Abteilung 2, 741–766.

Shevell, S. K. The dual role of chromatic backgrounds in color perception. *Vision Research*, 1978, *18*, 1649–1661.

Stromeyer, C. F., III Further studies of the McCollough effect. *Perception & Psychophysics*, 1969, *6*, 133–137.

Stromeyer, C. F., III McCollough effect analogs of two-color projections. *Vision Research*, 1971, *11*, 969–978.

Stromeyer, C. F., III Edge-contingent color aftereffects: spatial frequency specificity. *Vision Research*, 1972, *12*, 717–733.

Stromeyer, C. F., III Form-color aftereffects in human vision. In R. Held, H. W. Leibowitz & H.-L. Teuber (Eds.), *Handbook of sensory physiology* (Vol. VIII) 7, *Perception*. Berlin: Springer-Verlag, 1978.

Stromeyer, C. F., III, & Dawson, B. M. Form-colour aftereffects: Selectivity to local luminance contrast. *Perception*, 1978, *7*, 407–415.

Van der Wildt, G. J., & Bouman, M. A. The dependence of Bezold-Brücke hue shift on spatial intensity distribution. *Vision Research*, 1968, *8*, 303–313.

Wiesel, T. N., & Hubel, D. H. Spatial and chromatic interactions in the lateral geniculate body of the rhesus monkey. *Journal of Neurophysiology*, 1966, *29*, 1115–1156.

Wooten, B. R. *The effects of simultaneous and successive chromatic contrast on spectral hue*. Ph.D. Dissertation, Brown University, Providence, Rhode Island, 1970.

Wyszecki, G., & Stiles, W. S. *Color science: Concepts and methods, quantitative data and formulas*. New York: Wiley, 1967.

Young, T. *A Course of Lectures on Natural Philosophy and the Mechanical Arts*. London: Printed For J. Johnson, St. Paul's Church Yard, by William Savage, 1807.

31

Size Interactions in the Perception of Orientation

Christopher W. Tyler
Ken Nakayama
Smith-Kettlewell Institute of Visual Sciences
San Francisco, California

ABSTRACT

To dissociate the roles of small and large receptive fields in the processing of line orientation, we devised a sawtooth line stimulus where local tilt of the sawtooth segments could be varied independently of overall tilt of the line. Perceived orientation of the overall line varied with the tilt of the segments in a biphasic manner. For small segment tilts (peaking between $5-15°$) overall orientation was shifted in the direction of the segment tilt, whereas for greater segment tilts (peaking between $30-45°$) there was a larger perceived shift in the opposite direction. The results suggest an interaction between orientation-specific neurons with small receptive fields and those with large receptive fields.

To explain these effects, we developed a model which illustrates that peak orientation shift for a population of large receptive fields is proportional to the slope of the population response profile for small receptive fields. Within this framework, small receptive fields show both excitatory and inhibitory influences on larger receptive fields, and it is possible to estimate the magnitude and orientation selectivity of these influences. The model can account for two powerful illusions of orientation, the Fraser and the Zöllner illusions.

INTRODUCTION

The perception of straightness and orientation in straight lines has been of interest since the earliest years of visual investigation. Purkinje (1819) observed that after prolonged inspection, straight lines were perceived as breaking into differently oriented segments, and many well-known illusions of the 19-century deal with deviations from perceived straightness (e.g., Zöllner, 1862; Hering, 1879/1942). Purkinje's (1819) observation is of particular interest, because it suggests that straight lines might be processed in terms of small segments whose orientation may be dissociated from that of the line as a whole.

The discovery of orientation- and size-selective cells in the visual cortex offers a fresh approach to the problem. For any given retinal region, there exist many cortical units with different receptive field sizes as well as different preferred orientations (Hubel & Wiesel, 1962). When a long straight line is projected onto the retina, orientation-selective cells with both large and small receptive fields will be stimulated (Fig. 31.1a). Because there is a congruence between local and global orientation in straight lines, the orientation associated with maximum response is the same for populations of neurons with small and large receptive fields. (Figs. 31.1b and Fig. 31.1d).

On the other hand, if the stimulus line is broken up into equal segments, with a local orientation different from that of the configuration as a whole (Fig. 31.2), the distribution of responses will differ for cells with small and large receptive fields. Thus, each group of cells would provide conflicting information as to line orientation (Fig. 31.2b and Fig. 31.2d).

To determine the interactions between orientation signals from cells with large and small receptive fields, we measured the effect of local segment angle

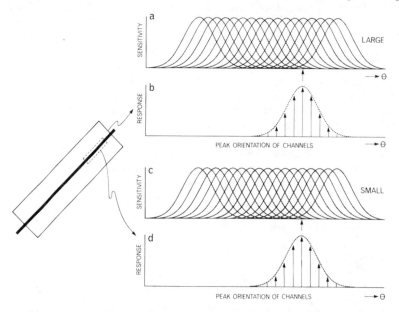

FIG. 31.1.   Single line stimulus and two sizes of cortical receptive field that will be preferentially stimulated by the oriented lines. a) Population sensitivity of a class of cells having large receptive fields. b) response of population a to single line stimulus. c and d) Same as in a and b except for small receptive fields.

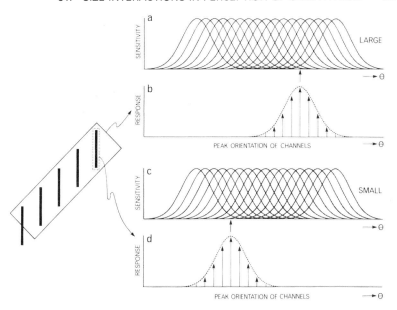

FIG. 31.2. a) Interrupted sawtooth stimulus used in this study. Note that in contrast to Fig. 1, the optimal orientation for large and small cortical receptive fields is different, and response profiles are shifted relative to each other (compare b and d).

on overall perceived orientation of a segmented line. This approach differs from previous studies of the Zöllner illusion (Gibson & Radner, 1937; Wallace, 1964; Carpenter & Blakemore, 1973; Oyama, 1975), which were concerned with interactions of orientation mechanisms for stimulus elements in *different* (but adjacent) retinal locations. In contrast, our stimulus is designed to examine interactions between orientation mechanisms for stimuli of different sizes in the *same* retinal location.

To anticipate our results, a demonstration of the basic findings are shown in Fig. 31.3. When the angle of tilted segments is small, the overall line appears to

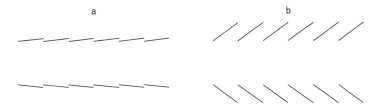

FIG. 31.3. Two pairs of parallel segmented lines where local orientation differs from the global orientation. a) Line segments are tilted by a small amount, causing a slight shift in perceived orientation of the segmented lines in the same direction as segment tilt. b) Same, except the segments are tilted by a much larger angle. In this case, perceived tilt of the segmented lines is in the opposite direction.

tilt in the same direction as the tilt of individual segments (Fig. 31.3a), while the reverse can be seen when the angle of the individual segments is larger (Fig. 31.3b).

A similar result was reported by Oyama (1975) in the classical Zöllner paradigm; although for most inducing tilts the test line was tilted in the opposite direction to the inducing lines, for small tilts the test line appeared to be tilted in the same direction as the inducing lines. While this result is interesting, it is potentially contaminated by assimilation from spread of excitation within the retina, rather than by interactions between cortical neurons. This supposition is in accord with another of Oyama's (1975) experiments, in which tilted segments were set at different distances from the test line. An assimilation effect at small tilts disappeared for separations greater than 6 arc min, although negative induction at large tilt angles was relatively unaffected by the distance to the test line.

METHODS

Either one or two segmented lines were generated on the face of an oscilloscope screen using an electronic function generator. Angle and number of segments per line could be controlled by varying the amplitude and frequency of a sawtooth waveform. Because the fast phase of the sawtooth was extremely rapid, it was possible to adjust the luminance of the trace so that only the tilted segments were visible. The lines subtended 10° in length and, unless otherwise noted, had a luminance of 1 cd/m² in a room with dim illumination. The screen had a circular surround and thus could not have been used as an orientation cue. Angle of the segments was related to the amplitude (A) and frequency (f) of the sawtooth by the following expression:

$$\theta = \tan^{-1} (k\ A\ f),\ \text{where k is a scaling constant.}$$

The angles used were limited to a range of ±60°, since beyond this range the sawtooth lines were wider than the gaps between them.

To measure the effect of segment angle two experiments utilized a cancellation procedure and one a matching procedure. In Experiment I, two horizontal configurations with oppositely tilting segments were presented (see Fig. 31.3) and the observer adjusted the angle between these configurations until they appeared parallel. For Experiment II, only one segmented vertical line was visible in an otherwise dark room. The observer had to set the segmented line to perceived verticality without the aid of any visual comparison. (Vertical orientation was used here because it has the best absolute orientation discrimination; Howard, 1981). In Experiment III, the observer set a straight, non-segmented comparison line to be parallel to a single segmented line, again in a horizontal orientation. One experienced and two naive observers were tested.

RESULTS

Experiment I: Pairs of Segmented Lines

In this experiment, two segmented lines with oppositely directed segments were varied in overall orientation until the observer judged them to be parallel. The number of segments was maintained at six and the distance between the centres of the two lines was 4°. The observer was instructed to move fixation freely over the display and to set the orientation of the global lines to be parallel, without attending to particular positions, and especially avoiding attention to the theoretical line joining the two end points. Four adjustments were made at each segment orientation.

The effect of segment angle on perceived orientation of the overall line is plotted in Fig. 31.4a. Note that there is a biphasic change in orientation of the overall line as the angle of segments is increased. This can be seen for all three observers in varying amounts. Between 5–20° there is a small but reproducible shift of orientation towards the angle of individual segments, whereas at larger angles (peaking between 33–45°), there is a much larger shift in the global orientation in the opposite direction. Similar results for the classical Zöllner illusion have been reported by Oyama (1975).

We were concerned that if judgments were made with regard to the theoretical line joining the extreme tips of the segmented line, judged orientation of the global line would be biased towards the tilt of the terminal segments. This might explain the first part (but not the second part) of the biphasic curve. We therefore conducted the same experiment with the outer halves of the terminal segments removed (see inset, Fig. 31.4b). In this condition the terminal points of the segmented pattern defined a line which always remained parallel to the overall pattern, regardless of the angle of the segments. Figure 31.4b shows that adding this restriction does not diminish the effect. Consequently, the data are in accord with the observer's impression that the judgment can be made without regard to the terminal points.

Experiment II: Single Segmented Line

Because the previous experiments used a pair of oppositely tilted lines, it is possible that the results could be contaminated by an interaction between the tilted segments of one line and corresponding regions of the other line 4° away (see Discussion). To deal with this issue, we repeated the experiment with a single vertical segmented line in a dark room where no other visual orientation cues were available. Residual stray light in the room was kept below visibility by light-adapting the observer between trials. Thus, the only available orientation references were gravitational and proprioceptive.

For observer KN the results (Fig. 31.5) are similar to those obtained with the pairs of segmented lines in Experiment I. The curve has the same biphasic

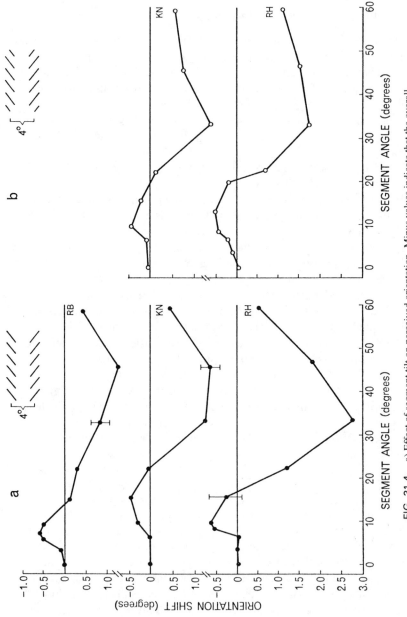

FIG. 31.4. a) Effect of segment tilt on perceived orientation. Minus values indicate that the overall line appears to be tilted in the same direction as the segments, whereas plus values indicate the opposite. b) Similar data obtained with the outer halves of the terminal segments removed, thereby excluding any cues as to the end point of the lines. The distance between the lines was 4°.

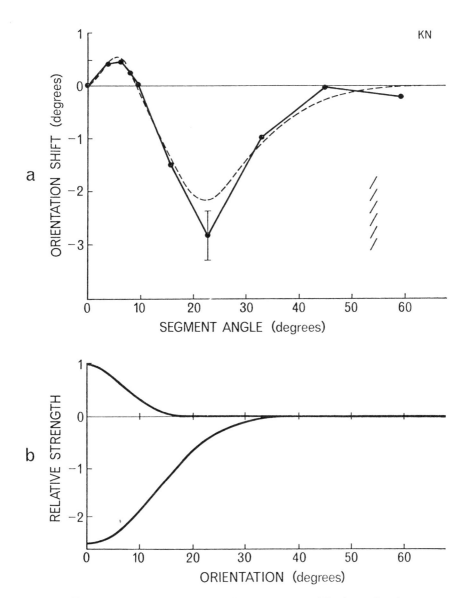

FIG. 31.5.   a) Perceived orientation of a single segmented line in an otherwise dark room. The fact that these results are similar to those using pairs of segmented lines (see Fig. 4) indicates that the previous results are not due to spatial interactions between the configurations. b) Relative magnitude and orientation tuning of hypothetical excitatory and inhibitory signals from a population of small receptive fields impinging upon a similar array of large receptive fields. Dashed curve in (a) shows the computed fit of this theoretical model to the observed perceptual shifts (see Theoretical Model).

relationship with segment tilt, although each aspect of the curve occurs at slightly lower inducing tilts than in Experiment I. By providing a control for contour repulsion effects between segments, this experiment supports the view that orientation rather than position is the determining sensory variable for both positive and negative induction effects. The small differences in peak orientations relative to Fig. 4 suggest that there may be a small degree of interaction between the two segmented lines in Experiment I, which is eliminated in the single segmented configuration. The latter is therefore considered to be the purer case of size/orientation interactions, and the one that is modeled in the Theoretical section.

Experiment III: Effect of Segment Spatial Frequency

The relation obtained between segment angle and perceived orientation of the segmented line suggests an interaction between size and orientation mechanisms; signals from smaller receptive fields can affect those from larger receptive fields. Therefore, we examined the effect of size directly. The strength of both positive and negative tilt induction was measured as a function of the spatial frequency of

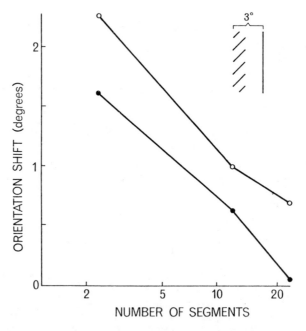

FIG. 31.6.   Effect of number of segments on the magnitude of the positive (filled circles) and the negative (open circles) effects for observer KN. Both magnitudes are plotted as positive to aid comparison of the slopes. The stimulus had segment angles of 15° for the positive effect and 40° for the negative effect.

the segments (reciprocal of segment length in degrees, or number of segments per degree of visual angle).

For this experiment, the tilt angles of the segments that yielded the greatest positive and negative effects in Experiment I were selected and the number of segments was varied. For KN these peak values were about 15° for the positive and 40° for the negative effect. As in the second part of Experiment I, the outer halves of the endmost segments were removed to avoid end effects. The observer set the global orientation of the segmented line so that it appeared parallel to a straight comparison line placed 3° away. Figure 31.6 shows the effect of spatial frequency on both positive and negative induction effects. The major finding is that perceived tilt increases directly with length of the segments. Greatest amounts of induction occur at 5° per segment, where there are only two complete segments. Oyama (1975) reported related results for the classical version of the Zöllner illusion, in which tilted segments were adjacent to a straight test line, but for his data the length effect saturated at a segment length of about 2°, whereas in Fig. 31.6 the length effect continues up to at least 5°.

DISCUSSION

The results indicate that local orientation of a series of line segments affects the orientation of the ''line'' formed by those segments. For segment angles from 0° to about 20° (depending on the observer), the global orientation is tilted in the same direction as the local tilt. On the other hand, beyond about 20° the opposite result occurs. In this case, the results are analogous to the apparent contour repulsion seen in figural aftereffects (Köhler & Wallach, 1944), but the present data show ''repulsion'' with respect to orientation rather than distance.

The results are similar in many respects to those of previous investigators (see Introduction), with the difference that in our stimulus the orientation interactions must be occurring between cells responding to different sizes of oriented stimuli, rather than between cells responding at different retinal locations.

Relation to Fraser and Zöllner Illusion

The biphasic nature of the tilt response appears to relate two illusions of orientation which have not been previously considered under the same rubric, namely, the Fraser (1908) and Zöllner (1862) illusions. In the Fraser illusion, segments with a small angle of tilt induce a perceived global tilt in the same direction, as is the case for small angles of tilt in our sawtooth line. This result is an important control for the possible artifact that local retinal interactions may be responsible for the small angle assimilation effects reported in previous studies (Oyama, 1975).

In the Zöllner illusion, segments with a large angle of tilt usually induce the opposite direction of tilt in an overlaid test line. We have shown that it is not necessary to have a separate test line. The global orientation of the line formed by the segments themselves is similarly affected by the segment tilt.

It may be noted that the original Fraser illusion (and our equivalent tilted letter illusion, Fig. 31.7) is more powerful than the segmented line version (Fig. 31.3). This is probably due to relatively weak stimulation of cells with large receptive fields (as in Fig. 31.2) in the original illusion, as a result of the presence of both dark and light patches in the summation region of such receptive fields. With this qualification, both the Fraser and Zöllner effects can be considered manifestations of the interaction between oriented receptive fields of different sizes processing the same stimulus.

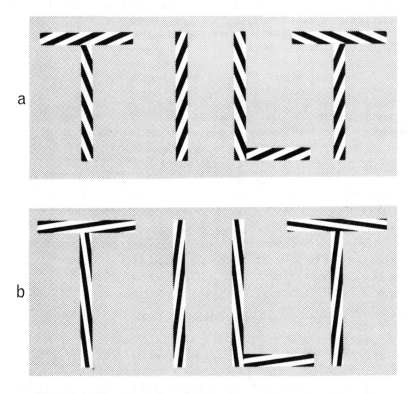

FIG. 31.7.   Zöllner (a) and Fraser (b) effects illustrated by segmented letters. In the Zöllner illusion the apparent orientation of each bar of the letters is in the opposite direction as the segments, which are tilted at 30° to the horizontal and vertical bars. The tilt direction alternates in alternate letters. For the Fraser effect the segment tilt is at 10° to the bars. Note the opposite directions of perceived tilt in the two cases.

Theoretical Model

In order to understand the tilt induction data in terms of psychophysical and neurophysiological information on orientation selectivity, they should be placed in the framework of a general model for the perceptual shifts. Our model is based on the idea that the induced shift is a function of the rate of change of inducing signal across the relevant perceptual dimension (which is orientation in the present case, but the analysis is generally applicable to any perceptual dimension).

To begin, we assume a population response of orientation channels similar to that suggested by Blakemore (1970), Anstis (1975), and Howard (1981), based on much neurophysiological (Hubel & Wiesel, 1962, 1968) and psychophysical (Campbell & Kulikowski, 1966) evidence. Each local region of visual space is processed by a set of cortical neurons with overlapping receptive fields, each tuned to a narrow range of orientation by means of the relationship of excitatory and inhibitory subfields. The half-bandwidth of these orientation tunings is from 12–15°, assuming a Gaussian envelope for each tuning. For a stimulus of a given orientation, the pattern of excitation across this array of orientation channels is assumed to be proportional to the sensitivity of each channel at the stimulus orientation. The pattern of excitation across a population of channels, therefore, is also Gaussian with the same bandwidth as that of the individual channels.

In this study, we have explored the dimension of size as well as orientation specificity. Consequently, we must consider separate arrays of orientation channels for different sizes of stimulus. What is the form of the interaction from small to large receptive field arrays of orientation channels, beyond the level of interactions that determine the orientation specificity of each channel? This higher level interaction might be purely excitatory (i.e., a form of direct crosstalk), it might be purely inhibitory, or it might be a combination of both excitation and inhibition. (The question of corresponding interactions from the large to the small orientation channels is not considered in this chapter, because the observers judged only the orientation of the global configuration, not the local segments.) For simplicity, only two size tunings of orientation array were considered, but the argument would apply equally across a range of sizes. In that case, the interactions would be some function of the size difference between the tunings of arrays (as suggested by Fig. 31.6).

We now analyze how tilt is affected by the interaction between arrays. Suppose there is an added pattern of excitation from the small orientation channels to the large orientation channels. In the simplest case, this added excitation might have a uniform slope (Fig. 31.8b). Such a slope will alter the resultant excitation pattern so as to shift the peak in the direction of increasing amplitude of the added signal (Fig. 31.8c). We assume that perceived orientation of the stimulus is determined by the position of the peak of the distribution of excitation. Clearly, the degree of peak shift will depend on the slope of the added excitation. If

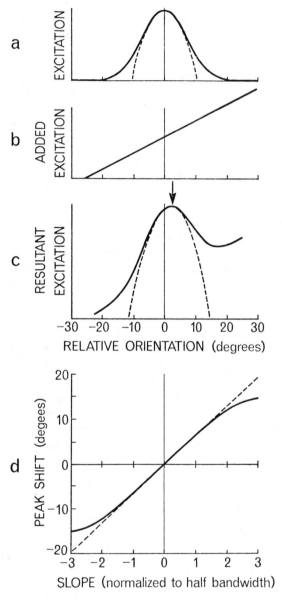

FIG. 31.8. a) Theoretical analysis of orientation interactions assuming Gaussian (continuous lines) or parabolic (dashed lines) sensitivity profiles for the population response of orientation selective mechanisms. For a linear distribution of added excitation from the interaction input (b), the peak of the resultant excitation (arrow) shifts towards the higher added excitation (c). The bottom panel (d) shows that for a parabolic population response profile, the peak shift is a linear function of the slope of added excitation (dashed line). For a Gaussian profile of population response (continuous line) the profile is approximately linear up to 2 times the half bandwidth.

the slope were zero, there would be no peak shift, whereas a steep slope would induce a large peak shift.

How can the degree of peak shift be quantified? For purposes of mathematical simplicity consider that the population response profile is parabolic (dashed lines in Fig. 31.8) with a linear slope of added excitation. In this case the peak shift is directly proportional to the slope of added excitation, as derived in the Appendix. For a more realistic Gaussian distribution the peak shift is close to that of the parabola for shallow slopes and progressively deviates from proportionality as slope is increased. The amount of peak shift as a function of slope is shown for the parabola (dashed line) and the Gaussian (continuous line) in Fig. 31.8d. These relations are general, but the degree of peak shift for the case of orientation channels with a full bandwidth of 24° is shown on the ordinate of Fig. 31.8d. It can be shown that even for the Gaussian, peak shift is a linear function of added slope within 10% for peak shifts up to 10°, which exceeds the range of induced tilts obtained in most studies of orientation interactions.

Suppose the added excitation is also Gaussian. Since the addition of two complex distributions is analytically unwieldy, we determine merely the degree of departure from the simple linear slope model. The pattern of added excitation being Gaussian rather than a linear slope will cause some further distortion in the peak shift function. However, this distortion can be neglected to the extent that a Gaussian distribution of added signal approximates a parabola. This is a good approximation for small peak shifts, as shown in Fig. 31.8d.

This analysis of orientation interactions shows that the peak shift of the combined excitation pattern should be approximately proportional to the slope of the added excitation but of the opposite sign, because the shift is measured in terms of effect on the global orientation. Thus, in the orientation domain, the expected degree of peak shift should correspond to the inverse of the first derivative of the added excitation distribution.

Three possible effects of the added signal from the small orientation channels on the peak for the large orientation channels are diagrammed in Fig. 31.9. If the interaction signal were purely excitatory, with a Gaussian distribution (Fig. 31.9a), the peak shift would first increase and then decrease back to zero tilt as the orientation difference between the small segments and the global line increased from zero (Fig. 31.9b). (The opposite function for orientation differences in the other direction is indicated by the dotted line).

Thus for excitation only, the expected tilt function is a single-humped, positive curve (solid curve in Fig. 31.9b). Similarly, for inhibition only (Fig. 9c), the first derivative gives an expected tilt function in a single-humped negative curve (solid curve in Fig. 31.9d). Neither case resembles the biphasic curve that was obtained in Fig. 31.3 and Fig. 31.4 for the measured data. In order to match this form, one needs the presence of both excitatory and inhibitory interactions, as shown for the response function in Fig. 31.9e and for its derivative, the expected tilt function in Fig. 31.9f. This last function is a good match to the qualitative features of the measured data. An example of the theoretical fit to one set of data

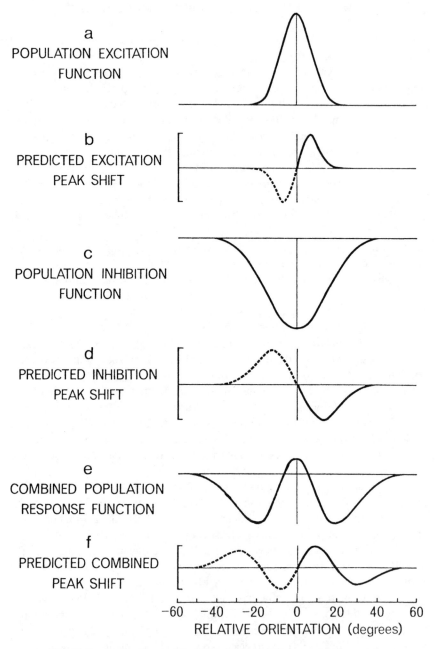

FIG. 31.9. Predicted peak shift (b, d, and f) for different types of population interaction: Purely excitatory (a), purely inhibitory (c), or a combination of the two (e). Note that peak shift changes sign from positive (upward) to negative (downward) with type of interaction.

is shown in Fig. 31.5 (dashed line), derived as in Fig. 31.9. The parameters used for this curve are a half bandwidth of 8° for the excitation function and 16° for the inhibition function, with relative amplitudes of 1:2.5 (as depicted in lower panel of Fig. 31.5). Although the fit is quite good, it should be mentioned that the four parameter fit allows other choices of parameter values with similar results. Thus, while the model is an acceptable description of the data, it should not be regarded as a unique solution.

CONCLUSION

This analysis suggests that the "assimilation" effect of the Fraser illusion is due to excitatory "crosstalk" between arrays of cells with small and large receptive fields and different orientation preferences. The Zöllner illusion, on the other hand, is a result of the inhibitory interactions between these same arrays of cells. The analysis is consistent with physiological recordings showing the existence of both size and orientation selectivity (Hubel & Wiesel, 1962), as well as interactions between orientation selective neurons (Blakemore & Tobin, 1972; Nelson & Frost, 1978). Furthermore it adds weight to previous psychophysical evidence for the interaction of orientation signals (Carpenter & Blakemore, 1973; Magnussen & Kurtenbach, 1981). It appears that the signals conveying orientation information are segregated as to size, although the effect of size is graded rather than abrupt, as was shown in Fig. 31.6. Furthermore, the analysis suggests that the inhibitory interaction has about twice the strength of the excitatory interaction. Thus, the segmented line approach may provide new insight into the mechanisms processing orientation, and suggest an analytic approach for use in other perceptual domains.

ACKNOWLEDGMENTS

Supported by Grants 5R01-EY-03884, 5P30-EY-01186 and the Smith-Kettlewell Eye Research Foundation. A preliminary abstract of these results was published in the *Journal of the Optical Society of America, 66,* 1090, 1976.

APPENDIX

Derivation of Proportionality of Peak Shift to Slope of Added Excitation

If the population response profile (y) with respect to orientation (θ) is parabolic, it has the equation:

$$y = a - b\theta^2 \qquad (1)$$

where a is an amplitude constant and b is the steepness parameter.

Adding an excitation signal with a constant slope (m), gives a resultant response profile of

$$y = a - b\theta^2 + m\theta \tag{2}$$

The peak of this distribution (θ) will occur at the orientation where its slope is zero, that is,

$$\frac{dy}{d\theta} = 0, \theta = \hat{\theta} \tag{3}$$

This occurs when

$$\frac{d(a - b\theta^2 + m\theta)}{d\theta} = 0 \tag{4}$$

$$m - 2b\theta = 0 \tag{5}$$

From equation 5 the peak orientation (θ) is directly proportional to the slope of added excitation

$$\hat{\theta} = \frac{m}{2b} \tag{6}$$

as shown by the dashed line in Fig. 30.8d. Similarly, for a Gaussian excitation profile the resulting distribution is

$$y = e^{-b\theta^2} + m\theta \tag{7}$$

The slope is zero when

$$-2b\theta e^{-b\theta^2} + m = 0 \tag{8}$$

when θ is small, $e^{-b\theta^2} \approx 1$

$$\text{and } \hat{\theta} = \frac{m}{2b} \text{ , as before.} \tag{9}$$

Therefore, the peak shift for a Gaussian direct excitation function approximates that of a parabola when θ is small, as shown by the full line in Fig. 30.8d.

We next show that if the *added* excitation has a parabolic profile, peak shift is proportional to the orientation difference ($\Delta\theta$) between the population profiles. If the equation for the added excitation is

$$y = c - k(\theta - \Delta\theta)^2 \tag{10}$$

The resultant response distribution is

$$\begin{aligned} y &= a - b\theta^2 + c - k(\theta - \Delta\theta)^2 \\ &= a + c - b\theta^2 - k\theta^2 + 2k\theta\Delta\theta - k\Delta\theta^2 \end{aligned} \tag{11}$$

For which

$$\frac{dy}{d\theta} = -2b\theta - 2k\theta + 2k\Delta\theta \tag{12}$$

When $\frac{dy}{d\theta} = 0$, $\theta = \hat{\theta}$

and hence

$$2(b + k)\, \hat{\theta} = 2k\Delta\theta$$
$$\hat{\theta} = \frac{k\Delta\theta}{b + k} \tag{13}$$

Thus the peak orientation shift ($\hat{\theta}$) is directly proportional to orientation difference ($\Delta\theta$) between the two populations of orientation detectors, for any fixed values of the widths of response profiles (b and k). More importantly, it should be noted that the slope (m_θ) of a parabolic added excitation is directly related to distance ($\Delta\theta$) from the peak.

Consider that, for $y = c - k\theta^2$

$$m_\theta = \frac{dy}{d\theta} = -2k\theta \tag{14}$$

When $\theta = \Delta\theta$, $m_\theta = -2k\Delta\theta$

or

$$\Delta\theta = -\frac{m_\theta}{2k} \tag{15}$$

We can substitute this into equation 13, giving

$$\hat{\theta} = \frac{-m_\theta}{2(b + k)} \tag{16}$$

Thus the peak shift ($\hat{\theta}$) is directly proportional to the slope of added excitation, at the peak of the direct excitation function. Since this result was obtained both for a linear slope (equation 6) and a continuously varying function (equation 16), it will be taken as a general result for well-behaved profiles of added excitation, as long as the direct excitation profile approximates a parabolic form (see Fig. 30.8d).

In summary, the mathematical derivations indicate that the *peak shift* of the resultant excitation function may be considered to be directly proportional to *local slope* of the added excitation function at the peak, for the class of well-behaved orientation tuning functions:

$$\hat{\theta} \propto m_\theta$$

REFERENCES

Anstis, S. M. What does perception tell us about perceptual coding? In C. Blakemore & M. Gazzaniga (Eds.), *Handbook of psychobiology*. New York: Academic Press, 1975.

Blakemore, C. The baffled brain. In R. L. Gregory & E. H. Gombrich (Eds.), *Illusion, art, and nature*. London: Duckworth, 1970.

Blakemore, C., & Tobin, E. A. Lateral inhibition between orientation detectors in the cat's visual cortex. *Experimental Brain Research*, 1972, *15*, 439–440.

Campbell, F. W., & Kulikowski, J. J. Orientational selectivity of the human visual system. *Journal of Physiology*, 1966, *187*, 437–445.

Carpenter, R. H. S., & Blakemore, C. Interactions between orientations in human vision. *Experimental Brain Research*, 1973, *16*, 287–303.

Fraser, J. A new visual illusion of direction. *British Journal of Psychology*, 1908, *2*, 307–320.

Gibson, J. J., & Radner, M. Adaptation, aftereffect, and contrast in the perception of tilted lines. I. Quantitative studies. *Journal of Experimental Psychology*, 1937, *20*, 453–467.

Hering, E. Der Raumsinn und die Bewegungen der Augen. In L. Hermann (Ed.), *Handbuch der Physiologie*. Trans. C. Radde, American Academy of Baltimore: Optometry, 1879/1942.

Howard, I. P. *Human visual orientation*. New York: Wiley, 1981.

Hubel, D. H., & Wiesel, T. N. Receptive fields, binocular interaction, and functional architecture in the cat's visual cortex. *Journal of Physiology*, 1962, *160*, 106–154.

Hubel, D. H., & Wiesel, T. N. Receptive fields and functional architecture of monkey striate cortex. *Journal of Physiology*, 1968, *195*, 215–263.

Köhler, W., & Wallach, H. Figural aftereffects: An investigation of visual processes. *Proceedings of the American Philosophical Society*, 1944, *88*, 269–357.

Magnussen, S., & Kurtenbach, W. Adapting to two orientations: Disinhibition in a visual aftereffect. *Science*, 1981, *207*, 908–909.

Nelson, J. I., & Frost, B. J. Orientation selective inhibition from beyond the classic visual receptive field. *Brain Research*, 1978, *139*, 359–365.

Oyama, T. Determinants of the Zöllner Illusion. *Psychological Research*, 1975, *37*, 261–280.

Purkinje, J. *Beobachtungen und Versuche zur Physiologie der Sinne*. Prague: J. G. Calve, 1819.

Wallace, G. K. Measurements of the Zöllner illusion. *Acta Psychologica*, 1964, *22*, 407–412.

Zöllner, F. Über eine neue Art anorthoskopischer Zerrbilder. *Poggendorffs Annalen*, 1862, *117*, 477–484.

32

Illusory Line Rotation in Expanding and Contracting Displays

N. J. Wade
University of Dundee
Dundee, Scotland

M. T. Swanston
Dundee College of Technology
Dundee, Scotland

ABSTRACT

Head movement towards and away from a display consisting of a stationary grating with a superimposed inclined line leads to the apparent rotation of the line. This phenomenon has been investigated using a television system with a motorized zoom lens to effect such transformations. The direction and magnitude of the apparent rotation depend upon the orientation of the line to the grating, reaching a maximum at a relative orientation of 45°. The shape of the angle function can be described by a simple formulation based on a vectorial analysis of the changes in the display. It is suggested that the apparent rotation is a consequence of a discrepancy between the perceived transformations of the line and the grating. The magnitude of apparent line rotation is influenced by the gravitational orientation of the background grating and by the phase and duration of zooming. The spatial characteristics of the line and grating have relatively little effect on the amount of rotation observed.

INTRODUCTION

In the course of many experiments, Professor Kohler has described the perceptual adaptations consequent on exposure to certain classes of modification of the optic array. Prolonged experience of inversion or chromatic bias leads eventually to perceptual adaptation, and to a range of aftereffects on the return to normal optical conditions.

While such transformations need to be imposed by some external optical intervention, others are natural consequences of the geometry of the environment and of our motion within it. The human visual system is adapted to the occurrence of these both by evolution and by experience. Such transformations are important sources of information for spatial perception (Gibson, 1950; Johansson, 1978, pp. 675–711), but little is known of the processes by which this information is used, or of the origin of stable percepts in the presence of conflict or ambiguity. Here we describe some phenomena that arise from the expansion and contraction of the optic array, as would result from approach or recession in a normal environment.

FIG. 32.1.   A vertical squarewave grating. If a matchstick or some other thin linear object is placed over the center of the grating at an inclination of 45°, then the apparent line rotation can be seen by moving the head towards and away from the display. The effect of line orientation can be examined by inclining the line at different orientations to the grating. If the line is placed at 45° to the background and the page is rotated to make the line vertical and the background oblique, then head movement still produces rotation, but its magnitude may well appear smaller than that produced with a vertical background and an oblique line.

Viewing a display consisting of a grating and a superimposed inclined line results in the apparent rotation of the line, but not the grating, when the head is moved towards and away from it. This phenomenon was initially observed accidentally when looking at a grating over which a pencil was lying, and moving the head towards and away from it. Since the orientation of the pencil with respect to the grating could be readily adjusted, a number of additional observations could be made. The reader is encouraged to check these personally by placing a matchstick, or some such appropriate linear stimulus, over the center of Fig. 32.1. The figure should be viewed from about 30 cm, and the head should be moved steadily back and forth through about 10 cm. Fixation of the center of the superimposed line is advantageous. The direction of apparent rotation will be seen to depend upon the direction of the superimposed line: If it is placed at 45°, i.e., clockwise to the vertical, then approach results in counterclockwise (CCW) rotation; if it is placed in the opposite oblique, at 135°, then approach yields clockwise (CW) apparent rotation. No rotation occurs when the line is either in the same orientation as the background or orthogonal to it.

METHOD

In order to quantify these observations it is necessary to obtain some index of the amount of apparent rotation. One convenient method is that of magnitude estimation, since observers can report the number of degrees through which the line appears to rotate during approach or recession. However, there remains the problem of controlling or quantifying the rate of head movement. Because of the difficulties inherent in such control or measurement we decided to use an analogous, though not identical, means of generating the necessary transformation. Suppose an observer views a screen at a fixed distance and the display on the screen is subject to radial expansion or contraction about its center. This would result in transformations similar to those occurring with head movement towards or away from a display. The differences relate to : (a) the variations in accommodation and vergence that occur with head movement but are not necessary when viewing the screen; (b) the variations in the angular subtense of the display; and (c) the possible distinction between active movement of the head and passive variation on the screen.

Our initial experiments made use of the apparatus shown in Fig. 32.2. A video camera with a motorized zoom lens was aligned with its optical axis directed at the center of a grating, on which a line was superimposed. The output of the camera was displayed on two monitors; one observed by the subject in a dark chamber and the other by the experimenter. The subject's display subtended 12° at the eye. At maximum zoom-out the spatial frequency of the square-wave grating was 2.6 cycles per degree (cpd) and the line subtended 4.8° in length; following 2 sec zoom-in the values were changed to 1.1 cpd and 11.2°, respectively. The motorized zoom lens and the shutter for exposing the display were

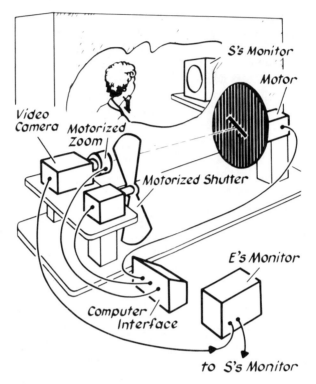

FIG. 32.2.   The experimental arrangement for generating radial transformations on a television screen.

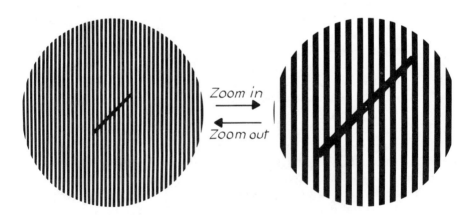

FIG. 32.3.   The display was transformed continuously between these two terminal states.

controlled by a microcomputer (see Swanston & Wade, 1981 for a more detailed description of the apparatus). Such transformations would have been more difficult to generate using conventional oscilloscope techniques for the presentation of gratings. Therefore, the subject saw a display of fixed size that was radially expanded or contracted as shown in Fig. 32.3. This is analogous to head movement towards and away from a grating viewed through a fixed aperture.

Subjects were required to report verbally the extent and direction of any apparent line rotation. They were asked to use a scale of degrees, but it was found that there was considerable variation between individuals in the range of values employed. Accordingly, less weight should be placed on the averaged values reported than on the variations between the different conditions within an experiment. For any given condition individual subjects were consistent in the values they reported. For all the experiments, unless it is stated otherwise, the transformation observed was zoom-in or expansion.

EXPERIMENTAL RESULTS AND DISCUSSION

We found that appreciable apparent rotation occurs with this arrangement, and that the directions were equivalent to those consequent on head movement. Viewing a single line on a blank background yielded no rotation, nor did a line zoomed on a display of random dots. However, varying the angle of the line relative to a vertical grating yielded an apparent rotation of the line which was maximal when it was at 45° relative to the background (Fig. 32.4, solid curve); the magnitude at other inclinations declined systematically. In this experiment the maximum rating of apparent rotation following a 2 sec zoom-in was about 6°, and no apparent rotation occurred when the line was at 0° or 90°.

This pattern of results is quite unlike those found for other orientation distortions like the Zöllner and Poggendorff illusions (Robinson, 1972). It is possible to interpret these results in terms of the differences between the perceived transformations of the background grating and the line. Since the aperture for viewing the display remains constant, the background appears to be moving horizontally outwards from the central point. That is, although the optical expansion is radial, the absence of any texture in the vertical lines renders only the horizontal displacements detectable. The superimposed line, on the other hand, expands both in length and in width. Therefore, there is a discrepancy between the path of movement perceived for the background and for the line. This discrepancy can be given a simple mathematical description as a result of vector analysis: If the line is at an angle α to the vertical grating than the "discrepant vector" is proportional to $\cos\alpha$ (Fig. 32.5a). In general, this describes the discrepancy along a vertical axis of any point along the line with respect to the vertical background adjacent to it. A "rotation vector" corresponding to the perceived motion for the line can be derived by determining the component of the vertical

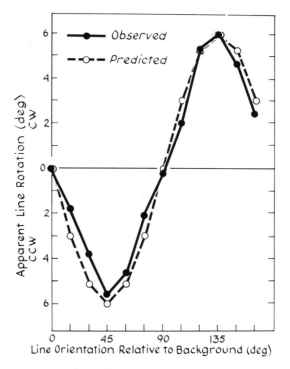

FIG. 32.4.   The angle function relating the rated magnitude of apparent rotation
to line orientation with a vertical background (solid line), and that predicted by an
analysis of the rotation vector (dashed line). The values of sinα. cosα have been
calculated with respect to the maximum CW apparent rotation.

discrepancy that operates perpendicularly to the line orientation. Such a rotation
vector is proportional to sinα · cosα (see Fig. 32.5b). If this analysis is valid it
should describe the angle function obtained. Figure 32.4 (dashed curve) shows
the predicted values for this experiment, and they are in good agreement with the
data actually obtained.

A grating that is expanded radially behind an aperture is perceived to expand
in the direction orthogonal to its orientation, since there is no texture to be seen
moving along the length of the lines. Wallach (1935, 1976, pp. 201–216) has
described a range of perceptual effects which arise from similar discrepancies
between the perceived path of motion and that objectively present. The illusory
rotation of a line superimposed on a grating is due, we have argued, to a
discrepancy between the *perceived* transformations of the line and of the background. This would account for the absence of apparent rotation of a line zoomed
on a uniform background or a randomly textured background. In the latter case,
there is sufficient textural information in the background to perceive the radial
expansion. Consequently, no discrepancy is perceived between the motions of
the background and the line.

There are, however, certain aspects of the phenomenon that pose problems for the above interpretation. We noted informally that when moving the head back and forth with respect to the display the apparent rotation appeared to be larger with recession, i.e., when the pattern is contracting. Also, the apparent rotation seemed to be dependent upon the absolute orientation of the display, being greater with a vertical background and an oblique line than vice versa. Both of

For Radial Motion at α Degrees to Vertical Background

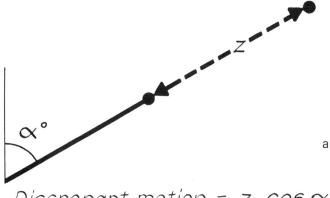

a

Discrepant motion = z . cos α

Line at α Degree to Vertical Background

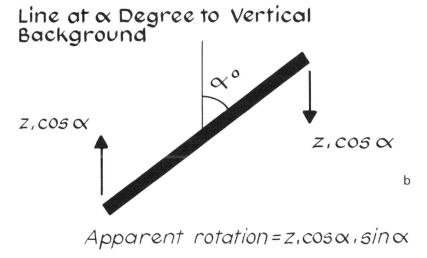

b

Apparent rotation = z . cos α . sin α

FIG. 32.5.   A summary of the parameters involved in the calculation of the magnitude of apparent rotation. (For details see text.)

these aspects have been investigated with the television zooming apparatus. Zoom-in produced smaller ratings of line rotation than zoom-out: the value for zoom-in was 86% of that for zoom-out. This result could be accounted for by a difference in the perceived lateral displacements in the two conditions. That is, the movement perceived in the background could be greater for zoom-out than zoom-in. If ratings of the perceived movement of the background alone could be obtained, then these should be greater for zoom-out than zoom-in. As yet, we have not examined this issue.

The influence of overall pattern orientation has been studied in two experiments utilizing zoom-in. In the first, ratings were obtained with respect to four background orientations: vertical, horizontal, 45° and 135°. The line was always presented at 45° *relative to the background*. The results are shown in Fig. 32.6. Larger rotations were perceived when the background was vertical or horizontal than when it was at either oblique setting. This anisotropy cannot be readily encompassed within the formulation presented above, as the apparent rotation would be predicted to be equivalent under each condition. The results could be interpreted in terms of differences in the perceived transformations of the backgrounds, as was the case for the zoom-in/zoom-out difference. That is, the

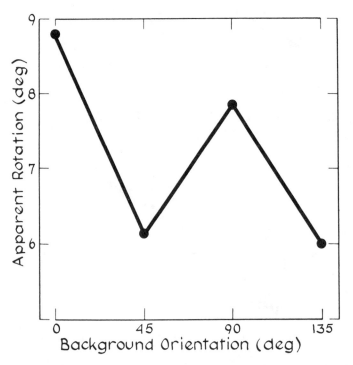

FIG. 32.6.   The magnitude of apparent rotation for different background orientations, when the superimposed line was inclined at 45°.

backgrounds might appear to expand by different amounts when oriented in different directions, with vertical or horizontal displacements appearing larger.

One way of examining the anisotropy is to separate the influences of orientation with respect to either the retina or gravity, by tilting the head so that the eye is in alignment with an oblique grating. In the second experiment, this was done for a vertical and 45° background (with 45° or vertical superimposed lines) both with the head vertical or tilted, so that the eye was inclined at 45° (the ocular countertorsion occurring with lateral head tilt was taken into consideration). With the head upright or tilted the apparent rotation for the vertical background was larger (12.6° and 13.3°, respectively) than that for the 45° background (8.4° and 8.3°). Accordingly, it is the orientation of the background with respect to gravity that determines the anisotropy of apparent rotation and not the orientation on the retina. Moreover, since the gravitationally vertical background would have been perceived as vertical in both head positions, due to orientation constancy (see Howard & Templeton, 1966), the perceived rotation of the background may be said to be dependent upon its perceived orientation.

ADDITIONAL EXPERIMENTS

In other experiments some temporal and spatial parameters have been varied. We have examined two zoom durations: the value for 1 sec zoom was approximately 65% of that for 2 sec zoom. In contrast, line length did not influence the magnitude of line rotation, nor did line width. The size of the background pattern had no effect either. Therefore, the spatial characteristics of the line and grating are not defining variables of the phenomenon, whereas zoom duration is (see Wade, Swanston, Ono & Wenderoth, in press, for a more detailed account of these experiments).

The experimental results discussed so far utilized a television display on which subjects observed patterns transformed by zooming. The mask on the display was circular and of constant visual subtense, so that the lines either disappeared laterally from the display during zoom-in or they appeared during zoom-out. As indicated initially, these transformations are not precisely the same as those consequent on head approach or recession, where the whole display is constantly visible. Since we wished to relate the effects observed using the television display to those occurring with head movements, a closer correspondence was obtained by zooming a display so that the whole pattern remained continuously visible, as shown in the Fig. 32.7 (lower). The experimental arrangement employed in the previous experiments is shown in Fig. 32.7 (upper), and the amount of apparent line rotation was measured for both conditions. The direction of line rotation was the same for both conditions, but the extent with a variable mask was only about 25% of that with the fixed mask. That is, the condition most similar to head movement produced a smaller effect than the display utilized in the earlier experiments. This could be due to the additional

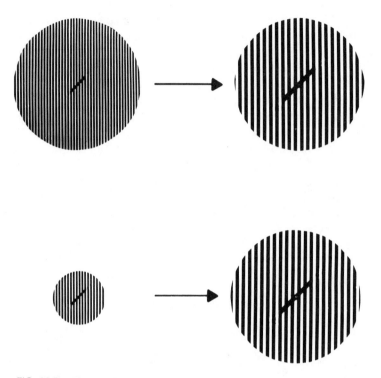

FIG. 32.7.   The transformations of the display in the fixed (upper) and variable (lower) mask conditions. The variable mask corresponds more closely to the changes occurring with head movement relative to a stationary display.

information resulting from the expansion of the circular border concerning the radial transformation imposed. Since the apparent line rotation occurs very clearly with head movements, it is possible that size constancy mechanisms may be in operation here in a manner that was not evident for our variable mask condition.

We have argued that the apparent rotation is a consequence of perceiving a lateral movement in the parallel lines of the background which does not conform to the radial transformation imposed by zooming. It becomes a matter of interest to examine whether all backgrounds that give the appearance of being formed by parallel components induce the same effect. For example, if a pattern is perceptually organized (i.e., "grouped" in the Gestalt sense) into parallel units, it can still contain textural information within the grouped lines. Such texture would provide cues for any radial transformation imposed on the pattern, i.e., a given physical discontinuity in such 'lines' would be displaced both vertically and horizontally during zooming. This information about texture could conflict with that from the perceived lateral movement of the background. Figure 32.8 shows examples of two such patterns. The superimposed line can be observed during head movement towards or away from the pattern in order to see the resulting rotation.

Since this is the case then there are problems for the approach we have proposed, as the perceived lateral movement of the grating has been attributed to the absence of any texture in the lines to allow the detection of any vertical displacements. With such perceptually organized backgrounds it would be the global structure that would influence the perceived transformation, rather than any specific physical features of the background. Accordingly, it would be predicted that any pattern that had a clear perceptual organization into parallel units would induce apparent rotation of a superimposed line during radial expansion or contraction.

The apparent rotation is not confined to gratings with single inclined lines, as can be seen in Fig. 32.9. In each of the displays four lines are inclined to the grating, arranged in the forms of a diamond and a cross. Head movement towards and away from these displays distorts the superimposed figures. Perhaps the most marked rotation can be seen in patterns that are geometrically repetitive, but comprise lines varying in orientation. Figure 32.10 is an example of one such design: Head movement towards and away from this pattern produces apparent rotation most particularly at the inflection points of the radiating curves. Moreover, rotations in opposing directions can be seen at the same time for those parts in which the inflections are in different directions. The illusory rotations attendant upon the dynamic transformations described above are of greater magnitude than those traditionally studied in static displays.

It will be instructive to determine the precise relationship between the apparent rotation consequent upon the television display transformations, and those

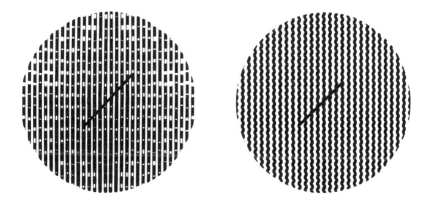

FIG. 32.8.   Two displays in which there is texture in the parts of the displays that are aligned vertically. The question of interest is whether the apparent line rotation still occurs, since the transformations of texture during head movement will provide information for the radial changes taking place. Each superimposed line appears to rotate in the same direction as on a conventional grating.

FIG. 32.9. A vertical grating on which a diamond is superimposed and an oblique grating with vertically and horizontally aligned pairs of lines. Head movement towards the diamond elongates its apparent vertical dimension, whereas recession leads to apparent horizontal elongation. For the other figure the pairs of orthogonal lines appear to rotate independently during head movement.

FIG. 32.10.   "Chrysanthemum" by Nicholas Wade. Head movement towards and away from this pattern produces apparent rotation at the inflection points of the radiating curves.

under the conditions of head movement with which the phenomenon was initially observed.

ACKNOWLEDGMENTS

We thank Hiroshi Ono and Peter Wenderoth for their collaboration in some of the experiments reported here. Hiroshi Ono also made many constructive comments on drafts of this article. The research was supported, in part, by a grant from the Medical Research Council of Great Britain.

REFERENCES

Gibson, J. J. *The perception of the visual world.* Boston: Houghton-Mifflin, 1950.
Howard, I. P., & Templeton, W. B. *Human spatial orientation.* New York: Wiley, 1966.

Johansson, G. Visual event perception. In R. Held, H. W. Leibowitz, & H.-L. Teuber (Eds.), *Handbook of sensory physiology* (Vol. 8), *Perception*. Berlin: Springer, 1978.

Robinson, J. O. *The psychology of visual illusion*. London: Hutchinson, 1972.

Swanston, M. T., & Wade, N. J. Apparent rotation of a line superimposed upon radially expanding and contracting backgrounds. *Perception*, 1981, *10*, 265–271.

Wade, N. J., Swanston, M. T., Ono, H., & Wenderoth, P. M. Factors influencing the apparent rotation of a line on radially transformed backgrounds. *Perception*. in press.

Wallach, H. Über visuell wahrgenommene Bewegungsrichtung. *Psychologische Forschung*, 1935, *20*, 323–380.

Wallach, H. *Hans Wallach on perception*. New York: Quadrangle/The New York Times Book Co., 1976.

33 Visual Motion Aftereffects: Adaptation and Conditioned Processes

Claude Bonnet
Michel Le Gall
Jean Lorenceau
Laboratoire de Psychologie Expérimentale
Université René Descartes
Paris, France

ABSTRACT

Residual movement aftereffects (MAE) can be observed long after inspection of real motion. They are contingent upon the features of the stationary test figure and upon its similarity to the features of the figure in real motion. A neurosensory adaptation process explains the noncontingent aspects of immediate MAEs. An associative conditioning process is proposed in order to explain the contingent aspects of the residual MAEs. In particular, these effects show extinction and spontaneous recovery.

Five experiments are presented. Experiment I proposes a taxonomy of the MAEs phenomena. Experiment II demonstrates that no recovery is obtained for a noncontingent MAE. Experiment III shows that the frequency of reports of residual MAEs varies curvilinearly with the duration of the rest period introduced between the observation of the real motion and the test of the residual MAE. Experiments IV and V examine the role of the distribution of the trials during the acquisition of the effect. It was found that a better acquisition is obtained when the noncontingent MAEs are observed during acquisition.

INTRODUCTION

After a century of research on the motion aftereffect (MAE), the theoretical significance of the basic phenomena is still controversial. The present chapter attempts to review the proposed mechanisms of the MAE and assess their the-

561

oretical significance. A two-process model appears to be necessary to explain most of the results: a neurosensory adaptation process and an associative conditioning process.

After prolonged inspection of real motion, three classes of MAE-phenomena can be distinguished:

(a) On a uniform field, a "ghostly" motion is seen in a direction opposite to that of the inducing stimulus (Wohlgemuth, 1911). A further effect following the prolonged inspection of a real motion is to be emphasized: An increase in the modulation contrast threshold for detecting the motion of a grating pattern drifting in the same direction as during the inspection period (Sekuler, 1975).

(b) An apparent motion is seen in the opposite direction if a stationary test pattern equal or similar to the inspection pattern is presented immediately at the end of the inspection phase. Such a MAE will be termed "immediate."

(c) An apparent motion analogous to the previous one is observed when a delay is introduced between the inspection and test periods. Such a MAE will be termed "residual" and refers to an MAE contingent on a stationary test pattern regardless of any delay between adapation and test.

Basically, the MAE has been attributed to differential neurosensory adaptation occurring in classes of neurons responding to visual motion in opposite directions (Barlow & Hill, 1963; Bonnet, 1978; Bonnet, Le Gall, & Lorenceau, 1982; Sekuler & Pantle, 1967; Sutherland, 1961). During the inspection period, the rate of firing of the neurons responding to the direction of the moving stimulus declines exponentially (Barlow & Hill, 1963; Vautin & Berkeley, 1977). Correspondingly, the apparent velocity of this real motion declines as a function of the inspection duration (Bonnet, 1973, 1978; Mashhour, 1964; Matsuda, 1970). This supports the view that neurosensory adaptation is the basis for the "ghostly" MAE (a) and the related threshold elevation (Barlow & Hill, 1963; Sekuler, 1975; Sekuler & Pantle, 1967; Sutherland, 1961).

On the other hand, neurosensory adaptation cannot explain the residual MAE (c) or contingent aspects in the immediate MAE (b). The existence of a residual MAE has rather suggested a "storage" process (Spigel, 1962) as invoked by Ivo Kohler (1951) to explain the aftereffects of prism adaptation. Such a process has been assumed to be of an associative conditioning type (Bonnet, 1973, 1975; Mayhew & Anstis, 1972). A similar process was proposed in the explanation of the McCollough effect (1965) by authors such as Leppmann (1973), Skowbo, Timney, Gentry, and Morant (1975), Murch (1976), MacKay and MacKay (1977), Schmidt, Pinette, and Finke (1978).

The proposed model postulates that the motion and the spatial characteristics of the stimulus pattern are coded in different neurosensory subsystems. The motion per se would be the unconditioned stimulus (UCS) that, by means of neurosensory adaptation, elicits an unconditioned response (UCR), called a noncontingent MAE. The "ghostly" MAE and the threshold elevation (a) are such non-contingent MAEs. During the test period, the stimulus pattern which has been combined with the UCS would assume the role of a conditioned stimulus (CS) in eliciting a conditioned response (CR). For this reason, a residual MAE (c) may be said to be contingent on the features of the test figure. Residual MAEs show the main characteristics of a conditioned response: contingency, acquisition, generalization, extinction, and spontaneous recovery (Bonnet, 1975). The last two characteristics, demonstrated in the following experiments, cannot be explained by neurosensory adaptation.

EXPERIMENT I

The aim of the first experiment is to provide directly comparable data for three classes of MAE-phenomena (a, b, and c). The results serve to illustrate a taxonomy of MAE-phenomena based upon the two processes described above.

Material and Procedure

Stimuli were presented in a two-field mirror-tachistoscope. One field served for inspection and the other for testing. Each field subtended 15×13 deg at a distance of 60 cm from the subject's eye. The mean luminance of each field was 100 cd/m^2 with stimulus contrast of .90. The motion presented in one field was provided by the rotation (120 rpm) of a 5-turn arithmetic spiral of 8 deg diameter.

A trial consisted of fixating the center of the test field for about 2 sec, then looking at the center of the rotating spiral for 30 sec, followed by one of four test conditions:

Condition 1 ("ghostly" motion) The test field was a piece of white paper, the texture of which was barely visible. It contained a faint fixation-point in its center and appeared immediately at the end of the inspection phase.

Condition 2 (interrupted "ghostly" motion) At the end of the inspection period, a 5 sec dark-interval was interposed. This duration was chosen as half the mean duration of the MAE obtained in Condition 1. After this time, the blank, white test field was presented. The aim was to show that the duration of the "ghostly" MAE is independent of the change of luminance of the test field.

Condition 3 (immediate MAE) A stationary test figure appeared immediately at the end of the inspection period. On every trial, one of three test figures was presented. They were made of concentric black circles of the same thickness (9 min) as the inspection spiral, but varied in the number of circles and in the related spacing inside the 8 deg diameter of the central test field. These test figures contained either three (*T3*), five (*T5*) or eight (*T8*) circles.

Condition 4 (residual MAE) At the end of the inspection period, a dark interval of 20 sec was interposed before the stationary test figures used in Condition 3 were presented.

The offset of the inspection field started a clock which was stopped by the subject when the MAE could no longer be seen. A two-min rest was given before the next trial.

Two experienced subjects took part in the experiments (one being the first author). Two additional subjects were used in Conditions 3 and 4. Each condition was presented in separate sessions. Conditions 1 and 2 were presented first and in that order. Conditions 3 and 4 were counterbalanced between subjects. Within a session, each condition was repeated four times. All experiments were done monocularly using the subject's preferred eye.

Results

Figure 33.1 presents the mean durations of the MAE for the two experienced subjects. In Conditions 3 and 4, durations refer to five circles of the test figure which is equal to number of turns of the inspection spiral ($T5$).

The results show that interposing a dark period does not influence the duration of the MAE observed on a blank field (Conditions 1 and 2). When tested on a spiral, the MAE lasts considerably longer (Conditions 3 and 4). With the interposed dark period (Condition 4), the MAE occurred when in Condition 3 it had already stopped. During the dark interval of Conditions 2 and 4, a "ghostly" MAE was seen.

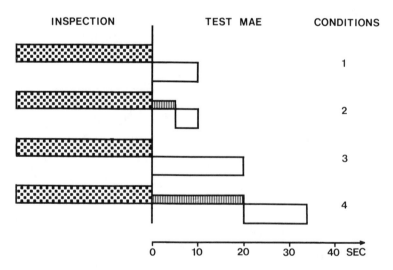

FIG. 33.1.   Mean duration of MAE (white rectangles) following inspection of a spiral (120 rpm) for 30 sec MAE was tested under four conditions. 1: with a uniform, white test field; 2: with a uniform white field presented after a 5 sec dark interval; 3: with a stationary spiral; and 4: with a stationary spiral presented after a 20-sec dark interval. (2 $Ss \times 4$ replications).

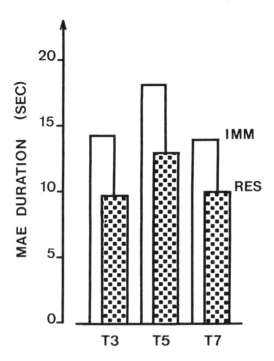

FIG. 33.2.   Mean duration of MAE following inspection of a five turn arithmetic spiral (120 rpm) and tested with three, five, and seven circles of the test figure. IMM= immediate-contingent MAE (condition 3), RES= residual MAE (condition 4). (4 Ss × 4 replications).

Figure 33.2 shows the mean results of the four subjects for Conditions 3 and 4. Here the MAE-durations are given from the beginning of the appearance of the test figure (T3, T5 or T8).

The duration of the MAE in Condition 3 is clearly longer than in Condition 4 $[F(1, 15) = 25.75, p < .01]$. The duration of the MAE varies curvilinearly with the number of circles in the test figure $[F(2,6) = 12.99, p < .01]$. It is greatest for T5.

Discussion

Our data confirm the findings of Wohlgemuth (1911) that a MAE can be observed on a spatially homogeneous test field, whether it is dark or light. Such a noncontingent MAE immediately follows the inspection period and has the same duration regardless of the changes in luminance (Conditions 1 and 2 in Fig. 33.1). The perceived velocity declines as a single exponential function (Bonnet, 1973; Taylor, 1963). When a patterned test figure is used, completely different results are obtained. First, the total duration of the MAE measured from the end of the inspection period is longer. Second, this duration increases with the spatial similarity between inspection and test figures. This indicates that the MAE of Conditions 3 and 4 are texture-contingent (Bonnet & Pouthas, 1972; Mayhew, 1973; Walker, 1972). MAEs obtained in Condition 3 will be called "immediate-contingent." It has been shown that the apparent velocity of such an immediate-contingent MAE decays according to two successive exponential functions (Bonnet & Pouthas, 1972; Masland, 1969; Taylor, 1963). The first phase of the decay is believed to be noncontingent whereas the second phase is clearly contingent (Bonnet, Bouvier, & Petiteau, 1976).

The MAE obtained in Condition 4 will be called "contingent-residual," or in short "residual." This condition suggests that there is some "storage" of the MAE as already proposed by von Szily (1905) and Spigel (1962). It is well known that a residual MAE is contingent upon the spatial features of the test figure. The decay function of its apparent velocity consists of only one phase resembling the second phase of the immediate-contingent MAE. This is true when the dark interval that was interposed between inspection and test phases lasted at least as long as the duration of the noncontingent MAE elicited by the same inspection stimulus (Bonnet et al., 1976). As a matter of fact, the noncontingent MAE observed in Condition 4 during the interposed dark interval lasted about as long as the one measured in Condition 1.

Hence, our proposed taxonomy of MAEs contains three classes of phenomena:

1. There are noncontingent MAEs which result from a neurosensory adaptation process. They may be observed directly as in Conditions 1 and 2, or indirectly by using a threshold elevation technique.

2. There are immediate-contingent MAEs which are mixed phenomena (Bonnet, 1973; Bonnet et al., 1976). They are noncontingent in their first phase of decay and contingent in their second phase of decay.

3. There are residual MAEs which are contingent on the features of the test figure and on their similarity to the features of the inspection figure. They are thought to result from an associative conditioning process. A further distinction between "simple" and "contingent" MAEs as proposed by Favreau (1979) is not necessary. Both effects she referred to are residual and consequently contingent.

The next experiments have been designed within the framework of an associative conditioning process for residual MAEs. They will emphasize some characteristics of these effects which are analogous, but not necessarily identical, to classical conditioned responses. The nature of what we consider to be the conditioned stimulus (or feature), i.e., the kind of contingency, will be systematically varied from one experiment to the next in order to ensure the generality of our theoretical conclusions.

EXPERIMENT II

If the residual MAE is to be considered a conditioned response, it should manifest phenomena analogous to extinction and spontaneous recovery, i.e., its decay should show a nonmonotonic time course. On the other hand, threshold elevation, understood as a measure of recovery from neurosensory adaptation (Sekuler, 1975), should show a monotonic time course. This is tested in the next experiment.

Material and Procedure

Stimuli were sinewave gratings with a spatial frequency of 3.5 cycles per degree (cpd). Gratings had a modulation contrast of .50, a mean luminance of 3 cd/m^2 and a drift rate of 3 Hz. They were generated on a cathode ray tube (P31 phosphor) using standard techniques. Gratings appeared in a circular aperture of 6 deg diameter surrounded by a background matched in luminance and chromaticity. Throughout the experiment the orientation of the grating was alternated from vertical (drifting rightward) to horizontal (drifting downward) every 15 sec.

The experiment was done in two sessions 1 week apart. Each session contained four periods:

1. Pre-inspection Period. Subjects repeatedly adjusted the modulation contrast of the grating until the direction of its drift could just be detected. Every 15 sec a click signaled the beginning of the trial. Only ascending adjustments were used. Vertical and horizontal motions were alternated. Ten settings were made for each direction.

2. Inspection Period. After a 1-minute rest, *drifting* gratings were presented with a contrast of .50. They alternated in orientation and direction of drift every 15 sec while the subject fixated a black dot in the center. Each direction of drift was shown 15 times. This inspection period is analogous to a learning period.

3. Extinction Period. At the end of the inspection period the field was uniformly illuminated for 30 sec, followed by the test or extinction period. Two types of extinction were used in different sessions. In session *T,* 20 contrast thresholds were measured for each direction of the drifting grating with a procedure similar to the one used in the pre-inspection period. In session *R, stationary* gratings with a contrast of .50 alternated in orientation every 15 sec. At every presentation, the subject was asked to press a key when a MAE was first observed and to release it after the MAE had stopped. Twenty measurements of the latency and duration of the MAE were taken for each orientation.

4. Spontaneous Recovery. Four hours after the last trial of the extinction period, a further test period was conducted. In session *T,* threshold measurements were made first followed by the assessment of residual MAEs. This order was reversed for session *R*. As in the extinction period, 20 measurements were taken for each orientation and each kind of measurement.

Four practiced subjects took part in the experiment, the order of sessions *T,R* being counterbalanced across subjects.

Results

1. Threshold Measurements.

The mean results of the threshold measurements are shown in Fig. 33.3. Because thresholds for the vertical motion were systematically higher than thresholds for the horizontal motion, they have been plotted separately.

Results of the extinction period are averaged in blocks of four trials. For the

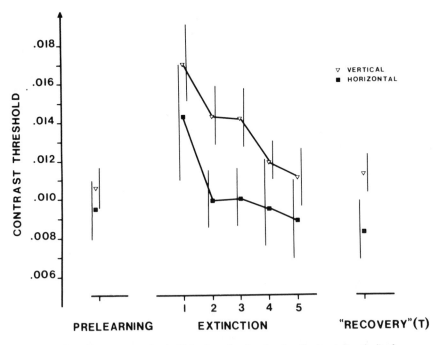

FIG. 33.3.   Contrast threshold for detecting the direction (horizontal/vertical) of a drifting grating. Pre-learning = thresholds measured before the inspection period. Extinction = thresholds measured (in five successive blocks of four trials each) after 7.5-min inspection of drifting medium-contrast gratings. Recovery (T) = thresholds measured 4 hours after extinction. Bars show ± standard error of the mean. Each point is the mean threshold for four *Ss* × four trials.

first block following the inspection period, thresholds were elevated by a mean value of 68.5% with respect to their pre-inspection levels. Thereafter, thresholds declined from block to block. There is no difference between the mean threshold in the fifth block of the extinction period and the threshold obtained in the recovery period, nor is there any difference to the threshold found during the pre-inspection period.

2. Residual MAEs.

Latencies and durations of the residual MAEs were analyzed (not shown). Whereas latency increased from block to block during the extinction period, duration is approximately constant. This result may be specific to small sample size.

The number of reports of MAEs declined from block to block (Fig. 33.4) and approached zero by the end of the extinction period. However, 4 hours later, in the recovery period *R,* the MAE was restored to a significant extent before declining again. Note also that a small number of MAEs were still obtained at a time when no detectable threshold elevation was observed (*T,* see Fig. 33.3).

Discussion

As expected, the present experiment shows that during the extinction period both threshold elevation and number of residual MAEs declined in parallel from block

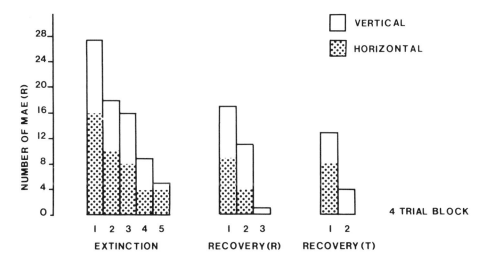

FIG. 33.4.   Total number of reports of MAEs (summed across four subjects) for the extinction period and for the recovery periods (R and T). There were four trials per block.

to block. During the recovery period (since no more inspection was given), thresholds remained at their pre-inspection level as would be predicted if one assumed neurosensory adaptation. However, residual MAEs that had been previously extinguished during the extinction period reappeared during the recovery period. Such a reappearance cannot be accounted for by a neurosensory adaptation process, but would be expected if a conditioning process were at work.

The next three experiments were done in order to clarify some procedural aspects of the residual MAEs and their theoretical implications. Since McCollough's demonstration of the color-contingent aftereffect in 1965, the procedure commonly used for measuring residual aftereffects can be characterized by the following aspects:

1. Two complementary unconditioned features such as two opposite directions of a motion are linked to two complementary conditioned features such as two orthogonal orientations (see Exp. V). In other words, two complementary conditioned responses are learned.

2. A massed inspection (or learning) period in which the presentation of one pair UCS1 + CS1 alternates with a complementary pair UCS2 + CS2 (see Exp. II and IV).

3. A rest interval between the end of the learning period and the beginning of the test period (see Exp. III). The argument for such an interval is generally to allow the immediate noncontingent MAE to vanish.

EXPERIMENT III

The aim of Experiment III was to evaluate the effect of the duration of the time interval introduced between the inspection period and the test (or extinction) period on the number of reports of residual MAEs.

Material and Procedure

The experiment was performed in four successive sessions at 1-week intervals. In each session there was a different interval between the inspection and test periods. These intervals were 15 sec, 3, 6, and 9 min. The last three intervals were spent looking around the lighted room.

Two spirals were shown continuously alternating during the inspection (or learning) and the test periods. They were presented in a two-field mirror-tachistoscope. The spirals had seven turns and were 6 deg in diameter. One spiral was black (B) on a white background. The other was white (W) on a black background. The width of the spiral line was 9 min. The modulation contrast was .90, the luminance of the white areas 100 cd/m^2, and the speed of rotation was 120 rpm.

Each session consisted of three successive periods:

1. Inspection Period.   One spiral was presented in centrifugal motion, the other in centripetal motion. The inspection period lasted 15 min. It consisted of alternate presentations of the white-centrifugal spiral with the black-centripetal spiral, or the reverse combination. Each type of motion was observed for 30 sec at a time and was seen a total of 15 times. Subjects were asked to fixate the center of the spiral.

After each session, the direction of motion for a given spiral (*W* or *B*) was reversed. Half of the subjects began with one combination of a given spiral with a given direction of motion, the other half with the complementary one.

2. Extinction Period.   At the end of the inspection phase, one of the four time intervals was used. Then the two stationary spirals were presented alternating every 10 sec. On every trial, the subject pressed a key to indicate when the residual MAE had stopped. The extinction period continued until no MAE occurred for 10 successive trials.

3. Recovery Period.   Eight days later, the session started with a recovery period during which trials were presented as in the extinction period. After the extinction of the effect learned one week before, a 5-min rest was given. Thereafter, a new cycle was started: inspection, extinction, and recovery.

Four practiced subjects took part in the experiment. The order of presentation of the inspection-test intervals was counterbalanced in a Latin square design across subjects.

Results

Duration of the residual MAE did not prove a reliable measure and is not shown here.

The total number of reports of a residual MAE for the extinction and for the corresponding recovery periods is shown in Fig. 33.5. The number of reports is largest for the 6-min interval. Such a result holds for the extinction period ($\chi^2 = 7.96$, $df=3$, $p<.05$) as well as for the recovery period ($\chi^2 = 65.05$, $df=3$, $p<.01$). A subsidiary result (not shown) was that after inverting the relation between the contrast of the spirals (*W/B*) and the direction of their motion, there was a decrease in the number of MAE-reports in the second session.

Discussion

The presence of a peak for the 6-min interval, also reported by Favreau (1976), is consistent with the assumption of some kind of reactive inhibition (Hull, 1943)

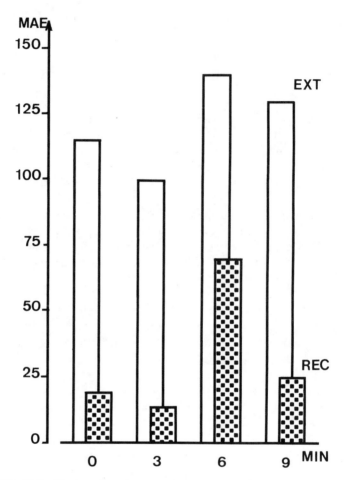

FIG. 33.5. Total number of reports of MAEs (summed across four subjects) following 15-min inspection of a white centrifugal spiral alternating with a black centripetal spiral, MAE is plotted as a function of the time interval between the end of the inspection period and the beginning of the test period during which a white stationary spiral alternated with a black stationary spiral. EXT = extinction period REC = recovery period 8 days later.

produced by the massed practice during the inspection period. Using the immediate-contingent MAE, Holland (1965) has shown that the duration of successively observed MAEs in a massed presentation is progressively reduced. He explained his data as resulting from reactive inhibition provoked by the massed practice. Such an inhibition dissipates with time, a fact which explains the increase in the number of residual MAEs with the length of the time interval. However, a forgetting (or extinction) process that combines with the reactive inhibition should also be at work. As a consequence of such a combination, longer time intervals should reduce the number of residual MAEs.

EXPERIMENT IV

The learning procedure used in Experiments II and III may be questioned with respect to the assumption of a conditioning process. In effect the trials are massed in such a way that no manifest "response" (noncontingent or immediate-contingent MAE) can be observed. One may suggest that such a conditioning procedure is less efficient than a procedure in which the unconditioned response would be produced (see Hilgard & Bower, 1975). The latter necessitates the trials to be more distributed in time. The following experiments examine the question of how massed versus distributed practice interacts with the structure of the test field interposed between successive inspection periods.

Material and Procedure

Stimuli used in the present experiment were four-arm logarithmic spirals, often termed Exner-spirals. Two such spirals rotating in opposite directions were alternately presented in the two fields of a mirror tachistoscope. Colored filters were interposed between the spiral and the subject's eye. One was green (Wratten No. 53), the other one was magenta (Wratten No. 32). A similar contingency was used by Favreau, Emerson, and Corballis (1972). The spirals were 6 deg in diameter with a mean luminance of about 30 cd/m^2 and a modulation contrast of .90. They were shown on a dark surround. During the inspection period they rotated at 100 rpm. The experiment consisted of three sessions spaced by 1-week intervals.

There were three periods within each session:

1. Inspection Period.   One direction of motion (for instance centrifugal) was seen with one color (for instance green) and the opposite direction (centripetal) with the complementary color (red). Each motion was observed 20 sec at a time. The pairing between a direction of motion and a color was reversed in each successive session. Fifteen presentations of each of the two combinations were made within a session, using one of the three following procedures:

(a) IS: The two complementary pairs of directions of motion and colors alternated in immediate succession, i.e., no time interval.

(b) T(ic): After each presentation of a motion in one direction with one color, a 20-sec test period was given during which the stationary spiral was presented with the same color. Subjects were to observe the immediate-contingent (ic) MAE and to indicate its duration.

(c) T(nc): All the temporal aspects of this procedure are identical to those of T(ic). However, during each of the interposed test periods the colored test field was uniform. Consequently, a noncontingent MAE was observed at every trial and its duration was recorded.

2. Extinction Period.   A 3-min rest was given at the end of the inspection period. Thereafter, a stationary green spiral was presented for 10 sec alternating with a stationary magenta spiral. At every presentation, the subject pressed a button as soon as he detected a residual MAE. The extinction period continued until in 10 successive trials no MAE occurred.

3. Recovery Period.   Eight days later a recovery period was introduced. Trials were presented as in the extinction period. A 5-min rest was given before the beginning of the new inspection period.

Six subjects took part in the experiment and were asked to fixate during the all period length.

Results

Figure 33.6 shows the total number of residual MAEs. For the extinction period, the largest number of MAEs is reported with procedure T(nc), i.e., in a condition in which a noncontingent MAE was observed on every inspection trial. A lower number of MAEs is reported with procedure T(ic), i.e., in a condition in which an immediate-contingent MAE was observed on every inspection trial. Finally, the lowest number of MAEs is reported with procedure IS, i.e., in a condition in which no immediate MAE was observed during inspection.

The overall difference in the number of MAEs is significant both for the extinction period ($\chi^2 = 26.46$, $df=2$, $p<.01$) and for the recovery period ($\chi^2 = 21.10$, $df=2$, $p<.01$). There is no significant difference in the number of reports of MAEs between procedures T(ic) and T(nc) in the recovery period.

Again a smaller number of reports of MAEs was obtained in session 2.

Discussion

Two interpretations can explain the lower number of reports obtained with the IS procedure. Such a procedure is characterized by a massed practice which may generate reactive inhibition. In that respect, the rest period of 3 min introduced between the inspection and the extinction periods is likely to be too short for such an inhibition to vanish (see Experiment III). Another factor in the IS procedure is that a MAE was not perceived on every trial since the successive stimuli are both complementary and spatially superimposed. The most effective procedure was the one in which the noncontingent MAE is observed on every trial of the inspection period (T[nc]).

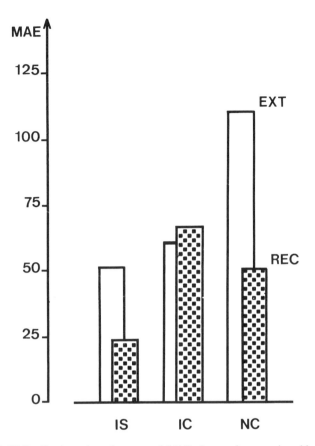

FIG. 33.6. Total number of reports of MAEs (summed across six subjects) during the extinction period (EXT) and the recovery period (REC) for the three inspection conditions of a rotating spiral (100 rpm) in Experiment IV: IS = immediate succession of the complementary pairs of motion and color (magenta/green); T (ic) = after each combination of motion and color the stationary spiral was shown and an immediate-contingent MAE measured; T (nc) = after each combination of motion and color, a uniform colored field was shown and a noncontingent MAE measured.

EXPERIMENT V

Since the problem is to separate the effect of massed practice from the fact that the subject did not observe any MAE during the inspection, a fifth experiment was designed. A new kind of contingency will be used to clarify the relative importance of these two factors.

Material and Procedure

A seven-turn arithmetic spiral with a white line on a black background was used. A white screen was placed in front of the spiral. The screen had a bow-tie cut-out through which only half of the surface of the spiral was seen. The cut-out was aligned either along the vertical diameter (*V*) of the spiral or along the horizontal diameter (*H*). These two bow-ties were spatially complementary. The experiment was conducted in three sessions at 1-week intervals. The inspection procedures were identical to those used in Experiment IV. During the inspection periods, one direction of the rotating spiral was paired with one orientation of the bow-tie cut-out and the complementary direction was paired with the complementary orientation. These pairings were reversed from session to session.

Aside from the nature of the conditioned stimulus, the main difference between Experiments IV and V lay in the IS procedure. Because the inspection figure of one trial did not overlap spatially with the inspection figure of the next, the subject observed a noncontingent MAE. At Trial 1 the subject was presented with a centrifugal motion in a horizontal bow-tie. At Trial 2 he would see a centripetal motion in a vertical bow-tie. Then, the subject could observe, at the same time, a centripetal MAE in the empty part of the figure corresponding to the centrifugal motion previously seen on Trial 1. Six new subjects took part in the three sessions of the experiment.

Results

Results are presented in Fig. 33.7. Contrary to what is shown in Fig. 33.6, the IS procedure now gives a larger number of MAEs than the T(nc) procedure both in the extinction and in the recovery periods. The IC procedure gives the smaller number of MAEs.

There is a significant difference in the number of reports of MAEs across procedures during the extinction period ($\chi^2 = 30.78$, $df=2$, $p<.01$) as well as during the recovery period ($\chi^2 = 19.01$, $df=2$, $p<.01$), although the difference between procedures T(ic) and T(nc) is not significant. However, the superiority of the T(nc) procedure over the T(ic) procedure is significant for the recovery period ($\chi^2 = 3.86$, $df=1$, $p<.05$).

As in the preceding experiments, the second session led to a smaller number of MAEs than the other sessions.

Discussion

It should be emphasized that a greater number of residual MAEs were obtained when a noncontingent MAE was observed on every trial during the inspection or learning period. Whether this period consisted of massed or more distributed trials is ot critical. Although their durations were not measured, noncontingent MAEs were reported in every trial in the present IS procedure.

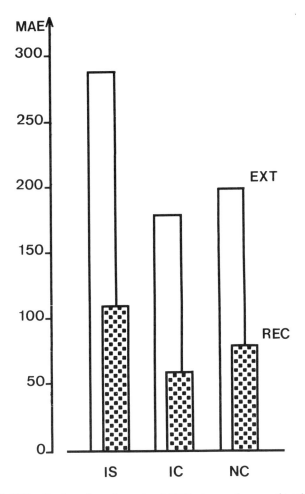

FIG. 33.7. Total number of reports of MAEs (summed across six subjects) during the extinction period (EXT) and the recovery period (REC) for the three inspection conditions of a rotating arithmetic half-spiral in Experiment V. IS = immediate succession of the complementary pairs of motion (centrifugal/centripetal) and orientation (vertical/horizontal) of the bow-tie cut-out, a noncontingent MAE could be seen; (ic) = after each combination of motion and orientation the stationaty half spiral was shown and an immediate-contingent MAE measured; T(nc) = after each combination of motion and orientation, a uniform field was shown and a noncontingent MAE measured.

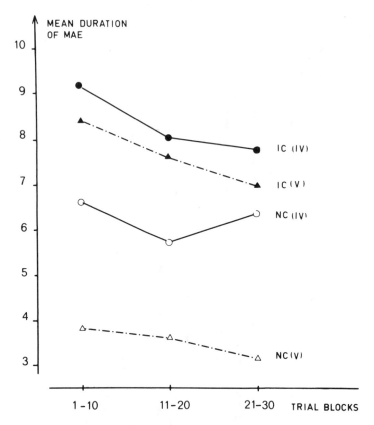

FIG. 33.8.   Mean duration (six Ss) of the immediate-contingent MAEs (IC) and
the noncontingent MAEs (NC) during the inspection periods of Experiments IV
and V for conditions T(ic) and T(nc). There were 10 trials per block.

Nevertheless, there may be an overall effect of massed practice. Durations of
the noncontingent MAEs and of the immediate-contingent MAEs were measured
in the T(nc) and in the T(ic) conditions of both experiments. The mean results are
shown in Fig. 33.8, averaged in blocks of 10 successive trials.

As already shown in Experiment I, each noncontingent MAE was shorter than
the corresponding immediate-contingent MAE. Plateau (1849) and Holland
(1965) have reported that the duration of immediate-contingent MAEs declines
with the rank of the trial when massed practice is given. A similar effect is
observed in Experiments IV and V. The slopes for both effects are −.7. The
changes in duration of noncontingent MAEs with the rank of the trials were not
significant. However, this does not allow us to conclude that a massed practice
has no effect on noncontingent MAEs. In effect, each test trial lasted 20 sec.

Since noncontingent MAEs lasted less than their corresponding immediate-contingent MAE, the T(nc) situation is more distributed than the T(ic) situation.

GENERAL DISCUSSION

The main experimental results are summarized in the following way:

1. Experiment I emphasizes that a taxonomy of MAEs distinguishes three classes of phenomena: First the noncontingent MAEs attributed to a neurosensory adaptation process; second, the immediate-contingent MAEs that are distinguished because they are attributed to both the neurosensory adaptation process and to the conditioning process (Bonnet et al., 1976); third, the residual (and contingent) MAEs attributed to an associative conditioning process.

2. Experiment II emphasizes the fact that the recovery from the neurosensory adaptation, as measured by threshold elevation, is a monotonic process. In contrast, residual MAEs demonstrated extinction and spontaneous recovery. The latter phenomenon is strong evidence for an associative conditioning process.

3. Experiment III demonstrates that the number of MAEs during the extinction period varies nonmonotonically with the duration of the rest interval introduced between the end of the inspection (or learning) period and the beginning of the test (or extinction) period. It has been suggested that such an effect can be explained by a combination of reactive inhibition and extinction processes (see Hilgard & Bower, 1975).

4 Experiments IV and V show that the greatest number of residual MAEs is obtained with the procedure that produced a noncontingent MAE on every trial of the inspection period. The contiguity between UCS - CS and UCR had the greatest reinforcing value. The next most effective procedure is the one in which the immediate-contingent MAE is observed on every trial of the inspection period, i.e., the contiguity between UCS - CS and UCR - CR has a lower reinforcing value. The absence of any observed response during the inspection period does not prevent the residual MAE from appearing, although it is less common. Such a result can be explained on the basis of Guthrie's theory (see Hilgard & Bower, 1975).

5. In most instances the differences in performance observed during the extinction period are preserved in the recovery period that was 8 days later. Such a result confirms that these differences in the number of residual MAEs mostly depend upon the level of learning reached during the inspection period. It also shows the relevance of such a dependent variable in the study of residual MAEs within the framework of a conditioning process.

Another aspect of the results deserves some comment in that respect. It has been mentioned that the second sessions of Experiments III, IV and V lead to a lower number of residual MAEs than any other session. This result holds both for the extinction and for the recovery periods. In each of these experiments, from session 1 to session 2, the pairing between the direction of motion and the feature (contrast, color, orientation) upon which it is contingent is reversed for the first time. A conditioned process might easily show such a detrimental effect of a counter-pairing. Because of the 1-week interval between successive sessions, a neurosensory adaptation process would not predict such a result. As a matter of fact, further unpublished experiments on this question demonstrated that the detrimental effect of inverting the pairing diminished rapidly with replications of the procedure. The latter result would be expected on the basis of a conditioning process.

The question remains as to the exact nature of the conditioning process involved here. Although the classical Pavlovian conditioning is taken as a model, we do not assume that it is a precise description. Some differences are obvious. The "response" we are referring to here is a sensation and has no motor component. Actually, both stimuli and responses belong to the same sensory modality. The conditions for generating a residual MAE are the simultaneous presentation of the UCS and CS. More experiments are necessary before the conditioned process, assumed to underlie residual MAEs and to be responsible for the color-contingent aftereffects, can be fully characterized.

ACKNOWLEDGMENTS

The authors thank L. Harvey, A. Pantle, M. Ritter, L. Spillmann, C. Stromeyer III, C. Tyler and B. Wooten for their helpful criticisms and for improving the English of our manuscript.

REFERENCES

Barlow, H. B., & Hill, R. M. Evidence for a physiological explanation of the Waterfall phenomenon and figural after-effects. *Nature*, 1963, *200*, 1345–1347.

Bonnet, C. Facteurs temporels dans le mouvement consecutif visuel. *Vision Research*, 1973, *13*, 1311–1317.

Bonnet, C. Le conditionnement sensori-sensoriel dans les analyseurs visuels d'attributs. *Psychologie Francaise*, 1975, *20*, 35–43.

Bonnet, C. Time factors in the processing of visual movement information. In J. Requin (Ed.), *Attention and Performance* VII, Hillsdale, N.J.: Lawrence Erlbaum Associates, 1978.

Bonnet, C., Bouvier, A., & Petiteau, H. Phases in movement after-effects and their relationship to the kinetic-figural effect. *Psychological Research*, 1976, *38*, 267–282.

Bonnet, C., Le Gall, M., & Lorenceau, J. L' adaptation neuro-sensorielle au mouvement visuel. *L' Année Psychologique*, 1982, *82*, 7–17.

Bonnet, C., & Pouthas, V. Interactions between spatial and kinetic dimensions in movement after-effect. *Perception & Psychophysics*, 1972, *12*, 193–200.

Favreau, O. E. Interference in colour-contingent motion after-effect. *Quarterly Journal of Experimental Psychology,* 1976, *28,* 553–560.

Favreau, O. E. Persistence of simple and contingent after-effects. *Perception & Psychophysics,* 1979, *26,* 187–194.

Favreau, O. E., Emerson, V. F., & Corballis, M. C. Motion perception: a color-contingent after-effect. *Science,* 1972, *176,* 78–79.

Hilgard, E. R., & Bower, G. H. *Theories of learning* (4th ed.). Englewood Cliffs, N.J.: Prentice-Hall, 1975.

Holland, H. C. *The spiral after-effect.* Oxford: Pergamon Press, 1965.

Hull, C. L. *Principles of behavior.* New York: Appleton-Century-Crofts, 1943.

Kohler, I. Über Aufbau und Wandlungen der Wahrnehmungswelt. Insbesondere über 'bedingte Empfindungen'. *Österreichische Akademie der Wissenschaften, Philosophisch-historische Klasse; Sitzungsberichte,* 227. Band, 1. Abhandlung. Wien: Rohrer, 1951.

Leppmann, P. K. Spatial frequency dependent chromatic after-effects. *Nature,* 1973, *242,* 411–412.

MacKay, V., & MacKay, D. M. Multiple orientation-contingent chromatic after-effects. *Quarterly Journal of Experimental Psychology,* 1977, *29,* 203–218.

Mashhour, M. Psychophysical relations in the perception of velocity. Stockholm: Almqvist & Wiksell, 1964.

Masland, R. H. Visual motion perception: experimental modification. *Science,* 1969, *165,* 819–821.

Matsuda, F. Developmental study of time, space and velocity estimations: III. Velocity estimations. *Japanese Journal of Psychology,* 1970, *40,* 297–303.

Mayhew, J. E. W. Movement after-effects contingent on size: evidence for movements detectors sensitive to direction of contrast. *Vision Research,* 1973, *13,* 1789–1795.

Mayhew, J. E. W., & Anstis, S. M. Movement after-effects contingent on color, intensity and pattern. *Perception & Psychophysics,* 1972, *12,* 77–85.

McCollough, C. Color adaptation of edge-detectors in the human visual system. *Science,* 1965, *149,* 1115–1116.

Murch, G. H. Classical conditioning of the McCollough effect: Temporal parameters. *Vision Research,* 1976, *16,* 615–619.

Plateau, J. Quatrième note sur de nouvelles applications curieuses de la persistance des impressions de la rétine. *Bulletin de l'Académie royale des Sciences et des Beaux Arts de Belgique,* 1849, *16,* 254–260.

Schmidt, M. J., Pinette, P. R., & Finke, R. A. Further evidence for conditioning processes in the McCollough effect. *Journal of General Psychology,* 1978, *99,* 117–132.

Sekuler, R. W. Visual motion perception. In E. C. Carterette & M. P. Friedman (Eds.), *Handbook of perception* (Vol. V), *Seeing.* New York: Academic Press, 1975.

Sekuler, R. W., & Pantle, A. A model for after-effects of seen movement. *Vision Research,* 1967, *7,* 427–435.

Skowbo, D., Timney, B. N., Gentry, T. A., & Morant, R. B. McCollough effects: experimental findings and theoretical accounts. *Psychological Bulletin,* 1975, *82,* 495–410.

Spigel, I. M. Contour absence as a critical factor in the inhibition of the decay of a movement after-effect. *Journal of Psychology,* 1962, *54,* 221–228.

Sutherland, N. S. Figural after-effects and apparent size. *Quarterly Journal of Experimental Psychology,* 1961, *13,* 222–228.

Szily, A. von Bewegungsnachbild und Bewegungskontrast. *Zeitschrift für Psychologie und Physiologie,* 1905, *38,* 81–154.

Taylor, M. M. Tracking the decay of the after effect of a seen rotary movement. *Perceptual and Motor Skills,* 1963, *16,* 119–129.

Vautin, R. G., & Berkeley, M. A. Responses of single cells in cat visual cortex to prolonged stimulus movement: neural correlates of visual after-effects. *Journal of Neurophysiology*, 1977, *40*, 1051–1065.

Walker, J. T. A texture contingent visual motion after-effect. *Psychonomic Science*, 1972, *28*, 333–335.

Wohlgemuth, A. On the aftereffect of seen movement. *British Journal of Psychology Monograph Supplement*, 1911, No. 1.

34 Aftereffects of Form, Motion, and Color

Stuart Anstis
York University
Downsview, Ontario, Canada

ABSTRACT

Following inspection of a slowly rotating disc, a stationary test disc appears to rotate in the opposite direction. Also, following adaptation to a light that grows gradually brighter (or dimmer), a steady test light appears to be growing gradually dimmer (or brighter). These aftereffects are probably caused by adaptation of neural channels sensitive to motion and to gradual luminance change, respectively. The nature and physiological site of these aftereffects was investigated. It was found that motion aftereffects could be made contingent on color, intensity and pattern.

Other studies explored spatial and temporal interactions between colored patterns. A grey spot on a green background looked faintly pink; but after prolonged fixation its afterimage was a brilliant green. Where did the green come from? We found that it had two independent sources: (1) the apparent pink induced into the adapting spot by simultaneous contrast led to a green afterimage, and (2) the pink afterimage of the surround spatially induced an apparent green into the spot's afterimage.

We also examined the spatio-temporal interactions between a pair of similar, overlapping patterns which were exposed in rapid succession to give apparent motion, like two successive frames of a movie. We asked how similar the successive pictures must be in order to give apparent motion. We found that the visual system could detect local, point-by-point correlations between the pictures to give local apparent motion. More subtle global correlations could also give rise to apparent motion, by means of a second, long-range perceptual mechanism. Various new illusions of motion illustrate these findings.

INTRODUCTION

This chapter presents a brief overview of some of my research in vision on topics related to Professor Kohler's interests. Most of these experiments were on the interactions between two visual stimuli. The first set of experiments are on visual aftereffects, in which exposure to an adapting stimulus temporarily changes the state of the visual system and alters the perception of the subsequent test stimulus. These changes in the visual system are probably adaptive, rather than a design fault, but their function is not really understood. I describe aftereffects of motion and of brightness, which typically last only a few seconds, and also contingent aftereffects, which can last for days or weeks.

I also describe experiments on apparent motion, in which two stimuli were flashed in quick succession, like consecutive frames of a movie. I ask how the visual system compares or correlates the successive pictures in order to extract apparent motion.

1. THE MOTION AFTEREFFECT AND RELATED PHENOMENA

1.1. Stimulus Conditions and Site of the Motion Aftereffect.

Retinal Image Motion, Not Eye Movements. If a slowly rotating disc is inspected for half a minute or so, and then stopped, the stationary disc will appear to rotate back the other way. This is the well-known aftereffect of seen motion. Although known since the time of Aristotle and much studied during the last century (see Boring, 1942, p. 59), this effect has only recently been explained. It is almost certainly caused by adaptation of neural channels which are sensitive to motion in a preferred direction: Sekuler and Ganz (1963) showed this psychophysically by finding direction-specific threshold elevation following adaptation, and Barlow and Hill (1963) showed that adaptation could slow the firing rate of motion-sensitive neurons in the rabbit retina. The aftereffect was studied by Helmholtz (1866), who in one of his rare slips attributed the effect to eye movements. Gregory and I showed that this was not so (Anstis & Gregory, 1965). We had an adapting field of stripes moving slowly to the right. If we adapted to these with the eyes fixed on a stationary point, the subsequent motion aftereffect was to the left, as expected. If we fixated on a moving stripe, followed it to the end of its travel, then turned our eyes quickly back to pursue another stripe, our eyes moved at the same speed as the stripes but there was almost no image motion across the retina. Result: no motion aftereffect. Next, we tracked a moving spot which moved to the right faster than the stripes, so that it was overtaking the stripes. This produced the same retinal image motion as would have occurred had the eyes been stationary and the stripes moved to the left. Result: a motion aftereffect to the right. We concluded that the direction of the motion aftereffect depended not upon eye movements, nor upon the perceived or judged direction of motion. It was determined only by the direction in which contours moved across the retina. (But see the section below on aftereffects from induced stimuli.)

Site of the Motion Aftereffect: Monocular Versus Binocular.   Is the motion aftereffect retinal or cortical? Papert (1964) found a component which must be central to the point of binocular fusion. He generated dynamic random-dot stereograms, which seen with one eye looked like the contourless electronic snow on a detuned TV receiver, but which when fused binocularly showed horizontal bars that drifted downwards. Inspection of these moving stereoscopic contours gave rise to an upward motion aftereffect. For related experiments see Julesz and Payne (1968) and Julesz (1971).

We cannot determine the site of the motion aftereffect by means of a naive experiment on interocular transfer. If one inspects a rotating disc with the left eye only, and then views a stationary test disc with the right eye only, a motion aftereffect is seen, but of about half normal strength. But this experiment, which at first view suggests a post-retinal site for the aftereffect, in fact tells us very little. It might be that when the adapted left eye is closed, it still sends up an aftereffect message which the brain combines with the message of the stationary test disc which is coming up from the right eye, Moulden and I (Anstis & Moulden, 1970) improved on this naive experiment, first by repeating an old experiment of Wohlgemuth (1911). Looking with both eyes open into a haploscope, we viewed one disc rotating clockwise with the left eye and simultaneously viewed a second superimposed disc rotating anticlockwise with the right eye. Result: When the discs were stopped, we saw no motion aftereffect if we kept both eyes open, but with only the left (right) eye open we saw an anticlockwise (clockwise) aftereffect. This shows that two opposite aftereffects can be built up simultaneously in the monocular pathways from each eye and are capable of canceling each other.

In a second, new experiment, Moulden and I devised a stroboscopic display of spots which flashed in sequence around a circle or clock face (Anstis & Moulden, 1970). This was especially arranged so as to share out the motion information between the two eyes in a way which ensured that each eye on its own would see clockwise motion, but the two eyes together would see anticlockwise motion (Fig. 34.1). First, the display was viewed with only one eye, left or right, and the intended clockwise motion was seen. Afterwards, a static test field showed an anticlockwise aftereffect. Then, for the main experiment, both eyes viewed the adapting and test stimuli. Result: The brain combined the two interleaved, monocular clockwise messages into a single dichoptic anticlockwise message, and the apparent rotation reported was anticlockwise. Afterwards, a

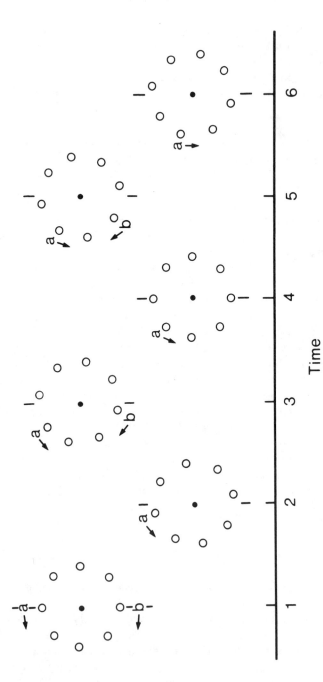

FIG. 34.1. Rotary motion shared out between the eyes. Using left eye only, subject saw clockwise rotation (top row, follow the lamps marked b). Right eye alone also saw clockwise rotation (bottom row). Using both eyes, subject saw anticlockwise rotation (both rows, reading zigzag, follow the lamps marked a). (From Anstis & Moulden. 1970. Reprinted by permission from *Quarterly Journal of Experimental Psychology*, 1970, 22, 222–229.)

clockwise motion aftereffect was seen, not only when the test field was viewed with both eyes open, but even when the test field was viewed monocularly. This aftereffect must be central to the point of binocular combination. It may be that the monocular cells feed into the binocular cells, and are in turn inhibited by them: This would explain both the combination of the monocular messages to produce a binocular aftereffect, and also the lack of monocular aftereffects.

Recently, Duncan and I have returned to this problem (Anstis & Duncan, in press). During a single adapting period subjects inspected a rotating disc with one eye or both eyes open, in the following sequence: Left eye saw clockwise motion, right eye saw clockwise motion, both eyes saw anticlockwise motion. Each stimulus was exposed in turn for 5 seconds, for a total adapting time of 2 minutes. Afterwards, the disc was stopped and viewed by the left eye, the right eye, or both eyes. Result: The left eye on its own saw an anticlockwise aftereffect, and so did the right eye, but both eyes together saw a clockwise aftereffect. So the procedure built up three independent aftereffects, two anticlockwise monocular effects and a clockwise binocular effect. Notice that each eye considered on its own saw equal amounts of clockwise and anticlockwise adapting motion, which would have canceled out if the visual system were linear, giving no net aftereffects. It follows that the visual system does not act linearly here. We conclude that the binocular effects resided in neural channels which were excited greatly by inputs from both eyes, but only minimally by monocular inputs. The monocular aftereffects must reside in channels which are excited by one eye and inhibited by the other eye.

1.2. Contingent Motion Aftereffects

In 1965, McCollough discovered the first contingent aftereffect. She exposed her subjects to orange and black vertical stripes, alternating in time with blue and black horizontal stripes. After adapting to these stimuli for a few minutes, subjects found that vertical black and white test stripes appeared to be tinged with blue (i.e., complementary to orange), and horizontal black and white test stripes appeared tinged with orange. She attributed this aftereffect to color adaptation of orientation-selective visual channels. She also compared it to the complementary phantom fringes, reported by Professor Kohler, that replace the colored fringes of chromatic aberration along the edges of objects produced by the wearing of prismatic spectacles (Kohler, 1962).

Her seminal paper percipitated a rush of investigations, my own included, to find further contingent aftereffects. A dozen or more were quickly discovered, and were summarized in a table whose rows were labeled with the adapting visual dimension (color, orientation, motion, binocular disparity) and whose columns were labeled with the dimension showing the aftereffect (also color, orientation, motion, binocular disparity). This table appeared in an article by

Mayhew and me (1972) entitled "Movement aftereffects contingent on color, intensity and pattern." Within a couple of weeks of our submission of this paper for publication, we were most surprised to learn of two other papers which were also in press, entitled "Motion perception: a color-contingent aftereffect" by Favreau, Emerson and Corballis (1972), and "A texture-contingent visual motion aftereffect" by Walker (1972). These three papers were almost identical in content. As sometimes happens when the time is ripe for a certain discovery, none of the three groups of authors was even aware until then of each other's work.

Mayhew and I (1972) found that motion aftereffects could be made contingent on color. We adapted our subjects to a textured disc which rotated clockwise under red illumination, alternating with anticlockwise rotation under green illumination. A stationary test disc now looked stationary under white light, but under red illumination it appeared to rotate in an anticlockwise direction and under green illumination, clockwise. Note that any given retinal region had been exposed to equal and opposite amounts of clockwise and anticlockwise rotation, so any simple motion aftereffects would have canceled out. Also, each retinal region had been exposed to equal amounts of red and green illumination, so any simple colored afterimages would also have cancelled out.

Harris and I showed that motion aftereffects could also be made contingent upon depth (Anstis & Harris, 1974). We adapted our subjects to a textured disc, rotating clockwise, which lay in a depth plane closer than the fixation point. This alternated with a disc, rotating anticlockwise, which lay in a depth plane behind the fixation point. A stationary test disc now looked stationary if it lay in the fixation plane, but it gave an anticlockwise (clockwise) motion aftereffect when it was in front of (behind) the fixation point.

In looking for new contingent aftereffects, we noticed that all the dimensions which gave contingent aftereffects when paired, such as color and motion, could also give simple aftereffects when presented singly. Adaptation to color alone or to motion alone gives rise to colored afterimages or to motion aftereffects. But, although this is necessary, it was not sufficient. For instance, neither we nor anybody else has succeeded in producing color aftereffects contingent on binocular disparity. Nor could we obtain motion aftereffects contingent on gradual change of luminance. We do not know why this is so, but it may be that connections cannot be set up between the visual channels which respond to stereo depth and those which respond to color, and so on.

Thus, the search for new contingent aftereffects leads to diminishing returns. Much more interesting is the question of why contingent aftereffects occur in the first place, and what neural mechanism underlines them. The two main theories are that the aftereffects represent adaptation of "double-duty" neural units, selective both to color and to orientation, or to depth and motion (McCollough, 1965: Stromeyer, 1969). The other theory attributes the aftereffects to some kind of associative conditioning or sensory learning (Mayhew & Anstis, 1972). Clearly, there is a link between color and orientation (or depth and motion) following adaptation. The crucial question is whether such a link exists before adaptation. The adaptation theory would say yes; the learning theory, no. To my mind, nobody has yet devised a satisfactory experiment to answer this crucial question. Of course, both processes might occur.

An alternative suggestion (Anstis, 1975) is that the different visual properties such as color and motion are transmitted to different cortical regions, but they might be contaminated by accidental neural "crosstalk." Crosstalk is a common problem in telephone engineering, when a conversation on one cable is accidentally induced into a neighboring cable. It can be detected and eliminated by running a cross-correlation on neighboring cables. It may be that the function of contingent aftereffects is to reduce visual crosstalk, but the underlying mechanism could equally well be adaptation or learning.

1.3. Ramp Aftereffects

While I was studying the motion aftereffect I discovered a new kind of visual aftereffect. I had noticed that the spiral aftereffect becomes invisible, as if suppressed, if one adapted to a rotating spiral in ordinary room lighting or daylight, and then tested on a stationary spiral which was lit intermittently by a stroboscope at 3 to 8 Hz (Anstis, Gregory, MacKay, & Rudolf 1963). It turned out that this apparent suppression was probably trivial, since the strobe flashes were much too short to allow the perception of any motion, but at the time it seemed important. I varied the properties of the stroboscopic illumination to see what aspect of the flashing was responsible for the suppression of the motion aftereffect. A stroboscope produces very short flashes or pulses of light. I lengthened the flashes by turning a light on and off in squarewave fashion at about 5 Hz, so that the on-periods or flashes had the same duration as the dark intervals. The supposed suppression was much less obvious, suggesting that the on or off transients of the flash were important. I decided to produce a flash with an off transient but no on transient, by arranging for the light to brighten gradually and then turn off sharply. In other words the luminance was to be modulated by a repetitive ramp or sawtooth. Nowadays one would do this with an oscilloscope or a light-emitting diode, but neither happened to be available to me at that time. So I used a fluorescent tube as the light source, built a power supply to drive it, and varied the current by shunting the lamp with an old potentiometer, 10 cm in diameter, whose wiper I rotated continuously with an electric motor. This proved quite satisfactory.

I let the motor run for about 30 sec and then switched it off. The lamp remained on, but to my dismay it appeared to be dimming markedly as I looked at it, even though the potentiometer was no longer being rotated. I spent the rest of the day trying to track down what had gone wrong with my power supply. Nothing had gone wrong. The dimming was taking place in my visual system, not in the equipment. A new visual aftereffect was trying to force itself upon my attention, but it took me all day to realize it. There are none so blind as those who will not see.

I soon established that following adaptation to a brightening (or dimming) light, a steady test light appeared to be dimming (or brightening). The effect did not transfer from one eye to the other, so it presumably involved monocular neural channels sensitive to gradual luminance change. The effect was not an artifact of pupil change, since a strong aftereffect could be produced by adapting to a checkerboard whose black squares gradually turned white while its white squares were gradually turning black. The space-average luminance of the display remained constant, yielding no net change in pupil diameter, but afterwards half the squares in a static test checkerboard appeared to be dimming and the other squares appeared to be brightening (Anstis, 1967).

Arguing that there may be analogies between vision and hearing, I searched for auditory adaptation to a loudening or softening sound. I attached a loudspeaker to a white noise generator and attempted to modulate its amplitude with a repetitive ramp, by taking hold of the volume control knob and turning it gradually up and then flicking it sharply down by hand. No aftereffect was forthcoming. It was not until some years later that I tried it again properly, by electronically modulating the amplitude of a 1 KHz tone with a 1 Hz rising or falling ramp. This gave a very clear aftereffect, which proved to be tuned to the carrier frequency. After adaptation to a 1KHz loudening (or softening) tone, a test tone of the same frequency showed a large aftereffect of apparent softening (or loudening). Test tones of different frequencies such as 900 or 1100 Hz showed progressively reduced aftereffects, and the tuning curve of the aftereffect was about $+-1$ octave (Reinhardt-Rutland & Anstis, 1982).

1.4. Aftereffects from Induced Stimuli

Most aftereffects are sharply localized to the retinal area which has been adapted. A colored afterimage has exactly the size and shape of the stimulating object, although (usually) the complementary color. When a stationary window of stripes moving upwards is projected on the retina, it will lead to a downward motion aftereffect whose size and shape is usually exactly the same as the adapting window.

This generalization is usually true, but we have found a special situation where it fails. Moreover, the failure occurs for aftereffects of motion, color, gradual luminance change, and possibly for other aftereffects too. Consider first a colored afterimage. As Hering (1920) pointed out, a small grey spot on a green surround will look pink by simultaneous contrast. If you stare at the spot to adapt to it and then transfer your gaze to a blank sheet of white paper, you will see a colored afterimage. The colors in this afterimage are unexpected; instead of a colorless spot afterimage on a red surround, you will see a brilliant green afterimage of the spot centered in a pale pink afterimage of the surround.

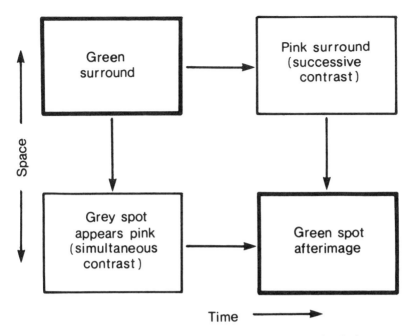

FIG. 34.2.   After adapting to a grey spot on a green surround, the afterimage seen on a white test field consists of a brilliant green spot (bottom right) on a faintly pink surround. This could be an afterimage of the previous contrast (bottom left), or else it could be induced color from the afterimage of the surround (top right). See text. (From Anstis, Rogers & Henry, 1978. Reprinted by permission from *Vision Research*, 1978, *18*, 899–911.)

How did the green color get into the afterimage of the grey spot? There are two possibilities. (1) The green adapting surround induces some pink into the adapting spot by simultaneous contrast, so you see the afterimage of an effectively pink spot. This would be an afterimage of a contrast-induced color. (2) The pink afterimage of the surround induces some apparent green into the grey afterimage of the spot during the test period: This would be a color change due to simultaneous contrast induced by an afterimage (i.e., successive contrast). The question is whether the simultaneous contrast between spot and surround occurred during the adapting period or during the test period between the afterimages of spot and surround (Fig. 34.2). We teased these possibilities apart (Anstis, Rogers, & Henry, 1978) in the following way. First, we established that whereas a grey spot looks pink on a green surround, a jet-black spot does not. It goes on looking black, or even faintly green. We used this fact to permit simultaneous contrast to operate between the adapting stimuli but to exclude it between afterimages during the test period. Two adapting fields were presented to the same retinal area in alternation. The first field consisted of a green surround, with a grey spot on the left (which looked pink) and a black spot on the right

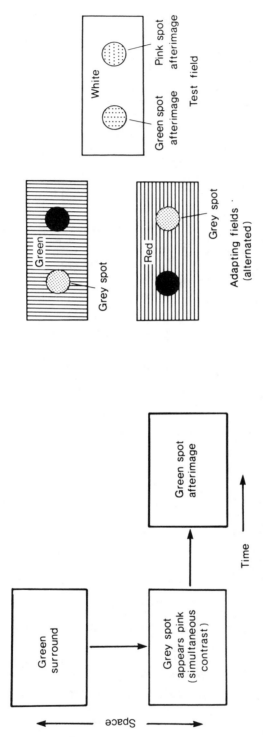

FIG. 34.3. Interactions between simultaneous contrast and afterimages. Afterimages from previous contrast were produced by eliminating any colored afterimages from the surround. Two adapting fields were presented in alternation, so that the left spot was alternately grey on a green surround (looking pink by contrast), and black on a red surround. The right spot was alternately black on a red surround, and grey on a red surround (looking green by contrast). (From Anstis, Rogers & Henry, 1978. Reprinted by permission from *Vision Research*, 1978, *18*, 899–911.)

(which did not). The second field consisted of a red surround, with the grey spot now on the right (so it looked greenish) and the black spot now on the left (which went on looking black) (Fig. 34.3). Notice that, owing to simultaneous contrast, the left-hand adapting spot looked alternately pink and black, whereas the right-hand adapting spot looked alternately black and green. Result: On a test field with a grey background, the afterimage of the left-hand spot looked green, and the afterimage of the right-hand spot looked pink. These must be afterimages caused by contrast colors induced during adaptation, because the adapting surround alternated between red and green, whose afterimages canceled out, giving a colorless afterimage for the surround. The colorless appearing surround could not have induced any colors into the spot afterimages during the test period.

Conversely, we showed that simultaneous contrast can induce apparent colors into afterimages, by allowing contrast between afterimages during the test period while preventing contrast between the physical stimuli during the adapting period. Before, we partitioned the adapting fields in time, but now we partitioned them in space (Fig. 34.4). As before, we relied on a convenient difference between grey and black. It turns out that any colored negative afterimage will be strongly visible on a grey or white test field, but is almost invisible on a jet-black test field. The adapting field consisted of a small grey spot on a surround which was partitioned into two red and two green quadrants. The two colors "fought" to induce contrast into the grey spot, but both failed because they canceled each other out, so the spot went on looking grey.

The test field was a grey spot centered on four black and white quadrants, congruent with the adapting quadrants. Result: When the previously red quadrants were white, a strong green negative afterimage was seen. This induced an apparent pink into the afterimage of the test spot. The black and white test quadrants were suddenly interchanged, so that the previously green quadrants were now white. The white test quadrants now revealed a red negative afterimage which induced an apparent green into the afterimage of the test spot. So, changes in the brightness of the test surround were sufficient to reverse the apparent color of the spot afterimage. This must be color contrast induced by the surround afterimages, and could not have been an afterimage of any color previously induced into the adapting spot.

Reinhardt-Rutland and I have used similar techniques with the motion aftereffect (Anstis & Reinhardt-Rutland, 1976). If a small patch of stationary random dots is centered in a large textured surround which is drifting slowly to the left, the patch will appear to drift to the right by induced motion, like the moon seen through drifting clouds (Duncker, 1929). If the patch is fixated for about half a minute, and the surround then stopped, the patch will show a motion aftereffect of apparent drift to the left, while the surround shows very little motion aftereffect. We were able to show that this secondary motion aftereffect in the test patch has two components. First, the induced motion perceived in the adapting patch produces its own aftereffect (aftereffect from induced motion). Second, the

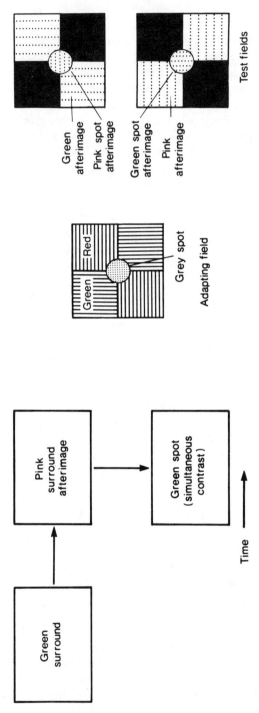

FIG. 34.4. Interactions between simultaneous contrast and afterimages. The pink afterimage of the surround was shown to induce color into the spot afterimage, by eliminating contrast-colors from the adapting spot. Adapting grey spot was surrounded by two red and two green quadrants, which, being in complementary colors, failed to induce any apparent color into the spot. Two test fields were used on different trials. On the upper test field, the previously red quadrants fell on white test quadrants, giving a strong green afterimage which spatially induced pink into the afterimage of the test spot. On the lower test field, previously green quadrants fell on white test quadrants, giving a strong pink afterimage which spatially induced green into the spot afterimage. (From Anstis, Rogers & Henry, 1978. Reprinted by permission from *Vision Research*, 1978, *18*, 899—911.)

motion aftereffect in the surround, while not easy to see itself, induced a secondary aftereffect in the opposite direction into the static test patch during the test period (apparent motion induced by an aftereffect).

The same experiment can be done with the aftereffect from gradual luminance change (Anstis, 1978b). A grey spot of constant luminance was centered in a surround which was gradually dimming, driven by a repetitive ramp. Simultaneous contrast made the central spot appear to be repetitively brightening. Following an adaptation period, the whole field was switched to a constant intermediate luminance, and the central spot now showed an aftereffect of apparent dimming, even though its actual luminance had never changed throughout the experiment. Once again, this aftereffect proved to have two components: an aftereffect of the apparent brightening which had occurred during the adapting period, and also a secondary aftereffect induced by the surround aftereffect into the test spot during the test period. No doubt the same experiments could be carried out on other types of visual aftereffects.

2. APPARENT MOVEMENT

Two spots flashing in alternation at suitable intervals of time and space can give the impression of a single spot jumping to and fro. This is the well-known phenomenon of apparent movement. Instead of two separated spots one can use two overlapping pictures, as in successive frames of a movie. Rogers and I have investigated the "correspondence problem" and asked: How similar must two successive pictures be in order to give an impression of apparent movement? (Anstis & Rogers, 1975). A running man bends his limbs into different configurations in each frame, but his overall shape remains sufficiently the same to carry the impression of movement. In two recent review articles (Anstis 1978a, pp. 655–673: Anstis, 1980) I have discussed the minimum correlation between frames which is necessary to produce apparent motion.

2.1. Reversed Apparent Movement

In 1970 I was studying apparent motion, exposing two slides in alternation on a screen, when I discovered a new visual phenomenon (Anstis, 1970). Both slides happened to be of the same random dot pattern, and I accidentally used a positive slide in one projector and a negative in the other. (Random dots look very much the same in negative as they do in positive. If I had been using a normal picture such as a landscape I would never have made such a "mistake.") To begin with, the slides were superimposed on the screen in exact registration. I realized that one picture was the negative of the other when I noticed that the two superimposed pictures formed a uniform bright field. To obtain apparent movement, I set the pictures a few minutes of arc out of exact registration, and then I used dimmers to alternate from one picture to the other, with the first picture fading down as the second picture faded up. To my surprise, the direction of apparent movement was in the direction towards the earlier stimulus, opposite to the physical displacement. It made no difference whether the positive or the negative picture was exposed first; in fact it is quite an arbitrary decision which of two random-dot pictures is called the positive. I called this phenomenon "reversed apparent movement." This effect is not related to delta movement, in which a dim positive stimulus is followed by a bright positive stimulus, and due to a physiological delay is seen later. Instead, it is probably caused by neural blurring. When a positive edge is superimposed on a slightly displaced negative edge a contour is formed, and if this contour is blurred by the point-spread function of the visual system, it becomes shifted in a direction away from the negative edge (Anstis & Rogers, 1975). Subsequently we have found analogous effects of reversed stereoscopic depth and apparent reversals of vernier offsets (Rogers & Anstis, 1975).

Continuous presentation of reversed apparent motion by means of a series of displaced frames can give rise to a motion aftereffect in a direction opposite to the illusory direction of motion, which indicates that the illusion arises early enough in the visual system to stimulate, and adapt, neural motion detectors (Anstis & Cavanagh, 1981). This is supported by physiological findings: When cortical cells in area 17 of an anaesthetized cat were presented with a positive and a negative picture alternating on a screen, they showed the same reversed, "illusory" responses as did human observers who were looking at the same screen (Blakemore & Anstis, unpublished results). Recently we have discovered a closely related illusion of motion in which a pattern oscillating through only a few minutes of arc appears to be drifting continuously in one direction only (Anstis & Rogers, in press).

2.2. Ambiguous Split Motion

Recently, while studying two well-known effects of visual motion, I discovered another effect which appears to be new. A pair of carefully selected random-dot patterns are presented in alternation, giving apparent motion. Seen from a distance the motion back and forth appears to be nearly vertical, but as one walks towards the display the apparent direction of motion gradually inclines, becoming first oblique and finally horizontal. A full report is forthcoming shortly.

I discovered this effect while studying the apparent motion of random-dot patterns and split motion. If a pattern of random dots makes a sudden jump from left to right, it will be seen in apparent motion provided that each dot in the first picture is correctly seen as jumping to its corresponding dot in the second picture, However, if the jump is made too big, incoherent random motion is seen because each dot is perceived as jumping towards whatever dot in the next picture happens to be closest. The visual system seems to lose track of the correlation between the two pictures. I was trying to determine the conditions that made a dot "choose" to jump either to its corresponding dot or else to its nearest neighbor. (See Pantle and Petersik, 1980, for an interesting experiment on this question).

Starting with the simplest display I could think of, I flashed up a single spot and followed it by a simultaneous pair of spots of which one was near to the first spot and to its right, while the other was further away from the first spot and above it. The three dots together were like a letter L. I had expected that proximity would win, and sideways motion would be seen without upward motion. However, the actual result was split motion, as already reported by De Silva (1926), Kolers (1972, p. 69) and Ullman (1980). The first spot appeared to split into two fragments, one jumping to the right and the other jumping upwards. Viewing distance made no difference. I then made a multiple version of this display. The first dot was replaced by a field of numerous sparsely distributed random dots, and the pair of dots in the second picture was replaced by a double image containing two identical, shifted versions of the first random-dot picture. One copy was shifted slightly to the right, and the other copy was shifted about twice as far upwards, so I expected to see each dot in the first picture splitting into two fragments as before, with one dot jumping sideways and the other upwards. That is not what happened.

While my computer was plotting the points, which took about 5 minutes, I went to get a cup of coffee. When I came back into the room the display had already started alternating. I glanced at it casually as I walked towards it, noting that the whole field appeared to move in one direction without splitting. I was startled to see the axis of the apparent motion changing steadily from almost vertical to horizontal as I walked forward. I sat down and found that the direction of motion remained steady as long as I sat working at the keyboard. The dot density was not critical, since the direction of motion was approximately the same whether there were 200 or 2000 dots on the screen, but the dot spacing, which was controlled by the viewing distance, was critical.

I do not yet understand this effect, but there are at least two possible explanations. The visual system may be tuned to some preferred jump size, which at short viewing distances may coincide with the short horizontal jump I used, but at longer viewing distances may match the longer vertical jump. Such a preferred jump size may reflect the receptive field size of motion-sensitive neurons. Alternatively, the ambiguity of the motion comes from selective visibility of different spatial frequency components in the random-dot display. Viewed from close up, the small horizontal jumps are easily seen, but the large vertical jumps are lost in the "noise," since the visual system loses track of which dots in the two pictures belong together. At greater viewing distances the visual system tends to blur out or attenuate the individual dots and to respond to clumps or galaxies of dots, which represent the low spatial frequencies of the random-dot patterns. This is supported by the fact that close viewing of an optically blurred pattern is just as effective as distant viewing in emphasizing the low spatial frequencies and enhancing the vertical motion. These two explanations, in terms of spatial distance and spatial frequency respectively, are not incompatible and could both be true.

2.3. Adaptation to Apparent Motion

Two spots flashing in alternation at a suitable rate are perceived as a single spot jumping back and forth in apparent movement. If the alternation rate is too slow, the spot is seen in two successive positions without seeming to move, and if it is too fast one sees two spots flickering in place. When the alternation rate is set approximately in the range between 2 Hz and 5 Hz, apparent motion is seen. However, on prolonged inspection the impression of apparent movement deteriorates and is replaced by an impression of two spots flickering in place (Kolers, 1972). Cogan and I (in press) have investigated this adaptation to apparent movement, and found that it is strongly dependent upon the frequency of alternation. At 2 Hz the impression of apparent motion is very stable and never degenerates into flicker. A 3 Hz alternation decays away into apparent flicker over a period of about 20 or 30 seconds, and 4 Hz alternation decays within only a few seconds. Moreover, two spots which are actually flickering, that is, turning on and off together in simultaneous phase, are much less effective as adapting stimuli than a pair of spots in apparent motion, that is, flickering in antiphase with one spot turning on as the other turns off. This is interesting, because each spot on its own has exactly the same history when it flickers as when it participates in apparent motion. The only stimulus difference lies in the relative timing or phase of the two spots. This shows that the visual channels which are being adapted have a receptive field which looks at both spots, not just at one. Furthermore, these channels are responsive to motion as such and not merely to flicker.

CONCLUSIONS

In most of my visual experiments I presented two stimuli at a time, to see how they interacted perceptually. When the stimuli were similar, the visual system could extract correlations between them, seeing apparent motion if the patterns were exposed in succession to one eye, or stereo depth if they were exposed simultaneously, one to each eye. On the other hand, if the two stimuli were different, as in the case of an adapting and a test field, then the visual system enhanced the differences between them, seeing aftereffects if the patterns were exposed in succession as an adapting and test field, or simultaneous contrast if they were exposed together as an inducing surround and a test patch.

In the case of apparent motion, the brain acted like a statistician looking for correlations. The brain's task is to compare two successive pictures, and I asked what types of correlation are, or are not, detected by the brain, or, to put it another way, how similar must successive pictures be to give a percept of apparent motion. If the pictures are identical, then no change or motion is seen because there is no change to see. If they are dissimilar, a complete changeover is perceived, like a cut from one shot to another in a movie, but there is no apparent motion. So the two pictures should be sufficiently alike without being identical. The changes between the pictures, or departures from perfect correlation, determine the perceived motion, while the similarities between the pictures, or the aspects which remain unchanged, determine the object which is seen as moving. In other words, the invariance specifies the object while the transformation specifies the movement. It seems that two broad classes of correlation between pictures could be extracted. Local, point by point correlations led to local motion of individual pixels (picture elements), and more subtle global correlations led to long-range, global motion of zones or regions within the pictures. Possibly, the local and global correlations are handled by different perceptual mechanisms.

My simple two-frame movies presented two similar pictures in succession. Stereograms present two similar pictures simultaneously, one to each eye. The challenge to the visual system is much the same, to compare two pictures and extract correlations. The invariance between the stereo pictures specifies the objects, but the slight differences or disparities between them specify not motion but depth. Motion detection probably developed very early in the history of evolution, while stereo vision did not appear until much later, in animals with forward-facing eyes. It is an interesting though unproven speculation that once stereo vision was "invented" it may have developed very rapidly, because the brain had already solved nearly all the perceptual problems beforehand for the very similar task of motion detection. The design of the neural circuits which already existed for seeing motion could easily be copied, with only slight modifications, to produce new circuits which would respond to stereo disparity.

Stimuli interact very differently in the case of simultaneous contrast or successive contrast (aftereffects). Here, the brain emphasizes not similarities but differences between stimuli, over space or time. It is not known why the brain does this, although many speculations have been put forward: Simultaneous contrast may be a way of enhancing edge information, or of compressing the dynamic range of stimuli, or of eliminating redundancies to transmit signals more efficiently. Successive contrast, or aftereffects, may be a valuable form of automatic gain control which keeps the visual system calibrated and matched to its inputs. These ideas, drawn mostly from electrical engineering, are no more than intriguing possibilities, since none has been established beyond doubt. But I have found them helpful in thinking about how the brain works, and why it works as it does.

ACKNOWLEDGMENTS

This research was supported by Grant A 0260 from the National Science and Engineering Research Council of Canada (NSERC).

REFERENCES

Anstis, S. M.   Visual adaptation to gradual change of intensity. *Science*, 1967, *155*, 3763, 710–712.

Anstis, S. M.   Phi movement as a subtraction process. *Vision Research*, 1970, *10*, 1411–1430.

Anstis, S. M.   What does visual perception tell us about visual coding? In M. Gazzaniga & C. Blakemore (Eds.), *Handbook of psychobiology*, ch. 9. New York: Academic Press, 1975.

Anstis, S. M.   Apparent movement. In R. Held, H. Leibowitz & H. L. Teuber (Eds.), *Handbook of sensory physiology* (Vol. 8), *Perception*. New York: Springer-Verlag, 1978. (a)

Anstis, S. M.   Interactions between simultaneous contrast and adaptation to gradual luminance change. *Perception*, 1978, *8*, 487–495. (b)

Anstis, S. M.   The perception of apparent movement. *Philosophical Transactions of the Royal Society, London*, Series B, 1980, *290*, 153–168. Reprinted in: *The Psychology of vision*. London: The Royal Society, 1980.

Anstis, S. M. & Cavanagh, P.   What goes up need not come down: moving flicker edges give positive motion aftereffects. In J. Long & A. Baddeley (Eds.), *Attention and performance* (Vol. 9). Cambridge: Cambridge University Press, 1981.

Anstis, S. M., & Duncan, K.   Separate motion aftereffects from each eye and from both eyes. *Vision Research*, in press.

Anstis, S. M., & Gregory, R. L.   The after effect of seen movement: the role of retinal stimulation and of eye movements. *Quarterly Journal of Experimental Psychology*, 1965, *17*, 173–174.

Anstis, S. M., Gregory, R. L., MacKay, D. M., & Rudolf, N.   Influence of stroboscopic illumination on the after effect of seen movement. *Nature*, 1963, *199*, 99–100.

Anstis, S. M., & Harris, J. P.   Movement aftereffects contingent on binocular disparity. *Perception*, 1974, *3*, 153–168.

Anstis, S. M., & Moulden, B. P.   After effect of seen movement: evidence for peripheral and central components. *Quarterly Journal of Experimental Psychology*, 1970, *22*, 222–229.

Anstis, S. M., & Reinhardt-Rutland, A. H.   Interactions between motion aftereffects and induced movement. *Vision Research*, 1976, *16*, 1391–1394.

Anstis, S. M., & Rogers, B. J.   Illusory reversal of depth and movement during changes of contrast. *Vision Research*, 1975, *15*, 957–961.

Anstis, S. M., & Rogers, B. J.   Oscillating positive-negative patterns give illusion of continuous apparent motion. In press.

Anstis, S. M., Rogers, B. J., & Henry, J.   Interactions between simultaneous contrast and coloured afterimages. *Vision Research*, 1978, *18*, 899–911.

Barlow, H. B., & Hill, R. M.   Evidence for a physiological explanation of the waterfall illusion and figural aftereffects. *Nature*, 1963, *200*, 1434–1435.

Boring, E. G.   *Sensation and perception in the history of experimental psychology*. New York: Appleton-Century-Crofts, 1942.

Cogan, A., & Anstis, S. M.   Adaptation to apparent movement. *Vision Research*, in press.

DeSilva, H. R.   An experimental investigation of the determinants of apparent visual movement. *American Journal of Psychology*, 1926, *37*, 469–501.

Duncker, K.   Über induzierte Bewegung. *Psychologische Forschung*, 1929, *12*, 180–259. Excerpted and translated in W. D. Ellis (Ed.), *A source book of Gestalt psychology*. London: Routledge & Kegan Paul, 1939.

Favreau, O. L., Emerson, V. F., & Corballis, M. C.   Motion perception: a color-contingent after-effect. *Science*, 1972, *176*, 78–79.

Helmholtz, H. von.   *Physiological optics* (Vol. 3, 3rd ed.). Hamburg: Voss, 1896. Translated by J. Southall. New York: Dover Publications, 1924–1925.

Hering, E.   *Grundzüge der Lehre vom Lichtsinn (Outlines of a theory of the light sense)*. Berlin: Springer, 1920. Translated by L. M. Hurvich & D. Jameson. Cambridge: Harvard University Press, 1964.

Julesz, B. *Foundations of cyclopean perception*. Chicago, Ill.: University of Chicago Press, 1971.

Julesz, B., & Payne, R. A. Differences between monocular and binocular strobocopic movement perception. *Vision Research*, 1968, *8*, 433–444.

Kohler, I. Experiments with goggles. *Scientific American*, 1962, *206/5*, 63–72.

Kolers, P. A. *Aspects of motion perception*. New York: Pergamon Press, 1972.

Mayhew, J. E. W., & Anstis, S. M. Motion aftereffects contingent on color, intensity and pattern. *Perception & Psychophysics*, 1972, *12*, 77–85.

McCollough, C. Color adaptation of edge-detectors in the human visual system. *Science*, 1965, *149*, 1115–1116.

Pantle, A., & Petersik, J. T. Effects of spatial parameters on the perceptual organization of a multistable perceptual display. *Perception & Psychophysics*, 1980, *27*, 307–312.

Papert, S. Stereoscopic synthesis as a technique for localizing visual mechanisms. *MIT Quarterly Progress Reports*, 1964, *73*, 239–243.

Reinhardt-Rutland, A. H., & Anstis, S. M. Auditory adaptation to gradual rise or fall in intensity of a tone. *Perception & Psychophysics*, 1982, *31*, 63–67.

Rogers, B. J., & Anstis, S. M. Reversed depth from positive and negative stereograms. *Perception*, 1975, *4*, 193–201.

Sekuler, R., & Ganz, L. A new aftereffect of seen movement with a stabilized retinal image. *Science*, 1963, *139*, 419–420.

Stromeyer, C. F. Further studies of the McCollough effect. *Perception & Psychophysics*, 1969, *6*, 105–110.

Ullman, S. *The interpretation of visual motion*. Cambridge, Mass: MIT Press, 1980.

Walker, J. T. A texture-contingent visual motion aftereffect. *Psychonomic Science*, 1972, *28*, 333–335.

Wohlgemuth, A. On the aftereffect of seen movement. *British Journal of Psychology Monograph Supplement*, 1911, No. 1.

35 Aftereffects from Motion Parallax and Stereoscopic Depth: Similarities and Interactions

B. J. Rogers
M. E. Graham
Psychological Laboratory
University of St. Andrews
St. Andrews, Scotland

ABSTRACT

Prolonged inspection of three-dimensional depth surfaces was found to produce large aftereffects of depth, such that a physically flat test surface appeared to be corrugated in depth but with the opposite phase to that of the adapting pattern. This was true when the adapting depth surface was specified by motion parallax information and when it was specified by binocular disparities. The strengths of the parallax and stereoscopic aftereffects were measured using a nulling technique and were found to be comparable. Evidence was also obtained for possible interactions between the parallax and stereo systems. It was found that prior adaptation to a 3-D corrugated surface specified by binocular disparities, biased the interpretation of an ambiguous corrugated surface specified by relative motion. Conversely, adaptation to an unambiguous parallax surface was found to bias the interpretation of an ambiguous stereoscopic surface. Together, these results suggest that not only are there similarities between the parallax and stereo systems, but also interactions at some level in the processing hierarchy.

INTRODUCTION

Prolonged stimulation along a particular sensory dimension has been shown to produce a number of different perceptual consequences (Anstis, 1975; Blakemore & Sutton, 1969), but the most striking of these must be the perceptual

603

aftereffect. One of the best known examples is the waterfall illusion or movement aftereffect, where sustained viewing of a particular direction of motion (e.g. downward) produces the impression of the opposite direction of motion (upward) on a subsequently viewed stationary pattern (Wohlgemuth, 1911). In this example, the aftereffect is negative in the sense that the neutral test stimulus is perceived as having opposite or complementary properties to those of the adapting stimulus (Favreau & Corballis, 1976). For other sensory dimensions, aftereffects can be demonstrated as a *shift* in the perceived value of a neighboring point on the stimulus dimension after sustained viewing of the adapting pattern (Blakemore & Sutton, 1969; Gibson, 1933). In both cases the characteristics of these perceptual aftereffects have been used to speculate on the properties of the underlying mechanisms in the visual system (Anstis, 1975; Frisby, 1979; Sutherland, 1961).

In the field of depth perception, a number of studies have demonstrated the effects of prolonged adaptation to 3-D figures and surfaces. Köhler and Emery (1947) reported that prior viewing of a figure sloping in depth affected the perception of a subsequently presented figure in the frontoparallel plane, such that it appeared to slope in the *opposite* direction. Other authors have shown that a figure or surface can appear to be *displaced* in depth as a result of prior adaptation to a figure with a slightly different depth value (Ames, 1935; Howard & Templeton, 1964). However, it is not clear whether these aftereffects resulted directly from the adaptive characteristics of the underlying depth processes, or indirectly from the adaptation of some local size or orientation mechanisms (Blakemore & Julesz, 1971). In order to demonstrate that the effects were a consequence of adaptation within depth processes per se, it would be necessary to use an adapting stimulus which did not contain any of these other confounding variables. The development, in the early sixties, of random dot techniques for investigating stereopsis provided the necessary paradigm (Julesz, 1960; 1971). Since the shape of the depth surface in a random dot stereogram is not visible in either monocular view alone, and the depth relationships are specified *only* by binocular disparities, any aftereffects produced by prolonged viewing of these stereograms must result from the adaptation of mechanisms at the level of stereopsis or beyond (Blakemore & Julesz, 1971; Papert, 1964).

In the experiment by Blakemore and Julesz, subjects adapted to a random dot stereogram portraying two squares lying in front of a surround. The upper square contained 4 min arc more crossed disparity than the lower square, and was therefore seen to lie closer to the observer. The test stereogram was similar except that the two squares had the same disparity values. After viewing the adapting stereogram for a minute, the depth relationship between the two squares in the test stereogram appeared opposite to that in the adapting pattern, such that the lower square appeared to lie closer to the observer. Moreover, Blakemore and Julesz (1971) reported that these stereoscopic aftereffects could be nulled by introducing a physical disparity difference between the squares in the test stereo-gram. Their data indicate that the squares appeared to lie at the same depth when the upper square contained approximately 1 min arc more crossed disparity than the lower. Expressed as a percentage, these results imply that some 25% of the depth in the adapting stimulus was needed to null or cancel their aftereffects.

These experiments clearly demonstrate that disparity processing mechanisms in the human visual system can be adapted and can generate depth aftereffects. What of the mechanisms involved in the processing of other sources of depth information such as motion parallax? Do these show similar adaptive properties and if so, how do the strengths of the aftereffects compare with those generated from binocular disparities? These issues are the subject of the first part of this chapter.

Our own work over the past few years has been concerned with the perception of depth based on motion parallax or relative motion information (Rogers & Graham, 1979). More recently, we have looked at the consequences of adapting to 3-D corrugated surfaces, where the depth information is specified *only* by motion parallax (Graham & Rogers, 1982a; Rogers, Graham, & Anstis, 1981). In the experiments reported here, we investigated aftereffects of parallax depth and compared the strength of the aftereffects with those produced by adaptation to stereoscopic surfaces. The existence of these depth aftereffects raises the further question of whether there might also be *interactions* between the different sources of depth information, or their perceptual consequences. Specifically, we have looked at: (1) whether the perception of an ambiguous depth surface in one domain can be biased by prior exposure to depth specified by the other and (2) whether cross-modal cancellation of depth aftereffects between the two domains is possible (Graham & Rogers, 1982b; Rogers & Graham, in preparation).

The decision to compare the characteristics of the parallax and stereo systems was not entirely arbitrary, but derived from the fact that the two systems are quite closely related. Formally, the task for the stereo system is to compare the relative positions of any corresponding object in the two retinal images *simultaneously* and to compute any differences or disparities, whereas for motion parallax it is to compare the relative positions of any corresponding object in *successive* retinal images and to compute any changes in position (Rogers & Graham, 1982). Moreover, we have found that the empirical characteristics of the two systems are closely related. In particular, the sensitivity curves for detecting 3-D surfaces as a function of the spatial frequency of the depth corrugations were very similar in shape for both motion parallax and stereopsis. In both cases, the maximum sensitivity for detecting depth modulations occurred when the spatial frequency of the corrugations was between .3 and .5 cycles/deg visual angle. In addition, the absolute sensitivity of the two systems was comparable for most observers, although the thresholds for perceiving stereoscopic corrugations were often somewhat lower (Rogers & Graham, 1982a; Rogers, Graham, & Anstis, 1980).

MOTION PARALLAX AND STEREOSCOPIC
AFTEREFFECTS

Method

To study aftereffects from parallax depth it is important to isolate motion parallax as the only source of depth information. The technique used was directly analogous to the use of random dot patterns in stereopsis, where there is no information in either half of the stereogram to specify the shape of the 3-D surface. In the motion parallax display, the depth information was specified by the patterns of relative motion in a single retinal image, rather than the binocular disparities between two binocular images. The overall aim was to simulate the motion parallax transformations that would normally be produced by a real 3-D surface during lateral movements of the observer's head. To achieve this, a single random dot pattern (viewed monocularly) was displayed on an oscilloscope screen and systematically "distorted" with each movement of the observer's head. The distortion signal, which was amplitude modulated according to the position of the subject's head, was fed to an additional X-input on the display oscilloscope. The subject's head position was monitored by a potentiometer attached to his chinrest. The information specifying the shape of the three-dimensional surface was therefore present as a pattern of relative velocities between different parts of the display screen, but *only* when the observer's head was in motion. Under these conditions, subjects typically reported that the random dot pattern appeared as a *stationary* and rigid 3-D surface which was viewed from different positions as the head was moved to and fro (Rogers & Graham, 1979). The shape of the simulated 3-D surface was determined by the waveform of the distortion signal and the amount of relative movement between different parts of the display pattern (and hence the amount of perceived depth) was determined by the gain of the amplitude modulation.

To generate aftereffects from parallax depth using this technique, subjects adapted to a sinusoidally corrugated depth surface of low spatial frequency (Fig. 35.1a). Subjects tracked a horizontal fixation line across the center of the screen, thereby preventing the build-up of conventional afterimages but at the same time ensuring that each retinal area was stimulated by the same depth value throughout the adaptation period. The adapting surface was then briefly replaced by a test pattern which contained no relative motion and would therefore be perceived as flat by an unadapted observer. However, we found that after as little as 8 sec of adaptation, the test pattern appeared corrugated in depth, but with the opposite sign to (180 deg out-of-phase with) the adapting surface (Fig. 35.1b). Since the only information specifying the shape of the 3-D adapting surface was given by the relative motion between different rows of dots on the display screen, the apparent corrugations seen during the test period represent a true negative aftereffect of parallax depth.

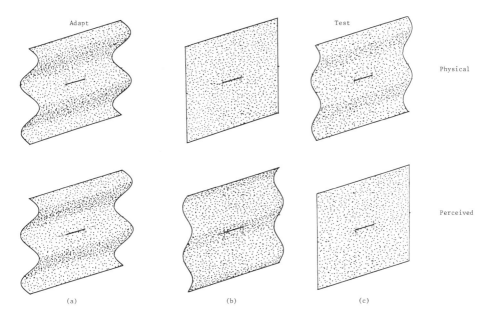

FIG. 35.1. Subjects adapted to a corrugated depth surface (a) while tracking a horizontal line in the center of the display. After adaptation a physically flat test surface (b-upper) appeared to be corrugated in depth with the opposite phase to the adapting surface (b-lower). The aftereffect could be nulled by "adding in" either disparity or relative motion to the test surface (c-upper) until it appeared flat (c-lower). (From Graham and Rogers, 1982a. Reproduced by permission of Pion Ltd.)

The strength of these parallax aftereffects was measured using a nulling technique. During the brief test period, the adapting pattern was replaced by a test surface containing parallax motion to specify a 3-D surface with the *same* phase as the adapting surface, but reduced in amplitude. The subject's task was to adjust the amount of relative motion in the test pattern until the physical depth specified by that motion exactly canceled the apparent depth of the parallax aftereffect (Fig. 35.1c). The amount of relative motion that had to be introduced to null the aftereffect was taken as a measure of the strength of the aftereffect. The strength of these parallax aftereffects was measured as a function of the amount of depth in the adapting surface. This was manipulated by altering the gain of the amplitude modulation in the parallax distortion signal (Rogers & Graham, 1979). Hence for the same extent of head movement, there could be more or less relative motion between the simulated peaks and troughs of the corrugations. The amount of depth in the parallax surface could therefore be expressed in terms of the relative displacement for every centimeter of head movement or, more conveniently, converted into units of *equivalent disparity* by integrating the amount of relative displacement over the interocular distance (Rogers & Graham, 1982). For example, a parallax surface which produced 1 min arc of relative movement for each cm of head movement would be equivalent to a surface having a binocular disparity of 6.5 min arc. This transformation into equivalent disparity units facilitated the comparison of the parallax aftereffects with the stereoscopic aftereffects described later.

Results

Strong negative aftereffects of depth were obtained as a result of adaptation to parallax surfaces. In all cases, a subsequently viewed flat test surface appeared corrugated in depth with the same spatial frequency but with the corrugations opposite to (180 deg out-of-phase with) the adapting surface. The build-up of the aftereffects was rapid and the effects could usually be seen after a single adapting period of only 8 sec duration. The decay of the aftereffects was also rapid such that they grew significantly weaker after viewing the flat test surface for only a few seconds. Moreover, the apparent corrugations could still be seen if the subject stopped moving his head from side to side during the test period.

Aftereffects were also obtained over a wide range of spatial frequencies of the adapting surface, but were largest after adapting to low spatial frequency corrugations. Quantitative measurements were made with .1 cycles/deg adapting surfaces (one complete corrugation spanning 10 deg of visual angle). Subjects were presented with a sequence of adapt and test displays lasting for 8 sec and 1 sec, respectively, for a maximum period of 2 minutes. The subject's task was to adjust the amount of parallax motion present during the test period so that it just canceled out the apparent depth of the aftereffect and the test surface appeared flat. For the two authors, five settings were made at each of three different values of depth in the adapting surface in a randomized sequence. In addition, depth aftereffects were measured with an equivalent adapting depth of 4.5 min arc, for six naive subjects.

In general, the parallax depth aftereffects were very large, requiring some 35–50% of the equivalent disparity in the adapting pattern to be added into the test surface for it to appear flat. The amount of relative motion (equivalent disparity) needed to null the aftereffect, as a function of the amount of depth in the adapting surface, is shown in Fig. 35.2a for the two authors as well as the mean results for 6 other subjects (♦). The upward slope of the functions shows that the size of the aftereffects *increased* with increasing amounts of depth in the adapting surface. However, when the same data are replotted in terms of the proportion or percentage of the depth in the adapting surface needed to cancel the aftereffects, the functions slope downward indicating that the largest *percentage* aftereffects (~50%) were obtained with the smallest peak-to-trough depths in the adapting pattern (Fig. 35.2b).

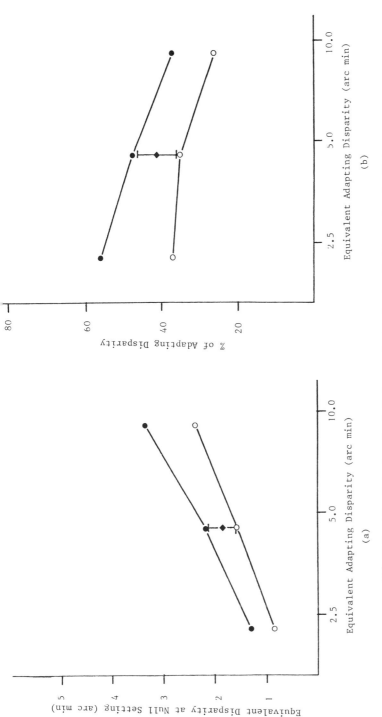

FIG. 35.2. Aftereffects of parallax depth: these graphs show the strength of the parallax aftereffects measured using the nulling technique, as a function of the amount of peak-to-trough depth in the adapting surface (that is as a function of the equivalent adapting disparity). The data for two subjects, MEG (open circles) and BJR (filled circles), indicate that the size of the aftereffects increased with the amount of depth in the adapting surface (a) but decreased when plotted as a *percentage* of the depth in the adapting surface (b). The mean setting and the standard deviation of the results for six subjects at an equivalent adapting disparity of 4.5 min arc are also shown (diamond). (From Graham and Rogers, 1982a. Reproduced by permission of Pion Ltd.)

These results clearly demonstrate that powerful depth aftereffects can be obtained when motion parallax is the only source of depth information. But how do the sizes of these aftereffects compare with those following stereoscopic adaptation? The largest percentage aftereffects calculated from the data of Blakemore and Julesz (1971) were around 25% and from the data of Long and Over (1973), less than 20%. However, the conditions and psychophysical procedures used in those studies are not strictly comparable with the procedures used here. Our own observations suggest that much larger aftereffects of stereoscopic depth can be produced using methods similar to those described previously for motion parallax (Graham & Rogers, 1982a; Rogers, Graham, & Anstis, 1981).

To generate stereoscopic aftereffects, subjects adapted to low spatial frequency corrugations as before, but with the depth information specified by binocular disparities. Two separate display oscilloscopes presented random dot patterns to the two eyes with the disparity between the two patterns sinusoidally modulated from the top to the bottom of the screen, to produce horizontal corrugations (Tyler, 1974). A sequence of 10-sec adapting periods and 2-sec test periods was presented to subjects, as in the parallax experiments, and subjects were asked to null any perceived depth aftereffect in the test pattern with physical disparity until the surface appeared flat.

Strong negative aftereffects of depth were obtained following adaptation to stereoscopic surfaces. The quantitative results obtained for the two authors with .1 cycles/deg adapting surfaces are shown in Fig. 35.3, as well as the mean results for six naive subjects at an adapting disparity of 10 min arc (diamond). The absolute size of the depth aftereffects, expressed in terms of the physical disparity needed to cancel the perceived aftereffect, *increased* with increasing amounts of depth in the adapting surface (Fig. 35.3a). When the same data are expressed in terms of the percentage of the depth in the adapting pattern needed to cancel the aftereffect, the functions *decrease* with larger amounts of depth in the adapting surface (Fig. 35.3b).

If the results for the stereoscopic aftereffects are compared with those for motion parallax, it is clear that the relationship between the strength of the aftereffect and the amount of depth in the adapting surface is similar in the two cases. However, the size of the stereo aftereffects was generally larger under comparable conditions. This might reflect a greater degree of adaptability in the stereoscopic system or might have resulted from the fact that good tracking of the fixation line (which was essential to obtain these aftereffects) was more difficult in the parallax experiments where the subject had to move his head to and fro continuously.

Discussion

The existence of large negative aftereffects of depth for both motion parallax and stereopsis leads to the question of what adaptive processes might be involved? In

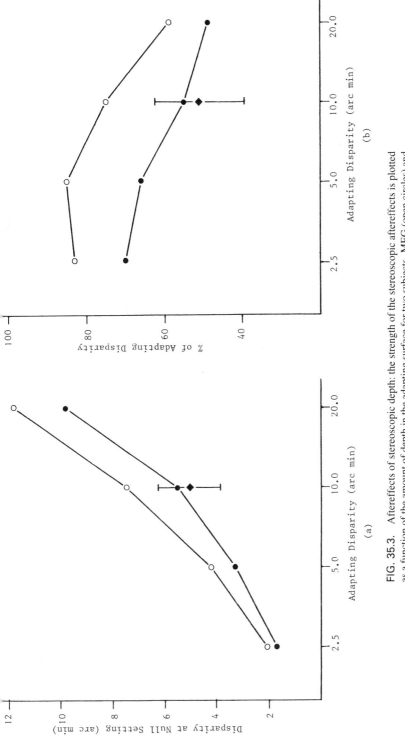

FIG. 35.3. Aftereffects of stereoscopic depth: the strength of the stereoscopic aftereffects is plotted as a function of the amount of depth in the adapting surface for two subjects, MEG (open circles) and BJR (filled circles), and the mean for six observers at 10 min arc adapting disparity (diamond). The results were similar to those found for the parallax aftereffects (Fig. 35.2) with the absolute size of the aftereffects increasing with the amount of depth in the adapting surface (a) but decreasing when plotted as a percentage of the adapting surface disparity (b). (From Graham and Rogers, 1982a. Reproduced by permission of Pion Ltd.)

611

the case of the parallax aftereffects, they cannot be accounted for in terms of simple movement aftereffects, since each region of the retina is stimulated equally by opposite directions of motion as the subject moves from side to side. Neither do they appear to be aftereffects contingent on head movement or head position, since the aftereffects could still be seen when the subject's head is kept stationary during the test period. Instead, it would appear that the aftereffects result from adaptation at the level of depth processing itself. The fact that the aftereffects are negative or complementary for both parallax and stereopsis might imply the existence of opponent or inhibitory links between mechanisms subserving crossed and uncrossed depth values. Alternatively, the opponent links might be between mechanisms detecting *changes in depth* or depth gradients across space. Our own demonstrations of powerful simultaneous contrast (or induced depth) effects in the parallax and stereo domains are probably better accounted for by such a model (Graham & Rogers, 1982a).

INTERACTIONS BETWEEN MOTION PARALLAX AND STEREOPSIS

The existence of similar and powerful depth aftereffects from motion parallax and stereopsis led us to question whether, in addition to adaptation within the separate motion parallax and stereo mechanisms, there might also be adaptation within some more central depth processing mechanism which receives inputs from both the parallax and stereo systems. Some initial observations indicate that there could be interactions between the two systems at a higher level. First, it was found that after adapting to a corrugated stereo surface for several seconds, a small depth aftereffect could be seen if only *one* eye viewed a random dot pattern. In other words, adaptation to a binocular depth cue produced a *monocular* aftereffect. Second, it was found that after monocular adaptation to a motion parallax surface, a small depth aftereffect could be seen when a flat test surface was presented to the unadapted eye, and also when a correlated zero disparity test surface was presented to *both* eyes. To explore the possible interactions between the stereo and parallax systems in more detail, two experiments were carried out. The aim in both cases was to see whether prior adaptation in one domain (e.g. stereo) would bias the interpretation of an *ambiguous* depth surface specified in the other domain (parallax), and vice versa.

Biasing of Ambiguous Motion Parallax Depth

In the first experiment, subjects adapted to a low spatial frequency (.2 cycles/deg) corrugated surface specified by stereoscopic information for 10 sec. The test surface, however, was only presented to one eye and contained a pattern of relative motion between the elements of the random dot pattern specifying a 3-D corrugated surface. The subject's head (and the oscilloscope) remained stationary, which rendered the phase of the depth corrugations ambiguous (Rogers & Graham, 1979). The assumption behind the experiment was that if there were interactions between the processing of stereo and parallax information, these might be revealed in the biasing of the ambiguous test surface in favor of one particular phase.

The ambiguous test pattern was generated in the following way. An additional sinewave signal was added to the X-input of the display oscilloscope and its amplitude was steadily increased over 2 sec. This signal progressively "dis-

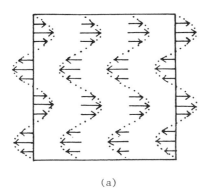

(a)

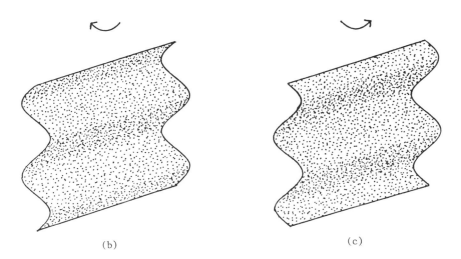

(b)   (c)

FIG. 35.4.   An ambiguous depth surface specified by patterns of relative motion. The arrows in (a) represent the velocities of the dots in the random dot pattern during the two second test period. These varied sinusoidally from the top to the bottom of the pattern. This pattern was perceived by subjects *either* as a corrugated surface in one phase rotating clockwise through a few degrees (b) *or* in the opposite phase rotating anticlockwise (c).

torted'' the random dot pattern producing the pattern of relative velocities illustrated in Fig. 35.4a. The lengths of the arrows indicate the relative velocities of the dots in different rows of the pattern. When viewed by a stationary observer, this pattern appears to most observers to be a 3-D corrugated surface which rotates around a vertical axis in the center of the screen, through about 30 deg (Rogers & Graham, 1979). However, the direction of rotation about the axis and the perceived depth of the corrugations are ambiguous. In other words, the same stimulus pattern can be seen as a corrugated surface in one phase rotating anticlockwise (Fig. 35.4c), or as a corrugated surface in the opposite phase rotating clockwise (Fig. 35.4b). Note that like the related kinetic depth effect (Wallach & O'Connell, 1953), a particular depth interpretation is always linked to a particular direction of rotation. This fact was exploited to reduce the possibility of bias in the subjects' responses. Instead of asking the subjects to report the phase of the perceived corrugations in the test surface, they were asked to report the apparent direction of rotation of the corrugated surface about the central axis. Furthermore, the amplitude of the ''distortion'' signal was randomly reversed so that a given interpretation of the surface was not always associated with the same direction of rotation.

As an additional control, subjects were presented with a series of trials containing an uncorrugated, zero disparity adapting surface to test whether subjects showed any bias towards reporting one phase of the test surface rather than the other, in the absence of prior depth adaptation. Cycles of 10-sec adaptation were alternated with 2-sec test periods containing the ambiguous depth surface. On each test presentation, subjects were asked to report the apparent direction of rotation of the corrugated surface.

Results

The mean results for four individual subjects are shown in Table 35.1. In the control condition where subjects adapted to a *flat* stereoscopic surface, the two possible phases or depth interpretations were perceived equally often, although some subjects showed a slight bias in favor of one or the other interpretation. However, after adapting to a corrugated stereoscopic surface of a particular phase, the subsequent interpretation of the ambiguous depth surface was strongly biased towards the *opposite* phase. Specifically, the results show that without prior exposure to the stereoscopic corrugations, phase A was perceived on 47% of the trials, phase B on 53% of the trials. However, in the experimental conditions, the ambiguous surface was seen in the phase *opposite* to that of the adapting surface, on average, 95% of the time (Table 35.1). Overall, these results demonstrate that adaptation to depth surfaces specified by binocular disparities can overwhelmingly bias the interpretation of an ambiguous depth surface, where the depth is specified by relative motion.

TABLE 35.1
Biasing of Ambiguous Parallax Depth

Adapt – Unambiguous Disparity
Test – Ambiguous Relative Motion

		Perceived Phase of Test	
	Mean %	*Phase A*	*Phase B*
	Control	47	53
Adapt	Phase A	0	100
	Phase B	91	9

The mean results for four subjects show that in the control condition, after adapting to a flat stereoscopic surface, the ambiguous surface was perceived as frequently in one phase as in the other, whereas in the experimental condition, after adaptation to an unambiguous stereoscopic surface, the perceived phase was consistently biased *away* from the phase of the adapting surface.

Biasing of Ambiguous Stereo Depth

The final experiment investigated the converse possibility that prior exposure to an unambiguous motion parallax surface would bias the interpretation of an ambiguous stereo surface. As in the previous experiment, subjects adapted to a low spatial frequency corrugated surface, but in this case, the depth was specified by the patterns of relative motion on the display screen. As the observer viewed the adapting surface, the display oscilloscope was moved laterally to and fro across the observer's line of sight. With this concomitant motion of the display oscilloscope, the perceived depth is powerful and *unambiguous* and similar to the parallax depth seen with lateral movements of the observer's head described earlier (Rogers & Graham, 1979).

The test pattern in this experiment was a random dot stereogram, viewed binocularly, specifying a corrugated depth surface with two alternative depth interpretations. This ambiguous test stereogram was derived from the familiar wallpaper illusion (Brewster, 1844) where it is possible to perceive a surface composed of identical, repetitive stripes in a number of different depth planes. In the simplest case, if the wallpaper stripes in one half of the stereogram are shifted horizontally through 180 deg with respect to the fixation point, the pattern may be perceived as lying *either* in front of the plane of fixation *or* an equal distance behind. In the present experiment, the stereograms were made up of horizontally repetitive clusters of random dots rather than black and white stripes. The spacing of the repetitive clusters determined the disparity difference between the potentially crossed and uncrossed fusions (Julesz, 1971). By varying the spatial

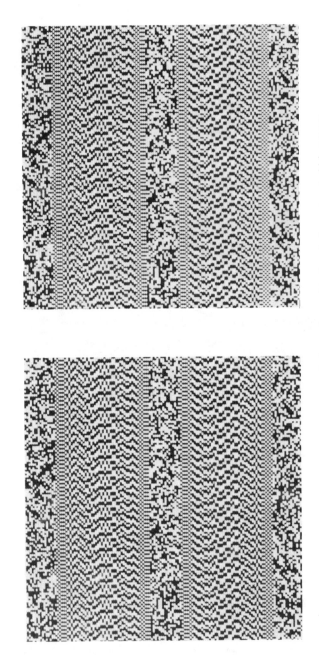

FIG. 35.5. A random dot stereogram similar to that used in the actual experiment which portrays ambiguous (crossed or uncrossed) depth corrugations. In order to determine possible biasing effects, subjects viewed this ambiguous figure after prior adaptation to an unambiguous parallax surface.

repetition rate from the top to the bottom of the pattern, it was possible to produce an approximation to an ambiguous sinusoidal depth corrugation (Fig. 35.5).

Using a procedure similar to that of the previous experiment, subjects adapted to the unambiguous motion parallax surface while scanning their eyes along a horizontal fixation line in the center of the display. After 15 sec, the monocular parallax surface was replaced by the ambiguous stereo surface. Subjects were asked to report the phase of the perceived corrugations with respect to the fixation point. Thirty adapt-test sequences were presented to subjects in blocks of five, with the phase of the adapting surface alternating between each block. Randomly interspersed with the experimental trials were a series of catch trials in which the ambiguous stereoscopic surface was highly biased in favor of the *same* phase as the adapting surface. These catch trials were introduced to avoid any possibility of response bias on the part of subjects, to report that the ambiguous corrugation was opposite in phase to the adapting surface. A further control condition was carried out in which the adapting surface contained no relative motion and therefore appeared flat. Any individual bias towards reporting a particular phase for the ambiguous test pattern without prior exposure to the corrugated surface could be measured in this way.

Results

The mean results for four individual subjects are shown in Table 35.2. For all subjects, prior exposure to a monocular motion parallax surface biased the per-

TABLE 35.2
Biasing of Ambiguous Stereo Depth

	Adapt – Unambiguous Motion Parallax *Test – Ambiguous Disparity*	
	Perceived Phase of Test	
Mean %	*Phase A*	*Phase B*
Control	52	48
Phase A	13	87
Phase B	93	7

The mean results for four subjects show that in the control condition, after adapting to a flat surface, each phase was perceived equally often, whereas in the experimental condition the perceived phase of the ambiguous surface was consistently biased *away* from the phase of the adapting surface.

ception of the ambiguous stereo surface in favor of the *opposite* phase. In the control condition, the ambiguous stereoscopic surface was seen in phase A on 52% of the trials and in phase B on 48% of the trials. However, in the experimental conditions (after adaptation to the parallax corrugations), the phase *opposite* to that of the adapting surface was perceived, on average, 90% of the time. These effects of adaptation were evident even for subjects who had strong individual biases towards seeing a particular depth interpretation in the control condition.

Discussion

The results of these two experiments lead us to conclude that prior exposure to stereoscopic depth corrugations can bias the perception of a subsequently presented ambiguous surface specified by relative motion. Conversely, adaptation to depth corrugations specified by motion parallax information can bias the interpretation of a subsequently presented ambiguous stereoscopic surface. In both cases the effect of prior adaptation was to bias the depth interpretation in a direction *opposite* to that of the adapting surface. These results strongly suggest that the motion parallax and stereoscopic systems do interact at some stage in the processing hierarchy. This interaction might take the form of inhibitory links between two principally autonomous systems, or alternatively, there might be some higher level depth process which receives inputs from both parallax and stereo mechanisms. If the latter possibility is correct, we might predict that the depth aftereffects obtained as a result of adaptation in one domain could be nulled or canceled with physical depth from the other domain.

Our most recent results support this possibility. We have found that, although these cross-modal effects are relatively small, it is possible to null the effects of adaptation to surfaces specified by stereoscopic information with depth specified by motion parallax and, conversely, aftereffects of parallax depth can be nulled with depth specified by binocular disparities (Graham & Rogers, 1982b). When seen together, these results suggest that not only are there both formal and empirical similarities between the motion parallax and stereoscopic systems but also links between the underlying mechanisms which allow depth information from one domain to interact quantitatively with information from the other.

REFERENCES

Ames, A. Aneisikonia—a factor in the functioning of vision, *American Journal of Ophthalmology*, 1935, *28*, 248–262.

Anstis, S. M. What does visual perception tell us about visual coding? In C. Blakemore & M. S. Gazzaniga (Eds.), *Handbook of psychobiology*. New York: Academic Press, 1975.

Blakemore, C., & Julesz, B. Stereoscopic depth aftereffects produced without monocular cues. *Science*, 1971, *171*, 286–288.

Blakemore, C., & Sutton, P. Size adaptation: a new aftereffect. *Science*, 1969, *166*, 245–247.

Brewster, D. On the knowledge of distance given by binocular vision. *Transactions of Royal Society of Edinburgh*, 1844, *15*, 663–674.

Favreau, O., & Corballis, M. Negative aftereffects in visual perception. Scientific American, 1976, *235*, 42–48.

Frisby, J. P. *Seeing*. Oxford: Oxford University Press, 1979.

Gibson, J. J. Adaptation, aftereffect and contrast in the perception of curved lines. *Journal of Experimental Psychology*, 1933, *16*, 1–31.

Graham, M. E., & Rogers, B. J. Simultaneous and successive contrast effects in the perception of depth from motion parallax and stereoscopic information. *Perception*, 1982a, 11.

Graham, M. E., & Rogers, B. J. Interactions between monocular and binocular depth aftereffects. *Investigative Ophthalmology & Visual Science*, 1982b, *22*, Supplement, p. 272.

Howard, I. P., & Templeton, W. B. The effect of steady fixation on the judgment of relative depth. *Quarterly Journal of Experimental Psychology*, 1964, *16*, 193–203.

Julesz, B. Binocular depth perception of computer-generated patterns. *Bell System Technical Journal*, 1960, *39*, 1125–1162.

Julesz, B. *Foundations of cyclopean perception*. Chicago: University of Chicago Press, 1971.

Köhler, W., & Emery, D. A. Figural aftereffects in the third dimension of visual space. *American Journal of Psychology*, 1947, *60*, 159–201.

Long, N., & Over, R. Stereoscopic depth aftereffects with random-dot patterns. *Vision Research*, 1973, *13*, 1283–1287.

Papert, S. Stereoscopic synthesis as a technique for localizing visual mechanisms. *MIT Quarterly Progress Report*, 1964, *73*, 239–243.

Rogers, B. J., & Graham, M. E. Motion parallax as an independent cue for depth perception. *Perception*, 1979, *8*, 125–134.

Rogers, B. J., & Graham, M. E. Similarities between motion parallax and stereopsis in human depth perception. *Vision Research*, 1982, *22*, 261–270.

Rogers, B. J., & Graham, M. E. Aftereffects from motion parallax and stereoscopic depth: Evidence for higher level interactions. (In preparation).

Rogers, B. J., Graham, M. E., & Anstis, S. M. Depth perception with motion parallax and disparity gratings. *Investigative Ophthalmology & Visual Science*, 1980, *19*, Supplement, p. 106.

Rogers, B. J., Graham, M. E., & Anstis, S. M. Simultaneous and successive contrast effects in depth from stereopsis and motion parallax. *Investigative Ophthalmology & Visual Science*, 1981, *20*, Supplement, p 223.

Sutherland, N. S. Figural aftereffects and apparent size. *Quarterly Journal of Experimental Psychology*, 1961, *13*, 222–228.

Tyler, C. W. Depth perception in disparity gratings. *Nature*, 1974, *251*, 140–142.

Wallach, H., & O'Connell, D. N. The kinetic depth effect. *Journal of Experimental Psychology*, 1953, *45*, 205–217.

Wohlgemuth, A. On the aftereffect of seen movement. *British Journal of Psychology Monograph Supplement*, 1911, No. 1.

VI NEUROPSYCHOLOGICAL EVALUATION OF CENTRAL VISUAL DEFICITS

36

The Spatial Organization of Stereopsis in Strabismus

Clifton Schor
Bruce Bridgeman
Christopher W. Tyler*
University of California at Berkeley
*The Smith-Kettlewell Institute for Visual Sciences

ABSTRACT

The effects of strabismus, considered as a long-term adaptation of the visual system to a monocular shift in visual direction, were studied for the spatial organization of stereoscopic depth perception. The minimum and maximum disparities for stimulating stereopsis in strabismus were examined as a function of spatial separation of disparate stimuli. Disparities and their spacing were produced by spatial modulation of two vertical lines viewed dichoptically. Most strabismics had normal upper disparity limits but elevated stereothresholds. Moderate stereothreshold elevations (100 arc sec) occurred independently of spatial separations of less than 15 arc min. A spatial crowding effect upon stereopsis resulted from the elevated lower threshold in several cases and a reduced maximum disparity limit for stereopsis in another case. Clinical tests of stereopsis that crowd stimuli closer than .25 degree underestimate the patients' optimal stereoacuities between two and fourfold. The results indicate that the spatial organization of stereopsis had not compensated for the monocular directional shift represented by the strabismic condition.

INTRODUCTION

Manifest strabismus is an oculomotor condition in which one eye is deviated from the position of appropriate correspondence from the fellow eye. Whether the basic cause of the strabismus is a muscular imbalance, inappropriate innervation, or a failure of sensory fusion, the net result is a shift of binocular retinal

623

stimulation away from the range of optimal correspondence between the two eyes. The horizontal or vertical binocular disparity of points in space depends on the angle and direction of the strabismic deviation. In concomitant strabismus, which is the focus of this study, the angle of deviation remains fixed for different directions of gaze.

Concomitant strabismus produces a natural stimulus for long-term visual adaptation in terms of the range of environmental disparities presented to the two retinae. The pioneering work of Stratton (1897) and Kohler (1964, pp. 116–133) showed considerable plasticity of the perceptual and perceptuomotor apparatus to certain types of reorganization, particularly image inversion and shift of the visual direction of environmental inputs. It is of interest to study the visual effects of a monocular shift in visual direction (such as occurs in concomitant strabismus) on the organization of visual processing. One aspect of visual perception which is likely to be affected by such monocular shifts is stereoscopic depth perception. We therefore asked to what extent stereoscopic depth perception is disrupted by long-term adaptation in the form of early concomitant strabismus.

Some aspects of the answer are already known. There appears to be plasticity of the binocular visual direction system in that the same visual directions are reported for binocular stimuli at the angle of deviation in cases of early concomitant strabismus, which would seem diplopic in the normal observer. This is known as anomalous retinal correspondence (Burian, 1947; Flom, 1980; Hallden, 1952). It is accompanied in some cases by anomalous fusion at the angle of deviation, in addition to fusion at the angle of normal correspondence.

In order to determine whether any kind of plasticity was exhibited by the stereoscopic system, we measured stereopsis for a full range of stimulus patterns of the form introduced by Tyler (1973, 1975). These consisted of two vertical sinusoidal lines which subtended, when viewed dichoptically, horizontal disparities that varied sinusoidally along the vertical meridian. This sinusoidal disparity modulation is perceived as a vertical line that curves sinusoidally in depth along the midline (see Fig. 36.1, inset). The spatial frequency of the vertical line determines the spatial disparity modulation and it provides a means of defining the spatial crowding or proximity and the gradient or rate of change of horizontal disparity variations along the vertical meridian. Varying the spatial frequency of the disparity modulation allows examination of both upper and lower disparity limits across a full range of disparity patterns. This method should, therefore, be very sensitive to the precise nature of any changes in stereoscopic sensitivity and to the extent of disruption by early adaptation to the range of environmental disparities produced by childhood strabismus.

METHODS

The lower and upper thresholds for stereoscopic depth perception were measured along the midline passing through the fovea in seven strabismic and two nonstrabismic observers as a function of spatial frequency of disparity modulation about the fovea. Spatial variations of disparity were produced on two CRT's with dichoptic vertical sinusoidal lines (12.5° long and 1.5' thick) having a luminance of 5 cd/m^2 whose spatial phase differed by 180° (Fig. 36.1, inset). When these vertical sinusoidal lines (one on each CRT) were fused haploscopically, observers perceived a single line curved sinusoidally in depth, with the plane of curvature passing through the midline between the eyes. The methods for producing these lines are described elsewhere (Tyler, 1975). Horizontal and vertical vergence errors were controlled by adjusting the mirrors of a haploscope to the observer's angle of strabismus or to an angle where the targets could be fused easily. The boundaries of the 8 × 13 degree rectangular test field served as sensory fusion locks. Horizontal nonius lines were placed to the left and right of the vertical sinusoidal line. The observer could detect vertical vergence errors by observing a misalignment of the horizontal nonius lines. The targets were viewed at a distance of 57 cm on a background screen with a luminance of 5 cd/m^2.

Stereoscopic thresholds were determined for spatial disparity modulation frequencies ranging from .1 to 3 cycles/deg. The lower stereoscopic thresholds were obtained in the same manner for squarewave variations in disparity as a control condition to distinguish between monocular vernier judgments as opposed to binocular stereoscopic judgments. Tyler (1975) has shown that for normal subjects, the lower threshold is independent of spatial frequency for square but not sinewave variations in disparity, whereas vernier judgments vary similarly for sine and squarewave variations as a function of spatial frequency.

The maximum sinusoidal disparity which could elicit a depth response (upper disparity limit) was also determined by the method of adjustment. Usually depth was perceived beyond Panum's fusional limit, i.e., where diplopia was present (Ogle, 1952; Schor & Tyler, 1981). Subjects were instructed to maintain the same criterion of absence of depth difference, although diplopia was clearly present in the display. Comparison of the upper and lower thresholds for stereopsis provided a measure of the range of disparities, as a function of spatial disparity modulation, that could be perceived as depth differences. The points for maximum spatial frequency were obtained by adjusting the frequency for a fixed amplitude rather than the reverse.

Observers

Two normal and seven strabismic observers participated in the study. All were experienced psychophysical observers; six of the clinical observers had congenital nonaccommodative esotropia and the seventh had congenital exotropia. The angle of strabismus for all cases exceeded 10 degrees during childhood and was reduced surgically or by orthoptic exercises and optical prescription such that five of the observers became intermittent exotropes and two others were constant postsurgical exotropes. Age of onset of strabismus for all observers was before the age of 3 years. At the time of this study, three of the observers were

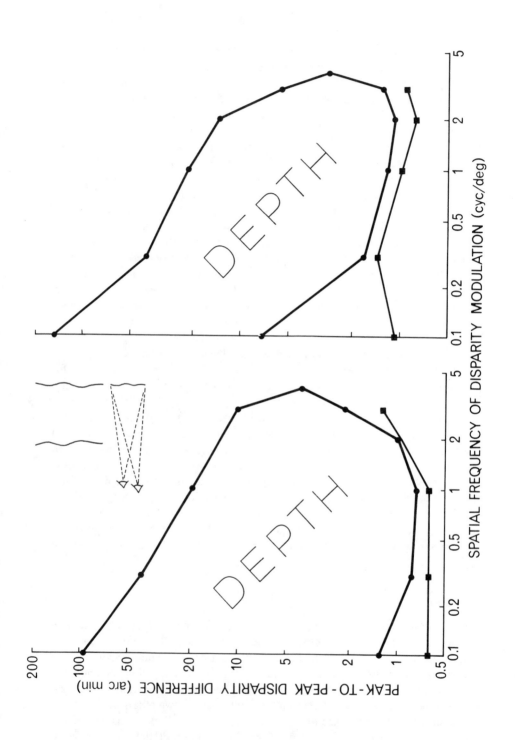

intermittent exotropes and two were constant postsurgical exotropes. No observer had amblyopia and all but two postsurgical exotropes had normal binocular correspondence. All acuities were at least 20/20 with refractive corrections in place as assessed by a multiple E chart which controlled for crowding effects (Flom, 1966). Stereoacuity was assessed using the clinical Wirt test which consists of a series of rings that subtend disparities ranging from 600–15 arc sec. Stereoacuities of the seven clinical observers ranged from 600 to 100 arc sec, whereas the two normal observers had stereoacuities of 15 and 20 arc sec. In the cases of constant strabismus, stereoacuity was assessed with the angle of strabismus corrected by a prism. Graphs are shown for four of the seven observers.

RESULTS

The limits of stereoscopic resolution are plotted on log-log coordinates in Fig. 36.1 for the two normal observers, in Fig. 36.2 for three observers with raised stereothresholds (100–600 arc sec clinical stereoacuity), and in Fig. 36.3 for one observer with a reduced upper disparity limit. Circles and squares represent thresholds for sinewave and squarewave stimuli, respectively. The standard errors of the mean were less than 5%, which usually fall within the width of the plotted symbols. In Fig. 36.1 the region of stereoscopic sensitivity labeled "DEPTH" replicates that reported by Tyler (1975). There is an approximately inverse linear relationship between the upper disparity limit and the spatial modulation frequency of disparity over a large range. This represents a disparity scaling effect since the ratio of disparity to period of the disparity modulation remains constant for the maximum depth. As shown in the data plot of Fig. 36.1, the upper disparity limit for maximum depth varies inversely with spatial frequency such that the product of these two variables is a constant. Thus the inset sinusoidal lines in Fig. 36.1, which subtend a disparity equal to the upper disparity limit for a viewing distance of 40 cm, will also subtend the upper disparity limit for depth at other viewing distances. For example, as viewing distance is reduced to 20 cm, the spatial frequency is reduced by half and the disparity is doubled. The product of the upper disparity limit and spatial frequency, however, is the same for both viewing distances. The lower stereothreshold does not show the scaling effect except at the lowest spatial frequencies tested. Stereosensitivity is greatest at approximately 1 cpd and it is reduced at higher

FIG. 36.1.   Complete region of depth perception as a function of spatial disparity modulation frequency of vertical sinusoidal disparity variations for two observers with normal stereopsis. (Inset shows the stimulus.) Upper portion—left and right eye views of a sample anti-phase stimulus. Lower portion—depiction of stimulus as seen by the observer.

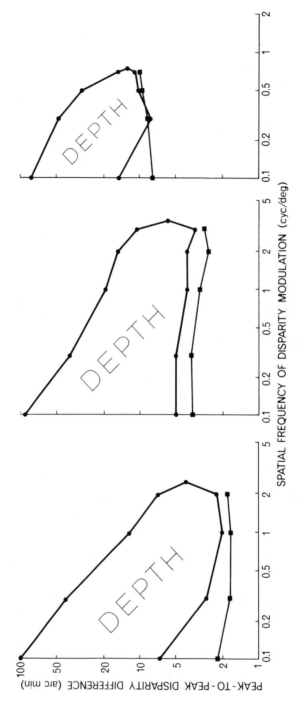

FIG. 36.2. Complete region of depth perception as a function of spatial disparity modulation frequency of vertical sinusoidal disparity variations for three observers with moderate elevations of their lower threshold for stereopsis.

spatial frequencies probably due to a crowding effect (Westheimer & McKee, 1980), which is an elevation of the stereothreshold resulting from surrounding contours within 10 arc min of the test target. Some observers also showed reduced sensitivity at lower spatial frequencies perhaps as a result of a disparity gradient limit. The disparity gradient refers to a threshold limit for stereopsis which increases as the separation of disparate contours is increased. Similar

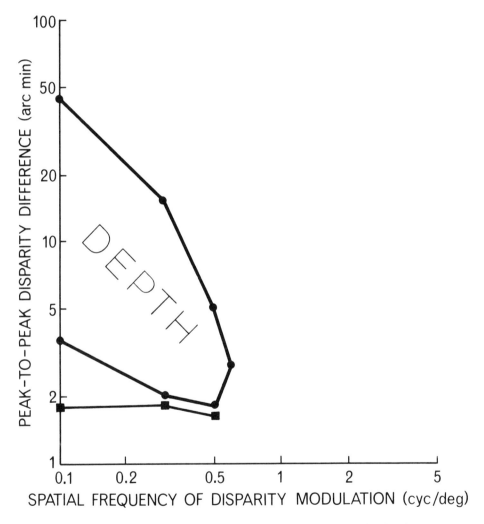

FIG. 36.3. Complete region of depth perception as a function of spatial disparity modulation frequency of vertical sinusoidal disparity variations for an observer with a threefold reduction of the upper disparity limit for stereopsis, although the reduced limit still shows disparity scaling.

gradient effects have been shown to limit the upper disparity limit for binocular fusion (Burt & Julesz, 1981; Schor & Tyler, 1981; Tyler, 1975). Since the disparity gradient in squarewave stimuli is independent of spatial frequency, the reduction of stereosensitivity at low spatial frequencies is not found with the squarewave stimulus.

The limits of stereoscopic resolution for strabismics with raised stereothresholds are shown in Fig. 36.2. The upper stereo limits of these observers are indistinguishable from those of normal observers shown in Fig. 36.1. They differ from the normal function by the elevation of the lower threshold at all spatial frequencies to a value proportional to the clinically assessed threshold measured with the Wirt Stereo test. The higher sensitivity to squarewave than sinewave disparity modulation at low spatial frequencies indicates that in strabismus there is a disparity gradient limit for stereopsis, as was observed in the normal observers.

Figure 36.3 shows the results of a fourth observer with a clinical stereoacuity of 400 arc sec. Unlike the results of observers shown in Fig. 36.2, he demonstrated an abnormal upper disparity limit, reduced by about a factor of three relative to the normal range. The reduction is uniform across spatial frequency of disparity modulation indicating that disparity scaling with spatial frequency is still obtained. This observer also shows a slight elevation of stereothreshold relative to the normal observers, but no greater than a factor of two (in the range of spatial frequencies where it is measured). The combined effect of the reduction of the upper disparity limit and the increase in stereothreshold is to produce a dramatic reduction in the maximum frequency of stereoresolution by a factor of five.

DISCUSSION

The limits of stereoscopic resolution in strabismus are abnormally restricted for small disparities, and in one case for large disparities as well. Thus, although these observers have elevated stereothresholds, most of them perceive suprathreshold disparities within the range of normal observers and their reduction of stereosensitivity appears to be fairly uniform across spatial frequency. If there are multiple channels sensitive to disparities correlated with the retinal size of a stimulus (Marr & Poggio, 1979; Tyler, 1975) all channels must be affected equally. If there is a single broad band channel (Richards, 1970) then the uniform stereoscopic reduction could also be explained by reduced sensitivity of a single mechanism.

The effect of elevated thresholds upon resolution of high spatial frequency disparities in severe stereoscopic loss has certain implications concerning the design of clinical tests of stereopsis. The spacing between disparate figures must be great enough to include the range of spatial variations of disparity that can be resolved by these patients. It is also important for tests of normal stereopsis that small disparities be spaced according to the 1 cycle/deg optimum for highest stereoacuity.

For the observers with clinical stereoacuities raised by factors of about 5, 10, 15, 20 and 25, the sinusoidal stereothresholds are raised by factors of only about 2.5, 5, 5, 2 and 10, respectively. Thus, data from this small sample of patients suggest that the Wirt test seriously underestimates the stereoscopic capabilities of stereoanomalous observers. This is probably due to the crowding effects of having a number of disparate stimuli presented in close proximity (less than 15 arc min). Redesign of the clinical stereotests could therefore provide a more accurate estimate of stereopsis in people undergoing treatment for strabismus. Patients with low stereoacuity should be tested at several low spatial frequencies, for clearly the high spatial frequencies involved in the current clinical tests are inappropriate in some cases.

Finally, viewing the strabismic condition as a type of long-term adaptation to monocular shift of visual direction, it is clear that the stereoscopic system has not fully compensated for the monocular shift that occurred in childhood, even though the condition was corrected for several years in some of the patients within the 4-year human critical period for the onset of amblyopia (Awaya, Sugawara & Miyake, 1979; von Noorden, & Maumenee, 1968). Furthermore, the nature of the stereoscopic loss seen in Figs. 36.2 and 36.3 is quite different from that found in the normal periphery (Tyler, 1975). Peripheral observation produces a high spatial frequency loss without affecting either the lower or upper disparity limits at low spatial frequencies.

It is evident that there is no long-term adaptation of the spatial organization of stereoscopic depth perception to monocular shifts of visual direction caused by strabismus. In many cases, however, the upper stereothresholds remain normal despite increased lower thresholds. The elevated lower disparity threshold is considered an anomalous condition rather than an adaptation. This threshold remains elevated even in persons who have adapted their binocular correspondence to match their angle of ocular deviation. The elevated stereothresholds appear to represent a disturbance peripheral to the motor adjustments to prism observed by Kohler which must occur at a more central or higher cortical level. Variations in the angle of anomaly observed in anomalous binocular correspondence may also represent adaptations at a higher cortical level than the permanent disturbance of the lower stereothreshold. The normal upper disparity threshold may represent an adaptation to strabismus but more likely it represents a retention of suprathreshold stereopsis when the angle of strabismus is artificially corrected by our haploscope. The reduced upper disparity threshold observed in one of our subjects may result from the reduced accuracy of vergence eye movements associated with strabismus since voluntary vergence movements normally contribute to depth perception with suprathreshold disparities (Foley & Richards, 1972; Saye & Frisby, 1975).

ACKNOWLEDGMENTS

This project was supported by NEI Grant No. EY03532 to Clifton Schor, NSF Grant BNS 79–06858 to Bruce Bridgeman and NEI Grant EY03622 to Christopher W. Tyler and the Smith-Kettlewell Eye Research Foundation. Experimental work was conducted while Bruce Bridgeman was on sabbatical leave from the University of California, Santa Cruz.

REFERENCES

Awaya, S., Sugawara, M., & Miyake, S. Observations in patients with occlusion amblyopia; results of treatment. *Transaction of the Ophthalmological Society of the United Kingdom*, 1979, *99*, 447–454.

Burian, H. M. Sensorial retinal relationships in concomitant strabismus. *Archives of Ophthalmology*, 1947, *37*, 336–368, 504–533, 618–648.

Burt, P., & Julesz, B. A disparity gradient limit for binocular fusion. *Science*, 1981, *208*, 615–617.

Flom, M. C. New concepts on visual acuity. *The Optometric Weekly*, 1966, *57(28)*, 63–68.

Flom, M. C. Corresponding and disparate retinal points in normal and anomalous correspondence. *American Journal of Optometry*, 1980, *57*, 656–665.

Foley, J. M., & Richards, W. Effects of voluntary eye movements and convergence on the binocular appreciation of depth. *Perception & Psychophysics*, 1972, *11*, 423–427.

Hallden, U. *Fusional phenomena in anomalous correspondence*. Uppsala: Almquist and Wiksells, Boktryc keri, 1952.

Kohler, I. The formation and transformation of the perceptual world. *Psychological Issues*, 1964, *3*, (4), Monograph 12. 28–46, 116–133, New York: International Universities Press.

Marr, D., & Poggio, T. A computational theory of human stereo vision. *Proceedings of the Royal Society London B*, 1979, *204*, 301–328.

Ogle, K. N. On the limits of stereoscopic vision. *Journal Experimental Psychology*, 1952, *44*, 253–259.

Richards, W. Stereopsis and stereoblindness. *Experimental Brain Research*, 1970, *10*, 380–388.

Saye, A., & Frisby, J. P. The role of monocular conspicuous features in facilitating stereopsis from random dot stereograms. *Perception*, 1975, *4*, 159–171.

Schor, C. M., & Tyler, C. W. Spatio-temporal properties of Panum's fusional area. *Vision Research*, 1981, *21*, 683–692.

Stratton, G. M. Vision without inversion of the retinal image. *Psychology Review*, 1897, *4*, 341–360, 463–481.

Tyler, C. W. Stereoscopic vision; cortical limitations and a disparity scaling effect. *Science*, 1973, *181*, 276–278.

Tyler, C. W. Spatial organization of binocular disparity sensitivity. *Vision Research*, 1975, *15*, 583–590.

von Noorden, G. K., & Maumenee, A. E. Clinical observation on stimulus deprivation amblyopia (amblyopia ex anopsia). *American Journal of Ophthalmology*, 1968, *65*, 220–224.

Westheimer, G., & McKee, S. Stereogram design for testing local stereopsis. *Investigative Ophthalmology & Visual Science*, 1980, *19*, 802–809.

37 Uses and Abuses of Assessing Contrast Threshold Functions for Anomalous Vision

Robert F. Hess
The Physiological Laboratory
University of Cambridge
Cambridge, England

ABSTRACT

The contrast sensitivity approach has enjoyed much success in its recent applications to anomalous vision. The uses, abuses, limitations and extensions of this approach are detailed using examples of amblyopias from acquired (organic) as well as developmental (functional) origin. This approach is seen to extend our assessment of visual function and to have greater sensitivity than acuity. We are, however, severely limited in what we can say of the perceptual consequences using this approach for two reasons. First, sensory thresholds are rather special points on our sensory scale and second, they monitor a rather peripheral aspect of visual function.

INTRODUCTION

The visual stimuli that are displayed in the first figure are typical of those used for assessment of normal and anomalous vision up to 20 years ago. Each is used to indicate the limit of the resolving capabilities of the eye and as such they have been able to catalog a number of conditions of both developmental failure and acquired pathology that result in anomalous resolution. A more complete assessment of our visual capabilities would include an estimate of how well we can detect and perceive objects within our resolving capacity. Contrast thresholds for a variety of stimuli have been used for this purpose; these include spots, squarewave gratings, and sinewave gratings. Since there are cells in the visual

a   b

FIG. 37.1.   Examples of the stimuli used for visual assessment two decades ago.
These high contrast stimuli assess the *limit* of our resolving capabilities but tell us
nothing of the *quality* of vision *within* this range.

cortex that are tuned to different sinusoidal spatial frequencies and different
stimulus orientations (having band pass characteristics for both), a good stimulus
for discretely probing visual sensitivity (at threshold) is the unidimensional sinusoidal grating. This stimulus allows discrete assessment of these mechanisms
along the dimensions of spatial frequency, temporal frequency, and orientation.
Our reasoning has not yet been constrained by any assumptions about whether
the visual system itself does a harmonic analysis of its visual image. If future
research suggests that this is likely, then we can add this to our list of advantages.

This approach, which I refer to as the contrast sensitivity approach, has been
shown to be useful for research into normal and anomalous visual function and it
is now being suggested by many of its protagonists that clinicians should use it
for routine diagnosis and monitoring of treatment for developmental and acquired anomalies of vision. It is thus appropriate to discuss the uses and abuses,
the limitations and the extensions of this approach. I endeavor to do this by
referring to my own results on anomalous vision: These may not turn out to be
the best examples of the points that I make but they are at this time the examples
that I know best. The scope of this review does not permit me to reference all the
major contributions, so I limit myself to certain very specific examples.

THE APPROACH

According to this approach the relationship between contrast threshold (its inverse being called contrast sensitivity) and spatial frequency is defined by the

inverted U-shaped function shown in Fig. 37.2. This is thought to represent the envelope of the sensitivities of more discrete spatially selective mechanisms or channels that have been shown to exist neurophysiologically in animals (Maffei & Florentini, 1973) and psychophysically in man (Blakemore & Campbell, 1969; Stromeyer & Julesz, 1972).

The contrast sensitivity function is similar in its overall shape and fine structure to the function relating tone frequency and sound pressure level in audition. Its fine structure differs from its auditory counterpart in that there are fewer visual channels and their bandwidth is wider resulting in our pitch discrimination (0.3%), being an order of magnitude better than our size discrimination (3%).

Anomalies of vision perturb this normal sensitivity profile (Fig. 37.2) in a number of different ways. Let us first consider the developmental (functional) anomalies of vision: strabismus, anisometropia, and monocular pattern deprivation. The general pattern of disruption to this curve is seen in the next figure (Fig. 37.3). Similar results can be derived from the data of other workers (Gstalder &

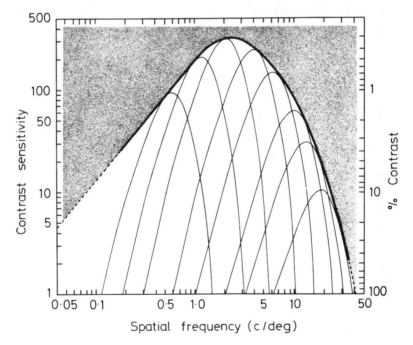

FIG. 37.2.   The threshold sensitivity function describes the relationship between the reciprocal of contrast threshold and the spatial frequency for a sinusoidal grating. It is seen to exhibit a maximum (in sensitivity) for intermediate spatial frequencies. The high frequency limit is at 50–60 c/deg and corresponds to our clinical acuity when measured with the stimuli depicted in Fig. 37.1. The overall curve is made up of a number of more spatially discrete mechanisms or channels which underlie our spatial discrimination.

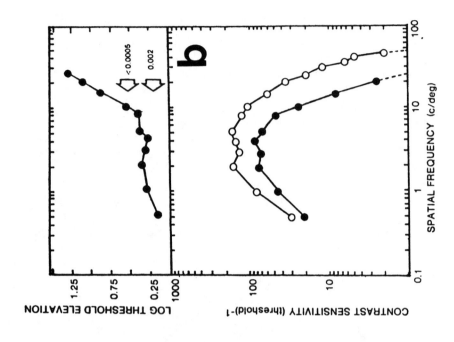

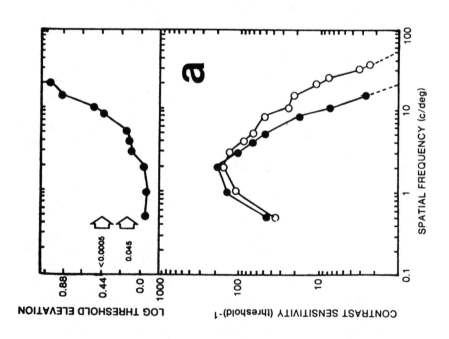

Green, 1971; Hilz, Rentschler, & Brettel, 1977; Levi & Harwerth, 1977; Mitchell, Freeman, Millodot, & Haegerstrom, 1973; Rentschler, Hilz, & Brettel, 1978; Sjostrand, 1978). Contrast thresholds are either raised for just high spatial frequencies or for all spatial frequencies (Hess & Howell, 1977). Both of these types of loss occur in strabismic and anisometropic amblyopia whereas only the second type occurs in pattern deprivation amblyopia. Even though these patterns of dysfunction are obvious, they do not in themselves allow us to differentially diagnose one type of amblyopia from another; there is too great a variation within each group.

In the acquired anomalies of vision (due to acute pathology), the same types of losses can occur as shown in Fig. 37.3 together with three extra categories which are displayed in Fig. 37.4. The threshold contrast loss can be evenly distributed across the spatial frequency spectrum, involve only the low spatial frequencies or involve only a restricted mid-frequency range. These results are for patients with optic neuritis secondary to demyelinating disease. Similar results have been reported previously by Bodis-Wollner (1972); Bodis-Wollner and Diamond (1976); Regan, Silver, and Murray (1977). This approach has undoubtedly extended our previous assessment from just acuity for these conditions to one involving the sensitivity of mechanisms within the resolution limit. Its usefulness, however, lies not in the area of differential diagnoses as much as it does in early detection of visual loss and its subsequent monitoring. For example, it would be very difficult to subdivide contrast threshold losses in terms of developmental and acquired with 100% success, let alone into the different developmental or acquired subgroups. It is only in the case of the notch (mid-range) and low frequency-only losses (Fig. 37.4) that the first coarse division can be made. On the other hand, the rapid fall-off in sensitivity at high spatial frequencies for normal and anomalous eyes makes the measurement of contrast thresholds (and thus its perturbation) a more sensitive measure than acuity. The slope of the high frequency sensitivity fall-off can be approximated by a straight line with a slope of five on this log/log plot, indicating that changes in contrast thresholds (vertical axis) are approximately five times more sensitive than changes in acuity (horizontal axis). This fact makes this approach very useful clinically for early detection and sensitive monitoring of neural dysfunction.

FIG. 37.3.   There are two basic types of visual loss in the different forms of developmental amblyopia. For one group of amblyopes (anisometropic and strabismic), threshold contrast sensitivity is only abnormal at high spatial frequencies (a). For the other group of amblyopes (anisometropic and strabismic), threshold contrast sensitivity is abnormal for all spatial frequencies (b). In these figures the normal (unfilled symbols) and fellow amblyopic eye (filled symbols) are compared for two amblyopes who each represent one of these two types of visual loss. In the upper figures the ratio between the results for the normal and amblyopic eye is plotted with significance levels indicated. (From Hess & Howell, 1977. Reprinted by permission from *Vision Research*, 1977, *17*, 1049–1055.)

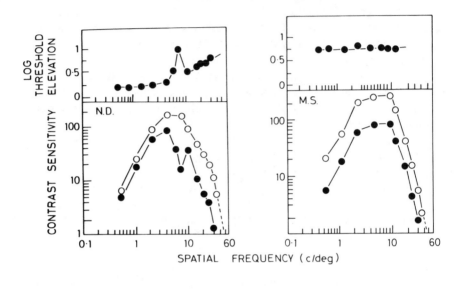

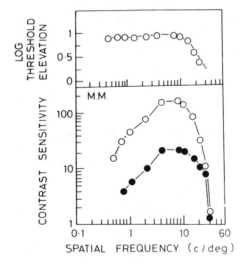

FIG. 37.4. Besides the two types of visual loss displayed in Fig. 37.3, patients with acquired (organic) amblyopia can display three other varieties of loss which are illustrated in this figure. Visual loss may involve mainly intermediate spatial frequencies (A), all spatial frequencies equally (B) or just low spatial frequencies (C). These results are for uniocular examples of optic neuritis and are plotted in an identical way to those of Fig. 37.3.

The results shown in Figs. 37.3 and 37.4, however, give us very little information about another important parameter; the distribution of the anomaly across the visual field. This important information is lost when thresholds are set for large-field grating targets. If thresholds are raised for high spatial frequency targets we can deduce that the central region of the visual field is affected, but unfortunately the relationship between low spatial frequency loss and the peripheral field being affected is not so clear. It has been shown that our low spatial frequency sensitivity is relatively constant across the visual field (Hess, Jacobs, & Vingrys, 1978; Hilz & Cavonius 1974; Lie 1980; Pöppel & Harvey 1973; Watson, unpublished data). In order to investigate the visual field locus of any anomaly we need to restrict our stimulus to a smaller patch of grating (wider bandwidth). When this is done and sensitivity retested for the various types of visual anomaly previously described, the results indicate (Fig. 37.5) that in strabismic amblyopia only the more central aspects of the field are affected. Even though the contrast threshold elevation shows considerate variation in the different subgroup of acquired loss, the visual field distribution is identical.

These results highlight one of the disadvantages of using a large periodic pattern. The visual system need only detect part of the pattern and so it can apply different strategies under different conditions for the same pattern. One result that puzzled me for some time was why strabismic amblyopia disappeared at mesopic luminances yet anisometropic amblyopia and those of the acquired varieties did not. The obvious explanation involved a selective photoreceptor abnormality yet why should such an abnormality vary with spatial frequency? It was only by using a restricted pattern (patch) that it was eventually shown that as luminance was reduced vision was biased towards more peripherally located detectors (in the visual field) and since these were normal only in strabismic amblyopia (unlike the other amblyopias) the anomaly disappeared (Hess, Campbell, & Zimmern, 1980).

So far we have seen that this approach has the dual advantage of higher sensitivity (gain) and of extending our acuity assessment. It suffers from the disadvantage of localization (if a large patch of grating is used) and differential diagnosis. We have not yet, however, considered our threshold results in terms of their possible visual significance. Before we are faced with deciding which frequency bands are of more visual importance, we need to ask whether raised contrast thresholds have any significance for our contrast perception of suprathreshold stimuli. This leads us to one of the more important limitations of any sensory threshold approach.

THE LIMITATION

If amblyopes need more contrast to set thresholds at a particular spatial frequency, does this mean that they see these targets when they are above threshold as a reduced contrast with their amblyopic eyes? If the answer is yes, then our

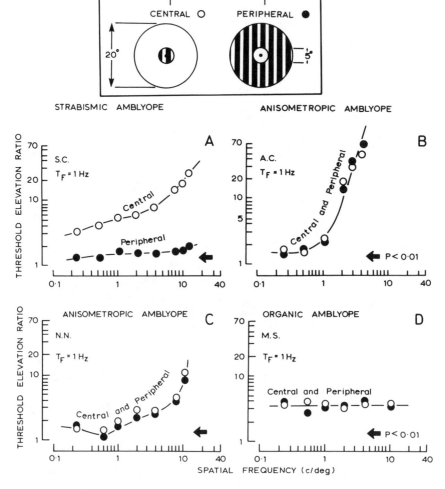

FIG. 37.5. The ratio of the contrast threshold for the normal and amblyopic eye of a number of different amblyopes (strabismic, anisometropic and organic) are compared for two types of stimuli: one probing central function and one probing peripheral function (see upper inset). The results show (see text) that only strabismics have an abnormality that is distributed differently in different parts of the visual field. (From Hess, Campbell, & Zimmern, 1980. Reprinted by permission from *Vision Research*, 1980, *20*, 295–305.

threshold findings directly indicate the quality of contrast perception in the suprathreshold range. The easiest way to test this is to present stimuli to the amblyopic eye and ask them to equate these with an identical stimulus seen by the fellow normal eye. Initially, this would begin with contrast thresholds being set for each eye and then contrasts above threshold are set in front of the amblyopic eye and matched to an identical stimulus by the normal eye. The results which are different for the two main types of developmental amblyopia are shown in Figs. 37.6 and 37.7 (Hess & Bradley, 1980). The results for normal observers fall along the diagonal sloping line, indicating that the contrast perception of both eyes is similar. In all types of developmental amblyopia, the contrast anomaly at threshold is always much greater than it is in the suprathreshold region. The most extreme example of this is the result for the strabismic amblyope whose anomaly at threshold was not present at all at contrasts 3 dB above

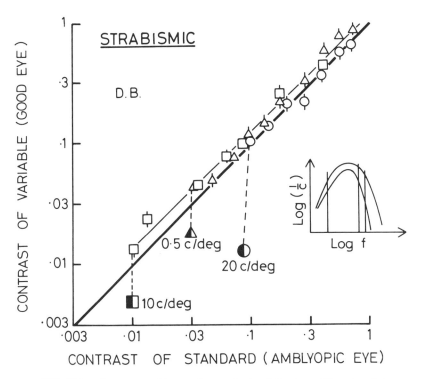

FIG. 37.6. Contrast matching results are displayed for three different spatial frequencies. The standard was shown to the amblyopic eye. Contrast thresholds are shown by half-filled symbols. The result for strabismics show a rapid change from the raised threshold to the normal contrast matching line. (From Hess & Bradley, 1980). This illustrates one severe limitation of the contrast sensitivity approach (see text). (Reprinted by permission from *Nature, 287,* 463–464. Copyright © 1980, Macmillan Journals Limited.)

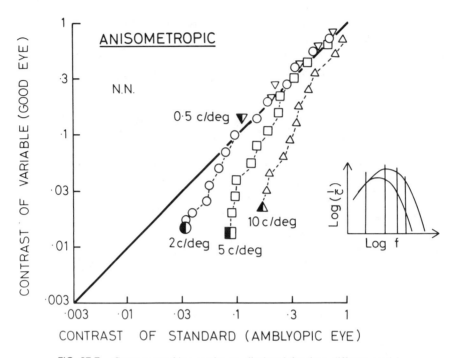

FIG. 37.7. Contrast matching results are displayed for three different spatial frequencies. The standard grating was presented to the amblyopic eye and the half-filled symbols represent threshold data. The result for anisometropes show a gradual return from the raised threshold to the normal matching line. (From Hess & Bradley, 1980). This illustrates one severe limitation of the contrast sensitivity approach (see text). (Reprinted by permission from *Nature, 287,* 463–464. Copyright © 1980, Macmillan Journals Limited.)

threshold. The anisometrope displays a more gradual recovery. Thus the contrast sensitivity losses at threshold that we have previously discussed either do not exist or have diminishing significance for everyday, suprathreshold image. This sets a limit on what we can conclude from our threshold results concerning the vision of these patients and it also questions the use of the commonly used term, contrast sensitivity. We should more correctly consider thresholds as thresholds (or its inverse as sensitivity at threshold) and parallel displacements from the matching line in Figs. 37.6 and 37.7 as an indication of our "contrast sensitivity."

Similar experiments on eyes with acquired anomalies, especially that of optic neuritis, show the opposite effect. The results in Fig. 37.8 are for a patient with a uniocular optic neuritis. The contrast matching results for the amblyopic eye are displaced evenly below that of the normal eye's results (e.g. matching line) for each of three different spatial frequencies. This indicates that contrast perception is just as anomalous at threshold as it is at any suprathreshold level; the "contrast sensitivity" has truly been reduced in this case. For these subjects we can speculate that their visual disability must be similar to seeing blurred imagery because blur would displace the results in just this way. They have "blurred" detectors, however, not blurred images!

These results complement the initial and important studies of Kohler (1951, 1964) on distorting the visual input. They show that such distortions in the contrast domain may not merely follow the input restrictions and may result in profound, permanent changes to perception. These results also point out that visual thresholds represent special points on our sensory scale and cannot be assumed to represent the situation in the suprathreshold domain. The contrast threshold approach assumes also that we have some predictive power for more complex perception by knowing the detectability of different, spatial frequencies in isolation. This leads on to another question. Does the detection of a spatial

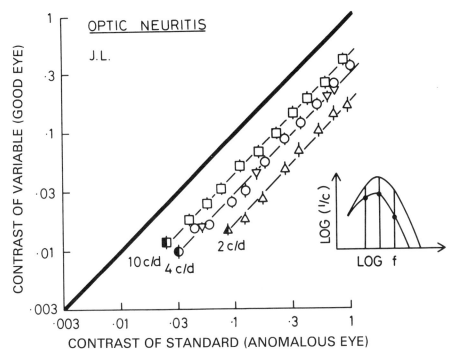

FIG. 37.8.   Contrast matching results are displayed for three different spatial frequencies for a patient with an essentially uniocular optic neuritis. The half-filled symbols represent the contrast thresholds. All the results are displaced parallel from the normal matching line (diagonal line). These results, which are similar to those for a blurred stimulus, differ dramatically in the high contrast range from those of developmental amblyopes (Figs. 37.6 and 37.7).

frequency target necessarily mean that it can be used as a basis for more complex perceptions? The answer to this question, as far as developmental amblyopes are concerned is not a simple one, but as we will see shortly it is an important one.

AN EXTENSION

The contrast threshold approach has enjoyed considerable success in anomalous vision because most of these conditions affect the more peripheral aspects of visual processing, acquired anomalies of the retina and optic nerve being a good example. Developmental amblyopia has not fared so well, for although contrast threshold abnormalities are present these do not explain the amblyopes' visual problems for two reasons.

1. These contrast sensitivity and grating acuity abnormalities are completely out of step with the amblyopes' visual problems. Normals with simulated defects similar to those typically seen in developmental amblyopia would not find much reason to complain.

2. Contrast thresholds may be raised but contrast perception is normal in the higher contrast range typical of everyday images.

One striking and, we believe, important aspect of amblyopic vision that is completely overlooked by this approach is that of spatial distortions. Amblyopes see these periodic patterns at and above their detection threshold as distorted when viewing with their amblyopic eye. A good example of how misleading the contrast threshold approach can be is seen in the next figure (Fig. 37.9). This amblyope has reduced letter acuity yet normal contrast thresholds at all spatial frequencies and orientations. A diagrammatic representation (made by the amblyope) of the spatial distortions seen by the amblyopic eye when viewing these gratings (for which normal thresholds were set) is seen in the upper frame of this picture. This illustrates an important point: The detection of simple spatial targets may not always form a useful basis for more complex perception. It is also a good example of one of the important limitations of the contrast threshold approach, for it may assess a function which is peripheral to the site of the main disturbance.

If an attempt to quantify these rather subjective reports of spatial distortions, Hess, Lawden, and Campbell (1981) asked the following question, "If amblyopes can detect two gratings of different spatial frequency, does that mean that they can discriminate between targets that are composed of different mixtures of these two components?" In other words, if amblyopes can detect two different spatial frequencies, does this mean that these two frequencies can be used as a basis for more complex perceptions?

Consider the example shown in the next figure (Fig. 37.10). Here we have two component frequencies, f and $3f$. These can be mixed in various phases to produce the other compound waveforms shown. Let us direct our attention to just the two extreme examples, that is the peaks-add version, the triangle wave $(f+3f)$

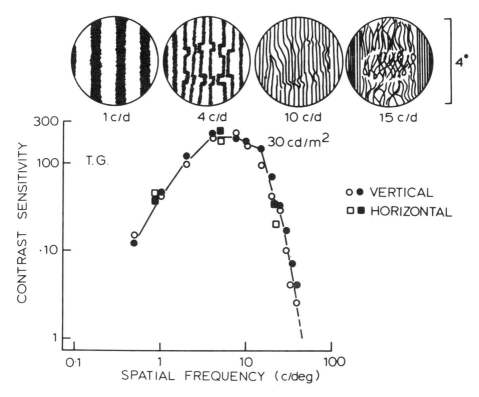

FIG. 37.9. Contrast threshold measurements are compared at a high luminance (300 cd/m²) for a number of grating orientations. These results show no difference between the normal and amblyopic eye of this subject. This should be contrasted with the reported suprathreshold appearance of these targets (upper diagrams) and the letter acuity (⁶/12). Contrast thresholds are normal yet suprathreshold spatial vision is anomalous. (From Hess, Campbell, & Greenhalgh. Reprinted by permission from *Pflügers Archiv,* 1978, *377,* 202.)

and the peaks-subtract version, the squarewave $(f+3f)$. We can distinguish between these two compound waveforms where their difference lies only in the mixing phase of the $3f$ component. In Fourier terms we are distinguishing patterns apart that have the same amplitude spectra but different phase spectra. Our question now simplifies to, "At contrasts at which amblyopes can detect the $3f$ components can they also distinguish these two compound waveforms apart as normals can?"

To test this ability (see Acknowledgments), our minimum requirement is to compare the contrast needed to detect the $3f$ component with that of the contrast of the $3f$ component (when added to a fixed contrast f) to reliably distinguish the $f+3f$ pattern from the $f-3f$ pattern. We used a 3 alternative forced-choice paradigm for both estimating the detection of the $3f$ *alone and for estimating the*

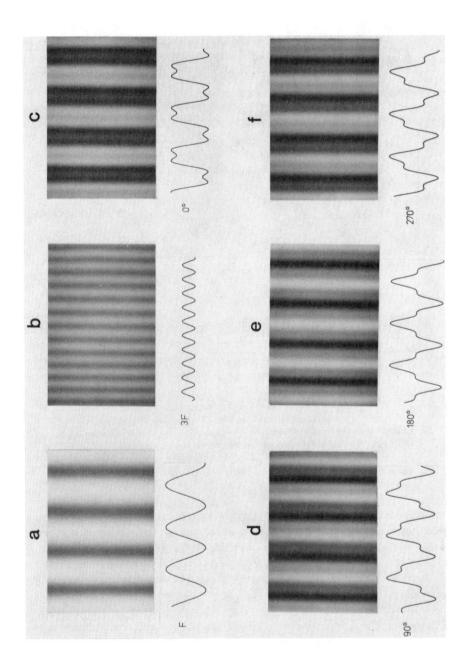

contrast of the 3f component required for the phase discrimination. In the latter case three targets were generated side by side on a video monitor; $f+3f$, $f+3f$; $f-3f$. The task was to tell the odd one out. This ensured that our subjects did not have to recognize the individual waveforms concerned. The results for a normal and an amblyopic eye are displayed in the next two figures (Figs. 37.11 and 37.12).

Normals are seen to need less contrast in order to make the phase discrimination under these conditions than they do to detect the 3f component when presented alone. One standard deviation is equivalent to twice the symbol size. This facilitatory effect is about a factor of eight and gradually declines towards the resolution limit. Thus normals are particularly sensitive at making these judgments and it is only near the resolution limit that the contrast needed to detect the 3f component and discriminate its phase in the compound are comparable. These results for normals disagree with those of Holt and Ross (1980). These workers suggested that our phase discrimination only extended to about 15 c/deg in the normal for such a task (marked with a vertical dashed line).

The result for an amblyopic eye is quite different from that of the eyes of normals (Fig. 37.11) or the normal fellow eye of amblyopes. Detection of the 3f component alone for different frequencies of 3f is shown in Fig. 37.12 by solid symbols and the solid curve. This is just the high spatial frequency limit of the contrast threshold function and we see that it is reduced by only a small amount compared with normal (see Fig. 37.11). The dashed curve in Fig. 37.12 represents the contrast of the 3f component needed for phase discrimination and it is distinctly abnormal (compare with Fig. 37.11 for normals). These results indicate the amblyopic eye can detect gratings in the upper frequency range that cannot be used as a basis for more complex perceptions even at contrasts of up to a log unit above their individual thresholds. Also over the mid-frequency range where normals are so sensitive at phase discrimination, requiring as little as 1/8 the contrast needed to detect the 3f component, amblyopes (strabismics and anisometropes)[1] need dramatically more contrast than necessary for 3f detection (Hess, Lawden, & Campbell, 1981). The dashed curve in Fig. 37.12 represents a more functional limit of the amblyopic eye than that of the conventional threshold curve (solid line).

These results indicate that our contrast threshold approach, while being a useful one, represents only the first step in visual assessment. It gives a more

---

[1] We have replicated this finding on five strabismics and six anisometropes.

FIG. 37.10.   When frequencies f and $3f$ (a and b) are mixed in different phases, a number of resultant compound waveforms result ($c-f$). The two extreme varieties are the triangle wave ($f+3f$ in *e*) and the "square" wave ($f-3f$ in *c*). These waveforms have the same amplitude spectra (f and $3f$) but different phase spectra (From Hess, Lawden, & Campbell, 1981).

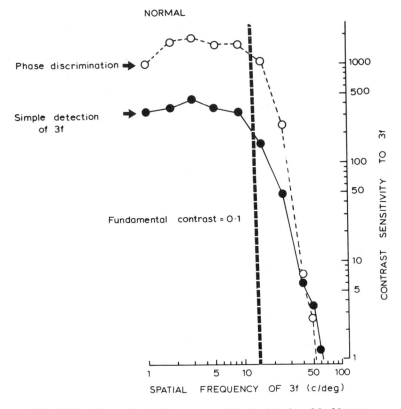

FIG. 37.11.   Contrast thresholds are compared for the detection of the 3f component alone (filled symbols) and the contrast of the 3f component when mixed with
a fixed contrast f to discriminate $f+3$ from $f-3f$ (see text). Contrast needed for
phase discrimination in the midfrequency range is less than for detection in normal
subjects (From Hess, Lawden, & Campbell, 1981). The dashed line represents the
phase limits of Holt & Ross (see text).

complete picture than acuity for conditions in which the abnormality occurs in
the peripheral processing and primary transmission of information from retina to
cortex such as retinopathies and optic nerve pathology. It represents only a
fraction of the picture when the abnormality involves later, cortical processing of
information such as may occur in developmental amblyopia. For these conditions
we need to test in rather more specific ways that the information that is detected
and transmitted from more peripheral sites is also processed correctly at these
more central sites. These results do not necessarily mean that amblyopes have
anomalous phase processing although this remains one of the possibilities. What
it does mean is that amblyopes exhibit a selective abnormality when distinguishing between targets that have the same amplitude spectra and different phase
spectra. We are at present investigating other possible candidates to explain this
phenomenon. For example whether it can be modeled by loss of foveal function.

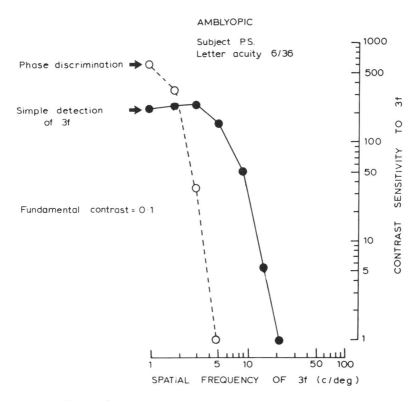

FIG. 37.12.   Contrast thresholds are composed for detection of the $3f$ component when presented alone (filled symbols) and for phase discrimination ($f+3f$ as compared with $f-3f$). Amblyopes can detect stimuli whose phase they cannot discern. Compare these results for amblyopes with those (Fig. 37.11) of normal subjects. (From Hess, Lawden, & Campbell, 1981).

Kohler (1951, 1964) showed how plastic the mature visual system is to distortions of its inputs and how beneficial (in the sense of adaptation) this is for the adult. We see here the other side of the coin, how susceptible the developing visual system is to restrictions or distortion of its input. Unlike Kohler's examples these restrictions lead to rather complex and permanent processing anomalies that are also cortically based but of no benefit.

ACKNOWLEDGMENTS

I gratefully acknowledge financial support from the Medical Research Council of Great Britain, the Wellcome Trust and St. John's College, Cambridge. I am especially grateful to Mark Lawden who allowed me to mention some of our more recent, yet unpublished, collaborated results on phase discrimination. I am also very grateful to Fergus Campbell for establishing an environment in which this work could be done.

REFERENCES

Blakemore, C., & Campbell, F. W. On the existence of neurones in the human visual system selectively sensitive to the orientation and size of retinal images. *Journal of Physiology*, 1969, *203*, 237–260.

Bodis-Wollner, I. Visual acuity and contrast sensitivity in patients with cerebral lesions. *Science*, 1972, *178*, 769–771.

Bodis-Wollner, I., & Diamond, S. P. The measurement of spatial contrast sensitivity in cases of blurred vision associated with cerebral lesions. *Brain*, 1976, *99*, 695–710.

Gstalder, R. J., & Green, D. G. Laser interference acuity in amblyopia. *Journal of Pediatric Ophthalmology*, 1971, *8*, 251–255.

Hess, R. F., & Bradley, A. Contrast perception above threshold is only minimally impaired in human amblyopia. *Nature*, 1980, *287*, 463–464.

Hess, R. F., Campbell, F. W., & Zimmern, R. Differences in the neural basis of human amblyopias: The effect of mean luminance. *Vision Research*, 1980, *20*, 295–305.

Hess, R. F., & Howell, E. R. The threshold contrast sensitivity function in strabismic amblyopia: Evidence for a two type classification. *Vision Research*, 1977, *17*, 1049–1055.

Hess, R. F., Jacobs, R. J., & Vingrys, A. Central versus peripheral vision: evaluation of the residual function resulting from a uniocular macular scotoma. *American Journal of Optometry and Physiological Optics*, 1978, *55*, 610–614.

Hess, R. F., Lawden, M. C., & Campbell, F. W. Amblyopes exhibit a phase discrimination abnormality. *Investigative Ophthalmology and Visual Science (Suppl)*, 1981, *20* (3), 124.

Hilz, R., & Cavonius, C. R. Functional organization of the peripheral retina: sensitivity to periodic stimuli. *Vision Research*, 1974, *14*, 1333–1337.

Hilz, R., Rentschler, I., & Brettel, H. Myopic and strabismic amblyopia: substantial differences in human visual development. *Experimental Brain Research*, 1977, *30*, 445–446.

Holt, J. J., & Ross, J. Phase perception in the high frequency range. *Vision Research*, 1980, *20*, 933–935.

Kohler, I. Über Aufbau und Wandlungen der Wahrnehmungswelt. Insbesondere über 'bedingte Empfindungen'. *Österreichische Akademie der Wissenschaften, Philosophisch-historische Klasse; Sitzungsberichte*, 227. Band, 1. Abhandlung. Wien: Rohrer, 1951.

Kohler, I. The formation and transformation of the perceptual world. *Psychological Issues*, 1964, *3*(4), Monograph 12. New York: International Universities Press.

Levi, D., & Harwerth, R. S. Spatio-temporal interactions in anisometropic and strabismic amblyopia. *Invest. Ophthal.*, 1977, *16*, 90–95.

Lie, I. Visual detection and resolution as a function of retinal locus. *Vision Research*, 1980, *20*, 967–974.

Maffei, L., & Florentini, A. The visual cortex as a spatial frequency analyser. *Vision Research*, 1973, *13*, 1255–1267.

Mitchell, D. E., Freeman, R. D., Millodot, M., & Haegerstrom, G. Meridional Amblyopia: Evidence for modification of the human visual system by early experience. *Vision Research*, 1973, *13*, 535–557.

Pöppel, E., & Harvey, L. O. Light-difference threshold of subjective brightness in the periphery of the visual field. *Psychologische Forschung*, 1973, *36*, 145–161.

Regan, D., Silver, R., & Murray, T. J. Visual acuity and contrast in multiple sclerosis: Hidden visual loss. *Brain*, 1977, *100*, 7563–579.

Rentschler, I., Hilz, R., & Brettel, H. Interactions of sustained and transient channels in amblyopia. *Invest. Ophthal.*, 1978, *17*, 293–298.

Sjostrand, J. Contrast sensitivity in amblyopia; a preliminary report. *Journal of Metabolic Ophthalmology*, 1978, *2*, 135–140.

Stromeyer, C. F., III, & Julesz, B. Spatial frequency masking in vision: critical bands and spread of masking. *Journal of the Optical Society of America*, 1972, *62*, 1221–1232.

38 Phase Lag in Human Contrast Evoked Potentials

Ingo Rentschler*
Donatella Spinelli
Laboratorio di Neurofisiologia del C.N.R.
Pisa, Italy

ABSTRACT

Cortical potentials (VECP) evoked by visual grating stimulation were recorded. The dependence of VECP amplitude and phase on spatial frequency, quality of the retinal image, and grating preadaptation was investigated. A linear dependence of phase on the logarithm of spatial frequency was found. Significant effects of optical blur on amplitude, but not on phase, occurred above 5 cycles per degree. Grating preadaptation of the eye caused a loss of amplitude and induced phase-shifts. These effects showed interocular transfer, as occurs in psychophysical studies. More specifically, a decrease in latency was observed when the ipsilateral eye was preadapted, whereas an increased in latency was observed when the contralateral eye was preadapted. No subjective counterpart of such effect is known.

The visually evoked cortical potential (VECP) is the electrical brain response to visual stimulation. Amongst other variables, the amplitude of the evoked response depends on the quality of the retinal image (Harter & White, 1968; Millodot & Riggs, 1970; Rentschler & Spinelli, 1978). It also depends on preceding adaptation to high contrast patterns such as gratings (Mecacci & Spinelli, 1976). These findings are consistent with the psychophysically observed effects of optical blur (Campbell & Green, 1965) and spatial frequency adaptation (Blakemore & Campbell, 1969) on contrast sensitivity.

This work was aimed at investigating another property of the steady-state VECP (for a review see Regan, 1975), namely the phase lag. More specifically, we asked the question as to the effects of optical blur, ipsilateral grating adaptation, and contralateral grating adaptation on the phase lag of the VECP.

---

*Now at Institut für Medizinische Psychologie, Universität München.

We found that the phase lag of the VECP linearly increases with the logarithm of spatial frequency. This increase is the same whether the grating stimulus is in focus or not. VECP phase also closely correlates with the latency of neuromagnetic cortical responses (Williamson, Kaufman, & Brenner, 1978) and psychophysical reaction time data (Breitmeyer, 1975). Grating adaptation of the eye, on the other hand, not only reduces VECP amplitude but induces phase shifts as well. These effects show interocular transfer as they are known from psychophysical results (Blakemore & Campbell, 1969). We observed a decrease in latency when preadapting the ipsilateral eye and an increase when adapting the contralateral eye. No subjective counterpart of this effect has yet been described.

We used gratings as stimulus patterns for the following reasons:

1. Grating patterns are suitable to measure the state of refraction and visual acuity (Rentschler & Spinelli, 1978).

2. With band-pass filtering at twice the stimulus frequency, the VECP elicited by a counterphased grating is a sinusoidal waveform thus permitting an easy analysis of both amplitude and phase (Campbell & Maffei, 1970; Pirchio, Rentschler, Spinelli, & Berardi, 1976).

3. A close relationship has been demonstrated between the amplitude of potentials evoked by counterphased gratings and psychophysical contrast sensitivity (Campbell & Maffei, 1970).

METHOD

The grating patterns were generated on the screen of a Hewlett-Packard 1300A oscilloscope with a P31 phosphor. Sinewave gratings were used in the adaptation experiments whereas squarewave gratings served as targets in all other experiments. The fundamental spatial frequency, i.e., the reciprocal of the period-length (in degrees), will be called the spatial frequency of the gratings. The spatial phase of the gratings was reversed by 180 deg, i.e., counterphased, at a fixed temporal frequency of 8 Hz. The contrast of the gratings is given by the quotient $(I_{max} - I_{min}) / (I_{max} + I_{min})$ where I_{max} and I_{min} are the luminance maximum and minimum, respectively. It could be varied by means of potentiometers, while keeping the average luminance constant at a level of 6 cd/m^2. Usually, grating contrast was 40%. The subject sat in a moderately illuminated room and faced the screen at a distance of 5m. The circular target subtended 4 deg in diameter. Accommodation was controlled by use of homatropin and pupil size was kept constant by means of a 4 mm diameter artificial pupil. Retinal images were blurred by putting appropriate lenses in front of the eye. Author D.S. served as a subject. No fixation target was used and the subject was allowed to freely gaze at the oscilloscope screen.

For recording the VECP one electrode was placed 2 mm above the inion in the midline and the other 2 cm laterally to the left of the first electrode. The potentials were amplified and then led through a Krohn-Hite 3750 active filter. A band-pass with corner frequencies of 2 Hz and 20 Hz (24 dB/octave) was used. The output was fed into a computer of averaged transients (CAT). Summed responses ($n=200$) were displayed on an oscilloscope and recorded on an X-Y plotter. Throughout the experiment the EEG was also monitored.

Amplitude and phase of VECP responses were gauged by eye. The response at 3.2 cycles per deg (cy/deg) was arbitrarily chosen as a reference for measuring the phase lag.

RESULTS

As has been reported before (Rentschler & Spinelli, 1978) the VECP amplitude is maximal in an intermediate range of spatial frequencies, centered at about 7 cy/deg. At higher and lower frequencies the amplitude falls off rapidly. Figure

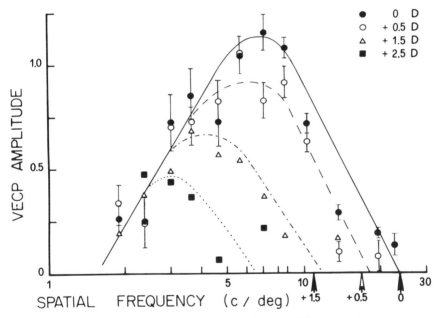

FIG. 38.1. VECP amplitude as a function of the spatial frequency of square-wave gratings. Contrast level was 40%. Subject D.S. (corrected to 20/20) viewed the test grating monocularly through a 4 mm diameter artificial pupil. The eye was homatropinized to eliminate effects of accommodation. Additional spectacle lenses were used to change the refractive power of the eye: filled circles (no lens), empty circles (+.5 D), triangles (+1.5 D). Individual data points are the average of four (0, +.5 D), two (+1.5 D), and one (+2.5 D) VECP records, each being the summation of 200 signals. Vertical bars represent ± 1 S.E. ($n=4$). Arrows indicate the psychophysical grating resolution for the well-corrected eye and for the eye +.5 D and +1.5 D out of focus, respectively. Data reproduced from Rentschler and Spinelli (1978). (Reprinted by permission from *Acta Opthalmology*, 1978, *56*, 67.)

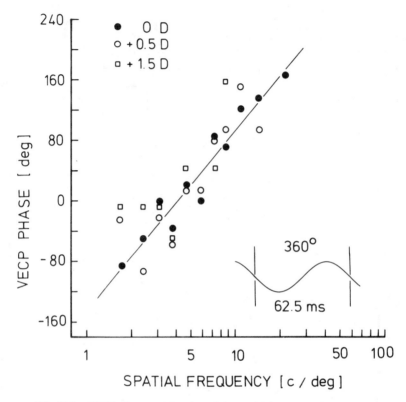

FIG. 38.2. VECP phase as a function of the spatial frequency of squarewave gratings, derived from the same VECP records as in Fig. 38.1. The arbitrary reference signal is the VECP response at 3.2 c/deg. The period length of the fundamental Fourier component of the VECP response is 62.5 ms. Subject D.S.

38.1 shows that an artificial myopia of +.5 D is sufficient to produce a significant decrease in amplitude provided the spatial frequency is greater than 4 cy/deg. Artificial myopias of 1.5 D and 2.5 D reduce the response amplitude even more severely, especially at high spatial frequencies. The psychophysically determined grating resolutions for the corrected eye and for the eye +.5 D and +1.5 D out of focus are indicated by means of arrows. In Figure 38.2 the phase lag of the VECP is plotted as a function of spatial frequency. Contrary to the results for amplitude, phase is not significantly affected by blurring the retinal image.

In Figures 38.3 and 38.4 the effect of changing the power of the lens added to the eye is shown for hypermetropic and myopic values. A squarewave target of a fixed spatial frequency of 8.8 cy/deg was used. At this frequency the VECP amplitude falls by about 50% for 1 D of defocusing (Fig. 38.3). In comparison, the VECP phase changes are relatively small (Fig. 38.4).

Figure 38.5 shows the effect of grating adaptation on VECP amplitude and phase. As a control, each eye was first tested with a sinewave grating of 40% contrast and 7.3 cy/deg spatial frequency. In the pre-adaptation condition the right eye (O.D.) was then exposed to the same grating but at 85% contrast and for a period of 15 min. Thereafter, each eye was again tested with 40% contrast.

There is a clear spatial frequency specific reduction in amplitude after adaptation to a high contrast grating as has been reported before (Mecacci & Spinelli, 1976). Moreover, there is an almost complete transfer of this effect to the unadapted eye. An unexpected result is the phase shift induced by grating adaptation. Here an average decrease in VECP phase of −98 deg occurs following ipsilateral adaptation whereas an increase in phase of + 72 deg is observed following contralateral adaptation.

DISCUSSION

We found that the phase lag of steady-state evoked potentials monotonically increases with the spatial frequency of the grating stimulus whereas it varies

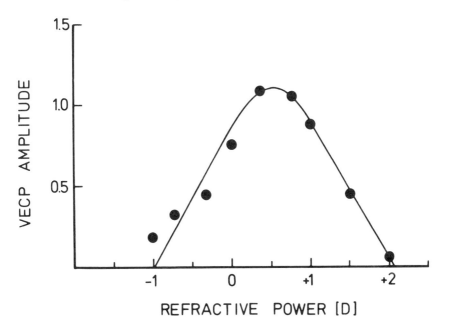

FIG. 38.3. VECP amplitude as a function of the power of a lens added to the homatropinized eye. The spatial frequency used was 8.8 c/deg. Each data point is the average of three records (each record 200 sums). Subject D.S. Data reproduced from Rentschler and Spinelli (1978). (Reprinted by permission from *Acta Opthalmology*, 1978, *56*, 67.)

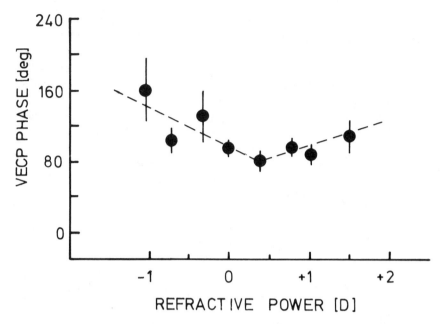

FIG. 38.4.   VECP phase as a function of the power of a lens added to the homatropinized eye. The spatial frequency used was 8.8 c/deg. Each data point is the average of nine measurements taken from the same three records as in Fig. 38.3. Vertical bars indicate ± 1 S.E. (*n*=9). Subject D.S.

relatively little with the quality of the retinal image. On the other hand, grating adaptation of the eye affects both VECP amplitude and phase and this effect shows almost complete interocular transfer.

Previous research has established that the speed of the visual system for flashed stimuli is related to the cube root of luminance. This seems to be true for psychophysical reaction times, the implicit time of all of the waves of the VECP, latency data on the *Limulus* optic nerve fibers, and frog optic nerve discharges (for a review see Riggs & Wooten, 1972, pp. 690–731).

Williamson, Kaufman, and Brenner (1978) recently reported that the latency of neuromagnetic responses to temporally varying gratings depends on spatial frequency. At a response frequency of 16 Hz (i.e., a stimulus frequency of 8 Hz), they found a latency increase of about 50 ms between the spatial frequencies of 1 cy/deg and 10 cy/deg. These data agree with Breitmeyer's (1975) reaction time data if a constant is added to the neuromagnetic response latency. Our VECP data (Fig. 38.2) confirm these results by revealing a phase-shift of 260 deg between 1 cy/deg and 10 cy/deg corresponding to an increase in latency of 45 ms.

When grating stimulation is used the latencies of VECP components seem to be functions of the pattern contrast as are the VECP amplitudes (Kulikowski, 1977, pp. 168–183). More specifically, a decrease in contrast generally produces an increase in latency. This may be why in our experiments the phase lag of the VECP shows a tendency to increase at large amounts of optical blur (Fig. 38.4).

A direct relationship between the mechanisms subserving contrast analysis in the human visual system and the activity of cortical neurones selectively sensitive to spatial frequency is suggested by the results of single-unit recordings in cat and monkey (for a review see Maffei, 1978, pp. 39–66). Of particular interest is that the response of simple cells in the cat's visual cortex is depressed after adaptation to a high contrast grating (Maffei, Fiorentini, & Bisti, 1973). It

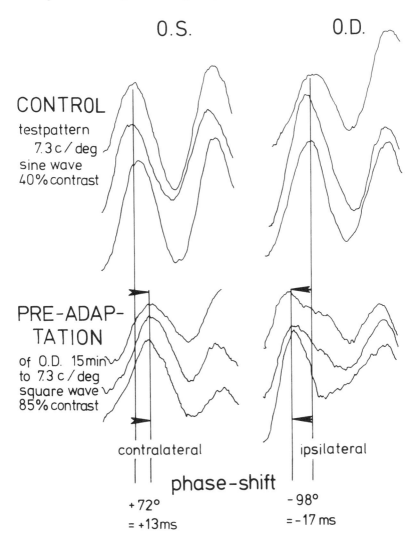

FIG. 38.5.   The effect of grating adaptation of VECP amplitude and phase. 200 responses averaged for each record. Subject D.S.

seems possible, therefore, that the reduction of the VECP amplitude following grating adaptation is related to this. Temporal phase-shifts in the VECP response may result from the interaction between excitatory and inhibitory regions within simple cell receptive fields (Maffei, 1978, pp. 39–66). The interocular transfer of the adaptation effect may be readily explained by the fact that the majority of these neurones are binocularly driven. The distinctly different phase-shifts, i.e., the difference in sign following ipsilateral and contralateral grating adaptation, however, are not accounted for by this hypothesis.

ACKNOWLEDGMENTS

Supported by Sonderforschungsbereich 50 "Kybernetik" of the Deutsche Forschungsgemeinschaft and Scuola Normale Superiore, Pisa/Italy

REFERENCES

Blakemore, C., & Campbell, F. W. On the existence of neurones in the human visual system selectively sensitive to the orientation and size of retinal images. *Journal of Physiology (London)*, 1969, *203*, 237–260.

Breitmeyer, B. G. Simple reaction time as a measure of the temporal response properties of transient and sustained channels. *Vision Research*, 1975, *15*, 1411–1412.

Campbell, F. W., & Green, D. L. Optical and retinal factors affecting visual resolution. *Journal of Physiology (London)*, 1965, *181*, 576–593.

Campbell, F. W., & Maffei, L. Electrophysiological evidence for the existence of orientation and size detectors in the human visual system. *Journal of Physiology (London)*, 1970, *207*, 635–652.

Harter, R. M., & White, C. T. Effects of contour sharpness and check-size on visually-evoked cortical potentials. *Vision Research*, 1968, *8*, 701–711.

Kulikowski, J. J. Visual evoked potentials as a measure of visibility. In J. E. Desmedt (Ed.), *Visual evoked potentials in man: new developments*. Oxford: Oxford University Press, 1977.

Maffei, L. Spatial frequency channels: neural mechanisms. In R. Held, H. W. Leibowitz, & H. L. Teuber (Eds.), *Handbook of sensory physiology* (Vol. 8), *Perception*. New York: Springer-Verlag, 1978.

Maffei, L., Fiorentini, A., & Bisti, S. Neural correlate of perceptual adaptation to gratings. *Science*, 1973, *182*, 1036–1038.

Mecacci, L., & Spinelli, D. The effects of spatial frequency adaptation on human evoked potentials. *Vision Research*, 1976, *16*, 477–479.

Millodot, M., & Riggs, L. A. Refraction determined electrophysiologically. *Archives of Ophthalmology*, 1970, *84*, 272–278.

Pirchio, M., Rentschler, I., Spinelli, D., & Berardi, N. Metodo di analisi dei potenziali visivi evocati. *Atti del 4° Congresso di Cibernetica e Biofisica*, Siena, 1976, 239–242.

Regan, D. Recent advances in electrical recording from the brain. *Nature*, 1975, *253*, 401–407.

Rentschler, I., & Spinelli, D. Accuracy of evoked potential refractometry using bar gratings. *Acta Ophthalmologica*, 1978, *56*, 67–73.

Riggs, L. A., & Wooten, B. R. Electrical measures and psychophysical data on human vision. In D. Jameson & L. M. Hurvich (Eds.), *Handbook of sensory physiology* (Vol. VII/4), *Visual psychophysics*. New York: Springer Verlag, 1972.

Williamson, S. J., Kaufman, L., & Brenner, D. Latency of the neuromagnetic response of the human visual cortex. *Vision Research*, 1978, *18*, 107–111.

39

Clinical Observations of Palinopsia: Anomalous Mapping From Retinal to Nonretinal Coordinates of Vision

Ivan Bodis-Wollner[1,2]
Morris B. Bender[1]
Sidney P. Diamond[1]
Departments of Neurology[1] and Ophthalmology[2]
The Mount Sinai School of Medicine
New York, New York

ABSTRACT

In certain patients with visual hallucinations, a relationship can be established between the hallucinated images and an actual primary visual stimulus. In palinopsia the image of the primary stimulus persists and sometimes recurs after the stimulus is no longer present. We considered (a) the separation of the palinoptic image and the primary stimulus in time, (b) whether they occurred at the same point in the visual field, (c) whether the palinoptic image moved with the eye or could be examined by circumspection. Patients' reports suggest that palinoptic experiences represent different stages in the transfer of visual signals tied to a retinal coordinate system to a store which remains accessible over long periods of time and has no retinal coordinates.

INTRODUCTION

Uncommon sensory experiences are not infrequently reported by patients with neurological disorders and particularly "subjective visual sensations" (Gowers, 1895) continue to receive the attention of neurologists and psychiatrists. Yet the pathophysiology of these sensations is not understood and even their classification is problematic.

A distinction is commonly made between the spatial or temporal distortion of real visual events on the one hand, and the perceptual experiences arising without an obvious physical referent, on the other. The former type of disturbance is classified as illusions, the latter as hallucinations. However, the distinction between hallucinatory experiences and illusions is not always simple to establish in practice. In some patients, careful questioning reveals a relationship between "seeing" an image and an actual visual stimulus. When the patient reports a persistent or recurrent image of the visual stimulus after that stimulus is no longer present, the experience is called "palinopsia" (Critchley, 1951). In polyopia (Hoff & Pötzl 1937) patients report seeing simultaneously several images of the same object. In some cases of palinopsia there is only unusual persistence of images; in others, a distinct time lag intervenes between primary stimulus and palinoptic image. There is no critical image duration which will distinguish palinoptic phenomena from normal afterimages and, as we shall show in this chapter, palinopsia cannot be regarded only as a temporal distortion of vision. It is necessary to take into consideration spatial properties of palinoptic images not previously analyzed.

Aim of Study

In order to discuss these phenomena, we distinguish between retinal and nonretinal coordinates of the visual system. By this we imply a division between visual information coded by the retinal locus of stimulation and vision existing in a reference system not related to the retinal coordinates of the stimulus. We describe simple bedside tests of palinopsia in four selected cases and discuss the continuum of palinoptic phenomena between "retinal" and "non-retinal" coordinates of vision.

CASE MATERIAL AND METHODS

In the last decades over 40 cases of palinopsia were encountered among patients treated and followed up in the Neurology Department of the Mount Sinai Hospital. Some cases were described in earlier communications (Bender, Feldman, & Sobin, 1968; Feldman & Bender, 1970; Jacobs, Feldman, Diamond & Bender, 1973). Of the new patients, four are described in detail.[1] Patients had standard neurological and neuro-ophthalmological evaluations and special interviews concerning their visual sensations.

Interviewing

Most patients need to be questioned about various forms of subjective visual sensations. This is most important since we found that patients are often hesitant

---

[1]One of these patients was seen by I. B-W. at the Massachusetts General Hospital, Boston, Massachusetts.

to complain of unusual or altered visual sensations for fear of being considered mentally ill, and some patients simply do not feel that these visual complaints are pertinent. Therefore patients were explicitly asked whether they noted objects to appear altered in size, shape, or color, and whether they had experienced persistent or spatially multiple images. A typical question was, "Did you ever look at an object and after looking away, no matter where you looked, continued to see the object or parts of it?" Patients were asked whether they observed "shimmering spots," "flashing lights," "wavy lines," or "checkerboard patterns." They were asked whether they experienced "flashbacks" of familiarity with their environment.

We tried to ascertain whether the visual experiences were altered by eye closure, covering one eye, blinking, or changes in the ambient illumination. When possible, patients were asked to draw images they had seen, on paper and in the air with outstretched arm to indicate the size of the image. They were asked about the distance and location in space at which they saw these images. Patients were also asked whether they were aware of the unreal nature of their visual sensation at the time of the experience and in retrospect. There were a few patients in our series who complained of seeing persistent images and who sought medical help for relief from them. Since the majority of patients whom we saw had palinopsia but did not reveal these symptoms spontaneously in the anamnesis, we concluded that palinopsia is not as rare a condition as might be estimated from the small number of reported cases.

Testing for Palinopsia

Only a few patients had palinoptic phenomena during testing. If a patient reported palinopsia, he was asked to perform a few tasks, such as fixating the tip of a flashlight for 20 seconds or fixating objects for 30 seconds and describing the subsequent after-sensations. We encountered a few patients who did not experience visual afterimages, although the majority described normal afterimagery and one reported afterimages which were prolonged in comparison to the examiner's. Objects which were fixated included colored signs, black and white patterns, or generally "contrasting" patterns. Patients were asked to look at pictures, at the examiner's face, tie, or common objects, and to report if they experienced symptoms of palinopsia, polyopia, dyschromatopsia, or dysmorphopsia.[2] We routinely tested the effects on the ongoing palinoptic images of an active or passive head and eye movement with and without ocular fixation, rapid changes in the room illumination, and eye closure and frequent blinking. These tests were developed over the last decade; they are similar to, but less

---

[2]Polyopia: spatial multiplication of a single image usually due to cerebral lesion. (Hoff & Pötzl 1937) Dyschromatopsia: a monocular or binocular change of color of a complete visual scene or partial visual scene following a retinal or cerebral lesion. Dysmorphopsia: changes in the shape of images as a result of retinal or cerebral lesion. (Critchley, 1949)

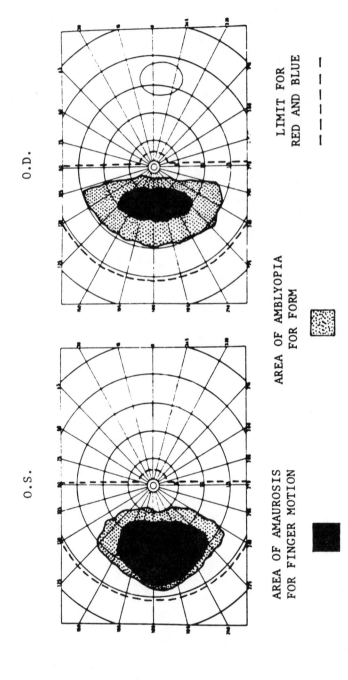

O.D.

O.S.

LIMIT FOR
RED AND BLUE

AREA OF AMBLYOPIA
FOR FORM

AREA OF AMAUROSIS
FOR FINGER MOTION

FIG. 39.1. Visual fields in patient I.G. (case no. 1) with geometric hallucinations and palinopsia showing a left homonymous paracentral absolute scotoma surrounded by a larger amblyopic zone for form and color.

extensive than those used by Jung (1979). The patients were also asked to perform these maneuvers unassisted whenever they experienced palinopsia in the absence of an examiner. One patient (case no. 2) was especially cooperative, and his observations are described in greater detail.

ILLUSTRATIVE CASES

Case 1

Persisting Geometric Hallucinations, Monocular Diplopia, Polyopia, and Palinopsia.   I. G., a 52-year-old man, had noted for a period of 2 months that objects appeared blurred and colorless ''to the left.'' The neurologic examination disclosed no deficits in mental, language, motor or sensory functions. The neuro-ophthalmological examination revealed a left homonymous paracentral scotoma which was absolute for motion, form, and color in between 5° and 20°, measured from the fixation point (Fig. 39.1). Between fixation and 5° away from it there was a relative defect for color. Fundi, pupils, and eye movements were normal. Afterimages were tested with a flashlight and with high contrast grating patterns. Their duration was no different for the patient than for the examiner. Optokinetic nystagmus was symmetrical when tested with an OKN tape. Eye movements were normal. A right brachial angiogram demonstrated an aneurysm at the origin of the right posterior communicating artery.

Subjective Visual Phenomena.   While reading a newspaper, he noticed that a checkerboard pattern (Fig. 39.2) of green and white repeatedly floated across the

FIG. 39.2.   Drawing by I.G. of his geometric hallucination which appeared recurrently in his ''blind'' field. See Fig. 39.1 for his visual field.

newspaper on the left side. This pattern appeared to move with his eyes. Sometimes it looked like wallpaper with fancy, flowery designs in different colors. At
times it would remain stationary in his left field of vision and then disappear in a
few moments. On occasion while he was watching television, the image he saw
on the TV would appear on the wall. If he shifted his gaze, instead of being
single, the image multiplied and then disappeared as he turned away. He described one such experience in great detail:

> "I was watching a basketball game on the television. It was a colored set with a 16-
> inch screen. I watched it from about a 3–4 meter distance. Suddenly, something
> like a snapshot of the scene appeared to the left of the screen." With his out-
> stretched arm he demonstrated the second image to be about 10° from the center of
> the screen. "For a moment there were two screens, the one in color straight ahead,
> the other in black and white to my left. There were two images with either eye
> alone. A player was just putting the ball in the basket. There were three other
> players on the screen. The game went on in front of me, but I kept seeing the same
> scene constantly in black and white to my left. I could see the background in the
> room. This 'replay' scene was very vivid. I kept seeing the same men in the
> 'snapshot.' The outline of the figures was very marked, jet black. I could not see
> their eyes or noses well. At the same time, I could see what happened on the real
> screen. The snapshot remained stationary for a while but then a new 'slide' came
> into view."
>
> This happened to him on several occasions. He stated that he saw the TV scene
> in the same location in his field of vision as the flowering pattern which occurred on
> "dozens" of occasions, even when he was traveling on the train. "Thank heavens
> it did not happen recently."

Comments.   In addition to geometric hallucinations and polyopia, monocular
diplopia occurred. This was immediately followed by a very detailed and persistent "false" image. All images moved with the eye.

Case 2

*Palinopsia Without Monocular Diplopia Occurring Seconds to Days After Stim-
uli.*   S. Y., a 37-year-old man, noticed on awakening that he had difficulty
seeing to his left. Later that day there was no improvement and he kept bumping
into objects on his left side. Over the following days he felt that the region of
visual impairment spread considerably closer to the midline, but he could still see
slightly to the left of the center. The neurological examination disclosed no
abnormalities except in visual functions. There was an incomplete left incongruous homonymous hemianopsia with selective sparing of 6°–8° central
vision in the right eye and 1°–2° in the left eye, tested with .2° white stationary
targets. A red match subtending roughly .05° at the eye looked redder to the right

of the midline than it did at the center of fixation. This was interpreted as relative central field involvement although his visual acuity was 20/20. Static perimetry of the central 3° was performed during his acute palinoptic phase; 6 days later there was no change. Afterimages were tested as in the first case, and also with a projector lamp at half-bleaching (approximately 6.8 log scotopic troland sec.) intensity (Rushton, 1965). They could not be evoked from his left fields. Foveal afterimages lasted as long as those of the experimenter. Fundi, eye movements, and pupillary reactions were normal. There was no nystagmus. The electroencephalogram was normal. Brain scan and brachial angiogram demonstrated a vascular mass over the convexity of the right occipital lobe extending almost to the occipital pole. On the basis of these findings, surgery was done. Following craniotomy no tumor was found by inspection or palpation, and no further surgical maneuver was attempted. Postoperatively, he did well. On the 6th postoperative day, he reported visual hallucinations. There was no change in his neurological status, and he remained mentally clear.

Interview

Walking down the corridor he saw a woman in green uniform, such as hospital personnel wear. "I have seen such a uniform on the floor, sitting in a chair to my left about 2 feet away from me. She was normal size. Couldn't see her features. None of the people I have hallucinated [*sic*] had distinct facial features. Only clothing texture and colors were clear. She was sitting in a chair, brown wood, no padding, arm rest. First I thought she was real. But as I went further (couple of steps) she moved with me. As I tried to look at her, she floated away in slow motion to my left and behind. When I came back to my bed, I saw towels along the floor, three or four of them, about 5 feet from the edge of the next bed to the middle of my bed. These were white towels, hospital towels, no markings, made of terry cloth. They were slightly soiled, had been used. Looked damp and wet, not fresh. Have seen similar pictures lots of times in the locker rooms, I go to gyms, massage parlors. They just lay there, not all of them overlapped." He denied having experienced polyopia. "Lasted 5 seconds. I could look at them, they were still there. I could look at them by moving my eyes and head. I knew they weren't real because they could not be here. Also because of the previous experience. When I saw the towels I knew that in the surround there were beds. First I saw the towels when I walked into the room straight in front of me. Then I walked to my bed. I did not step on the towels, they were not in my path, they were to my left. Then I sat on my bed, the towels were to the left. They drifted off in slow motion to the left." He said that, in general, things which come into view appear suddenly and move away slowly.

He had several simple palinoptic experiences, some of which he could reproduce in drawing (Fig. 39.3a,b,c). Some more complicated ones he described in detail.

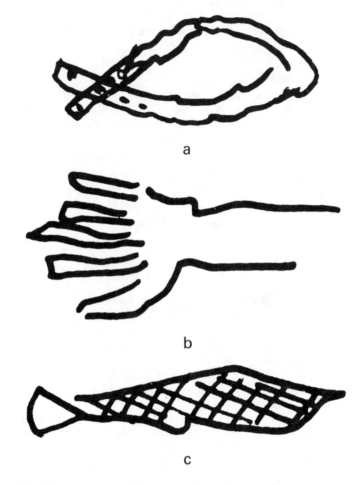

FIG. 39.3. Drawings by S.Y. (case no. 2) showing his palinoptic images.
(a) A tanned leather strap which he saw around his neck while he closed his eyes. The experience lasted 2 or 3 sec. He had no pressure sensation around his neck connected with this image.
(b) A hand which he saw as motioning him to go to it. He stated that it was "blurry," although he could distinguish individual fingers. He could see to the middle of the forearm. "I have seen thriller-chiller hands like these in a spook movie," he said.
(c) Drawing of the tie he saw "knotted around his neck." He described it as being blue-checkered, similar to those he had seen in "Mr. Frank's and Miffit's Men's Shop."

"I saw a woman down at the elevator when I walked to it. She was standing to my left. As I started to turn around to look at her she turned around with me and floated away to the left, after I completed a 360° turn. I couldn't discern her features. She had on a purple dress, little yellow and green flowers (he thinks about the size of the blunt end of a pencil, 7 mm.). She was almost on my left shoulder. The length of her dress was to her knee. She had a belt. The material was silk. I don't recall having seen the woman before, but I saw such material before, I don't know where."

"All the things I see I have seen before."

"There was a yellow napkin yesterday evening on my tray. It was unfolded lengthwise. It got up, floated away (like blown in the wind). I tried to grab it. It had a ripple in it (as if blown by wind) but did not change size or perspective during its flight. Its size stayed the same, only it got further away. There was in fact a napkin to my left, slightly damp (only it really did not float away). The floating experience started after I looked at the real napkin. I looked away to the left, looked back, and then it started to float away."

"The very first experience I had was this: as I was walking in the hall, the weighing scale on my left moved with me all the time. It happened after I first looked at the scale, then I looked away and as I walked away it came with me on my left. I have measured my weight a few times on it. I could see all the details of the scale. The big marker was around 100. I could see the height marker, pushed down. The bottom was floating above the ground. Behind the scale I could see the wall was there. I could not see details on the wall." He interrupted to report the sudden appearance of a hand in the middle of his field of vision, moving from his eyes to my chest. In fact several minutes before I had motioned with my hand exactly like that. He recognized the checks on my shirt sleeve. When he looked up at a chain above his head and then turned away, he reported that it appeared seconds later in his left field. He could not recall other experiences when he looked at something straight on with a later appearance to the left.

The patient had palinopsia for 3 days. Several times he experienced hands and arms performing some simple gestures in his left field of vision. As he walked away from the television lounge, he kept seeing the three-legged TV table, and described it in good detail from his palinoptic experience.

Following his own description of these phenomena he had been asked to perform some simple tests. He observed the following. Whenever he had a palinoptic image and fixated a point on the wall with his eyes while turning his head toward the image, it disappeared. When he tried to move his eyes toward the image while holding his head fixed, he was better able to look at the image; at other times, it disappeared with this maneuver. When he moved both his head and eyes toward the image, it seemed to move in the same direction and he could never catch up with it. He reported some sensations with closed, others with open eyes.

Comments.   This patient could describe palinoptic experiences in detail. These are given verbatim above to demonstrate that it is possible to draw inferences concerning (a) the absence of fine detail in palinoptic images, even though they were more precise than vague shapes, and (b) their relatively fixed position in reference to the patient's body axis. The first point is emphasized by the preservation of color experience and the ability to see the markers on the scale, but the absence of detail such as small letters, or reporting seeing fingers of a blurry hand (Fig. 39.3b).

Palinopsia occurred sometimes immediately following a stimulus, sometimes days later. Most images moved with the eyes, but some of them could be circumspected with free eye movements and shifted with body position.

Case 3

Palinopsia Occurring Months After the Primary Stimulus and not Moving with the Eyes.   M. L., a 56-year-old man, noted that while reading, words, letters, or pictures on his right side seemed to "drop off." He had some difficulty in recalling names or words he wanted to use in conversation. He occasionally noted shadows moving across from right to left in his field of vision. He was oriented, and his speech and mental functions as well as motor and sensory status were intact. The neuro-ophthalmological examination disclosed a right homonymous incongruous field defect with macular splitting. Visual acuity was 20/20 bilaterally. Eye movements and optokinetic nystagmus were intact. Afterimages, compared to the examiner's, were prolonged for contrasting targets but not for a flashlight stimulus. Among targets used were stripes, a tie, and a toothpaste label. A left carotid angiogram demonstrated an aneurysm at the branching of the left posterior communicating artery. Bilateral brachial angiogram did not demonstrate any other abnormality. The EEG was normal.

Interview

The patient reported seeing beige-colored geometric figures in motion in his right field. He reported seeing a moving row of small circles which he called "quarters" and rectangles ("pages") which moved from his left to his right. He experienced palinopsia in episodes, which sometimes lasted days. With his eyes closed he often saw a "mish-mash," a linear design looking like "hairs" to his right. Neither active nor passive motion of his eyes affected the location of the persistent images on the right. He saw in his right field a scene of "men," "animals," "fish," and "overgrowth of shrubbery." It was a scene from "pharaohs' times" that he had seen in biblical and historical studies before his hospitalization. Often images moved rapidly upward from the bottom to the top of his right field. He continued seeing daily the same scene all over again. The scene was always black and white, and every detail was "in excellent proportion." He reported some hallucinations with either closed or open lids but the "pharaohs' scene" was mostly present with closed lids. When a sketch of an eye was briefly shown to him, he could see it for more than a minute to his right, either by closing his eyes or looking to the right on the wall.

Follow-up

M. L. underwent surgical exploration. The aneurysm, however, was not accessible. His hallucinations disappeared after 2 years. His field defect first improved, then deteriorated. There was a gradual personality change. On a recent admission, he reported seeing geometric figures and sometimes an eye with eyelashes in his anopic right field. The image persisted only for 30 seconds. There was slight pallor of the left disc. His visual acuity was 20/300 O.S. and 20/20 O.D., and his eye movements were intact. Psychiatric examination disclosed evidence of depression with "some organic factors."

Comments.   On a bedside test there was evidence of allesthesia:[3] After M. L. looked at the foveal stimulus, it persisted in a projection in his right field. Palinopsia sometimes lasted for days, and the stimulus often preceded it by weeks or months. Neither active nor passive eye movements shifted the location of the palinoptic images: The patient always experienced them to the right of his body.

Case 4

Unformed Visual Hallucinations, Dysmorphopsia, Monocular Polyopia and Palinopsia Where a Primary Stimulus May Have Been Present 15 Years Preceding Palinopsia.   S. G., a 62-year-old man, noted increasing disability in his thinking process for 2 months prior to admission. He had often forgotten what he wanted to say and on occasion was disoriented in his home. He also noted defective vision and sometimes bumped into people on his right. He found that on reading, the right half of the page blended away. His condition fluctuated. On admission to the hospital he was oriented, his spontaneous speech was fluent, and his spelling was accurate. He had little difficulty with naming objects but had some trouble with calculations. There was a right homonymous hemiachromatopsia with macular splitting. He did not detect motion in the right homonymous fields beyond 15 to 20°. Within this limit he could detect moving objects but could not localize them. His neuro-ophthalmological examination, consisting of tests as in the previous cases, was otherwise negative. There were mild sensory deficits on the right side of the body elicited only by double simultaneous stimulation. There was no motor deficit. A left parieto-occipital malignant mass (with midline shift) was demonstrated on angiography.

---

[3]Allesthesia: displaced localization of a correctly perceived sensory stimulus to an untouched body part (somatosensory stimulus) or incorrect perception of the direction or origin in the extracorporeal space of an auditory or visual stimulus.

Interview

Just before admission he noted the following sensations all in the same day. ''I was watching the Johnny Carson show on TV when suddenly he did not appear to have a chin.'' See the patient's own drawing (Fig. 39.4). ''The chin seemed to have been elongated into the body. There was no chin line, the face was not demarcated. When I went into the kitchen I saw my wife and daughter also without chins. After I walked up the stairs to my bedroom I saw everything ''crawling.'' It was like in the rain, or as heat waves appear. It was all over my vision. All objects seemed to be in wavy motion. When I looked into the mirror in the bathroom it was horrible: There was a face without demarcation, the chin was down to the body. I knew that all these things were not real. I have seen faces similar to the faces I saw that night about 15 years ago in a Dick Tracy comic strip.'' While he was hospitalized, he once complained that he saw two images only in his left eye. He knew that it was only in one eye because he closed the other eye to test it. This monocular diplopia lasted about 30 minutes. He also complained that during this period he had pain in the socket of his eye. Furthermore, ''everything I looked at appeared to be two or

FIG. 39.4.   Drawing by patient no. 4 of a face he saw in the mirror and repeat-edly on walls. The face was not recognized by him as his own distorted face, but rather was attributed to a comic strip drawing he might have seen many years before this incident.

three. They were overlapping and appeared to be half normal size." This lasted for a short period. After his first hospitalization, he did not have any more visual hallucinations.

Comments. Besides unformed hallucinations, dysmorphopsia, micropsia, and monocular polyopia, the patient may have had palinopsia. The "palinoptic" image occurred 15 years after the primary stimulus. The image was not localized to either field; rather, it appeared in front of his body and he could examine it by moving his eyes around. This appears to be a case of palinopsia bordering on frank visual hallucination, and suggests the continuum between these entities.

DISCUSSION

For describing palinopsia and providing a framework for approaching the study of visual hallucinations, we make use of the concept of retinal and nonretinal coordinates of visual images. By retinal coordinates we do not mean the anatomical structure of the retina but rather all stages of the visual process where information is required about the retinal locus of stimulation (Turvey, 1977). In general, we consider images which are fixed by coordinates in reference to the center of regard (and thus by the position of the eye in the orbit) to have retinal coordinates.

During eye movements, a sequential sampling of various frames of a visible scene occurs. Whether or not a single anatomical region or structure is responsible for mapping the temporal sequence into a continuous spatial sequence, this mapping requires information about the retinal loci of restricted stimuli. In other words, each signal must be endowed with its retinal coordinates. At some later stage of processing, for instance in visual memory, retinal coordinates may not be necessary.

A parafoveal afterimage produced by a bright source of bleaching intensity disappears momentarily, depending on background illumination (Bodis-Wollner, 1971), but it can be evoked again by intermittent stimulation and it appears projected in reference to the fixation point in the same direction in the visual field where the primary light stimulus came from. Hence retinal locus must be coded for the sensation of an afterimage.

On the other hand, one is able to visualize even with closed eyes objects to either side of one's body, regardless of the momentary position of the eyes. We may consider that "mental" images are free of retinal coordinates because left, right, behind, etc., are related to the position of the body of the observer in the surrounding space and not to the relative position of his eyes.

A classification according to this division suggests that palinoptic experiences reported by our patients represent visual sensations in transition between retinal and nonretinal coordinate systems of the visual process. We described palinoptic experiences according to their relationship to stimuli which in the patient's own account may have preceded the hallucinatory phenomena. We considered (1) the separation in time between the primary stimulus and palinopsia; (2) the separation in space between the primary stimulus and palinopsia; whether the palinoptic image appeared at the same point in the visual field where the primary stimulus occurred; (3) whether the palinoptic image moved with the eye or could be circumspected with free eye movements.

In our first case, similar to other reported cases (Bekèny & Pèter, 1961; Bender, Feldman, & Sobin, 1968; Bender & Sobin, 1963; Lance, 1976; Michel & Troost, 1980; Pötzl, 1954; Swash, 1979), the patient simultaneously experienced a foveal and extrafoveal image of the same stimulus. The false image with the frozen basketball scene persisted while the game continued in the center of regard on the real television screen. This palinoptic image behaved as an image confined to the retinal space, showing in this respect similarity to migraine phosphenes (Jung, 1979). Indeed, this patient's geometric hallucination (Fig. 39.1) suggests a formal relationship between this type of palinopsia and migraine phosphenes. In one case of palinopsia, not reported hitherto, the patient experienced in a seizure flashing "rings" in the left visual field. Then the face of the examiner not only doubled, but multiplied, and appeared in each ring. When the examiner was no longer in view, these images persisted for minutes and moved with the patient's eyes.

In the second case no simultaneity of the palinoptic image and the primary stimulus was reported by the patient, although palinopsia most often occurred immediately after the patient looked at an object. It is likely that the *primary stimulus* utilized foveal pathways. One reason is because the palinoptic images were seen in a partially *blind* field. Another, perhaps more compelling reason, is the fact that while the palinoptic image did not contain the finest detail (see case 2), it was nevertheless too detailed to have been based on a primary stimulus falling on the extrafoveal retina (beyond 5°) which has low resolving capacity (Green, 1970). When compared to spatial frequency filtered pictures (Lundh, Derefeldt, Nyberg, & Lennerstrand, 1981), our patient's descriptions suggest that palinoptic images have a foveal bandwidth of 2 to 3 octaves up to about 12 c/deg. The case reports of Hoff and Pötzl (1937), Bender (1945), Bender and Sobin (1963), Bender et al. (1968), Critchley (1949, 1951), Gloning, Gloning, and Weingarten (1957), Bekèny and Pèter (1961), Kinsbourne and Warrington (1963), Jacobs, Feldman, Diamond, and Bender (1973), Cogan (1973), Lance (1976), Meadows and Munro (1977), and Michel and Troost (1980) also suggest that polyopia and palinopsia develop for many patients in the amblyopic eye or scotomatous area after central fixation. This spatial transfer in the genesis of the palinoptic image suggests that visual information is transferred to a "space" normally receiving input from the part of the visual field which has been deprived of normal input.

In the third case, palinopsia occurred many weeks after the stimulus. The primary foveal stimulus may have been transferred to an extrafoveal projection. This patient's images did not behave as ordinary afterimages: the level of illumination had not changed their appearance, nor had his eye movements changed their broad localization in the visual field.

In the fourth case, palinopsia may have been preceded by a primary stimulus some 15 years prior to it. The image was completely free of retinal coordinates: The patient could examine it while freely moving his eyes.

We see in these cases of palinopsia a progression from "retinal" to "nonretinal" spaces. This is characterized by (1) increasing separation in time between the "primary stimulus" and the palinoptic image; and (2) decreasing confinement of the palinoptic image to retinal coordinates.

Consideration within these spatial and temporal coordinates may offer advantages in classifying visual hallucinations in general. With simple bedside tests one should explore the influence of changing levels of illumination and the effects of eye, head, and body rotation on visual sensations. The "test" results described with the above considerations in mind could provide a useful framework for further investigations of the mechanism of hallucinations. When feasible, more rigorous vestibular testing, as performed by Jung (1979) in a case of migraine phosphene, could be of value to assess its role. Nevertheless, we believe that a detailed anamnesis and the described bedside tests can help in the differential diagnosis of palinopsia and other physiological forms of visual persistence. Differentiation could be based on the relative shortness of iconic memory (Dick, 1974; Sperling, 1960), the precise detail available in eidetic imagery (Stromeyer & Psotka, 1970), and the crucial effect of background illumination on the appearance of afterimages (Bodis-Wollner, 1971).

While there is an apparent phenomenologic continuum of palinoptic phenomena between the extremes of normal afterimages and frank hallucinations (Feldman & Bender, 1970), there is one interesting difference. In the normal, the time course for persistence is strikingly shorter for low than for high spatial frequencies (Meyer & Maguire, 1977). Yet, concerning the fine detail of their persistent images, the reports of our patients indicate an absence of very high spatial frequencies from palinopsia. This anomalous bridge between normal visual functions and hallucinations leaves us to wonder about the physiology and psychophysics of "retinal" and "nonretinal" coordinates of the normal visual process. There is ample clinical evidence for the relevance of the concept of a loosely retinotopic, piecewise "local" Fourier analysis to the processing of visual images (Bodis-Wollner & Bender, 1973; Bodis-Wollner & Camisa, 1981). The neuronal ensembles participating in this analysis have been defined (Andrews & Pollen, 1979; DeValois, DeValois, & Yund, 1979; Pollen & Ronner, 1980) but it is not known which neuronal ensembles cooperate to establish the egocentric coordinate system of vision (Hein & Diamond, 1972; Held, 1968). It is known that some parameters of ordinary afterimages are not immune to changes of body position (Gregory, Wallace, & Campbell, 1959). By using techniques pioneered by Kohler (1962), this observation may provide a clue for further psychophysical studies to explore whether short-term plasticity affects afterimages and ordinary vision similarly. Investigating the role of vestibular-visual interactions and roll vection (Dichgans & Brandt, 1978; Leibowitz, Post, Rodemer, Wadlington, & Lundy, 1980) on afterimages could be helpful, in addition to studies of patients, as outlined above. These may help to develop paradigms to study the nonretinal coordinate system of vision in man. Our feeling is that the egocentric space, as conceptualized by Richards (1975), may be one, perhaps the first of many "nonretinal" stages of imagery.

ACKNOWLEDGMENTS

This work was supported in part by grant no. EY01708 of the National Eye Institute; grant no. NS11631 of the Clinical Center for Research in Parkinson's and Allied Diseases; Core Center grant no. EY01867 of the National Eye Institute; and N.I.H. grant no. RR-00071, Division of Research Resources, General Clinical Research Center Branch.

Ivan Bodis-Wollner thanks Dr. D. A. Pollen for allowing him to examine his patient, Dr. N. Christoff for a critical review of an earlier version of the manuscript; and Dr. M. Barris for helpful suggestions on the final version of the paper.

REFERENCES

Andrews, B. W., & Pollen, D. A. Relationship between spatial frequency selectivity and receptive field profile of simple cells. *Journal of Physiology*, 1979, *287*, 163–176.

Bekèny, G., & Pèter, A. Über Polyopie und Palinopsie. *Psychiatrie und Neurologie Basel*, 1961, *142*, 154–175.

Bender, M. B. Polyopia and monocular diplopia of cerebral origin. *Archives of Neurology and Psychiatry*, 1945, *54*, 323–338.

Bender, M. B., Feldman, M., & Sobin, A. J. Palinopsia. *Brain*, 1968, *9*, 321–338.

Bender, M. B., & Sobin, A. J. Polyopia and palinopia in homonymous fields of vision. *Transactions of the American Neurological Association*, 1963, *88*, 56–59.

Bodis-Wollner, I. *Spatial discrimination of the rod afterimage*. A.R.V.O. Annual Meeting, Sarasota, Fla., 1971.

Bodis-Wollner, I., & Bender, M. B. Neuroophthalmology: Electrophysiology and psychophysics of acuity and contrast detection. *Progress in Neurology and Psychiatry*, 1973, *38*, 93–115.

Bodis-Wollner, I., & Camisa, J. Contrast sensitivity measurements in clinical diagnosis. In S. Lessell & J. van Dalen (Eds.), *Handbook of neuroophthalmology* (Vol. I). Amsterdam: Excerpta Medica, 1980.

Cogan, D. G. Visual hallucinations as release phenomena. *Albrecht von Graefes Archiv für klinische und experimentelle Ophthalmologie*, 1973, *185*, 139–150.

Critchley, M. Metamorphopsia of central origin. *Transactions of the Ophthalmological Society of the United Kingdom*, 1949, *69*, 111–121.

Critchley, M. Types of visual perseveration; "palinopsia" and illusory visual spread. *Brain*, 1951, *74*, 267–299.

DeValois, K. K., DeValois, R. L., & Yund, E. W. Responses of striate cortex cells to grating and checkerboard patterns. *Journal of Physiology*, 1979, *291*, 483–505.

Dichgans, J., & Brandt, Th. Visual-vestibular interaction: effects on self-motion perception and postural control. In R. Held, H. Leibowitz, & H. L. Teuber (Eds.), *Handbook of sensory physiology* (Vol. 8), *Perception*. Heidelberg: Springer, 1978.

Dick, A. O. Iconic memory and its relation to perceptual processing and other memory mechanisms. *Perception & Psychophysics*, 1974, *16*, 575–596.

Feldman, M., & Bender, M. B. Visual illusions and hallucinations in parieto-occipital lesions of the brain. In W. Keup (Ed.), *Origins and mechanisms of hallucinations*. New York: Plenum Press, 1970.

Gloning, I., Gloning, K., & Weingarten, K. Über occipitale Polyopie. *Wiener Zeitschrift für Nervenheilkunde und deren Grenzgebiete* 1957, *13*, 224–235.

Gowers, W. R. The Bowman lecture on subjective visual sensations. *The Lancet*, 1895, *1*, 1564–1625.

Green, D. G. Regional variations in the visual acuity for interference fringes on the retina. *Journal of Physiology*, 1970, *207*, 351–356.

Gregory, R. L., Wallace, J. G., & Campbell, F. W. Changes in the size and shape of visual after-images observed in complete darkness during changes of position in space. *Quarterly Journal of Experimental Psychology*, 1959, *11*, 54–55.

Hein, A., & Diamond, R. M. Locomotory space as a prerequisite for acquiring visually guided reaching in kittens. *Journal of Comparative Physiology and Psychology*, 1972, *81*, 394–398.

Held, R. Dissociation of visual functions by deprivation and rearrangement. *Psychologische Forschung*, 1968, *31*, 338–348.

Hoff, H., & Pötzl, O. Über Polyopie und gerichtete hemianopische Halluzinationen. *Jahrbücher für Psychiatrie und Neurologie*, 1937, *54*, 55–88.

Jacobs, L., Feldman, M., Diamond, S. P., & Bender, M. B. Palinacousis: persistent or recurring auditory sensations. *Cortex*, 1973, *9*, 275–287.

Jung, R. Translokation corticaler Migrainephosphene bei Augenbewegungen und vestibulären Reizen. *Neuropsychologia*, 1979, *17*, 173–185.

Kinsbourne, M., & Warrington, E. K. A study of visual preservation. *Journal of Neurology, Neurosurgery and Psychiatry*, 1963, *26*, 468–475.

Kohler, I. Experiments with goggles. *Scientific American*, 1962, *206/5*, 63–72.

Lance, J. W. Simple formed hallucinations confined to the area of a specific visual field defect. *Brain*, 1976, *99*, 719–734.

Leibowitz, H. W., Post, R. B., Rodemer, C. S., Wadlington, W. L., & Lundy, R. M. Roll vection analysis of suggestion-induced visual field narrowing. *Perception & Psychophysics*, 1980, *28*, 173–176.

Lundh, B. L., Derefeldt, G., Nyberg, S., & Lennerstrand, G. Picture simulation of contrast sensitivity in organic and functional amblyopia. *Acta Ophthalmologica*. 1981, *59*, 777–783.

Meadows, J. C., & Munro, S. S. F. Palinopsia. *Journal of Neurology, Neurosurgery and Psychiatry*, 1977, *40*, 5–8.

Meyer, G. E., & Maguire, W. M. Spatial frequency and the mediation of short-term visual storage. *Science*, 1977, *198*, 524–525.

Michel, E. M., & Troost, B. T. Palinopsia: cerebral localization with computed tomography. *Neurology.*, 1980, *30*, 887–889.

Pötzl, O. Über Palinopsie. *Wiener Zeitschrift für Nervenheilkunde und deren Grenzgebiete*, 1954, *8*, 161–186.

Pollen, D. A., & Ronner, S. F. Phase relationships between adjacent simple cells in the visual cortex. *Science*, 1981, *212*, 1409–1411.

Richards, W. Visual space perception. In E. C. Carterette & M. P. Friedman (Eds.), *Handbook of perception* (Vol. 5), *Seeing*. New York: Academic Press, 1975.

Rushton, W. A. H. Bleached rhodopsin and visual adaptation. *Journal of Physiology,* 1965, *181,* 645–655.

Sperling, G. The information available in brief visual presentations. *Psychological Monographs,* 1960, *74,* 1–29.

Stromeyer, C. F., III, & Psotka, J. The detailed texture of eidetic images. *Nature,* 1970, *225,* 346–349.

Swash, M. Visual preservation in temporal lobe epilepsy. *Journal of Neurology, Neurosurgery and Psychiatry,* 1979, *42,* 569–571.

Turvey, M. T. Contrasting orientations to the theory of visual information processing. *Psychological Review,* 1977, *84,* 67–88.

40

Abnormal Visual Threshold Functions in Subjects with Lesions of the Central Visual Pathways

K. H. Ruddock
Depts. Physics (Biophysics) and
Pure and Applied Biology
Imperial College
London, U.K.

ABSTRACT

Psychophysical studies on two subjects, each with a different lesion of the central visual pathways, are reviewed. One subject, G, suffers right homonymous hemianopia following accidental damage to the left optic radiation and/or visual cortex and the other, M, has a defect of a kind not previously described. The hemianope can detect and locate flashed or moving targets presented in his "blind" hemifield, but under the experimental conditions employed he exhibits no pattern or shape discrimination in response to such stimuli. G's threshold detection 30° off-axis in the "blind" hemifield is characterized by low sensitivity and large spatial summation and these features of his visual responses are examined in relation to a modified Fechner threshold function. The central feature of M's visual responses is a spreading inhibition elicited by chromatic, particularly red, stimuli, as a result of which his detection of high contrast targets located up to 12° from the inhibitory stimulus is suppressed. With the significant exception of fusion of two-color random dot stereograms, all of M's visual functions measured with colored lights are more or less abnormal, whereas those measured with white light are normal. Detailed incremental thresholds for the two subjects are presented and the factors which control their threshold functions are examined. The functional organization of the central visual pathways implied by the response characteristics of these two subjects is discussed.

677

INTRODUCTION

The mechanisms by which the brain interprets retinal images are still only partly understood, but considerable progress has been achieved in the analysis of the afferent pathways which perform the initial stages of visual image processing. Electrophysiological and anatomical studies on both cat and primates have shown that there is multiple mapping of the visual field onto the cortex (e.g. Hubel & Wiesel, 1968; Talbot & Marshall, 1941; Zeki, 1978) and that single neurons located in these areas exhibit considerable specificity in their responses to different kinds of light stimuli. For example, many neurons located in the striate cortex respond strongly only when stimulated by a bar pattern of specific width and orientation. There is also an ordered map of the visual field on the superficial layers of the superior colliculus (Cynader & Berman, 1972), the single cells of which respond selectively to transient stimulation and, in some cases, possess large receptive fields (Goldberg & Wurtz, 1972; Schiller & Körner, 1971). The projection to the superior colliculus is derived primarily from Y-type retinal ganglion cells (de Monasterio, 1978; Weller, Kaas & Wetzel, 1979).

Ablation of the visual cortex leads initially to loss of visual discriminations, but if the animal is subjected to visual testing, considerable recovery of function may occur (e.g. Cowey, 1967; Weiskrantz, 1972). Such recovery depends upon the integrity of the prestriate cortical regions (Pasik & Pasik, 1971), and it seems likely that it is mediated by retinal projections via the superior colliculus. Ablation of the superior colliculus alone causes somewhat subtle changes in the properties of visually controlled eye movements, but they are significantly impaired if corresponding projection areas of both the superior colliculus and the striate cortex are removed (Mohler & Wurtz, 1977). Thus, ablation studies indicate that the retinal projection via the LGN to the striate cortex mediates discrimination between retinal image parameters, whereas that to the superior colliculus controls visual spatial localization (Schneider, 1969; Sprague, 1966). The two projections operate in a complementary manner, however, and Mohler and Wurtz's results imply that if one is impaired, its function can be assumed, at least partially, by the other. Unfortunately, ablation techniques have not so far been sufficiently precise for the removal of areas in the prestriate cortex corresponding to a single field map, thus the intriguing proposal that independent parametric processing occurs in the different cortical maps has not been tested in this way.

In humans, damage to the visual cortex appears to give rise to permanent scotomata (Holmes, 1918; Teuber, Battersby, & Bender, 1960), which may cover the whole visual field (Brindley, Gautier-Smith, & Lewin, 1969). It was noted, however, that flashed or moving targets were detected by some subjects even when presented within an area covered by such a scotoma (Riddoch, 1917) and recently, several groups of investigators have shown that subjects with hemianopic field losses associated with cortical lesions can locate light stimuli presented to the "blind" hemifield (Perenin & Jeannerod, 1978; Pöppel, Held, & Frost, 1973; Weiskrantz, Warrington, Sanders, & Marshall, 1974). The subject studied by Weiskrantz et al. was able to discriminate the orientation, spatial distribution and, to a limited extent, the color of stimuli presented in his "blind" hemifield. There is clearly a parallel between visual function observed in animals following surgical ablation of the visual cortical projection area and the responses to "blind" field stimulation exhibited by human subjects, and this was reinforced by the finding that "blindsight" responses in humans improves with training (Zihl, 1980; Zihl & von Cramon, 1980). Visual functions elicited in the presence of blindness caused by cerebral damage are generally attributed to the activity of retinal projections to the mid-brain, although indirect cortical stimulation by signals transmitted from the mid-brain projection areas via the pulvinar may be essential for such functions.

In this chapter, psychophysical data are presented for visual threshold responses in two subjects, each with a different functional lesion of the visual pathways. One, a hemianope, has a lesion of the left optic radiation and the other exhibits response characteristics which suggest a lesion localized to a cortical region concerned with the representation of stimulus color.

METHODS

The incremental threshold data to be presented in the Results section were, in the main, obtained using a four-beam Maxwellian view optical system, which has been described in detail elsewhere (Barbur & Ruddock, 1980). The data presented in Fig. 40.3 and 40.4 were, however, measured using the tristimulus colorimeter designed by Prof. W. D. Wright (Wright 1927–28, 1946). In both instruments, the subjects viewed the stimuli through the fixed diameter instrumental exit pupil, and correct eye position was maintained by the subject's biting on a dental clamp. The same method was used throughout in the determination of threshold detection illumination levels. At the start of each measurement, the target illumination was set at a level such that the subject could readily detect it. The subject controlled the target illumination and was instructed to reduce it until the target could just no longer be detected. The target presentation was repeated until the subject obtained the required threshold setting. Both observers have been the subject of previously published reports and the principal conclusions of these earlier studies, which are essential to discussion of the new data, are reviewed briefly below.

Subjects

(A) G., a 23-year old male, suffered damage to the left optic radiation and/or visual cortex in a car accident which occurred when he was 8 years old. Specifically, a car bumper sliced into the brain behind the left ear and although brain scans of the damaged area are not available, the functional consequences are clear. Since the accident, he has exhibited a right homonymous hemianopia, with sparing of the right visual field for some 3° to 4° around the fixation point. The following are the principal features of G's psychophysical responses to stimuli located in his "blind" hemifield (see Barbur, Ruddock, & Waterfield, 1980, for details).

1. He can detect flashed and moving spots of light, and can locate flashed spots positioned up to 25° away from the fovea along the horizontal meridian with an accuracy of ± 1°. Such stimuli are perceived by G. as a shadow for near threshold illumination, and as a bright flash at higher levels.
2. Detection of stimuli presented to his "blind" hemifield is not due to light scattered into the normal hemifield, and indeed, he can detect and locate dark targets moving against a bright background, in which case there can be no light scatter associated with the moving stimulus.
3. For a given background illumination, his incremental thresholds for detection in the "blind" hemifield are much higher than the corresponding values for the normal hemifield.
4. His threshold sensitivity for the detection of moving targets increases with increase in target speed, up to some 50 deg/sec. His ability to discriminate between targets moving with different velocities in his "blind" hemifield is the same as for normal vision.
5. Critical fusion frequency for detection of a 100% modulated light stimulus is restricted to low frequencies (< 8 Hz).
6. With targets centered 30° off-axis in the "blind" hemifield, he is unable to discriminate target shape or size.
7. Responses to targets 30° off-axis in the "blind" hemifield are mediated by the scotopic response system.

(B) M., a 29 year-old male, has throughout his life suffered a severe color vision deficiency associated primarily with detection of red objects, but his visual responses are not characteristic of any previously described defect. He suffers no known ophthalmological or medical abnormality, and the defect has not been found in other members of his family. The origins of the defect are therefore unknown, but it has remained completely stable during 10 years of investigation at Imperial College. The principal features of M's visual responses which have been published elsewhere (Barbur, Ruddock, & Waterfield, 1979; Bender & Ruddock, 1974; Hendricks, Holliday, & Ruddock, 1981; Ruddock & Waterfield, 1978) can be summarized as follows:

1. A red ($\lambda > 610$ nm) object placed anywhere in the visual field elicits a grossly abnormal response, leading to the sensation of a blurred, greyish area which may spread for up to 12° from the stimulus edge. M's detection of high-contrast black and white targets is grossly impaired if such targets are placed within this blurred, greyish area. Red stimuli therefore appear to produce a potent spreading inhibitory response.

2. M's sensitivity for detection of near monochromatic stimuli is much lower than that of normal subjects, and for red ($\lambda \geq 620$ nm) stimuli, is some 10^5 less than the normal value.

3. Foveal color matching is dichromatic for both 2° and 10° bipartite fields, and two-color increment threshold measurements using the variable background method (Stiles 1959, 1978) reveal the activity of two mechanisms, corresponding to the π_1 and π_5 mechanisms of normal color vision.

4. Foveal spatial resolution for near-monochromatic targets is significantly reduced relative to that for normal subjects, and for stimulus wavelengths ≥ 600 nm, M can resolve square waveform gratings only when their bar-width is greater than about 1°.

5. Movement of red objects in M's visual field gives only a small increase in detection sensitivity.

6. M can fuse and identify two-color random dot stereograms (anaglyphs; Julesz, 1971), even though he is unable to resolve any structure in the image component seen through the red transmission filter (in our experiments, a 630 nm, narrow-band interference filter).

7. M's visual defect is bilateral and covers the whole of the visual field. The inhibitory effects elicited by red stimuli are transferred interocularly.

In this chapter, data are also given for a number of subjects with normal vision.

AIMS OF THE PRESENT INVESTIGATION

In the Introduction it was noted that the two subjects of the present study possess visual functional lesions and they may thus provide psychophysical data complementary to those obtained in animal ablation studies. G's lesion is well defined and his "blind" field responses reviewed above are restricted to detection and location of flashed or moving targets, without discrimination of other stimulus parameters such as spatial size or shape. Responses of this kind are consistent with vision mediated through pathways which possess an ordered visual field map and respond only to transient stimulation, properties which are characteristic of neuronal responses in the retino-collicular projection (see Introduction).

The cause of subject M's abnormal visual responses is not known, but the experimental data reviewed above suggest that they arise centrally in the visual pathways. Thus, M has very low spatial resolution for red stimulus patterns, but he can nonetheless identify correctly two-color random dot stereograms, even though he fails to resolve the images seen through the red filter. This implies that the inhibition elicited by red stimuli arises centrally with respect to the point at which signals from the two eyes meet to produce stereoscopic depth information. M's pupillary function is normal for all stimulus wavelengths which establishes that some signals leaving the retina are entirely normal. Furthermore, the inhibi-

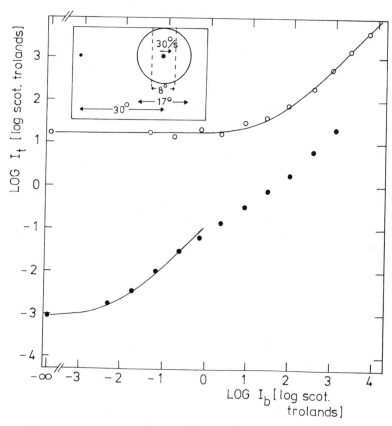

FIG. 40.1.   Log increment threshold illumination, log I_t, for detection of a moving target, plotted against log background illumination, log I_b. A 512nm, 3.5° diameter circular target moved at 30°/sec along the horizontal meridian, at the center of a 495nm, 17° diameter circular background field. The target moved through 8° of visual angle, from 26° to 34° off-axis along the temporal horizontal meridian (see inset). Each data point is the mean of five or more readings, with the typical standard error .02 log unit (subject G) and .01 log unit (subject I.H.) Open circles; subject G ("blind" hemifield);
full circles; normal subject I.H.
The curves represent the threshold function ($I_b + I_D$).

tory effect spreads over visual field areas considerably greater than the receptive field area of primate retinal ganglion cells.

The work presented here deals with the threshold detection characteristics of the two subjects. Detailed measurements of threshold detection illumination levels are presented in the Results section, and the significance of the data is examined in the Discussion section.

RESULTS

Threshold data for subject G were determined for targets centered 30° off-axis along the horizontal meridian, in the "blind" hemifield. The target was imaged onto the nasal retina of the right eye and fixation was maintained by means of a dim, red .6° diameter fixation target. Threshold illumination for G's detection of a circular target of 3.5° diameter, moving at 30 deg/sec along the horizontal meridian, is plotted against the illumination level, I_b, of the background field (Fig. 40.1; see inset for stimulus configuration). Corresponding values are also given for a subject with normal vision. For zero background illumination ($\log I_b \rightarrow -\infty$), threshold illumination, $\log I_t$, for G's "blind" hemifield is more than four log units greater than that for normal vision, and for the normal subject, $\log I_t$ starts to rise from its minimum level at considerably lower background illuminations than for the hemianopic subject. Despite these differences, the shape of the curve relating $\log I_t$ to $\log I_b$ is similar for both subjects, although the change of slope in I.H's data at $\log I_b$ equal to about $-.5$ indicates a change from one threshold response mechanism to another (Stiles, 1959).

The influence of stimulus *area* on G's "blind" field threshold for detection of a flashed target was investigated by measurement of $\log I_t$ as a function of both target area (Fig. 40.2a) and background field area (Fig. 40.2b). Both sets of data exhibit extensive spatial summation, with increase in the target area, A_s, causing $\log I_t$ to fall, and increase in the background field area, A_b, causing I_t to rise. Log I_t is related to $\log A_s$ by the straight line ($\log I_t = -1.07 \log A_s + $ constant) (Fig. 40.2a), which corresponds closely to Ricco's law of spatial summation, ($A_s I_t = $ constant) over the whole range of target areas investigated. The data presented in Fig. 40.2a refer to 512 nm stimuli and similar results have been obtained with white light (Barbur, Ruddock, & Waterfield, 1980). For the normal subject, J.B., the two variables are more nearly related by the line ($\log I_t = -\frac{1}{2} \log A_s + $ constant) which corresponds to Piper's law. In the case of the data for different background areas, $\log I_t$ for subject G increases more rapidly for small background field areas, A_b, than is predicted from the simple summation law ($\log I_t = \log A_b + $ constant), but follows this line for $\log A_b > .8$. In contrast, $\log I_t$ values for the normal subject I.H. are essentially independent of A_b, except when this is significantly smaller than the area of the test stimulus.

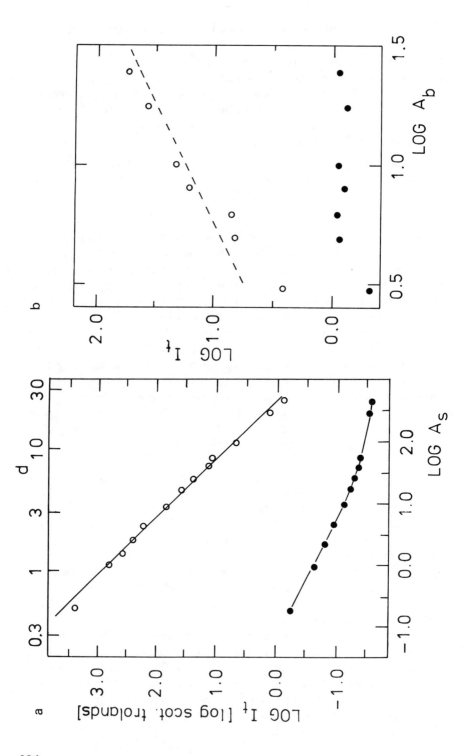

Subject M

M's increment thresholds were measured for foveally fixated targets and the experiments were concerned primarily with the influence of stimulus wavelength. Irradiation levels, (E_λ), for detection of a flashed (.5s on, .5s off) target were measured as a function of wavelength, λ. Spectral threshold sensitivity, S_λ, defined as $(E_\lambda)^{-1}$, is plotted against λ in Fig. 40.3. Values are given for M and for the normal subject, B.B., with the sensitivity scale normalized such that at λ = 570 nm, S_λ for B.B. is zero. M's low sensitivity for detection of all spectral stimuli but especially those in the long wavelength range, is clearly established by these data.

Increment threshold for detection of a 1° diameter circular target of wavelength λ, superimposed on a background of wavelength μ, is plotted as a function of log background illumination, log I_b, in Fig. 40.4. When the test and background wavelengths are the same ($\lambda = \mu$), there is, for long wavelength stimuli, a large fall in the increment threshold, I_t, as the background illumination, I_b, increases from zero (Fig. 40.4a). When the test and background wavelengths are different ($\lambda \neq \mu$), thresholds for detection of a red target (λ = 650 nm) show a similar fall for all background wavelengths though the value of I_b at which it occurs varies with μ (Fig. 40.4b). Threshold illumination, I_t, for detection of a circular white light target (diameter 3.5°; color temperature 3000 K) superimposed centrally on a white or red (636 nm) 17° diameter circular background field was determined as a function of log background illumination, log I_b.

FIG. 40.2.   Log threshold illumination, log I_t, for detection of a flashed target, plotted against stimulus area, A_s, in square deg. (lower scale) and stimulus diameter, d, in deg. (upper scale). The target was in each case centered 30° off-axis, along the temporal horizontal meridian. Each data point is the mean of five or more readings, with the standard error .03 log unit (subject G) and .01 (normal subject).

FIG. 40.2a.   Log I_t expressed in log scotopic trolands, plotted against log A_s, log of the area in square degrees of the circular test target. The test target was flashed for 10 ms every 2 s against a uniform 639 nm background field of illumination level .5 log scotopic troland.
Open circles   Subject G, "blind" hemifield, for a 512 nm test flash, with the line log $I_t = -1.07$ log A_s + (constant) drawn through the data points.
Full circles   Normal subject J.B.

FIG. 40.2b.   Log I_t, expressed in relative units, plotted against log A_b, log area of the circular background field expressed in square degrees. A 512 nm, 3.5° diameter circular test was flashed for 250 ms once every 3 s at the center of a 495 nm steady background field.
Open circles   Subject G, "blind" hemifield.
Closed circles   Normal subject I.H.
The broken line plots log $I_t = $ log A_b + (constant.)

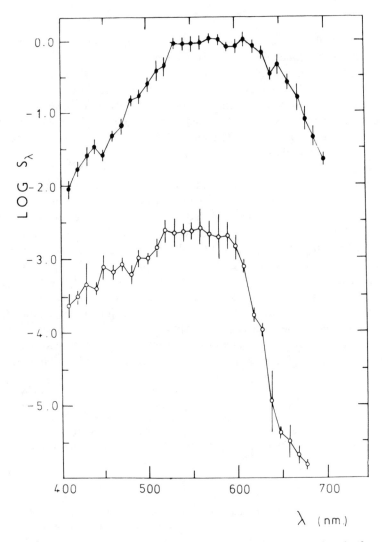

FIG. 40.3. Log relative foveal threshold sensitivity, log S_λ, for detection of a 1° diameter circular test, plotted against test wavelength, λ. The test was flashed for .5s. each s., and was fixated by means of four dim, white light spots located around it.

Open circles Subject M

Closed circles Normal subject B.B.

Each point is the mean of three readings, the spread of which is shown by the error bars.

Data for M and for a subject with normal vision, I.H., are plotted in Fig. 40.5a and show that for the white light target, the two subjects have similar thresholds for zero background illumination, whereas with white background fields, M's thresholds are slightly higher than I.H's. The red background field, however, produces a much greater increase in M's threshold settings than in those of I.H.

One of the principal features of M's visual responses (see Methods) is the spreading inhibition associated with detection of red stimuli and in order to obtain a quantitative measure of this effect, threshold was measured for M's detection of a circular green target (1.4° diameter, 524 nm) located at the center of a circular annulus (inner diameter 3°, outer diameter 8°). The data (Fig. 40.5b) establish that for subject M, threshold illumination, I_t, increases significantly with increase in the illumination level of the surrounding annulus, the effect being more marked for a 636 nm annulus (full squares) than for a 536 nm annulus (open squares). In contrast, threshold detection levels of the normal subject, I.H., are virtually independent of the annular illumination level.

DISCUSSION

The results show that each subject exhibits well-defined, but highly unusual threshold response characteristics. Consideration is given first to the data of subject G, who suffered a deep incision into the left cerebral hemisphere just to the rear of the left ear. G's response to flashed and moving targets presented in his "blind" hemifield are attributed, therefore, to retinal signals which project via the mid-brain and these responses are characterized by low threshold sensitivity (Fig. 40.1) and extensive spatial summation (Fig. 40.2). Incremental threshold illumination, I_t, for a target superimposed on a background of illumination, I_b, can be described, empirically, by the equation:

$$I_t = k \, (I_b + I_D) \tag{1}$$

I_D represents the dark noise which sets the value of I_t for zero background illumination and k is a constant which defines the "signal to noise" ratio for threshold detection. Equation 1 can be rewritten

$$\log I_t = \log k + \log I_D + \log (1 + I_b/I_D) \tag{2}$$

and when I_b is zero

$$\log I_t = \log k + \log I_D. \tag{3}$$

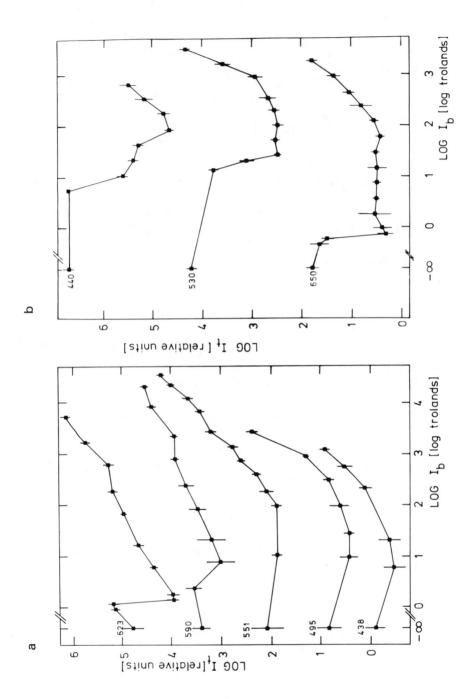

If I_D is increased by a factor K, the threshold illumination, I_t, is given by

$$\log I_t = \log k + \log K + \log I_D + \log (1 + I_b/I_D) \tag{4}$$

and with I_b equal to zero, this becomes

$$\log I_t = \log k + \log K + \log I_D. \tag{5}$$

Equations 3 and 5 show that for zero background illumination, a K-fold increase in I_D raises log threshold illumination by a factor $\log K$. Equations 2 and 4 establish that the shape of the curve which relates $\log I_t$ to $\log I_b$ is unchanged by an increase in I_D, because a K-fold increase in the background illumination, which corresponds to a shift of $\log K$ along the $\log I_b$ axis, gives Equation 4 the same form as Equation 2.

This analysis can be applied to the $\log I_t$ versus $\log I_b$ plots shown in Fig. 40.1. The function $\log (I_b + I_D)$ describes reasonably well both G's data and the normal data for $\log I_B < .8$, but at higher values of $\log I_b$, there appears to be a switch between threshold response mechanisms for the normal. Thus, qualitatively, the difference between the threshold data for the two subjects can be attributed to an increase in the dark noise, I_D, for subject G. Quantitatively, threshold at zero background field for subject G is 4.3 log units greater than for the normal, which corresponds to $\log K$ equal to 4.3 (Equation 5). The curve for subject G is shifted by 3.7 log units along the $\log I_b$ axis, which corresponds to $\log K$ equal to 3.7 (Equation 4). The two estimates of $\log K$ differ by .6, that is, the relative shift of G's data along the $\log I_t$ axis is .6 log unit greater than that along the $\log I_b$ axis. In terms of the threshold Equation 2, this means that the signal to noise ratio, k, for G's "blind" field is increased fourfold (i.e., an increase of .6 in $\log k$) relative to the normal value. An alternative analysis of incremental threshold data has been presented by Alpern, Rushton, and Torii (1970a,b). This involves two parameters, however, and predictions based on their analysis are therefore less specific.

FIG. 40.4.   Log threshold, $\log I_t$, for detection of a 1° diameter circular test plotted against log background field illumination, $\log I_b$. The test was flashed for .5s each s at the center of a steady, 7° diameter circular background field. Each point is the mean of three readings, with spread indicated by the error bars. Both sets of curves have been displaced along the $\log I_t$ scale for clarity. Subject M.

FIG. 40.4a.   Test and background wavelengths were the same, with the wavelength value indicated on the diagrams.

FIG. 40.4b.   The test wavelength was 650 nm and the background wavelength is given in the figure.

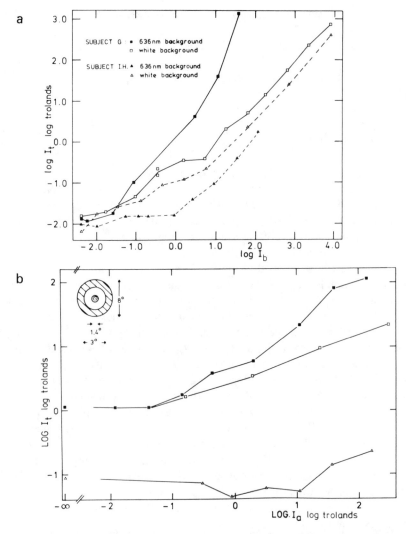

FIG. 40.5. Log threshold illumination, log I_t, for detection of a test field, plotted against log background illumination, log I_b. Each point is the mean of five readings, with typical standard error .02 log unit.

FIG. 40.5a. Data for a foveally fixated, 3.5° circular white light target, flashed for 300ms every 3 s in the center of a steady 17° background of illumination I_b trolands. *Full squares,* subject M, background field wavelength 636 nm, *open squares,* subject M, white light background; *full triangles,* normal subject I.H., background wavelength 636 nm; *open triangles,* normal subject I.H., white light background.

FIG. 40.5b. Data for detection of a 1.4° diameter, 524nm circular target, flashed for 300 ms every 3 s, at the center of an annulus (inner diameter, 3°, outer diameter 8°) of illumination level I_a trolands. *Full squares,* subject M, 636nm annulus; *open squares,* subject M, 536nm annulus; *open triangles,* normal subject I.H., 636 annulus.

For subject G, linear spatial summation corresponding to Ricco's law ($I_t A_s$ is constant, Fig. 40.2) extends to target illuminations of 3 log scotopic trolands (Fig. 40.2). The photoreceptor signals elicited by the test flashes are pooled to give the threshold signal and a linear relationship between test area and illumination level implies that the photoreceptor signals are proportional to the stimulus illumination. G's data show, therefore, that receptor signal linearity extends to at least 3 log scotopic trolands for the 10 msec flashes used in these experiments. Alpern, Rushton and Torii (1970a), evaluated the half-saturation constant, σ, for human rods as 200 scotopic trolands-s which for a 10 ms flash corresponds to a target illumination level of 4.3 log scotopic trolands. Signal linearity occurs for stimulus illumination levels significantly smaller than σ; thus the range of linearity implied by G's data is consistent with the σ value. The target area over which G's thresholds exhibit linearity, corresponding to circular fields of diameter .48° to 24°, far exceeds the normal Ricco summation area, which for circular fields extends at most to 2° diameter (e.g. Hallett, Marriott, & Rodger, 1962).

The retinal projection responsible for G's "blind" field vision must therefore possess mechanisms with much greater spatial summation capacity than the retino-cortical projection. It is noteworthy that some single units in the superior colliculus possess very large receptive fields (up to 225⁰², Marrocco & Li, 1977) which is one reason for attributing G's "blind" field responses to activity in the retino-collicular projection. The existence of such large receptive field summation does not, however, preclude G's observed ability to specify accurately the location of targets in his "blind" hemifield, as the superficial cells of the superior colliculus carry a well-defined visual field map (Cynader & Berman, 1972; Goldberg & Wurtz, 1972). It has been shown that G's visual thresholds imply an abnormally high dark noise, I_D, and this may arise because of spatial summation of the "dark current" arising in the small Ricco summation areas of normal vision. Both normal and hemianopic subjects exhibit spatial summation of background field illumination for small background fields (Fig. 40.2b), but only the hemianope, G, exhibits summation for large background fields. In this latter case, the experimental data follow Ricco's law and are, therefore, consistent with the existence of extended spatial pooling of signals by G's "blind" field response mechanisms.

In general, subject M responds normally to white light stimuli, but abnormally to colored lights (see Methods section) and this response pattern is reflected in the threshold data of Figs 40.3–40.5. These show that when used as test flashes, colored lights yield very low response sensitivity (Fig. 40.3) but when used as the background or as a masking surround annulus, they are abnormally effective in raising threshold for detection of a test flash (Fig. 40.5). In contrast, white test flashes superimposed on a white background elicit essentially normal responses (Fig. 40.5a). These observations imply that colored, and especially red, lights have an abnormally large inhibitory influence on M's visual responses. The resulting incremental threshold data, particularly those of the kind shown in Fig. 40.4, cannot be analyzed in terms of the generalized Weber-

Fechner law given by Equation 1, which predicts a monotonic relationship between I_t and I_b.

M's results therefore characterize an inhibitory response mechanism involved only in the detection of colored lights. The spread of inhibition revealed by incremental thresholds for an annular background field (Fig. 40.5b) establishes that this mechanism gives rise to extensive spatial interactions. M perceives a red stimulus as a diffuse, silvery-grey patch which covers an area much larger than the stimulus area and which in some cases extends up to 12° beyond the limits of the stimulus itself. Correspondingly, M's detection of high-contrast black and white targets located within this silvery-grey area is suppressed (Hendricks, Holliday, & Ruddock, 1981). Thus, it appears that inhibitory signals generate M's silvery-grey percept. The highly abnormal incremental responses observed for detection of red test flashes (Fig. 40.4) are, therefore, a property of the inhibitory mechanism.

Unlike G's "blind" field responses, which correlate reasonably well with single unit data recorded from the superior colliculus, M's visual responses cannot be readily related to the results of any electrophysiological investigation. Thus, although in primates color-selective response units with inhibitory receptive field areas are observed in the retina (de Monasterio & Gouras, 1975), LGN (Hubel & Wiesel, 1966), and striate cortex (Gouras, 1974), their inhibitory receptive fields are much too small to correlate with M's spreading inhibition. Further, it has been argued in the Methods section that M's abnormal function arises centrally relative to the site of stereoscopic fusion, which in primates is in the prestriate cortex (Hubel & Wiesel, 1970). A better candidate for the site of M's defect is the V4 prestriate area, in which some 60% of neurons exhibit color selective responses (Zeki, 1978). Receptive fields of V4 units are also relatively large, although not sufficiently large to explain the observed spread of M's inhibition (Zeki, 1980).

The data presented in this chapter illustrate the way in which studies on subjects with visual anomalies can provide novel information about the organization of the human visual system. A further example of this approach is the analysis of threshold data for amblyopic and albino subjects in terms of parallel X- and Y-type pathways (Barbur, Holliday, Ruddock, & Waterfield, 1980; Grounds, Holliday, & Ruddock, 1981).

ACKNOWLEDGMENTS

I am indebted to the two principal subjects of this study, G. and M., who have over a period of years voluntarily and generously devoted considerable periods of their spare time to carrying out experiments at Imperial College. I thank Dr. T. D. H. Gray for providing details about G's medical history and I also wish to acknowledge the collaboration of Dr. J. L. Barbur, now at City University, London; Dr. Vicki A. Barbur (Waterfield) now at the Research Laboratories, Kodak LTD., Harrow; Miss Isobel Hendricks and Mr. I. E. Holliday, both of this department, in the experiments which form the basis of this paper.

REFERENCES

Alpern, M., Rushton, W. A. H., & Torii, S. The size of rod signals. *Journal of Physiology, London*, 1970, *206*, 193–208. (a)

Alpern, M., Rushton, W. A. H., & Torii, S. The attenuation of rod signals by backgrounds. *Journal of Physiology, London*, 1970, *206*, 209–227. (b)

Barbur, J. L., Holliday, I. E., Ruddock, K. H., & Waterfield, V. A. Spatial characteristics of movement detection mechanisms in human vision III. Subjects with abnormal visual pathways. *Biological Cybernetics*, 1980, *37*, 99–105.

Barbur, J. L., & Ruddock, K. H. Spatial characteristics of movement detection mechanisms in human vision *I* Achromatic vision. *Biological Cybernetics*, 1980, *37*, 77–92.

Barbur, J. L., Ruddock, K. H., & Waterfield, V. A. A colour-dependent abnormality in the human visual detection of stimulus motion and spatial structure. *Neuroscience Letters*, 1979, *15*, 307–312.

Barbur, J. L., Ruddock, K. H., & Waterfield, V. A. Human visual responses in the absence of the geniculo-calcarine projection. *Brain*, 1980, *103*, 905–928.

Bender, B. G., & Ruddock, K. H. The characteristics of a visual defect associated with abnormal responses to both colour and luminance. *Vision Research*, 1974, *14*, 383–393.

Brindley, G. S., Gautier-Smith, P. C., & Lewin, W. Cortical blindness and the functions of the non-geniculate fibres of the optic tracts. *Journal of Neurology, Neurosurgery and Psychiatry*, 1969, *32*, 259–264.

Cowey, A. Perimetric study of field defects in monkeys after cortical and retinal ablation. *Quarterly Journal of Experimental Psychology*, 1967, *19*, 232–245.

Cynader, M., & Berman, M. Receptive field organisation of monkey superior colliculus. *Journal of Neurophysiology*, 1972, *35*, 187–201.

de Monasterio, F. M. Properties of ganglion cells with atypical receptive field organization in the retina of macaques. *Journal of Neurophysiology*, 1978, *41*, 1435–1449.

de Monasterio, F. M., & Gouras, P. Functional properties of ganglion cells in rhesus monkey retina. *Journal of Physiology, London*, 1975, *251*, 167–195.

Goldberg, M. E., & Wurtz, R. H., Activity of the superior colliculus in behaving monkeys I. Visual receptive fields of single neurons. *Journal of Neurophysiology*, 1972, *35*, 542–559.

Gouras, P. Opponent colour cells in different layers of foveal striate cortex. *Journal of Physiology, London*, 1974, *238*, 583–602.

Grounds, A., Holliday, I. E., & Ruddock, K. H. Selective modification of visual response mechanisms in amblyopes. *Abstracts of 4th European Conference on Visual Perception*, 1981.

Hallett, P. E., Marriott, F. H. C., & Rodger, F. C. The relationship of visual threshold to retinal position and area. *Journal of Physiology, London*, 1962, *160*, 364–373.

Hendricks, I. M., Holliday, I. E., & Ruddock, K. H. A new class of visual defect: spreading inhibition elicited by chromatic light stimuli. *Brain*, 1981, *104*, 813–840.

Holmes, G. Disturbances of vision by cerebrate lesions *British Journal of Ophthalmology*, 1918, *2*, 353–384.

Hubel, D. H., & Wiesel, T. N. Spectral and chromatic interactions in the lateral geniculate body of the rhesus monkey. *Journal of Neurophysiology*, 1966, *29*, 1115–1156.

Hubel, D. H., & Wiesel, T. N. Receptive fields and functional architecture of monkey striate cortex. *Journal of Physiology, London*, 1968, *195*, 215–243.

Hubel, D. H., & Wiesel, T. N. Cells sensitive to binocular depth in area 18 of the macaque monkey cortex. *Nature*, 1970, *225*, 41–42.

Julesz, B. *Foundations of cyclopean perception.* Chicago: University of Chicago Press, 1971.

Marrocco, R. T., & Li, R. H. Monkey superior colliculus: properties of single cells and their afferent inputs. *Journal of Neurophysiology*, 1977, *40*, 844–860.

Mohler, C. W., & Wurtz, R. H. Role of striate cortex and superior colliculus in visual guidance of saccadic eye-movements in monkeys. *Journal of Neurophysiology*, 1977, *40*, 74–94.

Pasik, T., & Pasik, P. The visual world of monkeys deprived of striate cortex: effective stimulus parameters and the importance of the accessory optic system. *Vision Research*, 1971, Suppl 3, 419–435.

Perenin, M. T., & Jeannerod, M. Visual function within the hemianopic field following early cerebral hemicortication in man. *Neuropsychologia*, 1978, *32*, 1–13.

Pöppel, E., Held, R., & Frost, D. Residual visual function after brain wounds involving the central visual pathways in man. *Nature*, 1973, *243*, 295–296.

Riddoch, G. Dissociation of visual perceptions due to occipital injuries with especial reference to appreciation of movement. *Brain*, 1917, *40*, 15–57.

Ruddock, K. H., & Waterfield, V. A. Selective loss of function associated with a central visual defect. *Neuroscience Letters*, 1978, *8*, 93–98.

Schiller, P., & Körner, F. Discharge characteristics of single units in superior colliculus of the alert rhesus monkey. *Journal of Neurophysiology*, 1971, *34*, 920–936.

Schneider, G. Two visual systems. *Science*, 1969, *163*, 895–902.

Sprague, J. M. Interaction of cortex and superior colliculus in mediation of visually guided behaviour in the cat. *Science*, 1966, *153*, 1544–1547.

Stiles, W. S. Colour vision: the approach through increment threshold sensitivity. *Proceedings of the National Academy of Science*, 1959, *45*, 100–114.

Stiles, W. S. *Mechanisms of colour vision: selected papers of W. S. Stiles, F.R.S. with a new introductory essay.* London: Academic Press, 1978.

Talbot, S. A., & Marshall, W. H. Physiological studies of neural mechanisms of visual localization and discrimination. *American Journal of Ophthalmology*, 1941, *24*, 1255–1264.

Teuber, H. L., Battersby, W. S., & Bender, M. B. *Visual field defects after penetrating missile wounds of the brain.* Cambridge, Mass.: Harvard University Press, 1960.

Weiskrantz, L. Behavioural analysis of monkey's visual nervous system. *Proceedings of the Royal Society London*, 1972, *B 182*, 427–455.

Weiskrantz, L., Warrington, E. K., Sanders, M. D., & Marshall, J. Visual capacity in the hemianopic field following a restricted occipital ablation. *Brain*, 1974, *97*, 719–728.

Weller, R. E., Kaas, J. H., & Wetzel, A. B. Evidence for the loss of X-cells of the retina after long-term ablation of visual cortex in monkeys. *Brain Research*, 1979, *160*, 134–138.

Wright, W. D. A trichromatic colorimeter with spectral stimuli. *Transactions of the Optical Society of London*, 1927–28, *29*, 225–242.

Wright, W. D. *Researches on normal and defective colour vision*, Chapters 2 and 3. London: Kimpton, 1946.

Zeki, S. M. Uniformity and diversity of structure and function in rhesus pre-striate visual cortex. *Journal of Physiology*, London, 1978, *277*, 273–290.

Zeki, S. M. Representation of colours in the cerebral cortex. *Nature*, 1980, *284*, 412–418.

Zihl, J. "Blindsight": improvement of visually guided eye movements by systematic practice in patients with cerebral blindness. *Neuropsychologia*, 1980, *18*, 71–77.

Zihl, J., & von Cramon, D. Registration of light stimuli in the cortically blind hemifield and its effect on localization. *Behavioural Brain Research*, 1980, *1*, 287–298.

41

Subkortikale Funktionen der visuellen Wahrnehmung

J. Zihl
Neuropsychologische Abteilung
Max-Planck-Institut für Psychiatrie
München, West Germany

ABSTRACT

In recent years the concept of the neural organization of visual perception has undergone rapid changes. Based on neurophysiological studies in primates, it has been shown that visual information is mediated not only by the geniculostriate pathway (the "*first*" visual system) but also by the midbrain (superior colliculus) and the thalamus (nc. pulvinar, the so-called *second* visual system). Considerable spared visual capacity has been found in monkeys blinded after striate cortex lesions; such animals are able to detect and to localize visual stimuli. The monkeys were not able, however, to identify these stimuli.

By using methods that depend upon forced-choice procedures (analogous to those used with monkeys), rather than on verbal responses, it could be shown that brain-damaged patients have similar capacities.

These patients had lost large parts of their binocular visual field after damage (mostly of cerebrovascular origin) to the geniculostriate pathway. The lesions had been verified by computerized tomography.

The patients were able to localize light targets presented briefly in their perimetrically blind hemifield by finger pointing or by shifting their gaze towards them. When forced to localize these targets repeatedly in different sessions, they showed a marked improvement in their localization accuracy.

In further experiments, the phasic electrodermal response was used as an indicator for the registration of a light target presented in the hemianopic field region. The experiments showed a significant correlation between the occurrence of the phasic electrodermal response and the presentation of a light stimulus in the perimetrically blind field. This response—a component of the orienting reaction—does, therefore, not depend on the intact geniculostriate visual system.

Hemianopic patients were also able to indicate the presence of a light target in their "blind" hemifield by voluntary motor responses such as lid closure and bar pressing after they underwent specific practice. In contrast, they were unable to indicate the presence of a light target by a verbal response. This observation suggests that the mechanisms for language are not associated with the neural substrate underlying the detection and localization of light stimuli in the absence of the geniculostriate pathway.

It is interesting to note that patients could localize light targets within their hemianopic field quite accurately after they were trained to indicate the presence of the light stimulus. It is concluded that both detection and localization of visual stimuli are subserved by the same or related neural mechanisms. These capacities in an otherwise blind field region can only be demonstrated, however, when the patient is forced to use them, even though he never can "see" any light stimulus, and does not have any conscious experience of it.

These observations suggest that patients possess some visual capacities in their perimetrically blind field region. These capacities are similar to those observed in destriated monkeys. Both humans and animals need specific practice in order to make use of these capacities. It seems plausible that they are mediated by the "second" visual system, since the geniculostriate pathway was completely damaged in the patients tested.

This suggestion could be strengthened if one were able to demonstrate the reverse effect after lesions had damaged these phylogenetically older retino-tectal pathways. One would expect that such damage would not lead to visual field loss, but would disturb the detection of visual stimuli and would also affect orienting reactions towards them. In monkeys, such effects were observed after tectal or pulvinar lesions. In patients, lesions affecting only the superior colliculus or the nc. pulvinar are relatively scarce. Single case studies of patients suffering a tectal or pulvinar lesion are, therefore, of high value. Reports on a few cases support the suggestion mentioned above. These patients have difficulties detecting light stimuli in the periphery of the visual hemifield contralateral to the lesion when presented simultaneously in either half-field. They also cannot easily shift attention to the side contralateral to the lesion, or shift their gaze towards targets presented there.

Summarizing the observations obtained in both monkeys and humans after damage to the "first" or to the "second" visual system, one might conclude that the detection and localization of visual stimuli is subserved by extrageniculostriate neural mechanisms, whereas the identification of these stimuli depends crucially on the geniculostriate pathway.

For visual perception both the "first" and the "second" visual systems are needed. The detection of visual events and the shift of gaze towards them could be termed prerequisites for the analysis of these events.

1. EINLEITUNG

Bis vor wenigen Jahren herrschte in der Neuroophthalmologie die Auffassung vor, daß eine Schädigung des genikulostriären Systems beim Menschen zu völliger Blindheit im betroffenen Gesichtsfeldbereich führt (Holmes, 1918; Teuber,

Battersby, & Bender, 1960). Diese Gesichtsfeldausfälle werden in der Regel perimetrisch bestimmt. Dabei wird der Patient aufgefordert, eine Taste zu drücken, wenn ein Licht auftaucht oder verschwindet. Ein erblindeter Bereich (absolutes Skotom) ist also dadurch gekennzeichnet, daß in ihm kein Licht wahrgenommen wird.

Beobachtungen an höheren Affen haben jedoch gezeigt, daß nach Entfernung beider Okzipitallappen Objekte weiterhin entdeckt und lokalisiert werden können (Humphrey, 1974; Klüver, 1942). Dieser Unterschied zum Menschen ist so interpretiert worden, daß bei diesem (im Gegensatz zum Affen) die visuellen Leistungen "kortikalisiert" sind. Eine Schädigung der genikulo-striären Sehbahn führt daher zum völligen Ausfall der visuellen Wahrnehmung im betroffenen Bereich (Weiskrantz, 1961).

Das klassische Konzept, demzufolge das genikulo-striäre System die Grundlage für alle wichtigen visuellen Wahrnehmungsfunktionen darstellt, wurde durch die Entdeckung von sogenannten kortikalen Merkmals-Analysatoren ("feature detectors") unterstützt. Durch Ableitung von Einzelzellen konnten neuronale Mechanismen im visuellen Kortex identifiziert werden, die die verschiedenen Merkmale der optischen Umwelt (z. B. Länge und Orientierung von Konturen, Farbe, Bewegungsrichtung, Geschwindigkeit) analysieren (Hubel & Wiesel, 1968, Zeki, 1978). In der visuellen Psychophysik und Wahrnehmungspsychologie versuchte man daher, subjektive Phänomene beim Menschen mit neurophysiologischen Befunden an höheren Affen zu korrelieren (Jung, 1961, 1973).

Die Analyse der Sehleistungen, die nach Abtragung des visuellen Kortex bei den höheren Affen intakt bleiben, sowie die mit Hilfe neuer Methoden erhobenen neuroanatomischen Befunde führten jedoch auch beim Menschen zu einem neuen Untersuchungsansatz. Dabei wurden die experimentellen Bedingungen für die Untersuchung von Patienten mit Läsionen der genikulo-striären Sehbahn den Testverfahren bei den höheren Affen so weit wie möglich angeglichen. Die Benützung solcher nichtverbaler Testverfahren ergab, daß die Unterschiede sehr viel geringer ausfielen als ursprünglich angenommen (Weiskrantz, 1977, 1980). Diese Vergleichbarkeit bildet eine wichtige Voraussetzung für die Zuordnung von Wahrnehmungsfunktionen zu Hirnstrukturen beim Menschen. Zwar kann von Befunden, die an höheren Affen gewonnen worden sind, nicht ohne weiteres auf analoge Grundlagen beim Menschen geschlossen werden, da sich die neuroanatomischen Voraussetzungen doch erheblich unterscheiden. Auch ist trotz der Entwicklung der Computer-Tomographie eine exakte (praemortem) Bestimmung der von der Schädigung betroffenen Hirnregion beim Menschen noch nicht möglich. Dennoch konnten auf der Grundlage der Tierexperimente Erkenntnisse am Menschen gewonnen werden, die zu einem besseren Verständnis der visuellen Wahrnehmung und ihrer neuronalen Mechanismen auf der Basis einer 'funktionellen Anatomie' führten. Das von Teuber (1955) entwickelte Konzept der doppelten Dissoziation von Funktionen erwies sich als sehr fruchtbar für diesen Ansatz, da es Rückschlüsse auf "funktionelle Systeme" bzw. zugrundeliegende Gehirnstrukturen zuläßt. Dabei wird angenommen, daß A und B Bestandteile eines Funktionssystems sind. Eine Funktion a, die zur Struktur A gehört, ist nur dann betroffen, wenn die Struktur A geschädigt worden ist; Funktion b, die einer Struktur B zugeordnet ist, bleibt dagegen intakt. Die gleiche Annahme gilt auch für den umgekehrten Fall. Für die neuroanatomische Zuordnung von visuellen Funktionen bedeutet dies folgendes: Eine Schädigung des genikulo-striären Systems führt zu einem Ausfall der davon abhängigen visuellen Leistungen (z.b. in Form von Gesichtsfeldausfällen), während bestimmte andere Funktionen erhalten bleiben. Diese können dann extrastriären Strukturen zugeordnet werden. Läsionen im Bereich der extrastriären retinalen Afferenzen (Retina-Mittelhirn-Thalamus-Kortex) führen dagegen zur Beeinträchtigung bzw. zum Ausfall der Wahrnehmungsfunktionen, die von dieser Afferenz abhängig sind; die genikulo-striären Sehfunktionen sollten jedoch intakt bleiben.

Eine Zuordnung von Sehfunktionen mit bestimmten Strukturen im ZNS kann für den Menschen nur unter Einbeziehung tierexperimenteller Ergebnisse erfolgen, da eine Schädigung eines einzelnen Abschnittes der Afferenz oder einer einzelnen Struktur (z.B. des Colliculus superior) sehr selten ist. Neurophysiologische Ergebnisse und Verhaltensbeobachtungen nach experimentellen Eingriffen bei höheren Affen erlauben zudem gewisse Voraussagen über die funktionelle Bedeutung der entsprechenden Strukturen beim Menschen. Das Tier dient also als Modell für den Menschen. In den folgenden Abschnitten werden die wesentlichen Ergebnisse der Neuroanatomie, der Neurophysiologie und der Verhaltensforschung übersichtsmäßig dargestellt. Im Anschluß daran sollen die Ergebnisse, die an Patienten erhalten wurden, beschrieben und diskutiert werden.

2. DAS SOGENANNTE "ZWEITE" VISUELLE SYSTEM UND SEINE BEDEUTUNG BEI HÖHEREN AFFEN

Neuroanatomische Befunde

Retinale Fasern projizieren zum Corpus geniculatum laterale und zum striären Kortex (genikulo-striäres System). Parallel zu dieser Projektion bestehen weitere Faserverbindungen zum Prätectum, sowie zu den oberen und mittleren Schichten des Colliculus superior (Hubel, LeVay, & Wiesel, 1975; Pollack, & Hickey, 1979; Wilson & Toyne, 1970; Abb. 41.1). Diese beiden colliculären Schichten projizieren ihrerseits zum inferioren und medialen Teil des ipsilateralen Nc. pulvinar, sowie zum inferioren Anteil des kontralateralen Nc. pulvinar, während die unteren Schichten im wesentlichen mit dem medialen und oralen Teil dieses thalamischen Kerns verbunden sind (Benevento & Fallon, 1975; Benevento & Rezak, 1976). Der inferiore Teil des Nc. pulvinar erhält außerdem genikuläre

(Trojanowski & Jacobson, 1975) und vermutlich auch direkte retinale Afferenzen (Campos-Ortega, Hayhow, & Clüver, 1970). Der mediale Anteil des Nc. pulvinar erhält zusätzliche Faserverbindungen vom Praetectum (Benevento, Rezak, & Santos-Anderson, 1977). Die einzelnen Anteile des Nc. pulvinar sind mit verschiedenen kortikalen Arealen verbunden; der inferiore Teil weist Faserverbindungen zum striären (Area 17) und peristriären visuellen Kortex auf (Area 18, 19; Benevento & Davis, 1977; Ogren, 1977; Wong-Riley, 1977). Der late-

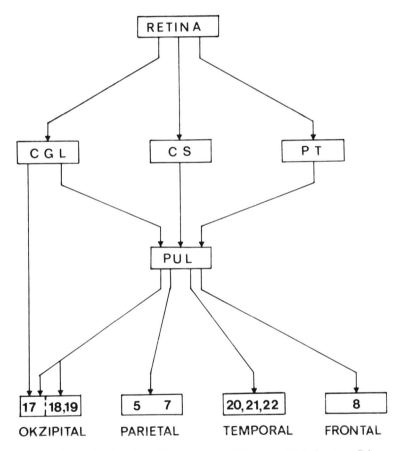

ABB. 41.1. Vereinfachtes Schema der Projektion von der Retina zum Colliculus superior (CS), zum Nc. pulvinar (PUL) und zu verschiedenen Arealen der Großhirnrinde. CGL: Corpus geniculatum laterale; PT: Prätektum. Nähere Beschreibung im Text.

FIG. 41.1. Simplified diagram of the retinal projections to the superior colliculus (CS), nc. pulvinar (PUL), and then to different cortical areas (numbers after Brodmann). CGL: lateral geniculate body; PT: pretectum.

rale Anteil projiziert zum peristriären visuellen Kortex (Ogren, 1977; Ogren & Hendrickson, 1977), zu den parietalen Arealen 5 und 7, sowie zum Temporallappen (Areale 20, 21 und 22). Der mediale Teil des Nc. pulvinar projiziert zum frontalen Kortex, vor allem zur Area 8 (Bos & Benevento, 1975; Trojanowski & Jacobson, 1976, 1977).

Zwischen verschiedenen kortikalen Regionen und dem Nc. pulvinar bzw. Colliculus superior bestehen wechselseitige Faserverbindungen (Ogren & Hendrickson, 1976; Wilson & Toyne, 1970); letzterer erhält auch Fasern vom parietalen Assoziationskortex und von der Area 8 (Astruc, 1971; Benevento & Davis, 1977; Künzle, Akert, & Wurtz, 1976; Petras, 1971).

Die sehr dichten und vielfältigen afferenten und efferenten Faserbeziehungen zwischen subkortikalen und kortikalen Arealen weisen darauf hin, daß eine einfache Zuordnung von Funktionen zu Strukturen nicht möglich ist (vgl. Chalupa, 1977). Eine Sehleistung, die in perimetrisch blinden Gesichtsfeldbereichen nachgewiesen werden kann (''Restsehen''), ist daher immer als Funktion des gesamten 'zweiten' visuellen Systems und nicht nur einer einzelnen Teilstruktur dieses Systems anzusehen.

Neurophysiologische Beobachtungen

Neurophysiologische Untersuchungen der oberen und mittleren Schichten des Colliculus superior beim wachen Affen haben ergeben, daß sie eine retinotope Abbildung der kontralateralen Gesichtsfeldhälfte aufweisen. Die colliculären Neurone zeigen aber im Gegensatz zu Neuronen im striären oder peristriären Kortex kaum eine Reizspezifität, außer daß ein geringer Teil der Neurone nur auf bewegte Reize in einer bestimmten Bewegungsrichtung antwortet (Wurtz & Albano, 1980).

Ein Lichtreiz, der in das rezeptive Feld eines colliculären Neurons fällt und von einer sakkadischen Zuwendebewegung gefolgt ist, löst eine deutlich stärkere neuronale Antwort aus als ein Lichtreiz, dem sich das Versuchstier nicht zuwendet (Goldberg & Wurtz, 1972a,b). Diese Ergebnisse wurden dahingehend interpretiert, daß der Colliculus superior eine wichtige Rolle für den Wechsel der visuellen Aufmerksamkeit auf bestimmte Bereiche im Gesichtsfeld spielt und eine Sakkade in Richtung auf den Reiz vorbereitet.

Uber die Eigenschaften der Neurone des Nc. pulvinar ist noch wenig bekannt. Der inferiore Teil des Nc. pulvinar weist eine retinotope Repräsentation der jeweils kontralateralen Gesichtsfeldhälfte auf (Gattass, Oswaldo-Cruz, & Sousa, 1978). Die Neurone besitzen ähnlich große rezeptive Felder wie sie für die oberen und mittleren colliculären Schichten gefunden wurden und antworten am besten auf bewegte optische Reize (Mathers & Rapisardi, 1973). Vermutlich spielen die medialen und lateralen Teile des Nc. pulvinar eine wichtige Rolle für spontane sakkadische Augenbewegungen und für okulomotorische Zuwendebewegungen zu optischen Reizen (Perryman, Lindsley, & Lindsley, 1980).

Verhaltensstudien

Nach Abtragung des visuellen Kortex bei Primaten kann die Entdeckung und Lokalisation von Lichtreizen intakt bleiben bzw. durch Training wiederhergestellt werden (Feinberg, Pasik, & Pasik, 1978; Humphrey & Weiskrantz, 1967; Weiskrantz, Cowey, & Passingham, 1977).

Eine operative Entfernung des Colliculus superior führt dagegen zu einem Verlust der Entdeckung und Lokalisation von optischen Reizen im peripheren kontralateralen Gesichtsfeld (Butter, Weinstein, Bender, & Gross, 1978). Eine einseitige colliculäre Läsion hat eine Erhöhung der Latenzen für sakkadische Zuwendebewegungen zur Gegenseite zur Folge (Latto, 1978; Wurtz & Goldberg, 1972). Die fovealen Sehleistungen bleiben dagegen unbeeinträchtigt (Anderson & Symmes, 1969; Cardu, Ptito, Dumont, & Lepore, 1975). Die Abtragung des visuellen Kortex und des ipsilateralen Colliculus superior zusammen führt zum völligen Verlust der Entdeckung und Lokalisation von Lichtreizen im betroffenen Gesichtsfeldbereich (Mohler & Wurtz, 1977), und zum Ausfall jeder Art von Zuwendebewegung (Denny-Brown, 1975). Eine ausgeprägte Verminderung von sakkadischen Suchbewegungen sowie von spontanen Sakkaden, und eine deutliche Verlängerung der Fixationsdauer werden auch nach bilateralen Läsionen des Nc. pulvinar beobachtet (Ungerleider & Christensen, 1977, 1979).

Zusammenfassend kann festgestellt werden, daß das extrastriäre, sogenannte "zweite" visuelle System eine wichtige Rolle für den Wechsel der selektiven Aufmerksamkeit im Gesichtsfeld und für die Auslösung von Augen- oder Kopfbewegungen zu neuen Objekten spielt, die im Gesichtsfeld auftauchen. Der Wechsel der Aufmerksamkeit geht dabei vermutlich dem Wechsel der Fixation voraus. Daraus ergibt sich, daß eine Schädigung im Bereich dieses Sehsystems zu einer Störung dieser Funktionen führen kann. Die Ausführung sakkadischer Augenbewegungen selbst bleibt ungestört, ihre Auslösung durch externe optische Reize erfolgt jedoch verzögert oder überhaupt nicht mehr.

3. EXTRASTRIÄRE VISUELLE FUNKTIONEN BEIM MENSCHEN

Visuelle Funktionen in perimetrisch blinden Gesichtsfeldbereichen

Den ersten wichtigen Hinweis für das Vorhandensein einer visuellen Wahrnehmungsleistung in perimetrisch blinden Gesichtsfeldbereichen beim Menschen erbrachten Pöppel, Held and Frost (1973). Sie fanden, daß Patienten in der Lage sind, Lichtpunkte in ihrem Skotom mit Hilfe *sakkadischer Augenbewegungen* auf ein akustisches Signal hin zu lokalisieren. Die Darbietungszeiten für die optischen Reize (100 ms) legen dabei deutlich unterhalb der sakkadischen Latenz (etwa 200 ms). Die Patienten konnten daher die Licht-

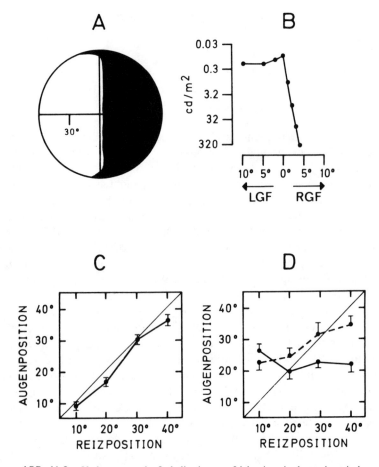

ABB. 41.2. Verbesserung der Lokalisation von Lichtreizen in der perimetrisch blinden, rechten Hälfte des Gesichtsfeldes. A: Binokuläres Gesichtsfeld (bestimmt durch kinetische Perimetrie; Testpunkthelligkeit: 320 cd/m^2, Größe des Testreizes: 116 Bogenminuten; Hintergrund: 3.2 cd/m^2). B: Profil der Helligkeitsempfindlichkeit entlang der Horizontalachse (statische Perimetrie: Testpunktgröße: 69 Bogenminuten; Darbietungszeit: .5 s, Hintergrund: 3.2 cd/m^2). LGF: linke, RGF: rechte Gesichtsfeldhälfte. C: Beziehung zwischen Reiz- und mittlerer Augenposition für die intakte linke Gesichtsfeldhälfte ($y = .76 \times {}^{1.06}$, $r^2 = .98$). D: Beziehung zwischen Reiz- und mittlerer Augenposition im perimetrisch blinden Halbfeld vor dem Training (durchgezogene Linie; $y = 32.15 \times {}^{-.11}$, $r^2 = .31$) und nach der systematischen Übung der Lokalisation (unterbrochene Linie; $y = 10.91 \times {}^{.31}$; $r^2 = .89$). Die senkrechten Linien in C und D geben den halben Standardfehler an ($n = 10$ je Reizposition).

FIG. 41.2. Improvement of saccadic localization of light targets presented at various eccentricities on the horizontal axis in the perimetrically blind hemifield. A: Binocular visual field as determined by dynamic perimetry; (target size 116 min arc; target luminance: 320 cd/m^2; background luminance: 3.2 cd/m^2). B: Profile of binocular threshold sensitivity along the horizontal axis (static perimetry; target size: 69 min arc; exposure duration .5 s; background luminance: 3.2 cd/m^2). LGF:

punkte nie bewußt sehen. Sie hatten vielmehr das Gefühl, rein zufällig auf verschiedene Stellen in ihrem ''blinden'' Gesichtsfeld geblickt zu haben. In Kontrollexperimenten konnten die Autoren Streulicht als mögliches Artefakt ausschließen. In weiteren Untersuchungen anderer Labors wurden diese Beobachtungen bestätigt. Außerdem konnte nachgewiesen werden, daß Patienten auch mit *Zeigebewegungen der Hand* den Ort im hemianopen Gesichtsfeldbereich angeben können, an dem ein Lichtpunkt kurzzeitig dargeboten wurde. Im Gegensatz hierzu konnten Patienten mit praechiasmatisch verursachten Gesichtsfeldausfällen, die unter den gleichen Bedingungen getestet wurden, Lichtpunkte in ihrem blinden Gesichtsfeldbereich nicht lokalisieren (Perenin & Jeannerod, 1975, 1978; Weiskrantz, Warrington, Sanders, & Marshall, 1974). Verglichen mit den Ergebnissen bei höheren Affen war jedoch die Lokalisationsgenauigkeit der Patienten deutlich geringer. Zwar zeigten auch die Affen unmittelbar nach der kortikalen Läsion eine geringe Lokalisationsleistung. Nach mehreren Trainingssitzungen nahm die Genauigkeit der Lokalisation jedoch deutlich zu (Weiskrantz, Cowey & Passingham, 1977). Wir fragten uns daher, ob die Leistung der Patienten durch eine systematische Übung ebenfalls verbessert werden kann.

Für des Training wurde ein Tübinger Perimeter benützt. Die Patienten wurden instruiert, einen roten Punkt in der Mitte des Perimeters zu fixieren, und, auf ein Signal hin, dorthin zu blicken, wo ''ihrem Gefühl nach'' der Lichtpunkt dargeboten worden war. Die Reizparameter waren dabei so gewählt, daß Streulicht-Effekte keinen Einfluß nehmen konnten. Die Darbietungszeit für die Lichtpunkte betrug 100 msec; der Durchmesser war 116 Bogenminuten, und die Leuchtdichte betrug 32 cd/m² bei einer Hintergrundleuchtdichte von 3.2 cd/m². Die sakkadischen Zuwendebewegungen wurden mit Hilfe des Elektrookulogramms auf einem Papierschreiber aufgezeichnet. Nach einer ausreichenden Übungsperiode von 800–1200 Durchgängen konnten die Patienten in der Regel die Lichtpunkte lokalisieren, d.h., die mittlere Amplitude der Blickzuwendebewegungen entsprach ungefähr der jeweiligen Reizposition (Zihl, 1980).

In Abb. 41.2 sind für eine Vp die Ergebnisse der Perimetrie (A,B), die Genauigkeit der Lokalisation von Lichtreizen auf der Horizontalachse im intakten linken Halbfeld (C), sowie die Übereinstimmung zwischen Reizposition und mittlerer Amplitude der sakkadischen Zuwendebewegungen im hemianopen Bereich vor und nach der systematischen Übung dargestellt (D; Patientenangaben

---

left visual hemifield; RGF: right visual hemifield. *C:* Mean eye position plotted as a function of target position for the intact left hemifield ($y = .76x^{1.06}$, $r^2 = .98$). *D:* Mean eye position as a function of target position for the perimetrically blind right hemifield before (continuous line:$y = 32.15x^{-11}$, $r^2 = .31$) and after practice with saccadic localization (broken line; $y = 10.91x^{.31}$, $r = .89$). Vertical bars in C and D indicate one-half standard error ($n = 10$).

TABLE 41.1

Clinical Details of the Patients Described in this Paper. The Time Between the Occurrence of Brain Damage and Their Participation in this Study Varied Between 3 Months (P4) and 5 1/2 Years (P2). During this Time, No Shift of the Visual Field Border Was Observed.

Patient	Age[1]	Sex	Visual Field Loss	Diagnosis[2]
P1	30	F	Right homonymous hemianopia	Embolic infarction in the territory of the left posterior cerebral artery
P2	57	M	Right homonymous hemianopia left lower homonymous quadranopia	Bilateral occipital haemorrhage (operated)
P3	48	M	Incomplete left homonymous hemianopia (residual field: 8 deg)	Ischemic infarction of the left calcarine artery
P4	29	M	Right homonymous hemianopia	Large brain defect in the left occipital lobe after removal of a haematogenous brain abscess
P5	19	M	Left homonymous hemianopia	Cerebral trauma with extensive right temporal contusion

[1]In years.
[2]Verified by computerized tomography.

unter P1, Tabelle 41.1). Im Verlaufe der 12 Trainingssitzungen führte diese Patientin 960 sakkadische Blickbewegungen in das perimetrisch blinde rechte Halbfeld aus. Der Unterschied in der mittleren Amplitude vor und nach der systematischen Übung ist statistisch signifikant (t-Test; $.05 < p < .02$).

Wenn ein optischer Reiz im Gesichtsfeld wahrgenommen oder "entdeckt" wird, so verfügt das ZNS sowohl über die Information, *daß* ein Reiz vorhanden ist, als auch *wo* (im Gesichtsfeld) dieser Reiz aufgetreten ist. Die Entdeckung des Reizes ist dabei vermutlich Voraussetzung für dessen Lokalisation. Wie die eben beschriebenen Ergebnisse zeigen, ist sie von der genikulo-striären Sehbahn unabhängig. In weiteren Experimenten wurde untersucht, ob der Patient im "blinden" Gesichtsfeld Reize bemerken und wie er diese angeben kann.

Ein gut untersuchter Indikator für das Bemerktwerden eines Reizes ist die phasische *Änderung der Hautleitfähigkeit* (sogenannte elektrodermale Reaktion, EDR). In den dazu durchgeführten Experimenten wurden die Lichtpunkte (Durchmesser: 116 Bogenminuten; Leuchtdichte: 32 cd/m^2; Hintergrund: 3.2 cd/m^2) auf der Seite des Gesichtsfeldausfalles bei 30 Grad Exzentrizität auf der Horizontalachse dargeboten. Die Expositionszeit betrug 200 ms. Die Hälfte der Darbietungen bestand aus Lichtreizen begleitet von einem Klick, die andere Hälfte aus Kontrollreizen (Klicks ohne Lichtreize). Test- und Kontrollreize wurden dabei in einer zufälligen, dem Patienten nicht bekannten Abfolge geboten. Die phasische elektrodermale Reaktion wurde mit Hilfe von Oberflächen-Elektroden registriert und auf einem Papierschreiber aufgezeichnet.

TABELLE 41.1

Patient	Alter[1]	Geschlecht	Gesichtsfeldbefund	Ursache des Ausfalles[2]
P1	30	W	Rechtsseitige homonyme Hemianopsie	Embolischer Infarkt im Versorgungsgebiet der hinteren linken Hirnarterie
P2	57	M	Vollständige rechtsseitige homonyme Hemianopsie. Homonyme Quadrantenanopsie links unten	Bilaterale okzipitale Massenblutung (operiert)
P3	48	M	Unvollständige rechtsseitige homonyme Hemianopsie (Restgesichtsfeld rechts: 8 Sehwinkelgrad)	Ischämischer Infarkt im Stromgebiet der linken A. calcarina
P4	29	M	Rechtsseitige homonyme Hemianopsie	Ausgedehnter Hirnsubstanzverlust im linken Okzipitallappen nach Entfernung eines Hirnabszesses
P5	19	M	Linksseitige homonyme Hemianopsie	Schädel-Hirn-Trauma mit ausgedehntem temporo-okzipitalen Kontusionsherd links

[1] In Jahren zum Zeitpunkt der Untersuchung.
[2] Verifiziert durch das kraniale Computer-Tomogramm.

Die Patienten wurden wiederum aufgefordert, in der Mitte des Perimeters zu fixieren, aber ihre Aufmerksamkeit auf die Seite des Gesichtsfeldausfalles zu richten. An den Experimenten nahmen zwei Patienten teil (Tabelle 41.1, P2 und P3). Die Versuche wurden an drei verschiedenen Tagen durchgeführt.

In Abb. 41.3 sind die Gesamthäufigkeit der elektrodermalen Reaktionen auf die Lichtreize und die (akustischen) Kontrollreize (A) sowie die mittlere Amplitude dieser Reaktionen dargestellt (B). Beide Maße unterscheiden sich signifikant für die beiden Bedingungen (Zihl, Tretter, & Singer, 1980). Diese Ergebnisse deuten darauf hin, daß sich (entgegen der Annahme von Sokolov, 1960) die Verarbeitung eines Lichtreizes im perimetrisch blinden Feld mit Hilfe der phasischen elektrodermalen Reaktion selbst dann nachweisen läßt, wenn die genikulostriäre Sehbahn unterbrochen ist.

In weiteren Experimenten wurden die *Lidmotorik* und die Handmotorik als Indikatoren für die Registrierung verwendet. Hierbei sollten die Patienten immer dann ihr Augenlid schließen, wenn sie ''das Gefühl hatten'', ein Lichtpunkt sei in der Peripherie der perimetrisch blinden Gesichtshälfte aufgetaucht. Die willkürlichen Lidbewegungen wurden mit Hilfe des Elektrookulogramms aufgezeichnet. Die experimentellen Bedingungen entsprachen denen der oben darge-

stellten Experimente. Die Darbietungsdauer betrug 100 msec; die Abfolge der
Test- und der Kontrollreize erfolgte zufällig. An diesen Experimenten nahmen
drei Patienten teil. Zwei von ihnen wiesen eine komplette homonyme Hemianop-
sie auf; beim dritten war auf der Seite des Ausfalles ein Restgesichtsfeld von 12
Sehwinkelgrad erhalten. Die Ursache für den Gesichtsfeldverlust war eine
Schädigung des Okzipitallappens auf der Gegenseite (Zihl & von Camon, 1980).
In Abb. 41.4 und 41.5 sind Original- und Verlaufsprotokolle für einen Patienten
wiedergegeben (P4 in Tabelle 41.1). Nach 8 Sitzungen mit jeweils 60 Durch-

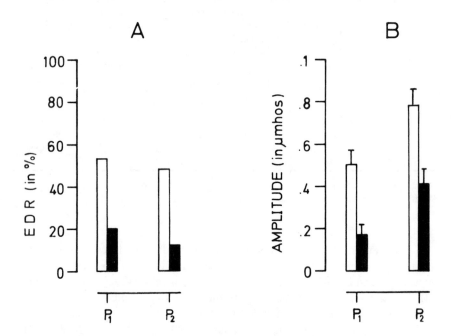

ABB. 41.3.   A: Häufigkeit des Auftretens einer phasischen elektrodermalen Reaktion (EDR, in Prozent) nach optischer Reizung in der Peripherie des hemianopen Bereiches (weiße Säulen) und auf Kontrollreize (schwarze Säulen) bei 2
Patienten (P1, P2). B: Mittlere Amplitude (in μmhos) der elektrodermalen Reaktion auf optische Reize und auf Kontrollreize. Die senkrechten Linien geben den
halben Standardfehler an. Übrige Angaben wie in A.

FIG. 41.3.   *A:* Frequency of the occurrence of phasic electrodermal responses (n
= 60, in %, 60 trials) after visual stimulation in the hemianopic region at 30°
eccentricity on the horizontal axis (white bars) and after ''blanks'' (black bars) for
two patients (P1, P2). *B:* Mean amplitude (in μmhos) of the electrodermal responses to light flashes (n = 60) and to blanks (n = 60), respectively. Vertical
bars indicate half the standard error. Other details as in A.

gängen (30 Test- und 30 Kontrollreize) konnte dieser Patient die Anwesenheit des Lichtreizes relativ sicher angeben.

Diese Leistung übertrug sich auch auf die *Handmotorik*. Die Patienten drückten dabei auf eine Taste, wenn ihrem "Gefühl" nach ein Lichtpunkt im perimetrisch blinden Halbfeld dargeboten worden war. Der Unterschied in der Reaktionshäufigkeit auf Test- und Kontrollreize war für alle Patienten statistisch signifikant. Dagegen konnten die Patienten nicht unterscheiden, ob ein Lichtreiz vorhanden war oder nicht, wenn sie dies verbal mit "ja" angeben sollten (Zihl & von Cramon, 1980). Diese Dissoziation zwischen verbaler und lid- bzw. handmotorischer Reaktion weist darauf hin, daß die neuronalen Mechanismen der Sprache offensichtlich keinen Zugang zu dieser extrastriären Form des "Sehens" besitzen.

Die Meldung eines Lichtreizes mittels der lidmotorischen Reaktion und seine Lokalisation mittels sakkadischer Blickzuwendung werden möglicherweise von denselben neuronalen Mechanismen vermittelt. Nach dem Üben der Blinkantwort lokalisierten die Patienten nämlich erheblich genauer als vorher, ohne daß es dazu einer weiteren spezifischen Übung bedurft hätte (Zihl & von Cramon, 1980). Der Colliculus superior könnte eine der Strukturen sein, die für diese beiden Funktionen verantwortlich ist, da er nach Abtragung des striären Kortex eine kritische Rolle für die Entdeckung und sakkadische Lokalisation von optischen Reizen beim Affen spielt (Mohler & Wurtz, 1977).

Die Bedeutung des 'zweiten' visuellen Systems für die Steuerung der selektiven Aufmerksamkeit beim Menschen geht aus Beobachtungen über die Beeinflußbarkeit der *Helligkeitsempfindlichkeit* in der Peripherie des Gesichtsfeldes hervor. Diese ist normalerweise dann am größten, wenn man die Aufmerksamkeit in Richtung des erwarteten Reizes lenkt (Aulhorn & Harms, 1972). Sie nimmt aber um etwa 0.4 log Einheit ab, wenn der Lichtreiz bei wiederholter Schwellenmessung in rascher Abfolge an derselben Stelle (z.B. bei 30° Exzentrizität auf der Horizontalachse im linken Gesichtsfeld) dargeboten wird, während die Versuchsperson in der Mitte des Perimeters fixiert. Diese Empfindlichkeitsabnahme zeigt interokulären Transfer, d.h. sie findet an einem zentralen Ort im visuellen System statt. Sie kann jedoch aufgehoben werden, wenn im spiegelsymmetrischen Bereich der kontralateralen Gesichtsfeldhälfte (also 30° rechts) die Schwelle ebenfalls mehrmals bestimmt wird, oder wenn die Versuchsperson eine sakkadische Zuwendebewegung dorthin ausführt. Diese Wechselwirkung zwischen den beiden Gesichtsfeldhälften wurde auch bei Patienten mit einer Hemianopsie beobachtet, wo die Schwellenerhöhung im intakten Gesichtsfeld durch optische Reizung im 'blinden' Halbfeld (bzw. durch eine visuell ausgelöste Sakkade) rückgängig gemacht werden konnte (Singer, Zihl, & Pöppel, 1977; Zihl, von Cramon, Pöppel, & Singer, 1979). Eine ähnliche Interaktion zwischen spiegelsymmetrischen Arealen haben auch Pöppel und Richards (1974) und Torjussen (1978) beschrieben.

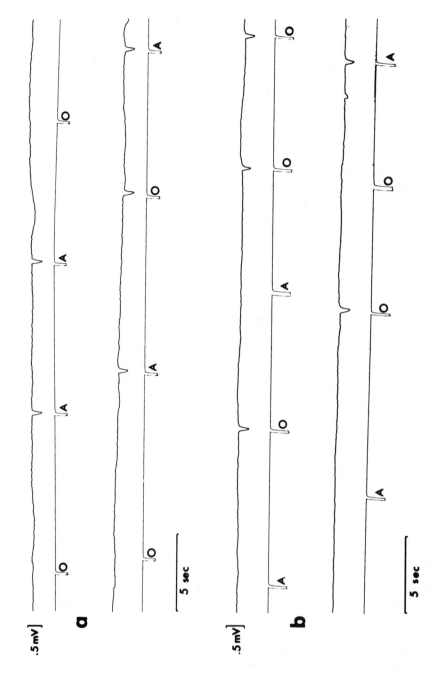

ABB. 41.4. Original-Aufzeichnung willkürlicher Lidbewegungen auf optische Reize (O) in der Peripherie des perimetrisch blinden Gesichtsfeldes und auf akustische Kontrollreize (A), zu Beginn (a) und am Ende der Übungsperiode (b).

FIG. 41.4. Registration of voluntary eyelid closures to light flashes (O) presented at 30° on the horizontal axis of the hemianopic field, and to 'blanks' (A) at the beginning (a) and end of practice (b).

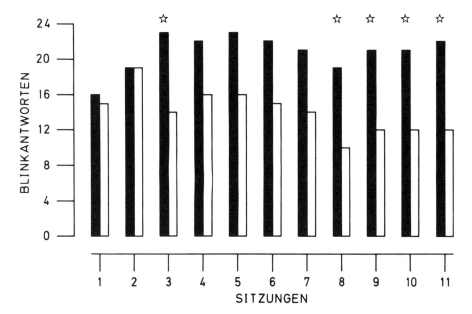

ABB. 41.5.   Blinkantworten auf Lichtreize (wie in Abb. 41.4) bei einem Patienten mit einer kompletten linksseitigen homonymen Hemianopsie. Ver-
laufsprotokoll von 11 Sitzungen. Die schwarzen Säulen stellen die Anzahl der
Blinkantworten auf Lichtreize dar, die weißen die Antworten auf die akustischen
Kontrollreize (30 Darbietungen je Bedingung und Sitzung). Die Sternchen über
den schwarzen Säulen bedeuten, daß in der betreffenden Sitzung der Unterschied
in den Antworten zwischen Test- und Kontrollreiz mindestens auf dem 2 %-
Niveau signifikant ist.

FIG. 41.5.   Eyelid responses to light stimuli (see Fig. 41.4) of a patient with a
complete left homonymous hemianopia in 11 consecutive sessions. Black bars
indicate the number of correct responses to light flashes (30 presentations per
session), and white bars indicate the number of responses to "blanks" (false
positive responses; 30 trials per session). Stars at the top of the black bars indicate
a significant difference between the number of responses to lights and to blanks (*p*
< .02).

Den Einfluß der *selektiven Aufmerksamkeit* auf die Helligkeitsempfindlichkeit
zeigt Abb. 41.6 (P5, in Tabelle 41.1). Wenn der Patient seine Aufmerksamkeit
auf den Bereich richten kann, in dem der Lichtreiz erscheint, so liegen die
Schwellenwerte niedriger als wenn er zufällig an verschiedenen Orten erscheint
und eine Ausrichtung der Aufmerksamkeit daher nicht möglich ist. Dieser
Einfluß der Aufmerksamkeit auf die Unterschiedsschwelle ist im
Übergangsbereich zwischen Gesichtsfeld und Skotom besonders auffällig.

Es gibt Hinweise dafür, daß im perimetrisch blinden Halbfeld auch eine
"Wahrnehmungskapazität" für die *Unterscheidung der Tiefe,* sowie für *einfache Mustermerkmale* vorhanden ist. Richards (1973) fand eine primitive Form

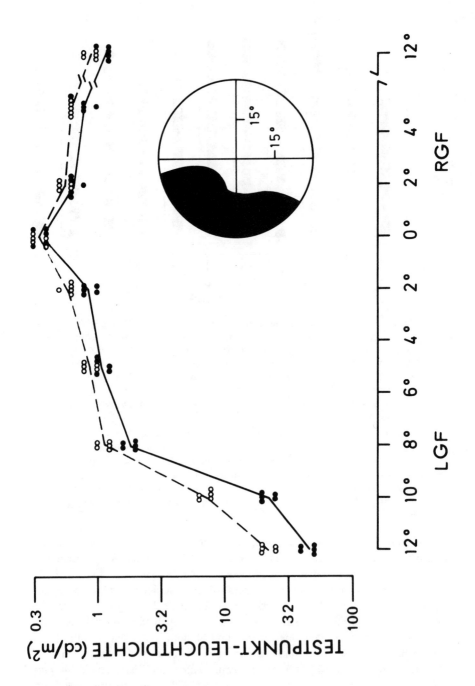

710

der Stereopsis; Weiskrantz et al. (1974) beschrieben einen Patienten, der einfache Muster, z.B. X vs. O, innerhalb des 'blinden' Gesichtsfeldareals unterscheiden konnte.

Die Untersuchungen von visuellen Funktionen in perimetrisch blinden
Gesichtsfeldbereichen haben gezeigt, daß das Bemerken und die Lokalisation
von Lichtreizen nicht an die genikulostriäre Sehbahn gebunden sind. Auch die
retinotop organisierte Kontrolle der selektiven Aufmerksamkeit im Gesichtsfeld
dürfte eine Funktion des ''sekundären'' visuellen Systems darstellen. Diese drei
Funktionen sind jedoch wesentliche Komponenten der visuellen Wahrnehmung,
da sie die Voraussetzung für die Identifizierung von neu auftauchenden Objekten
darstellen.

Für die Untersuchung von extrastriären visuellen Funktionen ergeben sich
daher zwei wichtige Forderungen: das Fokussieren der Aufmerksamkeit des
Patienten auf sein 'blindes' Gesichtsfeld, wo der Reiz dargeboten wird, und die
Auswahl einer geeigneten Reaktion, mit deren Hilfe der Patient den Reiz melden
und ''mitteilen'' kann, da seine Wahrnehmung der bewußten subjektiven Erfahrung und der Sprache entzogen ist (siehe auch Weiskrantz, 1980).

Die Auswirkungen einer Schädigung im Bereich des "Zweiten" Sehsystems auf Sehfunktionen

Läsionen des Colliculus superior oder des Nc. pulvinar haben keinen
Gesichtsfeldausfall zur Folge. Die kritische Flimmerverschmelzungsfrequenz ist
jedoch in der Peripherie des kontralateralen Gesichtsfeldes bei einer Schädigung

---

ABB. 41.6. Einfluß der selektiven Aufmerksamkeit auf die Helligkeitsempfindlichkeit bei einem Patienten mit einer unvollständigen linksseitigen Hemianopsie (die inneren 30 Grad des Gesichtsfeldes sind im Teilbild dargestellt). Die
Werte liegen - vor allem im Übergangsbereich zwischen erhaltenem Gesichtsfeld
und Skotom deutlich niedriger, wenn der Patient seine Aufmerksamkeit dorthin
richten kann, wo die Messung stattfindet (offene Kreise, unterbrochene Linie).
Man vergleiche dagegen die Werte, wenn der Ort der Messung nicht bekannt ist
(geschlossene Kreise, durchgezogene Linie). Die Kreise stellen die originalen
Meßwerte von 5 Meßwiederholungen pro Reizposition dar. LGF: linke, RGF:
rechte Gesichtsfeldhälfte.

FIG. 41.6. Effect of focusing attention towards a particular field region on
perimetric threshold measurements in a patient with an incomplete left homonymous hemianopia (as shown in the right lower part of the figure). Increment
difference thresholds are lower, especially along the visual field border, when the
patient could focus attention on that field region within which thresholds were
determined (open circles). In the second condition, the patient could not focus
attention (i.e., he was not informed about the field region where measurements
were to be taken). In this condition, threshold values were markedly increased
(closed circles). In both conditions, the patient fixated the center of the perimeter.
LGF, RGF: left and right hemifield, respectively.

des Nc. pulvinar oder des Colliculus superior und vermindert (Zihl & von Cramon, 1978, 1979b).

Auch die Entdeckungsleistung bei Patienten mit einer Schädigung im Bereich des "sekundären" visuellen Systems für unilateral oder bilateral dargebotene Lichtreize ist beeinträchtigt. Bei einer Patientin mit einer Läsion des rechten Nc. pulvinar (unter Beteiligung des ipsilateralen Parietallappens) ergab sich bereits ab 20° Exzentrizität eine deutliche Verminderung der Entdeckungsleistung schon bei unilateraler Darbietung (Zihl & von Cramon, 1979b). Bei dieser Patientin waren auch die sakkadischen Zuwendebewegungen zur linken Seite vermindert und die Latenzen erhöht. Dagegen wurde bei einer Patientin mit einer Schädigung des linken Colliculus superior nur unter sehr restriktiven Bedingungen (Testgröße: 0.15 Grad; Testpunkthelligkeit: 0.6 cd/m^2; Darbietungsdauer: 3 ms) ein 'Neglect' für die Peripherie des rechten Gesichtsfeldes jenseits von 35° Exzentrizität beobachtet. Diese Patientin zeigte keine Latenzerhöhung zur Gegenseite und keine Asymmetrie der spontanen lateralen Augenbewegungen.

Das bei Normalpersonen und bei Patienten mit einer Hemianopsie beobachtete Ansteigen der Lichtunterschiedsschwelle nach wiederholter Messung, und die Wechselwirkung zwischen spiegelsymmetrisch zur Vertikalachse gelegenen peripheren Gesichtsfeldbereichen wurden bei Patienten mit einer Schädigung im Bereich des Colliculus superior bzw. des Nc. pulvinar nicht gefunden (Zihl & von Cramon, 1978, 1979a).

Abschließende Bemerkungen

Die Ergebnisse der Untersuchungen der visuellen Funktionen bei Patienten mit Läsionen entweder der genikulo-striären Sehbahn oder der retinalen Projektion zum Colliculus superior und Nc. pulvinar stimmen mit den Beobachtungen an höheren Affen gut überein und unterstützen das Konzept einer 'Zweiteilung' des visuellen Systems (Ingle, 1967; Schneider, 1969; Trevarthen, 1968). Nach diesem Konzept ist das phylogenetisch ältere "sekundäre" visuelle System mit dem "Wo", d.h. mit der Entdeckung und Lokalisation von optischen Reizen, sowie mit Zuwendebewegungen (sakkadische Augenbewegungen, Kopfbewegungen, Handbewegungen) zu diesen Reizen befaßt. Diese Komponenten stellen eine notwendige Voraussetzung für die Erkennung von Objekten (dem "Was") dar. Die Identifizierung von Objekten erfolgt dann durch die Mechanismen des genikulo-striären Systems, die die Voraussetzungen für eine detaillierte Objektanalyse besitzen.

Natürlich sind beide "Funktionssysteme" für die Erkennung von Objekten, Personen etc. notwendig. Die Intaktheit nur eines der beiden Systeme reicht nicht aus, da das Wahrnehmungsergebnis entweder der bewußten subjektiven Erfahrung nicht zugänglich ist (im Falle eines Reizes im 'blinden' Feld), oder keine Entdeckung bzw. Zuwendebewegung erfolgt (z.B. bei der sogenannten optischen Ataxie; Balint, 1909).

Für die Kontrolle der Aufmerksamkeit spielt wahrscheinlich auch der hintere Parietallappen eine wichtige Rolle. Neurone in dieser Region weisen Eigenschaften auf, die die Bedeutung von externen optischen Reizen in Abstimmung mit dem internen Zustand des Organismus analysieren. Die selektive Aufmerksamkeit wird daher vermutlich durch interne Faktoren (z.B. 'Motivation') und durch Veränderungen in der Umwelt kontrolliert. Diese Abstimmung zwischen inneren Zuständen (z.B.Erwartung) und der Aktualität der Umgebung (und umgekehrt) ermöglicht ein Verhalten in Übereinstimmung mit der "inneren" und "äußeren" Welt (Mountcastle, 1975, 1978).

ACKNOWLEDGMENTS

Diese Arbeit wurde von der Deutschen Forschungsgemeinschaft unterstützt. Der Autor bedankt sich bei Frau G. Lorenz und Frau I. Hein für das Schreiben des Manuskriptes.

REFERENCES

Anderson, K. V., & Symmes, D. The superior colliculus and higher visual functions in the monkey. *Brain Research*, 1969, *13*, 37–52.

Astruc, J. Corticofugal connections of Area 8 (frontal eye field) in macaca mulatta. *Brain Research*, 1971, *33*, 241–256.

Aulhorn, E., & Harms, H. Visual perimetry. In D. Jameson & L. M. Hurvich (Eds.), *Handbook of sensory physiology* (Vol VII/4), *Visual psychophysics*. New York, Berlin, Heidelberg: Springer-Verlag, 1972.

Balint, R. Seelenlähmung des 'Schauens', optische Ataxie, räumliche Störung der Aufmerksamkeit. *Monatsschrift für Psychiatrie und Neurologie*, 1909, *25*, 51–81.

Benevento, L. A., & Davis, B. Topographical projections of the prestriate cortex to the pulvinar nuclei in the macaque monkey: An autoradiographic study. *Experimental Brain Research*, 1977, *30*, 405–424.

Benevento, L. A., & Fallon, J. H. The ascending projections of the superior colliculus in the rhesus monkey (Macaca mulatta). *Journal of Comparative Neurology*, 1975, *160*, 339–362.

Benevento, L. A., & Rezak, M. The cortical projections of the inferior pulvinar and adjacent lateral pulvinar in the rhesus monkey (Macaca mulatta): An autoradiographic study. *Brain Research*, 1976, *108*, 1–24.

Benevento, L. A., Rezak, M., & Santos-Anderson, R. An autoradiographic study of the pretectum in the rhesus monkey (Macaca mulatta): Evidence for sensorimotor links to the thalamus and oculomotor nuclei. *Brain Research*, 1977, *127*, 197–218.

Bos, J., & Benevento, L. A. Projections of the medial pulvinar to orbital cortex and frontal eye fields in the rhesus monkey (Macaca mulatta). *Experimental Neurology*, 1975, *49*, 487–496.

Butter, C. M., Weinstein, C., Bender, D. B., & Gross, C. G. Localization and detection of visual stimuli following superior colliculus lesions in rhesus monkeys. *Brain Research*, 1978, *156*, 33–49.

Campos-Ortega, J. A., Hayhow, W. R., & Clüver, P. F. de V. A note on the problem of retinal projections to the inferior pulvinar nucleus of primates. *Brain Research*, 1970, *22*, 126–130.

Cardu, B., Ptito, M., Dumont, M., & Lepore, F. Effects of ablations of the superior colliculi on spectral sensitivity in monkeys. *Neuropsychologia*, 1975, *13*, 297–306.

Chalupa, L. A review of cat and monkey studies implicating the pulvinar in visual function. *Behavioral Biology*, 1977, *20*, 149–167.

Denny-Brown, D. The physiology of visual perception and behavior. *Transactions of the American Neurological Association*, 1975, *100*, 1–14.

Feinberg, T. E., Pasik, T., & Pasik, P. Extrageniculate vision in the monkey. VI. Visually guided accurate reaching behavior. *Brain Research*, 1978, *152*, 422–428.

Gattass, R., Oswaldo-Cruz, E., & Sousa, A. P. B. Visuotopic organization of the cebus pulvinar: A double representation of the contralateral hemifield. *Brain Research*, 1978, *152*, 1–16.

Goldberg, M. E., & Wurtz, R. H. Activity of superior colliculus in behaving monkey. I. Visual fields of single neurons. *Journal of Neurophysiology*, 1972, *35*, 542–559. (a)

Goldberg, M. E., & Wurtz, R. H. Activity of superior colliculus in behaving monkeys. II. Effect of attention on neuronal responses. *Journal of Neurophysiology*, 1972, *35*, 560–574. (b)

Holmes, G. Disturbances of vision by cerebral lesions. *British Journal of Ophthalmology*, 1918, *2*, 253–384.

Hubel, D. H., LeVay, S., & Wiesel, T. N. Mode of termination of retinotectal fibers in macaque monkey: An autoradiographic study. *Brain Research*, 1975, *96*, 25–40.

Hubel, D. H., & Wiesel, T. N. Receptive fields and functional architecture of monkey striate cortex. *Journal of Physiology*, 1968, *195*, 215–243.

Humphrey, N. K. Vision in a monkey without striate cortex. *Perception*, 1974, *3*, 241–255.

Humphrey, N. K., & Weiskrantz, L. Vision in monkeys after removal of the striate cortex. *Nature*, 1967, *215*, 595–597.

Ingle, D. Two visual mechanisms underlying the behavior of fish. *Psychologische Forschung*, 1967, *31*, 44–51.

Jung, R. Korrelationen von Neuronentätigkeit und Sehen. In R. Jung & H. Kornhuber (Eds.), *Neurophysiologie und Psychophysik des visuellen Systems*. Berlin, Göttingen, Heidelberg: Springer-Verlag, 1961.

Jung, R. Visual perception and neurophysiology. In R. Jung (Ed.), *Handbook of sensory physiology* (Vol. VII/3 A), *Central processing of visual information*. New York, Berlin, Heidelberg: Springer Verlag, 1973.

Klüver, H. Functional significance of the geniculo-striate system. *Biological Symposia*, 1942, *7*, 253–299.

Künzle, H., Akert, K., & Wurtz, R. H. Projection of area 8 (frontal eye field) to superior colliculus in the monkey. An autoradiographic study. *Brain Research*, 1976, *117*, 487–492.

Latto, R. The effects of bilateral frontal eye-field, posterior parietal or superior colliculus lesions on visual search in the rhesus monkey. *Brain Research*, 1978, *146*, 35–50.

Mathers, L. H., & Rapisardi, S. C. Visual and somatosensory receptive fields of neurons in the squirrel monkey pulvinar. *Brain Research*, 1973, *64*, 65–84.

Mohler, C. W., & Wurtz, R. H. Role of striate cortex and superior colliculus in visual guidance of saccadic eye movements in monkeys. *Journal of Neurophysiology*, 1977, *40*, 74–94.

Mountcastle, V. B. The world around us: Neural command functions for selective attention. *Neurosciences Research Program Bulletin 14 (suppl.)*. Cambridge: MIT Press, 1975.

Mountcastle, V. B. Brain mechanisms for directed attention. *Journal of the Royal Society of Medicine*, 1978, *71*, 14–28.

Ogren, M. P. Evidence for a projection from pulvinar to striate cortex in the squirrel monkey (Samiri sciureus). *Experimental Neurology*, 1977, *54*, 622–625.

Ogren, M. P., & Hendrickson, A. Pathways between striate cortex and subcortical regions in Macaca mulatta and Samiri sciureus: Evidence for a reciprocal pulvinar connection. *Experimental Neurology*, 1976, *53*, 780–800.

Ogren, M. P., & Hendrickson, A. The distribution of pulvinar terminals in visual areas 17 and 18 of the monkey. *Brain Research*, 1977, *137*, 343–350.

Perenin, M. T., & Jeannerod, M. Residual vision in cortically blind hemifields. *Neuropsychologia*, 1975, *13*, 1–7.

Perenin, M. T., & Jeannerod, M. Visual function within the hemianopic field following early cerebral hemidecortication in man. I. Spatial localization. *Neuropsychologia*, 1978, *16*, 1–13.

Perryman, K. M., Lindsley, D. F., & Lindsley, D. B. Pulvinar neuron responses to spontaneous and trained eye movements and to light flashes in squirrel monkeys. *Electroencephalography and Clinical Neurophysiology*, 1980, *49*, 151–161.

Petras, J. M. Connections of the parietal lobe. *Journal of Psychiatric Research*, 1971, *8*, 189–201.

Pöppel, E., Held, R., & Frost, D. Residual visual function in patients with lesions of the central visual pathways. *Nature*, 1973, *256*, 489–490.

Pöppel, E., & Richards, W. Light sensitivity in cortical scotomata contralateral to small islands of blindness. *Experimental Brain Research*, 1974, *21*, 125–130.

Pollack, J. G., & Hickey, T. L. The distribution of retinocollicular axon terminals in rhesus monkey. *Journal of Comparative Neurology*, 1979, *185*, 587–602.

Richards, W. Visual processing in scotomata. *Experimental Brain Research*, 1973, *17*, 333–347.

Schneider, G. Two visual systems: Brain mechanisms for localization and discrimination are dissociated by tectal and cortical lesions. *Science*, 1969, *163*, 895–902.

Singer, W., Zihl, J., & Pöppel, E. Subcortical control of visual thresholds in humans: Evidence for modality specific and retinotopically organized mechanisms for selective attention. *Experimental Brain Research*, 1977, *29*, 173–190.

Sokolov, E. Neuronal models and the orienting reflex. In M. Brazier (Ed.), *The central nervous system and behavior*. New York: Josiah Macy Foundation, 1960.

Teuber, H.-L. Physiological psychology. *Annual Review of Psychology*, 1955, *6*, 267–296.

Teuber, H.-L., Battersby, W. S., & Bender, M. B. *Visual field defects after penetrating missile wounds of the brain*. Cambridge: Harvard University Press, 1960.

Torjussen, T. Visual processing in cortically blind hemifields. *Neuropsychologia*, 1978, *16*, 15–21.

Trevarthen, C. B. Two mechanisms of vision in primates. *Psychologische Forschung*, 1968, *31*, 299–337.

Trojanowski, J. Q., & Jacobson, S. Peroxidase labeled subcortical afferents to pulvinar in rhesus monkey. *Brain Research*, 1975, *97*, 144–150.

Trojanowski, J. Q., & Jacobson, S. Areal and laminar distribution of some pulvinar cortical efferents in rhesus monkey. *Journal of Comparative Neurology*, 1976, *169*, 371–392.

Trojanowski, J. Q., & Jacobson, S. The morphology and laminar distribution of cortico-pulvinar neurons in the rhesus monkey. *Experimental Brain Research*, 1977, *28*, 51–62.

Ungerleider, L. G., & Christensen, C. A. Pulvinar lesions in monkeys produce abnormal eye movements during visual discrimination training. *Brain Research*, 1977, *136*, 189–196.

Ungerleider, L. G., & Christensen, C. A. Pulvinar lesions in monkeys produce abnormal scanning of a complex visual array. *Neuropsychologia*, 1979, *17*, 493–501.

Weiskrantz, L. Enzephalization and the scotoma. In W. H. Thorpe & O. L. Zangwill (Eds.), *Current problems in animal behaviour*. London and New York: Cambridge University Press, 1961.

Weiskrantz, L. Trying to bridge some neuropsychological gaps between monkey and man. *British Journal of Psychology*, 1977, *68*, 431–445.

Weiskrantz, L. Varieties of residual experience. *Quarterly Journal of Experimental Psychology*, 1980, *32*, 365–386.

Weiskrantz, L., Cowey, A., & Passingham, C.: Spatial responses to brief stimuli by monkeys with striate cortex ablations. *Brain*, 1977, *100*, 655–670.

Weiskrantz, L., Warrington, E. K., Sanders, M. D., & Marshall, J. Visual capacity in the hemianopic field following a restricted occipital ablation. *Brain*, 1974, *97*, 709–728.

Wilson, M. E., & Toyne, M. J. Retino-tectal and cortico-tectal projections in Macaca mulatta. *Brain Research*, 1970, *24*, 395–406.

Wong-Riley, M. T. T. Connections between the pulvinar nucleus and the prestriate cortex in the squirrel monkey as revealed by peroxidase histochemistry and autoradiography. *Brain Research*, 1977, *134*, 249–267.

Wurtz, R. H., & Albano, J. E. Visual motor function of the primate superior colliculus. *Annual Review of Neuroscience,* 1980, *3,* 189–226.

Wurtz, R. H., & Goldberg, M. E. Activity of superior colliculus in behaving monkey. IV. Effects of lesions on eye movements. *Journal of Neurophysiology,* 1972, *35,* 587–596.

Zeki, S. M. Functional specialization in the visual cortex of the rhesus monkey. *Nature,* 1978, *274,* 423–428.

Zihl, J. "Blindsight": Improvement of visually guided eye movements by systematic practice in patients with cerebral blindness. *Neuropsychologia,* 1980, *18,* 71–77.

Zihl, J., & von Cramon, D. Perimetrische Funktionsprüfung des Colliculus superior. *Nervenarzt,* 1978, *49,* 488–491.

Zihl, J., & von Cramon, D. Midbrain function in human vision. *Experimental Brain Research,* 1979, *35,* 419–424. (a)

Zihl, J., & von Cramon, D. The contribution of the 'second' visual system to directed visual attention in man. *Brain,* 1979, *102,* 835–856. (b)

Zihl, J., & von Cramon, D. Registration of light stimuli in the cortically blind hemifield and its effect on localization. *Behavioral Brain Research,* 1980, *1,* 287–298.

Zihl, J., von Cramon, D., Pöppel, E., & Singer, W.: Interhemispheric modulation of light difference threshold in the periphery of the visual field. In J. S. Russell, M. W. van Hof, & G. Berlucchi (Eds.), *Structure and function of cerebral commissures.* London: The Macmillan Press Ltd., 1979.

Zihl, J., Tretter, F., & Singer, W. Phasic electrodermal responses after visual stimulation in the cortically blind hemifield. *Behavioral Brain Research,* 1980, *1,* 197–203.

Author Index

X,Y,Z

Subject Index

RETURN OPTOMETRY LIBRARY
TO⟶ 490 Minor Hall   642-1020

LOAN PERIOD 1	2	3
4	5	6

HOME USE

ALL BOOKS MAY BE RECALLED AFTER 7 DAYS
RENEWALS MAY BE REQUESTED BY PHONE

DUE AS STAMPED BELOW

DEC 1 9 1984		
MAY 2 0 1985		
MAY 2 1 1986		
DEC 1 6 1987		

UNIVERSITY OF CALIFORNIA, BERKELEY
FORM NO. DD 23, 2m, 3/80   BERKELEY, CA 94720